Imprisoned by the Past

IMPRISONED BY THE PAST

Warren McCleskey, Race, and the American Death Penalty

Jeffrey L. Kirchmeier

OXFORD
UNIVERSITY PRESS

Oxford University Press is a department of the University of Oxford. It furthers the University's objective of excellence in research, scholarship, and education by publishing worldwide.

Oxford   New York
Auckland   Cape Town   Dar es Salaam   Hong Kong   Karachi   Kuala Lumpur   Madrid
Melbourne   Mexico City   Nairobi   New Delhi   Shanghai   Taipei   Toronto

With offices in
Argentina   Austria   Brazil   Chile   Czech Republic   France   Greece   Guatemala   Hungary
Italy   Japan   Poland   Portugal   Singapore   South Korea   Switzerland   Thailand
Turkey   Ukraine   Vietnam

Oxford is a registered trademark of Oxford University Press in the UK and certain other countries.

Published in the United States of America by
Oxford University Press
198 Madison Avenue, New York, NY 10016

First issued as an Oxford University Press paperback, 2016
ISBN: 9780190653002 (paperback ; acid-free paper)

Library of Congress Cataloging-in-Publication Data
Kirchmeier, Jeffrey L.
   Imprisoned by the past : Warren McCleskey and the American death penalty / Jeffrey L. Kirchmeier.
      pages cm
   Includes bibliographical references and index.
   ISBN 978-0-19-996793-3 ((hardback) : alk. paper)
1. Capital punishment—United States. 2. McCleskey, Warren—Trials, litigation, etc.
3. Discrimination in criminal justice administration—United States. I. Title.
   KF9227.C2K57 2015
   364.660973—dc23
                                                                                                    2014024275

Note to Readers
This publication is designed to provide accurate and authoritative information in regard to the subject matter covered. It is based upon sources believed to be accurate and reliable and is intended to be current as of the time it was written. It is sold with the understanding that the publisher is not engaged in rendering legal, accounting, or other professional services. If legal advice or other expert assistance is required, the services of a competent professional person should be sought. Also, to confirm that the information has not been affected or changed by recent developments, traditional legal research techniques should be used, including checking primary sources where appropriate.

(Based on the Declaration of Principles jointly adopted by a Committee of the American Bar Association and a Committee of Publishers and Associations.)

For Alfred, Helen, and Georgie, who started my ongoing education to understand justice, fairness, and mercy.

"[W]e ignore [Warren McCleskey] at our peril, for we remain imprisoned by the past as long as we deny [racism's] influence on the present."
—Justice William Brennan, dissenting in *McCleskey v. Kemp*, 481 U.S. 279, 344 (1987)

CONTENTS

PREFACE TO THE PAPERBACK EDITION

Since the publication of *Imprisoned by the Past*, the significance of Warren McCleskey's case has only grown. His case continues to provide important lessons for modern society about race, the death penalty, and our criminal justice system.

The recent historical trends explored in the book persist. For example, the death penalty abolition period discussed in Chapter 22 continues, as states such as California consider whether or not to keep capital punishment. Also, in May 2015, Nebraska's unicameral leg'slature voted to abolish the death penalty by overriding the governor's veto.

Similarly, in August 2015, the Supreme Court of Connecticut held in *State v. Santiago*, 122 A.3d 1 (Conn. 2015), that the death penalty violates the state's constitution. And other previous death penalty advocates, such as former North Carolina Supreme Court Chief Justice I. Beverly Lake, have changed their minds and now oppose the death penalty.

As explained in the book, historically, during periods of death penalty abolition, supporters of the death penalty often become more active also. In Nebraska, the state's governor is campaigning for a referendum to retain the death penalty. And capital punishment supporters in other states are working to speed up executions.

Still, only a limited number of counties and states actually execute prisoners in the United States. These executions continue at a relatively slow rate as lethal injection problems persist and as states face challenges in obtaining execution drugs. For example, in May 2016, pharmaceutical company Pfizer announced new restrictions to prevent its drugs from being used for lethal injection executions.

As in McCleskey's case and other past Supreme Court cases, some justices still struggle with issues about the constitutionality of capital punishment. In *Glossip v. Gross*, 135 S. Ct. 2726 (2015), Justice Ruth Bader Ginsburg joined Justice Stephen Breyer's dissenting opinion that discussed several reasons why it is "highly likely" that the death penalty violates the Eighth Amendment of the U.S. Constitution. In that opinion, Justice Breyer supported his argument with references to statistical studies about race similar to the one used in Warren McCleskey's case.

Those two justices continue to question the death penalty. For example, in May 2016, the two dissented from a denial of a petition for writ of certiorari in *Tucker v. Louisiana*, 135 S. Ct. 1801 (2016). In that dissenting opinion, Justices Breyer and Ginsburg discussed the geographic arbitrariness that occurs because a murder's location affects whether or not a person is sentenced to death.

Additionally, as in McCleskey's case, the Supreme Court continues to consider problems with the administration of capital punishment and the role that race plays in the criminal justice system. For example, in 2016, the Court accepted review of the case of Duane Buck, whose trial was mentioned in the first edition of this book. At Buck's capital sentencing hearing, a psychologist testified that because Buck was black, he was more likely to be dangerous in the future.

Those concerned about injustice in our legal system have seen important developments in the last few years. Some developments have not been positive ones. For example, new studies are still finding a connection between race and the death penalty, as was found in the Baldus study discussed in Chapters 12 and 13. And there continue to be too many young African-American men killed by police.

On the side of positive progress, the Black Lives Matter movement and other groups are helping educate the public about the way African Americans and others are treated by police and the criminal justice system. Further, representatives from across the political spectrum recognize problems with the U.S. system of mass incarceration. They have taken some measures to address the issues, but only time will tell whether there will be lasting changes or whether fears about crime will prevent reasonable reform.

Recent social movements have led to other changes. The Confederate flag, which as part of Georgia's state flag had flown over Warren McCleskey's trial and execution, is being taken down across the American South. In July 2015, South Carolina removed the Confederate flag from the state's Capitol grounds. And, in May 2016, the U.S. House of Representatives approved a proposal prohibiting the display of large Confederate flags at national cemeteries operated by the Department of Veterans Affairs.

The nation is grappling not only with the meaning of the Confederate flag. A young generation is helping to raise questions about other symbols connected to the country's racist past.

For example, the statue of Thomas Watson pictured in this book's epilogue no longer stands on the Georgia State Capitol grounds in Atlanta. The statue of the man who helped instigate Leo Frank's lynching and the rise of the KKK, however, did not disappear completely. Officials moved the statue to a park across from the Capitol.

We can find hope in many of these changes. The statehouse grounds where Watson's statue once stood will be getting a statue of Martin Luther King, Jr. Similarly, many are planning for a King memorial on Stone Mountain.

We do not know where we will be in the next few decades regarding race, criminal justice, incarceration, and the death penalty. As in Warren McCleskey's case, the same dark forces that drove Thomas Watson still continue to lurk around our criminal justice system, just as Watson's statue has relocated but not completely disappeared.

Many of the recent changes do constitute progress, even if the nation has yet to fully consider the significance of the issues connected to Warren McCleskey's death sentence and execution. It is hoped that this slow march of progress will continue to help us better understand the imprisonment of the past.

Jeff Kirchmeier
June 2016

PREFACE

As a young lawyer, I heard an experienced capital defense attorney explain how reading the newly decided United States Supreme Court opinion in *McCleskey v. Kemp* constituted the most depressing moment in his career. I wondered how someone who had watched clients being executed could compare that experience with reading a court opinion. Similarly, other attorneys claim that the Supreme Court's opinion is one of the worst of all time, and even the author of that opinion came to regret his decision. But only after I learned more about the death penalty in America would I begin to fully comprehend the importance of Warren McCleskey's case.

When I teach criminal law to first-year law students, I skip over McCleskey's case in our book. I do so not because the case is unimportant, but because I fear I cannot do justice to it in a limited time for new law students. Only after learning about the history of the death penalty can one begin to understand why the case affects attorneys and Supreme Court justices so much. This book attempts to put the important case in its proper historical context.

This book resulted from research that goes back decades before I knew I would write it, so it is impossible to thank everyone who contributed in some way. I will, however, attempt to thank many of those who helped directly with *Imprisoned by the Past: Warren McCleskey and the American Death Penalty*.

I greatly appreciate the many people who provided information about Warren McCleskey and his litigation, including Laura Berg, John Charles ("Jack") Boger, Steve Bright, Rev. Murphy Davis, William ("Billy") Moore, Mary Sinclair, Robert Stroup, Rev. George Wirth, and George G. Woodworth. Thanks also to the wonderful people of Marietta, Georgia, who provided assistance.

Although any errors are my own, several people helped improve this book by reading drafts, including Deborah Denno, Barbara Hamilton, Sid Harring, Evan Mandery, Andrea McArdle, Ron Tabak, George G. Woodworth, and Deborah Zalesne. Sid Harring, Evan Mandery, Russell Miller, and Ruthann Robson provided additional valuable guidance at various stages of the process.

Thanks to the faculty, administration, and staff at CUNY Law School for various forms of support, and in particular thanks to colleagues who attended a presentation on the topic of this book and to Jenny Rivera for additional suggestions. I appreciate the guidance from Tony Lim and David Lipp at Oxford University Press for their efforts to get this book published; also thanks to Balamurugan Rajendran, Brooke Smith, and the folks at Newgen Knowledge Works for their efforts on this book.

Through the years, a number of CUNY Law School students provided outstanding research work that contributed to this book, including Andrea Barrow, Tillman Clark, Thea Delage, Michelle Edson, Everett Hopkins, Kimberly James, Eric Kushman, Mark Maher, Justyna Mielczarek, Sara Molinaro, and Virginia Wilbur. Additionally, thanks to Sarah Lamdan for her outstanding help in tracking down many of the photos used in this book, and thanks to the other hard-working staff and librarians of our school's library, including Alex Berrio Matamoros, Douglas Cox, Raquel Gabriel, Yasmin Sokkar Harker, Julie Lim, Nancy Macomber, Ricardo Pla, Jonathan Saxon, and Kathy Williams.

For other help with research leading me to historical documents and photographs, thanks to the Library of Congress, Tricia Gesner at the Associated Press, Lisa Harris at the Georgia Bureau of Investigation, Steve Petteway at the Office of the Curator of the Supreme Court of the United States, and Terry Zinn at the Oklahoma Historical Society. Ricardo Lewis, Jackie Williams, and the staff at the Fulton County Superior Court in Atlanta, Georgia were a great help with court records. Thanks for other assistance from Richard C. Dieter, William Erlbaum, Midiam Fernandez, Eric M. Freedman, Michael Laurence, Nereida Molina, Rick Rossein, and Maggie Ruperto.

The book includes with permission some research and rewritten excerpts from some of my law review articles: "Aggravating and Mitigating Factors: The Paradox of Today's Arbitrary and Mandatory Capital Punishment Scheme," 6 *William & Mary Bill of Rights Journal* (1998): 345–459; "A Tear in the Eye of the Law: Mitigating Factors, Disease Theory, and the Progression toward a New Theory of Criminal Justice," 83 *Oregon Law Review* (2004): 624–730; "Dead Innocent: The Death Penalty Abolitionist Search for a Wrongful Execution," 42 *Tulsa Law Review* (2006): 403–435; "Another Place beyond Here: The Death Penalty Moratorium Movement," 73 *Colorado Law Review* (2002): 1–116; and "Casting a Wider Net: Another Decade of Legislative Expansion of the Death Penalty in the United States," 34 *Pepperdine Law Review* (2006): 1–40. Thank you to the past and current staff of those journals.

Finally, my ongoing education about the death penalty and about justice has spanned across my lifetime and is part of my own past. During that time, I have had many more teachers than I can list here, but they include lawyers, friends, students, victims' families, clients, clients' families, my own family, educators, activists, authors, colleagues, judges, and many others. So thank you to everyone who helped make this book possible, and finally a special thanks to those close to me who tolerated my immersion in this project.

Jeff Kirchmeier
New York City
December 2014

INTRODUCTION

The history of the American death penalty, like the history of America itself, is one of big events and big concepts, but it is also made up of the stories of individuals. If one wishes to understand the American death penalty—its history, its present, and its future—a good place to begin is with Warren McCleskey. And similarly if one wishes to understand Warren McCleskey's case, one must begin with the history of the death penalty.[1]

The progression of the death penalty in the twentieth century from a political issue to a legal issue and back to a political issue is reflected in the history of the case of Warren McCleskey. The public consciousness about the death penalty revolves around memorable unusual crimes as in the cases of Ted Bundy or the Rosenbergs. But the reality is that an overwhelming number of those executed are names that you have never heard. Many of these executed men and women committed crimes comparable to many others who were sentenced to prison instead of to death. The people who are executed usually are not "the worst of the worst." They are the unluckiest of the "worst" or in some cases the unluckiest of the unlucky.

Warren McCleskey's case began as one of those anonymous cases. On a spring afternoon in 1978, Warren McCleskey and three other men botched the robbery of a furniture store in Atlanta, Georgia, resulting in the tragic death of a young police officer. At the time, it was a homicide whose significance mainly mattered to people close to those touched by the crime. But the incident ultimately developed into a historically significant case.

McCleskey merely would have been another black man executed in a southern state for killing a white person, but because of the timing of his case and the work done by lawyers and others, his case is a mirror of the modern American death penalty both because it is typical and because it is unique. First and foremost, it is significant for the decision by the United States Supreme Court in *McCleskey v. Kemp*. In the twentieth-century history of the death penalty, that decision looms large because it is the final time, as of today, that the Court decided a case that had a realistic chance of ending the U.S. death penalty. The Court's decision against McCleskey thus ended a long-term strategy to get the courts to abolish the death penalty and began a new era for the American death penalty.

The *McCleskey* case also illuminates today's death penalty and its problems, while also reflecting the past. McCleskey's attorneys compelled the Supreme Court to directly confront the issue of race that permeates the history of the death penalty in the United States. As Justice Brennan wrote of McCleskey's evidence of racism in the criminal justice system, "[W]e ignore him at our peril, for we remain imprisoned by the past as long as we deny [racism's] influence on the present."[2]

Although Warren McCleskey's case played its largest role in death penalty history because of its Supreme Court decision on race, the case also touches on other problems with the modern death penalty. The case is a window into several failures of a system that makes life-and-death decisions. McCleskey's case shows some of the inadequacies of the legal system—through failures of lawyers and through unfair procedural requirements that may determine whether one lives or dies. His "other" Supreme Court case, *McCleskey v. Zant*, created one of the many procedural hurdles for capital defendants to have their issues heard in the courts. Additionally, his case raises questions about rehabilitation, the causes of crime, inadequate funding for defense counsel, accuracy of verdicts, the humaneness of executions, and other issues.

Ultimately, McCleskey's case brought change. Death penalty lawyers and abolitionists had to adapt to the losses that occurred in his court decisions. The early years after *McCleskey v. Kemp* were ones where the death penalty seemed unstoppable. But death penalty abolitionists adapted to the decision by placing less hope in the courts, emphasizing their focus on another legal strategy while expanding their ongoing political strategy. Similarly, after *McCleskey v. Kemp*, policy makers began to understand that the Supreme Court was not going to resolve all of the problems with the American death penalty. Thus, the years after McCleskey's execution in the electric chair wrought some of the most significant changes to the death penalty in U.S. history.

Warren McCleskey and the decisions in his case hover over everything about today's death penalty, whether it has been the chipping away of the punishment at the edges in the courts or whether it is modern legislative victories in several states. Where the death penalty will be in thirty years is hard to predict, but it will remain connected to Warren McCleskey's case.

This book ties together three unique American stories. First, the book considers the changing American death penalty across centuries, including the drastic changes in the last fifty years. Second, the book addresses the role that race played in that history. And third, the book tells the story of Warren McCleskey and how his life and legal case brought together the other two narratives.

Because of the multiple stories, I have structured the stories in a way that makes sense for each of the tales, following a chronological approach for most parts of the book with some exceptions. Parts A and B explain the facts of Warren McCleskey's case, beginning with an overview of McCleskey's hometown of Marietta, Georgia, to plant the story in its American setting and to set the stage for the landmark litigation of Warren McCleskey's case. Specifically, Part B includes the story of McCleskey and his crime. It also addresses *McCleskey v. Zant*, even though the Supreme Court decided that case after *McCleskey v. Kemp*, because the later case is closely tied to the facts of the trial discussed in this section.

Part C provides an overview of the history of the American death penalty from before the nation's founding up to the first time McCleskey's attorneys argued before the Supreme Court. Although describing every single murder and execution in American history is beyond the scope of the book, the history section discusses some of the more notorious cases as well as some of the less notorious ones. The history section also gives context to the role played by Warren McCleskey's case and his case's evidence connecting race and the death penalty.

Part D is the story of race, lynching, the criminal justice system, and one of the most important Supreme Court decisions in U.S. history. Part E describes the final steps in McCleskey's case and his trips to the electric chair, connecting his electrocution to the history of U.S. execution methods.

The sections in Parts F and G follow through to examine the legacy of Warren McCleskey's case and how the American death penalty changed after his execution. Part F addresses a transformation that occurred with the moratorium movement, while Part G examines today's death penalty and the legacy of Warren McCleskey's case in the early twenty-first century. Finally, the Epilogue updates several of the major players in McCleskey's case along with more recent death penalty studies, thus bringing the book to a close.

Imprisoned by the Past is aimed at general readers as well as those with legal education, but different readers may use the book in different ways. Those who want a chronological story of the development of the modern death penalty may jump to Part C, which begins with the first uses of capital punishment in America. Those interested in Warren McCleskey may begin by focusing on the chapters about his life and his case. Some readers without legal training may decide to read the book in order but skip or skim the chapter on *McCleskey v. Zant*, which deals with the relationship between habeas corpus and capital punishment. In most cases, though, the author hopes that readers will discover that the best way to get the complete story of the American death penalty is to start at the beginning and read the book in order.

When the courts evaluated Warren McCleskey's case, the judges focused on the legal issues. They did not fully examine the person, and they did not consider his connection to history. This book attempts to fill in those connecting lines to provide a deeper understanding of his case and how the American death penalty remains imprisoned by the past.

PART A

Prologue

Prologue: America's Marietta

Warren McCleskey grew up in the Atlanta suburb of Marietta, Georgia. The city's connection to the Civil War, civil rights, and an infamous lynching reverberated in the area during McCleskey's youth.

The story of Warren McCleskey's hometown of Marietta, Georgia, reflects much of the history of the United States. The area has been home to Native Americans, settlers, slaves, war, violence, peace, and prosperity.

Marietta sits tucked away fifteen miles northwest of Atlanta not far from the North Georgia Mountains in a state that was one of the original thirteen colonies. The town is the county seat of Cobb County, named after Senator and Judge Thomas W. Cobb. Cobb's wife Mary may have provided the basis for Marietta's name.

Before white settlers arrived to the area, in the early 1800s, Cherokee Indians lived on the land that is now Marietta and the surrounding Cobb County. By 1833, nearly one hundred new white settlers were living in Marietta and the area was growing. As new pioneers came to the land with its fertile soil, conflicts soon arose between the whites and the Native Americans.

In 1838, the federal government ordered the Cherokee be resettled in the western United States, and the Cherokee from Marietta were forced with other Native Americans from Georgia and other states to relocate out west. Many of the Cherokee died as they made the long trip largely on foot and by wagon, facing exposure, hunger, and illness. Because of the sorrow and death caused by the removal of several tribes living in the southern United States, the forced march to current-day Oklahoma became known as the Trail of Tears.[1]

In the 1800s, cotton was a major crop in the area, and in 1860, there were 1,175 slaves in Marietta, with only thirteen free persons of color.[2] But soon the Civil War brought drastic changes to the area.

During the war, Marietta sat along the railroad route destroyed by General William Tecumseh Sherman on his way to Atlanta. Yet, even Sherman had to pause to admire the area on his march across Georgia. He described his view of Cobb County in early June 1864: "The scene was enchanting, too beautiful to be disturbed by the harsh clamor of war; but the Chattahoochee lay beyond, and I had to reach it."[3] Later that month, armies fought a major Civil War battle near Marietta on June 27, 1864, when Sherman ordered an assault on Kennesaw Mountain. During that hot day with temperatures exceeding one hundred degrees, the Confederate soldiers held off the Union attack. Sherman's army suffered 3,000 killed and wounded, the largest Union loss at the time in Georgia. More importantly for the South, the victory amplified Southern morale and support for Confederate General Joseph E. Johnston.

The Confederate success at Kennesaw Mountain held off the Union soldiers from advancing to Atlanta for a while. But within months, the Yankee soldiers entered Marietta. Then, for months, the federal soldiers occupied the town, confining citizens of Marietta under martial law. Later in the fall, the federal soldiers burned most of the town on their way to Atlanta and marching to the sea, destroying more than a hundred buildings both intentionally and accidentally. General Sherman left no federal troops behind in Marietta. So that November as the smell of smoke encompassed Marietta, citizens had no means of communication by train or telegraph.[4]

Following the Civil War, Marietta worked to rebuild from the destruction of the war and to survive through Reconstruction. Former soldiers and others from the North had been charmed by the town when they had traveled through, so they spread the word about Marietta. Thus, the resort town began attracting people from across the United States.[5]

After the war, Marietta became host to one of the largest cemeteries for Confederate soldiers.[6] At that time, Confederate soldiers often ended up buried apart from the Union soldiers because the U.S. government did not provide for proper burials for the Confederates. A donor offered the citizens of Marietta a private cemetery where Union soldiers and Confederate soldiers would lie in peace together. But Marietta citizens remained bitter about the invasion and so rejected the privately donated cemetery.[7] In the Confederate cemetery, a Confederate battle flag still flies above the 3,000 fallen soldiers, and some of the graves have a small version of the flag placed in the ground. A much smaller cemetery, called "Hangman's Hill," features the unmarked graves of several convicted criminals.[8]

At the turn of the twentieth century, approximately 30 percent of the people in Cobb County had African roots. Although they were no longer slaves, the African-Americans still had only limited rights. As in much of the South, following brief Republican governance during Reconstruction, white-supremacist Democrats reestablished power in the area. The new local governments limited the rights of African Americans for nearly one hundred years after the Civil War. W.E.B. Du Bois observed in 1903, "Not only is Georgia...the geographical focus of our Negro population, but in many other respects, both now and yesterday, the Negro problems seem to have been centered in this state."[9] Although slavery had ended, its effects remained. Racism and oppression partly explains why the county's African-American population dropped from 30 percent in 1900 to only about 4 percent by the time McCleskey lived in the town.[10]

Early in the twentieth century, violence again touched Marietta when citizens of the town lynched Leo Frank on August 17, 1915, less than thirty years before McCleskey was born. Frank, who was Jewish and a Northerner, managed an Atlanta pencil factory when he was accused of killing a thirteen-year-old employee from Marietta named Mary Phagan. The girl's battered dead body was found in the factory's basement after she had gone to the factory to pick up her pay on Saturday, April 26, which was Confederate Memorial Day. She was buried in the Marietta City Cemetery adjacent to the Marietta Confederate Cemetery.

A jury convicted Frank of the murder, and he was initially sentenced to death. Eventually, because questions were raised about Frank's guilt, the governor commuted Frank's sentence to life imprisonment. As racist and anti-Jewish propaganda inflamed emotions about the case, a group of esteemed citizens from Phagan's home town of Marietta—including a former Georgia governor and former Marietta mayor—began planning to abduct and hang Frank.[11] (See Figure Prologue.1.)

As temperatures swelled to more than ninety degrees on Monday, August 16, 1915, twenty-five men left Marietta in several cars on a staggered schedule to avoid attention. They drove to the prison farm that held Frank in Milledgeville, Georgia. That night, they broke into the prison and seized Frank. When he asked to change out of his nightshirt, the men told him he did not need clothes where he was going. They managed to get in and out of the prison with Frank in ten minutes without firing a shot. During the nighttime drive back toward Marietta, one of the men asked Frank, "Is there anything you would like to say before your execution?" Frank only responded, "No."

The men from Marietta then drove Frank back to a location near Phagan's childhood home in a Marietta grove. The former sheriff who owned the grove also tied the noose for the men. Frank remained calm though the ordeal, and after being allowed to write a note to his wife, he made his final statement: "I think more of my wife and my mother than I do of my own life."

As the morning light started to come through the trees, the men blindfolded Frank and tied his feet together. They then put a khaki cloth around his exposed lower body and put him up on a table set up in the area earlier for this purpose. One of the men placed a noose around Frank's neck. At 7:05 am, one of the leaders, a judge named Newt Morris, announced the sentence and kicked over the table.[12]

Word quickly spread about the lynching, and a crowd gathered with many taking pictures of the body swinging from the tree. One photograph of the scene shows Frank's dead body hanging from a tree next to several men who look into the camera with serious faces and without shame. As time passed, around 3,000 people gathered in the area, with some trying to ravage Frank's corpse. In the book *And the Dead Shall Rise*, author Steve Oney explained that "the gamut of emotions ranged from jubilation to rage to something approaching sexual rapture."[13]

Frank's body was taken to an Atlanta funeral home, and more than 15,000 people waited in the hot August afternoon to view it. At the same time, another crowd gathered in the Marietta town square to celebrate the work of the local men.

After Frank's body was transported back to Queens, New York, for burial in Mount Carmel Cemetery, other crowds gathered up North. But these crowds

Figure Prologue.1
Leo Frank (Library of Congress)

assembled to protest the lynching, as many saw Frank as an innocent victim of a lynch mob.

Not long after the lynching, an unexpected crowd of more than 20,000 people showed up at New York's Cooper Union for a conference on the persecution of Jewish Europeans. The crowd lined the streets for blocks in all directions. As Northern newspapers argued for justice for the lynchers and organized boycotts, crowds gathered at several places up North, including a crowd of 8,000 at Boston's Faneuil Hall.

In Marietta, the lynchers were never brought to justice. Several of those involved continued to have successful careers, including the judge who pronounced "sentencing" at the lynching. Citizens reelected Judge Newt Morris to his position in 1916, and he later became the chair of the Marietta School Board. Another participant in some of the events of that night went on to serve in the U.S. Congress and chair the House Un-American Activities Committee.[14]

Other men from Marietta who were involved in the lynching of Leo Frank soon became involved in the re-establishment of the Ku Klux Klan, which had been dormant in Georgia for fifty years. A former Populist Party presidential candidate and a future U.S. senator, Tom Watson—whose newspaper editorials helped inflame the Frank lynching—wrote another editorial in the month after the hanging. He responded to the North's critiques of the South over the Frank case. He wrote that if the North "doesn't quit meddling with our business and getting commutations for assassins and rapists who have pull, another Ku Klux Klan may be organized to restore HOME RULE."

Watson's call, along with other factors that included the release of D.W. Griffith's movie The Birth of a Nation earlier in the year, led to a meeting in Atlanta on November 23, 1915. The meeting included several of the Frank lynchers, and it resulted in the men making a trip up nearby Stone Mountain to light a wooden cross that signaled the resurrection of the Klan.[15] In the 1930s, a bronze statue of Watson was erected in front of the Georgia State Capitol in Atlanta.

In the legal system, Leo Frank's case laid the groundwork for courts to expand a state defendant's ability to seek relief in federal court through habeas corpus.[16] As in the Civil War's conflict involving states' rights and federal rights, courts responded to the Frank tragedy in Marietta by expanding the federal courts' ability to review decisions by state courts. However, the case of another Marietta resident, Warren McCleskey, later would result in limitations on those federal rights.

The aftereffects of the Civil War continued to linger in Georgia and the country through the twentieth century. When McCleskey was a teenager, the nation finally ratified the Twenty-Fourth Amendment to the U.S. Constitution, prohibiting the Reconstruction-era poll taxes that were used to keep African Americans from voting. Georgia, however, did not vote to ratify the amendment and has not done so to this day.[17]

In 1956, in rebellion against integration, Georgia adopted a new state flag incorporating the Confederate battle flag of the red and blue St. Andrew's Cross. Georgia adopted the flag as part of the state's resistance to the 1954 Supreme Court decision of Brown v. Board of Education, which had held that separate schools for blacks and whites violated the U.S. Constitution.

As part of Southern resistance to the Supreme Court decision, Georgians increased their adherence to the state's Confederate heritage. Not long after the Supreme Court's decision in Brown, Georgia Gov. Marvin Griffin stated in 1956 that "the rest of the nation is looking to Georgia for the lead in segregation." In the governor's State of the State address, he promised "there will be no mixing of the races in public schools, in college classrooms in Georgia as long as I am Governor."[18]

It was in this environment, as one court described, "that the Georgia General Assembly...chose as an official state symbol an emblem that historically had been associated with white supremacy and resistance to federal authority."[19] Officials raised the new state flag over the state capital while Warren McCleskey was eleven years old attending a segregated school.

By 1963, the flag still flew and the racial issues that prompted the Georgia Legislature to adopt it were still raging across the country. In mid-1963, spurred by recent events, President John F. Kennedy warned Americans they faced a "moral crisis" as he called for civil rights legislation. He pointed out that society treated blacks and whites in different ways, where blacks had significantly less access to education and employment. President Kennedy paraphrased Supreme Court Justice John Marshall Harlan in stating that blacks "have a right to expect that the law will be fair, that the Constitution will be color blind."[20]

Despite the hope created by the president's call for federal civil rights legislation, many dark clouds hovered on the horizon for the country and the civil rights movement. That spring in Alabama, Birmingham's commissioner of public safety Eugene "Bull" Connor and his officers used police dogs and fire hoses on peaceful demonstrators. On Good Friday, the officers arrested Rev. Martin Luther King Jr. and put him in the Birmingham jail, where he wrote about laws that discriminate directly or in their application.[21]

Earlier on the day of President Kennedy's Civil Rights Address, Alabama governor George Wallace had stood on the steps of the University of Alabama trying to prevent two black students from registering, continuing his inauguration promise to support "segregation now, segregation tomorrow, segregation forever." The following day in Jackson, Mississippi, a fertilizer salesman who was a Ku Klux Klan member shot and killed Medgar Evers in his driveway.

In August, the Atlanta-born King addressed the March on Washington for Jobs and Freedom, speaking of his dream and calling for freedom to ring throughout America, including through "Stone Mountain of Georgia," where the Ku Klux Klan had revived in 1915 following the Frank lynching controversy. But a little more than two weeks after King's speech, Klan members bombed a black church in Birmingham, killing four young girls. And then, less than six months after President Kennedy's speech, on November 22, 1963, the president was killed in Dallas.

Amid the nation's chaos, a few weeks after President Kennedy's assassination, a young African-American teenager returned from his segregated all-black high school to his home in Marietta, Georgia, which was less than an hour drive from the Stone Mountain mentioned in King's speech. Upon arriving home, the teenager, Warren McCleskey, discovered his mother had just killed his stepfather. The incident was not the only violence in the life of the young man, whose name would one day become associated with another setback for those who advocated for equal treatment of different races.

PART B

A Killing in Georgia

CHAPTER 1

A Death in Dixie

Warren McCleskey grew up surrounded by violent acts in his family and his neighborhood. Although the young man showed potential to have a good life, some misfortune and bad choices with unfortunate associates led to his participation in a trip from Marietta to Atlanta that resulted in a robbery and a murder at the Dixie Furniture Company.

Around thirty years after the Frank lynching in Marietta and the gathering of the new Ku Klux Klan at Stone Mountain, Willie Mae McCleskey gave birth to Warren McCleskey in Marietta, Georgia, on March 17, 1946. The baby would never know his natural father.

The racial changes McCleskey would see throughout his life were in the air on the date of his illegitimate birth. For example, no African Americans were playing Major League Baseball, but that was changing. On the date of McCleskey's birth, the Georgia-born Jackie Robinson was in the neighboring state of Florida playing his first game for a minor league team. The Daytona Beach exhibition game featured Robinson's Montreal Royals playing its parent club Brooklyn Dodgers, for which Robinson would eventually play starting that April.[1]

A small African-American population lived in Marietta during McCleskey's youth.[2] McCleskey grew up with six brothers and sisters in a part of town known as the "Skid Row" area of Marietta. McCleskey later described his childhood vicinity as having "terrible and never-ending" violence. He explained, "About every weekend, someone in the neighborhood was shot and killed. Fights all the time. A dog-eat-dog world where only the strong survive."[3]

The fights and violence intruded into the McCleskey household, too. For about five years of McCleskey's early childhood, his mother could not take care of the boy so she sent him to live with an aunt. The aunt, however, often beat McCleskey. McCleskey's sister Betty remembered her brother returning home timid and acting "like he had been cowed."[4]

When McCleskey was eight years old, his mother Willie Mae married John Henry Brooks.[5] Brooks physically abused his stepchildren and Willie Mae, and many times John beat Willie Mae until she bled.[6] Every weekend McCleskey's parents had physical battles, usually when John drank alcohol. Often, the police were called to break up the fights, and sometimes the young Warren McCleskey called the police to come save his mother.

During McCleskey's childhood, his parents supported the family with illegal activities. Willie Mae sold bootleg corn liquor. John Henry Brooks, meanwhile, ran an illegal gambling casino in their home while listing his official occupation as a "Dry Cleaner." Although the dilapidated house had a leaky roof, it became a neighborhood hangout for people buying moonshine. When the customers arrived, McCleskey and his siblings waited on them and served alcohol.[7]

McCleskey escaped the violent home life during the days when he went to his segregated school in Marietta. While McCleskey was in grade school in 1955, the U.S. Supreme Court in *Brown v. Board of Education* ordered that public schools be desegregated "with all deliberate speed."[8] But during McCleskey's school years, local residents argued about how to respond to the Supreme Court's desegregation decision. Many whites in Marietta supported the integration of the schools, but others did not.

In March 1960, the Cobb County White Citizens for Segregation took out a full-page ad in the *Marietta Daily Journal*, where they asserted they were working "to stop the forces that are trying to mix the races in our schools, churches, theatres and restaurants." Later in the month, several of the White Citizens group joined Ku Klux Klan members carrying Confederate flags in a car rally through Cobb County to support a boycott of local merchants who opposed segregation.[9] A few years later, while McCleskey was in high school, some local African Americans unsuccessfully attempted to desegregate the downtown Marietta lunch counters by having a sit-in. As in many other places, it ultimately took more than a decade for Marietta to desegregate the schools, so McCleskey spent all of his school years segregated from white students.[10]

Warren McCleskey completed his time at the all-black Lemon Street High School, which had opened as the city's first high school for black students in 1930. Despite his troubled home life, McCleskey showed some promise in school, serving as a co-captain of the football team and playing right offensive end for his eighth- and ninth-grade teams. In 1962, the Lemon Street High School Hornets dominated the league, not losing a game until losing the regional final by one point. Throughout the season, the team racked up lopsided wins, including an 81-0 victory where sophomore McCleskey scored three touchdowns. With McCleskey on the team, the Hornets won the 1961 and 1963 North Georgia Championships. McCleskey also did well in his classes, eventually graduating with a B grade-point average.[11]

Then, on a cool day early in December 1963, during McCleskey's junior year of high school not long after his football team's final game of the year, he came home from school to find his stepfather dying. Earlier in the day, after Brooks threatened to kill Willie Mae during an altercation, she grabbed a pistol out from under a mattress in the living room and shot the thirty-five-year-old Brooks in the chest. The young Warren McCleskey walked in the door a few seconds after the gun went off. An ambulance took Brooks to Kennestone Hospital, where he died.[12] Police charged

McCleskey's mother with the homicide, but after the authorities determined she had suffered from abuse and acted in self-defense, they allowed her to avoid prison by pleading guilty to lesser charges.[13]

The stepfather's death was not the only violent death near the family. Not long after Brooks's death, a neighbor killed Willie Mae's new boyfriend. In 1972, another boyfriend of Willie Mae's killed a man in the McCleskeys' kitchen.[14]

Despite the violent and abusive home environment, McCleskey completed high school and graduated. A photo of McCleskey on the day of his graduation in 1964 shows a smiling young man with some hope for the future, dressed in a suit and vest, well-groomed with short hair and a trace of a moustache.

After McCleskey graduated from high school, a few black students finally began attending the formerly all-white Marietta High School. White officials allowed the few black students to attend Marietta High School so they could claim that the school was now "integrated." Finally, by 1967, all of the Lemon Street High School students were integrated into Marietta High School. Officials briefly considered integrating both buildings, but white parents did not want to send their children to the dilapidated Lemon Street building, which they considered a firetrap. So, after the final all-black Lemon Street High School graduates received their degrees, the city quickly demolished McCleskey's former high school building during the summer.[15]

Not long after McCleskey's graduation, he married his high school sweetheart, Gwendolyn Carmichael. A few years later in 1966 when McCleskey was twenty years old, Gwen gave birth to their daughter Carla. From 1964 to 1969, McCleskey supported his young family by working for Lockheed Aircraft Company. By 1970, though, Lockheed had laid him off, and he then had trouble finding work. The stress of the financial problems began taking a toll on McCleskey's marriage as the two argued and his wife began talking about leaving him.[16]

McCleskey's solution to his financial and family woes led him to committing robberies to get money. He had limited success in his new illicit career, and police soon arrested him. One of the detectives who worked investigating the robberies, John Dean, noted that some of the officers thought McCleskey was so reckless in the robberies that he had the potential to commit murder in the future. After the arrest, McCleskey pleaded guilty to nine armed robberies around Atlanta. He later claimed he was only guilty of some of those robberies and pleaded guilty because he wanted a deal. The court sentenced McCleskey to three terms of life imprisonment, although the sentence was reduced on appeal.

Ultimately, McCleskey spent seven years and four months in prison, and then he went to a halfway house and participated in a work release program. The state paroled McCleskey in late 1977.[17]

After being paroled, the ex-con McCleskey struggled to turn his life around and to adapt back to life outside prison. His 1977 reunion with his wife Gwen and daughter were the happiest time of his life. But within about a year of his release from prison, his life started spiraling out of control. He and his wife divorced and he began seeing another woman named Brenda Hardy. If he had trouble finding work before he went to prison, the ex-con found it even more difficult to find a job now that he had a prison record. His problems helped lead to drug abuse and a return to robbing stores.[18]

During this period, McCleskey worked different jobs and connected with three men with long criminal records: David Burney, Bernard Depree, and Ben Wright. McCleskey met Burney in 1977 while they both worked at a restaurant and pub called Oliver's Place. One day while McCleskey talked to a busboy, the busboy mentioned that he lived at a halfway house with a man named Ben Wright. McCleskey knew Ben Wright from prison, so he soon got in touch with Wright. McCleskey and Wright began talking and became friends.

Wright soon introduced McCleskey and Burney to one of his friends, Bernard Depree, who sometimes spelled his name "Dupree." McCleskey remembered Depree from when they were both in Georgia State Prison, although he did not know him well.[19]

Even though the thirty-two-year-old McCleskey had three robbery convictions that had occurred in 1970–1971, his new associates had even longer records. David Burney, who was thirty-one and the youngest of the men, had been charged with a long list of crimes throughout his life, including murder, rape, escape, assault and battery, and many robberies. Ben Wright, who was thirty-six, had been convicted of burglary and a number of robberies. Ben Wright's girlfriend, Mary D. Jenkins, also had a criminal record and aliases.[20]

The oldest man in the group was the forty-three-year-old Bernard Depree, who had crimes that included pimping, pandering, armed robberies, aggravated assault, and burglary. Depree was born in Brooklyn in November 1934 and never knew his mother or father because both died while Depree was very young. Depree was raised in a mental institution until he was eight and then later lived at a school for children with an intellectual disability until he first went to prison at the age of seventeen.[21]

McCleskey and his new friends began planning to rob some local stores. The robberies were not focused on any type of stores, and the men generally robbed whatever seemed available. For example, in April 1978, McCleskey, Wright, and Burney robbed a Red Dot Grocery Store. During that robbery, they stole a .38 nickel-plated pistol they would use in another robbery in May.[22]

On Saturday morning, May 13, 1978, Warren McCleskey made a fateful decision to take part in a robbery that would result in many unfortunate consequences he did not foresee, setting in motion events that affect the American criminal justice system to this day. On that morning, as part of a plan to rob a jewelry store in Marietta, McCleskey drove his 1971 Pontiac Grand Prix to pick up Ben Wright, Bernard Depree, and David Burney. They stopped at Mary Jenkins's house to pick up weapons, gloves, and other supplies for the robbery.[23]

The four men then drove to the Marietta jewelry store and parked the car at around 10 am. They had planned to rob the store when it first opened, but because McCleskey was late picking up the other men, they arrived at the store after it had been open awhile. Wright, the leader of the group, went into the store to look around. While he perused the store, he bought a watchband. Then, Wright left the jewelry store and walked to a shoe store where he bought a pair of shoes.

After McCleskey picked up Wright near the shoe store, the men decided to find another place to rob. They did not have much of a plan, so they drove around Marietta trying to find another target. But they could not agree on a place. Finally, they decided to drive to the larger city of Atlanta where there would be more options.[24]

Throughout history, a number of bad results came from the journey from Marietta to Atlanta. Gen. Sherman's trip from Marietta to Atlanta resulted in the destruction of the city. Mary Phagan's trip from Marietta to Atlanta for her job resulted in her murder. On this Saturday morning, nothing good would come from the trip that Wright, Depree, Burney, and McCleskey made from Marietta to Atlanta.

Once they arrived in Atlanta in the early afternoon, they decided to rob a furniture store called "Dixie Furniture Company," which Wright had scoped out on another occasion. After they drove to the store, David Burney went inside to check out the security situation. After he returned to the car, McCleskey parked the car near the store on Marietta Street and the group sent him into the store to check it out. After McCleskey returned to the car, the four planned the robbery. Each took a gun when he got out of the car.

One of the robbers, later identified by some store employees as McCleskey, ran in the front of the store and quickly secured the area. According to later witness reports, this man had a "bumpy" face with festered facial hair bumps and a blister scar on the left side of his face. The man wore blue pants, a rust-colored shirt, and pink-shaded glasses, and he carried a silver gun later thought to be the same one taken earlier by a robber at a Red Dot store.[25]

As the one robber secured the front of the store, the other three men put on stocking masks and entered the back of the store through the loading dock. They rounded up employees in the area and started tying them up with tape and blindfolding them. The robbers made the manager turn over the store receipts totaling somewhere between $500 and $1,500. They also took the manager's watch and six dollars from his pockets.[26]

In the front of the store, a secretary-bookkeeper named Classie Barnwell saw the robbers, and unknown to them, she set off a silent alarm. The robber at the front of the store took the gun from the store's private security guard and made him, his brother, Ms. Barnwell, and another Dixie employee named Mamie Thomas lie on the floor and close their eyes.[27]

Meanwhile, the police responded to the silent alarm. Officer Frank Robert Schlatt, a young police officer who had been with the Atlanta Police Department for five years, was driving in the area on patrol by himself. (See Figure 1.1.) The police station notified him on his radio about the alarm at the Dixie Furniture Company. He drove his patrol car to the store and parked, arriving only a few minutes after the alarm had been set off. He quickly entered the building with his gun drawn to check things out. After he walked about fifteen feet down the main aisle, a voice called at him to stop and then two shots suddenly rang out. The first shot hit his eye and entered his brain. A second shot glanced off a pocket lighter in his chest pocket, ricocheting into a sofa in the store.[28]

Figure 1.1
Officer Frank Schlatt (Atlanta Police Department Public Affairs Office)

Meanwhile, Everett New and his wife were driving on the street outside the Dixie Furniture Company, and they saw some of these events transpire from their car. While stopped at a red light, they watched Officer Schlatt park his squad car at the store, pull his gun, and run into the store. About thirty seconds later, they heard two shots and saw "a black man running out toting a pistol" and running down the street. Mr. New noted that the fleeing man's handgun had a pearl handle and, inconsistent with other descriptions, that the man wore brown pants.[29]

After the two shots rang out, all four robbers ran from the store. In the rush to flee, though, Wright left behind his black jacket, which had been used to cover a sawed-off shotgun when they entered the store. Back in the car, the robbers debated going back inside to get the jacket. Soon, they realized they needed to flee immediately because a police officer had been shot.

After the crime, the robbers drove back to Marietta, where they divided the money and split up. McCleskey and Wright dropped off some of the weapons at the home of McCleskey's girlfriend, Brenda Hardy.

Wright kept the watch they took from the manager. He later gave the watch to Mary Jenkins's brother, but then took it back after worrying someone would trace it to the robbery and him. Instead of throwing the watch away, however, Wright threw it on the roof of David Burney's sister's house. He planned that if he were caught, he would be able to lead police to the watch to prove he was in the back of the Dixie Furniture Company when someone shot the officer in the front of the store.[30]

Officer Schlatt died at the hospital about three hours after he was shot. The thirty-one-year-old man had a young wife and, like McCleskey, a young daughter. The officer's daughter, Jodie, was nine years old.

The community recognized Officer Schlatt as a hero who died in the line of duty. Georgia governor Lester Maddox, several police commissioners, and other high-ranking officials attended Officer Schlatt's funeral. A large number of officers attended as well, as did newspaper writer Lewis Grizzard and Officer Schlatt's parents. During the funeral, one of the officers promised, "We'll find the animals who did this, no matter how long it takes." The young Jodie tried to console her mother about their loss. A newspaper article recounted how the little girl had placed a flower on top of the U.S. flag lying on her father's casket. The honor guard thoughtfully folded the flower into the flag, and then they presented the flag with the flower in it to Officer Schlatt's widow and daughter.[31]

Meanwhile, the police began closing in on their suspects. At the crime scene, they had found Wright's leather jacket, which had a laundry ticket stapled to the sleeve. Police recognized that Wright led a group of ex-cons in committing robberies in the area. Although they had not been able to find him, they soon found his girlfriend, Mary Jenkins, and began asking her questions. Eventually, Mary Jenkins gave a four-page statement to the police about the robbers.

The police connected the Dixie Furniture Company crime to other robberies they had been investigating, including a Red Dot market robbery. Using information they had connecting McCleskey to the Red Dot market robbery, police went to a judge to request a warrant. The judge issued an arrest warrant for McCleskey and a search warrant for his home. The police believed the search would lead them to evidence connected to the Dixie Furniture Company robbery and the killing of their fellow officer.

Hours before dawn on May 30, 1978, fifteen police officers swarmed into McCleskey's house, got him out of bed, and arrested him. The officers also arrested McCleskey's girlfriend Brenda Hardy in the bedroom. As the officers searched through the house for items related to the Red Dot robbery, they found $600 in

Hardy's purse, another $260 in the bedroom, $665 under a pillow, some marijuana, and a .38 caliber gun. Officers also looked for rings and specific items taken in the robbery, as well as other weapons, but they did not find them in McCleskey's home. When Cobb County officers in Marietta interrogated McCleskey that day, he denied being involved in the furniture store crime.[32]

The following day, officers arrested David Burney, who also denied being involved in the Dixie Furniture Company crime. While detectives interrogated Burney, they soon realized that Burney was terrified of Wright, who was still at large. To encourage Burney to talk, they promised to protect Burney and his family against Wright. The next day Burney confessed and named the three other robbers. As the police pressed Burney for information about Officer Schlatt's killer, Burney said that in the car after the robbery, McCleskey claimed he had shot the officer twice.

On May 31, 1978, McCleskey again made the trip from Marietta to Atlanta when Marietta officers transferred him to Atlanta officers in Fulton County. During the day, police Detectives W.K. Jowers and Welcome Harris Jr. interrogated McCleskey. At one point, Det. Jowers called in someone to record a statement from McCleskey, and the interrogation continued for about six more hours. During this time, McCleskey admitted to participating in the robbery, but he claimed someone else shot the officer. McCleskey explained to the detectives that during the robbery he became nervous and decided to leave the furniture store. When he saw the police car, he hid under a sofa until Officer Schlatt entered the store. Then, McCleskey said he walked to the back of the store. McCleskey claimed that as he was then leaving, he heard two shots. Thinking the officer was shooting at him, he ran to his car.[33]

Police officials announced to the media that they had arrested McCleskey and claimed he was the person who had shot and killed Officer Schlatt. Bernard Depree soon turned himself in, although he denied being involved in the robbery. The police and the FBI continued to search for Ben Wright. Finally, later in the summer, they tracked down Wright after police in Arkansas arrested Wright for another robbery.[34]

The assistant district attorney on the case, Russell Parker, worked on putting together the information on the crime with another attorney in the Fulton County District Attorney's office, Tom Thrash. Parker began to focus on the murder weapon, which was never found. Ballistic evidence revealed the murder weapon was probably a .38-caliber Rossi revolver that McCleskey and Wright had stolen in the earlier Red Dot robbery. The weapon stood out because it was silver with an ivory handle. But stories conflicted about whether Wright or McCleskey carried that gun in the Dixie store robbery. Burney claimed McCleskey carried a silver revolver, and the employee Classie Barnwell said that the robber at the front of the store, who she later identified as McCleskey, had a silver gun. Yet, Wright's girlfriend, Mary Jenkins, told police that Wright usually carried a silver .38 and McCleskey usually used a .45-caliber gun. In his statement, McCleskey reported he used a black .22 caliber gun.[35]

Parker recognized that a major challenge with his case was that none of the store employees saw who shot Officer Schlatt. McCleskey and Burney confessed to the robbery but each denied killing Officer Schlatt, while Burney told police that

McCleskey shot the officer. Based on Burney's statement and the information about the gun, Parker began to focus on McCleskey as the shooter. Still, another problem was that none of the witnesses could positively identify McCleskey, and some of the witnesses gave descriptions that were inconsistent with McCleskey's appearance.

Meanwhile, defense attorneys prepared to represent the accused men. McCleskey's sister did not trust public defenders so she hired John M. Turner Jr., an Atlanta solo practitioner and a former prosecutor. She did not have much money but could hire him for a total fee of $2,500, a low price considering the complexity of a capital case. When the court arraigned McCleskey on July 20, 1978, the judge set the trial for September 25, giving Turner only two months to investigate the case and prepare for a potential capital sentencing hearing. [36]

Turner believed the prosecutor had a strong case against his client, and he repeatedly advised McCleskey to plead guilty so he would not risk getting the death penalty.[37] McCleskey, however, thought he had a good case and wanted to go to trial. He also told Turner a different story than he told police. He explained to Turner that he was not at the Dixie Furniture Company when the crime occurred. He said Wright may have taken his car to the robbery because he had loaned Wright his car on that day. He then claimed he was playing cards with several people near his sister's apartment at the time of the crime.

Turner then asked McCleskey why he had confessed to the police that he was at the robbery if he were really playing cards. McCleskey explained that the police in their desire to find the person who killed a fellow police officer had coerced him to confess.

Turner did little investigation and did not review the prosecutor's case file— which included witness statements and police reports—until the Friday before the trial was to begin the following Monday. Largely because McCleskey claimed an alibi, Turner did not focus on the evidence regarding the shooting. Turner faced another challenge in that because McCleskey's family had little money, they had no resources to hire an investigator, experts, or consultants for the complex capital trial.[38]

On that Friday, Turner went to visit McCleskey in jail, again asking him to think about a guilty plea. Turner thought a plea would be the best option if they could get a deal. Turner had not engaged in concrete plea negotiations with the prosecutor because McCleskey wanted to go to trial. But Turner believed from his conversations with Parker that they might be able to work out a life sentence plea. McCleskey again refused to plead guilty and stressed his innocence. Turner asked him to at least think about it over the weekend.

So, as the trial approached, McCleskey's attorney did not focus on preparing to attack the prosecution's theory about the gun used, the location of the shooter, or other information related to the killing. Instead, he planned to argue that McCleskey played cards in Marietta when the robbery occurred in Atlanta.[39]

CHAPTER 2

The Trial of Warren McCleskey

McCleskey's trial began with the prosecutor arguing Warren McCleskey killed Officer Schlatt, while McCleskey's lawyer argued McCleskey was not present at the Dixie Furniture Company. But after the trial and a quick sentencing hearing, the court sent McCleskey to death row, where he would spend more than a decade.

In October 1978, Judge Sam Phillips McKenzie began Warren McCleskey's trial for armed robbery and murder in the Superior Court of Fulton County in Atlanta, Georgia. As McCleskey sat in the courtroom, he saw the American flag like the one used at Officer Schlatt's funeral. And next to that flag hung the Georgia state flag, which incorporated the Confederate battle flag from the Civil War.

The attorneys selected jurors for the trial. People who are categorically opposed to capital punishment are excluded from death penalty juries, so those ultimately selected for the jury had to state they were able to impose a death sentence. Beyond questions about whether or not the potential jurors opposed the death penalty, McCleskey's attorney and the prosecutor did little to explore the individual jurors' feelings about capital punishment.

In this jury selection process, the attorneys each had nine peremptory challenges to use their discretion to remove potential jurors. The prosecutor used seven of his peremptory challenges to remove seven blacks from the jury panel. The resulting jury at the start of the trial consisted of seven men and five women. Eleven of them were white, and one was black, and one of the alternates also was black. Many of the jurors were middle-aged or older with teenage or older children. The jurors included two housewives, a U.S. Postal Service employee, an IBM business planner, a public school building maintenance mechanic, two insurance agent office workers, and a Sears, Roebuck & Company employee. More than likely, many of them grew up in a racially segregated environment and attended segregated schools just as McCleskey had. The attorneys, however, did not explore whether any of the jurors might be biased based on a person's race[1]

After the trial began, the district attorney, Russell Parker, introduced two witnesses for the state from the Dixie Furniture Company store. Both witnesses now identified McCleskey as one of the robbers even though they were not able to identify him prior to trial. Classie Barnwell, the employee who set off the alarm, had previously been unable to describe the man at the front of the store or to pick McCleskey out of a lineup. But when she sat in the courtroom and saw McCleskey next to two sheriff's deputies, she said she recognized McCleskey from the robbery.

Similarly, Mamie Thomas, a cashier at the store, had previously been unable to identify McCleskey. Thomas told police that the man at the front of the store had bumps and a scar on his face—a description that did not match McCleskey. But, like Barnwell, Thomas testified at trial that she was certain the robber was McCleskey. She explained that she could not identify McCleskey earlier because she cannot recognize people in photos. And she was scared to identify him in person.[2]

The prosecutor introduced testimony from two witnesses who claimed McCleskey had admitted to the shooting, and he also introduced evidence that at least one of the bullets that hit Officer Schlatt came from a .38 caliber revolver, which was the type of weapon that some claimed McCleskey had during the robbery.

One of the two witnesses who asserted that McCleskey confessed to the killing was the alleged ringleader of the robbery, Ben Wright, who claimed McCleskey had admitted killing the officer.[3] Wright testified that McCleskey stayed at the front of the store, where Wright could see McCleskey during the robbery. The other robbers, he said, were at the back of the store away from where the shooting took place. Wright testified that McCleskey later told him that he hid behind a sofa when Officer Schlatt entered. Wright added that McCleskey explained that when he told Schlatt to "freeze," the officer turned around and McCleskey shot him.

On the witness stand, Wright told the jury that after the gun went off, the robbers all ran to the car. When they realized they had left Wright's jacket in the store, they debated going back inside until McCleskey told them they needed to flee immediately because he had just shot an officer. Wright responded to McCleskey, "Man, you done fucked up, you done killed the police." Then he got quiet and began thinking about the amount of trouble they faced if caught.[4]

Wright also was a key witness in claiming that McCleskey carried a .38 caliber silver revolver, which used the type of bullet that killed Officer Schlatt. Police never found the murder weapon, but both Wright and his girlfriend testified McCleskey carried the .38 pistol. During cross-examination by defense attorney John Turner, though, Wright admitted he had carried the .38 for weeks. Also, when police arrested Wright's girlfriend, she claimed Wright carried a .38 and McCleskey carried a .45 weapon.[5]

On the stand, Wright admitted that his testimony against McCleskey would help his own case. He revealed that the State planned to recommend twenty-year concurrent sentences in exchange for his testimony, despite the fact he was the leader of the robbery and had been a suspect for the killing. Wright was defiant through much of his testimony, admitting he would lie to keep from getting convicted of murder. He also revealed that he was testifying against McCleskey because McCleskey and Burney "broke the code" by implicating him in the robbery during their conversations with police. He believed that they hoped the police would kill him while trying to capture him: "Warren McCleskey and David Burney tried to get me killed. This is why I am testifying."[6] In later proceedings in the case, a U.S. district court judge reviewed Wright's testimony, calling it "obviously impeachable" and questioning whether his uncorroborated testimony should have been admissible.[7]

In response to the prosecutor's large number of witnesses, Turner presented a handful of witnesses in defense, including McCleskey. On the stand, McCleskey claimed that on the day of the robbery, he had loaned his car to Wright. And during the time of the robbery, he played a card game called "skin" with friends.

McCleskey explained that the reason he confessed to the police that he was present at the Dixie Furniture Company robbery was because he knew he was going to be convicted of other robberies. As he already faced a long prison sentence, one more robbery did not matter. He worried at the time that he did not have a strong alibi for the furniture store robbery and that his friends had used his car. So, he thought he would be convicted, and he figured he should cooperate with the police. During cross-examination, McCleskey admitted that he set up a fake alibi with his girlfriend Brenda at one point before deciding to tell the "truth."[8]

On cross-examination, the prosecutor Parker surprised Turner by leading McCleskey into questions about another confession. He asked McCleskey whether he had admitted to another jail detainee that he shot the officer. McCleskey denied it, but Parker knew he had a witness waiting outside the courtroom to impeach McCleskey's claims. Turner, McCleskey's attorney, objected to Parker's questioning and argued that if such a statement existed it should have been turned over to him. The judge overruled Turner.

Then, to rebut McCleskey's denials about the jailhouse confession, Parker put Offie Evans on the stand to show McCleskey lied by denying he had confessed to Evans in jail. Turner had let McCleskey testify to his version of events without knowing the prosecutor had a statement from Evans, who turned out to be a surprise key witness tying McCleskey to the murder.[9]

Offie Evans had a long criminal record and was already serving a six-year federal prison sentence for forgery. The jury learned that police held Evans in a cell next to McCleskey after McCleskey's arrest. Evans, who had spent three years hanging out with Ben Wright when both were in prison together, informed police that McCleskey confessed to shooting Officer Schlatt. Evans testified that McCleskey told him that he saw the police officer come into the store and then saw the officer heading toward the other three robbers. According to Evans, McCleskey told him that "he couldn't stand to see him go down there, and I think the police looked around and seen him and he said, 'Halt,' or something, and [McCleskey] had to—it was him or them one [sic], and said that he had to shoot."[10]

Evans also testified that McCleskey boasted he would still have tried to shoot his way out even if a dozen police officers were there. Additionally, Evans claimed that McCleskey said Mary Jenkins made him up with makeup and a disguise on the day of the robbery. His testimony about the makeup was important because McCleskey had a smooth face and store employee Mamie Thomas had claimed that the man who entered the front of the store had "rough facial features," a face that was "real bumpy," and had a scar.

But Evans's testimony conflicted with the testimony of prosecution witness Mary Jenkins. Although he testified Jenkins helped McCleskey with a disguise, she claimed not to have any involvement with the robbery.[11] Further, on the stand, the prosecution did not ask Evans about the extent of Jenkins's role, perhaps because she testified as a prosecution witness and they did not want to undermine her credibility with the jury.[12]

Finally, Evans explained that during the jailhouse conversation, a cell upstairs held another codefendant. At the time, Bernard Depree heard the conversation and yelled down to McCleskey to stop talking. But Evans worked to put Depree at ease too.

Evans's testimony helped convict McCleskey of capital murder. Not only was he the only witness besides the self-interested codefendant Wright who testified that McCleskey fired the fatal shots, his testimony supported the "malice" element of the murder charge. Further, he was the only witness who testified that McCleskey wore makeup, giving jurors a possible explanation for inconsistencies in identifications.[13]

By the time the trial went to closing arguments, Parker had presented thirty-nine witnesses for the prosecution's case in chief. For the defense, Turner presented only McCleskey and four witnesses. In rebuttal to the defense, Parker presented four more witnesses, including Evans, for a total of forty-three prosecution witnesses.

During closing arguments, Turner emphasized that eyewitnesses gave inconsistent descriptions of the robber at the front of the store, that is, the alleged killer. He stressed that the store employees were previously unable to identify that man as McCleskey until they saw him in the defendant's chair in court. He argued Ben Wright lied on the stand and that, in fact, Wright killed Officer Schlatt. Additionally, he attacked the truthfulness of Mary Jenkins's statements, arguing she probably took part in the crime.

In the prosecution's closing argument, Parker described McCleskey as a cold-blooded murderer, claiming McCleskey first shot the officer in the eye and then he walked over to Officer Schlatt's body on the ground and fired a second shot into the heart. Parker implored the jury to convict McCleskey of deliberate murder with malice. He asked them not to take "the easy way out" and convict McCleskey of felony murder, a crime that makes one guilty of murder by the fact that a killing occurred during the commission of a felony.

Parker continued by focusing on the two key witnesses and the gun. After arguing Wright told the truth, he recapped the testimony about the weapon. He noted that witnesses said Depree had a .22 handgun, Burney had a .38 dark blue Smith & Wesson pistol, Wright carried a sawed-off shotgun, and McCleskey carried the silver Rossi .38, which was the murder weapon.

Parker invoked Offie Evans's testimony to convince the jury McCleskey was a cold-blooded killer. He stressed that McCleskey "could have gotten out that back door just like the other three did, but he chose not to do that . . . and just like Offie Evans says, it doesn't make any difference if there had been a dozen policemen come in there, he was going to shoot his way out.... He deliberately killed that police officer on purpose."[14]

Regarding McCleskey's claim that he played cards in Marietta at the time of the Atlanta robbery, Parker reminded the jury that none of McCleskey's family or friends showed up at court to verify his alibi. Finally, Parker concluded by saying he hoped Officer Schlatt would have been satisfied with his work on the case. He hoped he did his duty in an honorable manner, just as Officer Schlatt had done.[15]

The jury then retired to evaluate if McCleskey were guilty of armed robbery and murder. Under Georgia law, armed robbery required a finding of "(1) a taking of property from the person or the immediate presence of a person, (2) by use of an offensive weapon, (3) with intent to commit theft." The "malice murder" that Parker sought was defined as: "A person commits the offense of murder when he unlawfully and with malice aforethought, either express or implied, causes the death of another human being." The "malice" in the statute included "express malice," which is the "deliberate intention unlawfully to take away the life of a fellow creature." The malice may be implied "where no considerable provocation appears and where all the circumstances of the killing show an abandoned and malignant heart."[16]

After deliberating for about two hours, the jury asked the court for further instructions on the meaning of "malice" in the murder charge. Not long after the additional instructions, the jury found McCleskey guilty of malice murder and two counts of armed robbery.[17] Observers were not surprised the jury found McCleskey guilty, considering his unbelievable claims on the stand that he was nowhere near the robbery while several others placed him at the scene of the crime.

Still, even though the jurors did not believe McCleskey's alibi, some of the jurors had doubts about McCleskey's culpability in the murder. At least some of the jurors based their vote on the murder on the testimony from Offie Evans. They discounted Wright's testimony because of his self-interest, but they assumed Offie Evans had little motive to lie, an assumption that would be questioned much later.[18]

* * *

After the jurors found McCleskey guilty of murder and robbery, the court immediately held a sentencing hearing. Some of the jurors were surprised to hear they were now going to have to decide whether or not to impose a death sentence.

In order to obtain a death sentence, a prosecutor must establish a statutory aggravating factor that separates the case from other murder cases. In McCleskey's case, the prosecutor sought to prove two aggravating factors: (1) the murder was during the course of a serious felony, and (2) the murder victim was a police officer. Considering that the jury had found McCleskey guilty of killing a police officer during a robbery, the jury would certainly find the aggravating factors making McCleskey eligible for death.

During the hearing, because Georgia allows prosecutors to argue other aggravating evidence in addition to the statutory factors, District Attorney Parker argued McCleskey should not receive mercy, asking the jury: "Have you observed any repentance by Mr. McCleskey? Has he exhibited to you any sorrow? Have you seen any tears in his eyes for this act that he has done?" He also asked the jury to consider McCleskey's prior convictions, noting McCleskey had previously received life sentences that were reduced to lesser sentences after he "went through the appellate process and somehow got it reduced." Finally, he compared McCleskey unfavorably to Ben Wright, who testified that his profession was to rob without killing. In contrast to Wright's description of himself, Parker warned the jurors that McCleskey would likely kill again.[19]

In response to the aggravating factors presented by the prosecution, defense attorneys usually present witnesses and mitigating evidence to argue why a capital defendant should be sentenced to life in prison instead of the death penalty. In McCleskey's case, his attorney could have presented testimony about McCleskey's troubled life, but he did not present such evidence, which he may not even have known about.

There are a number of possible explanations why no evidence was presented on McCleskey's behalf at his capital sentencing hearing. At the time of McCleskey's trial, the current death penalty system had not been in place for long, as only two years earlier, the Supreme Court had set new constitutional requirements for capital trials. So some attorneys at the time did not know how to adequately investigate and conduct capital sentencing hearings under the new developing system.[20]

Turner also encountered some high hurdles. Because McCleskey had argued he was not even present at the scene of the crime, it would have been a challenge for Turner now to present evidence to mitigate McCleskey's involvement in the murder. Additionally, McCleskey's family who had hired Turner had little money. Thus, he did not obtain resources to hire investigators and other assistance in developing a mitigation case. Years later, Turner claimed that neither McCleskey nor his sister gave him any names of people who would testify on McCleskey's behalf. He also claimed that McCleskey's sister would not testify and that she said that McCleskey's mother was too ill to testify. By contrast, McCleskey's sister later said Turner did not ask her for help in finding people to testify on her brother's behalf.[21]

For the sentencing hearing, then, Turner presented no mitigating evidence and no witnesses. Turner made only a few brief arguments on McCleskey's behalf. Thus, his entire sentencing case for his client, in what is often comparable to a trial in itself in most capital cases, merely resulted in a little more than four double-spaced pages of the trial transcript that exceeds one thousand pages.

Turner began his remarks by asking the jury to consider "the discriminatory application of the death penalty" because recently the state did not seek the death penalty against another defendant who murdered a police officer in Fulton County. Then, he spoke about deterrence and punishment, quoting the Bible's admonishment that "Thou shalt not kill." He argued that McCleskey was a human being, although he did not present any evidence to humanize his client. He concluded by talking about mercy, but he noted that the jurors might conclude that none of the robbers showed mercy in this case. Still, he claimed, the jurors could still show mercy. "Basically," he said, "at this stage of the case all I can do is plead to you."

Toward the end of his brief argument, Turner told the jurors that even if they gave McCleskey the death sentence, "the status of the law is such we don't know if they might change it tomorrow." The jurors might have heard those words as easing their conscience on a vote for death, believing the final responsibility for McCleskey's life rested elsewhere. Finally, Turner summed up his entire argument for why McCleskey should not be executed: "I ask you in the sake of humanity, in the sake of fair play, and for mercy to give Mr. McCleskey his life."[22]

After the sentencing hearing, the jury was out for only two hours before reaching a verdict. During deliberations, a number of the jurors struggled to find a reason to avoid a death sentence and sentence McCleskey to life in prison. Some jurors felt that the defense attorney did not do as good of a job as the prosecutor. So the jurors believed they were not given any reasons not to impose a death sentence. One juror, who had come from a broken home, wondered about McCleskey's background: "But no one in this case gave us any real reason to vote for life."[23]

When the jurors returned to the courtroom that night at 8:16 pm, they gave McCleskey two consecutive natural life sentences for the two counts of armed robbery and the death penalty for malice murder.[24] The jury found both aggravating circumstances. In light of the fact that the jury had already found McCleskey guilty of the crime that included the two aggravating factors and the fact that McCleskey's attorney presented no mitigating evidence and gave such little argument for life, the death sentence was not surprising.

In Judge McKenzie's sentencing order, he required officials to return McCleskey to jail and then to take him to the Georgia State Prison in Tattnall County. Although everyone knew the appeals court would grant a stay, Judge McKenzie set the first execution date for McCleskey in about a month. He ordered McCleskey to be executed by electrocution on November 17, 1978, adding the traditional execution order closing line, "AND MAY GOD HAVE MERCY ON HIS SOUL."[25]

After the jury and judge announced the death sentence, Turner was disappointed but believed the result helped vindicate his pretrial prediction. He asked McCleskey if he now wished he would have sought a plea deal. Despite the loss, Turner continued to work on the case for his client, filing an unsuccessful Motion for a New Trial on November 9, and later a Notice of Appeal. As is normal for criminal cases, eventually Turner would turn the case over to other attorneys. Not long after leaving McCleskey's case, Turner switched from doing defense work back to being a prosecutor, and he went to work as a trial attorney in the Fulton County District Attorney's Office.[26]

Meanwhile, in a separate trial, the state tried Depree and Burney together, and each received three life sentences for armed robbery and murder. Wright, the mastermind behind the robbery who testified against McCleskey, separately received a twenty-year sentence for armed robbery.

Those close to McCleskey believed he was innocent of the murder. His sister, Betty Myers, did not believe he would have shot the officer: "He is not the type of person that would do such a thing." McCleskey's ex-wife Gwen Sharpe also believed he could not have killed the officer: "Warren has always been a quiet, easy-going person, not the violent type at all."[27]

As the Dixie Furniture Company robbery cases came to a close, the convictions and death sentence for McCleskey made it appear there was some finality for Officer

Schlatt's family as well as for the families of the convicted men. But many of the cases would go through the courts for years. Because McCleskey received a death sentence, his case was guaranteed to continue for a long period. During that time, Officer Schlatt's family and McCleskey's family would repeatedly wonder when the case would show up in the news again and whether or not each new execution date would lead to McCleskey's death.

* * *

McCleskey returned to prison again, although unlike his previous stint, this time he went to death row. The judges, the lawyers, the jurors, Officer Schlatt's family, and Warren McCleskey himself likely did not know where the journey would end or whether or not he would eventually be executed. They had no idea how this typical murder case would eventually yield two important Supreme Court decisions and play a major role in the history of the American death penalty. For McCleskey, he had to focus on the immediate situation of returning to prison and adapting to a new environment on death row. (See Figure 2.1.)

Figure 2.1
Warren McCleskey being escorted back to his cell in Jackson, Georgia, 1983. (AP Photo/*Atlanta Journal-Constitution*)

Author Arthur Koestler in his book *Dialogue with Death* described the transition one makes to prison:

> Guilty or innocent, the prisoner changes form and colour, and assumes the mould that most easily enables him to secure a maximum of those minimal advantages possible within the framework of the prison system. In the world outside, now faded to a dream, the struggle is waged for position, prestige, power, women. For the prisoner these are heroic battles of Olympian demi-gods. Here inside the prison walls the struggle is waged for a cigarette, for permission to exercise in the courtyard, for the possession of a pencil. It is a struggle for minimal and unworthy objects, but a struggle for existence like any other.[28]

At the age of thirty-two, Warren McCleskey entered the last home he would ever know. But many struggles still stood between him and the electric chair.

CHAPTER 3

Offie Evans and *McCleskey v. Zant*

After jurors sentenced Warren McCleskey to death, McCleskey's lawyers appealed his case and then sought post-conviction relief in the state and federal courts. McCleskey's attorneys raised two claims regarding the key trial witness Offie Evans: (1) that Evans hid from the jury the fact that he had been promised help with his case, and (2) that the police violated McCleskey's right to an attorney by asking Evans to get information from McCleskey.

OFFIE EVANS

After the jury sentenced Warren McCleskey to death in 1978, Officer Schlatt's widow told reporters outside the courtroom that the death sentence revealed that justice really exists. But it would be more than a decade before McCleskey's case ended, as his case went through direct appeal, state post-conviction review, and federal habeas corpus proceedings.

Through his appeals and post-conviction proceedings, defense attorneys raised a number of claims regarding the trial and sentencing. John Turner appealed McCleskey's case to the Georgia Supreme Court, raising issues on the trial record, and in January 1980, the Georgia Supreme Court affirmed McCleskey's conviction and death sentence.[1]

In December 19, 1980, McCleskey's new attorney, Robert H. Stroup, filed an "Extraordinary Motion for New Trial." The motion included an affidavit from a prisoner who claimed that while in jail, he heard Bernard Depree say he shot Officer Schlatt. Before the judge could rule on the motion, though, Stroup withdrew his claim, apparently because of Judge Sam Phillips McKenzie's explanation that he believed from past experience that the prisoner was "mentally unstable."[2]

Stroup had volunteered to represent McCleskey pro bono out of his belief that lawyers should do public service. Because Stroup's usual practice involved handling discrimination cases, not capital appeals, he consulted with lawyers with death penalty experience at the NAACP's Legal Defense Fund (LDF). Soon, a young LDF attorney named John Charles ("Jack") Boger began working on the case with Stroup.

In 1981, a state court rejected a number of claims the attorneys had raised in a state habeas corpus petition, including Stroup's argument that Turner provided McCleskey ineffective assistance of counsel at trial. Later that same year, Stroup filed a petition for writ of federal habeas corpus in a United States District Court, using a procedure that allows federal courts to review state criminal trials for federal constitutional violations.

McCleskey's post-conviction attorneys reasoned that no reliable evidence indicated McCleskey fired the gun during the robbery. Even though McCleskey told police he participated in the robbery, he never stated to them that he shot the officer. The little physical evidence relating to the killing centered on a pearl-handled pistol used in the robbery. One witness saw someone run from the store with a pearl-handled pistol. And Ben Wright and his girlfriend claimed McCleskey used a pearl-handled pistol that had the same bullet caliber as the one that killed Officer Schlatt.[3] Police, however, never found the pistol allegedly linking McCleskey to the crime.

Thus, the key testimony against McCleskey regarding his role in the killing consisted of two witnesses with motivation to implicate him. Codefendant Ben Wright had a deal that the prosecutor would recommend a twenty-year prison sentence in exchange for Wright's cooperation in the case against McCleskey. Wright testified McCleskey had a white-handled handgun that used bullets the same caliber as the one that killed the officer. Wright also testified that McCleskey confessed to killing the officer to him.[4] Possibly, Wright told the truth and McCleskey did confess. But Wright also had incentive to lie because if a prosecutor and the court believed McCleskey did the killing, it exonerated Wright from the killing. Additionally, for cooperating, his testimony would further cut down his punishment.

The other key witness regarding the killing was Offie Evans. After McCleskey's arrest, police held Evans for another crime at the Fulton County Jail in a cell next to McCleskey. Evans claimed that while they were neighbors, McCleskey boasted he had shot the officer and would have shot his way through a dozen officers in getting out of the store. At trial, the prosecutor used Evans to testify in rebuttal to McCleskey, who had testified that he was not involved in the robbery and that he did not talk about it to anyone in the cell next to him.

One might raise several possibilities regarding the truth about McCleskey and the crime. First, possibly McCleskey committed the murder, and he told his jail neighbor Evans—as well as his codefendants—that he did so. Second, it is possible Evans told the truth about what McCleskey said, but McCleskey did not commit the murder. Instead, McCleskey may have falsely bragged to another person in jail. He may have made an untrue boast for several reasons, including an attempt to find camaraderie with another inmate or to spread the word that other prisoners should not mess with him. A third possibility is that Evans lied or embellished what McCleskey said, so as to curry favor in his own case and because of his friendship with Ben Wright.[5]

Evans's motivation to lie became an issue in several claims raised by McCleskey's attorneys. On appeal in 1980, Turner argued that Evans's statements surprised the defense at trial because the prosecutor failed to reveal the police statements prior to trial. Turner argued that the prosecutor's failure to give him the statement violated *Brady v. Maryland*,[6] a Supreme Court case requiring prosecutors to turn over exculpatory evidence of innocence. A unanimous Georgia Supreme Court agreed that the prosecution withheld the evidence, but the court concluded that the statements were not exculpatory, and so *Brady* and the U.S. Constitution did not require the prosecution to turn them over.[7]

After the direct appeal, Stroup and Boger continued to investigate the circumstances surrounding Offie Evans and his testimony. It would be nearly a decade before they discovered that the prosecution had more information about Evans than they revealed at trial. In post-conviction proceedings, McCleskey's attorneys focused both on: (1) whether the jury was misled about whether Evans had a deal for his testimony, and therefore a motive to lie; and (2) whether police were involved in Evans's attempts to get a statement from McCleskey on their behalf in violation of McCleskey's Sixth Amendment right to an attorney.

THE PROMISE TO OFFIE EVANS

Regarding the first argument about the secret deal, McCleskey's attorneys claimed the State violated McCleskey's due process rights because the prosecutor did not disclose the agreement with Evans.[8] At trial, in response to questions from the prosecutor, Evans claimed that the prosecutor did not offer any help with his pending escape charges. In the following exchange, Evans claimed no deal existed.

Q: Have you asked me to try to fix it so you wouldn't get charged with escape?
A: No, sir.
Q: Have I told you I would try to fix it for you?
A: No sir. [9]

Evans also claimed the only reason he revealed what McCleskey told him was because a deputy overhead the two talking and asked him about it.[10]

In 1981, McCleskey's lawyers filed a petition for a writ of habeas corpus in the U.S. District Court for the Northern District of Georgia. In one of the claims, McCleskey's attorneys argued police had made promises to Offie Evans before his testimony, and the prosecutor failed to disclose that information to McCleskey's trial attorney in violation of *Giglio v. United States*.[11] In contrast to what the jurors heard at trial, Evans revealed at the hearing in federal court: "I wasn't promised nothing by the D.A. but the Detective told me that he would—he said he was going to do it himself, speak a word for me. That was what the Detective told me."

McCleskey's attorney then asked, "The Detective said he would speak a word for you?" and Evans responded, "Yeah." After McCleskey's trial, the prosecutor did contact federal authorities to tell them about Evans's cooperation, and the escape charges were dropped. But jurors at the trial did not know that a detective had promised to "speak a word" for Evans.[12]

Based on this new revelation, on February 4, 1984, U.S. District Court Judge J. Owen Forrester held that the prosecution violated *Giglio* in McCleskey's case.

Judge Forrester noted that undisclosed promises to witnesses do not always require reversal, but in McCleskey's case, Evans's testimony was key evidence tying McCleskey to the homicide in a case based on non-substantial circumstantial evidence. Forrester also concluded that Evans appeared to lie at the trial about the nature of his escape charge. Finally, he held that "[b]ecause disclosure of the promise of favorable treatment and correction of the other falsehoods in Evans' testimony could reasonably have affected the jury's verdict on the charge of malice murder, petitioner's conviction and sentence on that charge are unconstitutional."[13]

Later investigation revealed Judge Forrester correctly concluded that at least some of the jurors were swayed by Evans's testimony and would have voted differently had they known the full story about Offie Evans and his motivations. Years after the trial, jurors Robert F. Burnette and Jill Darmer asserted that they would not have condemned McCleskey to death had they known the truth about Offie Evans. In an affidavit, Darmer wrote that the new evidence that Evans had a motivation to lie because of his pending federal escape charges changed her view of the whole trial. She noted that had she had known about Evans and what the police told him, "I would never have voted to impose capital punishment." She added that her belief was strong that she would have been able to hold out against any other jurors to prevent the death penalty. Both Darmer and juror Burnette noted they did not trust Ben Wright's testimony, so the whole issue about the actual murder came down to Offie Evans and the information they did not have about his bias.[14]

On January 29, 1985, though, the U.S. Court of Appeals for the Eleventh Circuit reversed Judge Forrester's decision on the *Giglio* claim and affirmed McCleskey's conviction and sentence. The court reasoned that the detective's promise to "speak a word" for Evans was not the type of promise that would motivate a witness or affect his credibility, and therefore the nondisclosure of the promise did not affect McCleskey's due process rights. Further, the court concluded that even if there were a constitutional violation, it did not affect the outcome of the case and hence, it was a harmless error. The court believed that Evans's testimony was not that important to McCleskey's conviction.[15]

When McCleskey had heard in early 1984 that Judge Forrester overturned his murder conviction and death sentence, he was thrilled. But he was stunned when within a year the U.S. Court of Appeals for the Eleventh Circuit reversed Judge Forrester. McCleskey would feel the roller coaster of relief and despair with court decisions several times while on death row, but as time went on, he strived not to let such news affect him so much.[16]

POLICE ROLE IN THE OFFIE EVANS CONVERSATION

Although the *Giglio* claim about the State's failure to disclose Evans's motive for lying on the stand ultimately failed, McCleskey's attorneys continued to try to find more evidence about Evans. One question they investigated was why Evans tried to get a statement from McCleskey in the jail. They wondered if the police, in their attempts to find the person who killed another officer, used unconstitutional tactics.

McCleskey's attorneys claimed the police violated McCleskey's Sixth Amendment right to counsel when Evans, working with the police, obtained the statements while McCleskey was represented by a lawyer. This Sixth Amendment claim became the focus of a Supreme Court decision in McCleskey's case. Under the Court's decision in *Massiah v. United States*, if a defendant is represented by counsel, the State cannot get around that right by planting an informant in a cell next to a defendant to deliberately elicit incriminating statements from the defendant.[17] The *Massiah* case stressed the importance of the Sixth Amendment right to counsel by finding that once a defendant has invoked that right and criminal proceedings have begun, the State should not be able to go around that right by tricking the defendant in the absence of counsel.

In McCleskey's case, the timing of his claim became as important as the claim itself. McCleskey's lawyers first raised a *Massiah* Sixth Amendment issue in post-conviction proceedings in state court in 1981. But when they filed McCleskey's first federal habeas corpus petition in the U.S. District Court in December 1981 raising the *Giglio* claim and others, they did not raise the *Massiah* claim. At that time, state officials denied that they planted Evans in the cell to get information, so McCleskey's attorneys recognized that they did not have enough proof that Evans was working with police.[18]

Eventually, though, McCleskey's lawyers obtained more evidence about Offie Evans from an unlikely source. In 1987, Stroup asked a friend at the county attorney's office to look through the old case files one more time, and his friend discovered a written statement that Evans had made prior to McCleskey's trial. So, in June 1987, almost nine years after the trial, a prosecutor gave McCleskey's attorneys a twenty-one-page statement that Evans had made to the police on August 1, 1978. The statement included further evidence Evans may have been working with the police to get information from McCleskey. It also revealed more details about Evans's questioning of McCleskey that the trial prosecutor did not disclose while Evans testified at McCleskey's trial. The statement implied Evans had a special relationship with the police, because it revealed that state officials were around when Evans made a phone call for McCleskey to McCleskey's girlfriend.[19] The twenty-one-page statement confirmed Evans played an active role in his discussion with McCleskey, supporting the argument that he worked at the request of the authorities.[20]

Based on the discovery of the statement, McCleskey's attorneys immediately went back to the U.S. District Court for the Northern District of Georgia with a second habeas corpus petition, and Judge Forrester held a new hearing in August 1987. Prior to the hearing, McCleskey's attorneys also discovered a new witness. So, in addition to Offie Evans's statement, McCleskey's attorneys presented as their final witness Ulysses Worthy, a jailer who worked at the jail where McCleskey had been held in the summer of 1978.

The newly discovered evidence created a dramatic hearing. Judge Forrester found Worthy's testimony confused on some issues, but Worthy revealed that at some point someone asked permission to move Evans near McCleskey's cell. Worthy did not remember specifically who asked him to make the move, but he recalled that a deputy sheriff made the request after a meeting among Evans, Atlanta police homicide detectives, and an assistant Fulton County district attorney. This testimony implied that the State intentionally planted Evans near McCleskey as part of an effort to obtain statements from McCleskey in his lawyer's absence.

Everyone recognized the impact of Worthy's testimony. Judge Forrester told Worthy, "I think [McCleskey's] life hangs on your testimony."[21] At the end of the hearing, McCleskey's attorneys believed that Worthy's testimony had saved their client's life.[22]

So, after nine years, McCleskey's lawyers finally obtained a document from the State supporting their Sixth Amendment claim and also found a state employee to testify about what happened in the jail. It seemed as though they at last had evidence that supported what they had always suspected: officials worked with Offie Evans to get an incriminating statement from McCleskey, thereby violating McCleskey's constitutional right to counsel.

On December 23, 1987, McCleskey received a Christmas present. Judge Forrester for the second time on an issue connected to Offie Evans ruled in McCleskey's favor, this time finding a Sixth Amendment violation. Based on the Evans document and Worthy's testimony, the judge found jail authorities had in fact placed Evans next to McCleskey's cell "for the purpose of gathering incriminating information" and "Evans was probably coached in how to approach McCleskey and eavesdropped on McCleskey's conversations with others."[23]

The district court reversal gave McCleskey hope, but he remained on death row. Unlike a trial acquittal, the State can appeal decisions made later in the process. So, Georgia did appeal this decision to the United States Court of Appeals for the Eleventh Circuit.

After more than a year of enjoying the victory in the district court, McCleskey had his victory reversed in 1989. The grounds for the reversal were not based on a disagreement about whether the State had violated the Sixth Amendment. The Eleventh Circuit court based its decision on the way McCleskey's lawyers had handled the claim and based on procedural rules. The issue went from whether McCleskey's Sixth Amendment rights were violated to whether his attorneys had raised the issue at the right time.[24]

THE SIXTH AMENDMENT CLAIM GETS LOST IN A HABEAS CORPUS PROCEDURE ISSUE

Following the Eleventh Circuit decision, McCleskey's lawyers then filed a petition for a writ of certiorari asking the United States Supreme Court to review the issue. The Court granted the writ, meaning that they agreed to review the claim. But at this point, the issue was no longer about the merits of McCleskey's Sixth Amendment argument. The Supreme Court asked the parties to brief and argue a single procedural issue: "Must the State demonstrate that a claim was deliberately abandoned in an earlier petition for a writ of habeas corpus in order to establish that inclusion of that claim in a subsequent habeas petition constitutes abuse of the writ?"[25]

As McCleskey's LDF attorney Jack Boger and Georgia Senior Assistant Attorney General Mary Beth Westmoreland argued before the Supreme Court, the justices peppered the attorneys with questions about whether or not the twenty-one-page statement by Offie Evans really revealed anything new, about when McCleskey's attorneys asked for the statement, and about why the State had not turned over the statement earlier.[26] The Court's consideration of the case, however, would have little to do with the impact of the statement or the question of whether the State violated the Sixth Amendment. Instead, it would rely upon procedural rules surrounding the doctrine of habeas corpus.

Habeas corpus—the Great Writ—is a right that has a long history in English and American law, going back centuries. Alexander Hamilton wrote about the importance of the writ in the Federalist Papers, and the U.S. Constitution protects the right. One of the most important early U.S. Supreme Court decisions on habeas corpus involved Leo Frank, the man who was lynched in Marietta. In 1915 in *Frank v. Magnum*, the Supreme Court noted that federal courts have jurisdiction to hear habeas petitions in state cases where the state's procedures did not provide an effective remedy to protect federal constitutional rights.[27]

In death penalty cases that are prosecuted in state courts, habeas corpus creates an avenue that allows capital defendants to have their cases reviewed by the federal courts. In a typical capital case that starts in state court, a defendant convicted at trial may appeal the case to a state appellate court. Then, the defendant may seek state post-conviction review in the state courts, where the defendant may introduce new claims such as that the trial attorney failed to discover important evidence. Following that, through filing a petition for a writ of habeas corpus, the defendant may ask the federal courts—the U.S. District Court and then the U.S. Court of Appeals—to determine whether any of the issues raised in state courts were incorrectly decided on federal constitutional grounds.

Part of the reason for habeas corpus in this context is to allow the federal courts to have a say about how the federal constitution should be interpreted. At various stages the U.S. Supreme Court may review a case, but such review is rare. So, lower federal courts play an important role through habeas corpus. As the Supreme Court noted in *Harris v. Nelson*, the Great Writ of habeas corpus is "the fundamental instrument for safeguarding individual freedom against arbitrary and lawless state action."[28]

Because in federal habeas corpus review courts re-evaluate state court proceedings, the courts and Congress have created a number of procedural requirements for petitioners. One of these procedural requirements became the focus in the U.S. Supreme Court's decision in *McCleskey v. Zant*.[29]

The problem for McCleskey was that his attorneys did not raise the Sixth Amendment *Massiah* claim in his first federal habeas corpus petition filed in 1981 but instead raised it later in his second habeas corpus petition filed in 1987. As noted earlier, although the attorneys had raised the claim in state court proceedings, they dropped it from their first habeas corpus petition due to a lack of evidence. At that point, the State still denied that Evans had been part of a scheme to get a jailhouse confession from McCleskey. The defense attorneys then raised the claim in the second habeas petition filed in 1987, approximately one month after officials finally gave McCleskey's attorneys the document.

Thus, his attorneys' delay in raising the claim might be considered an "abuse of the writ," that is, an abuse of the writ of habeas corpus. Prior to the Supreme Court's decision in *McCleskey v. Zant*, the standard for determining whether a defendant may bring a new claim in a second habeas corpus petition was that a defendant could do so as long as he or she did not "deliberately abandon" the claim. The courts were concerned that for some strategy purpose, a defendant may withhold a claim intentionally with the plan to bring it later. So, when attorneys intentionally withhold claims, they waste the court's time. Under that standard, McCleskey's attorneys thought they had a good explanation that they did not intentionally delay raising the claim because they were waiting to get more evidence from the State.

In the decision in *McCleskey v. Zant* of April 16, 1991, though, the Supreme Court by a vote of 6-3 changed the legal standard for McCleskey, as well as for future petitioners in the federal courts. The Court reasoned in an opinion by Justice Anthony M. Kennedy that courts should strongly encourage petitioners to file every claim in a first habeas petition. Therefore petitioners generally are not allowed to bring claims in a second habeas petition. The Court admitted that its previous decisions regarding abuse of writ were not precise, so it used McCleskey's case to create a new standard.

Under this new standard, the federal courts could refuse to review claims in a second habeas corpus petition even if the petitioner did not deliberately try to manipulate the process. Thus, in order for a habeas corpus petitioner to have a federal court consider a new claim in a second or subsequent habeas corpus petition, the petitioner must show cause for failing to raise the claim earlier and that the petitioner was prejudiced from the failure. Alternatively, a petitioner could have claims heard by showing a fundamental miscarriage of justice would result if the court does not hear the claim.

Justice Kennedy justified this new strict standard on several grounds. He stressed a strong interest in "finality" of criminal judgments, meaning that capital cases should not continue indefinitely. Allowing long litigation of capital cases would impugn the dignity of the courts, and the courts should be able to use their limited resources efficiently.[30]

The Court's new standard now ruined McCleskey's chances for relief. Under the standard in effect at the time his attorneys filed both his first and his second habeas petition, he had a very strong argument that the federal courts should hear his Sixth Amendment claim. Additionally, the only federal court that addressed the merits of his Sixth Amendment claim had held he should get a new trial. But under the new standard, the Supreme Court refused to even consider the merits of his Sixth Amendment claim.

The Court reasoned McCleskey could not meet the new high standard and could not show "cause and prejudice" for not raising the claim earlier. The Court concluded McCleskey's attorneys were on notice to raise the Sixth Amendment *Massiah* claim long before they received the twenty-one-page document from the State in 1987. The Court reasoned McCleskey and his attorneys knew that Evans resided in a cell next to him, that he claimed to be a relative of Ben Wright, and that he testified against McCleskey. Therefore, they should have brought the claim in the first habeas petition in 1981 even without the twenty-one-page document they obtained in 1987.

Finally, Kennedy noted that McCleskey's attorneys had not yet found the jailer Worthy before they raised the claim in the second petition. So the only justification McCleskey's attorneys had for raising the claim in the second petition was the twenty-one-page document, which merely verified evidence that McCleskey already knew. Thus, because McCleskey's attorneys could not show cause for failing to raise the claim in his first petition, the Court did not even address whether the failure to raise the claim prejudiced McCleskey.[31]

Three justices dissented from the decision rejecting McCleskey's claims. Justice Thurgood Marshall, in an opinion joined by Justices Harry Blackmun and John Paul Stevens, argued the Court changed from a good faith standard for successive petitions without justification. He disagreed with the majority's conclusion that the new standard strikes the proper balance between allowing petitioners to bring habeas corpus claims and the goals of finality and respecting state decisions.

Aside from the merits of the competing standards for future cases, Marshall claimed the Court's ruling created a manifest injustice for Warren McCleskey by applying a new standard to him retroactively. McCleskey's attorneys did not even get the chance to argue the abuse of the writ issue because it did not arise in the lower courts. Marshall noted that it was unclear through briefing and oral argument that the Court was considering this new standard. In fact, Georgia did not even argue for the "cause and prejudice" standard in briefing or in oral argument. So, in effect, the majority adopted a new rule that applied to McCleskey's detriment without giving his attorneys the chance to thoroughly address the new standard.

But what made the change even more egregious in McCleskey's case was that when his attorney filed the first habeas corpus petition, the standard for bringing a second habeas corpus petition was the "good faith" standard. So, at that time of his first petition, his attorneys believed that as long as they acted in good faith, any additional claims could be brought later in a successive habeas corpus petition. Had the attorneys known that the standard for bringing new claims would be a much more difficult hurdle, the attorneys would have had an incentive to bring all of the claims in the first petition in 1981.

The Court created a further injustice to McCleskey, according to Marshall, by holding that his attorneys raised the Sixth Amendment claim too late, when the State had withheld the twenty-one-page statement. When the jury heard and weighed Evans's testimony, Evans claimed he had no deals with the prosecution. Jurors also did not know he was planted in the cell to get a statement from McCleskey.[32] Justice Marshall asserted the delay in raising the claim was the State's fault, not McCleskey's. He recounted that "the State affirmatively misled McCleskey and his counsel throughout their unsuccessful pursuit of the *Massiah* claim" through the state court proceedings and through the first federal habeas proceedings.[33] McCleskey's attorneys interviewed or deposed the assistant district attorney, jailers, and other government officials, and they all denied knowing the State and Evans had a deal.

Although the majority concluded McCleskey still could have found Worthy prior to the first habeas petition, Marshall responded that McCleskey's attorneys had little motivation to continue talking to other jailers when everyone on the State's side had already denied a deal existed. Marshall concluded, "The sum and substance of the majority's analysis is that McCleskey had no 'cause' for failing to assert the *Massiah* claim because he did not try hard enough to pierce the State's veil of deception."[34]

Justice Marshall had used even stronger language in an earlier draft of his *McCleskey v. Zant* dissent, calling the majority's opinion "lawless." Upon seeing the draft, Justice Stevens, who planned to join Marshall's opinion, asked Marshall to consider removing the word. He said he would join the opinion either way, but he appealed to a sense of logic: "Even though I agree that the majority's opinion is outrageous, I wonder if the word 'lawless' is not too strong in the first sentence of your opinion. After all, when five members of the Court agree on a proposition, it does become the law." Marshall wrote back to Stevens, "I took out the word 'lawless' within a minute after receiving your note." And then the majority decision became law, and McCleskey became another step closer to Georgia's electric chair.[35]

A few days after the Supreme Court's decision in *McCleskey v. Zant*, an editorial in the *Atlanta Constitution* stressed that at the time of the first habeas petition, McCleskey's attorneys did not know Offie Evans had been a government plant. The paper argued the decision "makes a mockery of the judicial process by encouraging the prosecution to play dirty."[36]

Meanwhile, lawyers debated how the Supreme Court's decision in *McCleskey v. Zant* might affect other death row inmates. Defense attorneys predicted the case would result in an increase in executions. Georgia Attorney General Michael J. Bowers, a proponent of the death penalty, predicted, "The ruling in the McCleskey case...will cut years off the appeals of several death-row inmates."[37]

The Supreme Court's decision holding that McCleskey lost because his attorneys should have raised the *Massiah* claim earlier surprised McCleskey and his attorneys. McCleskey wrote to a friend and religious adviser: "The decision no doubt was very disappointing because we had hope of a favorable decision. Nevertheless my trust and faith in God remained unbroken."[38] But he also knew his time was running out.

Thus, almost thirteen years after a jury sentenced McCleskey to death, the Supreme Court's decision in *McCleskey v. Zant* essentially brought his case to an end. In 1991, Warren McCleskey began preparing for his death. His case had been heard by several judges, and the decision was actually the second time his case had gone to the U.S. Supreme Court. As he got closer to the electric chair he began receiving more attention from the media. The media focused on McCleskey not for *McCleskey v. Zant*, but for the earlier Supreme Court case and how his case had affected the history of the American death penalty. To understand how his case altered the future of the American death penalty, though, one first must visit the past.

American Death Penalty History and the Courts

CHAPTER 4

The First Limits: The Early American Death Penalty through the 1850s

The foundation for Warren McCleskey's execution began in the early years of America's history. A jury was able to sentence McCleskey to death because the United States evolved into one of the countries that maintained the death penalty through the twentieth century, and because Georgia became one of the states to retain the death penalty.

THEMES AND TRENDS IN AMERICAN HISTORY

When the Georgia jurors condemned Warren McCleskey to death, their vote added to the lengthy history of the death penalty in America. Long before the United States became a country, humans struggled to resolve how a society should deal with horrible crimes such as the killing of Officer Schlatt. Although the crime of murder is recognized as morally wrong throughout the world, the official government responses to crimes have changed over time. In the relatively short history of the United States, government responses to murder as well as other crimes have varied by jurisdiction through different time periods. Yet, one may see several themes and trends across the history of the American death penalty.

One trend is that the popularity of capital punishment fluctuates through history, with support and opposition affected by various factors. While the popularity of capital punishment varies across the country, some periods of U.S. history have been abolitionist, with states eliminating capital punishment, while other periods have seen a number of states reinstate capital punishment. Occasionally, abolitions and reinstatements have overlapped, such as during 1872–1887. Yet, one may identify significant periods of death penalty abolition in U.S. history roughly during 1846–1853, 1907–1917, 1957–1965, and the early twenty-first century starting in 2005. By contrast, the two most active periods of reinstatement occurred roughly around 1916–1920 and around 1972–1979 after the Supreme Court struck down existing death penalty statutes. Less active reinstatement periods occurred during 1935–1939 and 1994–1995.

Various factors contributed to the successful abolitions, but many of the abolition periods have similarities. For example, in many instances during these periods, governors were at the forefront of leading the call for abolition. Yet, throughout history, some politicians made decisions about the death penalty based on their perceptions of how the issue would affect their chances for election.

Specific cases affected the popularity of the death penalty through history. Concerns about executing the innocent can make the death penalty less popular while an especially egregious crime may have the opposite effect. As James Cristoph, writing about Great Britain's death penalty, noted: "The cause of abolition, for example, might be advanced by a series of murder cases in which it is suspected that an innocent person has been hanged; or it might be setback by one or more particularly heinous murders that arouse fears and disgust in the community."[1] This statement is equally true in the United States. Interestingly, rare and unusual cases often frame the death penalty debate while the majority of average cases have little effect on the policy discussion.

Although no one single event dictates the popularity of the death penalty, some historians have noted that opposition to the death penalty often drops during periods of war. When soldiers are dying on the battlefield, society members care less about the lives of criminals. Even though the carnage of war has often weakened the public's outrage against capital punishment, some of the greatest death penalty abolition periods have coincided roughly with American involvement in unpopular wars. One possible explanation is that unpopular wars motivate some in the public to take action on social issues. So, abolition movements showed some success during the early years of the Vietnam War, during the Iraq War, and during a period around World War I. The wars, of course, do not dictate the abolition movements, but wars and other large events affect society and people's views on social issues. Similarly, economic hard times and other societal events may result in less concern for convicted criminals.

Besides the trend of the fluctuating popularity of capital punishment, a second continuing historical shift is that the main setting for debate about death penalty laws changes over time. Throughout American history up until the 1960s, the most effective discussion about death penalty abolition occurred among legislators, governors, and the general population. But for a period starting in the 1960s through the 1970s, and to some extent continuing through Warren McCleskey's first trip to the U.S. Supreme Court, the courts became the main venue of the abolition issue.

A third death penalty trend is that states have changed the way they execute criminals. Starting in the 1830s, states moved away from public executions to private executions. Similarly, all states have changed their primary methods of execution, moving toward methods that appear to be more "humane."

A fourth trend is that over time, states have limited the number of capital crimes. While initially jurisdictions imposed the death penalty for a long list of crimes, American society gradually narrowed down that list.

Finally, a fifth trend is that states changed their procedures for sentencing defendants to death. Most jurisdictions initially had mandatory death sentences for certain crimes. Then, for various reasons, they changed to giving jurors complete discretion in imposing the sentence. Last, they changed to the system in place today where jurors are given instructions to guide their discretion in deciding whether or not to impose a death sentence. The role of those procedures and state's attempts to eliminate arbitrariness in their capital sentencing systems would come to a head when Warren McCleskey's case went to the U.S. Supreme Court in 1987.

The following chapters in this Part consider these trends and how the American death penalty has changed over time. This history provides the setting for how Warren McCleskey's case became a turning point in death penalty history.

COLONIZATION THROUGH THE AMERICAN REVOLUTION

The discovery and settling of the North American continent occurred during a time when most nations in the world used the death penalty. Many countries had a long history of executions through various methods for a large range of crimes. The original settlers, largely from Europe, brought with them a large part of this history.

The North American landscape at the time, of course, was not devoid of people. When the new settlers arrived, North America had "more than 700 separate cultural units with deep-rooted civilizations," made up of at least 8–12 million Native Americans, and some scholars suggest the number is much higher.[2] Their ways of life and own complex systems differed from the European legal systems and were largely ignored by new settlers who wished to take the land for themselves. So, these native systems, including some tribal laws that allowed for something comparable to the death penalty, were swept away by the new residents. Thus, foreign countries, including Great Britain, ultimately provided the foundation for what would evolve into the modern American death penalty.

Executions by settlers in the New World began almost as soon as they arrived on the continent. Within a year after settling in Jamestown in 1607, citizens of the colony of Virginia executed Captain George Kendall, one of the original councilors for the colony, for mutiny. At one time or another, almost all of the leaders of Jamestown were accused of mutiny, but the settlement executed only Kendall. The evidence supporting his execution was questionable. The witness against Kendall, a blacksmith named James Read, had himself earlier been sentenced to death for fighting with an official. After Read climbed the ladder to be hanged, he announced he had information for the colony's leader. Then, he made a deal to testify against Kendall in exchange for a pardon.

Scholars do not know many details about Kendall's life, but he was a man of some standing. Although the settlers had planned to hang the blacksmith, they executed Kendall using the more prestigious method of shooting him. Thus, in 1608 Kendall became the first Englishman tried by jury and condemned to death on the land that would become the United States.[3] As in McCleskey's case, the first settler executed on American soil went to his death largely based upon the testimony of someone else accused of a crime.

North of Virginia, the Pilgrims hanged John Billingham, one of the signers of the Mayflower Compact, on September 30, 1630, for murder. Before the hanging, though, the settlers had to first determine they had the authority to inflict capital punishment. The Massachusetts Bay Colony executed the first woman among the new settlers when in 1638 it hanged the mentally ill Dorothy Talby for killing her daughter.[4]

The settlers used capital punishment on the land's natives too. The first legally sanctioned execution of a Native American occurred in 1639, when the military beheaded a Pequot Indian named Nepauduck for the murder of a white man named Abraham Finch. In 1711, the first Native American woman to be executed under the laws of the white settlers, Waisoiusksquaw, was hanged in Connecticut for killing her husband.[5] The first legal execution in the colony of North Carolina occurred on August 26, 1726, when the colony hanged the Native American George Sennecca for murder.[6]

Although the settlers, like modern day states, mostly executed men, they sometimes used the noose on women. One of the most famous early executions took place in Salem, Massachusetts, in 1691–1692 when fourteen women and five men were hanged for being "witches." Another man, Giles Corey, was pressed to death under heavy stones in an attempt to get him to plea. Colonial Georgia had its first execution in 1735. That year, officials hanged Alice Ryley, who came to the colonies on an Irish transport ship, for the murder of her master, William Wise.[7]

During these years, the number of capital crimes was much greater than today. The first settlers did not have codified criminal laws, so the first written laws defining capital offenses by the settlers in the New World were the Capital Lawes of New-England, written in 1636 for the Massachusetts Bay Colony. The laws made several crimes punishable by death: witchcraft, idoltry, murder, blasphemy, assault in sudden anger, buggery, sodomy, adultery, rape, statutory rape, man-stealing, perjury in a death penalty case, and rebellion. The document cited a provision of the Old Testament as a source to justify capital punishment.[8]

People in other parts of the continent incorporated practices from their countries of origin. For example, when the Dutch controlled New York, the state used a broad death penalty. In some cases if the court could not determine the guilty party for a crime, men drew lots to resolve who would be executed. The British brought more organized capital punishment procedures when they took control of New York. During that time, New York continued to have a broad range of capital crimes, and a number of people were burned at the stake, but officials also often pardoned people who promised to leave the colony or enlist in the army.[9]

Although all Thirteen Colonies had the death penalty, some settlements opposed the English Crown's wishes for more capital crimes by enacting few such crimes.[10] The Colonies had considerably less capital crimes than the more than 200 capital crimes in England, but the Colonies maintained the death penalty for a range of crimes, including murder, robbery, treason, piracy, arson, rape, aiding runaway slaves, horse stealing, sodomy, and burglary. On average, colonies each had around twelve capital crimes, with one of the reasons for the lesser number than England being a need for more laborers in the New World.[11]

From early on, some early settlers expressed concerns about capital punishment. South Jersey, in its Quaker-influenced Royal Charter, banned executions, and William Penn's 1682 "Great Law" of the Colony of Pennsylvania limited capital punishment to murder and treason.[12] One may understand the Quaker opposition to capital punishment in light of the Puritan practice of punishing and hanging Quakers in the 1600s.

Many of the leaders who participated in the American Revolution used the new freedoms and philosophies to question the right of government to take life. Thomas Paine argued for the abolition of capital punishment. On one occasion, after a person assaulted Paine in a crime that could have been punished by death, Paine helped his attacker avoid prosecution and the death penalty by aiding him to leave the country. Later, Paine tried to persuade the French to not use capital punishment during the French Revolution.

Dr. Benjamin Rush, a signer of the Declaration of Independence in 1776, became one of the most vocal early American death penalty opponents. Dr. Rush described the death penalty as "an improper punishment for *any* crime" in his famous 1787 treatise, *An Enquiry into the Effects of Public Punishments upon Criminals and upon Society*, which he first delivered as a speech at Benjamin Franklin's home. Among various arguments, he asserted capital punishment had no place in a republic because the practice was a product of monarchical governments and the belief of the divine right of kings. In 1794, largely due to the efforts of Dr. Rush and Pennsylvania's attorney general William Bradford, Pennsylvania limited the death penalty to first-degree murder crimes. Other states followed with similar reforms of their own death penalty laws.[13]

Other leaders from the American Revolution era—such as James Madison, Benjamin Franklin, and John Jay—favored reform of death penalty laws, if not outright abolition. James Wilson, one of only six men to sign both the Constitution and the Declaration of Independence, often expressed concerns about capital punishment in his writings. John Hancock as Massachusetts governor argued for an end of the death penalty for burglary.[14] New York governor John Jay and Virginia governor Patrick Henry worked to limit the death penalty to fewer crimes. Benjamin Franklin made one of the most famous American quips about capital punishment when, as the Continental Congress discussed independence, he warned that the men must hang together or they would hang separately.

In the 1770s, Thomas Jefferson wrote a bill for Virginia that would have limited the death penalty to be used only as a punishment for murder and treason. As a member of the House of Delegates, James Madison led attempts to pass Jefferson's bill, "Proportioning Crimes and Punishments in Cases Heretofore Capital," which advocated for various degrees of punishment and was inspired by the Enlightenment. Jefferson based the bill on the equal retaliation doctrine of lex talionis and also included punishments such as castration for rapists and poisoning for murderers who used poison. Although the Virginia bill failed by one vote to pass in 1785, legislators passed a similar bill in Pennsylvania.[15]

One challenge for Jefferson and other early reformers was the question of how to revise criminal law and penal policy. If they were to eliminate the death penalty, they had to figure out a substitute punishment. At the time, county jails were inadequate for dealing with criminals, so officials usually addressed crime by death, mutilation, and fines.[16] Through the middle of the 1700s society generally dealt with criminal offenders by using the death penalty and forms of corporal punishment. By the late 1700s and the early 1800s, though, Western Europe's Enlightenment period helped change views about crime in the Colonies. Criminals were no longer seen as possessed by evil demons, meaning that officials saw the possibility an offender could reform. Thus, the use of prisons began to grow because they punished criminals and protected society in what society saw as a more humane way than capital or corporal punishments, allowing prisoners to reflect on their deeds.

Some ideas for alternatives eventually came from changes in Pennsylvania, including that state's experiment with using a penitentiary as a form of punishment.[17] These developments set the stage for the rest of the history of the death penalty in America, as Americans continued to use capital punishment but increasingly reserved it for the most serious crimes.[18]

While the ideas of the American Revolution inspired Dr. Rush and others to oppose the death penalty, some still saw a need for capital punishment to maintain order. During the first years after the Revolution ended in 1783, society was in turmoil as many wondered whether the new country would survive. Executions were a means to preserve order in a society in flux during a time that featured threats to stability, as in the case of 1786's Shays' Rebellion. For example, in 1799, future president James Monroe was governor of Virginia when the state executed a number of slaves for participating in an uprising led by a twenty-four-year-old blacksmith slave named Gabriel. After consulting with his friend Jefferson by letter, Governor Monroe recommended leniency for many of the accused slaves, but ultimately twenty-six men, including Gabriel, were hanged for participating in the conspiracy.[19]

As part of this ritual to preserve order, at public executions, pastors spoke to the crowds, warning the audience to obey their government and avoid vice. The tradition of using public executions for preaching went back to the early settlers, such as when Cotton Mather wrote in his diary in 1681 of his excitement at being able to preach at a hanging, which guaranteed a large crowd.[20]

During the early years after America won the War of Independence, lawmakers did not spend a lot of time on the death penalty. During the 1787 Constitutional Convention, the men in Philadelphia briefly discussed the death penalty, largely in the context of the punishment to be listed in the Bankruptcy Clause and the Treason Clause. When the Convention adopted the Bankruptcy Clause on September 3, 1787, the only vote against it came from Connecticut's Roger Sherman. He worried that the provision allowing Congress to establish bankruptcy laws might lead to following England's practice of punishing some bankruptcies with capital punishment.

In an important decision for death penalty jurisprudence, several years later, the Bill of Rights was added to the U.S. Constitution, including language prohibiting "cruel and unusual punishments." The concept of regulating punishments went back far in history, but this language of the Eighth Amendment derived from the English Bill of Rights of 1689, which had been incorporated in Virginia's

Declaration of Rights in 1776. Similarly, on July 13, 1787, the Continental Congress in New York City had passed the Northwest Ordinance as a law governing the territory northwest of the Ohio River. This law included a provision directed at punishments, including the language, "no cruel or unusual punishments shall be inflicted." The Northwest Ordinance's prohibition of "cruel or unusual punishments" was arguably broader than the language of Virginia's Declaration of Rights that barred "cruel and unusual punishments." But it would be the conjunctive version of "cruel and unusual punishments" adopted in the Eighth Amendment in the U.S. Constitution in 1791. Although later courts would focus on the "and" versus "or" language in the Constitution, many scholars believe the authors of the amendment gave little consideration to differences in meaning.[21]

Because Americans used the death penalty widely in the eighteenth century, most citizens did not view capital punishment as cruel or as unusual. There were criminal justice reforms in the late 1700s, including Philadelphia's opening of the Walnut Street Jail. But states continued using the death penalty even as they eliminated whipping, branding, and other physical punishments. Thus, when the country added the Bill of Rights to the U.S. Constitution in 1791, the Fifth Amendment included a reference to capital punishment in providing due process and indictment rights: "No person shall be held to answer for a capital, or otherwise infamous crime, unless on a presentment or indictment of a Grand Jury, except in cases arising in the land or naval forces, or in the Militia, when in actual service in time of War or public danger." Further, the amendment stated "nor shall any person be subject to the same offence to be twice put in jeopardy of life or limb . . . nor be deprived of life, liberty, or property without due process of law."[22]

Although George Washington generally thought the death penalty should only be used as a last resort,[23] during his first term as president of the United States, the First U.S. Congress in April 1790 passed a federal death penalty law allowing prosecutions for some capital crimes in federal court. The new law created a mandatory death penalty for murder, treason, piracy, forgery, and rescuing someone convicted of a capital offense. During the next thirty-six years, 138 defendants were tried for federal capital offenses, resulting in twenty-four executions.[24]

The federal government also employed executions to deter soldiers from deserting the military. The government generally used this punishment more frequently if a war became less popular over time. For example, as the War of 1812 dragged on, the use of the military death penalty increased. The Army shot thirty-two deserters in 1813 but then shot 146 deserters in 1814.[25]

Most executions, though, were under the jurisdiction of the individual states instead of under federal law. In the late eighteenth century, states often used the death penalty for serious offenses.[26] By the end of the eighteenth century, there had been more than 1,500 executions in America.[27] Most of these executions, per capita, were taking place in the southern states rather than in the northern states.

By the time the Eighth Amendment took effect in 1791, Georgia had fifteen executions. Between the first recorded execution in 1608 and 1791, most of the other colonies had more executions than Georgia, including Connecticut (25), Maryland (58), Massachusetts (193), New Jersey (80), New York (183), North Carolina (127),

Pennsylvania (192), Rhode Island (47), South Carolina (91), and Virginia (297). By contrast, Delaware had only ten executions and New Hampshire only five.

Generally, in the southern states, slaves were executed at a much higher rate than whites.[28] In both the North and the South the condemned were disproportionately African American, setting the precedent for the new country's use of capital punishment mainly for society's outsiders. Thus, as the eighteenth century came to an end, many in the new country saw capital punishment as a way to maintain order as they faced a questionable future.

A NEW NATION BEGINS A PERIOD OF CAPITAL PUNISHMENT REFORM IN THE NINETEENTH CENTURY

The years after the War of 1812 in the nineteenth century brought a number of changes to the American death penalty. Toward the middle of this century, the first U.S. states abolished the death penalty. Also, with a growing number of prisons, states began limiting the use of capital punishment while also moving away from public executions. During this time, states also began to think about developing fairer procedures for imposing capital punishment.

As the country expanded west in the nineteenth century, executions were one way to enforce order on the frontier, and some executions took place under territorial governments. Judge Isaac Parker became known as a "hanging judge" for the way he handed out death sentences as part of frontier justice while he was a U.S. District Court Judge for the Western District of Arkansas presiding over a large area that included the future state of Oklahoma. Also, as members of the Church of Latter-day Saints settled in what is now Utah, the territorial legislature in 1852 passed a criminal code permitting capital punishment. The new code adopted provisions passed a year earlier by the General Assembly of the State of Deseret, a failed attempt to get the U.S. government to approve a state that included large parts of modern-day Utah, Nevada, California, and Arizona along with other western states. The State of Deseret's capital punishment statute provided for execution "by being shot, hung, or beheaded." Although Utah initially included the beheading option, the state never employed that method. After Utah became a state in 1896, the firing squad became the state's main method of execution for more than a century.[29]

While western states were expanding the country's jurisdictions with capital punishment, efforts by death penalty opponents began to pay off when several movements to abolish the death penalty arose. By 1850, national and state organizations were formed to abolish the death penalty, including ones in New York, Pennsylvania, Tennessee, Ohio, Alabama, Louisiana, Indiana, and Iowa. The organizations participated in various activities, including circulating petitions, raising funds, lobbying state legislators, and writing editorials.

One success for reformers occurred when the Maine Legislature passed a procedural law slowing down the death penalty process. The 1837 Maine law, which resulted from a state legislative report in 1836, prevented the governor from issuing a warrant of execution until at least one year had passed since the defendant's sentencing. The required delay limited executive power and prevented executions taking place while emotions were high, resulting in fewer executions. And, as the law required the governor to affirmatively act after that delay to issue the warrant of execution, there were no executions in the state for decades. Other New England states copied the Maine law, which also encouraged some states to consider abolishing capital punishment.[30]

In the mid-nineteenth century, three states became the first ones to abolish the death penalty. Michigan had limited capital punishment crimes in 1820 and basically had halted use of the punishment since 1830. Then, in 1846, the Michigan Senate voted 9-2 and the House voted 21-14 to eliminate the death penalty for all crimes except treason. After Governor Alpheus Felch signed the bill, the new law went into effect the following year in March 1847. Michigan thus became the first state to abolish capital punishment for murder. The abolition stood, even though the legislature considered re-enacting the death penalty within a few years and throughout the next decade. Every time a new egregious murder occurred there, proponents of the death penalty cited the need for the punishment to stem the crimes. But state legislators steadfastly refused to reinstate the death penalty.[31]

Scholars do not know why Michigan, which joined the United States as a state in 1838, became the first state to abolish the death penalty. Prior to Michigan's abolition, other eastern states—such as New York, Massachusetts, and Pennsylvania—had come close to abolition. Professor David G. Chardavoyne, author of *A Hanging in Detroit*, notes that the 1846 Michigan Legislature featured men who had left their homes in the East for the frontier. These adventurous men, he reasons, may have been more likely to be opposed to capital punishment.[32] Yet, the efforts to abolish the death penalty in Michigan were not especially unusual.

After the Michigan death penalty abolition and not long after the controversial U.S. Mexican War (1846–1848), Rhode Island abolished the death penalty in 1852, having previously limited the death penalty to murder and arson in 1844. The year after Rhode Island's 1852 abolition, Wisconsin governor Leonard J. Farwell signed a bill on July 10, 1853 that abolished the death penalty for all crimes—an abolition still in effect today.[33]

A number of changes affected the American death penalty in the early and middle nineteenth century. Social reform movements during this period, including efforts at prison reform, questioned the law and the power of the state. In the first forty years of the 1800s, an influx of immigrants contributed to a number of social and political changes. The 1850s saw a religious revival and the start of the Third Great Awakening in U.S. history, with this revival often connecting faith to social issues. Reformers also worked against superstitious beliefs, poverty, slavery, and the subjugation of women, with the various efforts overlapping. A large number of women worked to abolish the death penalty, and a number of people worked against both the death penalty and slavery. For example, the antislavery activist Frederick Douglass opposed the death penalty. And in the years leading up to the Civil War, slavery abolitionists Wendell Phillips, Theodore Parker, and William Lloyd Garrison also worked against capital punishment as well as for other social causes.[34]

In the nineteenth century, simultaneously with attempts to abolish capital punishment completely, prison reformers also worked to limit the use of the death penalty in jurisdictions that retained the punishment. States continued to limit the number of crimes for which one could receive the death penalty, generally narrowing the offenses to those such as murder, rape, and treason.

Another area of debate in the early 1800s centered on public executions. Many citizens criticized the spectacle of public executions, such as New York's 1827 execution of Jesse Strang in Albany. Between thirty and forty thousand people attended the execution of Strang, who the state had convicted of killing his lover's husband. Other executions sometimes were so chaotic that people in the crowd were injured or killed.

The display at public executions turned some people against capital punishment. The Wisconsin abolition largely resulted out of disgust at a celebratory crowd at the public hanging of John McCaffary in 1851. Michigan's final execution under state law occurred when the state hanged Stephen G. Simmons on September 24, 1830, before a crowd of 1,200–2,000 people. Simmons, a tavern owner who was convicted of killing his wife while he was drunk, addressed the crowd about the evils of alcohol and about his remorse for killing his wife. He then asked the crowd to sing a hymn with him. According to some reports, the act of witnessing the hanging turned the large crowd into a mob that marched through the streets of Detroit and tore down the whipping post, throwing it into the Detroit River.[35]

Other states did not abolish capital punishment but instead eliminated public executions and put hangings behind prison walls, as Pennsylvania did in 1834 and New York in 1835. The transformation to private executions took longer in other states. Although North Carolina revised its state constitution in 1868 to stipulate executions must take place in private behind the walls of a state penitentiary, the state continued to execute prisoners in public until around the turn of the century.[36]

Around the same time states were moving executions out of the public, the English also were debating whether to continue with public executions. Charles Dickens and others advocated against public executions there. In an 1849 letter to the *London Times*, he wrote how watching a public hanging made his "blood run cold": "Fightings, fainting, whistling, imitations of Punch, brutal jokes, tumultuous demonstrations of indecent delight when swooning women were dragged out of the crowd with their dresses disordered, gave a new zest to the entertainment."[37]

Many opponents of capital punishment believed the shift to private executions would eventually lead to the abolition of the death penalty. By the 1840s, however, they realized they had been mistaken, as they discovered that the privatization of executions and the elimination of spectacle removed one of their arguments against the punishment.[38] And, around this time social reformers also became overwhelmed with issues besides capital punishment.

CHAPTER 5

Wars and Death Penalty Abolition: The Civil War through World War II

As American soldiers died on the battlefields of the Civil War, World War I, and World War II, many civilians had little concern for condemned criminals. But changes in society during this time period would lead to big swings in states abolishing and bringing back the death penalty.

The mid-1800s through the early 1900s became an important period for the American death penalty and the abolition movement. During these decades, major wars impacted the death penalty issue, while the Progressive Era saw the most active death penalty abolition period in the nation's history, followed by the most active death penalty reinstatement period.

THE CIVIL WAR AND THE LATE NINETEENTH CENTURY

During the years immediately leading up to the Civil War, efforts to abolish the death penalty dropped off. Politicians focused on the issues of slavery and war. For example, in 1858, two Senate candidates in Illinois, Senator Stephen Douglas and Abraham Lincoln, concentrated their debates on slavery and the Supreme Court's 1857 decision in *Dred Scott v. Sandford*, where the Court had stated that slaves were not citizens and Congress did not have the power to exclude slavery from federal territories.[1]

At the same time, executions sometimes were used as a response to fears of slave uprisings to help preserve the social order. For example, in August 1831, a slave named Nat Turner led other slaves in killing white slave owners, ultimately killing sixty-one white persons. As word spread of the uprising, state and federal troops stopped the rebellion, eventually capturing many of those involved. Virginia executed seventeen slaves and three free blacks who were involved in the insurrection. White mobs in Southern states responded to the insurrection and the fears it created by killing around 200 blacks, even though many of them were not involved in the uprising.

Turner eluded capture until October 30, 1831. Several days later, he was tried in Jerusalem, Virginia, and convicted and sentenced to death. After Turner's hanging on Friday, November 11, officials gave his body to surgeons for dissection. As recounted by John W. Cromwell in a 1920 article in *The Journal of Negro History*, "Turner was skinned to supply such souvenirs as purses, his flesh made into grease, and his bones divided as trophies to be handed down as heirlooms."[2]

Another famous hanging that occurred in response to fears of a slave uprising took place on the morning of December 2, 1859, when the government hanged abolitionist John Brown in Virginia for treason and for inciting a slave insurrection. That fall, Brown had led twenty-one men on a raid of Harpers Ferry Armory in what is now West Virginia with the hope others would join and there would be a slave uprising.

The unsuccessful raid at Harpers Ferry in a sense included the first shots of the Civil War, even though the Battle of Fort Sumter in April 1861 was less than two years away. Brown's case had several connections to the upcoming war, including the involvement of several future Confederate soldiers. At Harpers Ferry, Colonel Robert E. Lee led the U.S soldiers against Brown, and an army lieutenant named J.E.B. Stuart first tried to negotiate with the raiders. In the audience for Brown's December execution were John Wilkes Booth and Thomas Jonathan Jackson, who less than two years later would earn the nickname "Stonewall" on the battlefield.

One of America's most patriotic songs connects to this 1859 execution, starting with the song, "John Brown's Body." According to some accounts, "John Brown's Body" began as a fun song created by soldiers singing about a comrade named "John Brown," and when others heard the song they assumed the lyrics referred to John Brown the abolitionist and added verses to that effect. Words to the song included: "John Brown's body lies a'mouldering in the grave/...But his soul goes marching on." Julia Ward Howe heard the song and wrote new lyrics for the music to create the song for the Union, "The Battle Hymn of the Republic."

In these years leading up to and during the Civil War, social reformers devoted most of their time to slavery and war issues, turning their attention away from the death penalty, women's suffrage, temperance, and other issues. Capital punishment reform efforts dwindled through the war and Reconstruction because fewer people were sympathetic to the execution of criminals after so many young men died on the battlefield. As civilians saw photos by photographers Mathew Brady and Alexander Gardner of dead sons, brothers, and fathers on the battlefield, they found it difficult to care about the execution of a relatively small number of criminals. A young prison reform activist named Marvin Bovee explained to a Civil War veteran, "It is useless to talk of saving life when we are killing by thousands. Can't elevate mankind when government is debasing them."[3]

Meanwhile, during the war years of 1861 through 1865, Union authorities executed 275 men—executing more soldiers than U.S. authorities have done in all other U.S. conflicts combined. Only 0.19 percent of the 80,000 returned deserters were executed, but 54.31 percent of those executed were foreign-born or black.[4]

Although Lincoln was president during a large number of federal executions, he also often granted pardons to soldiers sentenced to be shot for deserting. In considering clemency requests, Lincoln may have remembered working as a lawyer for a condemned man. In 1839, Lincoln represented William Fraim, who ultimately was convicted for stabbing a man in a drunken brawl. After Lincoln exhausted the available legal remedies, Fraim was hanged.[5]

One federal mass execution during the war years had nothing to do with the Civil War. On the day after Christmas in 1862, the U.S. government hanged thirty-eight Native Americans near Mankato, Minnesota. The Sioux warriors were convicted of participating in war parties in the Minnesota settlements, killing hundreds of settlers. Originally, more than 300 of the Sioux were sentenced to death, but President Lincoln pardoned all but thirty-eight of them. The defendants were tried by a military commission without defense counsel, and with some trials lasting only five minutes. Prior to the executions, local citizens made two attempts to lynch some of the Sioux prisoners.

On the morning of the execution, the thirty-eight were led to a circular scaffold. Some of the condemned wore full tribal regalia and chanted and swayed while standing on the scaffold. The nooses were put around each of their necks, and then the executioner cut a rope release so the men all fell in unison. As the bodies dropped, the 3,000 observers cheered. But the rope holding Rattling Runner broke, and he fell to the ground unconscious. The executioners retrieved Rattling Runner's body and hanged him again.

After the hangings, the bodies were put in a hole and then covered with blankets and dirt. But as occurred after Nat Turner's execution, the bodies were not left to rest in peace. That night, several doctors from the area drove to the burial site and dug up bodies to use for teaching and studying anatomy. One of them, Dr. William Mayo, took the corpse of a warrior named Cut Nose, who had been one of the leaders. Dr. Mayo made Cut Nose's body into a mounted skeleton that he would use to teach his two sons about bones. The two sons, Charles and William, later grew up to found the Mayo Clinic in Minnesota.[6]

As John Brown's execution marked one of the early major steps toward the Civil War, another execution by the U.S. government helped mark the end of the Civil War and the start of Reconstruction. In response to the April 15, 1865 assassination of President Lincoln, the government executed five conspirators for participating in the plan to kill President Lincoln and other government officers. (See Figure 5.1.) After John Wilkes Booth died during his capture, Mary Surratt, John Surratt, George Atzerodt, David Herold, and Lewis Powell were tried by a military tribunal and hanged on July 7, 1865. Despite the growing popularity of the fallen president, the execution stirred some controversy. Mary Surratt may have had only a tenuous connection to the conspiracy beyond the fact that planning meetings took place in her home. So, many prominent citizens supported her and unsuccessfully lobbied President Andrew Johnson to stay her execution.[7]

In contrast to President Johnson, President Lincoln, and other presidents who merely have overseen executions as an executive, one future president actually served as an executioner in the late 1800s. In 1872–1873, future president

Figure 5.1
Officials adjust the ropes for hanging the Lincoln conspirators. (Alexander Gardner/Library of Congress)

Grover Cleveland worked as a sheriff in Erie County, New York, where he hanged two men.[8]

Although John Wilkes Booth escaped the noose, other presidential assassins have been executed. Less than twenty years after the hanging of the conspirators connected to President Lincoln's murder, officials hanged Charles J. Guiteau for assassinating President James A. Garfield. Guiteau shot Garfield in a train station, but the president lingered for eleven weeks battling infections before dying on September 19, 1881. Guiteau exhibited bizarre behavior during his trial, and he cursed the jury in an outburst when they found him guilty of murder. The government hanged him in the District of Columbia on June 30, 1882.

For a number of reasons, anti-death penalty activists made only limited progress toward abolishing the death penalty in the late nineteenth century. The hanging of the Lincoln conspirators, the Garfield assassination, a growing use of lynching, and executions in the West like the 1877 hanging of Jack McCall for killing the famous Wild Bill Hickok made many Americans believe society needed the death penalty. Also, when in 1868 the country ratified the Fourteenth Amendment, which would become essential to allowing the federal government to enforce rights in the various states, the new amendment contained language similar to the Fifth Amendment referencing the existence of the use of the death penalty taking human life: "nor shall any State deprive any person of life, liberty, or property, without due process of law."[9]

During the late 1800s, some efforts to end capital punishment continued, although the reformers met with little success. In Iowa, which joined the Union in 1846, the legislature considered a number of bills to abolish the death penalty, starting in 1851. Eventually, the *Des Moines Register* helped lead a successful campaign to abolish the Iowa death penalty in 1872. But the victory did not last long. Subsequently, citizens blamed a number of lynchings on the death penalty's absence, so the state reinstated the death penalty in 1878 to restore order.[10]

Similarly, other states went back and forth on the death penalty issue during this time. The Rhode Island General Assembly, which had abolished the death penalty in 1852, brought back a limited death penalty in 1872 for murders committed while a defendant was serving a life sentence. Maine abolished the death penalty in 1876, bringing it back in 1883 before abolishing it again in 1887. As in other states, Maine reinstated the death penalty in response to specific brutal murders, while the state abolished the death penalty in 1876 and 1887 partly due to gruesome hangings and low murder rates. As in Michigan's abolition, after Maine's last abolition in 1887, a variety of factors such as a cultural attachment to Enlightenment ideology and support from anti–death penalty newspapers helped ensure the state remained without the death penalty into the twenty-first century.[11]

When Utah became a state in 1896, the Utah state legislature rejected a proposal to abolish the death penalty, and the new state passed a capital punishment statute in 1898. In the same year Utah became a state, it executed Patrick Coughlin for killing two police officers. When officials asked Coughlin what method of execution he wanted, he responded, "I'll take lead." Thus, the new state used the firing squad, with one of the shooters firing Coughlin's murder weapon.[12]

In the decades after the Civil War, many in the country had their minds on other issues besides abolishing the death penalty. Tensions between the North and South lingered, and the country faced several financial crises between 1873 and 1893. During this era of instability, many politicians reacted to fears about the freed slaves and about immigrants. In May 1882, President Chester Arthur signed the Chinese Exclusion Act, the nation's first major law restricting immigration, and other immigration laws followed.[13]

Thus anti-death penalty activists had little success in abolishing the death penalty in the post–Civil War late nineteenth century. Despite that limited success, some significant changes to capital punishment occurred during this period. For example, after the Civil War and into the early twentieth century, partly out of concerns about lynchings, states began centralizing executions under state control instead of allowing local communities to supervise hangings.[14] Additional changes during this time period included ongoing efforts to eliminate public executions, the move away from mandatory death sentences, and the beginning of the use of the electric chair as a more "humane" method of execution than hanging.

Regarding the latter change, although hanging remained the nearly universal means of execution in the United States through most of the nineteenth century, by the end of the century, some politicians looked to new technologies for a more humane execution method. Thus, as the century neared the end, New York became the first state to use the electric chair as a means of execution, and other states followed. By 1915, twelve states had adopted the electric chair as a more humane method of execution.[15]

By contrast, the movement away from mandatory death sentences helped limit the use of capital punishment. When the Eighth Amendment's ban on cruel and unusual punishments was ratified with the rest of the Bill of Rights in 1791, all states followed the common law practice of making the death penalty the automatic sentence for anyone convicted of certain crimes. But the states eventually discovered that mandatory death sentences often resulted in jurors acquitting sympathetic guilty defendants because the jurors did not want to impose the automatic death sentence. So, the states responded with new laws that gave jurors discretion in imposing capital punishment. Once jurors found a defendant guilty of a capital offense, the jurors then had discretion whether or not to impose a punishment of death.

Although in 1846, only Tennessee, Alabama, and Louisiana had discretionary death penalties, between the Civil War and the beginning of the twentieth century, twenty jurisdictions moved from mandatory to discretionary capital punishment. While advocates for the discretionary statutes argued these laws were fairer and allowed mercy in the sentencing process, some historians have argued a less noble reason led to the change. They note that one of the reasons southern states first adopted these discretionary schemes was because the discretionary statutes allowed juries to impose death sentences for African Americans and lesser sentences for white defendants.[16]

Regardless of the justifications, American jurisdictions continued to move away from mandatory capital sentencing to discretionary sentences. The U.S. Congress passed a law in 1897 that, while limiting the federal death penalty to five categories of crimes, changed the federal death penalty from a mandatory system to a discretionary one. From the beginning of the twentieth century to United States involvement in World War II (1941-1945), eighteen more states moved to discretionary capital punishment sentencing. By 1963, the federal government and every state with capital jury sentencing gave juries the discretion to grant mercy to a capital defendant. Although this sentencing discretion solved the problem of the harshness of mandatory death sentences, it created new problems of arbitrariness.[17]

THE EARLY TWENTIETH CENTURY'S PERIOD OF SOCIAL REFORM AND ANOTHER PERIOD OF DEATH PENALTY ABOLITION

The early twentieth century brought a period of social reform, but the beginning of the century also brought the use of the new electric chair to execute another presidential assassin in 1901. Leon Czolgosz, thinking himself a heroic anarchist, approached President William McKinley at the Pan-American Exposition in Buffalo, New York, on September 6, 1901, and shot the president in the abdomen twice.

President McKinley survived for a number of days, eventually dying on September 14. As in the case of Garfield's killer twenty years earlier, some questioned Czolgosz's mental state. But in a swift act of justice the government tried him nine days after President McKinley died and the jury recommended the death sentence two days later. Within a little more than a month after the crime, Czolgosz was executed in the electric chair on October 29. Within a span of less than forty years from 1865 to 1901, three presidents were assassinated and the government executed the survivors who were involved in the assassinations.[18]

Despite the notorious execution of Leon Czolgosz in the early twentieth century, the Progressive Era and a growing focus on social reform brought widespread success for death penalty abolitionists for the first time since before the Civil War. Colorado abolished the death penalty in 1897, and then Kansas abolished it in 1907 under the leadership of Governor Edward W. Hoch, who had vowed to resign before he would sign a death warrant. Those states were followed by Minnesota (1911), Washington (1913), Oregon (1914), North Dakota (1915), South Dakota (1915), Tennessee (except for rape crimes) (1915), Arizona (1916), and Missouri (1917). The North Dakota law signed by Governor Louis B. Hanna, however, maintained the death penalty on the books for treason and for defendants who committed murder while serving a life sentence for murder. Those final two provisions were finally repealed in 1973 with overwhelming support and no debate.[19]

Many of these abolitions in the early 1900s were led by progressive governors. After Governor Ernest Lister signed the bill abolishing the death penalty in Washington State, the Anti-Capital Punishment Society of America made him an honorary vice president. South Dakota governor Frank M. Byrne recommended abolishing the death penalty at his 1913 inauguration, and the legislature passed the abolition bill 63-24 within two years.[20] Not all of the progressive governors during this time were successful in abolishing the death penalty, but some still did what they could. Governor Lee Cruce, Oklahoma's second governor, commuted all of the twenty-two death sentences given during 1911–1915 because he opposed capital punishment.[21]

Some of the abolitions were long-lived while others were not. For example, Colorado reinstated the death penalty in 1901 after only four years of abolition. After the state had abolished the death penalty, there had been two high-profile lynchings that increased support for legal executions. In one case, a mob hanged a "mulatto" as thousands watched. In the other one, a group burned at the stake a sixteen-year-old African American named Preston Porter for murder. After Porter's crime, the town voted that all "negroes of bad character" must leave town.

Similarly, Arizona brought back the death penalty in response to specific crimes. George W.P. Hunt worked for many years to rid Arizona of the death penalty as President of the Arizona Constitutional Convention and then as the state's first governor. He told the legislature he believed "that capital punishment is a relic of barbarism, that the legalized taking of life is a straining of Christ's law which has no place in modern civilization."[22] Through his efforts as governor, citizens of Arizona narrowly voted to abolish the death penalty for first-degree murder on December 8, 1916, although the death penalty remained for the crimes of treason and robbing a train. Subsequently, death penalty proponents worked to bring back the death penalty, arguing that the abolition increased violent crime. Two years later, they were successful in their efforts. On December 5, 1918, Arizonans voted by a large margin to bring back the death penalty for murder, largely in response to a couple of violent crimes, including a shoot-out and the lynching of a rapist-murderer.[23]

Similarly, Tennessee abolished capital punishment and then brought it back during this era. In 1915, Tennessee abolished the death penalty for the crime of murder, although the state kept the punishment for the crime of rape and for murders committed by life-sentenced prisoners. A retired grocery merchant named Duke C. Bowers led the successful abolition movement. But within two years, in 1916 the state brought back the death penalty for murder. During the short time that Tennessee had abolished the death penalty for murder, the state executed four people for other crimes. And, as in Colorado, lynchings of African Americans during the period of abolition raised concerns about the necessity of the death penalty. The three lynchings of African Americans included one where a group burned a man at the stake before a crowd of 1500 people after hot irons on his body were unsuccessful in getting a confession.[24]

Just as grisly murders prompted some states to reinstate or maintain capital punishment, some grisly executions prompted states to eliminate capital punishment. In February 1906, Minnesota executed William Williams, who was gay, for killing his former lover and his lover's mother. The sheriff, however, miscalculated the length of the drop for the hanging, and during the execution Williams fell through the trap all the way to the ground. So, three deputy sheriffs on the platform pulled on the rope to keep Williams's feet off the ground as he strangled to death for fifteen minutes. A 1895 law prohibited newspapers from publishing execution descriptions, but newspapers wrote about the hanging anyway. The state abolished the death penalty within five years.[25]

One prominent execution inspired activists for reasons besides a botched execution. In 1915, the same year a Marietta mob lynched Leo Frank, Utah executed Union organizer and Industrial Workers of the World songwriter Joe Hill for the murder of two storekeepers in Utah. In Hill's case, only limited circumstantial evidence supported the conviction that reportedly involved "collusion between the prosecution and the trial judge in an atmosphere of anti-union hostility." [26] Many, including President Woodrow Wilson and Helen Keller, supported Hill and requested reprieves on his behalf. Before Hill's execution, he wrote his union supporters with the advice, "Don't waste time mourning, organize."[27]

WARS AND ECONOMIC HARD TIMES

By 1917, twelve states had abolished the death penalty either in whole or for all but a few very specific crimes. Of the states with the death penalty, only twelve retained mandatory death sentences, with the rest allowing for discretion in imposing the punishment. Yet, as in the past, a war and a recession adversely affected the death penalty abolition movement. As the United States entered World War I in 1917, promising abolitionist movements in several states came to a halt. Five abolitionist states brought back the death penalty by 1920: Arizona (1918), Missouri (1919), Tennessee (1919), Washington (1919), and Oregon (1920).[28]

The death penalty abolition movement continued to stall during the war and through the economic recessions in the years after the war ended in 1918. Before long, all but two of ten jurisdictions that had abolished the death penalty during the previous era brought the punishment back.[29] Thus, America's greatest death penalty abolition period preceded its greatest death penalty reinstatement period. The end of this abolition period resulted from several fears connected to severe economic recession in the early 1920s, labor violence, unrest spreading from the Russian Revolution, racial tensions that grew into violence in several cities by the Red Summer of 1919, and a perception of increasing crime during the Prohibition years of 1920 to 1933. People's fears about crime grew during the 1920s and 1930s partly because of high-profile crimes by Al Capone, John Dillinger, Bonnie and Clyde, and others. As in the past, many in society felt a need for capital punishment to maintain social order, prevent a drastic increase in lynchings, and help control a growing minority population. Subsequently, no other states abolished the death penalty until the late 1950s well after World War II.[30]

Although the years between the world wars were not very successful for death penalty abolitionists, the activists saw a few bright signs. During the first half of the twentieth century, states continued following a trend toward humanizing the methods of execution, and the federal courts expanded their role in reviewing death sentences.[31] One abolitionist success occurred in April 1929, when Puerto Rico, a self-governing U.S. territory, abolished the death penalty.

Activists continued to struggle against capital punishment during the 1920s and 1930s. In August 1925, the League for the Abolition of Capital Punishment formed and started organizing a nationwide campaign. The organization promoted speakers ranging from Sing Sing's warden Lewis E. Lawes to attorney Clarence Darrow. In 1928, Warden Lawes released the book *Life and Death in Sing*, arguing that the death penalty is a travesty.

Like Lawes, another warden took a stand against the death penalty during this period. On January 1, 1924, Captain R.F. Coleman, the warden of the Texas prison in Huntsville, announced he was resigning effective January 15, the day before the state's scheduled first use of the electric chair. He explained in an interview that "[a] Warden can't be a warden and a killer too. The penitentiary is a place to reform a man, not to kill him." Former sheriff Walter Monroe Miller replaced Coleman as warden and soon oversaw the state's first use of the electric chair in the electrocution of five black men after midnight on Feb. 8, 1924.

Some famous death penalty cases in the 1920s helped shape public perception of capital punishment. As in the past, for good or ill, specific cases have drastically affected death penalty support. During the 1920s, several high-profile cases added to the debate.

In 1924, the media focused on the death penalty issue as a result of a high-profile crime and the "trial of the century." Two students from the University of Chicago—Nathan Leopold and Richard Loeb—were charged with the murder of fourteen-year-old Bobby Franks. Clarence Darrow, the attorney for the two students, put the death penalty itself on trial after Leopold and Loeb both pleaded guilty. When the sixty-seven-year-old Darrow argued for the students' lives, the local paper reported that a mob "fought like animals to...hear Darrow speak."[32] Several newspapers from around the country published Darrow's twelve-hour-plus plea in whole or in part. The attorney succeeded. The judge sentenced Leopold and Loeb to life for the murder and ninety-nine years for kidnapping, but no death penalty. Although after nine years another prisoner killed Loeb in prison, Nathan Leopold lived to be paroled in 1958 at the age of fifty-three. He moved to Puerto Rico, worked at a church-operated hospital helping others until his death, and eventually married and earned a master's degree at the University of Puerto Rico.[33]

One of the most famous American executions of all time took place on August 23, 1927, when Massachusetts executed Nicola Sacco and Bartolomeo Vanzetti.[34] The case received worldwide attention because of how prejudice and an unfair trial may have led to the conviction of two innocent men. Sacco and Vanzetti were two Italian immigrants who were convicted of the 1921 murder of a person during an armed robbery of a shoe company paymaster. The fish-peddler and shoemaker were admitted anarchists, and the xenophobic patriotism of the early 1920s fueled their conviction. Outside the courtroom, trial judge Webster Thayer stated one day, "Did you see what I did with those anarchist bastards the other day? I guess that will hold them for awhile."[35] In Vanzetti's speech on April 9, 1927, prior to his sentencing, he asserted his innocence: "Not only am I innocent of these two crimes, not only in all my life I have never stolen, never killed, never spilled blood, but I have struggled all my life, since I began to reason, to eliminate crime from the earth."[36]

The Sacco and Vanzetti case drew national and international attention, and at the time of the execution of the Italian immigrants, protests were held in several nations. American and international Communists rallied to use the case as propaganda about the problems with capitalism.[37] Liberal intellectuals and social activists also used the case to highlight problems in American society.

The evidence of guilt in the Sacco and Vanzetti case was questionable. Prior to the execution and before he became a Supreme Court justice, Professor Felix Frankfurter wrote a study of the problems in the case. The execution of Sacco and Vanzetti changed society and the criminal justice system for some time. The case inspired artists, poets, and writers, such as Edna St. Vincent Millay, John Dos Passos, and Upton Sinclair. Folksinger Woody Guthrie wrote songs about the two condemned men decades later. The case energized the American League to Abolish Capital Punishment, an organization that established an important link to later death penalty abolition movements.[38]

Another death penalty media event followed in 1928 when *The Daily News* in New York published one of the most famous death penalty photos after photographer Tom Howard witnessed the execution of Ruth Snyder for killing her husband. The photographer used a hidden miniature camera strapped to his ankle to capture a photo of Snyder in the electric chair.[39]

Despite these prominent cases in the 1920s, by the 1930s and 1940s an economic crisis and concerns about war made reformers less focused on death penalty issues. The death penalty rose in popularity through the 1930s and 1940s. Social progress suffered in other ways too in the wake of war, as illustrated by the Supreme Court's 1944 decision in *Korematsu v. United States*, holding that President Franklin D. Roosevelt's executive order allowing the internment of Japanese-Americans did not violate the constitution.[40]

After the Great Depression began in 1929 and through the early post–World War II years, states executed prisoners at the highest rate of the century. In 1935, states executed 199 people, the most during any year in the twentieth century. During 1930–1939, there were an average of 167 executions a year in the United States, and during 1940–1949, there were an average of 128 executions a year. Most of these executions—around 80–90 a year—took place in southern states.

Out of the many executions in the 1930s, Americans especially followed the drama of two high-profile executions. On March 20, 1933, Florida executed an Italian immigrant named Giuseppe "Joseph" Zangara in the state's electric chair. A little more than a month earlier, he had tried to kill president-elect Franklin D. Roosevelt but missed and instead shot five other people, including Chicago's mayor Anton Cermak, who died from the injury. The mentally ill Zangara called his sentencing judge a "crook," and he angrily yelled in the death chamber when he learned the execution would not be photographed. As the executioners put a black cowl over Zangara's face, he said, "Good-bye, adios to all the world." Then, under the cowl, in a muffled voice, he told the executioners how to proceed and taunted them to "push the button." The execution occurred only two weeks after the death sentence verdict and only five weeks after Zangara fired the gun at President Roosevelt.[41]

The other high-profile capital case in the 1930s began when Charles Augustus Lindbergh Jr.—the twenty-month-old child of national aviator hero Charles Lindbergh and his wife, Anne Morrow Lindbergh—was kidnapped from the second floor of their East Amwell, New Jersey home on March 1, 1932. Later, the child was found dead, perhaps killed when the ladder used by the kidnapper broke. More than two years after the Lindbergh baby disappeared, a payment with marked ransom money led police to arrest Bruno Richard Hauptmann, and his "trial of the century" began on the day after New Year's in 1935.

Due to Lindbergh's celebrity from his 1927 solo flight across the Atlantic Ocean and due to anti-German sentiment at the time, the nation followed the trial closely. Newspaper and radio commentator Walter Winchell bragged after the verdict, "I predicted he'd be guilty. Oh, that's another big one for me." The Hearst newspaper chain, which hoped for a conviction, unbeknownst to Hauptmann had hired his lead defense attorney Edward J. "Death House" Reilly. The condemned man claimed he could smell alcohol on his attorney's breath during the few times Reilly visited. At one trial recess, Reilly told an FBI agent he did not like Hauptmann and he "was anxious to see him get the chair." According to some reports, Reilly alienated the jurors during the trial, and not long after the trial, Reilly himself went into an insane asylum due to symptoms of tertiary syphilis.[42]

New Jersey ultimately executed Hauptmann in its electric chair, and many states expanded their laws to make kidnapping a capital offense. Executioner Robert G. Elliott, who also threw the switch for Sacco, Vanzetti, and the first woman to be executed by electricity, Ruth Snyder, presided over Hauptmann's execution on April 3, 1936, at 8:44 pm. Later, Elliott wrote a biography where he stated, "I believe that capital punishment serves no useful purpose and is a form of revenge...I hope the day is not far away when legal slaying...is outlawed throughout the United States."[43]

To the end, Hauptmann maintained his innocence, while many debated his guilt. Because of Hauptmann's possession of some of the ransom money and evidence connecting him to the ladder apparently used in the kidnapping, some commentators believe he was involved in the crime.[44] Others continued to speculate that Hauptmann was innocent, and, at the least, his trial was not fair. Among others, Hauptmann's widow, Anna, fought tirelessly to prove Bruno's innocence until her own death more than fifty years later. [45]

So many executions took place during this time period, though, that most of the stories behind the murders and the executions become mere footnotes buried among the world-shaking history of the times. Yet, each capital case was a major life-changing event to the families touched by the crime, the litigation, and the executions. The stories include that of Henderson Young, a sixteen-year-old African American executed for rape, in Texas's electric chair on May 6, 1938, becoming the youngest person in Texas to be executed by electrocution.[46] The youngest person executed in the United States during the twentieth century was George Stinney, Jr., a fourteen-year-old African American, who was electrocuted in South Carolina in 1944 for raping and murdering two white girls. In Kansas that same year, another black man was executed for armed robbery, resulting in the last execution of a man for killing a black victim for nearly half a century when the phenomena occurred again in 1991. This phenomenon of rare death penalties for cases involving black victims would eventually be at the heart of Warren McCleskey's legal case.

The 1930s also saw the final public execution in the United States. Public executions had disappeared in most northern states by the middle of the nineteenth century, but some southern states held onto public executions longer, especially for rape crimes where blacks were executed more often than whites. Kentucky, which had initially abolished public executions in 1880, forty years later brought back public hanging as an option for rape and attempted rape crimes. On August 14, 1936, Kentucky hosted the public hanging of the African-American Rainey Bethea for rape and murder. Hot dogs and popcorn were sold to the 10,000 people in attendance. Some people in the audience had to climb trees and telephone poles to get a good view. One reporter noted that within minutes of the hanging, "eager hands clawed at the black death hood" to tear off pieces of cloth to keep as souvenirs. Kentucky officially abolished public executions in 1938, and other state legislators responded in the same way so that the Bethea hanging is now the last public execution in the United States.[47]

One execution in the late 1930s created a conflict between an abolitionist state and the federal government. Although Michigan had abolished the death penalty in the previous century, the federal government prosecuted, convicted, and sentenced Anthony Chebatoris to be executed in that state for his role in a bank robbery where a bystander was killed. Residents of Michigan protested the planned execution in their state. The victim's widow and sister-in-law also opposed the execution, and the sister-in-law claimed that the victim's own wishes before he died had been that Chebatoris be spared the death penalty.

Michigan's governor Frank Murphy asked President Franklin D. Roosevelt to move the Chebatoris execution to another state. Roosevelt referred the issue to the U.S. Attorney General and a U.S. District Court Judge, and the federal officials decided to proceed with the execution in Michigan. As the execution neared, Governor Murphy spoke of Michigan's "pride in being the first commonwealth on this earth to abolish capital punishment." He added that moving the execution to Illinois would be appropriate because Illinois was like a neighbor who "was in the habit of chloroforming dogs in his backyard." Thus, the killing there would be appropriate because "one more or less probably wouldn't disturb him." But the execution proceeded, and the federal government hanged Chebatoris at a federal detention farm in Milan, Michigan, on July 8, 1938. The hanging is the only time in the twentieth century the U.S. government executed a capital defendant in a state that had abolished the death penalty.[48]

The next year, the execution of a possibly innocent man prompted questions about the capital punishment. In 1939, Colorado executed Joe Arridy, a mentally disabled twenty-three-year-old Syrian-American man, for raping and killing a fifteen-year-old girl named Dorothy Drain. Arridy, who had an I.Q. of 46, apparently gave a coerced confession, and at the time the girl was killed, he was in a different town. Further, officials found the murder weapon, a hatchet, in the home of Frank Aguilar, who was identified as the killer by Drain's sister and who had the motive that he had been fired by Drain's father. Aguilar, who also was executed, confessed to the crime and said he did not know Arridy.[49]

Another controversial execution during this time involved a faulty electric chair. In 1946, Louisiana's electric chair did not work properly during Willie Francis's execution, and it did not kill him. An all-white jury had convicted Francis, an illiterate sixteen-year-old African American, of murdering Andrew Thomas, a prominent white businessman. The sheriff in charge of the execution later explained that when the electricity started, Francis "groaned and jumped so that the chair came off the floor." Another witness reported hearing one officer yelling for "more juice" and the operator yelling "he was giving him all he had." The witness noted, "Then Willie Francis cried out 'Take it off. Let me breathe.'" Prison officials unstrapped Francis from the chair, and he survived the execution. Lawyers tried to prevent his return to the chair, but after the Supreme Court voted against Francis 5-4 in *Louisiana ex rel. Francis v. Resweber*, the state executed Francis for the second time a year later.[50]

The second execution successfully killed Francis, but several of the justices were troubled by Francis's case. Justice Robert Jackson ultimately voted with the majority, but the botched execution troubled him as someone who had recently returned from working as a prosecutor of Nazi war crimes at Nuremburg. In a draft concurring opinion, Jackson wrote that if he could vote his personal sense of decency, he would not have allowed Francis to go to the chair in the first place. He explained, "This is not because I am sentimental about criminals, but I have doubts of the moral right of society to extinguish a human life, and even greater doubts about the wisdom of doing so."

Similarly, Justice Felix Frankfurter felt bound by the law to allow the second execution to proceed, but he later wrote about how the case offended his personal standards of decency. Despite his vote with the majority, Frankfurter later sought help from a former Harvard classmate to try to obtain clemency for Francis from the Louisiana governor. The attempt failed. Future justices, however, would share in the agony felt by Justices Jackson and Frankfurter in allowing executions to proceed despite personal abhorrence at state killings.[51]

Other forgotten executions took place in the 1940s. In 1942, Florida executed the twenty-seven-year-old uneducated African-American Willie "Mayo" Williams without an appeal even though Williams claimed he acted in self-defense. Williams's letter to Governor Spessard L. Holland asked for a stay so his sister could get a lawyer to handle his appeal: "Please sir give them a little chance to try to save my life me, please sir to your honor; for I did not hit him to kill him I did it, in order to get away from him." The governor ignored the request.[52]

After Texas executed J.B. Stephens on December 19, 1944, the condemned man's financially strapped mother asked whether she could receive the discharge money usually given to inmates after they were released from prison. She wrote the warden, "When a boy leaves they give him 50 dollars and my dear boy is gone never to come back?" The prison denied her request.[53]

More than a hundred such stories took place each year during these decades, tragic crimes with unfortunate victims followed by defendants and families waiting for death. Little time usually passed between conviction and execution, and the prisoners had fewer constitutional rights and procedural protections than today. For example, defendants did not have to be told they had a right to an attorney before they were interrogated, and other appeal issues were limited.

In addition to the increase in number of executions, some abolitionist states brought back the death penalty in the 1930s due to concerns about violent crime during the Great Depression. Kansas reinstated the death penalty in 1935 after twenty-eight years of abolition. And in 1939, South Dakota reinstated the death penalty after twenty-four years of abolition. Although South Dakota had only four murders in 1938, one case especially outraged citizens when officials accused Earl Young of the kidnapping and sex-killing of seventeen-year-old Betty Schnaidt. The *Pierrre Daily Capital-Journal* published numerous editorials advocating for the return of capital punishment, with some articles advocating the use of lynching.[54]

Around this time, Georgia for the only time in its history executed a woman in its electric chair. In March 1945, the state executed an African-American woman named Lena Baker after an all-white, all-male jury convicted the maid of killing her white employer, Ernest Knight. The execution went forward despite Baker's claims that Knight had restrained her and threatened to kill her. Eventually, six decades later in 2005, the Georgia Board of Pardons and Paroles pardoned Baker, finding she acted in self-defense and that she should not have been executed.[55]

Although the number of U.S. executions remained high throughout the Great Depression and World War II, in the 1940s many other countries moved away from the death penalty. The mass killings of World War II and the Holocaust made many European countries question any state-sanctioned killings. Switzerland abolished the death penalty in 1942; Italy abolished it after the war in 1948; Finland and Germany abolished it in 1949; Austria abolished it in 1950. England moved toward abolition by the late 1940s and early 1950s. Until Stalinism took over the U.S.S.R., that country limited and then abolished the death penalty for a short period in the late 1940s. Also around this time, in 1948, the United Nations adopted the non-binding Universal Declaration of Human Rights, stating, "Everyone has the right to life."[56]

This progress toward abolition in other countries and at the United Nations did not reach the shores of the United States. During the forty years between 1918 and 1956, no U.S. state abolished the death penalty. Thus, from the end of World War I, through Prohibition, through the Great Depression, through World War II, through the first use of the atomic bomb, through the birth of network television, and through the postwar boom, no U.S. state abolished the death penalty. During this period, Woodrow Wilson, Warren G. Harding, Calvin Coolidge, Franklin D. Roosevelt, Harry S. Truman, and Dwight D. Eisenhower occupied the White House.

During these decades as well as through the first century and a half of America's existence, the U.S. Supreme Court did not play a major role in the history of the death penalty. Although the Court decided cases involving procedural rights in capital cases and had evaluated execution methods, the Court did not grapple with the constitutionality of the death penalty itself.

Some individual justices, though, were troubled by the use of capital punishment. For example, in 1948 in *Haley v. Ohio*, a majority of the justices voted to overturn the death sentence of an African-American fifteen-year-old by finding that an all-night interrogation resulted in an involuntary confession. In a concurring opinion, Justice Felix Frankfurter wrote about his views on the death penalty:

> A lifetime's preoccupation with criminal justice, as prosecutor, defender of civil liberties and scientific student, naturally leaves one with views. Thus, I disbelieve in capital punishment. But as a judge I could not impose the views of the very States who through bitter experience have abolished capital punishment upon all the other States, by finding that "due process" proscribes it.[57]

Thus, despite Justice Frankfurter's heartfelt beliefs from his experience, he concluded that the Constitution did not allow him to impose his personal perspective.

In the United States in the immediate years after the soldiers returned home from World War II in 1945 and in the early years of the Cold War, capital punishment remained popular in American society. But the country and its citizens' views on the death penalty started changing in the next decade. Those changes would lead to the Supreme Court paying more attention to the constitutionality of the death penalty. And one of Justice Frankfurter's former students from his Harvard law professor days would sit on the Supreme Court reflecting on his former professor's concurring opinion in *Haley*. During his own time on the Court, that former student, Harry A. Blackmun, would look back on his professor's words from 1948 as he felt the same troubled conflict between his personal beliefs and his reading of the U.S. Constitution.[58]

CHAPTER 6

A Time of Change: American Society and the Death Penalty in the 1950s through the 1960s

During the decades leading up to McCleskey's crime, opinions about the death penalty were chang-ing as attorneys raised new constitutional challenges in the courts. Events during this time would set the stage for death penalty issues to go the U.S. Supreme Court.

INDIVIDUAL CASES GAIN NATIONAL ATTENTION

While Warren McCleskey attended school, popular opinion began to again ques-tion the death penalty, as from the 1950s through the 1970s Americans struggled with the death penalty issue. Although polls indicated growing support for capital punishment through the 1930s and 1940s, including up to 68 percent support in a 1953 Gallup poll, support for capital punishment began dropping significantly to new lows over the next two decades.[1]

As states continued to consider whether or not they needed the death penalty, attorneys began raising new constitutional questions in the courts during these decades. Unbeknownst to the young McCleskey, his state of Georgia would play a sig-nificant role in the fall and resurrection of the death penalty in the United States. As in the years 1907–1917, the decades after the middle of the century would be a volatile period for the American death penalty. Unlike the earlier period, though, the changes in the 1960s–1970s occurred largely in the courts instead of in state legislatures.

But in the 1950s, appeals courts still gave minimal attention to the constitution-ality of capital punishment while defendants proceeded toward their executions. During this time, criminal defendants had few rights compared to today, with some proceeding through the criminal justice system without attorneys. Even in capital cases, attorneys were paid very little, if at all. Often, a capital defendant only would have a lawyer for appeals if an attorney volunteered to handle the case for free.[2]

Some death penalty cases during the 1950s did receive special attention, including a prominent death row commutation involving another attempt on a president's life. On November 1, 1950, Puerto Rican nationalists Oscar Collazo and Griselio Torresola planned to assassinate the president, and they went to Blair House where President Harry S. Truman was staying with his family. After an exchange of gunfire with White House police officers and U.S. Secret Service Agents, Torresola was killed, as was White House officer Leslie Coffelt. Collazo survived and was sentenced to death for his role in Coffelt's death, but in 1952 President Truman commuted Collazo's sentence to life in prison to avoid making Collazo a martyr.[3]

Some cases sparked outrage about the use of the death penalty, such as the federal execution of the Rosenbergs as Soviet spies in 1953. Ethel and Julius Rosenberg were executed on June 19, 1953, after being tried in the U.S. District Court for the Southern District of New York and convicted of conspiracy to commit espionage. The trial occurred during the Cold War in a time when the United States was gripped by fears of communists, and several aspects of the prosecution were troublesome, including the harshness of the sentence. Even as the appeals were pending, international support for the Rosenbergs grew. Pope Pius XII, Albert Einstein, and others requested clemency for the couple. As the time of execution approached, approximately 15,000 people gathered spontaneously in New York's Union Square to protest and hope for a last-minute reprieve from President Dwight D. Eisenhower.[4] The reprieve never came, and the two were executed.

Not everyone was outraged by the execution of the Rosenbergs. Early the following year, Texas governor Allan Shivers went on television and called on the Texas Legislature to pass a law making mere membership in the Communist Party punishable by the death penalty.[5]

Some executions in California garnered national attention, including the execution of Leandress Riley early in the 1950s, the execution of Burton Abbott in 1957, and the execution of Caryl W. Chessman in 1960.[6] Leandress Riley's case became notorious for the execution itself, rather than for the person or the typical crime. A jury convicted Riley of a 1949 robbery and murder where Riley had shot a bystander. Riley, a one-eyed African-American man who at thirty-two weighed about eighty pounds, had a troubled life. He grew up with an abusive father and mentally ill mother, and he ran away from home to live on his own at the age of fourteen. After he was sentenced to death, psychiatrists debated whether or not he was legally insane, but a majority of jurors at a special trial concluded he was sane.

Riley went to California's gas chamber on February 20, 1953, but he fought it all the way. He tried cheating the executioner by slitting his wrists, and the blood made it difficult to handcuff his skinny arms. On the way to the chamber, he fought and screamed. Once the execution team had him restrained in the chair in the gas chamber, right before the cyanide pellets dropped, Riley slipped his bloody wrists out of the restraints and began running around the room and pounding on the glass. Guards had to re-enter the chamber and strap him into the chair again, and by some accounts, Riley escaped the wrist straps a few more times. In the end, they restrained him. Although Riley held his breath as long as he could, he eventually inhaled the fumes and died.[7]

Another California execution in the 1950s did not go well for another reason. In "Reflections on the Guillotine," Author and philosopher Albert Camus wrote about Burton Abbott's execution in California's gas chamber on March 15, 1957. Abbott, a college student convicted on circumstantial evidence, claimed to be innocent of the crime of murdering a fourteen-year-old girl. A representative from the governor's office called the prison with news of a reprieve to stop the execution two minutes after Abbott had already started breathing the fumes from the gas. Although prison workers removed Abbott from the gas chamber in an effort to save him, it was too late. The call to the prison arrived late because of communication issues with Governor Goodwin J. Knight, who was out on a ship at the time.[8]

Although the Riley and Abbott executions horrified some, the California case that transformed the way many Americans viewed the death penalty involved Caryl Chessman, whose crime occurred before Riley's but who remained on death row many years longer. California authorities arrested Chessman for being the "red-light bandit," a man who had robbed several people parked in secluded areas by approaching with a red spotlight as if he were a police officer. On two occasions, the bandit took a woman into his car and forced her to perform fellatio and then released her. Chessman asserted his innocence, and although he had a criminal record, he had never been charged with a sex crime. In 1948, a jury convicted him of robbery, rape, and kidnapping. The court imposed a sentence of death under the "Little Lindbergh" kidnapping law the state passed in 1933 in response to the kidnapping of Charles Lindbergh's baby.

During Chessman's time on death row, he continued to maintain his innocence and tried to prove that he had reformed from his prior life of crime. He gained many supporters through his writing, which included a national best-selling book, *Cell 2455 Death Row*.

Chessman's lengthy stay on death row brought him much attention. His twelve years on death row, which included nine stays of execution issued by the courts, constituted the longest time on death row of anyone up to that time.[9] During those twelve years, the laws in California changed so that by the time of Chessman's execution, others convicted of the exact same crimes would not be executed. Three California governors signed off on execution dates for Chessman at different times, including Governor Earl Warren, who would later become Chief Justice of the United States Supreme Court and lead the Court in deciding *Miranda v. Arizona* and other cases that expanded the rights of criminal defendants.

Like Burton Abbott before him, Chessman might not have been executed but for a problem with a phone call. On a sunny morning on May 2, 1960, Chessman's appeals ran out and he was sent to the gas chamber. After guards strapped Chessman to the chair, though, Chessman's lawyers won a one-hour stay of execution, and the judge's secretary went to call San Quentin State Prison. After first dialing the wrong number, she got through to the assistant warden, who told her, "I'm sorry it's too late. The pellets have just been dropped."[10] The executioner had already released the bag of cyanide pellets in the chamber, and they could not open the door to rescue Chessman because the fumes would kill others.[11] After twelve years on death row, Chessman was executed when his final stay of execution came too late to save him.

The governor who sat in office at the time of Chessman's execution was Edmund "Pat" Brown. Governor Brown, who opposed capital punishment, did grant clemency to some men who had actually killed their victims, but he did not grant clemency to Chessman. In his memoir published many years after his service, *Public Justice, Private Mercy: A Governor's Education on Death Row*, Brown noted that as Chessman's execution approached, his future gubernatorial opponent, Richard M. Nixon, was already making an issue of the death penalty and the Chessman case. Nixon claimed capital punishment for kidnapping worked as a deterrent. Because Nixon made an issue of the death penalty, Brown thought he would lose his re-election bid in the 1962 election. After permitting the state to execute Chessman, Brown defeated Nixon and remained as governor.

Some, including Alan Bisbort in *When You Read This, They Will Have Killed Me*, have argued that Brown's record on the death penalty was somewhat ambiguous because thirty-six men were executed during his eight years as governor. During the year of the 1962 election, California's eleven executions were the most in the country. But after Brown's re-election, he pushed for a four-year moratorium on executions. When that effort was unsuccessful, starting in 1963 he granted clemency and stays of executions in all cases. Nobody went to California's gas chamber during the rest of his time as governor.[12]

A NEW DEATH PENALTY ABOLITION PERIOD BEGINS

The late 1950s and early 1960s constituted a time of change in the United States. After the Supreme Court struck down school segregation in *Brown v. Board of Education* in 1954, civil rights workers continued to strive toward what would become the federal Civil Rights Act of 1964. In the midst of these and other emerging social reforms, American society became more concerned about capital punishment. After some debate among civil rights leaders, they eventually connected capital punishment to the country's racial issues.[13]

Martin Luther King Jr. recognized the link between capital punishment and civil rights. He opposed the death penalty for the way it had been used against African Americans, but he also opposed it on practical and religious grounds. In June 1959, King wrote a letter defending his opposition to the death penalty for four white men charged with raping a black teenager, stating, "I don't believe in capital punishment for white people or Negro people." In November 1957 in "Advice for Living," King explained, "Capital punishment is against the best judgment of modern criminology and, above all, against the highest expression of love in the nature of God."[14]

The civil rights movement of the 1960s influenced the death penalty debate as the general public became more aware of racial discrimination's effects on the death penalty. Still, the death penalty debate differed from other social movements in the 1960s. Although many in the death penalty abolition movement might draw parallels with the civil rights movement of the 1960s, the anti-death penalty forces were never as strong as the civil rights movement for a number of reasons. In particular, the civil rights movement had a substantial foundation because people who were affected by the laws being challenged were able to stand up for the cause. By contrast, the people on death row constituted a much smaller group, and those on death row sat in their cells out of the public eye and could not participate in protests. Further, even if the condemned could march, they would not have generated much sympathy because of their crimes. The predominance of mental illness and other problems among death row inmates added to the difficulty in finding respected spokespersons among that group.[15]

During the 1960s, the antiwar movement and other significant social movements thrived in the United States, while the United States increased its involvement in Vietnam. These movements were not disconnected from capital punishment, so they generally invigorated the abolitionist movement. Activist and folk singer Phil Ochs wrote a song that appeared on his 1965 album *I Ain't Marching Anymore* called "Iron Lady," noting how the death penalty is a punishment for the poor, singing "And a rich man's never died upon the chair."[16] During the same decade, Bob Dylan and other folk singers touched on themes of justice and injustice, and Johnny Cash released two popular country music albums that were recorded inside Folsom Prison and San Quentin State Prison.[17]

Popular culture reflected this shift against the death penalty in other ways. In 1958, Susan Hayward starred in *I Want to Live!*, based on the life story and 1955 execution of Barbara Graham. Her sympathetic portrayal won an Academy Award.[18] In the 1960s, the television series *The Twilight Zone* presented several episodes touching on the death penalty, often illustrating the barbarity of the practice. In 1961's "Shadow Play," a condemned prisoner tries to convince his captors they are all dreamed characters in his real-world repeating nightmare. In the show's 1964 broadcast of the French film "An Occurrence at Owl Creek Bridge," Civil War soldiers prepare to hang a man at Owl Creek Bridge. When the man drops, the rope breaks, dropping him into the river below, where he escapes and returns to his family and loved ones. In the film, based on an 1890 short story by Ambrose Bierce, the escaped prisoner then discovers the escape was all a dream in the instant before death. Finally, in "I Am the Night—Color Me Black," broadcast in 1964, the sun fails to rise on the morning of the execution of a prisoner named Jagger, a black man who killed a bigot in self-defense.

The social changes and critiques of the death penalty contributed to some success for capital defense lawyers and death penalty abolition groups. As defense lawyers made new ground with their arguments in courtrooms, other capital defendants followed Caryl Chessman in spending longer periods of time on death rows. By the 1950s, the number of executions dropped, averaging 72 executions per year. After averaging more than 100 executions per year throughout the 1940s, by the first few years of the 1950s, the number of executions were in the low 80s, and in 1953, there were only 62 executions in the United States. By 1958, states executed only 49 people during the year.[19] (See Table 7.1.)

Consistent with earlier trends to limit death penalty crimes, states mainly used the death penalty for the crime of murder during this era, but some states also imposed the punishment for some non-homicide crimes as in Chessman's case. Of the ninety-seven total executions in 1958–1959, sixteen were for non-homicide crimes, mostly for rape, and fifteen of those sixteen men executed were African-American, all in southern states.[20]

Although not one state had abolished capital punishment between 1918 and 1956, several states did so in the following decade. Before they became states in 1960, the territories of Alaska and Hawaii abolished the death penalty in 1957. Hawaii has remained without the death penalty partly because of the memory of how whites used capital punishment against minority groups in the state.[21]

Following the actions in Hawaii and Alaska, from 1958 to 1965, the death penalty was abolished in Delaware, Oregon, Iowa, and West Virginia. In 1963, even though Michigan in the 1800s had already abolished capital punishment for all crimes except treason, the state strengthened its position against the death penalty by passing a new constitutional amendment that became effective January 1, 1964. The amendment stated, "No law shall be enacted providing for the penalty of death."[22]

Other states significantly limited the death penalty to fewer crimes. In 1965, Vermont limited the death penalty to those who murdered a prison officer or had an unrelated second capital crime. New York's state legislature considered a bill to abolish the death penalty every year between 1950 and 1962, but it instead eventually passed a law severely restricting the use of capital punishment. In May 1965 New York governor Nelson Rockefeller, who supported capital punishment, succumbed to pressure and signed a bill limiting the death penalty to cases where defendants killed a police officer or where a prisoner had killed a prison guard while serving a life sentence. The state, however, soon expanded the death penalty again in 1967.[23]

In states that abolished capital punishment, some worked to bring back the death penalty. After Governor J. Caleb Boggs on April 2, 1958, signed the law abolishing the death penalty in Delaware, the state brought back the punishment a few years later in 1961 soon after a notorious crime where Kermit West murdered a family on their farm. Other abolitions lasted longer. After West Virginia abolished the death penalty in 1965, state senators introduced bills to reinstate the punishment almost every year between 1969 and 1988. All of those attempts failed.

Southern states, however, generally kept the death penalty. Although McCleskey's state of Georgia maintained a death penalty through this time, the Georgia Legislature did reconsider one aspect of its capital punishment law. In 1963, the state repealed a provision authorizing the death penalty for "desecrating a grave."[24]

In addition to the social movements at the time, as in the past, various factors contributed to the abolitions. For example, when Iowa abolished the death penalty in 1965, the *Des Moines Register* and church groups played important roles. Additionally, Governor Harold Hughes advocated against the death penalty, proclaiming the abolition made Iowa a "more humane and wholesome society."[25]

Oregon abolished the death penalty after more than 60 percent of voters voted for abolition in a public referendum. Various factors in Oregon contributed to the large vote against capital punishment in 1964, including a recent governor who opposed the death penalty, a large political and public campaign (including ads by celebrities), and public attention on a sympathetic condemned female inmate.

Regarding the latter, local newspapers opposed the execution of a twenty-year-old woman, Jeannace June Freeman, who had been convicted of helping murder her lover's children.[26]

Several politicians of this period spoke out against capital punishment. Michael DiSalle, the governor of Ohio from 1959 to 1963, campaigned against capital punishment while in office and after his term. In the 1960s, North Carolina governor Terry Sanford similarly argued against capital punishment. In 1960, presidential candidate Hubert Humphrey also opposed capital punishment.[27]

The Quakers and other religious groups had opposed capital punishment for more than a century, but more religious organizations issued official statements against the death penalty in the 1950s and 1960s. Groups actively opposing capital punishment included the Methodist Church, the Lutheran Church, the American Baptist Convention, the Protestant Episcopal Church, the United Presbyterian Church, the Union of American Hebrew Congregations, and the Mennonite Church.[28] Secular groups also took up the cause, including the New York Committee to Abolish Capital Punishment, which was formed in 1957 to work toward abolition and to provide representation to capital defendants.[29]

The movements against the death penalty were not unique to the United States in the middle of the twentieth century. Many other countries abolished the death penalty during these years. In 1955, across the Atlantic Ocean, Arthur Koestler wrote "Reflections on Hanging," and the National Campaign for the Abolition of Capital Punishment was formed in Great Britain. Both events helped influence Great Britain to suspend the death penalty in 1965 on a trial basis and then abolish the punishment in 1969. While that country re-evaluated capital punishment, in 1966 singer Tom Jones had a hit song in the voice of a sympathetic death row prisoner dreaming of the "Green, Green Grass of Home." A year earlier, the song, written by Claude Putnam Jr., became a country hit in the United States for Porter Wagoner.

Across the United States, popular opinion turned against the death penalty. In 1966, more people were against the death penalty than were in favor of the punishment. Arkansas governor Winthrop Rockefeller ordered a moratorium on executions after he took office in 1967. In 1968, United States Attorney General Ramsey Clark asked Congress to abolish the federal death penalty. That same year, in *Witherspoon v. Illinois*, the U.S. Supreme Court observed that death penalty supporters were a "distinct and dwindling minority."[30]

In Pennsylvania in 1969, Attorney General Fred Speaker signed a legal opinion concluding the death penalty violated the U.S. Constitution, and he ordered a prison warden to dismantle the electric chair. Speaker, who earlier had supported the death penalty, became opposed to the punishment after visiting an execution chamber. Speaker timed his order after new governor Milton J. Shapp's inauguration but before Governor Shapp appointed Speaker's successor. Governor Shapp quickly responded by rescinding Speaker's order, but by then the electric chair had been taken apart and workers had converted the chamber into an office.[31]

As the 1960s neared its end, New Mexico in 1969 eliminated capital punishment for all crimes except for a second murder or murder of a law enforcement officer or prison guard. Even though New York and Delaware had gone back and forth during the decade, at the end of the 1960s, thirteen states had effectively ended using the death penalty or severely limited it: Michigan, Rhode Island (some exceptions), Wisconsin, Maine, Minnesota, North Dakota (some exceptions), Alaska, Hawaii, Oregon, Iowa, Vermont (some exceptions), West Virginia, and New Mexico (some exceptions).[32]

The death penalty was dying. Earlier in the decade, an article in *Time Magazine* had predicted, "If opponents of capital punishment were patient enough, they could just sit back and wait for it to fade away—in practice, if not on the statute books." The article noted, however, that "abolitionists try to hasten that fadeaway by argument."[33] The article correctly assessed the activists, who were soon making their arguments to get rid of the death penalty in front a new audience of nine men.

THE MAIN DEATH PENALTY ABOLITION FRONT MOVES TO THE COURTS

In the 1960s, as public opinion turned against capital punishment, abolitionists shifted much of their focus to the courts. Throughout the United States Supreme Court's history since the founding of the country through the 1960s, though, the Court had basically taken a hands-off approach to the death penalty.

Up to that time, the Court had addressed the cruel and unusual punishment clause of the Eighth Amendment only ten times. One reason for the dearth of Eighth Amendment cases was that for most of the early years of the country the Court did not apply the ban on cruel and unusual punishments to state prosecutions until after the Court incorporated the Eighth Amendment's cruel and unusual punishment prohibition through the post–Civil War Fourteenth Amendment. In the six cases where the Court considered the death penalty, it generally did so to affirm that the federal constitution did not prohibit the use of the death penalty, such as when in dicta it found no constitutional bar to executions by firing squad in 1879 in *Wilkerson v. Utah*.[34] Thus, until the late middle of the twentieth century, the Court did little with the Eighth Amendment's ban on cruel and unusual punishments or the Fourteenth Amendment's due process requirements in the context of the death penalty.

In 1958, though, in a noncapital case addressing revocation of citizenship as punishment, the justices wrote about the Eighth Amendment in a way that would influence future capital punishment cases. In *Trop v. Dulles*, Chief Justice Earl Warren, writing for the Court, stated that the Eighth Amendment "must draw its meaning from the evolving standards of decency that mark the progress of a maturing society."[35] This "evolving standards" language clarified that the meaning of the Eighth Amendment was not chained to the time of its writing, which was a time when Americans used the death penalty with little regulation. Instead, the meaning of "cruel and unusual punishments" can evolve over time. The Court's description gave hope to those who wished to argue the death penalty now violated the Constitution.

Not long after the *Trop* decision, the Court's hands-off approach to the death penalty began to change, sparked by a dissenting opinion written by Justice Arthur Goldberg. Goldberg had opposed capital punishment since he was a child. As a sixteen-year-old, he sat in a courtroom and watched Clarence Darrow make a case against the death penalty in the Leopold and Loeb murder trial. And, after World War II ended, he recognized a connection between the Holocaust and the use of capital punishment.

After President John F. Kennedy nominated Goldberg to the Court, Goldberg joined the Bench in the Court Term during the fall of 1962. Once on the Court, having had little experience with criminal cases, he discovered states applied the death penalty in an arbitrary manner and that the punishment often fell unfairly on blacks and other minorities.[36] (See Figure 6.1.)

Figure 6.1
Justice Arthur Goldberg (Collection of the Supreme Court of the United States)

Then, the Court received a petition for a writ of certiorari in *Rudolph v. Alabama*. In the Alabama case, Frank Rudolph, who was black, had been sentenced to death for the rape of a white woman. The Court also received a petition from another capital case involving a Virginia defendant, Frank Jimmy Snider Jr., who was convicted of raping a nine-year-old girl and who was one of the rare white men sentenced to death for rape.[37]

Even before the justices met to decide what to do with the *Rudolph* case and some other pending capital cases, Justice Goldberg circulated a memo to the other justices suggesting the Court address whether or not the death penalty was "cruel and unusual," even though none of the cases had raised the issue. In the memo, Goldberg informed his colleagues he wanted to raise questions about the constitutionality of the death penalty for further discussion. In proposing the death penalty might be unconstitutional under the Eighth Amendment, he also addressed policy concerns. The memo added that ending the death penalty for rape "would eliminate the well-recognized disparity" in the way the death penalty applied to nonwhite versus white defendants in sexual assault cases.[38]

When Goldberg first circulated his memo, even those inclined to agree with it wondered whether the country would accept the Court striking down the death penalty. Chief Justice Earl Warren discouraged Goldberg from publishing his memo, but they agreed Goldberg could issue a much more abbreviated dissent on the subject. Chief Justice Warren reasoned that the country found the issue of race and rape controversial; thus he also asked Justice Goldberg to cut back his discussion of race.[39]

Justice Goldberg agreed, and in October 1963 the majority denied the petitions for writ of certiorari in the two cases, in effect deciding—usually without any comment—not to address the merits of them. Goldberg issued his short dissenting opinion joined by Justice William O. Douglas and Justice William J. Brennan Jr. The three justices indicated some members of the Court were willing to hear arguments against the death penalty based upon the Eighth Amendment's ban on cruel and unusual punishments and based upon the Fourteenth Amendment's Due Process Clause.

Goldberg did not intend the four-sentence dissent to resolve the issues. Instead, he hoped to raise the questions. His first sentence explained that the dissenters would grant the petitions for certiorari in the two cases to address the question of whether the use of the death penalty for the crime of rape violated the Constitution. The remaining three sentences were questions about evolving standards of decency, proportionality, and policy. Specifically, the three questions focused on the use of the death penalty for a crime where the defendant did not kill.[40]

More broadly, the questions in the dissent sent out a message to capital defense attorneys across the country that at least some of the justices were open to constitutional arguments about the death penalty. For guidance, in seven footnotes to the four-sentence opinion, the dissenters provided authority from Supreme Court cases on the Eighth Amendment and information from a United Nations report.

After Justice Goldberg released his short dissent, he hoped it would inspire lawyers to concentrate on bringing more challenges to the nation's death penalty.

Goldberg had worked on his more-detailed original memo with his young law clerk, Alan Dershowitz, who would become a professor at Harvard Law School after finishing his clerkship. Goldberg gave Dershowitz permission to distribute the research from the memo to attorneys who might find it useful in raising claims about the death penalty.[41]

Justice Goldberg's hopes were realized when lawyers did respond to the *Rudolph* dissent. Capital defense lawyers and anti-death penalty lawyers wisely saw an opening to put more resources into attacking the death penalty in the courts.

Lawyers at the National Association for the Advancement of Colored People's Legal Defense and Education Fund (LDF) took the lead in organizing these constitutional challenges. As part of a concern about the unfair application of the death penalty, LDF lawyers had already been raising various constitutional challenges to the death penalty.

LDF's strategy to attack capital punishment in the courts during the 1950s and 1960s echoed the NAACP's earlier civil rights work starting in the 1930s fighting for legal rights for African Americans. In the 1930s, NAACP attorneys recognized Southern Democrats controlled Congress and would not pass remedial civil rights legislation, and President Franklin Roosevelt would not push for racial reforms that would jeopardize his New Deal programs. Thus, although the NAACP still worked for equality in other ways during the 1930s, a large part of its efforts focused on the courts and enforcing existing statutes that protected civil rights.[42] Also, the NAACP's work on capital cases was a natural progression from its work on lynching cases in those earlier decades. The leaders of the NAACP realized that cases involving race, sex, and violence were controversial and complicated. But they also realized that such cases grabbed headlines, helped bring in donations, and highlighted racial problems in the country.[43]

In the early 1950s, LDF began arguing that the death penalty for rape violated the Equal Protection Clause of the Constitution by focusing on the fact that in southern states blacks were more likely than whites to be sentenced to death for the crime of rape. Those arguments were not successful because courts required a showing of intentional discrimination for such claims. Still, while these race claims were losing in the courts, LDF continued to focus on the death penalty.[44]

Anthony G. Amsterdam, a University of Pennsylvania law professor, had started as a consultant with LDF around the time of Justice Goldberg's dissent in 1963, and he soon took charge of LDF's death penalty strategy. The tall and brilliant Amsterdam, who had clerked for Justice Felix Frankfurter, became legendary for his hard work and legal acumen, and he continued to play an important role in landmark capital cases for decades. Once he began working with LDF, he, LDF Director-Counsel Jack Greenberg, and other LDF attorneys recognized they were ethically required also to raise other claims besides race claims for their clients who were facing execution. Thus, LDF expanded its focus to a broad range of constitutional challenges to the death penalty, which also opened up their representation to white clients too.[45]

Following Justice Goldberg's dissent, by the mid-1960s, LDF lawyers attacked the death penalty using a courtroom strategy that included three tactics: (1) challenging cases in the Supreme Court, (2) developing and using social science evidence in the courts, and (3) attempting to block all executions while the litigation progressed. As part of this overall plan, LDF lawyers used a national strategy to enlist and work with lawyers around the country, just as they later worked with McCleskey's attorneys.[46]

Starting in 1965, LDF began coordinating federal constitutional challenges to the death penalty as part of a national effort. According to Amsterdam, LDF "developed a number of substantive constitutional arguments, embodied them in form pleadings that included applications for a stay of execution, instructed local lawyers on the arguments and the procedures for presenting them, and undertook to represent any condemned inmate for whom no other competent representation could be found."[47] In working with other attorneys, LDF struggled to control the overall strategy to make sure other lawyers did not raise claims or file class actions that would be inconsistent with LDF's plans.[48]

Justice Goldberg's *Rudolph* dissent led death penalty abolitionists to organize around a strategy that was unlike previous efforts to abolish the American death penalty. This new strategy did not focus on political discourse and popular sentiment. Instead, this new approach concentrated on using the courts to dismantle the death penalty. In an evaluation of the anti-death penalty movement, Professor Herbert Haines explained that therefore, "[t]raditional abolitionist arguments— for example, the failure of execution as a deterrent, the inhumanity of executions, the danger of fatal miscarriages of justice—...were recast as *constitutional* issues whose historical origins lay in the civil rights and civil liberties movements."[49] Haines noted this change made lawyers the leaders of the death penalty abolitionist movement.

This shift in control soon led to a decline in the strength of anti-death penalty organizations that worked through the political process. In effect, the death penalty abolitionists put much of their resources on the hope that the lawyers would end the American death penalty. So, efforts to abolish the death penalty through political means began declining in the mid-1960s. As the lawyers took the reins of the abolition efforts, some anti-death penalty activists went on to use their activist skills on other issues. For example, people associated with the Black Power Movement and the American Friends Service Committee, or Quakers, began placing more focus on general prison reform and other social movements.[50]

Similarly, even while activists continued to work on all fronts, significant anti-death penalty financial resources went toward the litigation strategy. For example, in addition to the work of LDF, the American Civil Liberties Union (ACLU) worked to end the death penalty in the United States. In 1965, the ACLU reversed its previous position that capital punishment was not a civil liberties issue and began an anti-death penalty strategy focusing on state legislatures. But the ACLU's legislative strategy received much less money than LDF, which was part of a tax-exempt organization.

This shift in the main focus from politicians to judges occurred while both courtroom action and legislative action showed encouraging signs for abolitionists. Public opinion in favor of abolition reached a high point, with a 1966 Harris

Survey showing 47 percent of the surveyed supporting abolition of the death penalty and only 38 percent supporting retention.[51] Some would wonder years later, in retrospect, what would have happened if a campaign that focused on state legislatures would have had the same resources that LDF and others spent on a courtroom campaign.[52]

But the litigation strategy dominated. LDF's litigation strategy eventually largely targeted two parts of the U.S. Constitution, the Fourteenth and the Eighth Amendments. The Fourteenth Amendment was added to the Constitution soon after the Civil War. After the Thirteenth Amendment's adoption in 1865 to ban slavery, several southern states responded by adopting Black Codes that denied blacks their new rights of citizenship. The post–Civil War Reconstruction Congress responded by passing the Civil Rights Act of 1866 and then, partly to ensure the constitutionality of that act, wrote the Fourteenth Amendment to protect the citizenship of blacks. The amendment, which was adopted in 1868, included the language "No state shall make or enforce any law which shall abridge the privileges or immunities of citizens of the United States; nor shall any state deprive any person of life, liberty, or property, without due process of law; nor deny to any person within its jurisdiction the equal protection of the laws."[53]

Initially, the LDF attorneys focused on the Fourteenth Amendment arguments because they believed that Eighth Amendment arguments would be unsuccessful. But they eventually added these other claims to their briefs and motions. The Eighth Amendment, which was added to the Constitution as part of the Bill of Rights in 1791, states, "Excessive bail shall not be required, nor excessive fines imposed, nor cruel and unusual punishments inflicted."[54] Although the country allowed executions at the time of the amendment's drafting, lawyers used *Trop v. Dulles* to argue the definition of "cruel and unusual punishments" could evolve over time. Thus, Amsterdam and the other LDF attorneys recognized, "Our only hope of getting the death penalty declared unconstitutional lay in arguing that something had changed."[55]

After LDF began its litigation strategy, LDF's racial disparity claims would not make it to the Supreme Court for more than two decades, when the Court decided to hear the claims in the case of Warren McCleskey. But other claims based on these amendments would soon find more immediate success in the courts.

While the capital defense lawyers were raising a broad range of constitutional claims, courts began to examine the constitutionality of the death penalty, and the federal courts became more sensitive to capital defendants' post-conviction litigation. As a result of this attention on the constitutionality of the death penalty, the number of executions in the country declined dramatically. Whereas executions in the United States had reached 199 in 1935, by 1963, the number of annual executions dropped to 21, followed by 15 in 1964, then 7 in 1965, then one in 1966 and two in 1967.[56]

Although executions were slowing down, states were still sentencing defendants to death. So, the execution slowdown meant that the population of state death rows throughout the country grew larger. In 1955, there were 125 people on death row, but by 1967, there were 435 condemned prisoners in the United States.

That number would continue to grow to 620 by 1972. The growing logjam made it less likely so many executions could ever be carried out.[57]

The executions finally ground to a complete halt by the middle of 1967. California and Colorado each performed one execution in 1967, constituting what would be the final two executions in the United States for a decade. California executed Aaron Mitchell on April 12, and then Colorado executed Luis Monge on June 2.

Mitchell had been convicted of killing police officer Arnold Gamble during a shootout at a 1963 Sacramento restaurant robbery. On the morning of the day before Mitchell's execution, correction officers found Mitchell lying on his back and banging his head on the concrete floor while screaming he was Jesus Christ. Although prison doctors declared Mitchell sane, the next day, they suggested sedation. San Quentin Warden Lawrence Wilson, however, rejected their suggestion. Guards dragged Mitchell to the gas chamber as he moaned and shouted, "I am Jesus Christ." According to Wilson, after prison officials strapped Mitchell in the chair and the gas pellets dropped, Mitchell continued to swing his head around violently and his body convulsed. Officials pronounced him dead twelve minutes after the pellets dropped.[58]

Unlike California's execution of Caryl Chessman seven years earlier, the state's execution of Aaron Mitchell received little national attention, even though the African-American defendant used statistics to argue that the death penalty was applied in a racially discriminatory manner. Only a few hundred people showed up at San Quentin to protest Mitchell's execution, while the same week in San Francisco 65,000 people participated in a march to protest the Vietnam War.[59]

Two months later in Colorado, Luis Monge gave up his appeals and ceased trying to prevent his execution for the murder of his wife and three of his ten children. As the doctor attached wires to monitor Monge's heart in the gas chamber, Monge asked the doctor, "Will that gas in there bother my asthma?" The doctor responded, "[N]ot for long." Monge donated his eyes to an eye bank, and his corneas were successfully transplanted.[60]

Monge could not know as he went to his death that he would be the last person executed in the United States for almost a decade. Had Monge continued to appeal his case, he probably would not have been executed. A major change to the American death penalty approached over the horizon.

The justice who had encouraged the constitutional litigation, though, would no longer be on the bench by the time the Court finally addressed the issues. Justice Goldberg, who wrote the 1963 dissenting opinion that sent a signal to capital defense attorneys, spent only three years on the Court. Although justices often serve decades as part of their lifetime appointment to the Court, Justice Goldberg retired after merely three years on the Court when President Lyndon B. Johnson persuaded him to step aside to create room for the president's friend Abe Fortas.[61] There would be several other changes on the Court as it began tackling the death penalty issue in the next decade.

CHAPTER 7

Into the Courthouse: The 1970s Abolition Strategy

*Capital defense attorneys continued their litigation attack on the American death penalty into the
1970s, eventually winning a major victory in the U.S. Supreme Court. But during this time, the
status of the American death penalty was rapidly changing.*

As in the mid-1800s and early 1900s, the 1960s period of anti-death penalty
sentiment occurred during a time of scientific progress and significant social
activism, including the civil rights movement. As executions ground to a halt, in
1968, Jack Greenberg, the director of LDF litigation, declared the organization's
legal strategy had accomplished a "de facto national abolition of the death penalty."[1]

Politicians also sensed the declining support for capital punishment. On December 29, 1970, outgoing Arkansas governor Winthrop Rockefeller commuted the
capital sentences of the fifteen inmates on death row in the state. Citizens of the
state supported the Republican governor's commutations by a 3-to1 margin. The
following year in the *Catholic University Law Review*, Rockefeller encouraged other
governors and legislators to take the lead in abolishing the American death penalty. Other governors who had commuted all or a large number of death sentences
during this period from the late 1950s to 1970 included Oregon governor Robert
Holmes (1957–1959), California governor Edmund G. (Pat) Brown (1959–1966),
and Massachusetts governor Endicott Peabody (1963–1965).[2]

But as the 1960s ended and the 1970s started, the main action regarding the
death penalty occurred in the courts. In courtrooms across the country, capital
defense lawyers argued against the American procedures used for imposing the
death penalty. In particular, they criticized the unlimited sentencing discretion
states gave to jurors and judges after jurisdictions abandoned mandatory death
penalty systems. In most death penalty jurisdictions, anyone found guilty of
first-degree murder became eligible for capital punishment, with Georgia and some
states using a broad common-law definition of murder.[3] Then, juries had complete

discretion for deciding which of the many murderers should be executed and which ones should serve life in prison. So defense attorneys invoked the Eighth and Fourteenth Amendments of the U.S. Constitution to challenge this capital sentencing process, claiming an unconstitutional arbitrariness resulted from the discretion given to juries in capital cases.

One of these cases almost resulted in a major victory for the anti-death penalty lawyers. During the Supreme Court's 1968–1969 Term, the justices heard argument in *Maxwell v. Bishop* to address the constitutionality of a death sentence imposed without a separate sentencing hearing. By a vote of 6-3 in the case of a black man sentenced to death for the rape of a white woman, the justices initially voted to strike down the procedures as unconstitutional. The six justices in the majority were Chief Justice Earl Warren, Justice William O. Douglas, Justice John Marshall Harlan II, Justice William J. Brennan, Jr., Justice Abe Fortas, and Justice Thurgood Marshall. But as the justices began drafting their opinions on issues surrounding the unitary capital trial where jurors had complete discretion, Harlan thought Douglas's majority opinion went too far, so he switched to join the dissenters. Although that still left a 5-4 majority, Fortas resigned due to an ethics investigation in May 1969 before the justices could issue an opinion. Thus, the remaining justices were equally split 4-4 on the case. And then Chief Justice Earl Warren resigned that summer.

As a few of President Richard M. Nixon's nominations to replace the departing justices failed in the Senate, and following a re-argument on the case, the justices decided to wait to address the death penalty issue until nine justices sat on the Court again. Eventually, the Court gained its two new members. Warren E. Burger replaced Chief Justice Warren as Chief Justice, and Justice Harry A. Blackmun took Justice Fortas's seat. The two retired justices, both who had voted against the death penalty in *Maxwell*, were now replaced by two friends from Minnesota with such similar conservative backgrounds that Blackmun and Burger were often called "The Minnesota Twins."

Ultimately the Court with the new justices wrote a short per curiam opinion in *Maxwell* that relied upon a narrow jury selection issue. Still, the previous back-and-forth among the justices on the case meant several members of the Court had now written drafts on death penalty issues that they would soon address.[4]

Then, in June 1970, the Supreme Court accepted review in *McGautha v. California* and *Crampton v. Ohio* to consider the constitutionality of the death penalty process.[5] The cases were an exception to the major cases at the time in that LDF did not represent the defendants. LDF, however, submitted amicus curiae briefs in the cases.

With two of the justices who were in the majority in *Maxwell* replaced by the two conservative justices, few were surprised that *McGautha* resulted in a defeat for the defense lawyers. The *McGautha* Court held that a sentencing procedure giving jurors absolute discretion in deciding to impose a death sentence did not violate the Due Process Clause of the Fourteenth Amendment. Writing for the Court, Justice Harlan, who had changed his vote during the drafting of opinions in *Maxwell*, wrote that the system needed jury discretion because it was impossible for legislatures in advance to define cases deserving of death. He explained, "To identify before the fact those characteristics of criminal homicides and their perpetrators which call for the death penalty, and to express these characteristics in language which can be fairly understood and applied by the sentencing authority, appear to be tasks which are beyond present human ability."[6]

In the 6-3 decision, Justices Douglas, Brennan, and Marshall dissented, finding a Fourteenth Amendment Due Process violation. Had the case been decided a year earlier before Fortas and Warren resigned, it may have had a different result. Their two replacements both voted with the majority. Even though Blackmun and Burger voted to uphold the death penalty on constitutional grounds and would do so many times through their careers, deep down they were both opposed to capital punishment on policy grounds.[7]

Although the *McGautha* case set back the litigation strategy to end the death penalty, the decision did not end the attacks in the courts. In the case, the Supreme Court did not address the issue of whether the discretionary capital sentencing process violated the cruel and unusual punishment ban in the Eighth Amendment. Thus, LDF continued to bring cases arguing death sentences violated the Eighth and Fourteenth Amendments due to the arbitrary and discriminatory manner in which states imposed the death penalty.

So, the attorneys did not give up on their litigation strategy, even though up to this point in American history, death penalty reform had come only through legislatures and not a single state or federal court had struck down the death penalty. Some LDF lawyers, including Tony Amsterdam, were skeptical that the Eighth Amendment arguments would win in the courts. They advocated for more focus on Congress, state governors, and public education. But soon anti-capital punishment lawyers finally saw some success with the litigation strategy, when the California Supreme Court struck down that state's death penalty on state constitutional grounds in 1972.[8]

After *McGautha*, the U.S. Supreme Court Justices recognized the Eighth Amendment challenges needed to be resolved and planned to look for cases to review the issue. Initially, Justice Brennan, who dissented in *McGautha*, suggested they should deny the pending petitions from death row defendants. He feared the Court would not find an Eighth Amendment violation.[9] Similarly, Justice Douglas objected to the plan to accept review of the Eighth Amendment issue. He recalled that in *Boykin v. Alabama* in 1967, the Court had considered the issue. In a secret vote of 6-3, the justices concluded the death penalty did not violate the Eighth Amendment, even though the vote never became public because the Court decided the case on other grounds. Justice Douglas argued the Court should not raise the hopes of the condemned by taking the issue when clearly the Court would not stop their executions. Justice Douglas, however, could not convince the other justices to cease their plan.[10]

Instead, the eighty-five-year-old Justice Hugo L. Black, who hoped the Court would clarify that the Eighth Amendment's original meaning permitted the death penalty, convinced the others to address the Eighth Amendment issue. So, Justices Brennan and Stewart took on the task of finding the cases for the Court to evaluate the Eighth Amendment issues.

Despite Justice Black's entreaty for the justices to review the Eighth Amendment issue, he would not be on the Court when it finally reached the issue. In September 1971, Black resigned from the Court and died a little more than a week later. Justice Marshall Harlan II retired around the same time as Black after learning he had spinal cancer and he passed away in December of that year. President Nixon appointed William H. Rehnquist and Lewis F. Powell Jr. to replace Harlan and Black, respectively. Capital defense lawyers saw the new Nixon appointments as making the Court even less likely to rule in their favor. Director-Counsel of LDF Jack Greenberg and other LDF attorneys such as Michael Meltsner began to see the Eighth Amendment claim as a losing argument.[11] (See Figure 7.1.)

Within a year, though, the Supreme Court did review the Eighth Amendment issue, and it became a victory for the capital defense lawyers. The decision involved the combined cases of two Georgia capital defendants, William H. Furman and Lucious Jackson, along with another defendant from Texas, Elmer Branch. All three of the defendants were black, and LDF represented the two Georgia defendants.

The twenty-six-year-old Furman, who had a sixth-grade education and mental problems, had been convicted of killing William Micke in Chatham County, Georgia. The killing occurred during a bungled burglary, and Furman claimed he accidentally fired his gun when he tripped. Superior Court Judge Earl Dunbar Harrison sentenced Furman to Georgia's electric chair after an all-white jury found Furman guilty of murder. Jackson's case also came from Chatham County but he was convicted of rape instead of murder. Under the Georgia statute, because Jackson's jury did not recommend mercy, the trial judge automatically sentenced him to death. Both Furman and Jackson lost their appeals to the Georgia Supreme Court in unanimous decisions upholding constitutional challenges to the state's death penalty.

In the third case, Elmer Branch had been sentenced to death in Texas for raping a sixty-five-year-old woman.[12] The Court also had selected a California case to review involving Earnest Aikins, Jr., and attorneys argued *Aikens v. California* before the Court with the other cases. But the U.S. Supreme Court dropped the review grant after the California Supreme Court struck down that state's death penalty laws, making the Supreme Court's review moot.

On Monday, January 17, 1972, the Court heard oral arguments on the death penalty cases. Among others, Tony Amsterdam, who in 1969 began teaching at Stanford Law School, argued the *Aikens* and *Furman* cases for LDF. Jack Greenberg argued the *Jackson* case for LDF. Dorothy Beasley argued the *Furman* and *Jackson* cases for the Georgia Attorney General's office, and Ronald George, a Deputy California Attorney General, argued *Aikens* for California. In the Texas case, Dallas attorney Mel Bruder represented Branch, while Charles Alan Wright, a University of Texas law professor and leading scholar on constitutional law and federal procedure, argued to uphold the death sentence.[13]

On June 29, 1972, the last day of the Court's term, the Court announced its opinion. In *Furman v. Georgia*,[14] the Court struck down Georgia's system of giving complete discretion to the sentencer. A majority of the justices found that

Figure 7.1
The *Furman v. Georgia* Supreme Court. Back row: Powell, Marshall, Blackmun, and Rehnquist. Front row: Stewart, Douglas, Burger, Brennan, and White. (Collection of the Supreme Court of the United States)

imposition of the death penalty in the cases before it constituted "cruel and unusual punishment" under the Eighth and Fourteenth Amendments. Beyond the conclusion, the reasoning of the 5-4 decision had no clear consensus, with each justice writing a separate opinion in what amounted to the longest Supreme Court decision ever.[15] There was not a majority of justices stating they would find capital punishment unconstitutional in all circumstances, but a majority of the justices raised concerns about arbitrariness in the capital punishment sentencing system.

Two of the justices—William Brennan and Thurgood Marshall—concluded the death penalty per se violates the Constitution. Justice Marshall, a former lawyer at the NAACP who had represented people sentenced to death, reasoned the death penalty was cruel and unusual punishment. In his analysis, he expressed concerns about the role of race and capital punishment, noting "[s]tudies indicate that while the higher rate of execution among Negroes is partially due to a higher rate of crime, there is evidence of racial discrimination."[16] Marshall based his finding that the death penalty violated the constitution on two grounds. First, he concluded the punishment was excessive and served no valid legislative purpose. Second, he found capital punishment was abhorrent to currently existing moral values.

Similarly, Justice Brennan listed four principles of the Eighth Amendment: (1) punishments must not be so severe that they are degrading to human beings, (2) punishments must not arbitrarily inflict severe punishment, (3) a severe punishment must be acceptable to contemporary society, and (4) a severe punishment must not be excessive and unnecessary. He then explained that the death penalty violated those principles, discussing how the punishment is arbitrary, how it does not deter, how it is used rarely, and how it degrades human beings. Both Marshall and Brennan would maintain their position on the death penalty in *Furman* throughout the rest of their careers, although many years earlier in 1962 as a judge on the U.S. Court of Appeals for the Second Circuit, Marshall had joined an opinion denying habeas corpus relief to a man sentenced to death.[17]

The other three justices in the majority were Justice William O. Douglas, Justice Potter Stewart, and Justice Byron White. They did not go as far as Justices Brennan and Marshall to say that the death penalty is always an unconstitutional punishment. But the three wrote opinions finding capital punishment unconstitutional in the way courts imposed it.

The first of the three, Justice Douglas, focused largely on the discriminatory results from the death penalty statutes. He found the system unconstitutional because it allowed discrimination against the underprivileged and minorities. He concluded the "cruel and unusual" punishment clause of the Eighth Amendment of the Constitution prohibited such discrimination. The purpose of the clause, he explained, "is to require legislatures to write penal laws that are even-handed, non-selective, and nonarbitrary, and to require judges to see to it that general laws are not applied sparsely, selectively, and spottily to unpopular groups." He reasoned, then, "the death penalty inflicted on one defendant is 'unusual' if it discriminates against him by reason of his race, religion, wealth, social position, or class, or if it is imposed under a procedure that gives room for the play of such prejudices." In considering the death penalty statutes before the Court, he noted "[t]hey are pregnant with discrimination" that was incompatible "with the idea of equal protection of the laws that is implicit in the ban on 'cruel and unusual' punishments."[18]

Although Douglas did not discuss specific statistics, significant racial disparities existed in the use of capital punishment. William Furman, like 80 percent of Georgia's death row, was African American. As were 81 percent of those executed in the state during the previous three decades, even though at the time of Furman's arrest, the African-American population in the state was only 27 percent. Finally, the fact that he had been convicted of killing a white man made it even more likely he would get a death sentence.[19] For now, though, the Court did not delve into these statistics but focused on the arguments about the system in general.

The other two justices of the five who voted to strike down the death sentence also focused on the arbitrariness of the death penalty system that gave complete discretion to jurors. Justice Stewart compared the selection of who receives a death sentence to being struck by lightning. He reasoned that the Eighth Amendment does not allow the death penalty "to be so wantonly and so freakishly imposed." Despite the randomness of the death penalty, Justice Stewart noted, "racial discrimination has not been proved, and I put it to one side."[20] Justice White found the death penalty unconstitutional because under current procedures, states imposed it so infrequently that it did not substantially serve the criminal justice system.[21]

The four dissenting justices who voted to uphold Furman's death sentence were also the newest members of the Court, all appointed by President Nixon. Chief Justice Warren Burger, Justice Harry Blackmun, Justice Lewis Powell, and Justice William Rehnquist each wrote separate opinions stating they would uphold Georgia's death penalty statute.

Several of the justices in both the majority and the dissent agonized over their decisions. In *The Brethren*, Bob Woodward and Scott Armstrong reported that some of the justices had trouble sleeping as the case weighed on them. Justice Powell recognized he did not know the law in the area so he increased his workload to read all of the past death penalty cases, giving up going to church and other activities. Ultimately, though, Justice Powell voted to uphold the death penalty. Although statistics showing racial discrimination concerned him, he felt that such discrimination in capital sentencing was largely a thing of the past and was rare in modern cases with procedural safeguards.[22]

As a result of the nine opinions and the 5-4 vote in the *Furman* decision, the Court reversed the death sentences in the three cases before it and entered similar orders in 120 other death penalty appeals. In effect, the Court's decision prevented the execution of all of the death row prisoners in the United States at the time, and 587 men and 2 women were taken off of death rows. At the time, Florida had the largest death row in the country, with 102 condemned. In Warren McCleskey's state of Georgia, the death row contained 43 inmates convicted of murder (29), rape (12), or armed robbery (2). Thus far into the twentieth century, Georgia had executed more people than any other state. During the years between 1924 and 1972, Georgia executed 412 people, with 337 of the condemned being black and only 75 being white.[23] But now executions ground to a halt. (See Table 7.1.)

In later years, 322 of the people who had been condemned to death at the time of the *Furman* decision were eventually paroled. Pro-death penalty advocates point out that five of those paroled and nine of those who remained in prison later committed homicides, including a man in Texas who raped and strangled several young women until authorities finally caught and executed him. Anti-death penalty advocates argue that the relatively low recidivism rate for the class does not support the death penalty for the entire group.

As for William Furman, the African-American defendant at the center of the litigation, Georgia resentenced him to prison for his felony-murder conviction for breaking into a house and killing a man. The state eventually released Furman from prison in 1984, but by the late 1990s he was having health and mental disabilities. In 2006, he pleaded guilty to a burglary charge and was sentenced to twenty years. Furman, who was 64 at the time of his plea, may spend the rest of his life in prison.[24]

Table 7.1. EXECUTIONS IN AMERICA PRIOR
TO *FURMAN V. GEORGIA*[25]

Years	U.S. Executions
1601–1700	169
1701–1750	388
1751–1760	94
1761–1770	184
1771–1780	238
1781–1790	275
1791–1800	230
1801–1810	192
1811–1820	231
1821–1830	379
1831–1840	380
1841–1850	330
1851–1860	616
1861–1870	526
1871–1880	695
1881–1890	1,002
1891–1900	1,104
1901–1910	1,309
1911–1920	1,069
1921–1930	1,342
1931–1940	1,648
1941–1950	1,255
1951–1960	697
1961–1970	136

A New Era: A New U.S. Death Penalty Returns in the Late 1970s

Had the Supreme Court's 1972 decision on the American death penalty survived, Warren McCleskey probably would have been sentenced to life in prison. But major changes began taking place in response to Furman v. Georgia *that would create a new death penalty scheme.*

I n 1972, many thought *Furman v. Georgia* had ended the death penalty in the United States. Jack Greenberg, the director of the NAACP Legal Defense Fund, and Chief Justice Warren Burger agreed that capital punishment in the United States was a thing of the past.[1] Justice Potter Stewart also believed the Court was finished with the death penalty issue. Perhaps recalling his early career as a politician on the Cincinnati City Council as well as his father's political career that included time as Cincinnati mayor and a candidate for Ohio governor, Stewart believed that the state legislatures would not pass barbaric mandatory death penalty laws to get around the Court's holding.[2] But in the written opinions in the case, a majority of the *Furman* justices left open the issue of the constitutionality of the death penalty. And change was in the air.

Although there had been a strong wind against capital punishment in the 1960s, by the end of the decade, public attitudes already were shifting. As the LDF's attacks on the American death penalty finally halted executions in the United States for the first time in 1968, American society was changing. Those that Richard M. Nixon called the "silent majority" were responding to what appeared to be a nation in chaos. In just the first half of the year, the United States faced heavy fighting in the TET Offensive in Vietnam, students were protesting, President Lyndon B. Johnson changed his mind about running for re-election, and Martin Luther King Jr. and Robert Kennedy were assassinated. In August, antiwar protesters and Chicago police confronted each other during the Democratic National Convention. Meanwhile, Nixon's presidential campaign focused on restoring order, including promises to address the high crime rate and to control the liberal Supreme Court.

The country overwhelmingly elected him as president in November. Former Alabama governor George Wallace also ran for president that year as an independent candidate on a law-and-order and segregationist platform, winning five southern states, including Warren McCleskey's Georgia.[3]

In the 1960s, as views on the death penalty were in transition, Richard Nixon became a trailblazer in using crime issues in his campaigns, sensing shifting popular opinion on the death penalty and law-and-order issues. Six years before Nixon became president, in the California governor's race in 1962, the former vice president attempted to use the delays in executing Caryl Chessman against incumbent governor Edmund "Pat" Brown. Theodore Hamm explained in *Rebel without a Cause* that at the time, Californians lived in an era of prosperity led by a successful governor, so Nixon had few issues from which to choose. With polls showing California citizens were increasingly concerned about crime, Nixon focused on the Chessman case and the death penalty in general in his campaign. Brown won the 1962 election, partly because of perceptions that Nixon was using California as a vehicle to get back into national politics. In his concession speech, Nixon famously stated, "You won't have Nixon to kick around anymore because, gentlemen, this is my last press conference." But the California loss did not end his career. Meanwhile, Nixon set a precedent of using the death penalty and crime issues in California politics, and he remembered the lesson for his own future campaigns for higher office.

After Governor Brown defeated Nixon in 1962, he lost his campaign for re-election to a third term in 1966, losing in a landslide to former actor Ronald W. Reagan. The new governor, like Nixon, was another up-and-coming Republican who used the law-and-order theme in the campaign for governor and continued to use it during a successful political career. The Watts riots during the summer of 1965 and other factors led the state's citizens to embrace the crime issue. Thus, by 1966, California polls showed citizens were most concerned about "racial problems" and "crime, drugs, and juvenile delinquency." Governor Reagan began his inaugural speech by discussing "lawlessness" and then another major issue, welfare. After Brown lost the race for governor, some hoped he would commute the sentences of everyone on death row. Instead, he commuted the sentences of only four death row prisoners, leaving sixty men on California's death row, with one-third of them African-American.[4]

Although in the early 1960s California elected a governor who opposed the death penalty, the state overwhelmingly chose the law-and-order Ronald Reagan in 1966. While the national rate of executions plummeted, one of the two 1967 executions occurred when Governor Reagan denied clemency to Aaron Mitchell, who was executed for killing a police officer during a robbery. Former governor Brown criticized the execution, saying, "Life is getting too cheap." Around the same time period, California juries started giving out more death sentences after 1966, and 65 percent of Californians supported the death penalty in a 1969 Field Poll.[5]

California's changing attitude about capital punishment reflected a nationwide trend as the 1960s ended and the 1970s began. Although a 1966 Gallup poll showed 47 percent of people supported abolition of the death penalty versus

42 percent supporting retention (similar to a Harris poll at the same time), by 1969 another Gallup poll found only 40 percent support for abolition of the death penalty versus 50 percent support for retention. As part of the overall change, a significant shift occurred among blue-collar workers, who earlier in the decade opposed the death penalty at a much higher rate than more affluent people. In 1966, 50 percent of blue-collar workers had opposed the death penalty with only 40 percent supporting it. But by the end of the decade they significantly increased their support for the death penalty, consistent with the New Right's politicians such as Nixon and Reagan who advocated for capital punishment as part of a law-and-order agenda.[6]

The political atmosphere continued changing in the early 1970s, and not long after *Furman v. Georgia*, the country entered a recession from 1973 to 1975 and unemployment rose. As in the past, such economic changes may have contributed to less concern about the use of the death penalty for convicted murderers.

Thus, even by the time the *Furman* Court invalidated the country's death penalty laws in 1972, the national anti-death penalty sentiment already was retreating. A new viewpoint developed out of frustrations over protests and social unrest, replacing the youthful rebellion of the 1960s on political and social issues. The writer Hunter S. Thompson described the early 1970s as "that place where the wave finally broke and rolled back."[7]

On top of all these societal changes, death penalty opponents, who had focused their resources on a court-based abolition strategy, were not fully prepared for the backlash to the *Furman* decision. Looking back on these years, Norman Redlich, an anti-death penalty lawyer and former New York University Law School dean, reflected, "As the emphasis in the fight against capital punishment shifted to the courts, we forgot the politics. We were lulled into believing that if we continued to win cases in court, it wouldn't matter what the public thought." Redlich conceded that death penalty opponents erred by focusing so much on the courts because public opinion and fear about crime affected politics and the men and women on the courts.[8]

One could see the political shift affecting the Supreme Court. By 1972, the *Furman* Court already included four justices appointed by President Nixon in his first three years: (1) Chief Justice Warren Burger, who had replaced Chief Justice Earl Warren; (2) Justice Harry Blackmun, who had replaced Justice Abe Fortas; (3) Justice Lewis F. Powell, Jr. who had replaced Justice Hugo Black; and (4) Justice William Rehnquist, who had replaced Justice John Marshall Harlan II. Nixon's four appointees were in the dissent in *Furman,* and the unanimous dissent of the new justices signaled that the Court and the country were heading in a new direction. Five months after *Furman,* the nation re-elected President Nixon.

In addition to the personnel changes on the Court, by the early 1970s, the Supreme Court as an institution had felt political pressure for many of its decisions for decades. Under Chief Justice Earl Warren from 1953 to 1969, the Court decided landmark cases on civil rights, which included *Brown v. Board of Education* in 1954, and on criminal rights, which included *Miranda v. Arizona* in 1966. These cases were met with open hostility from various parts of the country and particularly in the

South. For a time in the 1950s and 1960s, in the South one might see "Impeach Earl Warren" signs planted by the John Birch Society.

Additionally, around the same time the Court felt backlash from *Furman*'s intrusion on state's rights, the Court felt the political heat on another case involving questions about life and death. Seven months after deciding *Furman*, the Court decided *Roe v. Wade* in January 1973,[9] taking much of the abortion issue away from state legislatures by finding that laws banning abortions were unconstitutional. At the beginning of the decade, a large majority of both Republicans and Democrats had believed that abortion decisions should be left to a woman and her physician. But the abortion debate, like the death penalty debate, became highly politicized in the 1970s. One of the reasons for the political divide was that President Nixon followed the suggestions of advisers in 1971 to become an outspoken opponent of abortions as a strategy to divide Democrat voters in the South.[10]

With *Roe v. Wade* and *Furman v. Georgia*, the Court angered a significant segment of American society that opposed abortions and favored capital punishment. Critics of the decisions argued the Court used the Constitution to take political issues away from the people. These critics could do little immediately to get state legislatures to ban abortions outright because the Supreme Court in *Roe* stated that the Constitution prohibited such a ban. So people who wished to stop abortions had to go the difficult route of trying to change the Constitution, and representatives introduced a right-to-life amendment in Congress eight days after the Supreme Court decided *Roe*.[11] Additionally, movements on both sides of the abortion debate were organized and prepared to work on educating the public. By contrast, the division among the justices in *Furman* left open an option for state politicians to bring back the death penalty through simple legislation. And the anti-death penalty organizations that had used their resources for the court attacks were not prepared to respond in the political arena.

Because the Court did not abolish capital punishment per se and struck down only the existing death penalty statutes, state legislatures responded to the decision by attempting to write new death penalty statutes that would pass constitutional muster. The response was swift. One day after the decision in *Furman*, legislators were already promising to write new death penalty laws. Within days after *Furman*, Florida Governor Reubin Askew called the state legislature into a special session to work on a new death penalty law. Before 1972 ended, in December, Florida became the first state to restore capital punishment. Other states followed. In the general election of November 1972, Californians—led by Governor Ronald Reagan and his wife, Nancy Reagan—passed by a wide margin a proposition to amend the state constitution and restore the death penalty to that state.[12] Several states followed with new death penalty laws in 1973, and more followed. Many anti-death penalty activists were surprised by the quick backlash after *Furman*.

In McCleskey's home state of Georgia, the politicians reacted to the Supreme Court decision in *Furman* by starting work on a new death penalty law. Georgia's lieutenant governor and former governor Lester Maddox exclaimed that *Furman* gave a "license for anarchy, rape and murder."[13] Georgia Senator James L. Lester criticized some of the justices for claiming the death penalty was racially biased. Senator Lester responded that it was "ridiculous" for the Supreme Court to want to keep a "box score" on the race of the condemned in Georgia. He asked, "[I]s this going to be carried to the extreme where they will say that we have electrocuted 10 blacks and we can't electrocute any more blacks until we execute 10 whites?"[14]

In early 1973, two Georgia state representatives introduced House Bill Number 12, a new death penalty law to replace the one found unconstitutional the previous year in *Furman*. Another representative, Representative Bobby Hill, led African-American House members in an unsuccessful bid to stop the bill. The death penalty bill eventually passed in the House by a vote of 154 to 16, although representatives rejected a House member's proposed amendment to allow public hangings. African-American legislators cast fourteen of the sixteen votes against the death penalty reinstatement bill.[15]

Subsequently, in the Georgia Senate, the senators passed their version of the House Bill by a vote of 47-7. The Senate rejected an amendment proposed by Leroy Johnson, who was the first African American to serve in the Georgia Senate and who opposed capital punishment. Johnson, having failed in attempts to stop the capital punishment bill altogether, proposed that capital sentencing be mandatory for certain crimes. He later explained that he made his unsuccessful attempt to make death sentences mandatory because he wanted to make sure the law applied the same for blacks and whites. Senate majority leader Gene Holley argued the state needed the new death penalty law because without it, the people "will take the law into their own hands," as he may have recalled the lynching of Leo Frank by the group of men from Marietta.[16]

Another Georgia senator, Sen. Robert Smalley, questioned the constitutionality of the law and made a prediction later resolved with Warren McCleskey's case in the Supreme Court. He argued, "The simple fact of the matter is that when the Supreme Court keeps its box score, it will not pass muster because juries are not going to impose the death penalty indiscriminately. They are going to impose it on the poor and the black and it is going to be declared unconstitutional again."[17]

After both chambers of the Georgia General Assembly approved the bill, on March 28, 1973, Georgia Governor Jimmy Carter signed into effect the law, which eventually would be used to sentence Warren McCleskey to death. When a reporter asked Governor Carter whether or not the law might be constitutional, he stated, "I'm not going to predicate my decision on what a court might do if a challenge is filed." Like Georgia's previous death penalty law, this new one would soon go to the Supreme Court in another landmark case. More immediately, Georgia courts had to reverse some death sentences after anxious prosecutors sought death penalties for crimes that occurred prior to the effective date of the new Georgia law.[18]

As in Warren McCleskey's home state, in other states the legislative and courtroom responses occurred as support for the death penalty had been growing. Polls in the 1970s showed the late 1960s change continuing. A Gallup Poll taken in March 1972 before the *Furman* decision found 50 percent in favor of the death penalty with 42 percent opposed. By comparison, after *Furman*, a poll in November 1972 saw an increase to 57 percent in favor of capital punishment with 32 percent against it. Within four years, a 1976 poll found support for the death penalty rose to 65 percent with only 28 percent opposed. Thus, within a few years after *Furman*, the anti-death penalty sentiment that flourished in the 1960s fell back to its low early-1950s level.[19]

After the new laws went into effect, juries handed out a record number of death sentences. By 1974, more than 150 inmates had been sentenced to death in the United States under the new laws. By the spring of 1975, thirty-one states had new death penalty laws. In 1975 alone, courts put 298 people on death rows in the United States, more than any previous year of American history for which statistics were kept.[20]

* * *

As the state legislatures struggled to rewrite their statutes to address the Supreme Court justices' concerns about arbitrariness, they came up with different approaches. Some states took the capital sentencing task away from jurors and gave it to the trial judges, reasoning judges would be less arbitrary than juries. For example, Arizona's new law that became effective in August 1973 required that after a jury found a defendant guilty of capital murder, a trial judge would weigh aggravating and mitigating factors to determine the sentence.[21]

Beyond the question of who did the sentencing, the states for the most part came up with two different sentencing procedures. Many states responded to the *Furman* decision's arbitrariness concerns by rewriting their death penalty statutes to either give judges and juries guidance or to provide for mandatory death sentences. Sixteen states passed mandatory death penalty laws that automatically imposed the death penalty for certain crimes, such as murder of a police officer or murder-for-hire. Other states passed laws requiring judges or juries to consider aggravating factors or some other type of guidelines in imposing capital sentences.[22]

It was only a matter of time before the Supreme Court had to revisit the death penalty issue to resolve the confusion in the lower courts caused by the divided *Furman* decision. In April 1975, the Court heard oral arguments in *Fowler v. North Carolina* to address an Eighth Amendment challenge to North Carolina's mandatory death sentencing procedure.[23] LDF represented the prisoner Jesse T. Fowler. In addition to LDF and an attorney for the state, the U.S. government became involved in the case when Solicitor General Robert Bork filed an amicus brief and argued before the Court in favor of upholding the death penalty.

Another change on the Court, though, prevented the *Fowler* case from resolving the issue. Several months before the *Fowler* argument, Justice Douglas had a stroke and was in bad health. After the rest of the justices split 4-4 on their initial conference vote in the case, they believed Douglas too ill to participate in the case. Thus, they decided to hold the case over until the next term, ultimately resolving to take different cases to address the Eighth Amendment issues. Justice Douglas still hoped to participate in the new cases, but he reluctantly resigned in November 1975. President Gerald R. Ford nominated Douglas's replacement, John Paul Stevens, whom the Senate easily confirmed. Stevens then was sworn in during December.[24]

The next month, in January 1976, the Court accepted review of five capital cases from five different southern states: *Gregg v. Georgia, Jurek v. Texas, Proffitt v. Florida, Woodson v. North Carolina*, and *Roberts v. Louisiana*. The Court selected the five cases because together they represented the different types of laws passed after *Furman*, featuring variations on the mandatory and guided-discretion sentencing options. Georgia used a system that provided sentencing juries with guidelines, while the Florida system similarly provided guidelines but had judges doing the final sentencing. The cases from North Carolina and Louisiana reviewed mandatory death sentencing schemes. The case from Texas featured a variation on the guidelines approach, with juries given specific questions to answer.

The justices decided to take only murder cases, leaving the issue of capital punishment for non-murders for another day. They also selected cases that were relatively straightforward and avoided other issues such as claims that the death penalty discriminates based on race.[25] Then, the Court set an expedited schedule for the cases.

One of the cases, *Gregg v. Georgia*, again came from Georgia. It addressed the statute written to replace the one struck down in *Furman*. The defendant in the case was Troy L. Gregg, who had been convicted of murdering two men, robbing them, and stealing their car after they picked him up while he hitchhiked. The jury imposed four death sentences: two for the two murders and two for the two robberies. Before the case reached the U.S. Supreme Court, though, the Georgia Supreme Court struck down the death sentences given for the armed robberies, finding the punishment of death excessive for the crime of robbery.[26] Then, the U.S. Supreme Court granted review of the remaining two death sentences for murder in Gregg's case, along with the cases from the other states.

The oral arguments on the five cases were scheduled for two days on Tuesday, March 30 and Wednesday, March 31, 1976. A large number of attorneys argued for the five defendants and the five states, with U.S. Solicitor General Robert Bork also arguing in support of the states. LDF again represented some of these defendants, although other defense attorneys represented Gregg and Proffitt.

Tony Amsterdam, who had successfully argued against the death penalty statutes in *Furman* in an outstanding piece of advocacy, again appeared before the Court for LDF. But this time, he found himself making arguments far from what most of the justices now had the patience to hear. For the clients represented by LDF, he steadfastly maintained that the death penalty violated the Eighth Amendment in all cases, which prevented him from making compromises on questions from the Court such as whether someone who set off a hydrogen bomb in New York City should be given a prison sentence with the opportunity for parole. Amsterdam was a zealous advocate for his clients and steadfastly asserted his position that the death penalty differed from all other punishments. But some of the justices believed his argument's absolute position and his refusal to engage the Court in distinguishing the different statutes bordered on self-righteousness.[27]

Since the 1972 *Furman* decision, only one change had occurred on the Court, with Justice John Paul Stevens replacing Justice William Douglas. Douglas had been in the majority to strike down the death penalty statutes in the 1972 case.

After the justices accepted review of the 1976 cases, Justice Powell believed the Court would strike down the death penalty permanently. He expected the new justice, Stevens, or Justice Blackmun to join the other four justices remaining from the majority in *Furman*. But Powell was wrong, as both Stevens and Blackmun ended up voting to uphold the constitutionality of the death penalty.[28]

In opinions issued two days before the nation's bicentennial in 1976, the Court addressed the constitutionality of the new statutes. Before addressing the procedures in the new statutes for imposing capital punishment, the Court had to address whether or not capital punishment is a cruel and unusual punishment. By a vote of 7-2, with only Justices Thurgood Marshall and William J. Brennan, Jr., dissenting, a majority of the Court held the death penalty for murderers did not violate the Constitution.

In a plurality opinion, Justice Stewart reflected on the long history of the use of the death penalty in explaining that capital punishment is not cruel and unusual. In considering "evolving standards of decency" to interpret the Eighth Amendment, he reasoned that the fact that thirty-five states passed new death penalty laws did not show states had rejected capital punishment. Further, he reasoned the death penalty was not so inconsistent with penological goals of deterrence and retribution that the Court needed to substitute its judgment for the state legislatures.[29]

With the issue of the constitutionality of the death penalty in general resolved, the next issue was whether any states had devised constitutional procedures for imposing capital punishment. Among the five cases, the Court found that at least some states had come up with constitutional procedures for imposing the punishment. Although a majority of the Court upheld these statutes, a majority of the Court did not agree on the reasoning, so each of the three cases featured a plurality opinion. The Court in *Gregg v. Georgia*, *Jurek v. Texas*, and *Proffitt v. Florida* upheld systems where the sentencer followed statutory guidelines in using discretion.[30] These statutes were generally based on a model statute called the Model Penal Code, which was designed in 1963 by scholars, practitioners, and others. Under these state statutes, sentencing juries were given questions or factors to consider in deciding whether or not to sentence a defendant to death.

For example, the Georgia statute that the Court upheld in *Gregg v. Georgia* listed a number of aggravating factors about the crime. The sentencing jury had to find at least one of those factors before it could impose a death sentence. The aggravating factors in the Georgia statute included: (1) the offense was committed by a person with a prior capital felony conviction; (2) the offender created a grave risk of death to more than one person in a public place by using a weapon dangerous to more than one person; (3) the offender committed the murder for the purpose of receiving money; (4) the offender murdered a judge or district attorney; (5) the crime was "outrageously or wantonly vile, horrible, or inhuman in that it involved torture, depravity of mind, or an aggravated battery to the victim"; or (6) the murder was committed by a person who had escaped from custody or by a person interfering with an arrest.[31] If the jury found one or more of these statutory aggravating factors, the jury would then consider that finding along with the defendant's mitigating factors to determine whether or not to impose a death sentence.

The Texas statute, instead of listing factors, asked jurors to answer specific questions about the crime and the defendant before being able to impose a death sentence. The questions included consideration of whether or not the defendant was a future danger to society. This future-dangerousness question asked jurors to answer "whether there is a probability that the defendant would commit criminal acts of violence that would constitute a continuing threat to society."[32] As in the Georgia case, in *Jurek v. Texas* the Court upheld the statute, even though some believed the Texas statute should have been categorized as a mandatory death penalty statute. The justices found that the questions gave sufficient guidance to jurors to determine whether or not to impose a death sentence.

Thus, a majority of the Court upheld the statutes from Texas and Georgia that gave jurors sentencing guidelines. In *Proffitt*, a majority also upheld Florida's statute that gave guidelines for a judge to do the sentencing. The plurality reasoned that these new statutes sufficiently guided the sentencers' discretion.

In *Gregg*, the plurality explained the Georgia statute satisfied *Furman's* requirement that "discretion must be suitably directed and limited so as to minimize the risk of wholly arbitrary and capricious action."[33] The petitioner in *Gregg* argued arbitrary discretion still existed under the new guided discretion statutes due to prosecutorial discretion, a jury's ability to convict of a lesser offense, and the possibility of governor commutations. The plurality, however, responded that such situations involved removing someone from consideration as a candidate for the death penalty, while *Furman* was concerned with the decision to impose capital punishment. The plurality reasoned "the decision to afford an individual defendant mercy" does not violate the Constitution. "*Furman* held only that, in order to minimize the risk that the death penalty would be imposed on a capriciously selected group of offenders, the decision to impose it had to be guided by standards so that the sentencing authority would focus on the particularized circumstances of the crime and the defendant."[34] Thus, some level of discretion did not violate the Constitution.

At the same time the Court upheld these guided-discretion statutes, the Court issued opinions on the second group of death penalty statutes. In *Woodson v. North Carolina* and *Roberts v. Louisiana*, the Court struck down mandatory death sentence statutes.[35] A plurality of the Court explained that statutes that mandated a sentence of death under certain circumstances violated the Eighth Amendment because the statutes did not allow for consideration of the individual characteristics of a defendant. In order for a statute to be constitutional, the sentencer must be able to consider mitigating factors about the defendant. Noting "the penalty of death is qualitatively different from a sentence of imprisonment," the plurality found that the Constitution demands a higher standard of reliability than other sentences. Thus, the Eighth Amendment "requires consideration of the character and record of the individual offender and the circumstances of the particular offense as a constitutionally indispensable part of the process of inflicting the penalty of death."[36]

The Court also expressed concerns about the history of mandatory death penalty statutes. Historically, jurors had rejected mandatory death penalties by often refusing to convict guilty defendants when they did not want the defendant executed. Such a history of jury nullification revealed "that the practice of sentencing to death all persons convicted of a particular offense has been rejected as unduly harsh and unworkably rigid."[37]

Although there have been many cases after these 1976 cases that interpret the individualized sentencing and the guideline requirements of the Eighth and Fourteenth Amendments,[38] such a system remains in place today. For a death penalty to be constitutional, a jury must be given guidance in determining whether a defendant is eligible to be sentenced to death, and then a jury must have discretion to consider reasons not to impose the death sentence.

Thus, regarding death penalty procedures, these and later capital cases interpreting the Eighth Amendment stressed the underlying theme that "there is a significant constitutional difference between the death penalty and lesser punishments."[39] These early cases of modern death penalty jurisprudence established two important constitutional principles for capital cases: (1) the sentencing authority must be given clear and objective standards both to determine who is eligible for the death penalty and to narrow the group; and (2) the sentencer must be able to consider, as mitigating factors, all aspects of a defendant's character and record as well as the circumstances of the offense.[40]

* * *

In the 1976 cases, the justices split along three lines on the discretionary and mandatory statutes. Two groups of justices were at the extreme ends of either voting for or against all of the new laws. The four justices Rehnquist, White, Blackmun, and Burger voted to uphold the death penalty in all of the cases. Justices Thurgood Marshall and William Brennan voted to strike down the death penalty in every case, consistent with their stated belief that capital punishment is morally wrong and the death penalty violates the Constitution in all applications. (See Figure 8.1.)

Because neither of those two groups of justices at the extremes had a majority out of the nine justices, the key votes came from the plurality of Justices Lewis Powell, John Paul Stevens, and Potter Stewart. That group of three voted to strike down the mandatory death penalty statutes and to uphold the discretionary statutes that contained guidelines. The three justices were, in effect, the architects of the new death penalty, and they recognized the importance of their role. During deliberations, the three men met for lunch at The Monocle Restaurant on Capitol Hill to work out their positions on the five cases.[41]

These three men who worked together to fashion the modern American death penalty came from somewhat similar backgrounds. Powell, Stevens, and Stewart each grew up in a prominent family. And all three served their country during World War II, with Stewart and Stevens serving in the Navy and Powell serving in the Army Air Corps.

Of the three men, Potter Stewart had been on the Court the longest. Stewart came from a Cincinnati political family and served on the U.S. Court of Appeals before being appointed to the Court at the young age of forty-three by President Eisenhower, starting on the Court as a recess appointment on October 14, 1958.

John Paul Stevens also came from a prominent Midwestern family, growing up in Chicago. After law school and a clerkship with Supreme Court Justice Wiley

Figure 8.1
The *Gregg v. Georgia* Supreme Court. Back row: Rehnquist, Blackmun, Powell, Stevens. Front row: White, Brennan, Burger, Stewart, and Marshall. (Collection of the Supreme Court of the United States)

Rutledge in 1947–1948, Stevens worked at a large law firm and then as an Associate Counsel for a subcommittee of the U.S. House of Representatives. President Nixon nominated him to the Court in 1970.

Lewis F. Powell, Jr. was the most recent appointee of the three, having only begun his term on the Court on January 7, 1972 after President Nixon appointed him. Powell came from a prosperous Virginia family. Although all three men spent some time at a large law firm in private practice, Powell had spent the longest time at a firm, practicing corporate law as a partner.[42]

Considering the three men's record in prior death penalty cases, some may have been surprised the three united to form the heart of the 1976 decisions. Justice Powell dissented in the *Furman* case, voting to uphold the discretionary death penalty statute in that case. But now he voted against the mandatory death penalty statutes, showing his concern focused more on the harshness of automatic death sentences than on any arbitrariness in complete discretionary schemes.

Justice Stewart, by contrast, had voted to strike down the discretionary death penalty scheme in *Furman*, and with his rejection of the mandatory statutes too, he signaled he was satisfied only with the guided discretion statutes. He was the only justice to vote in the majority in all of these early key cases. He expressed special disquiet with the mandatory North Carolina statute, telling colleagues it was a "monster" that resulted in a "lawless use of the legal system."[43] But even his decision to uphold the death penalty in *Gregg* weighed on him. On the day when the Court announced the results, Stewart's voice cracked and his hand shook as he read his opinion that would allow executions to resume in the United States.[44]

Finally, Justice Stevens, who voted for the guided discretion statutes and against the mandatory statutes, was the only justice voting in the 1976 cases who did not sit on the Court on *Furman*. President Gerald R. Ford appointed him in 1975 to replace the retiring Justice Douglas, who was in the majority in *Furman*. Although Justice Douglas had voted to strike down the death penalty in *Furman*, this one change in the Court personnel since *Furman* likely did not affect the outcome of the 1976 cases. If Douglas would have voted differently than Stevens in the guided discretion cases, which is possible, it would not have affected the outcome, only making those 7-2 cases into 6-4 cases. His vote could have affected the 5-4 mandatory death penalty cases, but as a fairly liberal member of the Court who had been criticized for granting a stay to the Rosenbergs, Douglas most likely would not have voted to uphold those harsh statutes.

Although Justice Douglas no longer sat on the Court, the 1976 cases still impacted him. In their book *The Brethren*, Bob Woodward and Scott Armstrong described how before the Court heard oral arguments on the 1976 death penalty cases, the recently retired Justice Douglas showed up at the Court to hear the oral arguments. He had retired due to a stroke but he continued to try to participate on the Court. After he tried to participate in the 1976 death penalty cases, the justices got together and wrote a letter to Douglas, telling him he could not participate on the Court. The disappointed Douglas then stopped his requests.[45]

The 1976 capital cases took a toll on other justices who remained on the Court, especially on Justice Marshall, who as an attorney knew and represented clients on death row. On the morning the Court announced the results in the 1976 cases, it was Justice Marshall's sixty-eighth birthday. He stressed his displeasure at the cases upholding the death penalty by reading his dissenting opinion from the bench, an unusual practice reserved for when a justice feels strongly about a dissent. He showed emotion and anger while reading his dissent, stressing that under Eighth Amendment standards, "[T]he taking of life because the wrongdoer deserves it surely must fail, for such a punishment has as its very basis the total denial of the wrongdoer's dignity and worth." After the announcement, the justices quietly exited the courtroom. Marshall went home early and, that weekend, had a mild heart attack, which was followed by two more in the next several days.[46]

* * *

In *Gregg, Proffitt,* and *Jurek*, where the Supreme Court affirmed the death sentences in the three guided-discretion cases, the named capital defendants were never executed. Charles Proffitt continued to challenge his conviction and sentence, and a decade later Florida resentenced him to life in prison. Similarly, Jerry L. Jurek eventually won relief in a federal appeals court and Texas resentenced him to life in prison.

Troy Gregg became the first person who died after being resentenced to death under the post-*Furman* laws. But he met his death outside prison walls instead of in Georgia's electric chair. In July 1980, he escaped from Reidsville Maximum Security Prison in Georgia with three other inmates. After the escape, Gregg called a reporter and explained that the men would rather be killed than have to live under the horrible death row conditions at the prison. Within two days of the escape, all of the escapees were recaptured except for Gregg. Officials instead found Gregg's dead body near a North Carolina lake. While Gregg and other escaped inmates were trying to avoid capture by hanging out with a motorcycle gang, Gregg had made an unwelcome comment to one of the biker's girlfriends. One of the escaped inmates who had been a member of a biker gang, Timothy W. McCorquodale, joined the boyfriend in stomping Gregg to death for his offense against the girlfriend. McCorquodale was never tried for Gregg's murder, but authorities recaptured him and later executed him under his original death sentence.[47]

After the Court's decision in the five cases, *The New York Times* predicted that in the states that already had discretionary capital punishment statutes, executions would start again after several months. But it would take a much longer time for executions to resume. Soon after the decision, Tony Amsterdam filed a petition for LDF asking the Supreme Court to rehear the cases. Because the Court was in recess, the decision fell to Justice Powell as the circuit justice for the states where the cases were located. Chief Justice Burger tried to get Powell to deny the temporary stay. But Powell did not want states to start executing based only on his decision, so he granted a stay until the Court would be back in session in the fall.

When the Court reconvened in October, it denied Amsterdam's petition for rehearing without dissent. Lawyers for LDF, however, began filing other challenges to the new death penalty laws.[48] The death penalty battle in the courts was far from over.

CHAPTER 9

Starting Over: Executions Resume in the 1970s and 1980s

After states passed new death penalty statutes that were upheld by the Supreme Court in Gregg v. Georgia, *the popularity of the death penalty continued to increase. Meanwhile, as Warren McCleskey began his time on death row, executions in the United States slowly resumed.*

The litigation defeats in the 1976 Supreme Court cases were not the only losses for the abolition movement during this time. Popular opinion continued shifting away from the anti-death penalty sentiment of the early 1960s. Some death penalty opponents turned their efforts toward other social issues, such as the anti-war movement. At the same time, because anti-death penalty activists focused their resources on the courts of law, they were not sufficiently prepared to make their arguments in the court of popular opinion. Meanwhile, for those who favored the death penalty, the punishment became a major issue in political campaigns.[1]

Popular opinion in the mid-1970s reflected strong support for the death penalty. For example, national polls indicated two-thirds of Americans said that they favored capital punishment.[2] One death penalty scholar has noted, "Beginning in the mid-1970s, probably no other factor regarding the death penalty in America has been so prominent, important, and enduring as the popular support for capital punishment."[3] Commentators noted a large increase in support for the death penalty around the time the Court decided *Furman*. Thus, some suggest the *Furman* decision helped create popular support for the death penalty because the decision fueled popular resentment of the federal government imposing its will on the states.[4]

After *Gregg*, states continued using the new statutes to sentence defendants to death. A new era for the American death penalty began, as jurisdictions started over under the constitutional guidelines laid out by the Supreme Court in *Furman* and *Gregg*. States with statutes approved by *Gregg* continued to sentence defendants to death. Meanwhile, states with unconstitutional mandatory sentencing statutes rewrote their statutes to comply with *Gregg*. For example, in May 1977, the Delaware Legislature passed a new death penalty law modeled on the Georgia statute upheld in *Gregg*.[5] Although death penalty opponents were skeptical, the Court's decisions offered a promise of a new capital punishment scheme unconnected to the arbitrariness and discrimination of the past. Many death penalty advocates, as well as the justices, hoped the new statutes would create a fair capital punishment system.

Although it would take years, and in some cases decades, for the Court to clarify various aspects of this new Eighth Amendment jurisprudence, lower courts and attorneys struggled to understand this new developing death penalty system. Many encountered confusion about such things as the requirement of clear aggravating factors and the requirement that mitigating factors allow for individualized sentencing. So, some attorneys were not prepared for the complexity of the new capital sentencing requirements.

Warren McCleskey's jury sentenced him to death within a little more than two years of the Supreme Court's decision in *Gregg v. Georgia*. Not only did his trial take place during a time where the death penalty had grown in popularity, but it also occurred prior to many of the Court's decisions that clarified the standards for death penalty cases. McCleskey's defense attorney, like some other capital defense attorneys at the time, did not present any mitigating evidence on his client's behalf during the sentencing hearing.

The Supreme Court's new capital punishment procedural requirements led to substantial litigation as lawyers and lower court judges struggled to figure out the constraints of the U.S. Constitution. During the next several years, various constitutional challenges invalidated aspects of the capital punishment statutes in several states, including Texas, Alabama, and Georgia. These challenges largely focused on procedures, such as the jury sentencing process and other aspects unique to capital cases. For example, as it became clear defendants were constitutionally entitled to introduce mitigating evidence, several cases resulted in reversals for capital defendants. In 1978 in *Lockett v. Ohio* the Court stressed that the Constitution requires that each defendant receive individualized sentencing. Thus, *Lockett* held that jurors must "not be precluded from considering as a mitigating factor, any aspect of a defendant's character or record and any of the circumstances of the offense that the defendant proffers as a basis for a sentence less than death."[6]

Another area of litigation focused on the constitutionality of various aggravating circumstances that made defendants eligible for the death penalty. Courts evaluated whether some of the factors were vague and offered insufficient guidance, such as those similar to Georgia's aggravating factor allowing the death penalty when the murder was "outrageously or wantonly vile, horrible, or inhuman." *Godfrey v. Georgia* clarified that the aggravating factors "must channel the sentencer's discretion by 'clear and objective standards' that provide 'specific and detailed guidance,' and that 'make rationally reviewable the process for imposing a sentence of death.'"[7] Cases clarified that aggravating factors serve an important narrowing function that ensures only some murderers, and not all, are eligible for capital punishment.

While the Georgia statute at the time of *Gregg* included six aggravating factors, through the years state legislatures in death penalty states continued to add new ones that broadened the use of the death penalty. For example, aggravating factors include those related to the murder—such as when the murder connects to a felony or creates a risk for others. Aggravating factors may relate to the defendant's motivation, such as making the defendant eligible for the death penalty if the murderer is motivated by race or desire to avoid prosecution. Other aggravating factors may be based on the defendant's status, making defendants eligible for the death penalty if they commit a murder as part of a gang or while under a protective order. Aggravating factors may also be related to the victim's status, such as where the victim is especially young or old, or where the victim is a police officer or corrections officer. In many death penalty states, legislatures continued to expand their list of factors, making more and more crimes eligible for the death penalty. Some noted that these expansions seemed to gradually return states to an arbitrary system that was similar to the one in place prior to *Furman*.

* * *

As new capital trials continued in the United States and constitutional challenges to the new procedures were raised in the courts, many anticipated the first post-*Furman* execution, which eventually went forward when a Utah firing squad executed Gary Gilmore in early 1977. Gilmore, who grew up in an abusive home and spent much of his life in institutions, killed a gas station attendant named Max Jensen during a robbery in 1976, and on the next day killed a twenty-five-year-old motel manager named Ben Bushnell. After the Utah jury convicted Gilmore of murder and sentenced him to death for the Bushnell killing, Gilmore soon sought to drop his appeals so the execution could be carried out.

Gilmore's case became the focus of national attention, as his lawyers fought for the execution to go through while his mother and anti-death penalty lawyers tried to save him. Death penalty abolitionists tried to stop Gilmore's execution because they feared the first post-*Furman* execution would open the floodgates and lead to more executions. The U.S. Supreme Court, however, ruled the execution could proceed.[8]

The case became part of popular culture. Gilmore sold the rights to his story, which was eventually made into the book *The Executioner's Song* by Norman Mailer. The December 11, 1976, episode of *Saturday Night Live* featured a segment parodying the situation as the cast members sang a holiday song, "Let's Kill Gary Gilmore for Christmas."

Around 8:00 am on January 17, 1977, guards took Gilmore to a building and strapped him into a high-backed chair. A doctor attached a target to show the location of Gilmore's heart, and five anonymous volunteer police officers fired their rifles at the target. One of the weapons fired blanks as part of a tradition to relieve the conscience of the shooters, but the four other shooters did their job, firing the bullets that killed Gilmore. Norman Mailer reported the condemned's last words were "Let's do it," as the machismo author created a machismo legend. Gilmore's brother, writer Mikal Gilmore, later revealed he learned that his brother's last words were "There will always be a father," apparently a reference to their abusive father.[9]

As in the last pre-*Furman* execution nearly a decade earlier—of Luis Monge in Colorado—Gilmore both gave up his appeals and then donated his eyes. Volunteers for execution continued to make up a significant portion of the executed in the United States under the new death penalty laws. For the next two decades, more than 10 percent of those executed would be volunteers who gave up their appeals as Gilmore did.[10]

At the time of Gilmore's execution, Warren McCleskey was in prison in Georgia. Months after the historical execution, the state paroled McCleskey after he had served seven years for his armed robberies. In a little more than a year, McCleskey would be involved in the crime that would lead to his own death sentence.

In addition to Gilmore's 1977 firing squad execution, another event that year had a significant effect on the history of the death penalty. Dr. Stanley Deutsch, the chair of the Dept. of Oklahoma University Medical School, developed a new method of execution using lethal injection of chemicals. Later in the year, Oklahoma and Texas adopted lethal injection as their method of execution.[11]

Although in 1977, both Amnesty International and the United Nations became more active working toward their goals of abolishing capital punishment, popular opinion in the United States strongly supported the death penalty. For example, a poll by the Field Institute revealed 71 percent of Californians supported capital punishment with only 23 percent opposing it.[12]

This U.S. death penalty resurgence occurred while the worldwide decline in the death penalty that started prior to *Furman* continued outside the United States. For example, in 1978, Norway, Nicaragua, and Luxembourg abolished the death penalty. In 1977, as the United States resumed executions, France used its guillotine for the final time.[13]

By contrast, in the United States, a growing number of executions followed Gilmore's, although it took some time for the execution machine to get up to full speed. No one was executed in the year after Gilmore's execution, and then states executed only two people in 1979.

The first person after *Gregg* to be executed in the electric chair occurred in May 1979 when Florida electrocuted John Spenkelink. Unlike Gilmore, Spenkelink fought his execution in the courts, thus becoming the first non-volunteer executed post-*Furman*. Because Spenkelink became the first person in the new era executed while challenging his case in the courts, people around the country followed the execution in the news.

A jury convicted Spenkelink of the 1973 killing of Joseph Szymankiewicz. The two men were traveling across the country committing robberies, when one night they argued in a hotel room. Spenkelink claimed self-defense for shooting Szymankiewicz and beating him with a hatchet, alleging the murder victim had regularly beaten and sodomized him.

Spenkelink's case illustrated that even with the new death penalty laws, death penalty trials still might not be fair. At Spenkelink's trial, one of his trial attorneys was absent from jury selection and another one later admitted he did not have the training to try a capital case. The lawyers failed to raise mitigating factors in the case and let Spenkelink take the stand without preparation. The appellate courts did not offer any relief, even though LDF attorneys and Tony Amsterdam represented the condemned man at various stages.

Spenkelink's defense attorneys raised a legal claim that would reach the Supreme Court in Warren McCleskey's case almost a decade later. During Spenkelink's appeals, a paralegal in Jacksonville started reviewing the racial data on Florida's condemned. In her study, she hoped to find racial discrimination against black defendants, but instead she noticed that people who killed white victims were more likely to get the death penalty than people who killed blacks. One of Spenkelink's LDF lawyers, David Kendall, used the information and succeeded in obtaining a stay of execution in 1977 on the racial discrimination claim. But in the end the courts rejected the claim.[14]

Governor Bob Graham signed the death warrant for Spenkelink, as the country's attention waited for the first non-volunteer execution of the new era. At the signing, Graham explained, "I'm convinced there will be less brutality in our society if it is made clear that we value human life. It will take this kind of step."[15]

On the clear blue morning of May 25, 1979, in central Florida, Spenkelink had his final visits with his girlfriend, sister, and mother. Spenkelink's sister, Carol Myers, cried as she spoke to reporters after visiting her brother, and then in a nearby pasture she addressed the 75–100 death penalty opponents who showed up to protest the execution.

The Supreme Court voted 6-2 to deny Spenkelink's final request for a stay of execution, and then guards immediately took Spenkelink to the death chamber. The superintendent asked him if he had a last statement, and Spenkelink responded only, "I don't wish to be accompanied by a prison minister." Later, Reverend Tom Feamster reported his final conversation with Spenkelink and his last words: "Man is what he chooses to be. He chooses that for himself. I love you." Reverend Feamster replied, "I love you."[16]

As the execution began, at 10:11 am, prison officials raised a blind in the electric chair viewing area so the thirty-two witnesses could watch the execution. Witnesses watched an electrician lower the mask over Spenkelink's face, and some of them thought they saw the hopeless terror in the condemned man's eyes.

The first burst of electricity hit Spenkelink at 10:12 am and his chest heaved, one hand clenched, and his legs jerked. One witness claimed the electric chair seared the flesh on one of the condemned's legs. Two minutes later, a doctor used a stethoscope to check Spenkelink and then stepped back. The executioners administered another burst of electricity. The doctor checked again and stepped back again. The executioners applied a third burst of electricity. Officials then declared the prisoner dead, making the first execution of a non-volunteer after the Supreme Court decided *Furman*. Tony Amsterdam later revealed that the loss in the Spenkelink case was the low point of his long prestigious career because of how badly the case went.[17]

Jesse W. Bishop, another volunteer who gave up his appeals, became the only other person executed during 1979. Bishop was a decorated paratrooper in the Korean War who picked up a drug habit through the medicine he took for his war wounds. During the final thirty years of his life, Bishop spent twenty-two in prisons and much of the rest of the time robbing stores. Nevada executed Bishop in the state's gas chamber for a murder that occurred during a store robbery when David Ballard, who was in Las Vegas to get married, tried to stop Bishop from robbing a casino cashier. Bishop's last words were, "This is just one more step down the road of life that I've been headin' for all my life."[18]

After the electrocution of Spenkelink and the gassing of Bishop, the pace of executions remained slow and continued to consist largely of volunteers. No state executed anyone in the United States during 1980, and the only person executed in 1981 was Steven Judy, another volunteer. The year 1982 saw two executions, including another volunteer, Frank Coppola, who was executed in Virginia's electric chair in August. Coppola protested his innocence and initially worked with his lawyers to challenge his conviction for several years. But after being housed in Virginia's maximum security prison, which some labeled inhumane, Coppola fired his lawyers and gave up his appeals four months before he was executed. More than one in ten people executed continue to be volunteers who waived post-conviction review of their cases. Most of the volunteers are young white males who have a record of being suicidal and abusing drugs.[19]

Coppola's execution also revealed the U.S. Supreme Court's desire to speed up executions. After Coppola had decided to withdraw his federal habeas corpus petition and let his execution go through, his attorney filed a next-friend petition arguing issues that included ones about Coppola's mental competence. After the federal district court denied the petition and the request for a stay of execution, a judge on the court of appeals granted a stay eight hours and twenty minutes before the scheduled execution. Subsequently, for the first time, the U.S. Supreme Court vacated a stay of execution by the lower court to let the execution go forward despite a lower court's desire to have more time to review the case. After Coppola's case, the Supreme Court would regularly lift stays of execution in cases where lower courts wished to review the cases.[20]

The other 1982 execution occurred on December 7 when Texas executed Charlie Brooks, Jr., who became only the second non-volunteer to be executed since the 1976 *Gregg* decision. The execution was significant for a number of firsts too. Brooks became the first person executed in Texas in eighteen years, and he was the first to die by lethal injection in the United States. Also, the 40-year-old Brooks became the first black man executed in the United States since 1967.

Some believed Brooks's case illustrated that an unfair death penalty system persisted in the post-*Furman* era. Brooks, along with a fellow drug addict, Woodie Loudres, had been convicted of kidnapping and killing a twenty-six-year-old auto mechanic as part of a scheme to steal a car. Neither of the two men, who had injected heroin and drank alcohol on the day of the murder, said who shot the lethal bullet, and both initially were convicted of first degree murder and sentenced to death. But Lourdes won a new trial based on an error in his first one, and he then accepted a plea bargain where he would potentially be released in six-and-a-half years. Brooks, who while on death row converted to Islam and changed his name to Shareef Ahmad Abdul-Rahim, lost his appeals. So, the execution proceeded, even though the prosecutor from his trial supported Brooks's appeals, claiming it was unfair to execute Brooks while his co-defendant Lourdes served a sentence of imprisonment.[21]

Although the executions came slowly, the support for the death penalty in theory remained strong as states continued to pass new death penalty laws. In addition to the states that had reinstated the death penalty between *Furman* and *Gregg*, several states brought back the death penalty after *Gregg*, convinced from the Gilmore execution that the death penalty would remain as a national institution. For example, the same year as Gilmore's execution, Idaho reinstated the death penalty.

One illustration of the shift in death penalty popularity occurred in the state of Oregon. That state's citizens, who had voted to abolish the death penalty by a large majority in 1964, voted to restore the death penalty in 1978. And when the Supreme Court of Oregon held that statute violated the state constitution, Oregon voters in 1984 again passed a new death penalty law.[22]

Similarly, in 1979, New Mexico brought back capital punishment, apparently influenced by the nationwide reactions to *Furman* and *Gregg*. Throughout that litigation, New Mexico did not have a death penalty, having banned capital punishment in 1964 by a popular vote.

In 1981, Ohio reinstated the death penalty after the Supreme Court in 1978 found the state's statute unconstitutional. In 1982, Massachusetts voters responded to a court decision striking down the state's death penalty by passing a referendum amending the state constitution to allow capital punishment. The legislature responded immediately by passing a new death penalty statute.

Also in 1982, New Jersey adopted a new death penalty law.[23] In the late 1970s, the New Jersey Legislature had voted two times to bring back the death penalty, but the bills were vetoed by Governor Brendan Byrne. Byrne opposed capital punishment, and as a trial judge had once held the death penalty violated the constitution. But after Governor Byrne left office, Governor Tom Kean signed a death penalty bill into law on August 6, 1982.[24]

Despite these legislative responses, many death penalty supporters felt dissatisfied by the slow progress toward resuming executions around the country. On May 8, 1983, at an Eleventh Circuit Judicial Conference in Savannah, Georgia, Supreme Court Justice Lewis Powell complained about the backlog of capital cases in the courts. Powell, one of the three key justices in creating the current death penalty system in the 1976 cases, noted the problem that cruel and brutal murders continue while "[w]e now have more than 1,000 convicted persons on death row, an intolerable situation." He expressed frustration at the system of "repetitive review" of cases that allowed attorneys to file last-minute appeals, and he called for legislation limiting habeas corpus filings.

Within two months after Powell's speech, the Supreme Court decided a case cutting back on a capital defendant's ability to obtain a thorough habeas corpus review. Other decisions—and legislation—to similar effect would follow in subsequent years. These changes gradually allowed executions to speed up to some extent, while death penalty opponents claimed the changes also allowed for more injustices and mistakes.[25]

Georgia's first post-*Furman* execution on December 15, 1983, illustrated one of the injustices of the evolving habeas corpus law. In separate trials, juries convicted John Eldon Smith and his wife Rebecca Akins Machetti of murdering Machetti's ex-husband and his new wife in Bibb County, Georgia. They had planned the murder along with another man so Machetti would receive the insurance proceeds, among other reasons. Both Smith and Machetti were sentenced to death.

At Machetti's trial, the prosecutor argued she was the mastermind of the murders. But her attorney made a constitutional objection because women were unconstitutionally underrepresented in the jury pool. On appeal, Machetti won a new trial on the jury pool issue and was sentenced to life. The same constitutional violation existed in Smith's case, but because his attorney failed to raise the claim at the proper time, procedural rules barred the federal courts from reversing his case. Thus, he proceeded to the electric chair on a Thursday morning in December at the age of fifty-three.

By the time of Smith's execution, Rebecca Machetti was already eligible for parole. Many years later she would be released from prison. Thus, the actions of the attorneys made the difference between life and death in the first execution in Georgia under the new statute written to eliminate arbitrariness.[26]

After Smith became the first person executed in Georgia after *Furman*, the following year saw the execution of the state's first African American, Ivon R. Stanley. Stanley's attorneys had raised constitutional arguments based upon a study showing that racial discrimination affected capital sentencing decisions in Georgia. As Stanley got closer to his execution date, Warren McCleskey's attorneys were making similar arguments in the federal courts. The U.S. Court of Appeals rejected the claim in Stanley's case, and the twenty-four-year-old became the first African American executed in the state after *Gregg*. Other defendants in the state had received stays of execution on the same grounds, but Stanley's execution went forward. Warren McCleskey would continue raising similar claims.[27]

During the 1980s, the number of executions started creeping up. In 1983 when Georgia executed John Eldon Smith, the whole country had five executions, and then in 1984, twenty-one people were executed. In 1985, states executed eighteen people. A study of the eighteen executed in 1985 found they each spent an average of five years and eleven months on death row between trial and execution.[28]

The 1980s saw the first post-*Furman* execution of a person who was a juvenile at the time of the crime when on September 11, 1985, the state of Texas executed Charles Rumbaugh. South Carolina executed another person who committed the capital crime as a juvenile, James T. Roach, several months later on January 10, 1986.

Although in the 1980s many states were expanding their death penalties and sentencing more people to death, death penalty opponents found some bright spots. In 1984, the Rhode Island Legislature removed their death penalty statute, and Rhode Island joined the states without a death penalty. Several years earlier, the Supreme Court of Rhode Island already had struck down as unconstitutional its law that required a mandatory death sentence for inmates who killed another prisoner.[29]

Another victory for death penalty opponents occurred as Georgia prepared to execute Warren McCleskey's best friend on death row, Billy Moore. Three days before Moore's scheduled execution date of May 24, 1984, the guards allowed Moore out into the prison yard, where he noticed that other inmates did not want to be around him out of fear and awkwardness of being so near to death. In the yard, though, McCleskey, who had become religious with Moore's guidance, came forward to approach Moore. Soon, other members of the two men's Bible study group joined them. The men stood together while Moore led them in prayer. After guards called Moore back inside, he asked the other condemned men to be strong. With tears in his eyes, McCleskey said, "Man, I know, but it's so hard after watching the others go and never return."

Moore continued on death watch, waiting for his appointment with the electric chair. But three days before his scheduled execution, the U.S. Court of Appeals for the Eleventh Circuit granted him a stay of execution. McCleskey greeted Moore back on death row, and he saw an important message in the saving of his friend. "Especially with you being guilty and not having any legal issues to stand on, this really shows the mercy of God, and everyone has to see it." There would be a few other miracles in store for Moore.[30]

* * *

Politics continued to play a role in the new post-*Furman* death penalty cases, as in the Louisiana execution of Timothy Baldwin. Baldwin and his girlfriend, Marilyn Hampton, were both convicted of killing an elderly woman who had taken care of Baldwin's children. Hampton testified that Baldwin killed the woman, and she received a life sentence.

Baldwin, however, asserted his innocence, and after the trial, attorneys found a motel receipt showing at the time of the crime he was hundreds of miles away from the crime scene. The prosecutors argued Baldwin had time to drive that far to establish an alibi. Howard Marsellus, the Louisiana Pardon Board Chairman, decided to take the drive to see if Baldwin would have had enough time for the travel and the murder. But then Marsellus received a mysterious anonymous telephone call threatening him if he made the drive. Marsellus later explained, "To my shame, I didn't go," and he then led the Board in denying clemency.

Marsellus watched the execution on September 10, 1984. "The night Baldwin died, he looked into my face and said, 'You are murdering an innocent man.' That's what I did. I acted as Judas." Marsellus explained, "What I did was totally wrong. I lacked the courage to vote on the basis of how I felt and what I believed. I gave in to the prestige and power, the things that went with my job. I knew what the Governor, the man who appointed me, wanted: no recommendation for clemency in any death case."

Prior to the execution, the Louisiana governor met with the key witness, Hampton, and her lawyer. Two months after the execution, an "expedite" order was given on her case, and the state freed Hampton after she had served only seven years.[31]

The first execution of a woman since 1962 also featured a role for politics. On November 2, 1984, the state of North Carolina executed Margie Velma Barfield, a fifty-two-year-old grandmother. Barfield, who had become addicted to a range of drugs after taking medications after a nervous breakdown, poisoned five people, mainly so they would not discover she stole from them to buy drugs. While waiting for trial, Barfield became born again and spent her six years in prison counseling young women inmates, praying, and reading the Bible. In later appeals, lawyers presented evidence she had been battered and sexually abused and had an abusive husband.[32]

Barfield might have had a chance at having her sentence commuted were it not for bad political timing. As her execution approached, North Carolina governor Jim Hunt was running for U.S. Senate against the incumbent senator Jesse Helms. With the execution scheduled only four days before the election, Governor Hunt had to make his commutation decision right before the election in a strongly pro-death penalty state. Although he denied clemency, Hunt still lost the election.[33]

One of the most noteworthy examples of death penalty politics occurred in California in the 1980s. California in the 1970s had elected Jerry Brown governor. Brown, who opposed the death penalty like his father Governor Pat Brown had, angered many death penalty supporters by his choices for judges. Eventually, death penalty advocates succeeded by using their resources against judges they deemed too lenient on criminals. In 1986, death penalty supporters mobilized to vote Chief Justice Rose Bird and two other California Supreme Court justices off the bench after a political campaign against them that focused on their votes in reversing death sentences.[34]

Some politicians remained critical of the death penalty, but often, the politicians who took a stand against the death penalty did so when they faced little political risk, such as when they no longer planned to run for office. On Thanksgiving in 1986, the tenth year since *Gregg*, New Mexico's outgoing governor Toney Anaya commuted the death sentences of all five New Mexico condemned prisoners to life in prison sentences. In his statement announcing the commutation, Governor Anaya explained he wanted New Mexico to lead the country by abolishing the death penalty and replacing it with a "moral, just, and effective criminal justice system." He concluded, "Let us begin in earnest to prevent crime, to effectively fight crime to seek proper retribution from, and rehabilitation of criminals, to compassionately care for the victims. And let this effort begin today. Here."

In announcing the commutation, Anaya became the first governor to give a blanket commutation since the death penalty returned in 1976. The last such commutation had occurred in 1970 when Republican governor Winthop Rockefeller commuted the sentences of everyone on Arkansas's death row.[35] Although no governor immediately followed Governor Anaya's lead, in two months, on January 20, 1987, Maryland governor Harry Hughes used his powers on his final day in office to commute the sentence of the only woman on Maryland's death row, Doris Ann Foster.[36]

In addition to Governor Anaya's commutation, those concerned about the application of the death penalty scored another victory in 1986 that would have growing reverberations. In that year, Georgia became the first state to ban the execution of defendants with an intellectual disability.

The Georgia Legislature passed the bill in quick response to public outrage over the execution of Jerome Bowden, who had been diagnosed with an intellectual disability at the age of fourteen. As Bowden's execution date approached in June 1986, the Georgia Board of Pardons and Paroles granted a temporary stay as an appointed psychologist verified Bowden had an intellectual disability. But the Board lifted the stay after concluding Bowden still understood the nature of his crime and the punishment. Bowden's execution, however, left a legacy. Slowly the federal government and a number of states followed Georgia's lead in banning the execution of those with an intellectual disability.[37]

In 1986, then, Georgia and New Mexico gave the opponents of capital punishment some victories. But death penalty opponents had no time to celebrate. In December, two more executions took place in Texas of two volunteers, Michael Wayne Evans and Richard Andrade. The executions brought the number of executions to eighteen for the year, a number that would be exceeded in 1987, when twenty-five people were executed.

Although in the first decade after *Gregg* the number of actual executions remained low, states continued condemning people to death at a much higher rate. By October 1986, only sixty-eight people had been executed in the decade since *Gregg*, but the number of men and women on death rows in the United States waiting for execution neared 2,000.[38] (See Table 9.1.)

Table 9.1. EXECUTIONS AND SIZE OF DEATH ROWS IN AMERICA 1968–1988[39]

Year	U.S. Executions	Size of U.S. Death Rows
1968	0	517
1969	0	575
1971	0	642
1972	0	334
1973	0	134
1974	0	244
1975	0	488
1976	0	420
1977	1	423
1978	0	482
1979	2	539
1980	0	691
1981	1	856
1982	2	1,050
1983	5	1,209
1984	21	1,405
1985	18	1,591
1986	18	1,781
1987	25	1,984
1988	11	2,124

Even though many states now had death penalty laws and executions were beginning again, many questions remained about the procedures used in sentencing someone to death. The capital defense attorneys who had failed to get the Supreme Court to find the death penalty unconstitutional began focusing more on attacking portions of the death penalty laws, although they had been making such attacks all along. So, instead of putting so much work into arguing the death penalty violated the Eighth Amendment in all cases, they focused on crafting new arguments out of the language of the 1976 cases. For example, attorneys argued that statutes that did not allow consideration of mitigating evidence were cruel and unusual. Also, they argued that specific aggravating statutes failed to give clear and objective guidance to juries. To a large extent, these arguments were successful in slowing down the death penalty machine. Appellate courts often reversed death sentences as states struggled to understand the new procedural requirements that the Supreme Court imposed under the Constitution.

This shift in the main focus of the court tactics—from trying to get courts to find the death penalty unconstitutional to trying to get courts to find some aspect of a specific death sentence unconstitutional—has lasted for the most part through today. One exception, though, occurred with Warren McCleskey's case that would work its way up to the U.S. Supreme Court in 1987.

As 1986 drew to a close, even though the nationwide rate of executions remained low, it seemed McCleskey's time was running out. He had already spent eight years on death row, longer than most of the condemned prisoners being executed. The year 1986 ended with his waiting to hear word from the U.S. Supreme Court.

McCleskey's attorneys claimed that part of the reason he sat on death row was because he was a black man convicted of killing a white man. The Court was preparing to finally confront the fears Justice Douglas raised in *Furman* that race plays a part in capital sentencing. These issues connected to the United States' long past regarding lynching, race, and the death penalty.

Lynching, Race, and McCleskey v. Kemp

CHAPTER 10

Lynching and Race in America

*As Warren McCleskey's case made its way to the Supreme Court during 1986, his attorneys chal-
lenged the death penalty system created in the wake of* Furman v. Georgia. *McCleskey's claims
had their foundations in the United States' history of racial discrimination connecting back to
America's history of slavery and lynching, the latter of which was a practice used more in post–
Civil War Georgia than any other state during the period.*

LYNCHING CULTURE

Around the time of Warren McCleskey's birth, fears about lynching still existed in
the black community of his hometown. Many African Americans sensed lynchings
were still possible and that they had to be careful because even innocent men could
be lynched. One Marietta resident remembered during that time that her mother
taught her brothers, "If I send you to the grocery store…and you see a white girl
walking down the street, cross over to the other side. You can cross back after she
passes and then go onto the store." The warning came from a sense that whites
"were hunting black men to try and catch them doing anything wrong."[1]

The lynching fears in McCleskey's childhood home town came from a history of
the practice in the United States and in Georgia. As noted earlier, one of the most
famous lynchings occurred in McCleskey's hometown thirty years before his birth
when men from Marietta stirred by anti-Jewish sentiment lynched Leo Frank in
1915. But Leo Frank was not the only person lynched in the Marietta area.

In March 1900, a teenaged woman walked near her family farmhouse when she
encountered John Bailey, an African-American man who reportedly threatened
her and cut her nose with a knife. After Bailey was arrested, a mob of approximately 100 masked men surrounded the Marietta jail and broke into it, pushing
Sheriff A.A. Bishop aside. After they knocked the locks off the jail cell door, the
mob carried Bailey out into the Square in Glover Park. In the Square, members of
the mob realized they had lost their rope, so they found some wiring and put it

around Bailey's neck and attached it to a tree limb. After they lifted him up, though, the wire broke and Bailey fell to the ground. Members of the mob then fired their pistols at Bailey until they thought he was dead. The crowd then ran off as Sheriff Bishop and a deputy arrived.

Bailey was still alive and conscious, so officials took him back to the jail where a doctor unsuccessfully tried to treat his wounds, which included several shots throughout his body and a crowbar blow to the head. Later, those in attendance reported that Bailey confessed to the crime before he died two days later. After the lynching, *The Marietta Journal* reported that African-American women were angry about the lynching, hinting that they would burn down the town to retaliate. The newspaper reporter was surprised at the women's anger because the reporter thought they should have taken the side of protecting females rather than worrying about lynching a man of their race.[2]

A few months after the Bailey lynching, authorities accused another black man of assaulting a white woman in Cobb County. Fearing another lynching, authorities transferred the defendant, Sam Robinson, to Atlanta. At trial, Robinson's attorney put up little defense, and Robinson was convicted and sentenced to death. After sentencing, to avoid another lynching, officials used extra security measures to transfer the condemned man back to Marietta. Ultimately, some citizens were proud that they executed Robinson under law instead of using lynching. As Robinson's body fell through the trapdoor in the gallows, some members of the crowd exclaimed, "Hurrah for Cobb County!"[3]

Several years later, during the summer of 1912 near Columbus, Georgia, a mob of twenty-five armed men became upset when a jury found the teenaged T.Z. McElhenny guilty of involuntary manslaughter instead of murder. McElhenny's crime occurred when he and a young white friend were playing with a gun in some cotton fields and the gun accidentally killed the white boy. After the jury announced the involuntary manslaughter verdict, an angry mob grabbed McElhenny, whose nickname was "Cotton," from the court bailiffs. They took the scared black youth into a street car to escape. They later got off the car and shot the child fifty times. Four men were charged with the murder of McElhenny, including the father of the white victim, but they all were acquitted.[4]

Numerous other lynchings occurred throughout the United States and Georgia during the late nineteenth and early twentieth century. Between 1880 and 1930, Georgia residents lynched at least 441 blacks and 19 Caucasians, more lynchings than any other state. Only a relatively small number of 42 people were lynched in Cobb County, which includes Marietta, during the same period, perhaps because the county had a smaller African-American population than some other counties in the state.[5]

Although lynchings were most frequent in the South, they occurred around the country. Groups lynched at least sixteen people in North Dakota between 1882 and 1930, twice the number of the total number of legal executions in the region between 1680 and today. On June 16, 1920, approximately 5,000–10,000 citizens of Duluth, Minnesota, watched a mob lynch three black men for allegedly attacking a seventeen-year-old girl.[6]

A lynching in Oklahoma would later be remembered in song by one of America's greatest folk singers. On, May 25, 1911, a mob lynched an African-American woman and her teenage son near Okemah, Oklahoma. The mob acted in response to the death of a well-respected white deputy sheriff, George Loney. Earlier, Loney was investigating the theft of livestock when teenager Lawrence Nelson reportedly thought the officer reached for a gun. So, Nelson shot Loney, who bled to death. A posse then went to arrest the teen and his family, which included Lawrence's mother, Laura Nelson, and her infant son. Lawrence's father ended up in jail, but a mob took the teenager and his mother, who at one point tried to protect her son by saying she fired the fatal shot. Although historians debate what happened to the infant, the mob ended up hanging the teen and his mother.[7]

A photographer took a picture of the lynching, showing a group of adults and children standing on the bridge above the lifeless bodies hanging below. Others mailed the photo as a postcard. (See Figure 10.1.) Many photographers took pictures of the dead bodies after a lynching, often with the members of the lynch mob appearing in the photo with the body. In 1908, officials had amended the U.S. Postal Laws and Regulations to try to curtail the use of such postcards, although the language more generally forbade the mailing of "matter of a character tending to incite arson, murder or assassination."[8]

One of the members of the lynching crowd in Oklahoma that day was a man named Charley, who a year later would name his new son Woodrow after President Wilson. Woodrow would grow up to have a different view of the lynching than the

Figure 10.1
Lynching of Laura and Lawrence Nelson, May 1911 in Okemah, Oklahoma (George Henry Farnum Collection, Oklahoma Historical Society Research Division)

participants. And Woody, as we would come to know him, developed political views that diverged from his father, Charley Guthrie. As an adult, folk singer Woody Guthrie wrote the song, "Don't Kill My Baby and My Son" about that Okfuskee County lynching. Woody focused the song's title on the words of the woman begging for her children's lives rather than choosing the voice of his father in the crowd.[9]

While the victims of lynchings were sometimes accused of murder, rape, or attempted rape, sometimes mobs reacted to more minor infractions of the social code. One of Woody Guthrie's disciples, Bob Dylan, wrote one of his first songs about an extrajudicial killing of the fourteen-year-old Emmett Till. In 1955, Till was visiting relatives in Mississippi when he went to Bryant's Grocery and Meat Market to buy some candy. Reportedly, while in the store, the young black teen either whistled at or requested a date from Carolyn Bryant, who ran the store with her husband Roy, who was out of town. As word spread around town about the incident, Roy Bryant returned to town and contacted his half-brother J.W. Miliam. A few days after the encounter in the store between Till and Byrant's wife on August 28, 1955, Miliam and Bryant abducted Till from his great-uncle's home. Three days later Till's body was found in the river. Many were outraged at the murder, with a reported 50,000 people attending the funeral, where Till's mother had an open casket to show the world what the men did to her son.

Authorities arrested Miliam and Bryant, who were tried and acquitted by an all-white, all-male jury. Many were outraged with the acquittal, and some credit the events with helping inspire the civil rights movement. Several months later, on January 24, 1956, *Look* magazine published "The Shocking Story of Approved Killing in Mississippi" that featured Miliam and Bryant confessing to the murder. In the magazine article, they described how after beating and shooting Till, they used barbed wire to tie a heavy cotton gin fan around his neck to weigh down his body when they threw him into the Tallahatchie River. Miliam and Bryant claimed that throughout the ordeal, the two men were unable to break the teenager, who kept insisting he was as good as them and that he had dated white women.

More than half a century has passed since Till's murder, but the crime has not been forgotten. Although Miliam and Bryant both later died from cancer, fifty years later the U.S. Justice Department continued looking into the case about prosecuting others who aided the crime and were still alive.[10] In 2008, the U.S. Congress passed the Emmett Till Act of 2008, sponsored by Representative John Lewis of Georgia. The act established an Unsolved Crimes Section in the Civil Rights Division of the Department of Justice and an Unsolved Civil Rights Crime Investigative Office in the Civil Rights Unit of the Federal Bureau of Investigation. Additionally, the act provided funding for investigating unsolved cases such as Till's.[11]

While the killing of Emmett Till and other lynchings have remained in the public eye periodically, most lynchings have fallen to anonymity. For example, a case very similar to Till's involved the fifteen-year-old African-American Willie James Howard. Howard swept floors at a Florida dime store in 1943. In December of that year, the good-natured boy gave Christmas cards to his coworkers, including a fifteen-year-old white female cashier. The girl told her father, who became angry about the card. Howard then wrote a note to the girl trying to explain himself and apologizing while closing with "I love your name. I love your voice. For a S.H. [sweetheart] you are my choice."

A little while later on January 2, 1944, the girl's father and two other men captured Howard, bound his hands and feet with rope, and took him to the bank of the Suwannee River. There, in front of Howard's father, they told the young teenager that they would shoot him or he could go into the river himself. Crying, Howard toppled into the river where he drowned.

Authorities never punished the men who killed Willie Howard, and few remember the case. But it was remembered by Howard's father and by the attorney who unsuccessfully tried to get state officials and the federal government to do something about the killing. That young attorney, Thurgood Marshall, would later sit on the Supreme Court hearing Warren McCleskey's arguments about race and the death penalty.[12]

LYNCHING, RACE, AND GEOGRAPHY

The United States has a history of both non-lethal and lethal extralegal punishments meted out by mobs. Non-lethal extralegal punishments in the eighteenth and nineteenth century included whippings, beatings, and tarring and feathering. These tactics were used throughout the United States. The states with slavery had a long history of using extralegal punishments on slaves, and non-lethal punishments were often used instead of lethal punishments for slaves so the owners would not lose workers.

A "lynching" generally is defined as a killing done by a group of people without government authority to enforce some sense of justice or tradition. Similarly, the NAACP defined a "lynching" as an illegal killing that is done by at least three people who claim to serve justice or tradition.[13]

Such killings are accomplished through various means, such as shooting and burning alive. Hanging, however, was the most common method of mob violence in the United States. After a lynching spree in Vicksburg, Virginia, in 1838, Abraham Lincoln commented, "[D]ead men were seen literally dangling from the boughs of trees on every roadside; and in numbers almost sufficient, to rival the Spanish moss of the country, as a drapery of the forest."[14] One reason vigilantes adopted the common legal execution method of hanging, as well as other "punitive rituals" of the legal system, was that the connection to legal process strategically gave the extrajudicial racial violence a type of legitimacy.[15] But in other lynchings, the vigilantes sometimes used more extreme methods of killing and debasement that included burning, torture, and displaying the dead bodies.

Further, sometimes the lynching involved some type of mutilation ritual or cutting off parts of the body for souvenirs, stripping the lynching victim of humanity and, in some cases, sexuality. For example, in 1923 the only drugstore in Milledgeville, Georgia, displayed a large bottle filled with alcohol and the fingers and ears of two African Americans who were lynched for shooting a white grocer.[16] Similarly, as in the Nelson lynchings, photos often were taken of hanging bodies and sold as souvenirs. One scholar explained that these public lynchings that involved torture were taken from earlier times and used "to communicate impassioned sentiments that could no longer be expressed in the official idiom of the criminal law, and to inflict a level of suffering that had long since been officially disavowed."[17]

The term "lynching" became commonly associated with this period during Reconstruction and after federal troops withdrew from the South in 1877.[18] While lynchings have occurred around the world, the United States is relatively unusual in its widespread use of this type of mob violence over decades, as well as in the practice's connection to race. During the years 1882 to 1968, there were 4,743 people killed by mob violence in the United States, with 98 percent of those killings taking place during the 1882–1936 period.

Mobs often used lynching as a tool against those they saw as outsiders. The Marietta citizens who lynched Leo Frank in 1915 were instigated by those who stressed that Frank was Jewish. Latinos, particularly Mexican-Americans, were lynched in large numbers during 1846–1925, which began during the period before the War with Mexico. Although the number of Latinos lynched during this time in the Southwest—more than 597—is less than the number of African Americans lynched, fewer Latinos than African Americans lived in the United States at the time. So the rate of these often overlooked Latino lynchings compared to the rate of lynching of African Americans. The methods and rationales for the lynchings were similar too. For example, as with the lynching of African Americans, white mobs often mutilated or burned the bodies of Mexican-Americans as part of the lynching ritual.[19]

Similarly, although details of the large number of lynchings of Native Americans are not well documented, historians know of several recorded instances of the use of extrajudicial mob violence toward Native American victims in several places, including California, Texas, Washington, Wisconsin, and Wyoming. For example in 1898, a group of townspeople in the Oklahoma Indian Territory burned alive two young Seminole men named Lincoln McGeisey and Palmer Sampson after torturing them into confessing to the murder of a young white woman. Scholars have argued McGeisey and Sampson actually were innocent of the crime of killing Mary Leard, while also speculating that white Southerners who participated in the lynching saw the natives as just some more nonwhite scapegoats.[20]

Although the practice occurred across the country, most lynchings happened in the South, with other regions significantly behind. A study of the years 1889–1918 found that 88 percent of lynchings occurred in the South, with 7 percent in the Midwest, 5 percent in the West, and less than 0.5 percent in the Northeast. If one takes into account the populations of the various regions, the sparsely populated West had the second-most lynchings per million people in the population during this time, but it was still far behind the South.[21] In 1919, the National Association for the Advancement of Colored People (NAACP) reported that for the previous two decades Georgia had the most lynchings of any state, followed by Mississippi and Texas.

The NAACP study also found an overwhelming majority of lynching victims were African Americans in states that included South Carolina (97 percent), Mississippi (94 percent), Georgia (93 percent), and Florida (90 percent). During those thirty years, 140 African Americans were lynched without even being charged with a specific crime, compared to the lynching of six whites under similar circumstances. Overall, during those decades, 73 percent of the lynching victims were African American and a significant number were Native Americans, Latino, and other minority groups.[22] White mobs lynched blacks for a variety of accusations ranging from rape and murder to threatening to go to authorities.

So, although in the 1800s mobs used lynchings to punish whites, Native Americans, Latinos, and immigrants, by the early 1900s lynching became even more identified with its growing use against African Americans. Another study found that from 1882 through 1968 in the United States, there were 3,446 black men and women lynched, which was 72.7 percent of the total number of 4,743 persons lynched. Generally, blacks were much more likely to be lynched for rape or attempted rape than whites were for those crimes.[23]

Many societal reasons help explain why Southerners used mob violence more than Northerners, including the changes after the Civil War and the history of slavery. To a large extent, Southerners who lived in an environment haunted by slavery remained more imprisoned by that past and were slower to escape their legacy than people in the North, even as racial tensions continued in the North too. Racial lynching grew in the South during the Civil War as a means of terror against blacks partly because of fears of slave uprisings. After the war, during Radical Reconstruction, Southern whites rebelled against the changing system by using violence in support of white supremacy. Lynching increased after federal troops withdrew in 1877 as whites sought to reestablish parts of the old order and for other reasons. Further, the South was less urban than the North and therefore developed less court structures and law enforcement agencies to deal with their changing environment.

After Reconstruction through the 1870s and into the 1890s, Southern farmers suffered from declining prices and the 1893 recession. When whites on small farms and blacks joined together with the Populist Party, powerful and rich whites tried to stir up racial animosity to divide the poor whites and blacks. For example, one study of Louisiana parishes revealed lynchings significantly increased during election years when Populists were powerful. Similarly, around this time, industrialization caused changes to the social order, sometimes resulting in industry owners using racial fears to prevent white and black workers from organizing together.

Although most of the lynching victims were attacked because they were accused of serious crimes, more than 25 percent of lynchings of blacks in Georgia between 1880 and 1930 (the five decades following Reconstruction) were for small offenses such as not following the imposed racial norms. Despite regional variations on the use of lynchings throughout different areas of the South, during the sixty to seventy years after the Civil War ended, "[m]any, if not most, white Southerners either acquiesced to or openly celebrated mob violence."[24] Yet, in each individual case, most of the perpetrators of the mob violence, if asked, would not consciously have acknowledged an overall scheme but responded that they were acting out of a sense of individual justice for a specific case. Similarly, Professor of Law and Sociology David Garland has stressed that lynching in a region often depended on various local circumstances. For example, local factors such as politicians, race relations, and nearby incidents of violence led to some areas accepting lynching.[25]

Scholars conclude that the dominant group in the South used lynching primarily to keep African Americans oppressed and to assert white superiority. Professor W. Fitzhugh Brundage has explained, "Virtually all observers and scholars of lynching suggest that whites resorted to mob violence to shore up caste lines in the face of some perceived threat, or, more simply, to 'keep blacks in their place.'" [26] Professor of Law and Sociology David Garland similarly has concluded, "The central function of these rituals was to assert and celebrate a specific communal identity—sovereign, Southern, supremacist—by brutally responding to black crimes that challenged that self-image and, more obliquely, to any white reformist politics that would undermine it. [27]

There were additional secondary reasons for the practice of lynching in the South. Lynchings served an entertainment function, providing a community experience to the participants and observers. Finally, lynching also functioned as an outlet for those who did not trust government or the judicial process. Historians additionally reason that lynching grew out of both a culture of violence and a culture of protecting a Southern code of honor. [28]

Lynchings thus helped keep African Americans oppressed while maintaining white dominance. Of course, other means supported this function of lynching too, including segregation and discrimination. During the era of lynchings, much of popular culture endorsed stereotypical views of African Americans. The emerging film industry portrayed African Americans in ways that endorsed stereotypes, including its portrayals of African Americans in *Birth of a Nation* (1915), *The Littlest Rebel* (1935), *Gone with the Wind* (1939), and other movies. During this era white actors often appeared in blackface, including stars such as Al Jolson, Fred Astaire, Mickey Rooney, Judy Garland, Shirley Temple, and even Bugs Bunny. [29] When society endorsed views that African Americans were less than white Americans, it was not surprising that violence against African Americans would often go unpunished, especially where the victims of their alleged crimes were white.

Thus, long before attorneys made race a constitutional death penalty issue, race played a role in lynchings. Public lynchings continued to be an ongoing problem for almost a century after the Civil War. Groups used lynching for various purposes throughout the early history of the United States, including for controlling the western frontier. But by the end of the nineteenth century lynching was primarily a southern means used to protect white supremacy. Although mobs used lynching in individual cases to punish an alleged violator of some offense, the broader function of lynching included oppressing women, controlling poor whites, and serving as a means of sending a message to African-American Southerners that they were not politically, socially, or economically equal to the whites. [30]

THE DECLINE OF LYNCHING

During a time period, some states used lynching more than capital punishment. For example, between 1865 and 1940 in Kentucky, there were 229 legal executions and 353 lynchings. [31]

But lynchings eventually declined across the South. For the first decade of the twentieth century, lynchings declined to 93 a year in the United States from 188 in the previous decade. Into the early twentieth century, lynchings continued to average two to three a week with marked increases during the "Red Summer" race riots of 1919 and during the Great Depression.[32] As lynching declined nationwide, though, the proportion of lynch victims who were African American increased, and lynching further became even more of a Southern phenomenon. For example, by the 1920s, the total percentage of U.S. lynchings that occurred in the South rose to 95 percent, with only 9 percent of lynch victims being white.

A number of factors contributed to the overall decline in lynching, including education efforts, the work of activists, and economic changes that occurred in the South. Several organizations and activists worked to end the practice. For example, two prominent African Americans who worked in the 1890s to end lynching were Frederick Douglass and Ida B. Wells.[33] Similarly, W.E.B. DuBois kept the black community updated about the anti-lynching movement as editor of the official NAACP newspaper *Crisis*.

In the early 1900s when many white men saw lynching as a necessary tool to protect women from being raped, other women in addition to Wells were among the leaders of the campaign against lynching. For example, Jessie Daniel Ames, who directed The Association of Southern Women for the Prevention of Lynching, worked tirelessly to stop the practice. Other women's organizations who were key participants in the anti-lynching movement included the Women's International League for Peace and Freedom and the Young Women's Christian Association (YWCA).[34] Many of the activists recognized that white men used the violent practice as a means, under the guise of "protection," to assert control over women too.

In the years after World War I, the NAACP led a significant campaign to persuade Congress to pass a federal anti-lynching law. Additionally, the NAACP worked with local blacks in Georgia and other states to push for investigation and exposure of local lynchings. Others promoted the cause too. President Warren G. Harding supported the push for anti-lynching legislation and spoke out against lynching at an October 1921 speech in Alabama. In 1939, Billie Holiday drew further attention to the issue of lynching when she recorded Abel Meeropol's song "Strange Fruit" about black bodies hanging on southern trees.

As in other states, various groups in addition to the NAACP worked to end lynching in Georgia. A number of prominent white ministers, educators, and social workers in Atlanta formed the Commission on Interracial Cooperation in 1919. The organization consciously avoided any appearance of challenging white supremacy so it could work effectively to help end racial violence in the state. In the early part of the twentieth century, newspapers from Atlanta and other Georgia cities pushed for political officials to address mob violence. After the Leo Frank lynching in Marietta, the *Atlanta Constitution* noted "the people of Georgia are being branded as barbarians in the North" as well as being criticized strongly within the state. Starting in the 1920s, local church congregations became more vocal in their opposition to lynchings. Academics, activists, black organizations, and business leaders concerned about the state's reputation all hoped to end lynching in the state. Political and economic changes also helped contribute to a growing opposition to lynching.[35]

Although one of the main goals of anti-lynching activists was to obtain a federal law against lynching, the movement failed in getting Congress to pass such a law. But the movement succeeded in education and reform efforts. During the 1920s, popular culture and officials no longer glorified mob violence, and lynchings declined. For example, in Georgia, the years 1920–1922 saw forty lynchings, while the next four years had only ten lynching victims. The years 1927–1929 were the first ones in fifty years without any lynchings in the state. By 1939, anti-lynching efforts and changes in the South helped to limit the number of lynchings nationally to just a few per year, and finally, in 1952, no lynchings occurred.[36]

The anti-lynching activists had much in common with the later anti-death penalty activists. The NAACP[37] and religious organizations[38] played important roles in both movements. In her book on women in the American anti-lynching campaign, Professor Mary Jane Brown wrote about the victory of the anti-lynching movement: "The decline in lynching was the result of a convergence of events: in addition to the concerted efforts of the NAACP, the ASWPL [Association of Southern Women for the Prevention of Lynching] and other anti-lynching activists, social changes, such as radio, movies, and improved roads cut through the isolation of the rural South to erode folkways and allow new ideas to trickle in." She also cited local outrage at notorious lynchings and international criticism as other factors that contributed to the decline in lynching.[39]

Thus, public opinion, education, and international pressure played key roles in the anti-lynching movement. Additionally, a change in society's structure contributed to the success of anti-lynching activists: New Deal programs that modernized the South's system of agriculture and revolutionized the southern plantation system led to a decline in the socioeconomic roots of mob violence. Economic changes led farm owners to use machinery and pay workers higher wages. As a result, traditional methods of controlling labor, including mob violence, were replaced by more educated farming techniques. According to one economist, due to the modernization of the rural economy in the South, "The economic underpinnings and social glue that had kept the [southern] regional economy isolated were no longer present in 1940."[40]

Although some proclaimed the curtailing of public lynchings was a success for the anti-lynching movement, others believed it merely represented a shift. The NAACP argued lynchings merely moved from being public spectacles to being conducted by small groups of white men who did their planning and killing in secret, avoiding prosecution by officials. Additionally, as post-Reconstruction social structures were set up, white supremacy could be enforced through segregation, disfranchisement, and other means.[41]

Additionally, similar results still occurred in the courtroom where blacks could be given unfair trials and sentenced to death based on questionable evidence. In the 1930s, two-thirds of all executions were of black defendants.[42] History Professor William S. McFeely explained that even though many nineteenth-century judges tried to provide fair trials, legal executions began acting as a replacement for lynchings in the South, and critics referred to these new cases as "legal lynchings."[43]

Thus, although the anti-lynching movement succeeded in changing society's values and public violent behavior, it did not change institutional structure. Not only did the movement fail to get a national anti-lynching bill passed, it could not change the social structures that divided the races.[44] In 1957, when McCleskey was a young child, William F. Buckley Jr., the founder of *National Review*, could argue "the White community in the South is entitled to take such measures as are necessary to prevail, politically and culturally, in areas in which it does not predominate numerically" because "for the time being, it is the advanced race."[45]

A later generation of civil rights workers would have to go beyond the NAACP's anti-lynching strategy of education and legal reform to use nonviolent resistance and direct action. Many of the civil rights workers and blacks in the South during the 1950s and 1960s, though, would encounter another wave of racial violence. But their efforts helped bring about changes that the NAACP's earlier anti-lynching efforts did not accomplish. At the same time, the NAACP and other organizations recognized that the foundations of a lynching society remained embedded in a legal system imprisoned by the past.

CHAPTER 11

Race and the Courts

Lynching featured many similarities to the U.S. legal system for much of history, when many criminal laws expressly treated defendants differently based on their race. Although legislators eventually ceased writing criminal laws that were facially racist, that past still connects to the American death penalty.

CRIMINAL LAWS AND RACE

The historical mistreatment of African Americans outside of the law is consistent with the way legal institutions treated blacks throughout American history. Even as the country worked to improve its legal system, blacks were left behind. Of course, the disparity had much of its origins in the institution of slavery. Anthony Trollope's mother, Frances, noticed the hypocrisy between the country's ideals and the treatment of blacks when she traveled to America in the late 1820s: "Look at them at home; you will see them with one hand hoisting the cap of liberty, and with the other flogging their slaves."[1]

In one of Warren McCleskey's cases before the U.S. Supreme Court, Justice Brennan discussed Georgia's history of treating blacks and whites differently within its criminal justice system: "During the colonial period, black slaves who killed whites in Georgia, regardless of whether in self-defense or in defense of another, were automatically executed."[2] In 1861, the Georgia Penal Code mandated the death penalty for blacks convicted of raping a "free white female," while the punishment for a white man who raped a white female was a prison sentence of between two and twenty years. If the victim were a black woman, Georgia punished the crime of rape "by fine and imprisonment, at the discretion of the courts."[3]

Many states maintained official disparities based on the race of the defendant and the race of the victim. In 1712 after a slave revolt, New York passed the first statute creating capital crimes for slaves versus lesser punishment for whites.[4] But most of these disparate sentencing schemes were created in the southern colonies as an attempt to control a large slave population. An 1856 treatise reported that Virginia had sixty-six capital crimes for slaves but only one for whites. Similarly,

Mississippi had thirty-eight crimes that were death penalty offenses for slaves but not for whites.[5]

These statutes covered a wide range of capital crimes for black defendants. For example, in 1740 in South Carolina, slaves and free blacks could be sentenced to death for destroying grain or bruising whites. Due to fears of poisoning, Virginia made it a capital crime for slaves to prepare or give medicine.

These disparities in the law books applied in practice. For example, during 1800 to 1860 in Virginia, whites were executed only for murder, while about half of the hundreds of blacks hanged during that time were executed for crimes other than murder.[6]

All the way up to the Supreme Court, society sanctioned the different treatment of blacks from whites. For example, in 1847 a slave named Dred Scott sued for his freedom based on extended time spent in the free state of Illinois and the free territory of Wisconsin. In 1857, the case went to the U.S. Supreme Court, which held in *Dred Scott v. Sandford* that because Scott was black, he was not a citizen and not entitled to bring the lawsuit. Chief Justice Roger Taney reasoned blacks were "so far inferior, that they had no rights which the white man was bound to respect."[7]

The disparate treatment was not limited to black men. A total of approximately 400 women have been executed on American soil since 1632, with 230 of them black and at least 189 of those known to be slaves. The slaves were executed for arson, attempted murder, conduct unbecoming a slave, and other crimes. But the majority—61 percent—of the executed women slaves killed their slave master, their mistress, or another person in the slave master's family. Likely, many of these homicides occurred because the women were being sexually assaulted. For example, in Missouri, Robert Newsom repeatedly raped and sexually assaulted a young black slave named Celia after the sixty-year-old man purchased the fourteen-year-old. When Celia tried to end the sexual relationship and Newsom refused, she hit him with a club and killed him. Officials tried the nineteen-year-old and sentenced her to death. On December 21, 1855, she was hanged.[8]

Although the federal government attempted to end race-based laws through both the Civil Rights Act of 1866 and the equal protection guarantee of the Fourteenth Amendment, white citizens figured out ways to continue using the death penalty disproportionately against blacks. Sentencing procedures that gave jurors discretion and statutes that applied the death penalty to a broad range of crimes both permitted racial discrimination.

In the 1800s, southern states begin giving complete discretion to all-white capital juries in sentencing capital defendants. These discretionary schemes were first adopted in the 1830s and 1840s in Tennessee, Alabama, and Louisiana, and they were most likely created to allow jurors to consider race. After the Civil War, most southern states adopted discretionary capital sentencing schemes for at least some crimes. For example, in 1866, Texas gave jurors discretion in capital rape cases, while in the same year Georgia passed a law giving jurors discretion in cases for all capital crimes.[9] States across the country soon adopted discretionary sentencing laws. The laws appeared equal in the abstract and, as noted in Chapter 5, eliminated the harshness of mandatory death sentences for all capital offenses. But in practice the statutes assured that all-white juries would sentence black defendants to death much more often than white defendants. These discretionary capital sentencing statutes would be used throughout the United States until the Supreme Court found them unconstitutional in *Furman v. Georgia*.

As slavery ended and Reconstruction began, white Southerners not only turned to violence and lynching, but they passed Black Codes allowing them various "legal" mechanisms of enforcing a social order. In the post–Civil War years, many white Southerners saw the death penalty as serving the same function as lynching to restrain blacks. In a September 28, 1899, editorial in *The Christian Recorder*, Ada Cooper described how an outcry against extrajudicial executions forced would-be-lynchers to use other methods to achieve their goals. She described how Virginia officials arrested the African-American Noah Finley for robbing a white man. Instead of lynching him, they prosecuted him under a rarely used old law that allowed highway robbery to be prosecuted as a capital crime. The court convicted Finley of the crime and officials executed him. Then, officials publicly displayed Finley's body "to serve the double purpose of showing the organized lynchers of the state how easy it would be to give semblance of law to the execution of Negroes, and of showing to those Negroes that a legal way had been discovered to dispose of them which could not be effectually criticized even by their friends."[10]

Some lawmakers in the twentieth century still wished to assert control over blacks, so discriminatory criminal laws continued to exist. Governor George W. Hays of Arkansas warned in 1927, "If the death penalty were to be removed from our statute-books, the tendency to commit deeds of violence would be heightened owing to the negro problem." Because of such fears, southern states maintained their pre–Civil War approach of applying the death penalty to a large number of crimes while northern states limited capital punishment to murder. By 1954, rape was a capital offense in eighteen states and robbery was a capital offense in nine. In both cases, the states that retained those capital offenses were southern states except for Nevada. Similarly, the five states that retained the death penalty for arson and the four that retained it for burglary were all southern states. Georgia retained the death penalty for rape, robbery, and arson.

Although murder convictions in many states had sizeable racial disparities, the use of capital punishment for crimes besides murder allowed for bigger racial disparities. By 1977 when the U.S. Supreme Court held it violates the Constitution to execute a person for the rape of an adult woman where a death did not occur, studies revealed that of the 771 people executed between 1870 and 1950 with an identifiable race, 701 of them were black. During the same time period, 31 of the 35 executed for robbery were black, and 18 of the 21 executed for burglary were black.[11] Thus, throughout much of American history, blacks continued to be punished more harshly both inside and outside the legal system.

THE DEATH PENALTY'S CONNECTIONS TO LYNCHING

The legacy of lynching still hovers over modern society. For many, a noose still evokes a time when lynching was commonplace and where the mob used its power against the oppressed, and in particular, African Americans. For example, in 2007 after an altercation where black teenagers beat a white classmate regarding the right to sit under a tree in Jena, Louisiana, white students hung nooses on the tree as a message to the black students. Although none of those students had been around during the lynching era, they all knew the message from a noose could be used to threaten blacks.[12] And in late 2002, during a capital trial in Louisiana of an African-American defendant, as a "joke" a prosecutor wore to court a tie that featured a picture of a noose.[13] The legacy of lynch law cannot easily be purged from society, as it lingers in more subtle forms than its overt violent past.

In the 1970s, McCleskey's attorneys knew their case representing a black man accused of killing a white law enforcement officer connected to America's past. For example in the contemporary Utah trial of Pierre Selby and William Andrews for capital murder, one trial observer crudely invoked the past. Authorities accused Selby of killing three people during a 1974 stereo-shop robbery with his codefendant, William Andrews. During the robbery, Andrews had forced five people to drink Drano before he left Selby behind at the scene. Selby raped an eighteen-year-old hostage and left two survivors, including a sixteen-year-old boy who suffered from disabilities the rest of his life from being shot in the head. The brutal crime created an outrage in the community. During the trial of the two African-American defendants, an angry observer passed a note to one of the members of the all-white jury, encouraging them to "Hang the niggers." The judge denied the defense attorneys' motion for a mistrial. Utah executed Selby on August 28, 1987, and executed Andrews on July 30, 1992. When the Supreme Court declined to review the case, Justice Thurgood Marshall wrote a dissenting opinion that was joined by Justice William Brennan, calling the note "a vulgar incident of lynch-mob racism reminiscent of Reconstruction days."[14]

Before his days on the Supreme Court, Justice Thurgood Marshall had heard similar language as an attorney, including once from an unexpected source. While representing a man on death row as an attorney for the NAACP, Marshall listened to a phone conversation when the U.S. Attorney General called President Franklin Delano Roosevelt at his home in Hyde Park about the impending execution. Marshall recalled that Roosevelt, who did not know Marshall was on the line, chastised the Attorney General for disturbing his morning coffee about the African-American man in Virginia. Roosevelt ordered, "Don't you ever bother me about that nigger again."[15] While one may assume President Roosevelt would not have participated in a lynch mob in his youth, like many others of the time, he was not above dehumanizing a condemned man in Virginia.

Several parallels exist between lynching and the death penalty. The most obvious similarity between capital punishment and lynching is that both involve the killing of an individual for committing some type of crime. By contrast, the most obvious difference between the two is that the government explicitly sanctions the death penalty's killing.

Even though lynching was technically illegal, its practice had qualities similar to legal executions. Many whites either tolerated or accepted lynching. Further, although lynchings are by definition outside the law, the procedures and policies behind lynchings often reflected society's legal system. Professor Timothy V. Kaufman-Osborn has noted that lynching parties often invoked some rituals comparable to trial procedures before completing the lynching. For example, as noted earlier, when men from Warren McCleskey's home town lynched Leo Frank, an actual judge in attendance announced the "sentence." Correspondingly, in some cases where an actual trial preceded an execution, the trials often were run by members of a mob that preordained the outcome of the trial.[16]

Lynching and capital punishment have other historical connections. Death penalty advocates often linked the two by warning that capital punishment laws were necessary so mobs would not resort to lynching. Additionally, although both practices occur around the world, they each have a unique American legacy and history.[17]

Lynching mainly occurred in one region of the country—the South. Similarly, some note that "the most powerful predictor of differential imposition of the death penalty is...geographical region."[18] The fourteen states with 100 or more lynchings in the United States from 1882 to 1968 are Mississippi, Georgia, Texas, Louisiana, Alabama, Arkansas, Florida, Tennessee, Kentucky, South Carolina, Missouri, Oklahoma, North Carolina, and Virginia.[19] For the first several decades after *Gregg*, of the 1,320 executions between 1977 and 2012, more than 1,000 took place in southern states. Of the fourteen states that led the country in number of executions during this recent period, most are in the South and twelve of them are the same as the lynching leaders: Texas (492), Virginia (109), Oklahoma (102), Florida (74), Missouri (68), Alabama (55), Georgia (52), Ohio (49), North Carolina (43), South Carolina (43), Arizona (34), Louisiana (28), Arkansas (27), and Mississippi (21).[20]

The high rate of lynchings and executions in the southern United States occurred for a number of possible reasons. Some have argued that lynchings and executions occur from a cultural embracing of "a logic of exclusion." Under such reasoning, it becomes easier to extinguish a life when "the life being terminated is placed outside the security of the 'bonded' community." Thus, because of the history of treating blacks as outside the community, it may be easier culturally to accept practices such as lynching and the death penalty. UCLA professor of law Stuart Banner has argued that the geographic disparity in the use of capital punishment results from several factors, including that the South has a higher murder rate and that southern states generally provided less funding than northern states for capital defense, resulting in poor quality representation of capital defendants.[21]

Judicial executions generally do not directly result from overt racism in the same way as did lynchings, but many commentators argue racism still plays a role in capital sentencing. In the years leading up to *Furman v. Georgia* when many states gave jurors complete discretion in capital sentencing, 49 percent of executed murder defendants were black, while in Southern jurisdictions the rate climbed to 70 percent. When the death penalty applied to the crime of rape, 89 percent of those executed nationally between 1930 and 1967 were black.[22]

The connection between race and the death penalty is not limited to any regions of the country or to blatant racists. Numerous studies demonstrate how people across all geographic, education, and social spheres tend to be biased in various ways in their perceptions of African Americans. These biases may translate into death sentences in various ways, ranging from jurors' actions in associating blacks with future dangerousness, problems with witness identifications across different races, defense attorneys' unconscious bias affecting their relationships with their clients, prosecutors using racially biased reasons for excluding African-American jurors, and numerous other effects.[23] Similar biases regarding other characteristics, such as class and poverty, may also affect who gets executed.

Another similarity between lynching and capital punishment is that both are affected by the economy. Just as the death penalty increased in popularity during the hard times of the Great Depression, some have "claimed that high correlations existed between lynching rates in the South and indicators of economic performance such as the per acre value of cotton."[24] Advocates of such reasoning argue that poor economic conditions breed frustrations that are expressed in violence. In the case of lynchings, that frustration took the form of violence against African Americans. Similarly, economist Benjamin Friedman noted in *The Moral Consequences of Economic Growth* that in difficult economic times, people become more selfish.[25] It is difficult enough to have any compassion for someone accused of murder, and when members of the public are suffering economically, it is less likely they will worry about individuals accused of crimes.

Finally, the struggle between state and federal powers affected the histories of both lynching and capital punishment. Much of the debate about lynching in the early part of the twentieth century focused on whether the issue should be addressed by the states or the federal government. Some presidents, such as William Howard Taft, preferred to leave the issue to the states. Thus, Congress never passed an anti-lynching law, despite efforts by reformers that led to House passage of anti-lynching measures on three occasions.[26] Similarly, the states' response to *Furman* by enacting new death penalty statutes was to some extent a reaction to the federal court stepping on the toes of states' rights. Today, much of the debate surrounding the review of capital cases by federal courts centers on issues of states' rights and federalism, including several decisions by the Supreme Court as well as the Anti-Terrorism and Effective Death Penalty Act that have limited federal review of state capital cases.

Thus, the use of the death penalty parallels the use of lynching regarding severity, their American nature, geographical influences, racial issues, economic influences, and federalism. One might argue in some ways that legal executions—which rose sharply during the 1930s in many southern states as the number of lynchings dropped—replaced extralegal lynchings. Professor W. Fitzhugh Brundage has explained, "With the decline of lynching, many southern whites renounced the inhumanity of the mob, preferring instead to rely on the harsh justice of the state."[27]

The courthouse procedures were preferable to mob violence, but numerous legal executions maintained similarities with non-legal executions.[28] The famous Scottsboro case illustrates a transitional link between lynching and capital punishment. In 1931, nine black youths were arrested in Alabama and charged with rape. At another place or at an earlier time, they probably would have been lynched, but efforts of Governor Benjamin Meeks Miller and local officials kept the mobs away. Still, in an unfair trial with questionable evidence, eight of the youths were sentenced to death.[29] It would take many years, mass movements, and the Supreme Court's decision in *Powell v. Alabama*[30] to save the lives of the Scottsboro defendants, who were likely innocent of the charges. Thus, in many ways the Scottsboro case illustrates how qualities of lynching transitioned into

Figure 11.1
Justice Thurgood Marshall (Collection of the Supreme Court of the United States)

the courtroom, including the racial component, the southern locale, the lack of adequate trial procedures, and the issues regarding the role of the federal government in state trials.

One African-American capital defense lawyer who saw the connection between the death penalty and lynching visited Tennessee in November 1946, the year of Warren McCleskey's birth. The attorney, working for the NAACP, successfully represented several black men who were accused of rioting and of attempted murder of police in Columbia, Tennessee. When the jurors returned to the courtroom to announce their verdict, the attorney sensed the tension from the white officials and audience members.

After the jurors announced their verdict of "not guilty," the NAACP lawyer and his colleagues planned to leave town quickly because there had been threats on their lives. As they were leaving town that night, though, a police car pulled them over, arresting the attorney for driving while intoxicated, even though he had had nothing to drink. The officers took the attorney in their car, eventually driving down a dark dirt road toward a well-known site of several lynchings.

In the car, the attorney saw in the headlights that at the end of the dirt road a number of men were waiting for their arrival and the possible lynching. Fortunately, one of the attorney's colleagues followed the police car to the site and made a scene, refusing the officers' orders to leave. Eventually, the police put the attorney back in the car, leaving the lynch mob behind and taking him back to the courthouse, where a magistrate ordered the police to let him go.

The attorney, who had barely escaped being lynched, continued fighting against racial injustice in the South. And the attorney, Thurgood Marshall, would remember the other men who had been lynched in the South as well as his own close call with lynching after he became a U.S. Supreme Court justice and sat hearing the arguments in Warren McCleskey's case.[31] (See Figure 11.1.)

When the Supreme Court addressed a claim of racial discrimination in McCleskey's case in 1987, the justices addressed more than one condemned man. For Justice Marshall, McCleskey's Supreme Court case invoked the entire United States' history of slavery, race, discrimination, lynching, and capital punishment. Similarly, Justice John Paul Stevens later noted the evidence Warren McCleskey's lawyers presented in *McCleskey v. Kemp* "provides a haunting reminder of once-prevalent Southern lynchings."[32]

CHAPTER 12

Warren McCleskey and the Baldus Study

Warren McCleskey's case launched the final broad constitutional attack on the American death penalty. His case featured a landmark study researched and written by Professors David Baldus, Charles Pulaski Jr., and George Woodworth. This study and McCleskey's case carried the burden of the country's history of racism and capital punishment. And it would go all the way to the Supreme Court.

As lynchings dwindled in the South and criminal laws that overtly discriminated were taken off the books, racial prejudice took on other forms in criminal trials. During the middle of the twentieth century, officials continued to be creative in their criminal prosecutions of African Americans.

Officials rigged the system in various ways, such as excluding blacks from juries. During McCleskey's childhood in Cobb County, Georgia, the local court continued a historical practice of preventing African Americans from serving on juries. Respected jurists allowed this discriminatory system to continue in various ways. For example, because jury pools were drawn from a list of property owners in a tax digest, court officials gave white tax return forms to white citizens and yellow tax forms to African-American citizens. For jury selection, officials then removed a tab from the form with the taxpayer's name. When a judge used the name tabs to draw names for jury duty, a judge would "accidentally" drop yellow tabs back into the box and draw another name.[1]

When McCleskey was nine years old attending his segregated school in Cobb County, the U.S. Supreme Court evaluated the yellow-ticket practice in a capital case involving Amos Reece. A jury convicted the African-American Reece of raping a woman when he left a road gang while serving time at a prison farm. After a grand jury indicted Reece for the crime in October 1953, Reece's attorneys challenged the composition of the all-white grand jury. During hearings, court clerks admitted they did not remember an African American ever serving on a Cobb County grand jury. Attorneys pointed out that although blacks made up 10 percent of the population of Cobb County, and more than one thousand blacks were listed as landowners, only a few blacks were even on the jury list. After Judge James Manning rejected a motion to quash the indictment, the trial proceeded and the jury voted for a verdict of guilty without a recommendation of mercy so that Reece was sentenced to death.

The Supreme Court, however, ordered a new trial for Reece. Justice Tom C. Clark wrote the Court's opinion, holding that a defendant is denied equal protection under the U.S. Constitution when members of the defendant's race are systematically excluded from grand juries. The Court concluded that because of the large black population and because no blacks had served on juries, Cobb County's discrimination against African Americans was "ingenious or ingenuous." Because in the face of this evidence Georgia officials had not proved they did not discriminate, the Court reversed and remanded the case.[2]

After the Supreme Court decision, the case inflamed some of the state's open wounds still festering from Reconstruction. When the FBI began investigating the alleged discrimination in the Cobb County court system, local politicians criticized the federal government for getting involved. In the U.S. Congress, Georgia representative Henderson Lanham attacked the FBI for its "flagrant invasion of the rights of sovereign states." He also accused the NAACP of trying "to wipe out all racial lines in the South in the hope of seeing the blood of the two races mingled in future generations of Americans."[3] Meanwhile, Georgia did not stop executing other capital defendants with the same legal claim. On March 30, 1956, the state executed Aubry Williams, whose jury selection process used yellow and white tickets based on race.[4]

In Reece's case, ultimately, the FBI did not prosecute any officials in Cobb County, and the county retried Reece, found him guilty, and again sentenced him to death. Reece was sent to the prison in Reidsville, where Warren McCleskey would later serve a prison sentence. Attorneys argued that Reece had low intelligence and was not competent to be executed, but the execution date approached. On January 4, 1957, at 10:45 am, Georgia prison workers executed Reece in the state's electric chair, and officials returned Reece's body to Cobb County, where it was buried at Reece's church, Big Bethel.[5] At the time of Reece's execution and burial, Warren McCleskey was a ten-year-old living in the same county.

The racism in some capital cases came closer to the surface than in others. While McCleskey sat on death row, in the Georgia capital trial of William Dobbs, an African American tried for killing a white man, the judge and defense attorney referred to Dobbs as "colored" and as the "colored boy." Dobbs's attorney, who himself believed blacks were inferior to whites, did little work at Dobbs's sentencing hearing. The court sentenced Dobbs to death. Other post-*Furman* cases featured judges and lawyers using racial slurs in capital cases. A judge and defense attorney in Arizona used the term "wetbacks" in a capital case involving a Mexican-American. One may find other examples from across the country, some with the racial biases more out in the open than others.[6]

As part of a long-term legal strategy attacking capital punishment, capital defense lawyers had been arguing for decades that race corrupts the American death penalty. Since the 1950s the NAACP Legal Defense Fund (LDF) had been raising claims about the death penalty being racially biased. For example, LDF attorney Frank Heffron had interviewed Arkansas court clerks about race in capital rape cases and had tried to use the information in 1964 in the case of William Maxwell, a black defendant sentenced to death for raping a white woman.

After Maxwell's case, defense attorneys realized they needed more precise statistical studies. Thus, attorneys in early litigation challenges used a study by University of Pennsylvania criminologist Marvin Wolfgang of around 3,000 rape convictions in eleven states from 1945 to 1965. In that study, Wolfgang found black men were seven times more likely than white men to be sentenced to death, and black men convicted of raping white women were eighteen times more likely to be sentenced to death than any other racial combination.

Claims based on Wolfgang's study, however, were not successful. In 1968 in *Maxwell v. Bishop*, the U.S. Court of Appeals for the Eighth Circuit in an opinion by Judge—and future Supreme Court justice—Harry Blackmun rejected a constitutional challenge based on the Wolfgang study. Blackmun rejected the claim for several reasons, including that the study did not take into account every variable. Although the Supreme Court granted a writ of certiorari in the case from Arkansas, it reversed the Eighth Circuit decision on another issue and did not even mention race.[7]

Within several years, though, some justices discussed the race issue during the litigation of *Furman v. Georgia* even if the Court as a whole did not resolve the case on race grounds. Then, after the U.S. Supreme Court upheld the death penalty in *Gregg v. Georgia*, defense attorneys knew that the only way they might get the Court to strike down the death penalty was if they could prove that states used the death penalty in a racially discriminatory way.

As part of this strategy, Anthony Amsterdam, who had argued *Furman* and *Gregg*, and Jack Greenberg, who served as the Director-Counsel of LDF from 1961 to 1984, continued to work with LDF to develop an attack on the death penalty using statistical studies. As discussed in Chapter 9, in the 1970s, another LDF attorney, David Kendall, raised a constitutional race claim in the case of John Spenkelink even though Spenkelink was white. Building on the earlier important work of Professor Wolfgang, Kendall argued that the discrimination centered on the race of the victim because those who murdered whites were more likely to get the death penalty than those who killed blacks.[8]

The attorneys looked for other studies on racial discrimination in capital sentencing. William J. Bowers and Glenn L. Pierce found disparities based on the race of victims in a 1980 study of death sentences in Florida, Georgia, Texas, and Ohio. As with the Wolfgang study, courts criticized the work of Bowers and Pierce because they did not address every possible variable.[9]

Death penalty opponents and capital defense lawyers needed a more detailed study, and one soon came from University of Iowa College of Law professor David C. Baldus, who performed the work with George G. Woodworth, a University of Iowa professor of statistics and actuarial science, and Charles A. Pulaski Jr., who had been a professor of law at the University of Iowa College of Law and Arizona State University College of Law before going into private practice in 1986. Baldus and his colleagues obtained funding for their first study from the National Institute of Justice and the University of Iowa and Syracuse University Law Schools.

Although LDF approached Baldus to enhance the study and helped him obtain further funding, the researchers worked independently of LDF. Also, the publication of their results did not depend on LDF's interests.

The work by Baldus, Pulaski, and Woodworth came to be known as "the Baldus study," although it actually included two statistical studies. Initially, in the Procedural Reform Study they completed in 1982, they evaluated more than 200 variables for 594 defendants who were sentenced for murder in Georgia from March 1973 through July 1978. Baldus and his colleagues expanded on this work in their subsequent more-detailed Charging and Sentencing Study, which added data on the strength of the evidence of the defendant's guilt and was not restricted to murder convictions.

This second study covered more than 2,400 Georgia homicide prosecutions from 1973 through 1980 considering more than 400 variables. Using sources that included records of the Georgia Supreme Court and of the Georgia Board of Pardons and Paroles, six law students supervised by Edward Gates coded the cases based on variables over a number of decision points, including grand-jury decisions, prosecutor decisions, and jury decisions. Baldus, Woodworth, and Pulaski then focused more narrowly on 230 factors in 1,066 cases, analyzing the cases by considering the variables that could affect the outcome of the cases. They used multiple-regression analysis to examine factors that affected the nature of the offenses.[10]

Although attorneys introduced both studies in court proceedings, the courts generally referred to both together as "the Baldus study," while mainly using the information from the more thorough Charging and Sentencing Study. The Baldus study included a significant amount of data about both Georgia and Fulton County, the location of McCleskey's trial and sentencing. After the study became available in 1982, LDF lawyers, including the young Jack Boger, began looking for Georgia capital cases where they could use the study, and they encouraged other attorneys to use the information.

In the statistical analysis, Baldus and his colleagues concluded that counting for all of the nonracial variables, a black defendant charged with killing a white victim was significantly more likely to get the death penalty than a defendant charged with killing a black victim. Although the study found a small disparity based on the race of the defendant, the most influential racial factor was the race of the victim. The researchers found the effects from the race of the victim came both from the prosecution decisions and from the decisions of capital sentencing jurors.[11] In effect, the mostly white decision-makers in capital cases were more likely to sympathize with victims of their own race.

Among the findings, the Baldus study concluded that a capital defendant's odds of getting the death penalty are multiplied by 4.3 if the victim were white. A number of observers misunderstood the difference between "odds" and "probabilities" in this context. But Baldus, Woodworth, and Pulaski later explained the difference in their book *Equal Justice and the Death Penalty*. They noted, "A 4.3 probability multiplier increases a .20 probability to .86 (4.3 x .20). However, a 4.3 multiplier of the 1:4 odds (that are equal to a .20 probability) increases the odds to 4:4 (4 x .25), which is a probability of only .50."[12]

In other words, the 4.3 odds multiplier applies to the odds of getting the death penalty considering all of the other nonracial factors evaluated in the study. If based on the facts of a case, the odds in a black-victim case were 1:8 (11 percent probability), meaning that one defendant would get the death penalty for every eight defendants sentenced to life; one would apply the 4.3 multiplier to find the odds for white-victim cases. So, based on otherwise identical facts, a defendant with a white victim would have the odds 4.3:8, or a 35 percent probability, of getting the death penalty, compared to the 1:8 odds if the victim were black.[13]

Expressing relative risk of a death sentence as an odds multiplier means that the effect of a factor, such as the presence of a white victim, multiplies the odds on a death sentence in the reference group of similar cases with no white victim by a fixed multiple, regardless of the nonracial facts of the case. Mathematically, however, this factor does not multiply the probability of a death sentence by a fixed multiple.

Instead, the same odds multiplier can have quite different effects on probability depending on other facts in the case, such as the egregiousness of the murder. The example above shows the probability in some types of cases more than tripling from 11% to 35% based on the race of the victim. But if the nonracial facts of a case were such that almost everyone with those facts would get the death penalty, mathematically the presence of a white victim results in a smaller numerical increase in the probability. For example, if the case had an especially aggravated fact pattern that historically resulted in nineteen death sentences out of twenty nonwhite victim cases (the reference group), the odds of a death sentence would be 19:1 and the probability of a death sentence would be 95 percent (19/20). But the presence of a white victim on the same facts would multiply the 19:1 reference-group odds by the 4.3-fold odds multiplier, so that the white-victim group odds would be 81.7:1, so the probability would be 99 percent (81.7 death sentences out of 82.7 on those facts). Thus, in the more aggravated case, the fact that the victim was white would result in a smaller increase of 4 percent.[14]

So the odds multiplier illustrates how race has a variable effect on the likelihood of getting a death sentence based on the other facts of a case. Professors Baldus, Woodworth, and Pulaski determined McCleskey's case fell in a range where race had a material effect. More specifically, the researchers concluded that "in black defendant cases with a level of aggravation comparable to McCleskey's case, defendants with white victims faced an estimated death-sentencing rate of between .34 and .43." By contrast, black defendants with a similar level of aggravation but with black victims faced a much lower estimated death-sentencing rate of between .14 and .23.[15] A probability multiplier in McCleskey's case would average around 2 based on the studies, meaning that for cases with similar facts, McCleskey was twice as likely to get the death penalty because his victim was white instead of black. Thus, the race of the victim in McCleskey's case created a material risk of racial bias in his sentence.[16]

Considering other variables in the Georgia capital sentencing process, the Baldus study concluded that the race of the victim, with a "death odds multiplier" of 4.3, played a more significant role in death sentences than some other factors, including armed robbery (4.2), the victim was weak or frail (3.1), the victim was a police or corrections officer on duty (1.7), or the defendant had a pecuniary motive for the killing (0.80). Additionally, the study concluded that a black defendant had an odds multiplier of 1.1 and thus was more likely to be sentenced to death than a nonblack defendant.[17] Some factors, on the other hand, played a larger role than the race of the victim, including that the victim was twelve years of age or younger (4.8), the defendant killed two or more people (7.9), or rape was involved (12.8).[18]

The study examined the different stages of the legal process that could lead to a death sentence: the indictment, the prosecutorial decisions on plea bargaining, the jury's decision on the offense, the prosecutorial decision on whether to proceed to a capital sentencing hearing, and the jury's decision whether to impose a death sentence or life in prison. For example, the study noted prosecutors "sought the death penalty in 70% of cases involving black defendants and white victims; 32% of cases involving white defendants and white victims; 15% of cases involving black defendants and black victims; and 19% of cases involving white defendants and black victims."[19] According to these statistics, McCleskey, as a black man charged with killing a white man, fell into the category where he was more likely to receive a death sentence than another defendant merely because of his race and the race of his victim.

More narrowly, Baldus and his colleagues also considered comparable cases involving the deaths of police officers that had occurred in Fulton County, Georgia, between 1973 and 1979. Ten such homicides were committed during that time involving eighteen offenders. Of those eighteen, seven were triggermen, and of those seven, only one received the death penalty: Warren McCleskey. Baldus would testify in McCleskey's federal district court hearing: "What we do know [is] that there was nothing that looms in McCleskey's record that would clearly distinguish his case from these other cases. In a circumstance like that, it seems, it is my opinion that a racial factor could have been the consideration that tipped the scale against McCleskey in this case."[20]

The racial statistics were a far cry from the days when African Americans were lynched throughout the South, showing on the one hand how far America had come in its use of the death penalty. But courts had no more cleansed racial discrimination from the application of the death penalty than the country had cleansed it from the nation's history. The influence of race on condemning defendants to death differed from the past, but it remained directly connected to the past. From John Bailey, who was lynched in Marietta in 1900, to the trial of Marietta resident Warren McCleskey in 1978 was a long journey, but the road connected. The Baldus study showed race still mattered.

The racial disparity depending on the race of the victim occurs for a number of reasons. As in lynchings, a number of factors can help explain the results. At the core of the causes of lynching underlies a fear that "outsiders" threatened the lyncher's community. One may also see how lynching illustrates human empathy to protect those close to us, while at the same time we have less compassion for those who differ from us. Similarly, in the death penalty context, these human feelings are present, where decision-makers, who are mostly white, may find more compassion for victims who are similar to them. The result, though, is that the lives of minorities are devalued.

Once police accuse a defendant of a crime, each of the decision-makers in the process may be influenced by personal beliefs. In *Georgia v. McCollum*, Justice Sandra Day O'Connor explained that "conscious and unconscious racism can affect the way white jurors perceive minority defendants and the facts presented at their trials, perhaps determining the verdict of guilt or innocence."[21] In addition to the discretion of prosecutors and jurors, a case also may be affected by biases of the defense attorney, as well as by judicial bias. The composition of juries may influence the outcome of the case too, with the composition possibly affected by the exclusion of minorities from jury duty or with the votes affected by the discretion and racial biases of the jurors. Finally, the sentence for a black defendant convicted of killing a white victim may be affected merely by chance due to where the case is tried.

Yet, when a person is accused of racial bias, even unconscious racial bias, it carries a heavy stigma in today's society, where a former two-term U.S. president will confess that the low point of his eight-year administration was being called a racist by a musician.[22] Because of that heavy stigma, people are less likely to show their bias openly or to admit to it. So, it often makes it harder to establish racial bias directly. Similarly, people often do not recognize they do discriminate based on race. The way society treats race and the way racial discrimination is taboo also can make courts less likely to find that prosecutors or jurors were biased.

Regarding the Baldus study, lawyers, scholars, reporters, and others sometimes misstate the findings. Some incorrectly claim the study showed a significant disparity based on the defendant's race instead of the victim's race. They often incorrectly state the findings by confusing probabilities and odds.[23] Some death penalty supporters have pointed to these interpretation errors in an attempt to undermine the study's results. For example, Kent Scheidegger, the Legal Director of the Criminal Justice Legal Foundation, an organization with one of its goals "to assure that people who are guilty of committing crimes receive swift and certain punishments,"[24] has criticized the way lawyers, judges, and scholars perpetuate the confusion about "probability" and "odds."

Further, while even Scheidegger conceded a racial disparity exists in the result of who gets executed, as did the *Technology Review* article he relied upon, he has argued there is a benign explanation for the disparity.[25] Scheidegger, who also filed a Supreme Court amicus curiae brief against McCleskey on his informant issue in *McCleskey v. Zant*, has suggested any disparities from the race of the victim may be explained by reasons that are unrelated to intentional racial bias on behalf of jurors or prosecutors. He argued that members of a certain race may be unwilling to cooperate with law enforcement and prosecutors. And he also claimed crimes with black victims may be less likely to result in death sentences because black communities oppose capital punishment.[26]

Yet, unlike the detailed analysis in the Baldus study, critics offer no proof to justify the racial disparity. Even if Scheidegger's premise about cooperation varying by race were true, that reasoning or other unknown reasons might be hiding other disparities. For example, some commentators have argued that the greater race-of-victim disparity in capital cases masks and makes it impossible to prove existing race-of-defendant disparities.[27] Also, if one accepts his explanation for the cause of the disparity, the reasons that many in the black community oppose capital punishment show an understanding of the history of the death penalty and still may reflect underlying racial problems in the legal system.[28] Ultimately, Scheidegger concedes the Baldus study found a difference based on race, but he believes it is a justifiable difference.

In contrast to such justifications for the disparity, numerous statistical studies have duplicated similar results to the Baldus study, with other studies showing less benign reasons can lead to these racial disparities. A Capital Jury Project study found sentencing jurors either consciously or subconsciously factor in race when evaluating some capital sentencing factors.[29] Another study of murder cases in southwest Georgia in the Chattahoochee Judicial Circuit from 1973 to 1990 found prosecutors would often meet with the family of white victims to discuss whether to seek the death penalty. By contrast, prosecutors rarely met with the family of African-American victims, and many of those families were not even contacted about the case until after it ended. Additionally, prosecutors often used their discretionary peremptory challenges during jury selection to remove potential black jurors, resulting in a number of African-American defendants being tried by all-white jurors. During this time period, even though the victims of homicides in the circuit were African American 65 percent of the time, 85 percent of the capital prosecutions involved white victims.[30]

As with the causes of lynching, one may argue various reasons for the Baldus study results, including community opposition to the death penalty or jurors' psychological connection to victims who look like them. But considering the history of race and the death penalty, one should be skeptical of any justification to legitimize different treatment based on race. And the possible causes for treating different defendants differently based on race of the defendant or race of the victim do not negate the racial disparities that remain after removing a wide range of other factors.

In addressing arguments downplaying the study's results, Professor Baldus and Professor Woodworth explained that outcomes based on the race of the victim are immoral for a number of reasons. First, race-of-victim discrimination undervalues black lives. Second, the decision-making process is distorted based on race. Third, race ends up being a but-for cause of many death sentences. Fourth, the discrimination is unfair to black communities. And the discrimination sends an "unseemly message...that the overriding objective of capital punishment in America is the protection of white people."[31]

Thus, the Baldus study raised serious questions about the role of race in the capital punishment system, and in the 1980s the LDF attorneys looked forward to the courts evaluating the study. For decades, the Supreme Court largely had dodged arguments about race and the death penalty. Now, the capital defense attorneys believed the thoroughness of the Baldus study would force the Court to address their Eighth and Fourteenth Amendment challenges.

* * * * *

Warren McCleskey's case eventually became the vehicle that took the Baldus study to the U.S. Supreme Court. After the Atlanta jury convicted McCleskey of armed robbery and murder and sentenced him to death, he unsuccessfully sought relief in the Georgia state courts. After his lawyers lost in the state courts, lawyers at LDF—the same organization that led the 1960s and 1970s challenges to the American death penalty—began playing a larger role. Long before anyone knew McCleskey's case would be a landmark one on race and the death penalty, LDF became involved in his case when its lawyers, and in particular Jack Boger, began working with McCleskey's attorney Robert Stroup. Stroup, Boger, and other LDF attorneys continued working on McCleskey's case for more than a decade through the remaining state and federal court litigation.[32]

After capital defendants are unsuccessful in state court, they may file a petition for a writ of habeas corpus in federal court, asking the federal court to review the case. So after the losses in the state courts, McCleskey first went to the federal district court and then to the federal court of appeals. McCleskey's lawyers used the Baldus study in his first habeas corpus petition, and his case then became the leading one on the race issue for a few reasons.

One reason McCleskey's case became the leading one with the Baldus study was due to the facts of the crime. The Baldus study found race played the biggest role in cases that fell in the middle range of culpability. For aggravated crimes such as multiple murders or murders involving torture, juries gave a large number of defendants the death penalty. For less aggravated cases, such as homicides during a fight, defendants were less likely to get the death penalty. But Baldus classified McCleskey's crime in the middle, where the effects of race played the largest role.[33]

Another reason McCleskey's case became the leading Baldus study case was because his attorneys were successful in getting a federal court hearing on the study. Other Georgia capital defendants—including James L. Spencer, Willie X. Ross, and William "Billy" Mitchell—raised claims based on the Baldus study. But their district court judges refused to hold evidentiary hearings in those cases.[34]

By contrast, the district court judge in McCleskey's case recognized the potential impact of the evidence. U.S. District Court Judge J. Owen Forrester held an extensive evidentiary hearing to review the evidence, including testimony by Woodworth and Baldus. The state of Georgia also presented experts to dispute the findings of the Baldus study: Dr. Joseph L. Katz, then an assistant professor at Georgia State University, and Roger L. Burford, a professor of Quantitative Business Analysis at Louisiana State University.[35] Katz argued that one may explain the racial disparity by the fact that different races had different patterns of crime, and that interracial homicides were more likely to be the result of serious crimes that were more likely to be death penalty cases. For example, he noted that most cases with the combination of a black defendant and a white victim were armed robbery cases. By comparison, most cases with a black defendant and a black victim involved some kind of dispute. Assuming armed robberies are among the most aggravated murders, he argued that such cases justifiably resulted in more death sentences.[36] By contrast, McCleskey's attorneys responded that the Baldus study accounted for such factors.

After the hearing, in a February 1984 written opinion, Judge Forrester criticized the Baldus study and ruled against McCleskey, rejecting the Eighth and Fourteenth Amendment claims. Judge Forrester based his criticism of the Baldus study on several grounds, attacking the original Procedural Reform Study for not containing a "strength of evidence" factor while also conceding that the Charging and Sentencing Study did include information on the strength of evidence. Ultimately, Judge Forrester found the database for the studies was "substantially flawed." He concluded that the "statistics do not demonstrate a prima facie case in support of the contention that the death penalty was imposed upon [McCleskey] because of his race, because of the race of the victim, or because of any Eighth Amendment concern."[37]

McCleskey's attorneys appealed Judge Forrester's decision to the U.S. Court of Appeals for the Eleventh Circuit. The appeals court recognized the importance of the issue and took the unusual procedural approach of reviewing the case *en banc* on first review, meaning the full court reviewed it first instead of a panel of three judges.

The *en banc* court, perhaps realizing other experts respected the statistical study, did not try to reject the numbers as Judge Forrester did. Instead, the majority assumed the statistics were accurate and that "the factors of race of the victim and defendant were at work in Fulton County." But the majority concluded the level of discrimination found in the study did not rise to a constitutional issue, stating that "the statistics are insufficient to demonstrate discriminatory intent or unconstitutional discrimination in the Fourteenth Amendment context, [and] insufficient to show irrationality, arbitrariness and capriciousness under any kind of Eighth Amendment analysis."[38] Thus, nine of the appeals court judges ruled against McCleskey on his Baldus study issue while three dissenting judges reasoned that the Baldus study established a constitutional violation.

U.S. Court of Appeals Judge Robert S. Vance, who had been active in the civil rights movement during the 1960s and had stood up against Alabama governor George Wallace on such issues, voted with the majority against McCleskey on the constitutional race claims. Because the vote was not close, Judge Vance's vote did not affect the outcome of the 9-3 case, and one of his former clerks later speculated that Judge Vance must have felt helpless about the racial discrimination in the capital punishment system. Judge Vance, however, did conclude his concurring opinion by appealing to the Supreme Court to review the issue: "Claims such as that of petitioner are now presented with such regularity that we may reasonably hope for guidance from the Supreme Court by the time my expressed concerns are outcome determinative in a given case."[39] Judge Vance, however, would not live to see the final chapters in McCleskey's case. Within less than five years, a racist from Georgia who was disgruntled with his experiences before the courts sent a pipe bomb to Judge Vance, killing him in his Alabama home.[40]

Some court observers were disappointed with the lower court losses. The Lawyers' Committee for Civil Rights Under Law and the NAACP criticized the U.S. Court of Appeals result in McCleskey's case. The Congressional Black Caucus responded to the decision by stating it was astounded that any court today could "dismiss admittedly valid, comprehensive proof because it 'only' demonstrated that race is an influential factor in capital sentencing."[41]

After the loss in the Eleventh Circuit, McCleskey's attorneys persisted by filing a petition for writ of certiorari seeking review from the U.S. Supreme Court. On Thursday, June 26, 1986, the Supreme Court justices voted during their conference on whether to grant McCleskey's petition for a writ of certiorari for the Court to review the case. Four justices—Brennan, Marshall, Blackmun, and Stevens—voted for the Court to review some of the issues in the case. Five justices—White, Powell, Rehnquist, O'Connor, and Chief Justice Burger—voted to deny the petition. When the petition had first arrived at the court Justice Powell considered voting to review the claims, but by the time the justices voted, he had decided the Court should not take the case.

Although the vote was 5-4 against taking the case for review, under the Supreme Court's "Rule of Four" custom, it accepts cases for briefing and argument if four justices vote to hear the case. So, even though only a minority of the Court wanted to review the case, the Court officially issued an order granting the petition for certiorari on the Monday after the Independence Day weekend on July 7, 1986. McCleskey's case was going to the Supreme Court.[42]

When McCleskey's attorney Jack Boger heard the news, he saw it as a good sign for his client. Because the Baldus study was so thorough and well-respected, Boger believed it would be very difficult for the Court to rule against McCleskey.[43] Despite the losses in the district court and the U.S. Court of Appeals, McCleskey's attorneys hoped that when faced with the statistical proof in the Baldus study, the Supreme Court would directly address the role of race in the use of the death penalty.

The issue of race and the death penalty had finally made it to the Supreme Court. The issue had existed since the early days of the country, and it had been in the background of many of the landmark Supreme Court decisions leading up to *McCleskey v. Kemp*. Race underlay the issues raised in *Furman v. Georgia*, where Justice Douglas said the death penalty statutes were "pregnant with discrimination." [44]

Yet, the Court had repeatedly avoided directly addressing the connection between race and capital punishment. In *Coker v. Georgia*, attorneys asked the Court to consider the wide disparity between the number of African-American men executed for rape versus the number of white defendants, but the Court did not address that argument when it struck down the death penalty for rape. Some commentators criticized the Court for sidestepping the race issue in *Coker*, arguing that perhaps the Court intentionally chose a rape case with a white defendant to avoid the more complex issues.[45] A year before Justice Powell wrote the majority opinion in *McCleskey v. Kemp*, he wrote the majority opinion upholding the death sentence of Willie Darden Jr., where the defense attorney and the prosecutor referred to the African-American defendant Darden as an "animal" before an all-white jury.[46] But a majority of the Court did not consider race's relation to capital punishment in any of those cases. They would finally consider that history in *McCleskey v. Kemp*.

The Supreme Court justices accepted review of the case at a time when changes were occurring on the Court. Just before the Court granted review, Chief Justice Warren E. Burger announced in June 1986 he would resign at the end of that term after sitting on the Court since 1969. A new chief justice would be on the Court for the new era of the death penalty that began with Warren McCleskey's case. President Ronald Reagan, who had already appointed Sandra Day O'Connor to the Court, elevated President Nixon's appointed Associate Justice Rehnquist to the Chief Justice's chair.

President Reagan then nominated Judge Antonin G. Scalia for Rehnquist's former seat. Although Scalia was a known conservative, observers did not know his position on the death penalty. As a judge on the U.S. Court of Appeals for the District of Columbia Circuit, he had not had to deal with death penalty issues. Chief Justice Rehnquist and Justice Scalia were sworn in on September 26, 1986, less than three weeks before the oral arguments in McCleskey's case.[47]

The newly constructed Court was considering *McCleskey v. Kemp* when conservative law-and-order beliefs again dominated in the country. President Ronald Reagan was in his second term and he later would be succeeded by his Republican vice president, George H.W. Bush. As part of his conservative agenda, President Reagan pushed for a War on Drugs during his second term and continued a law-and-order strategy, following the Nixon approach that they both had used since their days in California.

In other ways, society had changed since the Supreme Court struck down capital punishment in 1972. When the Court addressed McCleskey's case, it knew that support for capital punishment had nearly doubled since it had struck down the death penalty fifteen years earlier. Most members of the Court had the faith that the Court's 1970s cases had eliminated much of the improper discrimination in the system. The justices also recognized that the civil rights movement of the 1960s had weakened, with many in society opposing affirmative action and criticizing the Court as being too protective of black citizens.[48]

In the wake of these events, while the Supreme Court considered Warren McCleskey's case, it granted stays of execution in several other cases from Georgia, Florida, Louisiana, and Texas raising similar claims about the role of race on capital sentencing. But on September 18, 1986, the Court denied a stay of execution to John William Rook who had raised a race claim, allowing North Carolina to execute Rook by lethal injection. Attorneys speculated about whether or not Rook's execution boded poorly for McCleskey's claims. But some noted that Rook's attorneys relied upon a study less detailed than the Baldus study, and so the Court might have denied his stay request based upon that ground or on a procedural ground. Because the Court did not issue any explanation about Rook's case, McCleskey's attorneys had to move forward hoping the stay denial was not a bad sign for their case and that the detailed Baldus study would save their client.[49]

As the Court considered the case, the litigation received so much media focus that McCleskey felt the attention in his prison cell. The Georgia prison's "Performance Recording Sheet" for McCleskey for the month of October 1986 noted, "Inmate continues to receive a lot of publicity because of his case. He appears to be handling it well. He has had no complaint or particular request. He continues to participate in crochet, . . . craft[s] and yard sports. He attends regular religious services. No problem noted."

CHAPTER 13

The Supreme Court and *McCleskey v. Kemp*

Although race had been an underlying issue in many of the Supreme Court's capital punishment decisions, the Court finally addressed the connection between race and capital punishment in Warren McCleskey's case. The decision in his 1987 Supreme Court case would help alter the future of the country's death penalty.

O n October 15, 1986, attorneys argued *McCleskey v. Kemp* before the nine justices of the U.S. Supreme Court in Washington, DC. During the oral argument, some justices expressed skepticism about the statistics showing race played a role in capital sentencing in Georgia. Similarly, an amicus brief by the state of California stressed that there were thousands or maybe millions of pieces of information that juries considered in sentencing. Thus, the state argued race could not be singled out with statistical analysis. During oral arguments, Assistant Georgia State Attorney General Mary Beth Westmoreland claimed "that there is simply no way to take account of all those variables." She argued that any disparity based on race of victims could be explained because the white victim cases were generally more serious than the black victim cases.[1]

By contrast, at oral argument, McCleskey's attorney Jack Boger—the director of LDF's Capital Punishment Project and Poverty and Justice Program—defended the studies and the research done by David Baldus, Charles Pulaski, and George Woodworth. As Baldus watched in the crowded courtroom, Boger also invoked the history of the role of race in capital sentencing going back to years before the Civil War.

Many of the questions from the bench, however, focused on practical concerns about the case. For example, Justice Sandra Day O'Connor expressed concern that the racial bias resulted from discretion in the capital punishment system, and she wondered if that meant the only alternative was to go back to mandatory death penalties. Yet, based on the justices' questions during oral argument, Boger walked away from the lectern with a strong impression McCleskey may have won.[2] Other defense attorneys were optimistic too, recognizing that McCleskey's case featured more proof of racial bias than the Court had when it struck down the death penalty in 1972.

When the justices met two days later in conference on the case, though, a majority of them were against McCleskey. The two Reagan appointees, Justices Sandra Day O'Connor and Antonin Scalia, joined Chief Justice William Rehnquist, Justice Byron White, and Justice Lewis Powell in the majority. The lineup did not surprise the justices. Even before the oral argument, White took the unusual step of sending a memo to the other justices who ended up in the majority, arguing they should reject McCleskeys' claims.

On the other side, on the first round of voting, Justices Thurgood Marshall, William J. Brennan, Jr., and John Paul Stevens voted to reverse the Court of Appeals in favor of McCleskey. Justice Harry Blackmun held off voting in a first round of voting so he could listen to the other justices explain their positions. Then, in a second round of voting, Blackmun announced he would join the three who voted to reverse. During the conference, Justice Powell kept notes of the views of the other justices, noting for Marshall, "Understandably, TM talked about the discrimination historically imposed on blacks." After the votes, Justice Powell wrote at the top of his notes: "Affirm 5-4."[3]

Because he was in the majority, Chief Justice Rehnquist decided who would write the majority opinion. He had no desire to write the opinion himself, but Justices White and Powell each were interested in tackling it. After the post-argument conference, Rehnquist assigned the majority opinion to Powell. (See Figure 13.1.)

When Justice Powell began his assignment to write the opinion, he already had struggled with racial and capital punishment issues. Powell had joined the Court in 1972 after President Richard M. Nixon appointed him. Before that, Powell had chaired the school board in Richmond, Virginia during 1952 to 1961, where he had addressed important race issues. During his first term on the Court, one of the first oral arguments Powell heard was *Furman v. Georgia*. In that case, he dissented when the Court struck down the death penalty, but he implied in that case that a black defendant would have an equal protection argument if the defendant "could demonstrate that members of his race were being singled out for more severe punishment than others charged with the same offense." But at the same time, in *Furman*, Powell stated his belief that the possibility of racial bias in criminal cases had diminished in recent years, noting "[b]ecause standards of criminal justice have 'evolved' in a manner favorable to the accused, discriminatory imposition of capital punishment is far less likely today than in the past."[4]

Not only had Powell thought about the issue, but he had previously encountered some of the research used in McCleskey's case. Several years earlier, Justice Powell reviewed a case using the initial Procedural and Reform Study by Baldus and his colleagues. At that time, Powell did not realize the extent of the study. In a dissent from a decision granting a stay of execution to Georgia capital defendant Alpha Otis O'Daniel Stephens in 1983, Powell wished to deny relief because Stephens had not raised his equal protection claim at the appropriate time in his first

Figure 13.1
Justice Lewis F. Powell, Jr. (Collection of the Supreme Court of the United States)

habeas corpus petition. In a footnote in the Stephens case, Powell noted that the Baldus study was not before the Supreme Court. But he questioned whether the Baldus study was just another "merely general statistical survey." In that case, he stated, "Surely, no contention can be made that the entire Georgia judicial system, at all levels, operates to discriminate in all cases.... [S]uch arguments cannot be taken seriously under statutes approved in *Gregg*."[5] In the *Stephens v. Kemp* case, the U.S. Court of Appeals for the Eleventh Circuit agreed with Justice Powell that Stephens's attorney did not submit the evidence at the proper time. So, after that court denied a rehearing, Stephens was executed in 1984 in Georgia's electric chair without any court evaluating the merits of the study.[6]

In McCleskey's case, though, his attorneys had introduced the evidence at the correct time, and the district court judge had allowed the evidence to be developed. So, Justice Powell now had to confront the detailed statistics and the arguments that racial bias still existed in the modern-day death penalty.

Even before oral argument, Justice Powell began writing his ideas about McCleskey's issues in a memo summarizing his initial thoughts. He started by noting the high quality of the opinions from the district court and the U.S. Court of Appeals for the Eleventh Circuit. He considered that of the twelve court of appeals judges who heard the case, nine rejected McCleskey's reliance on the Baldus study while three dissented. He wrote he had a high opinion of the dissenting judges, but he also noted those judges often sided with capital defendants.[7]

Justice Powell's law clerk Leslie Gielow initially thought McCleskey should prevail, but she did not push the issue with Powell. The 1985 law school graduate had only recently started working with Powell, and she sensed he had already made up his mind and would not change. But Gielow's research led her to believe the findings in the Baldus study could not be disputed. In one of her interoffice memos to Powell, she explained, "The experience of this country with race discrimination, especially in Georgia, makes the Baldus results believable.... It is entirely plausible that despite admonitions and jury selection safeguards, the individuals on a jury could value white life more than black life. Worded more benignly, individuals on a jury could identify more with individuals more like themselves."[8] In effect, the clerk reasoned that jurors appear to relate to the victim. So when the victim is of the same race as the jurors, they are more likely to impose a harsh sentence on the defendant.[9]

The other justices also sorted through their rationales with their clerks. Among the dissenters, Justices Marshall and Stevens and their clerks initially focused their reasoning on the Fourteenth Amendment, while Brennan and his clerks wanted to focus on the Eighth Amendment as a way of getting more votes. When one of Justice White's clerks wrote a bench memo supporting McCleskey's claims, White returned the memo and said, "This is a very nice memo recommending reversal. Now write one recommending affirmance." For a while, Justice O'Connor went back and forth on her view, and her clerk unsuccessfully tried to convince her to rule in McCleskey's favor and to limit prosecutor discretion as a remedy.[10]

Within a month after the oral argument, on November 13, 1986, Justice Powell circulated a draft of the majority opinion. That same day, Justice Sandra Day O'Connor sent Powell a short handwritten note praising his work, "You have written a splendid opinion in *McCleskey*. No one could have done better. You grappled fairly and appropriately with all aspects. We owe you our thanks."[11] The next day, she sent him an official memo joining his "excellent" opinion. Also on November

14, Justice Brennan notified Powell that he would be dissenting and noted it might take a little time because he regarded McCleskey's case as an especially important one. A little over a week later, after Powell had circulated an updated draft, Rehnquist and White signed on to the majority opinion.[12]

In early January after the holidays, Justice Scalia, the newest justice, circulated a memo to his colleagues stating his intent to join Justice Powell's draft but expressing some reservations. In his memo, he conceded unconscious racial factors probably play a role in capital cases, even as he believed such evidence should not constitute a successful constitutional challenge.

> I disagree with the argument that the inferences that can be drawn from the Baldus study are weakened by the fact that each jury and each trial is unique, or by the large number of variables at issue. And I do not share the view, implicit in the opinion, that an effect of racial factors upon sentencing, if it could be shown by sufficiently strong statistical evidence, would require reversal. Since it is my view that the unconscious operation of irrational sympathies and antipathies, including racial, upon jury decisions and (hence) prosecutorial decisions is real, acknowledged in the decisions of this court, and ineradicable, I cannot honestly say that all I need is more proof. [13]

Scalia's memorandum questioned whether a reversal would be in order even if evidence provided a strong indication that racial factors affected the sentence. But he eventually signed on to the majority opinion on February 27, 1987.

For almost two more months, Powell continued to work on the majority opinion and to make stylistic changes. He circulated a fourth draft on March 30, a fifth draft on April 1, a sixth draft on April 14, a seventh draft on April 17, and the final and eighth draft on April 20, a few days before the justices announced the result.

* * * * *

Six months after oral argument, the Supreme Court issued the opinion in *McCleskey v. Kemp* on April 22, 1987. Justices White, O'Connor, Scalia, and Chief Justice Rehnquist joined Justice Powell's majority opinion. The Court stated the issue at the beginning of the opinion as "whether a complex statistical study that indicates a risk that racial considerations enter into capital sentencing determination proves that petitioner McCleskey's capital sentence is unconstitutional under the Eighth or Fourteenth Amendment."[14] (See Figure 13.2.)

In the majority opinion, Powell began by assuming for the sake of the Court's analysis that the Baldus study findings were accurate, just as the Court of Appeals did. In making the assumption, Powell may have been inspired by his clerk's thorough analysis of how the district court judge had misread the statistically sound Baldus study.[15] The assumption allowed the Court to avoid delving into the methods used by Baldus and his colleagues. But it also meant that the Court could avoid discussing the reasons for the disparities found in the Baldus study or even to acknowledge explicitly that race affects capital sentencing, as Justice Scalia had done in his memo. Instead, by assuming the study was valid statistically and by not

Figure 13.2
The *McCleskey v. Kemp* Supreme Court. Back row: O'Connor, Powell, Stevens, Scalia. Front row: Marshall, Brennan, Rehnquist, White, and Blackmun. (Collection of the Supreme Court of the United States)

delving deeper into the findings, Justice Powell could state in a footnote that the Court did not assume the study proved "racial considerations actually enter into any sentencing decisions in Georgia." Such a sophisticated multiple regression analysis, he explained, could "only demonstrate a risk that the factor of race entered into some capital sentencing decisions."[16] Thus, the majority opinion merely acknowledged the Baldus study's statistical analysis and accepted it for argument's sake.

Next, even though the Court concluded that McCleskey had standing to assert his constitutional claims based on disparities related to the race of victims,[17] it ruled 5-4 against McCleskey on his substantive constitutional claims. Justice Powell first addressed McCleskey's claim that the Georgia death penalty statute violates the Equal Protection Clause of the Fourteenth Amendment, one of the amendments ratified after the Civil War to protect, among various rights, former slaves in the South. The Court concluded that when a defendant, such as McCleskey, alleges a violation of the Equal Protection Clause, the defendant has the burden of proving "the existence of purposeful discrimination" that "had a discriminatory effect" on him. Powell explained that discretion is a normal part of the criminal justice process, so there must be exceptionally clear proof a sentence resulted from discrimination. Probabilities are not enough. Thus, the statistical studies illustrating racial discrimination in Georgia's death penalty scheme were not enough because they did not show discrimination played a part specifically in McCleskey's sentence.

McCleskey's attorneys argued that the state of Georgia acted with discriminatory purpose because the state had continued to use a death penalty system that permitted the discriminatory results shown by the Baldus study. But the Court held that to show discriminatory purpose, the defendant must show the legislature acted "because of" these adverse effects, not "in spite of." And there was no evidence "that the Georgia Legislature enacted the capital punishment statute to further a racially discriminatory purpose."

Regarding the past, Justice Powell indicated McCleskey's attorneys did not establish that the history of racial discrimination in capital cases was relevant to McCleskey. Powell wrote, "Unless historical evidence is reasonably contemporaneous with the challenged decision, it has little probative value." Thus, he isolated Warren McCleskey's case from the recent history of the death penalty. But he also isolated McCleskey from Marietta's history, from Georgia's history, from America's history of racism and lynching, and from the state flag with the Confederate emblem that hung in the Atlanta courthouse when McCleskey was sentenced to death.

Powell then addressed whether or not the Baldus study showed Georgia's death penalty is cruel and unusual, violating the Eighth Amendment of the U.S. Constitution. The Court considered its previous cases where it held the Eighth Amendment required that punishments must be proportionate to the crime and that capital sentences must not be arbitrary and capricious.

The Court explained that its decisions since *Furman* set up a "constitutionally permissible range of discretion" for capital cases. The cases first created a required threshold below which the death penalty cannot be imposed. This component requires states to establish criteria that narrow the cases eligible for the death penalty, distinguishing those cases from those not eligible for the death penalty. Second, the Court's cases held that states cannot limit the sentencer's consideration of any relevant mitigating circumstances that would cause the sentencer to vote for a life sentence instead of death.

Under this Eighth Amendment framework of discretion, the Court next addressed two Eighth Amendment arguments by McCleskey's attorneys. First, the attorneys argued McCleskey's sentence was disproportionate to the sentences in other murder cases. Second, they argued McCleskey's sentence was arbitrary and capricious.

Regarding the proportionality argument, McCleskey's attorneys argued that because of racial differences, defendants similar to McCleskey in other aspects besides race did not receive the death penalty while he did. The Court, however, responded that McCleskey could not establish an Eighth Amendment violation by arguing that other similar defendants did not get the death penalty. Just because juries in other cases gave mercy to some white defendants with black victims, it did not create a constitutional violation for McCleskey. As long as Georgia's procedures were fair and required jurors to focus their discretion on the crime and the defendant, the Court presumed his sentence was not disproportionate. Although Justice Powell did not say so in his opinion, he later revealed that he might have seen the case differently had the Baldus study shown more of an effect based on the race of the defendant instead of on the victim's race.[18]

Regarding McCleskey's claim that his sentence was arbitrary and capricious and therefore excessive, the Court responded that juries need to have discretion and that such discretion may benefit a defendant. The Court stressed the Constitution is satisfied when a state provides sufficient safeguards to make the process as fair as possible. In other words, the Constitution requires the process to be fair, not the outcome. Thus, although the Baldus study showed some effects of race, it did not show a "constitutionally significant risk of racial bias" or that the system was unfair.[19]

After dismissing McCleskey's constitutional claims, Powell went further to give two additional practical justifications for that result based on a fear that a McCleskey win would open the floodgates of other litigation. The Court first noted that if it accepted McCleskey's Eighth Amendment claim, many other defendants could then claim racial discrimination invalidated other sentences besides death. Second, the Court worried that a victory for McCleskey would mean all types of criminal defendants would be bringing similar arbitrariness claims based on various factors, not necessarily even limited to minority groups or gender.[20]

Finally, the majority concluded McCleskey's claims are the type best reserved for legislative bodies. State legislatures may evaluate the studies and make changes to the law.[21] In such reasoning, the Court appeared to believe legislators are better equipped to evaluate complicated empirical evidence than judges. Similarly, some commentators believed the Court feared that federal judges would become overburdened with statistical social science evidence were the Supreme Court to give such studies constitutional significance.[22]

Justice Brennan wrote a dissenting opinion that was joined by Justices Marshall, Blackmun, and Stevens. Brennan, like Justice Marshall, had written in prior decisions that the death penalty always violated the Eighth and Fourteenth Amendments, but his opinion in this case focused his Eighth Amendment analysis on the specific evidence of racial disparity.

Brennan began the dissent with a compelling story, imagining McCleskey before the start of his trial, asking his attorney about his chances. The attorney would have to tell the client that the jury would be more likely to impose the death penalty merely because the client was a black man who killed a white person. "The story could be told in a variety of ways, but McCleskey could not fail to grasp its essential narrative line: there was a significant chance that race would play a prominent role in determining if he lived or died."[23]

Brennan invoked Georgia's history, noting how the state's criminal laws going back to the days of slavery distinguished between blacks and whites. Although he acknowledged Georgia's past did not automatically implicate it in ongoing discrimination, he argued that the history buttressed the relevance of the statistics presented in the Baldus study. He called on the Court to recognize the role of history and its effects on individuals and our culture: "[W]e ignore [Warren McCleskey] at our peril, for we remain imprisoned by the past as long as we deny [racism's] influence on the present."[24]

Brennan summarized the majority's analysis, noting that the majority claimed that the Baldus study cannot prove to a moral certainty that race influenced

McCleskey's death sentence, despite a "likelihood" that race entered the decision and that there is a "discrepancy that appears to correlate with race." Then, he noted the Court had four reasons for avoiding the implications from the Baldus study: (1) a desire to encourage sentencing discretion, (2) the existence of statutory safeguards, (3) a fear of encouraging widespread challenges, and (4) the limits of the judicial role.

In responding to the majority's reasoning, Brennan argued that since *Furman*, the Court has been concerned with the risk of imposition of an arbitrary sentence. In prior cases, in order to find a constitutional violation, the Court required only that the system pose a significant risk of impermissible considerations. Here, he claimed, the risk shown by the Baldus study is intolerable. Baldus, Woodworth, and Pulaski concluded a jury would more likely than not have spared McCleskey had the victim been black. Brennan further stressed the risk of racial prejudice is especially serious where dealing with the finality of a death sentence.

Brennan claimed the majority's fears that granting relief to McCleskey would open the floodgates of litigation constituted a fear of too much justice. If courts are discriminating on other factors, he explained, such discrimination also would be repugnant to conceptions of fairness. Also, the Court could limit such claims to race because of a long line of cases where the Court treated race differently from other constitutional claims.[25]

In response to the majority's claim that legislatures would better address the Baldus study than the Court, Brennan stressed that the Court must fulfill its role to protect those who the democratic process has not adequately protected in the past, such as minorities and criminal defendants: "Those whom we would banish from society or from the human community itself often speak in too faint a voice to be heard above society's demand for punishment."[26]

Justice Blackmun, who had been among the justices to uphold the death penalty in *Gregg*, dissented in *McCleskey v. Kemp*. The notoriously slow writer became the last of the justices to produce his opinion. While the justices were circulating their drafts for months, they were still waiting to see something in writing from Blackmun three weeks before the decision was eventually announced.[27] When he finally circulated his opinion, Blackmun argued that the Court deviated from its Fourteenth Amendment equal protection jurisprudence. He claimed the majority gave too little weight to the fact that part of the decision-making process is done by prosecutors, who are clearly state actors for Fourteenth Amendment purposes. He stressed that under previous cases, a defendant may establish a prima facie case of purposeful discrimination based on evidence such as the Baldus study. Then the burden shifts to the state to rebut the claim. Here, he argued, the Baldus study and other evidence were sufficient to support a prima facie case of purposeful discrimination.[28]

During his time on the Court, Justice Blackmun often agonized over cases and became emotionally involved with the issues.[29] Although he had voted to uphold the death penalty in *Gregg*, in that case he noted his personal opposition to the death penalty, and he continued to struggle with the death penalty issue throughout his time on the Court. Although the language of his dissent in *McCleskey* did not reveal it, the majority's decision in the case bothered him. Warren McCleskey would continue to haunt Justice Blackmun.

In another dissenting opinion, Justice Stevens claimed that "[t]he Court's decision appears to be based on a fear that the acceptance of McCleskey's claim would sound the death knell for capital punishment in Georgia." Stevens noted that if the Court had to choose between the "death knell" and allowing a racially discriminatory death penalty, the Constitution would require the "death knell." But he went on to argue that a ruling for McCleskey would not necessarily end the death penalty. The Baldus study indicated that race played less of a role in certain types of cases, and Georgia could limit its death penalty to those more aggravated cases.[30]

* * *

On the question of whether a ruling in favor of McCleskey would end the death penalty, Justice Blackmun agreed with Justice Stevens that the death penalty could survive such a ruling. Justices Brennan and Marshall, however, did not join Stevens's conclusion that the death penalty could survive a McCleskey victory.

While the justices were working on deciding the case, Justice Powell and other justices contemplated the feasibility of ruling for McCleskey in a way that would not abolish the death penalty. Many of the Supreme Court clerks suggested to the justices they could give relief to McCleskey by fashioning a narrow remedy. Options for a narrow remedy included remanding the case and requiring Georgia to rebut an inference that McCleskey's death sentence was based on race. Or the state could have granted relief only to capital defendants sentenced to death during the period studied in the Baldus report.[31]

The Baldus study itself did not conclude that the only cure for the racial disparities was to abolish the death penalty. The social scientists who created the study revealed they were "not yet convinced that arbitrariness and discrimination in death sentencing is inevitable." And they noted that in highly aggravated murders, race did not play the large role that it played in McCleskey's case.[32]

McCleskey's attorney Jack Boger similarly explained to the Court during oral argument that the death penalty could survive a ruling in favor of McCleskey. But it also was a smart strategic choice for Boger to maintain the Court could save his client without necessarily abolishing capital punishment. Similarly, another one of McCleskey's attorneys, Timothy Ford, earlier had explained to the *ABA Journal* that although the case had "some very broad implications," a victory would not "necessarily affect every case in the country, or even, for that matter, outside of Georgia."[33]

In the written briefs, LDF attorneys presented several alternatives to abolishing the death penalty. The Court could have issued a narrow ruling that the death penalty violates the Eighth Amendment only in states that have complete studies showing that race affects the decision of imposing death. Further, LDF argued that state legislators would have the option to try to cure the problem. States could work to eliminate the disparity by providing more guidelines for prosecutors. Also, the Baldus study found that race played a lesser role in cases with a high level of aggravating factors. Therefore, the Georgia Legislature could rewrite its statutes to limit the death penalty to such cases.[34]

Scholars similarly have argued that the death penalty could have survived if McCleskey had won. For example, Columbia Law School professor James S. Liebman has reasoned the Court could have focused on a narrow aspect of the Baldus study in reversing McCleskey's sentence. While the study revealed a sentencing disparity based on race, those patterns of disparity occurred in cases where aggravating evidence and mitigating evidence were nearly equal. So the Court could have struck down Georgia's capital sentencing statute, finding a violation only in cases where aggravating evidence does not greatly outweigh mitigating evidence.[35]

But had the Court found McCleskey's death sentence violated the Constitution, one might wonder what would have happened next. As LDF suggested, in Georgia the legislature could then rewrite its death penalty statutes. Similarly, after the 1972 decision in *Furman*, many thought the case ended the death penalty, but Georgia and other states responded by rewriting their statutes. The *Furman* opinions, though, made it clearer that the legislators could respond by curbing the complete discretion that existed in the unconstitutional statutes. After a *McCleskey* decision striking down the death penalty, the problem would still be discretion. But because the Court also had prohibited mandatory death sentences, legislators would not have an option to completely eliminate discretion. So the Georgia Legislature would have had to struggle to further curtail discretion to see if it could eliminate the racial problem shown by the Baldus study.

Other states also would have had to respond to a McCleskey victory. Defense attorneys in other states likely would have hired statisticians to evaluate the role of race in their death penalty systems. Since *McCleskey v. Kemp*, many studies have shown that race plays a role in the death penalty decisions all across the country, so there would have been ample evidence to make *McCleskey*-like challenges in other states.

Thus, a decision for McCleskey would have created significant hurdles to maintaining a death penalty in the United States. Georgia and other states could have rewritten their statutes. But, at minimum, there would have been a significant period of re-evaluation and new studies. There likely would have been an informal moratorium on the death penalty while the courts and legislatures worked everything out. Because the options for states would not be clear, the period after *McCleskey* would have looked more like the long period prior to *Furman* as the Eighth and Fourteenth Amendment challenges were first working their way through the courts, instead of looking like the short period between *Furman* and *Gregg*.

More likely, though, the impact would have been even more significant. Although states would have taken steps to limit racial discrimination, perhaps by eliminating certain broad aggravating factors, it would have been extremely difficult if not impossible to eliminate the racial factor in a system that gives human beings discretion. Therefore, although a decision in McCleskey's favor might not mean an end to the death penalty either immediately or in theory, it possibly would mean an eventual end to the death penalty in the United States in practice.

Some close to the case also saw its potential to end the death penalty in America. McCleskey's attorney Robert Stroup and a number of capital defense attorneys around the country believed that *McCleskey v. Kemp* could end the American death penalty. Justice Powell, who wrote the majority opinion, similarly wrote in an interoffice memo as the justices debated the case, "This case presents, as we know, an attack on capital punishment itself."[36]

The possibility existed that *McCleskey v. Kemp* might have come out in Warren McCleskey's favor and ended the death penalty in the United States. Years later in the *New York Review of Books*, Justice Stevens surmised that had Justice Potter Stewart, who retired in 1981 and died in 1985, still been on the Court, he would have voted to grant relief to McCleskey. Although Stewart had joined the *Gregg* majority, the death penalty troubled him and he had shown a willingness to stand up on racial issues. After his nomination to the Court, he defied southern senators in defending his support of *Brown v. Board of Education*, costing him the votes of senators in eight southern states. In *McCleskey*, Justice Stewart's vote also would have been enough to swing the Court in McCleskey's favor, as he was replaced by Justice Sandra Day O'Connor, who joined the majority opinion.[37] Therefore, due to the health of one former justice the death penalty in the United States continued.

Thus, the Court by a 5-4 vote preserved the American death penalty. Professor Herbert Haines has noted that the *McCleskey* decision, more than any other Supreme Court decision, "signaled the futility of continuing to place hope for abolishing the death penalty on the constitutional strategy that had once been so successful."[38] After the decision, *Time Magazine* noted it was a "stunning defeat" for death penalty opponents and that the case "may prove to be their final major challenge" to capital punishment.[39]

* * *

Anti-death penalty activists, capital defense lawyers, and other commentators felt despair after the Supreme Court announced the *McCleskey v. Kemp* decision. A newspaper editorial from the *Tallahassee Democrat* argued that blacks must accept a separate-but-unequal system of justice in capital cases. Six days after the decision, Anthony Lewis of *The New York Times* concluded the Supreme Court had "effectively condoned the expression of racism in a profound aspect of our law."[40]

Those who contributed to McCleskey's case criticized the result. Professor Baldus, one author of the study, noted that in the decades since the *Furman* Court attempted to erase the arbitrariness of the death penalty, the punishment survived but now with "the arbitrariness and discrimination still in place and beyond the reach of the law."[41] Anthony Amsterdam, the attorney who had argued *Furman* and *Gregg* and had worked on McCleskey's case, later claimed *McCleskey v. Kemp* "is the *Dred Scott* decision of our time," referring to the infamous pre–Civil War 1857 Supreme Court *Dred Scott v. Sandford* opinion written by Chief Justice Robert B. Taney that denied citizenship to blacks. Amsterdam noted, "It is a decision for which our children's children will reproach our generation and abhor the legal legacy we leave them."[42] Harvard Law professor Randall L. Kennedy wrote in the *Harvard Law Review* that "the majority in McCleskey repressed the truth and validated racially oppressive official conduct." Kennedy also argued that the Baldus study revealed a greater societal problem that we tend to sympathize only with people like ourselves.[43]

The media still focused on the case the following year when Steve Bright, the director of the Southern Prisoners' Defense Committee, told *The New York Times Magazine* that the decision was "an everlasting blight on the Supreme Court and a badge of shame for the state of Georgia." By contrast, Russell Parker, the Fulton County assistant district attorney who prosecuted McCleskey's trial, told the same *Times* reporter that he merely saw the case as one where McCleskey killed an Atlanta policeman, who just happened to be white.[44]

Other capital defendants who raised similar race claims in their appeals knew the Supreme Court decision presented an ominous sign for their cases. After the April 22, 1987 decision in *McCleskey v. Kemp*, courts followed that opinion in denying relief to Mississippi condemned Edward E. Johnson. A documentary filmmaker recorded the final days leading to Johnson's May 20, 1987 execution in *Fourteen Days in May*, an award-winning film shown on British television by the British Broadcasting Corporation.

The standard the Court created in the *McCleskey* decision not only preserved the death penalty, it also made it very difficult for capital defendants to bring race-based constitutional claims in the future. The Court created a standard where racism could not void a death sentence unless the defendant could prove a decision-maker in the case acted with discriminatory motive. The standard created in *McCleskey* contrasts with Supreme Court decisions involving jury selection, housing law, voting law, and employment law. In those situations, the Court allows a party to use statistical evidence of racial bias to make a prima facie case of discrimination without having to prove intentional discrimination.[45]

The Court, though, required more from McCleskey. In many cases, it is nearly impossible for capital defendants to prove a discriminatory motive. For example, a few years after the Supreme Court decided *McCleskey v. Kemp*, a U.S. court of appeals rejected an equal protection claim made partly based on the fact that the trial judge referred to the defendants as "colored" and that one of the defendants was represented by a trial attorney who admitted believing blacks are morally and intellectually inferior to whites.[46]

By contrast, some have argued *McCleskey* made the Court more defensive about its decisions regarding race in capital punishment, at least for a short time. During the same Court term as McCleskey's case, the Court issued an unusual number of opinions in favor of black capital defendants in cases involving white victims.[47] But even with new studies finding results similar to the Baldus study, the Court showed no willingness to reconsider its decision in *McCleskey v. Kemp*. Since that case, the Court has never come so close to eliminating the death penalty in the United States. As McCleskey's attorney Jack Boger recognized many years later in retrospect, "*McCleskey* was in some sense the culminating case of that whole era of constitutional challenges to the death penalty."[48]

* * *

McCleskey's attorneys were devastated by the Supreme Court loss. Jack Boger had been hopeful after the oral argument. At that time, he predicted McCleskey would win the votes of the four justices who did vote ultimately for McCleskey, but he hoped they would pick up at least one of Justices White, Powell, O'Connor, or the new justice Scalia. But none of Boger's "hopeful" justices voted for McCleskey, and he found the result "heartbreaking."[49]

Now, McCleskey's attorneys had to turn to other legal issues to try to save their client's life. And two months later, in June 1987, they received notice from the trial court setting July 14, 1987, for McCleskey's execution.[50] McCleskey's attorneys obtained a stay of execution because of other legal proceedings, and the litigation continued based on other claims. One other issue would eventually take them to the Supreme Court again in *McCleskey v. Zant*, based in part on the statement of Offie Evans that Georgia finally gave the defense attorneys this same year. On December 23, 1987, McCleskey's attorneys won a victory when the U.S. District Court overturned McCleskey's conviction, although that victory would be overturned less than two years later in the U.S. Court of Appeals.[51]

Meanwhile, one of McCleskey's former codefendants had an even better year. Ben Wright, the supposed ringleader of the robbery and key witness against McCleskey regarding the murder, was released from prison in 1987. But he soon went back to his old ways and committed several more crimes, subsequently being sentenced to life in prison.[52]

For McCleskey himself, *McCleskey v. Kemp* was a difficult loss, but he continued to try to keep himself busy on death row. Around the time the Court issued its ruling, prison officials only recorded normal activity for the prisoner: "McCleskey keeps a low profile and seems to depend on staff for nothing other than normal request[s]. Is involved in church service of G-House."

Not long after the Court decided *McCleskey v. Kemp*, McCleskey worked to earn several educational certificates. In 1988, he earned certificates from the United Christian International Bible Institute for General Bible Knowledge and was awarded a degree of Doctor of Bible Knowledge. Also, that spring, he completed a Bible correspondence course with Source of Light Ministries International. The following year, he completed several math courses through the Education Extension Program of the Georgia Baptist State Missions Program, earning A's in his courses.

In March 1988, the Georgia prison's "Performance Recording Sheet" for McCleskey noted, "Warren was in good spirits this period. He made reference to the fact [that] his case is being handled to his liking. He made no formal request nor did he make any complaint. He has continued to maintain a good attitude, continues regular participation in the Chaplain Bible Study program. It also appears that he has become a 'peace maker' in the cell-block according to different sources." A little later in the year he was disappointed "but not disrespectful" when the prison did not allow him to add "a Christian friend" to his visitation list. In August 1988, he still hoped his death sentence would eventually be overturned, and he sought counseling on programs that would be available to him if he were taken off of death row.

As the years went by, the holidays were difficult for McCleskey, but he also found comfort in the faith he had found on death row. A few days after Christmas in

1990, he wrote Reverend George Wirth: "I can't complain, for the Lord is truly good and merciful to me. Under the circumstances, the Christmas holidays were pretty nice. Although it doesn't in some respect compare to being with family and friends during this time of the year. But when we truly reflect on the purpose of Christmas and the majestic display of God's love for mankind it becomes very easy to rejoice and be thankful regardless of where we are physically positioned." McCleskey did not know, though, that it would be his final Christmas.[53]

PART E

Execution

CHAPTER 14

Mitigation and Reform

A capital defendant, like any other human, remains imprisoned by the past, and that past is con-stitutionally relevant. Defense attorneys ask sentencing juries to consider the person's entire life, and governors and clemency boards may also evaluate the condemned's life. As Warren McCleskey's execution neared, his attorneys hoped Georgia officials would consider aspects of McCleskey's life that his jury did not know about.

N ot long after McCleskey went to death row at the Georgia Diagnostic and Clas-sification State Prison in Jackson, Georgia in 1978, he met another inmate who would have a big effect on him. After McCleskey's arrival, one of the correction officers approached death row inmate William "Billy" Moore, asking him to look after McCleskey: "Moore, take care of him and look out for him, okay?" The officer knew Moore was a religious man who tried to look out for others on the row.

After Moore went to McCleskey's cell and introduced himself, McCleskey was impressed by how Moore seemed well adapted while living under a sentence of death. Moore explained that his faith helped him cope with the situation. McCleskey responded that he was not religious and that he questioned the exis-tence of God, considering where he now found himself. McCleskey asked Moore if he would get him some cigarettes. Moore promised to do so, but he also tweaked McCleskey's curiosity when he explained how his faith and prayers helped him to give up cigarettes.

In addition to finding some cigarettes for McCleskey, Moore gave him the book, *Dealing with the Devil*, by C.S. Lovett.[1] The book about the battle between Satan and the Holy Spirit made an impression on McCleskey, as did his conversations with Moore. Soon, McCleskey told Moore he wanted a change in his life and he wanted to accept Jesus Christ as his Savior. The two men soon started a Bible study group and invited other men on death row to join as they studied the New Testament verse by verse.

McCleskey devoted himself to the study group. But after some time passed, Moore often found McCleskey playing chess instead of attending the study group.

Eventually, after a few months, Moore noticed something change in McCleskey as he began faithfully attending and contributing to the group. He often talked about how he had made wrong choices in his life and discussed the lessons he learned. McCleskey explained to a pen pal, "When I found Jesus things in my life began to change and my situation just turn[ed] into a blessing."[2]

McCleskey and Moore helped others on the row. The two of them wanted to live an exemplary life, reading the Scriptures every day and living like the early Christian Community.

At one point, they learned about a program that inmates had started at Reidsville State Prison many years earlier, where prisoners kept a fund to help inmates who did not have any support. McCleskey and Moore decided to start a fund where they could provide necessities for inmates who did not have any money or anyone to help them. McCleskey and Moore put together whatever money they had to start the fund, and they bought items to have on hand to help other inmates.

They lived with common resources and created a cell block without violence. Moore and McCleskey inspired Reverend Murphy Davis, who counseled the men. She sent $20/month to McCleskey, and he used it so others in the cell block had access to what they needed if they did not have family or friends to help them. McCleskey would let her know if others were not getting visits, if they were having trouble or breaking down, or if they had other problems.[3]

In running their fund for poor inmates, McCleskey and Moore could see which inmates did not have outside support by noticing who did not have many possessions. The two men decided to keep their community resources in McCleskey's cell because McCleskey could best reason with inmates who might want to abuse the program by trying to get items to use for gambling. Throughout the rest of their time on death row, both Moore and McCleskey worked to affirm their faith and to help others on the row.[4]

In some capital cases, an inmate's transformation in prison has the potential to affect the inmate's sentence in a similar way that one's background prior to a crime may affect the capital sentencing process. Warren McCleskey grew up as a child in a violent and troubled environment, and then he entered into a pattern of drug abuse and crime. After the state sent him to death row, he worked to change himself and be a better person. None of it, of course, excuses his crimes. But the jurors did not know everything about McCleskey when they assessed his life.

Because jurors did not have that background information, or the information about how McCleskey would behave in prison, those facts weighed less in his sentencing than his race and the race of the murder victim. While the Supreme Court has held the Constitution requires that a defendant be allowed to present mitigating factors at sentencing, one may ask why such factors should be legally relevant to sentencing a convicted murderer. A long line of court decisions provide an answer.

* * *

The U.S. Constitution requires that juries and courts recognize that capital defendants, at least to some extent, are each imprisoned by the past. This constitutional mitigation requirement goes back to the cases the Court decided in 1976 with *Gregg v. Georgia.* At that time, the Court rejected the idea that the Constitution permits mandatory death penalty laws that automatically condemn a defendant to death upon conviction. The fact that a defendant committed a capital murder does not justify a death penalty by itself. After conviction, in a sentencing hearing, a prosecutor may present factors that argue for a death sentence, and a defendant's attorney may present mitigating factors.

In 1978 the Supreme Court held in *Lockett v. Ohio* that the U.S. Constitution entitles capital defendants to present evidence that may be used to argue against a death sentence, including information about a defendant's background that helps explain why the defendant ended up in a situation where he or she committed murder. In that case, the Court stated jurors must "not be precluded from considering as a mitigating factor, any aspect of a defendant's character or record and any of the circumstances of the offense that the defendant proffers as a basis for a sentence less than death."[5]

Thus, the Supreme Court requires courts and jurors to consider mitigating factors. In the following years—in an unexpected side effect of the Court's jurisprudence—judges have considered, and defense attorneys have struggled to set a record about, the causes of violent crime and the moral justifications for punishing certain individuals. For example, in *Williams v. Taylor,* the Supreme Court held that Terry Williams's trial attorney should have presented mitigating evidence such as the fact that Williams had an intellectual disability, that he grew up in a violent and neglectful environment, that his childhood home was littered with bowel movements and urine, and that his parents were either incarcerated or intoxicated for long periods.[6] Such information about the background of capital defendants does not excuse their later crimes, but it begins to help explain how they started down a path leading to criminal activity.

In Warren McCleskey's case, his attorney presented no mitigating evidence at the sentencing hearing, but mitigating evidence existed that might have helped his case. The jury might have been told about the violence and crime that surrounded McCleskey as a child, including that his mother killed his stepfather. The jury might have learned more about how drug abuse influenced McCleskey's actions. The jury might have learned he had family who loved him and did not want him to die. The jury might have learned McCleskey had a child who would lose a father if he were executed. The jury might have learned more about McCleskey's life and about him as a human. They might have concluded that none of those facts changed that he had taken the life of an officer acting in the line of duty. Or they might have latched onto a reason not to impose the death penalty and instead sentenced him to life in prison

Some of McCleskey's jurors found it difficult to decide in favor of death, but they felt the defense gave them no reason to choose another sentence. One juror later explained, "If we had found any valid reason not to give death, I am certain that I, and a number of other jurors, would never haven [*sic*] given McCleskey a capital sentence." Another juror who came from a broken home wondered what was McCleskey's background and how he might have ended up where he did, "[b]ut no one in this case gave us any real reason to vote for life."[7]

One should understand the reasons any mitigating evidence should be considered for such a horrible crime, and why McCleskey's background and apparent reform should have been considered in the decision of whether he should be executed or should spend the rest of his life in prison. Mitigating factors tell us much about the death penalty and the criminal justice system. But to understand why Warren McCleskey's background may be relevant requires an understanding of: (1) the reasons society punishes in the first place, and (2) why a defendant's background is relevant to whether or not the person should be executed.

* * *

Although in the abstract the suffering of individuals is not a desirable goal, "legal punishment involves deliberate infliction of suffering...beyond the suffering occasioned by stigma and censure."[8] Traditionally, there have been two main rationales for punishment: utilitarian theories and retributive theories. The theories of utilitarianism and retributivism are inconsistent to some degree, but lawmakers, judges, and scholars use a mixture of the two to justify punishments.

In 1843, Jeremy Bentham wrote about the utilitarian theory when he explained that because punishment itself is evil, "if it ought at all to be admitted, it ought only to be admitted in as far as it promises to exclude some greater evil."[9] Utilitarian theory reasons punishment should be used only if it benefits society, such as by protecting society from the individual, by deterring others from committing crimes, or by rehabilitating the criminal.[10]

In the United States, until the late twentieth century, rehabilitation was the "central professed goal" of the justice system. In the late twentieth century, however, rehabilitation became one of the least-professed goals of the American criminal justice system, while other utilitarian justifications such as incapacitation and deterrence became the dominant goals.[11]

As opposed to utilitarian justifications, retribution theory, such as that advocated by philosopher Immanuel Kant, justifies punishment because it is deserved, and it is deserved when a criminal freely decides to violate the rules of society. "A retributivist believes that the imposition of deserved punishment is an intrinsic good."[12] The classic formulation of retribution differs from vengeance in that it focuses on what the perpetrator deserves as an individual, not on the victim's desire for retaliation. Retribution has a proportionality component in that, as Kant stated, "Punishment ought to be 'pronounced over all criminals proportionate to their internal wickedness.'"[13]

Although there are variations on retributive theory, under Kantian moral philosophy, society not only is justified in punishing criminals, it has a moral obligation to do so. Kant explained this obligation: "Even if a civil society were to dissolve itself by common agreement of all its members.... the last murderer remaining in prison must first be executed, so that everyone will duly receive what his actions are worth and so that the blood-guilt thereof will not be fixed on the people because they failed to insist on carrying out the punishment."[14] In a 1992 U.S. Supreme Court capital case, *Morgan v. Illinois*, Justice Scalia quoted this passage in a dissenting opinion.[15]

In the United States, simultaneous with the growth of the death penalty in the latter half of the twentieth century, there was a "great philosophical revival of retributivism," reintroducing "ideas of moral agency and moral responsibility into the criminal law, abandoning the brute therapeutic psychologism of the mid-twentieth century."[16] Professor James Whitman has argued the major role retributivism plays today partly results from American democracy, because "[o]rdinary voters are never capable of the kind of routinized, sober, and merciful approach to punishment that is the stuff of the daily work of punishment professionals."[17] Thus, to gain popular support, American politicians push for retributive punishments, resulting in dramatically long prison sentences even for nonviolent offenses, "three-strikes-and-you're-out" laws, and one of the highest incarceration rates in the world.[18]

Others have connected retribution theories to the racial disparity evidence in McCleskey's case. They argue that the racial disparities found in the Baldus study have their root in arbitrariness resulting from ideas of retribution. They connect the modern death penalty to the history of lynching where citizens invoked ideas of retribution to avenge those who attacked white victims.[19]

When the Supreme Court addressed the constitutionality of the death penalty in the 1970s, it used utilitarian and retributive theories in its Eighth Amendment analysis. In *Furman v. Georgia*, Justice Marshall discussed these theories of punishment.[20] When the Court upheld the constitutionality of the death penalty in 1976 in *Gregg v. Georgia*, the plurality also looked at those factors. Quoting an earlier case, the plurality noted, "'Retribution is no longer the dominant objective of the criminal law.'"[21] However, the plurality added, "[N]either is it a forbidden objective nor one inconsistent with our respect for the dignity of men."[22] The plurality concluded retribution could justify the use of the death penalty.

The *Gregg* plurality also reasoned the death penalty must have some deterrent effect, though legislatures were best left to determine the extent of that effect. In dissent, Justice Marshall discussed several studies and concluded that the death penalty is not necessary as a deterrent. Additionally, he rejected the plurality's reliance on retribution by stating that under the Eighth Amendment, punishments must comport with human dignity, and "[t]he mere fact that the community demands the murderer's life in return for the evil he has done cannot sustain the death penalty."[23]

The Supreme Court continued to struggle with these foundational questions about punishment, and through that struggle, the Court developed the constitutional requirements allowing defendants to present mitigating evidence in capital cases. Courts and legislatures have found a significant number of factors that should be considered in capital cases as mitigating if a defense attorney presents evidence of them to the jury.

Mitigating factors may be grouped into four different categories: (1) mitigating circumstances unrelated to the crime that show the defendant has some good qualities, (2) mitigating circumstances that show the defendant had a lesser involvement with the murder, (3) mitigating circumstances related to the legal proceedings, and (4) mitigating circumstances that show less culpability and/or help explain why a defendant committed the crime.

The first group of mitigating factors, "Good Character" Factors, shows the capital defendant has some good qualities and includes factors such as the defendant has good character, the defendant cooperated with the police or the prosecutor, the defendant's family loves the defendant, the defendant is religious, or the defendant is remorseful. These factors are mitigating because they show a defendant is not completely evil and therefore, should not be executed. A court's consideration of these factors recognizes, for retributive purposes, that a person consists of something more than the murder that took place on one day of the defendant's life. For utilitarian reasons, the factors also are relevant to the defendant's future dangerousness. For example, if a defendant has done good things and has not committed crimes in the past, it shows the murder was not consistent with the defendant's usual behavior.

The second group of mitigating factors consists of "Culpability Factors," which show the defendant had a lesser involvement in the murder. These factors include various circumstances that reduce a defendant's culpability, such as that the defendant was convicted of felony-murder and did not actually do the killing or that the defendant had minor participation in the killing.

The third category of mitigating circumstances is the Legal Proceeding Factors category, which consists of factors relating to the legal proceedings. These factors include that the prosecutor or the victim's family recommended leniency and that a codefendant in the case did not receive the death penalty. These factors make the system fairer in several ways while also looking at specific aspects of the defendant's case.

The fourth category of mitigating circumstances consists of Nature-Nurture Factors. These factors show the defendant has lesser responsibility for the crime or help explain why the defendant committed criminal acts. These factors include youth, brain damage, head injury, childhood abuse, a deprived childhood, drug addiction, emotional problems, various family background circumstances, mental illness, alcohol and drug use, post-traumatic stress, and impaired capacity. These qualities are common among capital defendants, as one informal review of court records in one state found approximately 50 percent of the state's death row inmates had evidence they had been victims of childhood abuse or neglect, and the actual number was certainly higher due to underreporting.[24]

Most of the factors in this category are mitigating because they may show that the defendant is less able to exhibit self-control or they may be among the causes that led the defendant to be involved in criminal activity. Many of these factors relate to the development of the defendant's brain and the idea that neurological or psychological problems show that the defendant is not as responsible as someone acting under "normal" conditions.

These factors also help partly explain "why" the defendant committed the crime. The justification for allowing these factors to be mitigating raises questions about punishment, evil, and morality. These factors undermine the retributive theories for punishing certain individuals because the individuals are less deserving of punishment.

Another possible reason many of these factors are mitigating might be because they show the defendant has already suffered in life. Similarly, they may raise questions about how jurors with different life experiences are able to judge the life of another person with different experiences. Although viewing these factors as "pity factors" might be part of what goes on in jurors' minds, the analysis from court decisions is more consistent with the view that these are causal factors relating to the crime.

The Supreme Court justifies these factors by noting that defendants with these circumstances have less control over their actions and are less deserving of punishment. In a sense, the courts accept that these defendants acted with something less than free will. In *Eddings v. Oklahoma*, the Supreme Court reasoned that a young age constitutes a mitigating factor because minors are not as mature or as responsible as adults. Noting adolescents are less able to control themselves and contemplate repercussions, the Court concluded that on moral grounds such offenders are not completely to blame because the murder had other causes: "[O]ffenses by the young also represent a failure of family, school, and the social system, which share responsibility for the development of America's youth.'"[25] The Court also discussed the importance of family background to mitigation. The Court explained that Eddings, who was sixteen years old, had been raised "in a neglectful, sometimes even violent, family background," and that fact could show a defendant's "mental and emotional development were at a level several years below his chronological age."[26]

The U.S. Constitution, then, requires courts to allow attorneys to present mitigating evidence to ensure that capital sentences are based on the individual defendant and the person's crime. But the system does not work perfectly. Some critics argue that this sentencing process is too similar to the pre-*Furman* procedures that gave too much discretion to jurors, so that the current sentencing process still leads to arbitrary jury verdicts and allows jurors to consider improper factors, like race. Additionally, for various reasons, jurors may not get enough information to fully assess the value of the defendant's life and crime. Some of the evidence is difficult to find for various reasons, including because witnesses are reluctant to reveal past family abuse and trauma.

Similarly, defense attorneys may not find existing mitigating evidence, so jurors may never hear the mitigating evidence in the case. In McCleskey's case, his attorney did not tell jurors about McCleskey's difficult childhood or about his life beyond his crimes. The jurors also could not know how McCleskey would live his life in prison.

* * *

Similar to the idea that a person's behavior before a crime should be mitigating, a defendant's behavior after a crime might be relevant too. In considering whether these death row conversions should matter, one might argue that the victim never got the chance to experience life for all the years that the killer did get. But the legal system still has a responsibility to assess the living condemned person.

In most cases, the death penalty system gives little weight to death row conversions or mitigating evidence that develops while the condemned lives on death row. Unlike mitigation presented at trial, a death row inmate's reform occurs after the trial, so juries are rarely given the opportunity to evaluate post-conviction evidence of reform. Clemency boards and governors do evaluate such evidence, but they are often hesitant to give credence to it. There have been several cases where a defendant's life after conviction became an issue and created a drive for the person to receive clemency. In these cases, often the drive failed, as in those of Karla Faye Tucker and Wilbert Evans.

In February 1998, Karla Faye Tucker became the first woman executed in Texas since the Civil War. Her crime was especially brutal. The twenty-three-year-old and her boyfriend, Daniel Garrett, planned to steal a motorcycle from Jerry Dean, who had been physically abusive to his wife, who was Tucker's friend. After three days of taking pills, shooting crystal meth, and drinking alcohol, Tucker and Garrett went to Dean's house, seeking to steal the motorcycle in revenge for the abuse. During the theft, Dean confronted them and Garrett began hitting him with a hammer. Tucker discovered another woman hiding under a cover, and in a frenzy Tucker grabbed a pickax and began hitting the woman numerous times, killing her and hitting Dean's body too.[27]

The police easily caught Tucker and Garrett. Both were sentenced to death, but Garrett died in prison after a few years. While Tucker lived on death row, away from the drugs and the influences that had led her to become a prostitute at age fourteen, she began to change. She became religious, and she showed great remorse for her crimes. Her change prompted a large amount of media attention, fueled by the fact that she was a white woman, attractive, well-spoken, and thoughtful. Religious groups embraced her as a Christian and fought against her execution. People from around the world tried to stop her execution, but in the end, Texas governor George W. Bush denied a temporary reprieve and the state executed her by lethal injection.[28]

Wilbert Evans similarly argued that he had changed while living on death row. Virginia jurors convicted Evans of the shooting death of a deputy sheriff, and they sentenced him to death based upon the aggravating factor that he was a "future danger." However, on May 31, 1984, a few months after the sentencing, six other Virginia death row inmates escaped from prison. During the escape, the six, who were all later recaptured, released the locks on the housing unit for the other inmates, who then seized control of the area. The inmates took twelve prison guards and two female nurses as hostage. Evans, who was a large man, intervened to control the other inmates and protect the prison employees. He saved the lives of several hostages and prevented the rape of one of the nurses.

When Evans's attorneys argued that their client's actions negated the "future danger" finding of his jury, the Supreme Court held these post-sentencing actions could not be used in post-conviction proceedings to look back in time to challenge the jury's findings.[29] Before Evans made his final walk to the electric chair, he was given a copy of Supreme Court justice Thurgood Marshall's opinion voicing his opposition to the execution. Evans, after getting some help to spell "bury," wrote on the opinion, "Please bury this with me," and put the opinion in his pocket before going to the execution chamber.[30]

On October 17, 1990, Virginia executed Wilbert Lee Evans. Evans's attorney Jonathan Shapiro attended the execution but turned his back to the electric chair because he could not watch his client die. When the electricity hit Evans, an increase in blood pressure caused blood to spray from Evans's nose onto his shirt. Witnesses reported hearing moaning sounds during the execution.[31]

Political concerns may have contributed to Governor Douglas Wilder's decision to deny clemency to Evans in Virginia, a state where voters strongly supported the death penalty. As Wilder considered Evans's case, activists pressured the governor to grant clemency to another condemned inmate, Joseph Giarratano. The governor did ultimately grant clemency to Giarratano, a white inmate who unlike the African-American Evans had a claim of innocence and a substantial base of supporters, including conservative columnist James J. Kilpatrick, actor Mike Farrell, singer Joan Baez, and several members of the U.S. Congress. But to grant clemency to two death row inmates around the same time would have made Wilder appear soft on crime.

In the past, Wilder had been against the death penalty, but he became an advocate for capital punishment when he first ran for the statewide office of lieutenant governor. He became a stronger supporter of the death penalty during his 1989 campaign for governor against another candidate who wanted to paint Wilder as soft on crime. Two days after Evans's execution, Wilder went to Massachusetts as part of his new campaign for president in 1992.[32]

As in the Evans case, procedurally, courts usually are barred from considering evidence about how a death row inmate has changed since conviction. But governors and clemency boards may consider an inmate's life since conviction in determining whether or not to let an execution go through.

In Warren McCleskey's case, his attorneys argued to his clemency board that McCleskey had been a model prisoner during his time at the Georgia Diagnostic and Classification Center in Jackson, Georgia. Part of McCleskey's change in prison resulted from McCleskey's faith through his friendship with fellow death row inmate Billy Moore.

Although Evans and Tucker were executed, some reformed death row inmates have been spared from execution, including McCleskey's friend Billy Moore. Georgia sent Moore to death row for committing murder in 1974 as a twenty-two-year-old. Moore's crime occurred while he tried to break into the home of seventy-seven-year-old Fred Stapleton. Moore killed Stapleton after he fired a shotgun at Moore. Moore never denied his guilt and pleaded guilty to the crime. After a mere three-hour sentencing hearing, the jury sentenced him to death on July 17, 1974.

While on death row, Moore and McCleskey both hoped to make the best out of their time in prison, vowing to create a death row where the inmates in the section treated each other decently. Moore helped with education programs and ran prayer groups. He studied law and theology. He also began corresponding with the family of Stapleton, offering his remorse for the murder, and he found forgiveness.

In 1984, Moore came within seven hours of being executed, but he received a stay. In 1990, he faced the prospect of another execution date. In August 1990, the Georgia Board of Pardon and Paroles granted a rare death sentence commutation to Moore, changing his death sentence to life in prison. During his clemency hearing,

Moore's attorneys argued that Moore had been a positive influence on others in prison. His lawyer also presented statements from Stapleton's family members asking for clemency. Jesse Jackson and Mother Theresa appealed on Moore's behalf to the Board by telephone. The Georgia Board of Pardons and Paroles voted unanimously to commute his sentence, and within a few years, Moore left prison a free man. After his release, he became a Pentecostal minister.[33]

But death row inmates rarely leave prison by executive clemency as Moore did. So, as McCleskey's own execution approached, McCleskey kept his spirits up. He understood that when he allowed his attorneys to turn his case into the test case on the race issue they were taking risks with his life. He told friends he hoped he made the correct choice to let his attorneys make his case the vehicle for the Baldus study. He wondered if his case may have had a different outcome if it had not focused on the Baldus study issues. But he felt the race claim was an important issue that needed to be litigated.

On death row, McCleskey kept in touch with various friends. For example, in 1989 he became pen pals with a white teenager from his hometown of Marietta. Although the young Michael Albanese came from the same town, their upbringings were quite different. Albanese lived in a happy middle-class environment in contrast to McCleskey's childhood of poverty, segregation, and abuse. But the two still found a common ground in their letters, writing about baseball, friendship, and faith. Eventually, as McCleskey got close to being executed, Albanese finally got to meet his death row pen pal. The sixteen-year-old's mom snuck him out of his high school against his father's wishes, and she drove him to meet McCleskey. Albanese felt moved and changed from this meeting with the condemned man. Decades later, after Albanese became a writer, he wrote a screenplay and began working on a film about his friendship with McCleskey.[34]

Prison staff members noticed in the late 1980s that McCleskey exerted a positive influence on other inmates and that he acted as a "peace maker" in the cell block.[35] In November 1988, McCleskey's prison counselor Cheyenne Puckett wrote that the inmate "maintain[s] a working relationship with staff [and] appears to get along well with inmate peers and shows leadership role in cell-block." Puckett predicted that if McCleskey's' death sentence were overturned, he would be a good candidate for a pre-release program. In April 1991, another counselor wrote about McCleskey's "good attitude and behavior," noting the inmate was "cooperative with staff and gets along well with the other inmates."[36]

As McCleskey's execution date approached, McCleskey's friend Reverend Murphy Davis saw that McCleskey had "an unbelievable level of equanimity and balance." McCleskey knew his execution neared, but he kept his spirits up around friends and family.[37]

CHAPTER 15

Warren McCleskey and the Electric Chair

As Warren McCleskey's execution date approached, he came closer to taking a seat in Georgia's electric chair. The electric chair is an American method of execution that grew out of the country's unique history. The entire process in the hours leading to McCleskey's execution—including the execution secluded from public view and the final litigation delays—also reflected the country's past.

In 1991 after the losses in *McCleskey v. Kemp* and *McCleskey v. Zant*, Warren McCleskey's attorneys were running out of options as their client got closer to an appointment with the electric chair. Although the use of electricity to kill capital defendants often evoked the cruel burnings used during the lynching era, developers created the electric chair as a triumph of new technology to provide a more humane option to the noose.

The electric chair's history went back more than a hundred years earlier. On June 4, 1888, Governor David B. Hill signed a law making New York the first state to adopt the electric chair as a means of execution. At the time, the electric lighting industry was new and many of today's common household electrical devices had yet to be developed. The state chose to use the new technology for executions because legislators believed it was a better method of killing criminals. Following tests on animals such as dogs and horses, and after a recommendation by a commission authorized by the New York governor to find "'the most humane and practical method known to modern science of carrying into effect the sentence of death,'" the New York Legislature approved the new method of execution.[1] But, like most political decisions, it was not that simple.[2]

Corporate interests and profit motives in the growing electric industry played a significant role in the debate about the execution method. The discussion heated up a few years later as New York prepared to execute William Kemmler, a fruit-peddler who had been convicted of killing his common law wife Matilda "Tillie" Ziegler with more than twenty-five hatchet blows during a drunken argument. George Westinghouse, who hoped to make alternating current (AC) the standard for distributing electricity into homes, worried that people would fear electricity if it were used for an execution. Thus, he supported Kemmler in his appeals.

Meanwhile, America's great inventor Thomas Edison, who desired to make direct current (DC) the household standard for electricity, advocated for an electric chair based on alternating current instead of one based on his DC power. Edison hoped that once people saw the electric chair killing human beings, they would see the danger of Westinghouse's AC power and adopt Edison's DC power as the standard in their homes. Edison helped convince the New York Legislature to use AC power in their new electric chair. To help make his point about the deadliness of AC, Edison sponsored demonstrations electrocuting animals, including a circus elephant named Topsy.

Edison's advocacy for an electric chair with AC power won the day. Courts, including the United States Supreme Court in *In re Kemmler* in 1890, found no constitutional bar to the execution. The New York state courts held that the execution did not violate the state or federal constitution. The U.S. Supreme Court reviewed the case but based its decision on the later-reversed view that the Eighth Amendment did not apply to the states. So the Court essentially deferred to the New York legislature's decision on the method of execution.[3]

The Supreme Court, however, did note that New York adopted the electric chair to use modern science "in the effort to devise a more humane method" of execution.[4] Although the Court did not apply the Eighth Amendment to Kemmler's case, it explained, "Punishments are cruel when they involve torture or lingering death; but the punishment of death is not cruel, within the meaning of that word as used in the Constitution. It implies there something inhuman and barbarous, something more than the mere extinguishment of life."[5]

After the journey through the courts, William Kemmler sat down in the electric chair on August 6, 1890, and prison guards strapped him to the chair. New York had purchased three used generators to power the electrocution.[6] Officials applied the electricity for several seconds, during which Kemmler strained against the leather straps and curled one finger so tightly it dug into itself, resulting in a trickle of blood on the chair's arm.

When attending doctors thought Kemmler was dead, the warden had the electricity turned off. But Kemmler's body continued to twitch, causing observers to faint and call for the current to be turned on again. After doctors confirmed Kemmler was still breathing, the executioner sent 2,000 volts through Kemmler's body. Kemmler's mouth foamed and blood vessels ruptured, and the witnesses smelled burning flesh as Kemmler's body caught fire. After the electricity ceased, Kemmler's body went limp, and doctors confirmed his death.[7] One of the physicians said he never wanted to see such a thing again, and a newspaper reporter concluded that Kemmler was "slowly roasted to death."[8]

Following Kemmler's execution, about twenty newspapers in New York unsuccessfully called for a repeal of the electric chair law. Pro-death penalty advocates argued for a return to hanging as the state's method of execution, while anti-death penalty advocates tried to capitalize on the grisly execution to get the death penalty abolished. Both groups were unsuccessful in stopping the electric chair's use.

Less than a year later, on July 7, 1891, New York resumed executions in the electric chair by executing four men in the chair in one day at Sing Sing Prison. In response to the outrage over Kemmler's execution, though, prison authorities excluded the press from witnessing these executions.[9] (See Figure 15.1.)

For Edison and Westinghouse, the battle's victor lost the war. Edison won the argument to use AC power for executions, but ultimately he failed to reach his main goal. Westinghouse's alternating current still became the standard in our homes, despite the danger showed by the electric chair. At some point, Edison must have questioned his own role in Kemmler's case, as under it all he opposed capital punishment.[10] "I do not approve of any execution," Edison explained in 1888 even as he pushed for the use of the electric chair as a more humane execution method than hanging, "I think that the killing of a human being is an act of foolish barbarity."[11] After William Kemmler's execution, Edison became an outspoken opponent of the electric chair.[12]

Several states followed New York in switching from hanging to electrocution as their execution method, with Ohio adopting electrocution in 1897 and then Massachusetts adopting it in 1900. By 1915, eleven states in the North and the South had adopted the electric chair, including New Jersey (1907), Kentucky (1907), Virginia (1908), Tennessee (1909), North Carolina (1910), South Carolina (1912), Arkansas (1913), and Pennsylvania (1915). Other states continued to change from hanging to the electric chair, including Texas in 1923.[13]

Figure 15.1
Electric Chair at Sing Sing Prison, 1915 (T. Fred Robbins/Library of Congress)

A few years after the end of World War II, the Supreme Court considered another execution in the electric chair in *Louisiana ex rel. Francis v. Resweber*. In that case, a mechanical malfunction had interrupted Louisiana's first attempt to execute Willie Francis, an African American who had been arrested as a sixteen year old and then convicted by an all-white jury of killing a white pharmacist. After the failed execution, Francis's attorney challenged the state's attempt to try again at a later date. But in the 5-4 Supreme Court decision, the Court permitted Louisiana another attempt to extinguish Francis's life. A plurality of the Court noted another attempt would not violate the Eighth Amendment because "[a]ccidents happen for which no man is to blame."[14] A year after the failed execution, Louisiana successfully executed the teen-aged Francis in the electric chair.

For nearly a century, most states used electrocution for most executions, although other methods used throughout the twentieth century were hanging, firing squad, and lethal gas, with lethal injection added toward the end of the twentieth century. Several of the most infamous condemned criminals died in the electric chair, forever attaching society's image of the death penalty to "the chair" or "Old Sparky." People executed in the electric chair include Sacco and Vanzetti, Bruno Hauptmann, Ted Bundy, and Julius and Ethel Rosenberg. During Ms. Rosenberg's execution, officials had to apply jolts of electricity five times before she died.[15]

Georgia continued to use hanging as its method of execution for decades after Kemmler's execution in New York. In 1924, the state finally switched to using the electric chair, and Georgia's first execution by electricity took place on September 13, 1924, as three wardens flipped the switches at the same time. This execution occurred at the Georgia State Prison Farm in Milledgeville, the same prison where Leo Frank had been held when men from Marietta abducted and lynched him. The people in Milledgeville were not happy to be associated with the electric chair, and they objected to having the killing machine in their community.

The state moved the electric chair in 1938 to the new Georgia State Prison in Reidsville, where it remained until executions were suspended in 1964 during litigation challenges to the death penalty. When Georgia resumed using the death penalty in 1974, it used a new electric chair at the Georgia Diagnostic and Classification Center near Jackson, Georgia. By the time Warren McCleskey entered the execution chamber at that prison, 433 people had already died in Georgia's electric chairs.[16]

The change from hanging to the electric chair transpired at around the same time executions switched from being public affairs to private ones, partly because of the nature of the new execution method. Electrocutions, which required the chair, a generator, and other technological specifications, naturally fit indoors as opposed to hanging, which more readily could be carried out in public.

Some states, however, still managed to maintain some sort of public aspect of executions while using the electric chair. For a period, Mississippi used a portable electric chair so executions could be carried out in the county courtroom where the capital defendant had been sentenced to death. For example, on May 8, 1951, when Mississippi executed Willie McGee for raping a white woman, Jones County executed him in the county courthouse where he was tried. More than five hundred people stood on the lawn outside the courthouse as the midnight hour approached. Some men and boys climbed trees to see the electric chair inside the courthouse. When the crowd heard the portable generator go silent, they burst into cheers and closed in around the courthouse to try to see the black man's corpse.[17]

Even today, experts are uncertain about the precise way electricity kills a human being. Research indicates electricity causes cardiac arrest and also may cause death by destroying the central nervous system. In litigation about the method of execution, attorneys often focus on whether or not death is instantaneous. Those who advocate for the electric chair argue that where everything goes as planned, a painless death occurs instantaneously. On the other side, experts have argued that although the electricity paralyzes the inmate, the inmate remains conscious and feels severe pain. Some believe the human skull insulates the brain, making the death go slower to the person being electrocuted than it appears to observers. One expert, Dr. Orrin Devinsky, a professor of neurology at the New York University Medical Center, concluded that not only does a person being electrocuted feel intense pain, but the person loses perception of time, so the agonizing death appears to last a lifetime. Dr. Devinsky also argued that we cannot know the extent of the pain because those who are executed in the electric chair cannot report on what they experienced.[18]

In addition to any suffering that occurs when an electric chair execution goes well, the pain may be magnified if the process does not go well. For example, in 1990, Florida officials used the wrong type of sponge to attach to inmate Jesse J. Tafero's head to conduct the electricity. During the execution, witnesses observed flames and smoke coming out through the mask covering Tafero's head. After the power stopped and Tafero continued breathing, officials applied the electricity again and again until Tafero was dead.[19]

The electric chair as an execution method remains connected to the country's history of lynching, even though hanging is the execution method most often associated with the lynching of African Americans in the early 1900s. In many lynchings, the victims' bodies were often mutilated or burned before, during, or after the killing. For example, in 1920 in Paris Texas, a mob of about 3,000 watched as two brothers, Irving and Herman Arthur, who had killed their landlord in self-defense, were chained to a flagpole and "tortured, saturated with oil and burned to a crisp."[20] The electric chair evokes the spectacle of burning flesh in its execution process.

Much had changed since the lynchings earlier in the century when black men were burned alive by mobs. But in 1991, a black man, whose race may have been a deciding factor in his death sentence, waited to be burned to death in Georgia's electric chair.

* * *

Warren McCleskey encountered the electric chair as a forty-five-year-old man, nearly thirteen years after he had been sentenced to death. Although prison will wear down inmates, McCleskey had tried to keep himself in shape during his years on death row. In his final year there, he was still physically strong and had white teeth and short black hair. His blue-black eyes had not succumbed to aging, and he did not wear glasses. The older McCleskey looked healthier than when he was arrested as a young man abusing drugs. But the upcoming days would test his mental and emotional strength.[21]

On a Monday early in September 1991, five months after the Supreme Court's decision in *McCleskey v. Zant*, Fulton Superior Court Chief Judge William W. Daniel signed an order setting an execution date for McCleskey.[22] The order followed a common practice of setting a range of dates to give the state some flexibility in case delays prevented the execution going forward on the first one. Thus, the order announced the Georgia Department of Corrections could execute McCleskey between noon on September 24, 1991 and noon October 1, 1991.

As the execution date approached, prison officials at the Georgia Diagnostic and Classification State Prison in Jackson, Georgia, prepared to execute Warren McCleskey. Knowing the end neared, McCleskey gave his first interview since his 1978 conviction to *Atlanta Journal Constitution* staff writer Mark Curriden four days before the scheduled execution. McCleskey talked about how his faith had transformed him starting in 1984, and he admitted he participated in the Dixie Furniture Company robbery. But he stressed he did not shoot Officer Frank Schlatt, and he denied giving any confession to Offie Evans. He said he wanted his six-year-old granddaughter to know he took responsibility for his mistakes but he did not kill anyone. He explained that for a long time he had wanted to tell Mrs. Schlatt and her daughter that he was sorry for his role in the crime: "I deeply regret a life was taken." When asked what punishment he should have received, he said, "The appropriate punishment should be what the other co-defendants got—life in prison."[23] (See Figure 15.2.)

Early in the morning on a warm, clear day of the scheduled execution date on Tuesday, September 24, 1991, McCleskey's attorneys appealed to the five members of the Georgia Board of Pardons and Paroles, which included two police officers. McCleskey described himself as "hopeful but not optimistic" the board would grant him clemency.[24]

McCleskey's attorneys wanted the Board members to weigh evidence that the Supreme Court declined to consider in *McCleskey v. Zant* (as discussed in chapter 3). Two jurors from McCleskey's 1978 trial testified that if they had known Offie Evans was a government informant when he testified at McCleskey's trial, they would not have voted for the death penalty. Former juror Robert Burnette explained, "If we knew more about Offie Evans, his credibility would have been shot to hell." Former juror Julie Darmer said the legal proceedings had been "an outrage." Robert Stroup, one of McCleskey's lawyers, argued, "Jurors are supposed to be given the truth, the whole truth, and they just didn't get it."

In an interview with a reporter, Georgia Attorney General Michael Bowers claimed the jurors who changed their minds were influenced by the defense attorneys. He argued too much time had passed between the crime and the execution, noting "we wait so long, we forget the tragedy, the horror, and the barbarity of the crime in the first place." He also ridiculed the international attention on McCleskey's case: "We had a young policeman in the flower of his life gunned down

Figure 15.2
Warren McCleskey in Jackson, Ga. on Sept. 20, 1991. (AP Photo/*Atlanta Journal-Constitution*)

with no compunction whatsoever, and now we hail this guy as the poster child for Amnesty International. It's ridiculous."

Additionally, at McCleskey's hearing, Stroup and McCleskey's other attorneys presented records and statements showing McCleskey had been an exemplary inmate. Reverend George Wirth, pastor of the First Presbyterian Church in Atlanta, appealed to the Board, saying McCleskey was "a gentle man who is not violent and did not commit this crime."[25] Several people wrote the Board, including Minnesota senator Paul Wellstone, who raised the question about whether McCleskey fired the gun in the case. South African civil-rights leader and African National Congress president Nelson Mandela also wrote a letter to the Board of Pardons and Paroles. He explained, "To my mind, there is far more than reasonable doubt in the case of Warren McCleskey, and I believe that his execution would represent a tragic miscarriage of justice."[26]

Several former inmates wrote about McCleskey's faith and how McCleskey had helped them. For example, former death row inmate Mike Berryhill wrote: "I can't recall having ever seen him argue or fight with anyone, but countless times I did observe him help everyone who asked. He set an example for many on death row, myself included."[27]

In a separate hearing, the Board listened to appeals from family members and friends of Officer Schlatt who urged that the execution go forward. Family and friends said they were convinced McCleskey was the killer, and Officer Schlatt's twenty-four-year-old daughter Jodie Swanner explained, "All I want is justice." She said she believed McCleskey had become a Christian, "But Christians have to pay for their sins also."

Others expressed their anger at McCleskey. James William "Billy" Dukes Jr., who had owned the Dixie Furniture Company, told a reporter for *The Atlanta Journal* that he believed McCleskey was "guilty as sin." Dukes admitted he did not see McCleskey shoot Officer Schlatt, but he questioned why McCleskey had not pointed the finger at someone else. Dukes said business at his store suffered after the robbery, and he praised Officer Schlatt for giving his life to protect Dukes and his employees.[28]

Later in the day, the five members of the Georgia Board of Pardons and Paroles voted to reject McCleskey's appeal for clemency.[29] Parole board chairman Wayne Snow explained that the board gave little weight to the two jurors who said they would not have voted for the death penalty if they had known the two key witnesses were rewarded for their testimony. Snow said he believed the evidence clearly indicated McCleskey fired the gun that killed Officer Schlatt.[30]

When a member of the board called Officer Schlatt's daughter to tell her the execution would go forward, she prayed in thanks. For the execution, friends and family of Officer Schlatt planned to wear T-shirts saying, "Capital Punishment is Justice for the Unjust."[31]

Throughout the day, McCleskey spent his time visiting thirty-seven friends and family who came to see him at the prison. A large number of his family came to say goodbye, including nieces and nephews who had grown up knowing their uncle only on death row. McCleskey refrained from crying in front of his family, and he tried to keep their spirits up by telling stories.[32] The spokesperson for the Corrections department saw that at one point, McCleskey preached to five members of his family. "He's saying things like, 'Don't worry about me. I'm going to be with Jesus.'" The spokesman added, "He's more consoling them than they are consoling him."[33]

At 4:00 pm, as the 7:00 pm scheduled execution time approached, corrections officers moved McCleskey to a special holding cell near the electric chair. A half hour later, a doctor gave McCleskey a physical exam and checked dental records to confirm the condemned man's identity. Officials shaved McCleskey's head and leg to reduce resistance to electricity when wires were attached to him in the electric chair.[34]

Around this time, an official came to McCleskey's cell to allow him to make a recording of his final statement. As soon as McCleskey began recording, a phone rang and the official answered the phone, talking in the background throughout McCleskey's final statement. McCleskey apologized to those touched by his crime and asked for forgiveness for his role. He thanked his attorneys, friends, and religious advisers, and he continued to express his faith.[35]

At 5:00 pm, the warden came to McCleskey's cell with the final meal McCleskey requested. It consisted of pizza pockets, pinto beans, cornbread, and Kool-Aid. McCleskey declined to eat the meal.[36] Instead, while McCleskey's attorneys continued to file appeals in federal court, McCleskey made calls on a phone outside his cell to family and friends. He made one of his final calls to Rebecca Cope, a pen pal he had been writing since she had responded to an ad he placed in a magazine in 1986. During their correspondence, McCleskey wrote about his faith and always included a Bible verse to start his letters. During their final conversation, McCleskey told her, "I don't know why this has to be, and if it is necessary for my life to move in other ways, so be it."[37]

A chaplain who knew of the close bond between McCleskey and his friend Billy Moore arranged so the two inmates could talk one last time. Moore had spent three days on death watch himself before getting a stay, so he sensed what McCleskey felt. Since Moore's close encounter with the electric chair, his death sentence had been commuted to a prison sentence.[38] In his prison cell now he worried how his friend was handling the ordeal. Moore felt relief to hear McCleskey's voice saying "hello" and he responded, "How are you my brother and friend?" The two were able to talk for about thirty minutes, with McCleskey reaching out to support Moore even as he was hours away from his own death. Moore later wrote, "I thought it rather funny: here I was, expecting and desiring to support my brother hours before his execution, and as it ended up, he provided the blessings; he provided the encouragement."

The two men convicted of murder spent their last moments talking and supporting each other. McCleskey confessed to Moore, "Billy, I want you to know that the Lord has given me all the grace that is needed in this situation, and far beyond my own expectation. I never would have dreamed that I could be here and not be afraid, falling apart and scared." The two said goodbye, expressing their love and appreciation for their friendship and fellowship during their years together on death row.[39]

As the prison officials prepared for the execution, McCleskey's lawyers returned to the courts to raise claims about the fairness of McCleskey's clemency hearing. After the hearing earlier in the day, McCleskey met with his attorneys about a possible claim to challenge the clemency denial. McCleskey asked them to pursue the claim even if it were a long shot. McCleskey's attorneys returned to court to argue the hearing had been unfair because the Georgia Attorney General had pressured the Board, threatening to "wage a full scale campaign to overhaul the pardons and paroles board" if the Board were to grant clemency. In response, the Board's chairman had announced even before the hearing that they would not change McCleskey's death sentence.[40]

As the court challenges were pending, McCleskey repeatedly anticipated his death as his execution time changed six times during the next several hours. Fifteen minutes before the 7:00 pm scheduled execution, U.S. District Court Judge J. Owen Forrester, who in 1984 and again in 1987 had found constitutional violations in McCleskey's case before being reversed on appeal, granted a half-hour stay of execution. Then ten minutes before the new execution time, he granted another stay until 10 pm. At 9:30 pm, Judge Forrester granted a third stay until midnight while he continued to hear arguments from McCleskey's attorneys Clive Stafford-Smith and Michael Mears that the Board chairman had prejudged McCleskey's clemency application.

At 11:20 pm, Judge Forrester ruled against McCleskey, but the judge granted another stay until 2 am so McCleskey's attorney could appeal the case to the Eleventh Circuit Court of Appeals. The Court of Appeals, however, lifted the stay and officials at the prison set the new execution time as 2:15 am.

At 2:19 am, the execution team strapped Warren McCleskey into the electric chair as his attorneys frantically tried to fax their latest appeal to the U.S. Supreme Court. Then, their fax machine jammed. In the execution chamber, McCleskey began giving his final statement until Warden Walter Zant stopped him. The warden, whose name was already linked to McCleskey in the Supreme Court's recent decision in *McCleskey v. Zant*, announced that the U.S. Supreme Court had granted another stay. Officers unstrapped McCleskey from the chair and returned him to his cell, where McCleskey waited for further news about his fate.[41]

Having had stronger claims before the Supreme Court in the past, McCleskey's attorneys could not have had much hope for the stressful last-minute appeals arguing McCleskey had been denied an impartial clemency hearing. But McCleskey, exhausted in the late hour, remained calm as the minutes ticked away.

While McCleskey waited in his cell, the Supreme Court issued a ten-minute delay at 2:42 am so the justices could consider his clemency hearing claim. At the early morning hour, the Supreme Court justices were not at the Court or even in the same location. So they made their final vote about Warren McCleskey's life on the telephone. The resulting vote ended McCleskey's last hope. At 2:52 am, the United States Supreme Court denied McCleskey's final appeal by a vote of 6-3, with only Justices Marshall, Blackmun, and Stevens voting to stop the execution.[42]

A majority of the Court denied the stay of execution without comment, but in a somewhat unusual move, Justice Thurgood Marshall wrote a dissenting opinion from the Court's denial of a stay of execution. In his dissent, he not only addressed McCleskey's new clemency hearing claim, but looked back over the last several years at the Court's decisions in *McCleskey v. Zant* limiting habeas relief and in *McCleskey v. Kemp* rejecting McCleskey's race bias claim. Regarding the latter decision, Justice Marshall noted that in the several years since the Court heard McCleskey's race claim in *McCleskey v. Kemp* and tonight's scheduled execution, "the factual record has continued to show that the death penalty is not and cannot be administered fairly: white lives are routinely valued more than Afro-American lives."

In the 1940s and 1950s, as an NAACP lawyer representing blacks charged with capital crimes in the South, Marshall often strove to keep his clients alive so he could take the cases to the Supreme Court. He knew that in cases with black defendants in Southern courts, his best chance at getting a fair hearing lay with the Supreme Court. But on this night, as prison officials prepared McCleskey for his execution and Marshall sat on that Court, he felt frustration at the institution he once saw as a beacon of hope. He concluded his dissent by chastising his fellow justices: "Repeatedly denying Warren McCleskey his constitutional rights is unacceptable. Executing him is inexcusable."[43]

As Justice Marshall wrote his dissent, the eighty-three-year-old justice was less than a week from leaving the Court. The U.S. Senate was already holding confirmation hearings on then-Judge Clarence Thomas to replace the retiring Justice Marshall. In less than a month after Marshall highlighted the underlying racism in Warren McCleskey's case, his successor, Judge Thomas, invoked lynching and racism in a different context from the life-and-death stakes in McCleskey's case. After accusations surfaced alleging Thomas had sexually harassed a person he had supervised, Thomas connected the accusations to America's past, claiming the accusations made him the victim of a "high-tech lynching."[44]

But on this night in Georgia, guards returned McCleskey to the execution chamber at 2:53 am and again strapped him in the electric chair. Because of the work of reformers in the 1800s, the chair sat in a room isolated from the public and observed only by a small number of well-behaved witnesses watching through glass. At the command post in a room next to the execution chamber, one of the guards watched and narrated the events on the telephone to Department of Corrections officials in Atlanta.

McCleskey again read his final statement, and this time the warden did not interrupt him. McCleskey looked at many of the twenty-five witnesses and apologized for his role in the robbery that led to the murder of Atlanta police officer Frank Schlatt: "First of all I would like to say to the Schlatt family that I am deeply sorry and repentant for the suffering, hurt and pain that you have endured over the years. I wish there was something I could do or say that would give comfort to your lives and bring peace to it. I pray that you would find in your heart to forgive me for the participation in the crime that caused the loss of your loved one." He continued, "I am deeply sorry for the lives that have been altered the way they have because of my ignorance and stupidity." He asked for his family to be strong and not to be bitter, and he talked about his religious conversion while on death row, asserting, "This is not the end, but the beginning I hoped for—to be in the presence of my Lord."[45]

McCleskey's words, though, failed to reach the witnesses. The microphone installed to carry audio to the witnesses behind the heavy glass stopped working during his final statement. Among the witnesses stood one of McCleskey's attorneys, Jack Boger, who had left LDF in 1990 to teach law but who had continued working on the case. Boger had not wanted to witness an execution, but he decided to attend so McCleskey could look out and see a friendly face in the crowd that came to watch him die.[46] Boger watched his client making the final statement into the dead microphone even though McCleskey did not know that the audience could not hear his words. And Boger contemplated how the scene symbolized their case through the years, where judges and others had failed to hear their arguments about its injustices.[47]

The prison chaplain gave the final prayer, and guards then secured the chinstrap around McCleskey's face. The warden read the death warrant to McCleskey and the witnesses, as the guards finished preparing McCleskey for the execution.

The execution team placed a metal plate on McCleskey's head with a wet sponge between the metal and his head to help conduct the electricity. A metal attachment was placed on McCleskey's shaved left calf so the electricity would flow through his body between the metal connections. One of the guards wiped the perspiration off of McCleskey's face. Finally, they put a leather mask with nostril holes for breathing over McCleskey's face.[48]

A few minutes after 3 am, three members of the execution team each hit one of three red switches to start the execution. Two of the switches were not connected to anything. The prison provided the dead switches so each of the executioners could sleep believing they did not do the killing. The active switch began a sequence of three timing devices. The first timer triggered 1,800 volts of electricity through Warren McCleskey for four seconds, followed by a four-second delay. As this initial bolt of electricity circulated through McCleskey's body, he sat upright and clinched his hands as smoke rose from his right leg. Then, the second timer released 1,044 volts of electricity for seven seconds. Finally, the third timer provided 120 volts to the body for 109 seconds.[49]

During electrocution, the electric shock causes respiratory paralysis and cardiac arrest. Experts speculate the prisoner feels like he or she is being burned to death and suffocating. After the electricity starts, the shock paralyzes the prisoner who then cannot speak or scream. The current flows along a path through the body destroying tissue while vital organs struggle to continue functioning. Some experts have concluded that death occurs by the damage the electric charge does to the nervous system. Studies also reveal that the way the electrical current affects one's body varies among individuals, so that different execution equipment and different bodies affect the time between the initial jolt of electricity and the time of cardiac arrest, pulmonary arrest, and brain death.[50]

Officials turned off the electricity at 3:08 am. After doctors waited for McCleskey's body to cool, they then approached the lifeless body and pronounced Warren McCleskey dead at 3:13 am on what was now Wednesday, September 25. He thus became the 155th person executed in the fifteen years since the Supreme Court allowed the death penalty to return in *Gregg v. Georgia*.[51]

After the execution, the execution team and witnesses were exhausted. McCleskey's attorneys were drained, but the attorneys and many of McCleskey's friends and family also were inspired. After witnessing the execution, attorney Jack Boger later explained to Billy Moore, "Most people would think that I would be sad because of Warren's execution. But to see how God was moving in his life as they put him through the entire ordeal—being put into the chair, taken out of it, and then put into it again—where most others would have broken down, Warren did not waver in his faith. Warren remained noble, and I am proud to have been his friend."[52]

Throughout the day, death penalty supporters and death penalty opponents had gathered outside the prison, over which flew the Georgia flag incorporating the Confederate battle flag. Some gathered to remember Officer Schlatt and some came to support the death penalty. Earlier in the day, one death penalty supporter held a sign saying, "Lethal Injection is Not Fair ... Let's Keep the Electric Chair!!!" Another

Figure 15.3
Death penalty supporters outside the Georgia Diagnostic and Classification State Prison, Jackson, Ga., Sept. 24, 1991 (AP Photo/*Atlanta Journal-Constitution*, Kimberly Smith)

man stood nearby in his Ku Klux Klan uniform holding a sign that said "We Support the Death Penalty."[53] (See Figure 15.3.)

In the early morning hours, a group of protesters waited in the rain on the prison lawn to hear the news about the planned execution. One of McCleskey's supporters was Reverend Fred Taylor, an African-American pastor who had been a leader in the civil rights movement and had been active in that movement since he was thirteen years old in 1955, working with Ralph David Abernathy and handing out leaflets during the Montgomery Bus Boycott. He also directed one of the departments of the Southern Christian Leadership Conference in the 1970s, and he became active in the fight against the death penalty. He had seen a lot of suffering and discrimination in his life. This night at 3:30 am when a state official came out and announced to the crowd, "The condemned was pronounced dead at 3:13," Rev. Taylor walked away from the other protesters. Once he found an isolated spot, he stopped and bent over toward the ground. As his body shook, he sobbed.

After much of the small crowd dispersed, another one of McCleskey's friends, Ed Weir, waited around because he wanted to see McCleskey's body pass by. Around twenty minutes after the announcement of McCleskey's death to the crowd, the hearse went by as television cameras broadcast the vehicle's passing. Weir spoke out loud, "Goodbye Warren, You have been a good friend to us all. Now you are free."[54]

* * *

The execution ended the life of Warren McCleskey, the man whose case created what some consider the worst United States Supreme Court decision since the Court upheld the Fugitive Slave Law. But McCleskey's case also changed the death penalty in the United States, even though on the night of the execution few could foresee the full impact. After the execution, Stephen B. Bright, the Director of the Southern Center for Human Rights in Atlanta, said that in light of recent Supreme Court decisions and McCleskey's case, "[W]hat we're going to see in case after case is people going to the execution chamber in cases in which the jury did not know fundamental things about the case."[55]

When Americans awoke on the morning of September 25, 1991, some media outlets discussed the case, but most Americans paid little attention to the death of Warren McCleskey. A few days after the execution an editorial in the *New York Times* featured the simple headline "Warren McCleskey Is Dead."[56] But at the time of the execution, most national attention focused on the recent collapse of the Soviet Union and the previous day's death of Theodore Geisel, that is, Dr. Seuss.

The execution did reverberate for those who were close to McCleskey and those who were close to Officer Schlatt. Officer Schlatt's daughter, Jodie Schlatt Swanner –who was nine when her father died and was now twenty-four—still felt the pain of the loss of her father. She had grown from a child into a young woman without her father. During that same time, Warren McCleskey lived on death row waiting for his execution and hoping for his case to be reversed. After McCleskey's execution, Swanner told reporters, "I feel for his family, but he's had 13 years to say goodbye to his family and to make peace with God. I never got to say goodbye to my father. This has nothing to do with vengeance. It has to do with justice."[57] Similarly, Georgia Attorney General Michael J. Bowers told a reporter, "I'm human, and I recognize that any execution is an awesome undertaking.... We're not doing this for the joy of it, but because the law requires it."[58]

The morning after the execution, one of the key witnesses against McCleskey, Offie Evans, woke up as a free man after being released from prison the previous day while McCleskey prepared for his death. Evans, who was now fifty-six years old, had continued his life of crime that began in his teenage years. This time, he had just completed serving four-and-a-half months of a one-year sentence for shoplifting a box of knives. The State Pardons and Paroles Board Spokesman explained that they released Evans from the Georgia Diagnostic and Classification Center in Butts Country under the state's early release program because of prison overcrowding. The spokesman stressed that Evans's release on McCleskey's scheduled execution date was an "unexplainable fluke."[59]

Georgia governor Zell Miller had received many telephone calls during McCleskey's final day asking that he commute McCleskey's sentence even though he had no power to do so after the Board's clemency denial. But Governor Miller was disturbed throughout the night as he heard about McCleskey being taken in and out of the execution chamber. The next day, he told reporters, "It was just a very unpleasant situation, and I'm sure it repulsed a lot of people."[60]

After the sun rose in the morning hours after Warren McCleskey's execution, a man who was hundreds of miles away from Marietta reflected on the night's events.

Justice Harry Blackmun had joined a majority of the Supreme Court in 1976's *Gregg v. Georgia* decision upholding the new death penalty laws, but his inability to stop McCleskey's execution disturbed him. Justice Blackmun was deeply troubled by McCleskey's claims in *McCleskey v. Kemp* as well as in *McCleskey v. Zant*. So, the morning after McCleskey's execution, Justice Blackmun sat at his breakfast table thinking about Warren McCleskey. And he began dictating his ideas about why he now believed the death penalty violates the Constitution.

Justice Blackmun did not immediately use the notes he wrote that morning during breakfast. But Warren McCleskey's execution changed him, and in subsequent cases he used stronger and stronger language to criticize the death penalty. He eventually used the notes he wrote the morning after McCleskey's execution, incorporating them into a dissenting opinion to announce he no longer would uphold any death sentences.[61]

A few days later, on Saturday, September 28, 1991, Warren McCleskey's body returned to his hometown of Marietta, Georgia, for the first time since his 1978 arrest. His funeral took place at Zion Baptist Church, a church started in Marietta in 1866 after the Civil War as a church for African Americans. The church sat on the same street and within a few blocks of the all-black high school where McCleskey had been a football star. Many friends and family members came to mourn McCleskey. His mother, Willie Mae McCleskey Brooks, who had shot and killed her abusive husband many years ago, now came to bury her son whose own life was destroyed by violence. McCleskey's brothers—James P. McCleskey, Johnny O. Brooks, and John H. Brooks—and his sisters—Betty M. Myers, Emma Jo Ballard, and Lillie M. Brooks—also came. Additionally, his daughter, Carla, her husband, and McCleskey's two granddaughters, Ashley and Brittany, came to mourn their father and grandfather.[62]

* * *

After Warren McCleskey's execution, states continued to move away from using the electric chair. In 1999 the U.S. Supreme Court granted a petition for writ of certiorari to review for the first time the constitutionality of the electric chair under the Eighth Amendment. But the Court later dismissed the Florida case without reaching the issue when Florida switched its method of execution to lethal injection. The Court in 2000 granted a stay of execution in an Alabama case raising the same issue, but ultimately the Court allowed the execution to proceed.[63] Still, states continued to abandon the electric chair.

As for Georgia's electric chair, only eight more men and no women followed McCleskey to die in it. On October 5, 2001, the Georgia Supreme Court found the state's electric chair constituted cruel and unusual punishment under the state's constitution, ensuring no more Georgia prisoners would be executed by electrocution. The court, noting the state legislature had recently passed a law making lethal injection the method of death for new cases, reasoned that execution by the electric chair method "inflicts purposeless physical violence and needless mutilation that makes no measureable contribution to accepted goals of punishment."[64] The court referenced autopsy reports showing there was "some degree of burning of the prisoner's body . . . in every electrocution."[65] Although the Georgia Supreme Court made no mention of the connection between mutilation and the history of lynching, the court's analysis of the electric chair evoked memories of that past. The court found the evidence reveals uncontrovertibly, that the bodies of condemned prisoners in Georgia are mutilated during the electrocution process."[66]

By 2008, Nebraska remained the only state that had electrocution as its sole means of execution. Then, in February 2008, the Nebraska Supreme Court held that the electric chair—the state's only method of execution—violated the Nebraska constitution. The Nebraska Supreme Court ruled that because the electric chair creates a "substantial risk of unnecessary suffering," it was cruel and unusual punishment under the state's constitution.

The Nebraska court evaluated evidence that prisoners suffer in the electric chair. Noting that sometimes the electric current does not go directly to the condemned person's brain, the court found that sometimes prisoners "will retain enough brain functioning to consciously suffer the torture high voltage electric current inflicts on a human body." Further, prisoners who remain conscious experience pain from the contractions of their muscles, from the burning of their flesh, and from "air hunger" caused by the stopping of respiration. The state argued that any such suffering lasted only fifteen to thirty seconds and therefore was not constitutionally significant, but the court rejected the argument. The court compared execution in the electric chair to burning at the stake and concluded, "Electrocution's proven history of burning and charring bodies is inconsistent with both the concepts of evolving standards of decency and the dignity of man."[67]

The following year, a proposed bill to replace the method with lethal injection initially failed in Nebraska's unicameral legislature, but the state legislature eventually passed a bill to adopt lethal injection. In May 2009, Governor Dave Heineman signed the law adopting lethal injection, making Nebraska the last state to adopt that execution method.[68]

Although no state retains the electric chair as its primary method of execution, as of 2014, eight states keep electrocution as an alternative to lethal injection in certain circumstances: Alabama, Arkansas, Florida, Kentucky, Oklahoma, South Carolina, Tennessee, and Virginia. In 2014, Tennessee passed a new law that would allow the state to use its electric chair if courts find that lethal injection is unconstitutional or if the state cannot obtain the drugs for lethal injections.[69]

So while the electric chair is not as prominent as it once was, it still remains as an American execution method. For example, in January 2013, Virginia executed Robert Charles Gleason Jr. in the state's wooden electric chair. Gleason, who was sentenced to death for killing two other prison inmates, had the choice to opt for electrocution because he was sentenced before the state adopted lethal injection. Gleason, who gave up his appeals to let his execution go forward, requested the electric chair because of the pain associated with lethal injection and because he wanted to be sitting instead of lying down while the state killed him.[70] As of Gleason's 2013 execution, a total of 158 people died in the electric chair in the United States since capital punishment returned in 1976.[71]

During the twentieth century, more people were executed in the electric chair in the United States than were executed by all other methods combined. After the development of the method, more than 4,300 people died in the electric chair. In New York, where it all started with William Kemmler, the state executed 686 men and 9 women by electricity through the state's last execution in 1963.[72]

As for Georgia, the last person executed in Georgia's electric chair was David L. Cargill, who the state executed on June 9, 1998, for killing two people during a gas station robbery. Between the adoption of electrocution as an execution method in 1924 and the Georgia Supreme Court decision finding the electric chair unconstitutional, 440 men and 1 woman died in Georgia's electric chair.[73] Of those executed in the electric chair, 78 percent, like McCleskey, were black.[74]

CHAPTER 16

Other American Execution Methods

Since Warren McCleskey's execution, Georgia switched to using lethal injection as its method of execution. Just as the electric chair constituted one attempt to find a more humane method of execution, lethal injection became the predominant method of execution in the United States, following various states' earlier use of the gallows, the firing squad, the gas chamber, and the electric chair.

Although early settlers, colonists, and states predominantly used hanging as the method of legal execution, they sometimes used other methods. Historians record two bludgeoning executions, taking place in 1707 (Michigan) and in 1810 (Ohio), and there were a few instances of disembowelment. Twelve men were executed by breaking on the wheel from 1712 to 1754, with most done for a 1730 slave revolt in Louisiana. There were fourteen known gibbetings—or hanging in chains, where the condemned usually was killed by hanging and then authorities publicly displayed the dead body in an iron cage where it would decompose. These displays occurred from 1700 to 1759, with one more recorded use of hanging in chains in 1913 in West Virginia.[1]

As in the case of lynching, these harsh execution methods or displaying of bodies often were inflicted on African-American defendants to help enforce the racial social order. In the 1700s, Georgia authorities could condemn slaves to death by whatever methods they deemed the most effective to deter others. In various places around the country, burning was a method of execution for slaves who planned a revolt or who murdered their masters. For example, after the 1741 Negro Plot involving a number of slaves and poor whites in the colony of New York, thirteen of the black participants were burned at the stake while none of the whites were.

After hanging, burning was the second-most most popular form of execution in the continent's early history. From 1681 to 1825, there were sixty-six known executions by burning. Sixty of those executions were of blacks, including twelve women. Those executions were for a range of crimes, although a number of them involved slave uprisings. Of the six whites, four white men were executed by burning in 1712 for aiding a slave revolt.

The other two whites executed by burning were women. Maryland burned the servant Esther Anderson in 1746 for killing her master, even though the state merely hanged the two men who participated in the killing with Anderson. Delaware executed Catharine Bevan by burning in 1731 for killing her husband with her servant and lover. Although officials often strangled the condemned before the flames consumed the person, in Bevan's case the rope burned through before she was strangled, so she burned alive. Authorities generally used the horrible means of a burning death, whether for slaves or a wife who killed her husband, to enforce an established hierarchy through fear.[2]

Harsh slave executions were not limited to the South. In 1755, the slaves Mark and Phillis were publicly executed in Massachusetts. After the two put arsenic in their owner's food and drink, state officials strangled Phillis and burned her alive, while they hanged Mark. Mark's body was hung in chains in a cage for twenty years in Charlestown Common, where his body's remains became such a landmark that Paul Revere noted the location during his famous midnight ride.[3]

The United States Supreme Court has never found that a method of execution constitutes "cruel and unusual" punishment, partly because for a long time the Court did not apply the Eighth Amendment to state convictions.[4] The Court has stated in the abstract that "punishments of torture . . . and all others in the same line of unnecessary cruelty, are forbidden." As an example of such forbidden punishments that added a deliberate infliction of pain, the Court in 1879 described punishments where the condemned was "emboweled alive, beheaded, and quartered" or executions involving "public dissection in murder, and burning alive."[5]

In addition to the method of electrocution used to execute Warren McCleskey, since 1976 states also have executed prisoners by hanging, lethal gas, firing squad, and lethal injection. These other methods each have had their supporters and their critics.

HANGING

Early Americans mainly used the method of hanging to execute criminals through the end of the 1800s. The early settlers brought the practice from England. One benefit of the method was its convenience. Although a rope and a tree often worked, early communities soon began building gallows. Early gallows required the condemned to stand on a ladder, which would then be removed. But then in the early eighteenth century, communities used a horse-drawn cart as the device to be removed. Eventually, communities began using a scaffold with a trap door, although Boston had a trapdoor scaffold as early as 1694.[6] After the American Revolution, hanging remained the most common means of execution in the new country, even though officials sometimes ordered deaths that involved additional suffering.[7]

By the middle of the nineteenth century, forty-eight states and territories used hanging as a method of execution. Hanging continued to be the main method of execution in the United States until the electric chair surpassed it in the twentieth century.[8] For example, in Warren McCleskey's Georgia, the state used hanging as the legal method of execution from 1735 until 1924, when the state switched to the electric chair. During those years, more than 500 people were executed by hanging in Georgia.[9]

Many hangings were disasters. In 1931, Arizona hanged Eva Dugan for killing a Tucson chicken farmer. The executioner miscalculated the weight of the large woman whose body also had deteriorated from syphilis. After the executioner opened the trapdoor and Dugan's body dropped, her head snapped off. Because of the spectacle, Arizona never used hanging for an execution again. The state changed its method of execution to the gas chamber, effective in October 1933.[10]

Experts debate how a hanging usually kills the condemned and whether or not the hanged person suffers. Because officials usually place a hood over the condemned's face, witnesses cannot see the prisoner's face during the execution. Some explain that when the weight of the drop dislocates the cervical vertebrae and separates the spinal cord from the brain, it causes instantaneous death in most cases. But other experts argue that in most cases the condemned dies from strangulation or suffocation. Clinton Duffy, who was the San Quentin warden from 1942 to 1954, described one hanging taking ten minutes for the condemned to die while "wheezing, whistling, trying to get air," and urinating and defecating.[11]

As noted earlier, other execution methods began replacing hanging in the late nineteenth century. Even after switching to the electric chair, though, two southern states continued to use hanging for rape, the crime most associated with lynchings. Kentucky, which adopted electrocution in 1910, and Arkansas, which adopted electrocution in 1913, kept hanging as the method of execution for the crime of rape. Kentucky even went so far as to begin using public hangings again between 1920 and 1938 for rape crimes.[12]

Although hanging long ago stopped being a common execution method in the United States, after *Furman* three death row prisoners were executed by hanging as of 2014. Two of those executions were in Washington state. On January 5, 1993, Washington executed convicted child murderer Westley A. Dodd by hanging him inside the Washington State Penitentiary in Walla Walla. It was the first legal hanging execution in the United States since 1965, but Washington soon hanged another man. In 1994 in *Campbell v. Wood*, the U.S. Court of Appeals for the Ninth Circuit held Washington State's plan to execute a defendant by hanging did not violate the Constitution. On May 27, 1994, Washington hanged Charles R. Campbell. He resisted guards and did not go to the gallows willingly so guards had to pepper spray him, strap him to a board, and carry him to his execution.[13]

The only other post-*Furman* hanging in the twentieth century occurred a few minutes after midnight on January 26, 1996, when on the cold night Delaware hanged Billy Bailey from a tall 23-step wooden gallows for murdering an elderly couple.[14] After Delaware no longer had anyone left on death row sentenced prior to the adoption of lethal injection, the state tore down the gallows in 2003.

Today, no state keeps hanging as its primary execution method, although two states have hanging as an option as of 2014. In Washington, inmates have the option to select hanging. And in New Hampshire, hanging becomes an option only if lethal injection may not be used.[15]

Although states abandoned hanging as a method of execution because other methods appeared less brutal, one of the many reasons hanging fell out of favor is its connection to the lynching past of the United States. For example, Judge Stephen Reinhardt of the Ninth Circuit U.S. Court of Appeals wrote in a 1994 dissenting opinion arguing that hanging violates the Constitution: "Hanging is associated with lynching, with frontier justice, and with our ugly, nasty, and best-forgotten history of bodies swinging from the trees or exhibited in public places."[16]

FIRING SQUAD

In 1608, settlers used a firing squad to perform the first recorded execution in the New World. Since then, officials have executed more than 140 people by firing squad on American soil.

In one of the Supreme Court's first considerations of capital punishment, the Court upheld a territorial court's sentence of death by firing squad in 1879 in *Wilkerson v. Utah*. In the case, the plaintiff argued that the trial court could not sentence him to be shot because the Territory of Utah statute did not specify an execution method. Although the Court did not review evidence about the execution method and the defendant did not raise a constitutional challenge to the firing squad, the Court explained in dicta that execution by firing squad was not a "cruel and unusual" punishment under the Eighth Amendment because it did not include the deliberate infliction of pain beyond the death sentence. The Court also recalled that the government traditionally used the firing squad for execution of military officers. By contrast, the Court cited examples from England that would be forbidden by the Eighth Amendment, including those executions in which "terror, pain, or disgrace were sometimes superadded" to the death sentence as in where the condemned were emboweled or burned alive.[17]

The state most associated with the firing squad is Utah. During the pre-*Furman* years from becoming a state in 1896 to 1972, the state executed thirty-three men, all but three of them by firing squad. The three men who were not executed by firing squad used their option to choose hanging.[18]

Some executions by firing squad resulted in prolonged suffering. In 1951, Utah used a firing squad to execute Eliseo J. Mares, who was the son of a deputy sheriff from Colorado and was eighteen at the time of his crime. Five gunmen lined up to shoot Mares. As was the usual firing squad practice to sooth the consciences of the shooters, officials gave one of the men a rifle with blanks without telling the men which one. The gunmen then fired at a heart-shaped target on Mares's chest, but none of the four bullets hit the target. Mares bled to death from the wounds, with several minutes passing before he was pronounced dead. Reports differ on why the men missed the heart-shaped target. Some claimed the gunmen wanted Mares to suffer while others argued prison staff liked Mares so nobody wanted to be the one who fired the fatal shot.[19]

As of 2014, only three people have been executed by firing squad since 1976, including the first post-*Furman* execution of Gary Gilmore in 1977. In Gilmore's case, Utah officials bound him to a chair by leather straps with a black hood over his head. After a stethoscope found Gilmore's heart, a doctor pinned a white cloth target over it. As in the Mares case, five gunman fired at Gilmore, with each shooter using a .30-caliber rifle loaded with a single round, although one gun contained a blank. After the men shot Gilmore, he died in two minutes.[20] The other two-post *Furman* firing squad executions also occurred in Utah: John A. Taylor in 1996 and Ronnie L. Gardner in 2010.

Today, many see the firing squad as a violent, anachronistic form of execution that conflicts with more modern and civilized means of killing. Thus, no state has the firing squad as its primary method of execution. As of 2014, only Oklahoma and Utah still have the method on their books. Both retain the firing squad option if an inmate who was sentenced before the adoption of lethal injection chooses it. And Oklahoma also retains it for use in the case that lethal injection and electrocution are held to be unconstitutional. Recent problems with lethal injection, though, have some lawmakers in other states discussing a return to executing prisoners with rifles.

LETHAL GAS

Although states began using the gas chamber after the invention of the electric chair, the newer method never became as popular as the older one. After Nevada first adopted lethal gas in 1921 to replace hanging and the firing squad, states did not embrace the new method widely. So by 1973, only twelve states used the gas chamber compared to twenty states using the electric chair. After 1973, no state adopted lethal gas.

As of 2014, no state has the gas chamber as a primary method of execution, although four states maintain it as an alternative to lethal injection either as an option for defendants sentenced before the adoption of lethal injection or as an option if courts find lethal injection unconstitutional. These states that maintain a gas chamber are Arizona, California, Missouri, and Wyoming. The most recent execution in the gas chamber was Arizona's of Walter LaGrand in 1999.[21]

An army medical corps officer named D.A. Turner invented the gas chamber after World War I. As in the case of the electric chair, modern capitalism played a role in the execution method's development. After the war's demonstration of the horrors of chemical warfare, chemical companies and others began advocating for the ways that chemicals could play a beneficial role in modern society. Some argued that chemicals could be used to make executions more humane than hanging or the electric chair.[22]

Gas chambers generally are airtight rooms shaped like an octagon. During the execution, a stethoscope is taped to the inmate's chest with a long cord going outside the chamber to a physician who may pronounce the person dead. Officials strap the condemned person in a perforated metal chair with a bowl under the seat. The executioner adds sulfuric acid to the bowl through a tube, and then controls a lever allowing a gauze bag of cyanide to drop into the acid. The cyanide reacts with the acid to release poisonous gas into the room, and the prisoner is asphyxiated in a way that amounts to suffocation or strangulation, technically death by hypoxia, which is the lack of oxygen to the brain.

Doctors have described the gas chamber execution pain as similar to that felt by a person experiencing a heart attack when the heart is deprived of oxygen.[23] Some commentators claim that execution by lethal gas results in a more predictable death process than hanging, electrocution, and the firing squad. But the method is predictably painful, and the prisoner generally remains conscious for several minutes. The toxic gas burns the nose and lungs as the person asphyxiates, which in turn causes the condemned to lose control of bodily functions.[24]

The gas chamber was first used in the United States on February 8, 1924, when the state of Nevada executed Gee Jon. Prejudice against Asians infected the coverage of the case in the local Nevada press, and the case attracted added attention because of the new execution method. Although Governor James G. Scrugham denied clemency to Gee Jon, within the next year Governor Scrugham joined with Warden Denver S. Dickerson, who oversaw the execution, to ask the Nevada Legislature to repeal the law adopting the gas chamber. They were unsuccessful, and in 1926, Nevada executed its second person by gas—Stanko Jukich, a young Serbian immigrant.[25]

The most famous gas chamber sits on the grounds of California's San Quentin State Prison. In 1938, Robert Lee Cannon and Albert Kessell were the first two people executed in San Quentin's gas chamber. The designer of the California gas chamber had boasted that it would "snuff out life" in fifteen seconds, but when prison officials tested the gas on a pig, it took three minutes to die. After the Cannon and Kessell executions, San Francisco Health Director Dr. J.C. Geiger stated, "The idea that cyanide kills immediately is hooey. These men suffered."[26] California's gas chamber would later be used to execute Caryl Chessman in 1960, after which one reporter recounted that Chessman gasped and thrashed for five to eight minutes in agony.[27]

Although states adopted the gas chamber as a more humane alternative to the electric chair, many witnesses have described the horrors of the gas chamber. During Mississippi's execution of Jimmy Lee Gray in 1983, the condemned convulsed for eight minutes before officials ordered witnesses to leave the observation room while Gray continued banging his head on a pole. In a dissenting opinion in *Gomez v. United States District Court*, Justice Stevens recounted an eyewitness description of Arizona's gas chamber execution of Don Harding on April 6, 1992. The witness described violent convulsions, uncontrollable shuddering, spasms, and twitching for about nine minutes.[28] One witness ran to grab the hand of a minister in the room, while others were overcome with emotion.

A few years later on June 15, 1994, when North Carolina officials began putting a leather mask on David Lawson's face in the gas chamber, Lawson began yelling,

"I'm human, I'm human!" After the gas was released, Lawson continued yelling, although after three minutes he could no longer yell the full sentence and instead yelled "Human!" about every twenty seconds. His exclamations continued for two to three minutes, and then he continued grunting for a period of a minute or a minute and half before only his body was quivering for an additional minute. His execution took twelve minutes.[29]

Such descriptions, along with the association that the gas chamber established with Nazi Germany, partly explain why states used the gas chamber only eleven times since 1976. For example, after newspapers recounted Arizona's execution of Don Harding, voters by popular referendum overwhelmingly voted to switch the state's method of execution to lethal injection.

States also abandoned the gas chamber because it was a relatively expensive method, and legislators feared that court challenges to the brutal killing method would slow down executions. For example, in 1994, a U.S. District Court judge in California held in *Fierro v. Gomez* that California's procedures for executing by lethal gas constituted cruel and unusual punishment. The U.S. Court of Appeals for the Ninth Circuit then enjoined the state from using the gas chamber.[30] All states that used the gas chamber eventually switched to lethal injection as their main method of execution.

LETHAL INJECTION

After eight more men followed Warren McCleskey into Georgia's electric chair during a little less than a decade, the state in 2000 changed its method to lethal injection. Just as people debated the cruelty of the electric chair in the past, people argue whether lethal injection as practiced in the United States is humane. And in the early twenty-first century, states continue to experiment with which drugs to use.

Several people in the United States contemplated lethal injection as a method of execution long before it came to fruition. For example, before New York became the first state to use the electric chair, Governor David B. Hill in 1886 appointed a commission to consider execution methods. The commission considered lethal injection but concluded the electric chair would be more humane.[31]

Following the return of the death penalty in the United States after the Supreme Court's decision in *Gregg v. Georgia*, politicians began looking for a more humane method of execution than the electric chair and the gas chamber. In 1973, California governor Ronald Reagan, as well as others, suggested the idea of lethal injection as an execution method. Governor Reagan gave the example of how veterinarians give a shot to put horses to sleep, and then stated, "I think maybe there should be more study of this to find out, if there's a more humane way, can we still improve our humanity."[32]

Several years later, some men in Oklahoma put the idea into practice. In 1977, Oklahoma state senator Bill Dawson and Oklahoma House representative Bill Wiseman consulted with the chief medical examiner for Oklahoma, Dr. A. Jay

Chapman. Out of other inquiries and that consultation where Dawson and Wiseman wrote down their ideas for a new statute, the Oklahoma Legislature passed a bill adopting lethal injection as the state's method of execution.[33] Oklahoma adopted a three-drug method of execution that other states soon copied with little thought or scientific testing about whether those three drugs constituted the best combination for executing humans.[34]

After Oklahoma's adoption of lethal injection, other states followed, and no state has since adopted any other method of execution as of the early twenty-first century.[35] Texas adopted lethal injection as its method of execution on August 29, 1977, about one year after the Supreme Court had upheld Texas's death penalty sentencing procedures in *Jurek v. Texas*. When Governor Dolph Briscoe signed the new bill into law in Texas, he stated his desire that the new law would "provide some dignity with death."

Various challenges to the new laws followed. Lawyers appealed to the U.S. Department of Health and Human Services to ban the use of the drugs for execution. They also made legal challenges based on the grounds that the Food and Drug Administration (FDA) had not approved the drugs for executing humans. Although capital defendants won a victory with the FDA claim in 1983 in the U.S. Court of Appeals for the District of Columbia Circuit in *Chaney v. Heckler*, the U.S. Supreme Court unanimously reversed the decision, allowing lethal injections to continue.[36]

In the early twenty-first century, lethal injection is the primary method of execution in every U.S. death penalty jurisdiction, and federal and state governments have executed a total of more than one thousand inmates using lethal injection. Several states maintain other methods of execution as alternative options in certain circumstances, but these other methods are rarely used today, and possibly some of them will never be used again.

Attorneys for the condemned argue lethal injection is inhumane and unconstitutional for a number of reasons. First, they point to cases where officials had difficulty injecting needles into a vein in the arm of the condemned, such as where an inmate was obese or an inmate had a history of drug abuse. Second, they argue the improper dosage of the drugs can result in the inmate being paralyzed but still conscious during a prolonged painful death.

Some of the problems may result because of lethal injection's similarity to a medical procedure that ordinarily might require medical expertise. Yet, several medical organizations have proclaimed that it is unethical for a medical doctor to act as an executioner. For example, the American Medical Association (AMA) has taken the position that the medical profession is "dedicated to preserving life when there is hope of doing so"; therefore they "should not be a participant in a legally authorized execution."[37] The AMA states that a physician can certify death after an execution but should do no more. An ongoing debate focuses on whether or not medical licensing boards may discipline the physicians who do participate in executions. So, as a result, executioners may not have the necessary expertise and training for their task.

The needle insertion problem has been documented in a number of cases. For example, in 2009 Ohio officials had difficulty inserting a needle in Romell Broom, who had been condemned for raping and killing a teenage girl. Broom later revealed the execution team stuck him with a needle eighteen times or more while he felt severe pain. After the attendants failed in trying to insert the needles for two hours, Ohio's governor issued a temporary reprieve to cease the attempts. In subsequent years, Broom continued to challenge Ohio's attempts to try to execute him again.[38]

Other states have had similar needle insertion problems. During a 1996 Indiana execution, the executioners could not insert a catheter into either of Tommie J. Smith's arms. After trying other areas—near Smith's heart, his neck, and his groin area—they inserted the needle into an artery in Smith's foot. Smith was awake during the thirty-five minute process of trying to find a place for the needle. Similarly, during a 1997 South Carolina execution, the execution team delayed the execution for forty minutes while they tried to insert a catheter into Michael Elkins's arms, legs, and feet before successfully inserting the needle into his neck. In 1987, Texas officials had trouble finding a suitable vein in Elliot Johnson, so they spent thirty-five minutes sticking needles in different areas in Johnson's arms and ankles.[39] In 2005, after California officials spent eleven minutes trying to insert needles for the execution of Tookie Williams, an exasperated Williams looked up from the gurney and asked his executioners, "You guys doing that right?"[40]

In other cases, executioners have made errors. During John Wayne Gacy's 1994 execution, Illinois executioners failed to rinse out the intravenous tube between the sodium pentothal and the pancuronium bromide, so the two drugs created a solid that clogged the tube. During Raymond Landry's execution by lethal injection in Texas in 1988, the catheter came out of his arm and sprayed chemicals around the room. Officials reinserted the catheter, but Landry did not die for twenty more minutes.

In the course of a Missouri execution in 1995, execution personnel strapped Emmitt Foster too tightly to the gurney, unintentionally restricting the flow of drugs to his veins. Seven minutes after the chemicals began flowing, Foster began convulsing and gasping. Prison personnel closed the blinds so witnesses could not see what was happening. They opened the blinds twenty-six minutes later to reveal Foster's dead body. They claimed that when they loosened the straps Foster had died in a few minutes.

Some inmates have had allergic reactions to the chemicals used to kill them. During a 1992 Oklahoma execution, Robyn Parks had muscle spasms and then gagged for several minutes before dying. Similarly, an execution that same year in Texas resulted in Justin Lee May having a spell of coughing, groaning, and gasping. A similar result occurred when Stephen McCoy was executed in Texas in 1989.[41]

Executioners continue to encounter these and other problems in states that use lethal injection. After the 2006 execution of Joseph Clark took nearly ninety minutes and led to a lawsuit and Ohio revising its lethal injection procedures, an execution the following year of Christopher J. Newton took nearly two hours. During the execution, Newton appeared to be suffocated to death.[42]

In the early twenty-first century, defense attorneys throughout the country were challenging lethal injection as a method of execution with some success, so it appeared inevitable the issue would reach the Supreme Court. Professor Deborah

Denno has explained that historically, challenges to execution methods generally followed the same route. Once states understand that a method has a record of mistakes and faces constitutional challenges, the states would change to a new method of execution.

The history for lethal injection, however, has differed from the paths of older execution methods. As challenges mounted to lethal injection with some success in the lower courts and through governors, states did not change execution methods, perhaps because of a lack of an alternative. Professor Denno noted that challenges to lethal injection resulted in "a striking array of continually changing strategies, ranging from action in the courts in the form of the more frequent section 1983 challenges and less frequent administrative law claims to gubernatorial attempts to investigate lethal injection without court involvement and state legislative efforts to permit doctor participation in executions."[43] Soon, though, the Supreme Court attempted to resolve the questions about the constitutionality of lethal injection.

In 2008, the Supreme Court considered in *Baze v. Rees* whether or not the three-drug method for lethal injection as used in Kentucky constituted cruel and unusual punishment under the Eighth Amendment of the U.S. Constitution. By that time, lethal injection was the most prevalent method of execution in the United States, with all thirty-six states that maintained capital punishment and the federal government using lethal injection as the only or primary execution method. Of those thirty-six states, twenty-seven required lethal injection as the sole method of execution.[44]

The Court in *Baze* considered the method of lethal injection used in Kentucky specifically, but at least thirty of the thirty-six states with lethal injection used the same method. In the procedure, three drugs are used in a specified order. The first drug injected into the condemned is sodium thiopental. Sodium thiopental is a barbiturate sedative that acts to put the inmate in a deep sleep. This drug's purpose is to prevent the inmate from feeling any pain associated with the effects of the next two drugs. Then, officials inject the second drug of pancuronium bromide, a paralytic that stops muscular-skeletal movements. The pancuronium bromide paralyzes the diaphragm so the inmate ceases respiration. Finally, the third drug is potassium chloride, which "interferes with the electrical signals that stimulate the contractions of the heart, inducing cardiac arrest."[45]

One of the criticisms of this three-drug method is that the paralyzing effect of the second drug, pancuronium bromide, may allow the condemned to suffer before death because the paralysis covers up any sign of agony. In some cases, inmates may not receive adequate amounts of sodium thiopental, so they are conscious but paralyzed, which prevents them from revealing their pain when the second and third drugs are injected. Because of a similar risk, a number of states have banned the use of pancuronium bromide for euthanizing animals.[46]

In *Baze*, the Court held that execution by lethal injection employing the three-drug procedure as used in Kentucky does not constitute a "cruel and unusual" punishment under the Eighth Amendment of the Constitution. Despite the *Baze* petitioners' claims about a risk the drugs will be administered incorrectly and result in severe pain, a majority of the Court concluded such a possibility is not enough to find a punishment unconstitutional.

A majority of the Court, however, could not agree on a rationale for the outcome. In a plurality opinion joined only by Justices Anthony Kennedy and Samuel Alito, Chief Justice John Roberts explained, "Simply because an execution method may result in pain, either by accident or as an inescapable consequence of death, does not establish the sort of 'objectively intolerable risk of harm' that qualifies as cruel and unusual."[47] Chief Justice Roberts clarified that for an execution method to violate the Eighth Amendment, there must be alternatives that "effectively address a 'substantial risk of serious harm.'" Such an existing alternative "must be feasible, readily implemented, and in fact significantly reduce a substantial risk of severe pain." Only when a state fails to adopt such an alternative in the absence of a "legitimate penological justification for adhering to its current method of execution," would the state's failure to change execution methods constitute a constitutional violation.[48]

In the decision, the vote was 7-2 for finding no constitutional violation in the case, but of the seven in the majority for the outcome, four of the justices— Stevens, Scalia, Thomas, and Stephen Breyer—merely concurred in the result for various reasons. Justice Thomas wrote an opinion joined by Justice Scalia where he argued for a stricter legal standard than the plurality's standard. Thomas stated he would hold that a method of execution would violate the Eighth Amendment only if it were deliberately designed to inflict pain. He argued the drafters of the Eighth Amendment meant only to prohibit execution methods created to be painful, so as long as legislatures were not trying to inflict pain, their execution methods would be constitutional.

The only two justices who dissented were Ruth Bader Ginsburg and David H. Souter. In the dissenting opinion written by Justice Ginsburg, she argued that the Court should balance the severity of the pain risked, the likelihood of pain, and the extent to which alternative execution methods were feasible. She reasoned that the case should be remanded to assess Kentucky's lack of safeguards for making sure condemned inmates are unconscious after the injection of the first drug.[49]

Although the *Baze* opinion appeared to clear the way for lethal injections to begin again in Kentucky as well as other states, other issues arose. In Kentucky, the state supreme court kept in place a stay on executions into 2011 to address legal issues surrounding the state's lethal injection protocol and how it was put into place.[50]

Nationally, states did resume lethal injections, but other issues surrounding the execution method slowed the executions. Starting in 2009, a national shortage of the drug sodium thiopental led states to scramble for other sources and other drugs. Then, in January 2011, Hospira, the only U.S. company that made the drug, announced it would no longer manufacture it. The company had planned to make the drug near Milan, Italy, but Italy's parliament then pressured Hospira to guarantee its drug would not be used for executions. As a result, states and the federal government had to look for other sources of the drug.[51]

In some states, controversies arose about where the government obtained the rare drug. California, Arizona, and other states obtained sodium thiopental from a company in Great Britain. But then, Great Britain, which does not have the death penalty, required that future shipments of the drug from British sources not be used to execute inmates.[52] In March 2011, U.S. Drug Enforcement Administration agents confiscated Georgia's supply of sodium thiopental due to questions about the importation of the drug from an unlicensed London company.[53] In subsequent months, the agency seized the drug from several other states, and issues about the use of sodium thiopental and obtaining the drug continued.

Some states soon started turning to other drugs for lethal injections. Because of a shortage of sodium thiopental, some states began experimenting with pentobarbital, a drug often used for euthanizing animals. States tried two methods of using pentobarbital: (1) as a substitute for sodium thiopental in the three-drug protocol, or (2) as the only drug used in execution. The use of pentobarbital, however, was not without controversy or botched executions.

In 2010, Oklahoma became the first state to abandon the three execution drugs of sodium thiopental, pancuronium bromide, and potassium chloride. The state replaced sodium thiopental with pentobarbital. After legal challenges were unsuccessful in trying to stop the new execution process, Oklahoma began executing inmates with the new drug cocktail.[54] Then, in an attempt to prevent similar legal challenges, in April 2011 Oklahoma governor Mary Fallin signed a law that did not specify the drugs used in lethal injection, merely stating a lethal amount of a "drug or drugs" would be used.[55]

In March 2011, Texas, the state with the most post-*Furman* executions, followed Oklahoma's lead in deciding to use pentobarbital instead of the hard-to-find sodium thiopental.[56] Other states that similarly replaced sodium thiopental with pentobarbital included Alabama, Arizona, Mississippi, Ohio, and South Carolina.

In June 2011, Georgia tried the new three-drug combination using pentobarbital to execute Roy W. Blankenship, but the execution went gruesomely awry. Once the injection started, Blankenship's head began jerking and lurching. He lunged forward twice with his mouth open as if gasping for air, and then about a minute later his head came forward and he mouthed unidentifiable words. During the entire three minutes his body kept moving and his eyes remained open. After twelve minutes, officials declared Blankenship dead. After the execution, medical experts debated whether or not officials did something wrong in carrying out the execution. Defense attorneys in other cases raised the prospect that the use of pentobarbital caused the violent reaction. Earlier in the same month, Alabama's use of the same drug in the execution of Eddie D. Powell also resulted in the condemned making strange movements during the first minutes of the execution.[57]

The shortage of sodium thiopental led some states to abandon the three-drug method altogether. In *Baze v. Rees*, the petitioners had unsuccessfully argued the three-drug method violated the Constitution because a more humane execution might be done with one drug. Then, with the subsequent drug shortages, states began experimenting with one-drug executions. Ohio first tried using only sodium thiopental when it executed Frank Spisak in February 2011. A month later, on the morning of March 10, 2011, one day after Illinois abolished the death penalty, Ohio became the first state to execute an inmate using only pentobarbital, the same drug that was used by Oklahoma the previous year in a combination with other drugs.

So, Johnnie Baston, an African American whom an Ohio jury sentenced to death for the 1994 murder of Toledo store owner Chong Mah, became the first person executed by the new method of using only pentobarbital.[58] At Baston's execution, officials pronounced Baston dead around thirteen minutes after the flow of 5 grams of pentobarbital to his arms began. According to a newspaper report, a minute after the execution started, Baston "appeared to gasp, then grimace and wince, but then was quickly still." During the execution, though, Baston's brother became visibly upset as he watched his brother dying.[59]

In the states that continued to use sodium thiopental for executions, officials struggled to find sources for the drugs, while the FDA and the U.S. Drug Enforcement Administration addressed arguments about the regulation and import of the drugs. In several states, attorneys filed lawsuits against the FDA regarding the agency's decision not to regulate drugs used for lethal injection.

Not long after the shortage of sodium thiopental led some states to begin using pentobarbital, those states began running out of the new drug too. The Danish company Lundbeck, one of the leading manufacturers of pentobarbital, placed restrictions on the distribution of the drug in an attempt to keep it from being used in U.S. executions. For example, by March 1, 2013, Georgia's supply of pentobarbital was expiring and the state pondered how it could execute the ninety-three men and one woman who remained on its death row.[60]

Some states turned to other execution drugs. In 2012, Missouri announced plans to use propofol, an anesthetic most known because it reportedly led to the death of singer Michael Jackson. In 2013, Arkansas became the first state to announce it would use phenobarbital in its lethal injection executions (as opposed to pentobarbital), although executioners would first give inmates a pre-execution sedative of lorazepam to offset any side effects of the phenobarbital. These new drugs also were untested for the purpose of killing human beings.[61]

States continued to experiment in 2014, resulting in several controversial executions. On January 16, 2014, Ohio, which had run out of pentobarbital, used a combination of midazolam (a sedative) and hydromorphone (to suppress breathing) for the execution of Dennis McGuire, who took about 25 minutes to die. Witnesses reported that during that time McGuire moved around and made gasping, choking, and snorting sounds. Subsequently, a federal judge ordered a temporary moratorium on executions in Ohio until the state reviewed and implemented new lethal injection procedures. [62]

On April 29, 2014, Oklahoma planned to execute two men but cancelled the second execution after the first one did not go well. The state began the execution of Clayton Lockett using, for the first time, a combination of midazolam, vecuronium bromide, and potassium chloride. During the execution, Lockett appeared conscious and in pain so officials stopped the execution. But around forty-five minutes after the execution started, Lockett apparently died from a heart attack. The preliminary autopsy findings concluded that prison officials did not properly insert IVs into Lockett's veins.[63]

Although the Ohio and Oklahoma executions raised some concerns, Arizona proceeded with the execution of Joseph R. Wood III on July 23, 2014, using the same combination of drugs that had been used in Ohio's execution of Dennis McGuire (midazolam and hydromorphone). Witnesses reported that Wood snorted and gasped 600 times in a prolonged execution that took one hour and fifty-seven minutes for Wood to die. As in other recent executions, prior to this one, the courts had refused to grant Wood's attorneys access to the identity of the manufacturer of the drugs and the information about the qualifications of the executioners.[64]

States may continue to experiment with different variations on lethal injection. What is more surprising than the recent changes is the fact that the states went for so long without adjusting the three-drug protocol first selected in 1977 in Oklahoma. The states' lackadaisical acceptance of the status quo occurred partly due to the fact that capital defendants were losing their challenges to lethal injection in the courts. Since the method's adoption, capital defense attorneys had been challenging lethal injection as unconstitutional, but courts routinely dismissed such claims, and attorneys and experts were unable to get more information about the states' executions because prisons kept much of the information secret from the public. Additionally, because state laws kept several other execution methods on the books, courts gave more attention to those older methods, along with other issues, such as attempts to end the death penalty through the litigation that resulted in *McCleskey v. Kemp*.

States, claiming they need to protect the privacy of those involved in the execution process, are still able to keep much information about executions secret from the public, one of the side effects of the historical elimination of public executions. But in more recent years, attorneys have obtained some information through section 1983 actions, and defense experts have developed more understanding about the lethal injection process.

The states' scattershot approach to changing drugs based on drug availability without adequate scientific testing remains connected to the past history of the rushed development and adoption of lethal injection as an execution process in the 1970s. Beyond states' attempts to vary the method of lethal injection, at some point in the future, states may even adopt a completely new execution method, assuming the death penalty remains in use. Just as the country has moved through hanging, the firing squad, the gas chamber, the electric chair, and lethal injection, creative Americans will continue the search for what they think is a better way to kill human beings.

EXECUTIONS CONTINUE

The United States, which prides itself on its technological innovation, has long been on the forefront of developing modern methods of killing condemned prisoners. Most other countries that still use the death penalty rely upon methods largely abandoned or never used in the United States. For example, in the recent year of 2010, the only other country to use lethal injection for an execution besides the United States was China. During that year, other death penalty countries used beheading (Saudi Arabia), hanging (Bangladesh, Botswana, Egypt, Iran, Iraq, Japan, Malaysia, North Korea, Singapore, Sudan, and Syria), and shooting (Bahrain, Belarus, China, Equatorial Guinea, North Korea, Palestinian Authority, Somalia, Taiwan, Vietnam, and Yemen). During the same year, the United States also used shooting and the electric chair. Although actual executions by stoning are rare, in recent years death sentences by stoning were imposed in Iran, the Bauchi state of Nigeria, and Pakistan.[65]

Through the decades and the uses of different execution methods in the United States, some have wondered about how the acts of killing prisoners may affect prison officials, medical technicians, and executioners who participate in the process. Some former executioners have gone on to be strong opponents of capital punishment. For example, for seventeen years Jerry Givens worked as the chief executioner in Virginia, where he oversaw sixty-two executions, starting with his first in 1984. Later, after spending time in prison himself on charges of money laundering and being released in 2004, Givens became an outspoken opponent of capital punishment, presenting key testimony before the Virginia General Assembly in 2010 to help prevent the expansion of the state's death penalty.[66] Similarly, Albert Pierrepoint, who served as the Chief Executioner of the United Kingdom for twenty-four years and who hanged 435 people before he resigned in 1956, also spoke out against capital punishment toward the end of his life.[67]

In the United States today, though, executioners in many states around the country continue to do their job. In most instances, executioners continue using lethal injection, even as some have called for states to bring back firing squads in light of recent botched lethal injections.

While throughout history some executions like the recent botched executions have led states to pause in their use of the death penalty, it is not always the case. In the immediate aftermath of Warren McCleskey's execution in the electric chair, execution chambers around the country began operating at the highest rates since before the Supreme Court decided *Furman v. Georgia*.

CHAPTER 17

The Unstoppable Death Penalty after
McCleskey into the Early 1990s

Following Warren McCleskey's execution, the death penalty seemed more firmly entrenched in the United States than at any time since the 1950s. McCleskey v. Kemp had revealed that the courts were not going to abolish the death penalty, and anti-death penalty advocates had to focus on other strategies. While attorneys and activists struggled to adapt, the popular death penalty appeared as if it would remain an American institution indefinitely.

After Warren McCleskey's execution, the death penalty in the United States had few obstacles. Politically, the death penalty remained overwhelmingly popular, and politicians pushed to expand the use of capital punishment. At the same time, federal courts were becoming less likely to review claims by capital defendants. Following Supreme Court decisions that started in the early 1980s and continued through *McCleskey v. Zant* in 1991, capital defendants faced several substantive and procedural limits on what claims they could raise in habeas corpus proceedings. Thus, starting in the late 1980s, death penalty opponents encountered the most despair they had felt since the 1950s.

As discussed in Chapter 13, following the *McCleskey v. Kemp* decision, the American death penalty was firmly entrenched. The decades-long litigation strategy to abolish the death penalty appeared to suffer a final defeat. The *New York Times* reported in 1988 that the *McCleskey* decision "ended what may well have been the last sweeping challenge to the death penalty in our time." Thus, defense lawyers were left to look "for more routine points to argue—and perhaps before an increasingly skeptical judiciary."[1]

Some feared that the *McCleskey* opinion helped legitimize the death penalty in the minds of people. Professors Carol S. Steiker and Jordan M. Steiker have argued that the defense attorneys' unsuccessful attacks on the arbitrariness of the death penalty "contribute[d] substantially to the stabilization and perpetuation of capital punishment as a social practice."[2] Similarly, Professors Baldus and Woodworth, who coauthored the study presented to the Court in *McCleskey v. Kemp*, later recognized that the Court's decision holding their statistical evidence did not create a constitutional claim "significantly legitimated tolerance for race discrimination" in capital cases.[3]

Advocates for the death penalty also recognized that McCleskey's case had effectively ended any chance that death penalty opponents could abolish the death penalty through court attacks. After the Supreme Court decided *McCleskey v. Kemp*, Kent S. Scheidegger, the Legal Director of the Criminal Justice Legal Foundation, concluded in a 1987 law review article that the "machinery of a constitutional system of capital punishment" was finally nearing completion. And he proclaimed, "The opponents' strategic decision to focus on the courts instead of on public opinion has proven a disastrous failure."[4]

McCleskey v. Kemp defeated the litigation strategy to abolish the death penalty, but it also created a turning point. After *McCleskey*, abolitionists realized that the Supreme Court would not end to the American death penalty. Defense lawyers would successfully continue to work to limit the death penalty's use in practice, and their work contributed to the abolition efforts. Yet, death penalty lawyers were no longer leading the abolition movement in the courts. Out of the ashes of *McCleskey v. Kemp*, abolitionists knew they had to re-energize and focus their energy elsewhere.

Many saw the approach of this turning point, as the years between *Furman* and *McCleskey v. Kemp* were years of limited success in the Supreme Court. The justices on the Court at the time of *McCleskey* were more conservative and less likely to strike down the death penalty than were the justices at the time of *Furman* and *Gregg*. Still, the abolition movement appeared stalemated during the years between *Furman* and *McCleskey*. The public's support for capital punishment grew and fewer obstacles existed to prevent executions.

The defeat in *McCleskey* forced abolitionists to fully acknowledge they had to abandon hopes on a litigation strategy and return their main focus to where it had been for much of American history. Despite the popularity of the death penalty, abolitionists realized they needed to focus more on education and legislative action. Although activists had targeted legislatures throughout the 1970s and 1980s, the decision in *McCleskey v. Kemp* made them begin to re-energize that focus.

But it would take a while before this approach would pay off. One of the first uses of this strategy after *McCleskey v. Kemp* was the attempt to accomplish through legislation what that case failed to do through the Constitution. In 1988, the U.S. Congress considered passing the Racial Justice Act that would have allowed capital defendants to use statistics to support claims that racial bias unfairly influenced their cases. The bill did not pass, and a later attempt to pass the federal statute also failed. But the debate about the bill educated politicians and the public about the issues raised in McCleskey's case.[5]

Legislatures did change their death penalty laws during these years, but the changes generally broadened capital punishment. Because of the difficulty in predefining the "worst" crimes, legislatures around the country continued to expand death penalty statutes, adding aggravating factors that made more defendants eligible for the death penalty. Often, when a particular heinous murder did not result in a death penalty, politicians felt they could advance their careers by advocating for laws to expand the death penalty. [6]

For example, the same year Congress failed to pass the Racial Justice Act, it instead passed its first federal death penalty statute since *Furman*. Congress passed the Anti-Drug Abuse Act of 1988 in haste without congressional hearings before November elections, making drug kingpins eligible for the death penalty. In the rush, the lawmakers failed to specify the procedures for executions.

Although the 1988 law targeted specific crimes, several years later Congress inflated federal death penalty laws to include sixty crimes.[7] President Bill Clinton signed into law the Violent Crime Control and Law Enforcement Act of 1994, which included a number of death penalty provisions that constituted the Federal Death Penalty Act of 1994. During the drafting of the law, members of the Congressional Black Caucus fought for the bill to include a Racial Justice Act because of their concerns about the decision in *McCleskey v. Kemp*. Their efforts failed, and the new law significantly expanded the federal government's ability to seek death sentences. Then-Senator and later-Vice President Joseph Biden introduced The Federal Death Penalty Act, which was overwhelmingly supported by Democrats, who used their support to counter allegations they were soft on crime. When President Clinton ran for re-election, he boasted, "My 1994 crime bill expanded the death penalty for drug kingpins, murderers of federal law enforcement officers, and nearly 60 additional categories of violent felons."[8]

While death penalty statutes became broader, other changes led to courts giving less rigorous review of capital cases. In the first decade after *Gregg v. Georgia*, federal courts often reversed capital sentences on habeas corpus review, finding constitutional violations the state courts were not adequately addressing. These reversals were based on claims that included failures in state procedures and ineffective assistance of defense counsel. But gradually, the Supreme Court issued more and more rulings that made it much more difficult for habeas petitioners to get relief in the federal courts.

The Supreme Court decisions limiting habeas corpus began soon after *Gregg*. In 1977, in *Wainwright v. Sykes*, the Court held that where a defendant's attorney failed to follow state procedures for objecting to a constitutional violation in state court, the federal courts could not review the claim unless the defendant met a burden of showing cause for the failure and that the failure prejudiced the defendant. The Court created other hurdles in subsequent years. In 1982 in *Rose v. Lundy*, the Court held habeas corpus petitioners must "exhaust" or properly raise all claims in state court before federal courts will review the claims. In 1989 in *Teague v. Lane*, the Court significantly limited the ability of defendants to benefit from "new rules" of constitutional law in post-conviction review. As discussed in Chapter 3, in 1991 in *McCleskey v. Zant*, the Court added burdens to habeas petitioners filing a second habeas corpus petition. The Court added further constraints in *Coleman v. Thompson* the same year.[9] Thus, as Warren McCleskey went through the court system from his trial through the Supreme Court and then to his execution, the Supreme Court's evolving habeas corpus doctrine became more complex and more prohibitive of federal court review.[10]

As the Supreme Court was limiting federal courts' ability to review claims, the Court occasionally became frustrated with lower courts who wished to take a more expansive approach. For example, as California prepared for its first post-*Furman* execution in April 1992, individual judges on the U.S. Court of Appeals for the Ninth Circuit issued four stays of execution for Robert A. Harris, who was convicted of killing two sixteen-year-old boys for their car. After each stay of execution, the Supreme Court set it aside. Finally, the exasperated Supreme Court issued an order stating, "No further stays of Robert Alton Harris' execution shall be entered by the federal courts except upon order of this Court." Following the admonition from the highest court in the land, California executed Harris in San Quentin's gas chamber on the early morning of April 21, 1992.[11]

As throughout history where egregious crimes have often resulted in expansion of or adoption of death penalty laws, an egregious crime resulted in additional limitations on federal court access. On August 19, 1995, Timothy McVeigh set off a bomb in a truck destroying part of a federal office building in Oklahoma City, killing 168 people and injuring hundreds of others. Congress responded to the tragedy by passing bills that limited federal habeas corpus review of capital cases, with the goal to shorten the time between sentencing and execution. So, in 1996, in front of family members of victims of the Oklahoma City bombing and other terrorist incidents, President Bill Clinton signed into law the Antiterrorism and Effective Death Penalty Act (AEDPA). The new law had several effects, including that it expanded upon the Supreme Court's limits on federal habeas corpus review for ordinary crimes. For example, with AEDPA Congress further tightened the restrictions adopted in *McCleskey v. Zant* for petitioners filing a second habeas corpus petition. Although the law attempted to speed up executions, in some cases, a lack of clarity in drafting resulted in more litigation.[12]

During the same time President Clinton and Congress were working to expand the federal death penalty and to limit federal review of state capital cases, state courts also were limiting their review of capital cases. On April 10, 1995, Governor Zell Miller, the Georgia governor in office during Warren McCleskey's execution, signed the Death Penalty Habeas Corpus Reform Act of 1995 to speed up post-conviction review in the Georgia state courts.[13]

Meanwhile, as the number of crimes eligible for the death penalty grew and as the federal courts became less likely to review constitutional claims in capital cases, the number of executions increased. In the early years after *Gregg*, states executed prisoners at a slow pace, largely due to the logistics of the new post-*Furman* death penalty statutes. Because states had to start from scratch with their death penalty prosecutions under the new statutes, it took years for the prosecution, trial, appeals, and post-conviction process. Additionally, because *Furman* and *Gregg* changed the legal landscape significantly, those cases allowed for new constitutional challenges that had to be litigated before executions could begin.

Thus, although one execution occurred in the year following the *Gregg v. Georgia* decision, that execution went forward because the capital defendant, Gary Gilmore, was a "volunteer" for execution who gave up his appeals. The following year, in 1978, no executions occurred, and subsequent years saw few executions. (See Table 9.1.)

In the years following *McCleskey v. Kemp*, though, the number of executions grew significantly. This growth occurred partly because time had passed since states had started sentencing defendants to death after *Furman*. So, time allowed appeals to run out. Another reason for the increase in the number of executions was that *McCleskey* ended the broad attack on the death penalty that could slow down the rate of executions. Thus, the gradual acceleration that started after the decision in *Gregg v. Georgia* continued.[14] Judges could now allow executions to proceed without worrying that the death penalty would later be found unconstitutional.

After *McCleskey v. Kemp*, additional states began their own eras of post-*Furman* executions. States that resumed executions for the first time since 1976 in the 1990s included Arkansas (1990), Illinois (1990), Oklahoma (1990), Arizona (1992), California (1992), Delaware (1992), Wyoming (1992), Washington (1993), Idaho (1994), Maryland (1994), Nebraska (1994), Montana (1995), Pennsylvania (1995), Oregon (1996), Colorado (1997), Kentucky (1997), and Ohio (1999). Because most of the southern states had resumed executions in the 1980s, the majority of the states that became new executioners in the 1990s were western and midwestern states.[15]

Media outlets often focused on these firsts in the late 1980s and early 1990s while focusing less on subsequent routine executions. On September 10, 1990, at 12:35 am, Oklahoma executed Charles T. Coleman by lethal injection, marking that state's first execution since the execution of James D. French in 1966.[16] A few days after Coleman's execution, Illinois executed Charles Walker, who gave up his appeals, by lethal injection on September 12, 1990. It was Illinois's first execution in twenty-eight years.[17] When Arizona executed Don Harding in the gas chamber in April 1992, the case received extensive media attention and front-page local newspaper coverage leading up to the execution because it was the state's first post-*Furman* execution. But for the most part, individual executions received little attention, even locally, unless there was something unique about the case or execution. In the next several years after Harding's execution, as Arizona executed several more inmates, the executions began receiving less and less media attention.

Occasionally unusual cases garnered extra media attention. For example, on June 25, 1990, Arkansas executed Ronald G. Simmons, a volunteer for execution who had killed fourteen family members and two other people in 1987 in the largest mass killing of a family in U.S. history.[18]

Another early 1990s execution first that received some media attention occurred when Virginia executed Charles S. Stamper on January 19, 1993, marking the first wheelchair-bound person to be executed in the post-*Furman* era. Stamper, who was sentenced to death for killing three people during a 1978 restaurant robbery, became partially paralyzed after a fight with another death row inmate in 1988. Stamper's attorney argued Stamper no longer presented a danger to others, but Virginia governor Douglas Wilder did not grant clemency to Stamper. The inmate requested he be allowed to walk to his execution with leg braces and a walker. The state denied that request, so Stamper tried to walk on his own. But when his legs went into spasms, the guards had to drag and ultimately carry him into the execution chamber.[19]

Some cases revealed flaws in the capital punishment system. Randall Dale Adams had come within seventy-two hours of being executed before the U.S. Supreme Court overturned his death sentence in 1980, but he continued to languish in prison despite questions about his guilt. In 1988, filmmaker Errol Morris released *The Thin Blue Line*, a documentary about the case that revealed the injustice of Adams's conviction. Not much later, in March 1989, the Texas Court of Criminal Appeals set aside the conviction of Adams, finding a constitutional violation because the prosecutor failed to turn over helpful evidence and because the prosecutor knowingly used perjured testimony.[20]

While *The Thin Blue Line* raised questions about the criminal justice system, more often, the cases that received the most attention during the late 1980s and early 1990s were those that involved disturbed serial killers, helping to make the case for the death penalty. On January 24, 1989, Florida executed Ted Bundy in the state's electric chair. By the time of the execution, police suspected Bundy had killed more than thirty people. His case received widespread attention for a number of reasons. He was a handsome former law student who appeared intelligent and articulate. Yet, his crimes were frightening. He killed and raped a large number of young women, often initiated when he approached them feigning to ask for help or posing as a police officer. He often mutilated the bodies or decapitated them, and in several instances he kept the remains in his apartment. Other times he returned to the dead bodies and had sex with them.

Throughout his capital trials until his final days, Ted Bundy continued to try to manipulate the legal system, adding to the myths about his evil intelligence. Although he had dropped out of law school after doing poorly, and his lawyers questioned whether he was even competent to stand trial, he acted as his own attorney at his 1979 trial for bludgeoning to death Lisa Levy and Margaret Bowman, two sorority sisters at the Florida State University Chi Omega sorority house. He was convicted and sentenced to death for those crimes, and in 1980 he was convicted and sentenced to death for killing twelve-year-old Kimberly Leach. In his final days on death row in 1989, he unsuccessfully sought a delay in his execution in exchange for revealing the location of the bodies of victims of a number of other murders he claimed to have committed.[21]

Although there have been other heinous crimes, few capital defendants captured national attention the way that Ted Bundy did. But Bundy was white, he loved to attract media attention, and he looked like an intelligent middle class "boy next door." In short, one reason he became the poster boy for death row was because he was not the typical death row inmate.[22] Throughout his time on death row, many criminologists struggled to try to understand Bundy and his crimes. In the end, the experts had more questions than answers about how someone could commit such horrible acts.[23]

Many celebrated on the morning of Bundy's 1989 execution in Florida's electric chair. A large crowd gathered outside the prison in a carnival atmosphere, selling pins of the electric chair and bearing signs with slogans such as "Bundy BBQ." After officials announced Bundy was dead, some members of the crowd set off fireworks and sang, "Na Na Na Na, Na Na Na Na, Hey Hey Hey, Goodbye." Radio stations played songs with lyrics they thought relevant for the occasion, such as Peter Gabriel's "Shock the Monkey" and Eddy Grant's "Electric Avenue."[24] Soon after the execution, the supermarket tabloid *The Weekly World News* published a photo of Bundy's dead body.

Even after Bundy's death, his image lingered. Books, magazines, newspapers, and tabloids continued to invoke him. Wax museums created likenesses of him, and he inspired a ballet in Washington. As writer David Von Drehle explained in his book *Among the Lowest of the Dead: The Culture of Death Row*, "Bundy was such a powerful symbol that he lived beyond his physical death as a postmodern, suburban Lucifer."[25]

That description—with a clown costume—might describe John Wayne Gacy, another serial killer who came to national attention around the same time as Bundy did. Illinois officials tried Gacy in 1980, a year after Bundy's Florida trial. Unlike Bundy, whose victims were young women, Gacy was convicted of killing thirty-three young men and boys and burying many of their bodies in a crawl space under his home outside Chicago. During the six years that Gacy committed the murders, he simultaneously appeared to be a functioning member of society, working as a building contractor and participating in local politics. He also sometimes worked as a clown at children's parties, earning him the nickname from the media of "Killer Clown." While in prison, he painted a number of pictures, including some of his own clown character, Pogo the Clown, thus haunting everyone with a fear of clowns. Gacy spent fourteen years on death row before walking to his lethal injection gurney in May 1994.[26]

The majority of executions in the 1980s and 1990s did not receive the same attention as the executions of death row poster boys Bundy and Gacy. In the unusual cases of those two men, their crimes were horrendous, frightening, and random; their executions were widely celebrated. All murders are horrible, but the extent of the crimes and number of victims allowed the media to portray the two as evil monsters that needed to be destroyed. Throughout the 1980s and early 1990s, though, many others were executed who received much less attention because their crimes were less sensational. Yet, when one thought of the death penalty during the 1980s and early 1990s, the people who first came to mind were Bundy and Gacy.

Politicians recognized the power of such cases. When Florida governor Bob Martinez, ran for re-election in 1990, he stressed he had signed Bundy's death warrant. In one television ad, he focused on the death penalty issue, bragging, "I now have signed some 90 death warrants in the state of Florida." The commercial featured footage of a Florida crowd chanting "Burn, Bundy, Burn" outside the prison during Bundy's execution. Then, the commercial showed an image of Ted Bundy with a smirk on his face as Governor Martinez reminded the voters, "I believe in the death penalty...I believe it's the proper penalty for one who has taken someone else's life." Governor Martinez, however, lost the election.[27]

The number of executions continued to grow during this time, as did the size of death rows in the United States. Through the year 2000, the number of men and women on death rows in the United States continued to grow up to 3,593, the largest number of condemned in the post-*Furman* era. (See Table 17.1.)

Table 17.1. EXECUTIONS AND SIZE OF DEATH ROWS IN AMERICA AFTER *McCLESKEY V. KEMP*, 1988–2001[28]

YEAR	U.S. EXECUTIONS	SIZE OF U.S. DEATH ROWS
1988	11	2,124
1989	16	2,250
1990	23	2,356
1991	14	2,482
1992	31	2,575
1993	38	2,716
1994	31	2,890
1995	56	3,054
1996	45	3,219
1997	74	3.335
1998	68	3,452
1999	98	3,527
2000	85	3,593
2001	66	3,581

The growth in punishment in the 1980s and early 1990s was not limited to the death penalty. The prison population in the United States increased from 319,000 to 1.3 million during the years of 1980 to 2000. One of the reasons for the popularity of punishment, and in particular the death penalty, during much of the time period was an increase in crime. For example, as crack use peaked from 1987 to 1990, youth homicides dramatically increased around the country by 230 percent.[29]

By the time the Supreme Court decided *McCleskey v. Kemp*, the death penalty was already heavily politicized. As noted earlier, in California in 1986, Chief Justice Rose Bird and two other California Supreme Court justices were voted off the bench following a political campaign that focused on their votes in reversing death sentences.[30] Similarly, a decade later a number of groups in Tennessee campaigned against Justice Penny J. White of the state's supreme court because of one decision whereby she voted for a new death sentencing hearing. In a retention election, citizens then voted her off the bench.[31] One death penalty writer noted, "For several years it has been virtually impossible for any candidate for high elective office in the states—governor, attorney general, appellate court judge—to appear hesitant over (much less opposed to) the death penalty."[32]

The year after the Supreme Court decided *McCleskey v. Kemp*, race and capital punishment played a role in the U.S presidential campaign. In 1988, Vice President George H.W. Bush used Governor Michael Dukakis's opposition to the death penalty as part of Bush's campaign for president. Race and crime issues entered the campaign when a political group ran an ad condemning Dukakis as soft on crime. The television ad featured a mug shot of a black man with an afro, Willie Horton, who had escaped and raped a white woman while on a weekend pass as part of a Massachusetts furlough program. As governor, Dukakis had vetoed a bill to stop furloughs to convicted murderers such as Horton, so the ad effectively linked Dukakis to fears connected to race and violence. In this context, the TV ad also highlighted that Vice President Bush supported the death penalty and Governor Dukakis opposed capital punishment, linking his opposition to his act of releasing a dangerous black rapist from prison.[33]

Four years later, when President George H.W. Bush ran for re-election in 1992, the Democratic nominee for president made sure President Bush would not be able to use crime issues and the death penalty to his advantage. Arkansas governor Bill Clinton campaigned for president as a pro-death penalty candidate, and he one-upped President Bush by showing he would actually preside over executions.

In one Arkansas case during the campaign, Governor Clinton faced the decision of whether or not to allow the execution of a brain-damaged African-American inmate named Ricky Ray Rector. Rector had shot himself in the head after killing a police officer who was investigating another murder charge against Rector. Because Rector's self-inflicted shot caused permanent brain damage, Rector's attorneys argued the condemned should be granted clemency. Governor Clinton, who faced attacks about alleged extramarital relationships at the time, allowed the execution to proceed. Rector still claimed he planned to vote for Governor Clinton in the presidential election after his execution.

During Rector's execution on January 24, 1992, the execution team took more than fifty minutes to find a vein, while witnesses who could not see the proceedings could still hear Rector's moans during the process. Rector tried to help the medical team find a vein. Rector also had a practice of saving his desserts from his meals to eat some time after his dinner. After his execution, prison officials entered Rector's cell and discovered he had saved his dessert from his last meal to eat after his execution.[34]

Many politicians believed they had to support the death penalty if they wanted to stay in office. Andrew Young, a former civil rights activist, sought the Democratic nomination to run for governor of Georgia in 1990 on a platform supporting the death penalty, although he had previously opposed capital punishment.[35] He lost the nomination to Zell Miller, who would go on to win the general election. Had Young won, though, his devotion to civil rights and the death penalty would have been tested as he then would have been governor when Warren McCleskey went to the electric chair.

Politicians in state legislatures also showed support for the death penalty during this time period, as two abolitionist states passed laws bringing back capital punishment. In 1994, Kansas reinstated the death penalty. In 1995, after the election of a new governor who campaigned on a pledge to bring back the death penalty, New York reinstated capital punishment.[36]

The prejudices that were at work in the Baldus study used in *McCleskey v. Kemp* continued to operate. And biases and prejudices in death penalty cases also included factors outside the context of race. Just as anti-Semitism could be the basis for a lynching in Leo Frank's case, bias against other groups could operate in the courtroom in other cases. For example, in 1991, an Arizona jury found David Grannis guilty of capital murder and the judge sentenced him to death. Four years later, the Arizona Supreme Court reversed the conviction, finding the trial judge should not have allowed the prosecution to introduce photos owned by Grannis that showed homosexual activity because the jurors may have convicted him based upon his sexual orientation. On retrial in 1996, Pima County Superior Court judge Bernardo Valesco dismissed the murder charges because of insufficient evidence Grannis participated in the murder.[37]

During this period, as the death penalty thrived, defense lawyers and abolitionists attempted to slow down the growing use of capital punishment. The death penalty abolition movement had never stopped being active on all fronts, even if its emphasis had been on the courts for a period. For example, soon after the *Gregg* decision, the National Coalition Against the Death Penalty, later renamed the National Coalition to Abolish the Death Penalty, formed. Other organizations that fought against the death penalty included Amnesty International, the American Civil Liberties Union, the Southern Poverty Law Center, and the NAACP Legal Defense Fund. But while the death penalty abolition movement remained relatively small through the 1980s and early 1990s, the movement's activities slowly increased.[38]

Then, a shift occurred around the mid-1990s, and opposition to the death penalty began to grow. One study found that in the United States, support for the death penalty declined about 10 percent between 1993 and 1999,[39] and other studies found a similar trend.[40] This change resulted partly due to abolitionists and others adjusting their focus following McCleskey's execution, but other events also led to this swing. A new death penalty era was about to begin.

CHAPTER 18

New Abolitionist Voices in the 1990s

Warren McCleskey's execution haunted many people, including some of the Supreme Court jus-
tices. His execution and other factors prompted some to reconsider the death penalty. And as
death penalty lawyers and anti-death penalty activists evaluated the failures of the litigation
strategy, they began to focus on other approaches to limit the American death penalty.

After Georgia executed Warren McCleskey, capital defense attorneys continued to raise racial discrimination claims. Defense attorneys used the Baldus study and other similar studies to argue that the American death penalty is unfair and arbitrary. On the other side, death penalty proponents argued that a risk of racial bias did not mean that race dictated any specific individual outcome. And they continued to argue the racial discrepancies were a thing of the past.

But Warren McCleskey's case did not disappear. As new studies supported the results of the Baldus study, many people were troubled by the evidence of racial effects on capital sentencing. Although in *McCleskey v. Kemp*, the Supreme Court effectively rejected the use of such evidence for constitutional arguments, the case still disturbed many judges. More specifically, the decision in the case continued to haunt several of the Supreme Court justices who voted on McCleskey's case.

Many also recognized that *McCleskey v. Kemp* was the final blow for the litigation strategy to abolish the death penalty, so now much of the future of capital punishment would be determined outside the courtroom. In that case, Justice Powell had foreshadowed that abolition would need to come from legislatures when he noted, "McCleskey's arguments are best presented to the legislative bodies. It is not the responsibility—or indeed even the right—of this Court to determine the appropriate punishment for particular crimes."[1]

Attorneys and activists recognized the significance of McCleskey's case too. After the Supreme Court decided *McCleskey v. Kemp* in 1987, capital defense attorney David Bruck saw the decision as the final "ratification" that attempts to abolish the death penalty in the courts would fail. But he also predicted that *"McCleskey* will also prove to be the rebirth of abolition" as the anti-death penalty struggle would return to where it belonged: "in our legislatures, our churches, and our labor, professional and community organizations."[2]

Similarly, Richard "Dick" Burr, an LDF director who helped with McCleskey's case, addressed lawyers and law students in 1990, explaining that Supreme Court decisions like *McCleskey v. Kemp* meant that activist lawyers needed to target the political arena, an area "which we have eschewed for a long time." He advised, "We...have to begin to learn how to work in legislatures and advocate for people who are condemned to death."[3]

Many activists had been working outside the courtroom all along, but after *McCleskey v. Kemp*, they and other abolitionists began refocusing their efforts. At the same time, many policy makers also recognized that the Supreme Court was not going to solve all of the problems with the capital punishment system. So, in the next decade, debate about the death penalty began to grow outside the courtroom.

Starting in the 1990s, important voices began speaking about the problems with the capital punishment system. One group of voices came out of the ruins of the abolition litigation strategy, as judges and others in the legal system began targeting an audience outside the courtroom. These critics argued that the capital punishment laws created after *Furman* and *Gregg* did not create a fair death penalty. Another voice opposing capital punishment, consistent with Bruck's reference to churches, came from a nun with a surprise best-selling book.

* * *

Although authors have written many books about the death penalty, Sister Helen Prejean's 1993 book *Dead Man Walking* stands out. The book was unique, not only because of its unusual author—a nun—but because it did not languish in obscurity. Instead, it went on to become a bestseller. Then, director Tim Robbins made the book into a popular movie in 1995. Actress Susan Sarandon, who portrayed Sister Prejean in the film, appealed for a "way to nonviolently end violence and heal" when she won an Academy Award for Best Actress for the role.[4] In 2000, the book also was made into an opera.[5]

Dead Man Walking became one of the first post-*McCleskey* successes for the death penalty abolition movement. It helped show that even if the litigation strategy to abolish capital punishment had failed, other avenues existed.

In her book, Sister Prejean takes the reader on her personal journey as she goes from knowing nothing about capital punishment to becoming intimately involved as she gets to know capital defendants and the families of murder victims. She recalls driving to Angola Prison in Louisiana with a capital defense attorney who explained that the man they were going to visit probably would not be on death row had he killed a black person. She describes how she witnesses the role of race in the criminal justice system, and she uses *McCleskey v. Kemp* to educate her readers about problems with the death penalty.[6]

Sister Prejean's book ranks with a handful of other significant anti-death penalty books or essays. Cesare Beccaria's *Dei delitti e delle pene*, or *Of Crime and*

Punishments,[7] which condemned capital punishment, influenced France and the world after its publication in 1764.[8] Other influential publications include Victor Hugo's *Le dernier jour d'un condamne (The Last Day of a Condemned Man)*, which helped reopen the death penalty debate in nineteenth century France,[9] and the 1957 book *Reflexions sur la peine Capitale*, a symposium by Hungarian-British author Arthur Koestler and French author and philosopher Albert Camus.[10]

In the United States, on other topics, there have been similar landmark books, such as Upton Sinclair's *The Jungle*, a novel that exposed life in Chicago's stockyards, and Rachel Carson's *Silent Spring*, a book that raised the level of environmental concern in this country. In some ways, one might argue *Dead Man Walking* is to the current death penalty abolition movement what Harriet Beecher Stowe's *Uncle Tom's Cabin* was to the slavery abolition movement. When President Abraham Lincoln met Ms. Stowe, he reportedly greeted her by saying, "So this is the little lady who made this big war?"[11] Similarly, one might argue Sister Prejean helped change the perception of the American death penalty.

Some debated about the message of the film version of Prejean's book. Capital defense attorney Millard Farmer detected a pro-death penalty approach that would result in more executions and called the movie "More Dead Men Coming."[12] Professor Austin Sarat of Amherst College claimed the movie "legitimates capital punishment" because it does not ask the viewer "to do more than comfortably embrace the conceptual categories of responsibility and representation that justify the apparatus of criminal punishment and keep the machinery of state killing in place and operating."[13]

But both the movie and the book inspired debate about the death penalty issue. Where once many accepted the punishment as the unquestionable "law," the book and movie raised questions about capital punishment, as had the 1958 movie *I Want to Live*, which featured Susan Hayward's Academy-Award-winning performance about the life and execution of Barbara Graham. Also, perhaps because of the success of the book and movie, popular culture embraced the issue as one that would sell in subsequent movies and television shows. Thus, the death penalty debate continued to be out in the open, raising questions.

The *Dead Man Walking* book and movie were important to the anti-death penalty movement because conservatives could not easily dismiss the works as liberal arguments against the death penalty. Although death penalty advocates sometimes claim reformers are not sufficiently concerned with the victims of violent crimes, both the book and the movie devoted substantial time to the victims' families. The movie juxtaposed an execution with the murder of the victims. And the book ended by focusing on the father of one of the victims struggling to continue to forgive the murderer of his son. Thus, the works attempted to show the issue and the accompanying complex human emotions.

Although one could disagree with Sister Prejean's conclusions about the death penalty, one could not dismiss her honest personal experience. Because the book told a compelling story, it succeeded commercially and helped raise questions about the death penalty outside the courtroom.

Around the time of the release of the book and the movie, other people spoke out against the death penalty. Some of these voices, which came from judges and others involved in the legal system, had an impact similar to Sister Prejean's book.

* * *

When the United States Supreme Court first addressed the Eighth Amendment challenges to the death penalty in 1972, Justice William J. Brennan, Jr. and Justice Thurgood Marshall reasoned that the death penalty violated the Constitution. Throughout the rest of their terms—until Justice Brennan retired in July 1990 and Justice Marshall retired in June 1991, they each continued to dissent in every subsequent case that upheld a death sentence. The main ground for Justice Brennan's and Justice Marshall's opposition to the death penalty was that the punishment unnecessarily degraded human dignity. In *Furman*, three other justices did agree with them that states imposed the death penalty arbitrarily, but no other justices joined them four years later in dissenting in *Gregg v. Georgia* when the Court upheld the new death penalty statutes. Throughout the rest of their terms, no other justice matched them in their complete opposition to the death penalty.

Not long after the release of Sister Helen Prejean's book, however, another Supreme Court justice concluded the death penalty violated the Constitution. Justice Harry Blackmun had joined the majority in *Gregg* in upholding the death penalty and had overseen the development of the new death penalty laws for more than twenty years. But, in 1994 in *Callins v. Collins*, he changed his position. (See Figure 18.1.)

As Justice Blackmun neared retirement, he wrote several opinions critical of the death penalty. In 1986, Justice Blackmun became frustrated with several of his colleagues about the way the Court almost did not grant a stay of execution even after garnering enough votes to grant review of *Darden v. Wainwright*, a case where the prosecutor had called the African-American Darden an "animal." The case even prompted some arguments with his old friend Chief Justice Burger.[14] In *Sawyer v. Whitley*, published in 1992 not long after Warren McCleskey's execution, Blackmun criticized the Court's standards for habeas corpus review in capital cases. He noted his "ever-growing skepticism that, with each new decision from this Court constricting the ability of the federal courts to remedy constitutional errors, the death penalty really can be imposed fairly and in accordance with the requirements of the Eighth Amendment."[15]

In 1993 in *Herrera v. Collins*, Justice Blackmun addressed colleagues who reasoned that innocence by itself could not establish an Eighth Amendment claim in habeas corpus proceedings. He wrote: "I have voiced disappointment over this Court's obvious eagerness to do away with any restriction on the States' power to execute whomever and however they please....Of one thing, however, I am certain. Just as an execution without adequate safeguards is unacceptable, so too is an execution when the condemned prisoner can prove that he is innocent. The execution of a person who can show that he is innocent comes perilously close to simple murder."[16]

Figure 18.1
Justice Harry A. Blackmun (Collection of the Supreme Court of the United States)

But perhaps no single capital case had more of an impact on Justice Blackmun than Warren McCleskey's. McCleskey's 1991 execution disturbed Blackmun greatly. The morning after the execution, he sat at breakfast writing about problems with the death penalty. After McCleskey's execution, Blackmun began looking for the best case to use those notes.[17]

During the 1993 term, not long after McCleskey's execution, one of Justice Blackmun's law clerks, Andrew H. Schapiro, recognized that the justice's recent opinions had become critical of the death penalty and asked him to consider finding the death penalty unconstitutional. Justice Blackmun agreed, and then he and his clerks worked on the draft and looked for a run-of-the-mill capital case without any other issues.[18] So, when the Supreme Court declined review of a capital case in *Callins v. Collins*, Blackmun incorporated his work into a February 22, 1994 dissenting opinion for the case. And then he took the unusual added step of announcing his decision orally from the bench, proclaiming to the world, "From this day forward, I no longer shall tinker with the machinery of death."[19]

In *Callins*, Justice Blackmun explained that the post-*Furman* decisions did not adequately curb the arbitrariness and discrimination that were at issue in that case. "It seems that the decision whether a human being should live or die is so inherently subjective—rife with all of life's understandings, experiences, prejudices, and passions—that it inevitably defies the rationality and consistency required by the Constitution."[20] He concluded that *Furman*'s constitutional requirement to eliminate arbitrariness could not be reconciled with the *Lockett v. Ohio* constitutional requirement that each defendant be considered as an individual. Therefore, the system could not work. Additionally, he believed the Court had "retreated from the field" by limiting the power of federal courts to review death sentences.[21] He concluded by predicting that one day the death penalty will be abolished, warning "[t]he path the Court has chosen lessens us all."[22]

In his *Callins* opinion, Justice Blackmun directly referenced *McCleskey v. Kemp*. He reasoned that because juries in capital cases must be given some discretion in evaluating mitigating circumstances, capital cases allowed too much opportunity for discrimination on race and other improper factors. He recalled that despite the "staggering evidence of racial prejudice infecting Georgia's capital sentencing scheme, the majority turned its back on McCleskey's claims, . . . unable to stamp out the virus of racism."[23]

Although no other justice joined Justice Blackmun's opinion and Justice Antonin Scalia wrote a concurring opinion to respond to the dissent, one of the other justices told Justice Blackmun in private that he or she was proud of him for writing the opinion. Justice Brennan, who had been retired for four years, called and left a message for Justice Blackmun, thanking him for "the present." Later, after Texas executed Bruce Callins in 1997, the condemned man's sister wrote Justice Blackmun to tell him what his dissent had meant to her brother.[24]

Following *Callins*, Justice Blackmun dissented from every case affirming a death sentence until he retired later that term. The reason for his newfound conclusion that "the death penalty experiment has failed"[25] was not based upon his long-standing moral concerns about the death penalty, but upon the unfairness of the sentencing and legal review process.

Around the same time as the *Callins* decision, another former Supreme Court justice revealed he had changed his mind about the death penalty, and in particular about Warren McCleskey's case. Like Justice Blackmun, Justice Lewis Powell was one of the *Furman* dissenters and was one of the *Gregg* justices upholding the death penalty. When his biographer John Jeffries asked Justice Powell if he regretted any of his votes on the Court, Powell responded that he regretted his decision in *McCleskey v. Kemp*, where he was the deciding vote and authored the majority opinion. When Jeffries asked Powell if that meant Powell would make his decision based on statistics, Powell responded, "No, I would vote the other way in any capital case." After noting that meant he would now vote against the death penalty in *Gregg v. Georgia* too, Powell explained, "Yes, I have come to think that capital punishment should be abolished." Powell's biographer wrote, "Justice Powell's experience taught him that the death penalty cannot be decently administered."[26]

The statements by Blackmun and Powell were significant because the justices could not be dismissed as liberals who always voted against the death penalty. The truth was more complex. Although Justice Blackmun ended up as one of the more progressive justices on the Court at the time he retired, Justice Powell often voted with the conservative members of the Court. Both justices had been appointed by President Nixon as part of his campaign pledge to change the liberal Warren Court. As for Blackmun's appointment to the Court, "Nixon found Blackmun's moderate conservatism perfect.... He had academic credentials, practical legal experience in the Middle West, and a predictable, solid body of opinions that demonstrated a levelheaded strict-constructionist philosophy." [27] Before his term on the Court, Justice Powell had served on President's Johnson's Crime Commission, and wrote in a minority report that the Warren Court had "swung the pendulum too far" giving rights to criminal defendants.[28]

Ultimately, Justices Blackmun and Powell focused their death penalty attacks on issues besides moral arguments. Although Blackmun did express moral reservations about the punishment, the reasons that Blackmun and Powell now found the punishment unconstitutional were procedural. The death penalty system in the United States was unfair, discriminatory, and arbitrary. Although these attacks had been made on the death penalty before, they were often made as extraneous arguments by abolitionists who were morally opposed to the death penalty. Here, Blackmun's arguments were not tied to nebulous moral or philosophical grounds, but instead were connected to concrete legal concerns. Professor Austin Sarat wrote that Justice Blackmun made an important attack on the death penalty because it was not based on popular opinion or moral grounds, which may be debated, but derived from fairness concerns that came out of the litigation arguments made by capital defense attorneys. [29]

The media reported on the justices' conversions, often quoting Justice Blackmun's statement about no longer tinkering with the death machinery. Justice Blackmun had initially kept his planned repudiation of the death penalty from the other justices. He knew he could not win over his colleagues to his position, so he aimed his words at people outside the Court. Still, perhaps his words eventually did have some influence on his colleagues.

A number of years later, one of the justices who was serving her first term when Justice Blackmun wrote his *Callins* opinion announced that as a matter of policy she supported a moratorium on executions. In April 2001, in a lecture in Maryland, Justice Ruth Bader Ginsburg said she would be "glad to see" Maryland pass a moratorium bill, adding, "People who are well represented at trial do not get the death penalty."[30] Eventually, Justice Ginsburg went further in her public statements, when during a talk to law students at the University of California Hastings College of Law a decade later, she said before she retired she would like to see the Court return to its position in *Furman v. Georgia* that "the death penalty could not be administered with an even hand." She explained, though, that she did not follow other justices who ruled that the death penalty was unconstitutional, because she thought she could be more influential by participating in the capital punishment decisions.[31]

Similarly, in July 2001, Justice Sandra Day O'Connor revealed she believed there are "serious questions" about whether the death penalty is administered fairly. In a speech before the Minnesota Women Lawyers association, she noted the possibility that innocent persons have been executed, adding that the residents of Minnesota "must breathe a big sigh of relief every day" because that state does not have the death penalty.[32] Her statement was particularly compelling because unlike Justice Blackmun who often agonized over cases and would doubt himself, Justice O'Connor was one of the most decisive justices who stuck firm to her opinions. In her Court chambers, she had a pillow featuring the embroidered words, "Maybe in Error But Never in Doubt."[33] Apparently, the years of death penalty cases eventually did create some doubt.

These Supreme Court justices are not the only members of the bench to criticize the death penalty. Perhaps following the lead of Justice Blackmun, several lower court judges—including several chief justices of states' highest courts—began to speak out against the death penalty in the 1990s, usually targeting an audience outside the courtroom. Their statements impacted others because the judges were credible persons who had intimate knowledge of the death penalty process in the United States.

In 1998, the Chief Justice of the Florida Supreme Court began speaking out against the death penalty during his final six months on the bench. Chief Justice Gerald Kogan, a former prosecutor who had been appointed to the court by a pro-death penalty governor, came to believe the death penalty system was too cumbersome and took too much of the court's time. As a prosecutor and judge, he had been involved in about 1,200 capital cases. Chief Justice Kogan did not oppose the death penalty on moral grounds, but he noted, "There is always that doubt that lingers in your mind whether these people are innocent."[34]

Similarly, former chief judge of the North Carolina Supreme Court James Exum Jr. stated that the death penalty "cheapens the rest of us; it brutalizes the rest of us; and we become a more violent society."[35] Charles F. Baird, who served as a judge on the Texas Court of Criminal Appeals for eight years, spoke out against the death penalty by saying, "I saw cases where there were serious concerns as to the guilt or innocence...I saw cases where...lawyers were actually sleeping through portions of the trial."[36]

Ohio Supreme Court Justice Paul E. Pfeifer, who had co-written Ohio's death penalty law as the Republican chairman of the Ohio Senate Judiciary Committee in 1981, announced on February 17, 1999, that he questioned the effectiveness of the death penalty. Noting long delays in carrying out executions undermines any deterrence or retribution functions of the death penalty, Justice Pfeifer also said he had become sympathetic to arguments that the death penalty is immoral.[37] As Ohio prepared to execute Wilford Berry, whose sentence had been upheld by Justice Pfeifer, the justice stated, "I guess I've come to the conclusion the state would be better off without [the death penalty] and should impose a life sentence without the possibility of parole." Although he explained he would continue to vote to uphold death sentences in cases where warranted, he revealed, "Knowing what I know now, my name would not have been on" Ohio's death penalty statute.[38]

Justice Pfeifer continued to speak out against capital punishment and later wrote an editorial explaining he changed his mind about the death penalty because it does not function in practice as he had hoped. The state legislature intended the death penalty to apply narrowly, but instead it came "to be applied more pervasively" than the drafters intended. Additionally, the drafters had hoped the Ohio Supreme Court would ensure death sentences in the state were applied evenly and fairly, but that had not happened either. Finally, he reasoned that "life without parole now offers us a viable alternative to the death penalty" and that Ohio should abolish capital punishment.[39]

Other state court judges continued to enforce the death penalty while criticizing it. In 2000 another Ohio judge, Cuyahoga County Common Pleas Judge Daniel Gaul, denounced the death penalty to reporters a day after sentencing a man to death.[40] Chief Justice Thomas Zlaket of the Arizona Supreme Court stated he believed the death penalty system does not work, but like Justice Pfeifer and Judge Gaul, he still followed the law in upholding death sentences.[41] His experience with the death penalty, however, led him to state, "I have the feeling that life and death is something for God to decide, not man."[42]

Chief Justice Moses Harrison of the Supreme Court of Illinois opined that the death penalty system has so many problems that it violates the United States and Illinois constitutions. In *People v. Bull*, he voted to overturn a death sentence and wrote that "when a system is as prone to error as ours is, we should not be making irrevocable decisions about any human life."[43] Former Kentucky Supreme Court justice Joseph Lambert also criticized the punishment because the capital cases become "legal monsters." He explained "it's impossible to streamline death-penalty litigation to justify the cost, because doing so would dramatically increase the risk of wrongful executions."[44]

In 2001 in *State v. Timmendequas*, Justice Virginia Long of the Supreme Court of New Jersey called for a moratorium on the death penalty in that state. In condemning the state's proportionality review system, she stated, "It is time for the members of this Court to accept that there is simply no meaningful way to distinguish between one grotesque murder and another for the purpose of determining why one defendant has been granted a life sentence and another is awaiting execution."[45]

Federal judges in the lower federal courts criticized the death penalty too. In 1997 in *Singleton v. Norris*, Judge Gerald Heaney of the U.S. Court of Appeals for the Eighth Circuit joined the majority in upholding a death sentence, but he wrote a concurring opinion "to add my voice to those who oppose the death penalty as violative of the United States Constitution."[46] Although he stated he must follow the law, he announced his own view after thirty years on the court "that this nation's administration of capital punishment is simply irrational, arbitrary and unfair."[47] Similarly, U.S. District Judge Michael Ponsor wrote he would enforce the death penalty as law, but warned that problems in the system make it inevitable an innocent person will be executed.[48]

Conservative judge Alex Kozinski of the United States Court of Appeals for the Ninth Circuit supports the death penalty, but in 1995 he argued for limiting it. He explained, "We have constructed a machine that is extremely expensive, chokes our legal institutions, visits repeated trauma on victims' families and ultimately produces nothing like the benefits we would expect from an effective system of capital punishment."[49]

Unlike United States Court of Appeals for the Eleventh Circuit Judge Robert S. Vance, who opposed the death penalty but affirmed a number of capital convictions,[50] some judges believed the United States' capital punishment system was so flawed that they could no longer participate in that system. After Colorado changed its death penalty law to require judges instead of juries to do the sentencing of capital defendants, District Judge Michael Heydt resigned because he found the new law "manifestly unworkable."[51]

Also, Justice Robert F. Utter resigned from the Washington Supreme Court in 1995 after twenty-three years on that court because of concerns about the death penalty. Justice Utter explained that his experience convinced him that the death penalty applies unfairly to racial minorities and the poor. Although as a prosecutor he sought the death penalty for some defendants, Justice Utter began questioning the death penalty when he presided over a trial more than thirty years earlier as a superior court judge: "That was the beginning of my questioning whether any human being is wise enough to decide who should die. Everything I've seen in the system since then has convinced me that we're not." Justice Utter continued speaking out against the death penalty after he resigned from the bench, calling on the state of Washington to abolish capital punishment.[52]

While there always had been judges and other prominent people critical of the death penalty, the attacks in the 1990s and later years were the voices of people who had seen the new post-*Furman* death penalty in action. The critiques were important to those who wanted to limit the use of the death penalty. In 1996 in *Against Capital Punishment*, Professor Haines recognized that if abolitionists were to start making progress against the death penalty "[t]hey must gain at least certain minimum levels of support and participation from sectors of American society that have heretofore either supported capital punishment or have been apathetic about it."[53] In a relatively short period of time, a number of former death penalty supporters spoke out against the death penalty.[54]

Many prominent voices—some of which were surprising—joined the judges criticizing the death penalty. Around the same time Justice Pfeifer called for Ohio to abolish the death penalty, other leaders from the state joined him. Former state prisons director Terry Collins came out against the death penalty. Later, Ohio Catholic Church leaders requested the state abandon the use of capital punishment.[55] In addition to Reverend Jerry Falwell taking the position that Karla Faye Tucker should not be executed, other unexpected voices raised concerns about the death penalty. George Will, Bill O'Reilly, and other conservative journalists questioned the use of the punishment. Also, Reverend Pat Robertson, a death penalty supporter, advocated for a moratorium on executions.[56]

Similarly, in addition to the judges discussed above, politicians spoke out against the death penalty—perhaps because they no longer feared the political repercussions once thought to accompany an opposition to it. For example, legislators in various states supported bills imposing a moratorium on executions. In Maryland, two prominent Baltimore political figures—Mayor Kurt L. Schmoke and Delegate Howard P. Rawlings—took out an ad in the Baltimore Sun in May 2000 to urge Maryland governor Parris N. Glendening to impose a moratorium on the death penalty in that state.[57] In Virginia, a conservative Republican in the state legislature who once supported a bill to resume public hangings, in 2001 introduced a bill to abolish the death penalty. In New Hampshire, state representative Loren Jean, a former deputy sheriff who had been in favor of the death penalty, co-sponsored a bill to repeal it in that state.[58]

In New York, several prosecutors were critical of the state's decision to bring back the death penalty in 1995. Manhattan District Attorney Robert M. Morgenthau stated, "The death penalty will be a major impediment to law enforcement, because of the cost, time spent and diversion of resources away from the prosecution of other crimes."[59] Bronx District Attorney Robert T. Johnson expressed concern that innocent persons would be executed and that race would be a factor in sentencing. Other prosecutors worried about the role of politics in the use of the death penalty and the added economic cost of prosecuting capital cases.[60]

Other current and former law enforcement officers spoke out against the death penalty too. In February 2000, a group of twenty-five former and current Missouri law enforcement officials took a position against the death penalty, and identified more effective alternatives to capital punishment. In the same year, judges, former prosecutors, and victim advocates formed The National Committee to Prevent Wrongful Executions. The coalition was formed to study how to prevent the execution of the innocent and to examine proposals such as instituting a national moratorium or imposing standards for defense counsel.[61]

Other officials connected to the death penalty process also raised concerns. In October 2000, Ed Leyva, a former member of the Arizona Board of Executive Clemency who had denied clemency to several death row inmates, became opposed to capital punishment when he realized the death penalty does not deter crime and "[l]ife is precious."[62] Charles Terrell, a former chairman of the Texas Department of Criminal Justice, asked that his name be removed from the prison's Terrell Unit that houses death row because the association made him uncomfortable due to concerns with the way capital punishment is administered. The state changed the unit's name in July 2001.[63]

Although overall the death penalty remained popular, as some politicians spoke out against the death penalty in the 1990s and early 2000s, it signaled a shift regarding the politics of capital punishment. While in the 1980s many politicians feared political consequences if they opposed the death penalty, by 2000 many no longer believed death penalty opposition was a liability. Further, strong support for capital punishment might even be a liability. For example, as pro-death-penalty Texas governor George W. Bush ran for president, *The Wall Street Journal* imagined that the "national shift in the politics of capital punishment" had the possibility of creating "unexpected complications" for Governor Bush's presidential campaign.[64]

During this same time, other high-profile individuals added their voice to attacks on the death penalty, lending added credibility to critics of the punishment. One important statement appeared in March 1995, when Pope John Paul II criticized the death penalty in his *Evangelium Vitae*. In the encyclical, he clarified that the Catholic Church's position condemns capital punishment in modern times because the only time the death penalty would be acceptable would be if it were the only way to defend society. He also noted there was "a growing public opposition to the death penalty."[65]

Celebrities Harry Belafonte, Mike Farrell, Danny Glover, Kenny Rogers, Michelle Shocked, Bruce Springsteen, and other musicians and actors spoke out against the death penalty.[66] Musician Steve Earle wrote several songs about the death penalty. In one song about a death row inmate released the year before McCleskey's execution, "Billy Austin," he incorporated the racial discrimination argument highlighted in *McCleskey v. Kemp*. The song's condemned character notes that most of the men on death row with him are "black, brown and poor."[67]

Another important voice against the death penalty that grew louder during the post-*McCleskey* years came from families of murder victims. For example, a group of relatives of murder victims joined with relatives of death row inmates in Virginia in April 2000 to call for a moratorium on executions.[68] Further, the organization Murder Victims' Families for Reconciliation (MVFR), an abolitionist organization of the families of murder victims that formed in the 1970s, continued to speak out against the death penalty. MVFR acts as a support group for relatives of people who were killed by a person or by the state.[69] Throughout the 1990s, MVFR sponsored the Journey of Hope, which consisted of events focusing on the death penalty, in various states.[70]

A mini-opera used Warren McCleskey as its centerpiece. In the cantata, *The Final Statement of Warren McCleskey*, composer Scott Robinson set McCleskey's execution, including his final words, to music. Robinson noted that "McCleskey's style of speaking is lyrical; it has a liturgical rhythm." The composition featured a mixed chorus for McCleskey's words, a baritone soloist singing the part of the warden, and a tenor singing the part of the chaplain. In a February 1995 performance, the singers were accompanied by a piano, English horn, viola, and timpani. The mini-opera about McCleskey focused on themes of forgiveness and redemption.[71]

Overall, the death penalty still remained popular in most states through the 1990s and into the 2000s. Many politicians and others continued to support capital punishment, such as the Florida State senator who interpreted the cross-shaped bloodstain on an executed inmate's shirt as a sign God blessed Florida's execution policy.[72] But new critiques attacked the post-*Furman* death penalty system, often using the same arguments that had been used by capital defense attorneys from the 1960s through Warren McCleskey's case. Thus, while McCleskey's lawyers failed to get the Supreme Court to strike down the death penalty, the arguments from *McCleskey v. Kemp* and other cases began popping up in the public discussion of the death penalty outside the courtrooms.

In the 1990s and continuing to today, a number of judges, politicians, and others began questioning the modern American death penalty, expressing their concerns publicly. One attorney predicted that even more judges will develop doubts about capital punishment as they continue to recognize that the death penalty is not just a criminal policy issue but has become a political issue.[73] Thus, the new voices continue to affect others, and new discoveries of innocent people on death row would add fuel to the anti-death penalty fire.

CHAPTER 19

Innocence and the American Death Penalty

Warren McCleskey's attorneys raised questions about McCleskey's role in the Dixie Furniture Company murder, just as throughout American history many capital defendants claimed they were innocent. After McCleskey v. Kemp, *new scientific breakthroughs and diligent work exonerated some prisoners, adding to the debate about whether the American death penalty had ever led to the execution of an innocent person.*

When the Supreme Court justices were discussing the racial discrimination issue in Warren McCleskey's case, Justice Thurgood Marshall told the other justices a story. He recalled from his attorney days representing an innocent African-American man accused of rape in the South. Marshall knew his client did not commit the crime, but while the jury was deciding the case, the judge explained to the people in the courtroom what would happen when the jury returned. He told everyone that after the sentence was announced, the bailiff would take the defendant back to jail. Surprised by the assumption the innocent man would be taken away, Marshall asked the judge about the possibility the jury would find his black client not guilty. The judge looked at Marshall and asked, "Are you kidding?" The jurors convicted Marshall's client and sentenced him to death. While some of the justices were moved by Marshall's story, it did not change any votes.[1]

Although Justice Marshall's appeal to his colleagues failed, he recognized that even if people were not moved by stories of racial bias in the death penalty system, they might be outraged by stories about innocent people being sentenced to death. Other people opposed to the death penalty have reached the same conclusion.

After the capital defense lawyers lost in *McCleskey v. Kemp*, death penalty abolitionists realized the race claims alone would not eliminate the death penalty. Although death penalty litigation continued to play an important role in strategies to prevent executions, abolitionists understood that *McCleskey v. Kemp* ended any remaining hope the Supreme Court would stop executions. And, while racial discrimination continued to trouble many, the abolitionists recognized that when faced with news about a gruesome crime, many Americans would not care about racial discrimination.

The answer for the death penalty abolitionists rested in McCleskey's other claims and in his other Supreme Court case, *McCleskey v. Zant*. In that case, procedural rules barred the courts from reviewing arguments challenging McCleskey's guilt. Abolitionists wondered how many capital defendants on death row were innocent and how many had innocence claims that might otherwise be barred by procedural rules. Most important, science had advanced since the time of McCleskey's trial, and new scientific evidence could be used in some cases to prove innocence. Thus, cases in the 1990s and the early twenty-first century raised awareness and concerns about executing innocent capital defendants.

Even though new discoveries affected the death penalty debate starting in the 1990s, innocence arguments go back through world history. For centuries, execution opponents asserted there was a risk that innocent people could be executed, but others confidently disputed those claims. In 1935, a writer in *The New Yorker* discounted the risk of wrongful executions, noting, "The vision of American criminal law as a ravening monster, forever hounding innocent people into the electric chair, is one with which emotional persons like to chill their blood. It is a substitute for tales of ghosts and goblins."[2]

Although innocence has been a concern throughout U.S. history, the amount of emphasis on the innocence issue in comparison to other death penalty arguments has varied at different times. During some historical periods, other issues predominated. For example, in the early 1800s, much of the debate about capital punishment focused on whether or not executions should be done in public. In the early 1900s, arguments against the death penalty often focused on connections to prison reform and to broader political and social changes taking place during the Progressive Era.

The impact of the horrors of World War II led to increased concerns about the risk of executing innocent defendants in the years following the war, although much of the debate about the death penalty in the 1950s and 1960s focused on issues besides innocence. And when the Court decided *Furman v. Georgia* in 1972, the justices paid little attention to concerns about wrongful executions.[3] Arguments that predominated in the 1960s through the early 1970s included the issue of the arbitrary use of the death penalty and the issue of racial discrimination that would eventually be addressed by the Supreme Court in Warren McCleskey's case.

Innocence, however, never completely faded out of the death penalty debate. In the United States in the 1820s, Edward Livingston raised concerns about executing innocent defendants, and others raised similar fears throughout the nineteenth and twentieth centuries. Similarly, arguments relating to innocence did not disappear in the 1960s and 1970s and often were reshaped into constitutional issues instead of moral ones.[4]

As throughout history where unusual cases or executions often shaped the death penalty debate, innocence arguments often arose because of specific cases. A number of pre-*Furman* cases raised innocence issues, such as the Salem "witches," Lincoln assassination co-conspirator Mary Surratt, union organizer Joe Hill, and others. But the most famous U.S. wrongful execution case is the 1927 execution of Nicola Sacco and Bartolomeo Vanzetti, which was discussed in chapter 5. While scholars still debate whether one or both of the men were actually innocent, the execution of the two exposed problems with the capital punishment system.[5] After the execution of Sacco and Vanzetti, Massachusetts reformed its review procedures, and today, partly due to Sacco and Vanzetti, Massachusetts does not have the death penalty.[6]

Other famous pre-*Furman* American alleged wrongful execution cases include those of Bruno Hauptmann, who as discussed in chapter 5 was executed for the Lindbergh baby kidnapping in 1936, and Ethel and Julius Rosenberg, who as discussed in chapter 6 were executed in 1953 for conspiracy to commit espionage. While many today conclude that both Hauptmann and the Rosenbergs (or at least Julius) were guilty, both trials and convictions were tainted, respectively, by anti-German and anti-communist fears.[7] Thus, the Rosenbergs case and the Hauptmann case, like the Sacco and Vanzetti one, were marked by errors and prejudice so that even those who believe the defendants were guilty are still troubled by the unfairness and biases in the process that condemned them.

Innocence issues can play an important role in abolition of the death penalty. For example, an alleged wrongful execution helped Great Britain abolish the death penalty. Derek Bentley, a nineteen-year-old, was executed in 1953 for his role in the murder of a London police officer. After the officer caught Bentley during a robbery, Bentley shouted, "Let him have it!" to his robbery accomplice, who then shot and killed the officer. During the trial, lawyers debated whether Bentley meant that his accomplice should give the gun to the officer or whether he was encouraging him to shoot. Bentley was convicted and executed while the young accomplice who shot the officer received a prison sentence.[8] The case helped inspire Great Britain to abolish capital punishment during the following decade.

At the same time in the United States, the pre-*Furman* executions revealed a variety of problems with the American death penalty. Although many had more faith in the post-*Furman* death penalty, after *McCleskey v. Kemp*, innocence became an even bigger part of the American death penalty debate.

Beginning in the late 1980s, innocence issues grew in importance. In the year after *McCleskey v. Kemp* was decided, a 1987 law review article by Hugo Adam Bedau and Michael L. Radelet emphasized the risk of executing innocent capital defendants.[9] The article, and later their book with Constance E. Putnam, identified a large number of cases where defendants had been wrongly convicted of capital offenses. The authors concluded that twenty-three defendants in the twentieth century had been wrongfully executed.[10] Their research had a broad impact, sparking discussion and debate about their findings. Similarly, organizations such as the Death Penalty Information Center have continued to keep track of innocence cases.

* * *

Although the innocence issue in the 1990s connected to a long history, that decade's innocence arguments were also unique. After less than two decades since *Gregg*, enough people had been sentenced to death for opponents to find prisoners among them who were arguably innocent. Also, after the *McCleskey v. Kemp* loss for the litigation abolition strategy, activists recognized they should focus even more on innocence cases. And importantly, new DNA science along with a growth in Innocence Projects and other innocence-oriented groups led to important revelations.

Thus, society discovered inmates on death rows around the country who were innocent or likely innocent. Between 1973 and 2000, states released 91 prisoners from death row after new evidence indicated the prisoners were innocent, and by the end of 2013, that number grew further to 143 exonerated.[11] In 2012, a report by the National Registry of Exonerations, a joint project of the University of Michigan Law School and the Center on Wrongful Convictions at Northwestern University School of Law, concluded that U.S. courts have had an error rate in capital cases of between 2.5 percent and 4 percent for the last twenty years. Similarly, a 2014 study asserted that 4.1 percent of death row defendants are wrongfully convicted.[12]

In the 1990s, newspapers began reporting more on the innocence discoveries too. For example, in November 1999, the *Chicago Tribune* ran a series entitled "The Failure of the Death Penalty in Illinois." The series considered the reasons innocent people ended up on that state's death row. The *National Review* explained that the *Tribune* series "examined each of the state's nearly 300 capital cases and found these trials were routinely riddled with bias and error, including incompetent legal work by the defense lawyers, and that prosecutors relied on dubious jailhouse informants in about 50 of the cases."[13]

In Illinois, during the first twenty-three years after the state reinstated capital punishment, thirteen condemned inmates were cleared of capital murder charges while only twelve inmates were executed. Several of the inmates in Illinois were cleared though the work of Northwestern University journalism students working under Professor David Protess. One of those inmates, Anthony Porter, had been two days away from his execution in 1998 when he received a stay. Porter was later exonerated when the journalism students persuaded the real killer to confess on videotape.[14]

Another university group did similar work. The Innocence Project at Cardozo School of Law in New York, run by Barry Scheck and Peter Neufeld, obtained the release of many people from prison by using DNA evidence and other types of proof.[15]

Although by 2000, at least nine former death row inmates were exonerated through the use of DNA testing, as of that year only two states had laws that gave defendants the right to use the latest DNA testing. In subsequent years the number of states allowing post-conviction DNA testing grew. In 2004, Congress passed the Innocence Protection Act that created a system allowing states to set up procedures to access post-conviction DNA testing.[16]

DNA evidence exonerated a number of individuals for both capital and noncapital crimes. For example, in September 2012, Louisiana released Damon Thibodeaux from prison after he had spent twenty-three hours a day in solitary confinement on death row for fifteen years. Thibodeaux had been convicted of a brutal rape and murder of his fourteen-year-old step-cousin after he succumbed to police pressure to confess. After years of investigation and after expensive DNA testing, Louisiana released Thibodeaux, who became the eighteenth person released from death row and the 300th convicted person exonerated from any crime substantially due to DNA evidence.[17]

Although DNA evidence played a major role in many exonerations, other discoveries and old-fashioned investigations also helped reverse capital convictions. Additionally, in some cases defense attorneys were able to debunk "junk science" – such as unreliable fingerprint, arson, and hair analysis evidence -- that had mistakenly helped put some innocent inmates on death row.

Fortunately, many of these developments were discovered in time to allow innocent defendants to leave prison. But DNA evidence did prove innocence in one case where a prisoner was already dead, although that person had died of natural causes, not by state execution. A Florida court convicted Frank Lee Smith of murder based on an eyewitness who was certain she had seen Smith near the location where an eight-year-old girl was murdered. Smith's attorneys continually argued for DNA testing while prosecutors opposed the tests. Courts rejected Smith's arguments. Then, in 2000, DNA tests revealed another man had committed the crime and that Smith was innocent. Smith, however, had died of cancer in prison ten months before the DNA tests cleared him, having spent fourteen years on death row.[18]

As society discovered more innocent people on death rows than in previous decades, the debate about whether or not an innocent person had been executed intensified. For example, around the time of McCleskey's execution, media focused on coal miner Roger K. Coleman who went to Virginia's electric chair in 1992 for the rape and murder of his sister-in-law.[19] As his execution date approached, state and federal courts would not review some of his claims because his attorneys filed a notice of appeal in state court one day too late.[20] *Time* magazine, newspapers, and TV news shows focused on the case and Coleman's claims. The case stirred up discussion about innocence and the injustice of the procedural rules that barred review of his claims, although more than a decade later DNA testing in effect confirmed Coleman's guilt.[21]

In contrast to Coleman, there are a number of inmates who were executed where questions still remain. The *Chicago Tribune* argued that Texas executed an innocent man named Carlos DeLuna on December 7, 1989, and other experts continued to assert DeLuna's innocence more than two decades later. In 1983, police found DeLuna hiding underneath a parked truck near a gas station where the clerk, Wanda Lopez, had been stabbed to death. DeLuna, who had no blood on his clothes, explained that he hid because he was on parole and became scared when he heard the police sirens. Although police asked two witnesses if DeLuna were the perpetrator and they confirmed he was, the witnesses were not consistent in their beliefs.

More importantly, some believe they discovered the person who really committed the capital crime. Another man who also had the first name "Carlos" and who looked like DeLuna had been with DeLuna that night. The other man, Carlos Hernandez, had a record of similar crimes and later confessed to family and friends he had committed the crime. So, many believe this other Carlos committed the crime for which DeLuna was executed. After Texas executed DeLuna, Hernandez died in prison serving time for another assault with a knife.[22]

Further studies of the case supported DeLuna's innocence. Columbia Law School professor James S. Liebman published the results of his investigation in the case, concluding that DeLuna was innocent.[23] Additionally, the 2008 documentary *At the Death House Door* presented the case for DeLuna's innocence. The film focused on Texas death house chaplain Reverend Carroll Pickett who knew DeLuna and eventually came to be against capital punishment.[24]

Similarly, some argued that Ruben Cantu, who was executed in 1993 in Texas, was innocent. After the execution, the only witness to the crime recanted the identification of Cantu, and a codefendant revealed that under police pressure he falsely accused the seventeen-year-old Cantu. Cantu's case received a significant amount of attention because a series of articles in the *Houston Chronicle* and the *San Antonio Express-News* focused on his possible innocence.[25] More than a decade later, though, District Attorney Susan Reed from Bexar County, Texas, issued a report asserting Cantu's guilt. Some have debated the findings of her report, noting Reed previously sat as a judge who had heard Cantu's appeal and had set an execution date.

A few years after Cantu's execution, Missouri executed Larry Griffin on June 21, 1995, for the 1980 fatal shooting of a drug dealer. After the execution, an NAACP Legal Defense and Educational Fund investigation led by Professor Samuel Gross of the University of Michigan Law School questioned Griffin's guilt. Among other things, LDF's report raised questions about a key witness, the physical evidence, and the procedures used for identifying Griffin.[26] In response to LDF's report, however, the St. Louis Circuit Attorney's Office investigated the case and concluded that "no credible evidence exists to suggest that Larry Griffin was wrongly convicted."[27] In light of the conflicting conclusions, some advocated for an independent evaluation of the case.

In another possible wrongful execution case, in June 2000 Texas executed Shaka Sankofa, who was born with the name Gary Graham, despite questions about Sankofa's guilt for the murder of Bobby Lambert. Many argued that the case against Sankofa lacked physical evidence and was based upon one questionable and contradicted eyewitness. One side effect of the case was that the publicity surrounding the case inspired actress Susan Sarandon to contact Sister Helen Prejean about the nun's first death penalty book, leading to the making of the movie version of *Dead Man Walking*.[28]

Observers also debated about the guilt or innocence of Claude Jones, who was convicted of a 1989 crime and executed in Texas in December 2000. As in Warren McCleskey's trial, Jones's capital sentence resulted from a robbery-murder with questions about which one of the robbers fired the fatal shot. Jones and an accomplice robbed a liquor store, but one of the two men stayed in a pickup truck while the other went inside and killed the store owner during the robbery. A third accomplice who supplied the weapon used in the robbery claimed Jones later confessed to the shooting, although the accomplice later recanted. Because under Texas law a conviction cannot rest solely on an accomplice's testimony, then, the key piece of evidence against Jones was a single strand of hair that prosecutors claimed belonged to him. Scientific advances after Jones's execution, however, revealed that the hair did not belong to Jones.[29] Thus, in Jones's case, the evidence that sent him to death row has been negated.

In yet another Texas case, the state may have executed another innocent man when it executed Cameron Todd Willingham, but Texas officials created post-execution hurdles to resolving the question of Willingham's guilt or innocence. Willingham was convicted of murdering his three young daughters by setting their Corsicana, Texas house on fire in 1991, although Willingham claimed he was innocent. As in Warren McCleskey's case, prosecutors used a jailhouse informant to claim that Willlingham confessed to the murders, and one of the issues was whether or not officials gave the informant a deal in exchange for the testimony. Also, after the trial, the informant, Johnny Webb, went back and forth on whether he told the truth at trial, eventually explaining that he lied on the stand so the prosecutor would help get his sentence reduced. More importantly, new discoveries about the science of fire supported that an accidental fire killed the children.[30]

After Willingham's February 17, 2004 execution, defense attorneys struggled to find a forum to prove Willingham's innocence. In 2010, State District Court Judge Charlie Baird began holding hearings to review the case, despite protests by prosecutors. Around the same time, the Texas Forensic Science Commission started reviewing the case. The Commission encountered some controversy when Texas governor Rick Perry replaced three members of the Commission and named Williamson County District Attorney John Bradley as the new chair.

Still, in spring 2011, the Commission made recommendations for investigators, judges, and lawyers on how to handle future cases. The Commission found that arson investigators in Willingham's case used what are now discredited practices in concluding that the fire was intentional. But in summer 2011, Texas Attorney General Greg Abbott advised the Commission that it did not have jurisdiction to decide whether there was professional negligence in Willingham's case or any other cases prior to September 2005.[31] Thus, there remained serious questions about Willingham's innocence, and the case continued to receive national attention after being profiled in a 2011 documentary film, *Incendiary: The Willingham Case*.

Throughout these years, a number of other executed inmates similarly have had strong advocates for their innocence. Sister Helen Prejean, the author of *Dead Man Walking*, wrote another book, *The Death of Innocents*, about two men she claims were wrongfully executed: Joseph O'Dell, who was executed in Virginia in July 1997, and Dobie Williams, who was executed in Louisiana in January 1999.[32] Others assert the innocence of David Spence, executed in 1997 in Texas, and Leo Jones, executed in 1998 in Florida.

Proving the innocence of an executed person is even more difficult than proving the innocence of a living defendant, which itself is quite difficult because of various procedural hurdles to introducing new evidence once a trial is completed. Attorneys are appointed to represent living death row inmates, while courts do not provide resources for dead inmates. Professor Liebman noted in 2002 that in "the cases of perhaps forty to seventy-five among the 700 men and women who have been executed in the modern capital-sentencing era in this country" there are left police files where "lie untested, but potentially exonerative, biological samples."[33] And, as time passes, it becomes more difficult to find reliable witnesses and evidence, and many cases do not have DNA evidence at the crime scene. Further, in cases where there might be DNA evidence, in some states it may be difficult for defendants to get DNA testing, such as in those that take away the right to post-conviction DNA tests once a defendant pleads guilty.

Despite these hurdles, since the 1990s the exonerations of death row inmates and questions about the guilt of others contributed to a drop in support for the death penalty. The new discoveries of innocent people among the living condemned have led to a majority of Americans believing an innocent person has been executed recently in the United States.[34] In a dissenting opinion in *Kansas v. Marsh*, Justice David Souter noted the growing number of exonerations of death row inmates and concluded, "We are thus in a period of new empirical argument about how 'death is different.'"[35]

Not everyone agrees about the risks of executing innocent prisoners. In the same case where Justice Souter wrote that innocence cases were creating a new death penalty era, Justice Antonin Scalia challenged Justice Souter's reference to studies about wrongful death sentences by noting that Justice Souter could not identify a specific wrongful execution. Justice Scalia then reasoned that Justice Souter's reference to exonerated death row inmates "demonstrates not the failure of the system but its success."[36] Justice Scalia claimed that "with regard to the punishment of death in the current American system, [the possibility that someone will be punished mistakenly] has been reduced to an insignificant minimum."[37]

Despite Justice Scalia's assertion, new DNA technology and investigative work have raised questions about some executions and have resulted in innocent people being released from prison. These cases increased the public's awareness about injustices in our current system, such as the unreliability of eyewitness testimony. Thus, they helped create a foundation on which to build more support for a moratorium on executions. A columnist in the conservative *National Review* explained: "The right question to ask is not whether capital punishment is an appropriate—or a moral—response to murders. It is whether the government should be in the business of executing people convicted of murder knowing to a certainty that some of them are innocent."[38] Similarly, a 2006 article in *U.S. News & World Report* about the dropping number of executions and death sentences noted, "[n]othing has unsettled people more than the parade of prisoner exonerations based on DNA evidence."[39]

Thus, although Warren McCleskey's evidence of racial disparity failed to convince the Supreme Court the death penalty was arbitrary, in the decades since his execution, new discoveries of innocent people on death row changed the death penalty landscape. Politicians, judges, and the general population became aware that the legal system can convict an innocent person and sentence that person to death.

And, at a time where people such as Justice Harry Blackmun and Sister Helen Prejean were criticizing capital punishment, many claimed that the innocence cases highlighted other problems with the American death penalty. Capital defendants are often outcasts of society without resources to convince a jury of their innocence. And if innocent people are not getting fair trials, then injustices are occurring in other cases too. Systemic injustices, biased media attention, attorney errors, prosecutor misconduct, discrimination, unreliable witnesses, junk science, and human fallibility are problems in a range of cases, not just the genuine innocence ones. And starting in the 1990s, these discoveries of innocent people on death row helped change the way many viewed the American death penalty.

CHAPTER 20

A Moratorium Movement Emerges in the 1990s

In the 1990s, as new voices spoke out against the death penalty and society discovered innocent people among the condemned, Americans were changing their views about capital punishment. Out of these changes emerged a new movement advocating for a moratorium on executions and for a reassessment of the American death penalty.

After Justice Blackmun and Justice Powell changed their positions on the constitutionality of capital punishment in the years after Warren McCleskey's death, new discoveries of innocent people on death rows across the country led others to change their minds too. McCleskey's case reinforced the conclusion that arguments against the death penalty needed to be made outside the courtroom, and at the same time, some policy makers recognized their somber responsibility now that they knew that the Supreme Court was not going to end the death penalty.

So, in venues outside the courtroom, death penalty critics argued that states should impose a moratorium on executions. Those who advocated for a moratorium questioned the fairness of the death penalty process, just as Warren McCleskey's attorneys had done in courtrooms. So, in the 1990s, many began calling for a halt to executions and a re-examination of the system. Thus, was born the moratorium movement.

A number of factors contributed to the moratorium movement in addition to the discoveries of innocent people on death row, but one of the major driving forces came from a professional organization of attorneys, a group that included those who had seen the problems with the capital punishment system firsthand. In 1997, three years after Justice Blackmun published in *Callins v. Collins* the opinion he began writing after McCleskey's execution, the American Bar Association (ABA) adopted a resolution calling upon each death penalty jurisdiction to impose a moratorium on executions until that jurisdiction complied with ABA policies designed to "(1) ensure that death penalty cases are administered fairly and impartially, in accordance with due process, and (2) minimize the risk that innocent persons may be executed."[1]

The resolution did not take a position on whether or not the death penalty should be abolished. Instead, it focused on four areas of concern in the implementation of the modern death penalty: (1) ensuring competency of defense counsel, (ii) ensuring the ability of the state and federal courts to review the merits of constitutional claims in state post-conviction and federal habeas corpus proceedings, (iii) eliminating racial discrimination in capital cases, and (iv) preventing the execution of defendants with an intellectual disability and persons who were under the age of eighteen at the time of the crime.

The Chair of the ABA Section of Individual Rights and Responsibilities submitted a report to the ABA along with the proposed resolution, elaborating on the four areas of concern. The report discussed some of the same problems previously expressed by Justice Blackmun and Justice Powell, and it cited those two justices.[2]

With respect to legal representation, the report described several errors made by capital defense attorneys, such as a case where counsel later admitted he was so dependent on drugs during trial that he did very little on the case.[3] On the process issue, the report cited the Anti-Terrorism and Effective Death Penalty Act and cases such as *McCleskey v. Zant* that limited habeas corpus review of capital cases. The report also expressed concern that the Supreme Court had upheld the execution of juveniles and prisoners with an intellectual disability.

One of the main reasons for the ABA report's position calling for a moratorium came from Warren McCleskey's other Supreme Court case. The report explained that the Supreme Court rejected a constitutional challenge to racial discrimination in capital cases in *McCleskey v. Kemp*, and then Congress had failed to pass legislation to address the issue. For further support, the ABA cited the Baldus study and other research revealing the death penalty is more likely to be imposed in cases where the victim is white, noting that the race of the defendant also may affect the sentencing decision. The report stated the need for "effective mechanisms" to eliminate racial discrimination in death penalty cases.[4]

The ABA resolution, like Justice Blackmun's dissent in *Callins* and the discovery of innocent people on death rows, received extensive media coverage. One professor wrote that the ABA resolution was "quite significant" because it "legitimates arguments often dismissed as mere partisan attempts to erect 'technical' roadblocks on the path from death sentences to executions and lends important symbolic capital to death penalty opponents."[5]

After the resolution passed, courts, legislatures, and the media increasingly discussed the issues in the resolution. Within a few years, the ABA made the moratorium goal a priority, and the ABA President, Martha W. Barnett, called for a moratorium on federal executions and asked lawyers to work for moratoriums in the states.[6]

The moratorium strategy grew out of the failures and the successes of Warren McCleskey's case. The ABA lawyers recognized that after the Supreme Court rejected McCleskey's claims, the Court would not repair the problems with the American death penalty. But they also saw how the injustices of McCleskey's case and other issues could support an approach to attack the death penalty outside of the courts.

Despite the ABA Moratorium Resolution, the rate of executions in the United States continued to climb, and it did not appear any state would follow the ABA's recommendation in the near future. By 1998, one commentator concluded "there is little immediate prospect that [the ABA's] recommended moratorium will come to pass."[7]

Soon, though, the ABA's moratorium proposal began building momentum. In January 2000, the ABA reported that no U.S. jurisdiction had imposed a moratorium since it passed its 1997 resolution, but it noted that "developments toward that end are encouraging."[8]

One of those encouraging developments occurred when Nebraska's legislature became the first in the United States to vote for a moratorium since *Gregg*. In May 1999, the unicameral legislature voted 27-21 for the bill, which called for an extensive study of the fairness of the death penalty during a two-year moratorium. The prime sponsor of the moratorium was Senator Kermit Brashear, a Republican who favored the death penalty but was concerned about the fairness of the legal process. The victory for the moratorium movement did not last long; a few days later Nebraska governor Mike Johanns vetoed the proposed bill. Still, the legislative vote had national importance by giving momentum to the moratorium movement.[9]

Subsequently, the state legislature unanimously overrode the governor's objection to a study of Nebraska's death penalty. The study ultimately examined each of the approximately 15,000 criminal homicide cases since 1973 to determine whether in each case, race, gender, religious preference, or economic status of the victim or defendant played a role in the decision to seek a death sentence.[10]

The Nebraska study, released in August 2001, did not clearly find racial bias in the system, but it found "that criminals are nearly four times as likely to receive the death penalty if they murder someone who is relatively well-off financially instead of someone who is poor."[11] The author of the report was David Baldus, one of the authors of the report used in Warren McCleskey's case. His new report showed inconsistencies in Nebraska's twenty-seven post-*Furman* death sentences but found less inconsistency than in other states.[12]

While Nebraska debated a death penalty moratorium, people in Illinois became concerned about the large number of innocent defendants released from death row. Between 1976 and 1999, a time period where Illinois executed twelve people, thirteen death row inmates were exonerated and released from death row. The Illinois House of Representatives passed a non-binding moratorium bill in March 1999, and the Illinois Supreme Court and governor soon began studies of the state's death penalty.[13]

Then, on January 31, 2000, Illinois's Republican governor George H. Ryan ordered a moratorium on executions in that state and called for a special panel to study the state's death penalty system. Governor Ryan's action was especially significant because he was a Republican. Further—unlike actions such as Oregon governor Robert D. Holmes's policy in the 1950s of commuting all death sentences[14] or New Mexico governor Toney Anaya's 1986 commutation of all five inmates on New

Mexico's death row—Governor Ryan did not base his position on a moral opposition to the death penalty. Instead, he imposed the moratorium out of concerns about systemic problems. Perhaps because of Governor Ryan's conservative credentials and an increasing awareness about the problems with the death penalty system, 66 percent of Illinois residents approved of his action to impose a moratorium. The popularity of Ryan's action contrasted with the unpopularity of Governor Anaya's commutations as well as of Ohio governor Richard Celeste's 1991 commutations for eight death row inmates, both of which were done at the end of the governors' terms.[15]

The Illinois moratorium energized the moratorium movement. In addition to Illinois and Nebraska, by early 2000, at least fifteen other states were considering abolition, a death penalty moratorium, or studying their death penalty laws.[16] In early 2001, the Nevada Senate passed a bill requiring a two-year moratorium on executions, but the bill died for the session in the Assembly Judiciary Committee.[17]

Subsequently, a number of organizations and communities called for a moratorium on executions. By the American Bar Association's death penalty conference in October 2000, seven state and local bar associations had adopted death penalty moratorium proposals and three state bar associations had called for a review of the death penalty system. Between 1999 and 2001 in Virginia, several municipalities and organizations passed resolutions calling for a moratorium on executions. Similarly, around the same time, several communities in North Carolina adopted moratorium resolutions.[18]

A number of major cities passed moratorium resolutions. On March 20, 2000, the City of Atlanta, where Warren McCleskey was sentenced to death, adopted a resolution supporting a moratorium on executions. Baltimore, Philadelphia, San Francisco, and other cities also passed declarations supporting a moratorium on executions.[19]

Similarly, in 2000, Maryland governor Parris N. Glendening, influenced by the work of Professor Baldus and his colleagues in McCleskey's case, commissioned a study of race and the death penalty in Maryland. As part of that decision, Governor Glendening imposed a moratorium on executions while the study took place. Professors Raymond Paternoster and Robert Brame completed the study in 2003. They found black defendants whose victims were white were more likely to get the death penalty than other defendants of other racial combinations. Despite the findings, Governor Glendening's successor, Governor Robert L. Ehrlich Jr., lifted the moratorium.[20]

Meanwhile, New Hampshire's legislature went even further and passed a bill to abolish the death penalty. Although the governor of New Hampshire later vetoed the bill, the legislature's action constituted the first legislative vote to abolish the death penalty since *Gregg v. Georgia* in 1976.[21] In addition to the Illinois moratorium, the New Hampshire vote highlighted the growing concern about the necessity and the fairness of the death penalty at the turn of the century. Less than a decade after McCleskey's execution, abolitionists were finding success in the political arena instead of in the courts for the first time since the 1970s.

The Illinois moratorium led to further action within the state's borders. In 2003, during Governor Ryan's last week in office, he commuted the death sentences of everyone on death row. One of the condemned men who benefited from Ryan's moratorium and commutation, Danny Edwards, had kidnapped and killed a close friend of Ryan's family. Ryan's wife and Edwards, who wanted to executed, asked the governor to let the execution take place. Governor Ryan explained, "I concluded that the system was completely broken, so it wouldn't have been fair to choose between who lived and who died. Especially for personal reasons."[22]

Meanwhile, several other events contributed to the moratorium movement starting in the 1990s, including: (1) media attention on individual cases, such as those of Mumia Abu-Jamal, Shaka Sankofa (Gary Graham), and Karla Faye Tucker; (2) studies regarding errors in capital cases; (3) a decrease in the nation's crime rate; (4) many states adding the alternative punishment of life without the possibility of parole; and (5) growing international pressure to abolish the death penalty.

First, one of the factors contributing to the growth of the moratorium movement was that the media portrayed some sympathetic capital defendants during this time. Although one of the weaknesses of the anti-death penalty movement is that unusual high-profile crimes and executions can drastically affect public attitudes, during the 1990s several cases were helpful to the movement, including the innocence cases discussed in the previous chapter. The late 1990s brought new faces that made the public question the American death penalty.

One case that gained attention was the conviction of the activist Mumia Abu-Jamal, whose 1982 death sentence in Pennsylvania created a national movement on his behalf. As in McCleskey's case, a court convicted Abu-Jamal of killing a white police officer. But questions about his guilt and racial motivations for his prosecution led to a groundswell of support and extensive debate. Eventually, after a federal court of appeals reversed his death sentence, the state chose not to seek the death penalty again and Abu-Jamal was resentenced to life in prison.

Another death row inmate, Karla Faye Tucker, changed many people's perceptions about the death penalty too. Her case, discussed in more detail in Chapter 14, received international attention, and, as one person noted, "She put a human face on the inmates of death row."[23] The February 1998 execution of the apparently reformed Tucker made religious conservatives question the necessity of the death penalty. For example, following her execution, the evangelical magazine *Christianity Today* announced it would no longer support the use of the death penalty.[24]

At least one notorious capital defendant initially appeared to create a setback for the moratorium movement. The U.S. government had its first post-*Furman* execution when it executed Timothy McVeigh, the infamous "Oklahoma City Bomber," on June 11, 2001. The horrible crime and large number of victims attracted so much attention that more than 1,500 journalists asked to be among the execution witnesses.[25] Because of the nature of McVeigh's crime and the attention given to his case, many death penalty opponents found little to debate beyond a moral opposition to the death penalty. But McVeigh's case was an unusual one and far from the typical death penalty case in the United States. Additionally, some commentators noted that problems existed even in such a highly watched case, such as the discovery of documents the government improperly withheld from McVeigh's law-yers.[26] So, despite the overwhelming support for McVeigh's execution, other cases continued to lead many to question the fairness of the country's death penalty.

Second, several studies on the death penalty contributed to the growth of the moratorium movement in the 1990s. Just as the use of social science and statis-tics were important to the LDF's court-based abolition strategy, new studies were important in the moratorium movement outside the courts.

The Death Penalty Information Center issued several reports focusing on death penalty issues such as race, innocence, and the effects of politics.[27] A 2000 report from Columbia University studied the reversal rates in 4,578 capital cases, discov-ering that post-conviction and appellate "courts found serious, reversible error in nearly 7 of every 10 of the thousands of capital sentences that were fully reviewed" during 1973–1995. The report, which was extensively covered by the media, eval-uated the reversal rate in each state with capital punishment, concluding that "[c]apital trials produce so many mistakes that it takes three judicial inspections to catch them—leaving grave doubt whether we *do* catch them all."[28]

One report examined the use of the death penalty in the state with the most exe-cutions. *The Death Penalty in Texas: Due Process and Equal Justice or Rush to Execution, Regardless of Innocence*, released by the Texas Civil Rights Project, reported on sev-eral problems with the Texas system, including those in ensuring the competency of capital defense lawyers. For example, the report concluded that one-fourth of condemned inmates had been represented by attorneys who had been disciplined, disbarred, or suspended. The report also noted the national reversal rate for capital cases in state courts was 66 percent, but only 3 percent in Texas, implying the Texas appellate courts did not vigorously review claims made by capital defendants.[29]

Although the Baldus study did not save McCleskey's life, others learned from the famous research that such studies could have an impact outside the courtroom. These reports and others provided statistics and facts supporting the moratorium movement.

Third, dropping crime levels in the late 1990s contributed to the moratorium movement. In earlier time periods, jurisdictions were more likely to use the death penalty during poor economic times. Among other reasons, a healthy economy decreases criminal activity, which in turn results in society having less punitive attitudes.[30]

Fourth, a growing number of states adopted life without the possibility of parole (LWOP) sentences. The new sentencing option meant that people no longer saw the death penalty as the only way to permanently remove murderers from society. Further, in 1994 in *Simmons v. South Carolina*, the Supreme Court held that at least in some cases, the consideration of the option of LWOP is so important in capital cases, that the Constitution requires juries be told when a defendant has no chance for release. Popular support for the death penalty drops to around 50 percent and below when those surveyed are asked about the death penalty in comparison to life without the possibility of parole.[31] Thus, as people in death penalty states became more informed that a life sentence can really mean life in prison, overall support for the death penalty dropped because capital punishment was seen as unnecessary.

Fifth, growing international pressure on the United States to abolish the death penalty contributed to the moratorium movement in the 1990s. For example, in June 1995, a country with a long history of racial discrimination, South Africa, abolished the death penalty. The newly formed Constitutional Court of the Republic of South Africa in *The State v. T. Makwanyane and M Mchunu* held South Africa's death penalty violated the country's interim constitution, with the justices several times mentioning racial discrimination in the system.[32] Although a few abolitionist governments existed in 1945, by 1996, many more than half the countries in the world had abolished capital punishment de facto or de jure.[33] During the first twenty-five years after the United States reinstated the death penalty in 1976, more than seventy other nations had abolished the practice.[34]

In the public and political arena, abolitionist countries became more vocal in their criticism of the United States' use of the death penalty, influencing some politicians and the public. The United States' position on the death penalty forced the federal government to attempt to ratify human rights treaties with reservations that are internationally unpopular. In 1971, the United Nations adopted a resolution encouraging abolition of the death penalty, and the 1989 *Second Optional Protocol to the International Covenant on Civil and Political Rights Aiming at the Abolition of the Death Penalty*, which went into force in 1991, encouraged countries to take "all necessary measures to abolish the death penalty."[35]

Countries in Europe helped lead in the worldwide progress to ban capital punishment. All fifteen members of the European Union banned capital punishment, and the accession of new members was conditioned on their abolition of the death penalty. For the first time in history, in 1998, none of the forty member states of the Council of Europe executed anyone.[36]

Further, individual countries in Europe and elsewhere criticized the U.S. death penalty. For example, in 1999, Germany filed suit against the United States in the World Court regarding Arizona's execution of two German citizens.[37] Raymond Forni, the president of the French National Assembly, held a news conference in August 2000 to urge the United States to abolish the death penalty.[38] Mexican foreign minister Jorge Castaneda argued that many Mexican nationals on death rows in the United States are "an important strain on bilateral relations" between the two countries.[39] To mark Governor Ryan's imposition of a death penalty moratorium in Illinois, Rome lit up its ancient Colosseum with golden light. Further, officials planned to change the Roman Colosseum's lights from white to gold for two days whenever a condemned person was spared execution.[40] Meanwhile, international organizations such as Hands Off Cain worked to end the death penalty in the United States and worldwide.

Sometimes the international pressure had direct effects on individual cases. In early 2001, in *Minister of Justice v. Burns*, the Supreme Court of Canada, noting problems with the American death penalty and citing the 1997 ABA Report, refused to extradite two defendants to the United States without assurances that the death penalty would not be imposed. Similarly, other foreign countries refused to extradite fugitives to the United States if there were a chance they could be sentenced to death.[41]

The international death penalty trend continued into the twenty-first century. In June 2001, the Council of Europe's Human Rights Committee threatened to revoke the United States' observer status unless a death penalty moratorium was imposed in the United States within two years. In July 2010, the European Parliament and the 19th Session of the Parliamentary Assembly of the Organization for Security and Co-operation in Europe passed resolutions against the use of the death penalty.[42]

Death penalty abolition continues to progress around the world. In the mid-1990s, an average of forty countries carried out the death penalty each year. Into the first decade of the 2000s, that number dropped to an average of less than thirty countries. By 2010, only twenty-three countries carried out executions.

The number of countries in the world that have abolished the death penalty officially or in practice has also continued to rise. In 2001, there were 108 abolitionist countries. By the end of 2013, more than two-thirds of world's countries have abolished the death penalty in law or practice, with 140 countries abolitionist in law or practice while 58 countries retained the death penalty.

The countries that often use the death penalty continue to be aberrations. The only countries with more executions than the United States in 2013 were China, Iran, Iraq, and Saudi Arabia.[43]

* * *

Thus, during the 1990s, after two decades the post-*Furman* American death penalty machine showed signs of wear. The historical factors discussed above strengthened the abolition movement and helped ignite the moratorium movement. Additional factors also contributed to the moratorium movement. For example, as throughout history, a major contributor to the death penalty abolition movement has been the work of religious organizations and anti-death penalty organizations, such as the National Coalition to Abolish the Death Penalty. Throughout much of American history up through the current day, activists and organizations work against the death penalty. Protesters, as well as death penalty supporters, attend executions. Every year since 1994, activists in the Abolitionist Action Committee gather near the steps of the Supreme Court to fast and vigil on June 29, the date of the *Furman v. Georgia* opinion, and they remain until July 2, the anniversary of the *Gregg v. Georgia* opinion.

Additionally, the work of capital defense lawyers in creating a record of injustices was essential to the moratorium movement, leading to the Illinois moratorium and to judges and others criticizing the death penalty. For example, the attorneys and experts who presented evidence of racial disparity in McCleskey's case gave ammunition to the moratorium movement.

Ironically, actions taken by pro-death penalty persons to expand the death penalty in the first decades following *Gregg v. Georgia* also helped build the foundation for the moratorium movement. *McCleskey v. Zant*, other Supreme Court decisions, and Congress's passing of the 1996 Anti-Terrorism and Death Penalty Reform Act limited access to the courts. These limitations created injustices that were used to argue against the death penalty outside the courts. Similarly, inadequate funding for defense attorneys resulted in concerns about ineffective assistance of counsel.[44]

The growth of the Internet during this period also contributed to educating the public about the death penalty. In *Furman* and *Gregg*, Justice Marshall had commented on the public's ignorance about capital punishment and speculated that a more informed public would oppose the death penalty. And, around the same time the moratorium movement began to bloom in the early 1990s, Internet access also grew throughout the United States. So, as new information came out about innocent defendants on death row, more people had access to this information than ever before, making citizens more informed about capital punishment.

Each of the factors discussed above helped the growing moratorium movement, although reasonable minds might disagree about the importance of each event to that movement. The United States got to that point because of a unique blend of certain events that made support for the death penalty drop to the lowest it had been in the country in almost two decades.

Through the nineties and early into the twenty-first century, the moratorium movement continued to spawn small victories. Although as recently as August 1996, Arizona executed an inmate named Luis Mata who had an intellectual disability, five years later in 2001, Arizona's governor signed legislation banning the execution of any more defendants with an intellectual disability. Then, between June 2001 and August 2001, the governors of Florida, Connecticut, Missouri, and North Carolina signed into law similar bills that banned the execution of inmates with an intellectual disability.

Other changes resulted in part from the moratorium movement. Governors in several states signed laws giving capital defendants access to DNA testing. Finally, in July 2001, after twenty years of supplying the chemicals used for lethal injections in Oklahoma, the McAlester Regional Health Center, pressured by Human Rights Watch, announced it would no longer supply those chemicals used in executions.[45] Many of these changes would have an impact on the American death penalty in the following decades.

The moratorium movement that started in the 1990s could not be a permanent movement itself. The calls for moratoriums could have three possible long-term outcomes. First, the calls could become ignored and futile. The second possible result was that some states might adopt moratoriums for a period and then continue with executions. The third possible result would be that some states might evolve from focusing on moratoriums to working toward complete abolition. When speaking of fifty state governments in the United States, the result would not be uniform, but the question about the future remained as the country entered the twenty-first century: Would the moratorium movement merely die with a whimper, or would it evolve into something that would help the country escape from its death penalty past?

McCleskey's Legacy in the Early Twenty-First Century

CHAPTER 21

The Early Twenty-First Century Death Penalty in the Courts

Although Warren McCleskey lost in a final defeat for the court-based strategy to abolish the death penalty, capital defense lawyers continued to represent their clients and target narrower issues. These attacks did not have the potential to end the death penalty as in McCleskey v. Kemp, *but they helped limit its use as the new century began.*

The long legal journey taken by Warren McCleskey's case continues to have broad political and legal effects in the new century. When the Supreme Court struck down the death penalty statutes in *Furman* in 1972, the Court encountered a backlash. States responded immediately with new laws, and politicians attacked the Court for being too active in striking down laws and for reading the Constitution too broadly. Although the Court is isolated from politics in many ways, the justices were aware of the responses when they upheld the new death penalty statutes four years later in 1976.

So, when the Court heard Warren McCleskey's claims about race's impact on the death penalty in 1987, the justices knew they were addressing a case similar to *Furman* that might result in striking down capital punishment, resulting in another political backlash. Additionally, as noted in Justice Powell's opinion, the Court also feared that a decision in favor of Warren McCleskey would reverberate throughout the entire criminal justice system. The politics may not have affected the outcome of the case, but these concerns were present when the Court rejected McCleskey's Eighth and Fourteenth Amendment claims, leaving it to Congress and state legislative bodies to address McCleskey's evidence of racial discrimination.

Considering the current composition of the Supreme Court, the Court's prior rejection of McCleskey's evidence, and the states' responses to *Furman*, the Court probably will not strike down the death penalty in the immediate future. In light of the Court's interpretation of the Eighth Amendment as being guided by the "evolving standards of decency" dictated by society, this connection to popular and political response is not surprising.

Just because the Court will not strike down the death penalty completely in the near future, though, does not mean the Court will not limit some aspects of the punishment. And in the early twenty-first century that is what the Court did. Capital defense lawyers were already launching constitutional challenges to all aspects of the death penalty at the time of *Furman* and *Gregg*. But the process of chipping away at the death penalty around the edges became the main focus of litigation challenges after defense lawyers recognized the *Furman* and *McCleskey* strategy to completely eliminate the death penalty had failed. So, post-*McCleskey*, those who opposed capital punishment recognized the importance of the work in the courts, but they also recognized such work by itself would not end capital punishment.

In response to legal challenges, in the new century the Court decided a number of significant cases that broadened protections for capital defendants. In doing so, the Court reversed a number of decisions made during the first decades of the modern death penalty. These reversals partly resulted from the post-*McCleskey* abolition strategy that focused on education and legislative changes. Because the Court considers legislative decisions in interpreting the "evolving standards of decency" underlying the Eighth Amendment, those legislative victories translated into Court victories too.

Additionally, these changes likely were affected by many of the events that created the moratorium movement discussed in the previous chapter, including international condemnation of the American death penalty. In the new century, some of the justices of the Supreme Court began taking note of international opposition to capital punishment.

Although the Court virtually ignored foreign views on the death penalty for the late 1980s through the 1990s, it had not always been that way. When the Supreme Court first began closely examining the constitutionality of the death penalty, references to the laws in other countries and international law occasionally arose. When in 1963 Justice Arthur Goldberg signaled in his *Rudolph v. Alabama* dissent that the Court might be willing to examine the constitutionality of capital punishment, he cited a United Nations report.[1] In the 1970s in *Furman* and *Gregg*, the NAACP Legal Defense Fund lawyers used laws in other countries to argue the death penalty violates the Constitution, although only Justice Thurgood Marshall cited to an international law source. When the Court struck down the death penalty for rape of an adult in *Coker v. Georgia* in 1977, Justice Byron White's majority opinion noted it was "not irrelevant" that most major nations did not retain the death penalty for rape. Similarly, the Court recognized the relevance of international norms when it considered the application of the death penalty to the crime of felony murder in *Enmund v. Florida* in 1982.[2]

International law also appeared in Warren McCleskey's case. Although McCleskey's lawyers did not cite international law when they appeared before the Supreme Court in *McCleskey v. Kemp*, the International Human Rights Law Group submitted an amicus curiae brief arguing that capital sentences affected by racial discrimination violate a "peremptory norm of international law." The argument failed to win over the justices, but it was the first time attorneys argued in a capital case before the Supreme Court that international law by itself provides individual rights instead of just arguing international law could help interpret the U.S. Constitution.[3]

In 1988, the year after *McCleskey v. Kemp*, some of the justices debated the role of international law in *Thompson v. Oklahoma*, a case about the constitutionality of executing someone who committed murder at the age of fifteen. In finding the death sentence unconstitutional, Justice John Paul Stevens cited information on international law and the juvenile death penalty from an amicus brief submitted by Amnesty International. In contrast, Justice Antonin Scalia and the dissenting justices criticized the plurality's reference to international law.[4]

The use of international law to help interpret "evolving standards of decency" seemed to come to an end the next year in *Stanford v. Kentucky*, another case involving the juvenile death penalty, Justice Scalia wrote for the majority that international norms were not relevant to the interpretation of the Eighth Amendment because "it is *American* conceptions of decency that are dispositive."[5] Following *Stanford*, references to foreign law in capital cases were rare for the next decade until around the turn of the century.[6]

Then, international concepts began playing a larger role again for some justices in capital cases starting at the end of the 1990s. For example, in 1998 in *Breard v. Greene*, the Supreme Court addressed the effects of the Vienna Convention on Consular Relations on the rights of capital defendants.[7]

Justice Stephen Breyer illustrated an interest in international views on the death penalty in a 1999 case when the Court considered the constitutionality of keeping an inmate on death row for a period of time even longer than the nearly thirteen years that McCleskey spent waiting to be executed. In a dissenting opinion from a denial of certiorari in *Knight v. Florida*, where the Court declined to review a prisoner's claim that spending more than twenty years on death row constituted a cruel and unusual punishment, Justice Breyer cited legal opinions from several countries. He noted that an increasing number of foreign courts have held that excessive delays in carrying out a death sentence made the punishment inhumane, and he quoted legal opinions from India, Zimbabwe, Jamaica, and the European Court of Human Rights.[8]

Justice Breyer was not the only justice influenced by international law at the turn of the century. Following the Supreme Court's decision in December 2000 about the contested U.S. presidential election in *Bush v. Gore*, Justice Anthony Kennedy became more influenced by his exposure to foreign law and foreign judges. Author Jeffrey Toobin wrote in *The Nine: Inside the Secret World of the Supreme Court* that Justice Kennedy became a different justice at the time: "After 2000, in part to escape the political atmosphere in Washington, Kennedy deepened his commitment to the broader world, and his journeys changed him."

Justice Kennedy had traveled to other countries during his career, and the other justices maintained contacts with other judges from around the world. But in the new century, the dialogue with other countries significantly affected the Court, and in particular Justice Kennedy. These influences on Kennedy and Breyer from the world outside America were especially important in death penalty cases because most other democracies have abolished capital punishment.[9]

Although foreign and international views of the death penalty have not dictated the outcomes of cases, some justices considered them in expanding protections to capital defendants in the new century, including cases addressing prior decisions about executing juveniles and those with an intellectual disability. The Supreme Court had upheld these practices while McCleskey sat on death row, but activists worked with politicians to get a number of state legislatures to ban executions of individuals in those two categories.

Although the Supreme Court upheld the constitutionality of executing individuals with an intellectual disability in 1989 in *Penry v. Lynaugh*,[10] the Court reconsidered the issue in 2002. In *Atkins v. Virginia*, the Court reversed its 1989 holding and held the execution of individuals with an intellectual disability violates the Constitution. There had been some changes in Court personnel between the two cases, but Justices Sandra Day O'Connor and Kennedy, who both voted against the defendant in *Penry*, joined the majority voting for the defendant in *Atkins*. The change in outcomes occurred less due to changes in Court personnel and more because of educational efforts, activists' work with legislators, and changes in state laws.[11]

As discussed earlier, part of the Court's Eighth Amendment analysis considers "evolving standards of decency" as reflected by states' elected legislatures. When the Court decided *Penry* in 1989, only Georgia banned the execution of individuals with an intellectual disability. But by 2002, eighteen states and the U.S. government banned the execution of prisoners with an intellectual disability. This drastic legislative shift in a relatively short period of time occurred largely through organization and education. For example, University of New Mexico School of Law professor James W. Ellis learned the lessons of *McCleskey v. Kemp* and first worked for years with mental disability organizations educating legislators about the death penalty issue before he eventually argued *Atkins* before the Supreme Court.[12]

The Court in *Atkins* held by a vote of 6-3 that it violates the Eighth Amendment to execute individuals with an intellectual disability. Justice Stevens noted that various organizations, religious groups, and the world community were against executing such defendants. Considering this evolving standard, the justices also noted policy reasons supported such a ban. Individuals with an intellectual disability, they reasoned, deserve severe punishment less than other defendants and are less likely to be deterred by the death penalty. Also, because of their impairments, such defendants are less able to assist their attorneys.

In Chief Justice William Rehnquist's dissenting opinion, he stressed that nineteen states still permitted the execution of those with an intellectual disability, and therefore he argued contemporary America had not rejected such executions. He also criticized the majority for giving weight to the fact that foreign laws, professional and religious organizations, and opinion polls were opposed to executing people with an intellectual disability. Justice Scalia also wrote a dissenting opinion, arguing the majority's result merely reflected the personal views of the individual justices. Similarly, some commentators criticized the justices who cited laws from outside the United States.

The legislative changes and the Court's ruling came too late for individuals executed prior to 2002. But the decision arguably ensured that prisoners with an intellectual disability would not be executed in the future, even though the case also created more litigation for attorneys and courts to define which capital defendants were exempt from executions due to an intellectual disability.

The Court also left it to the states to figure out procedures to determine whether defendants have an intellectual disability, allowing states to develop a wide variety of standards. For example, although Georgia was on the cutting edge in instituting the execution ban on this class of defendants in 1986, in 2011 both the Georgia Supreme Court and the U.S. Court of Appeals for the Eleventh Circuit upheld the state's requirement for defendants to prove they have an intellectual disability "beyond a reasonable doubt." Georgia is the only state that maintains such a high burden for defendants to establish an intellectual disability.[13]

The Supreme Court, however, asserted in 2014 that the U.S. Constitution does not give complete free reign to states in evaluating whether or not a defendant has an intellectual disability. In 2014 in *Hall v. Florida*, the Court held that a Florida statute, as interpreted by the Florida Supreme Court, violated the Eighth Amendment because it required the defense to show that a defendant tested below a specific IQ score before other evidence of intellectual disability would be considered.[14]

Another victory like *Atkins* for capital defendants and the consideration of international law occurred in *Roper v. Simmons*, which addressed the issue of whether it violates the Eighth Amendment to execute someone who was under eighteen years old at the time the person committed the capital crime. In 1989, the Court had held by a vote of 5-4 in *Stanford v. Kentucky* that it did not violate the Constitution for states to execute sixteen- and seventeen-year old defendants. But fifteen years later, the Court reconsidered the issue in light of education efforts and changes in society.

At oral arguments for *Roper v. Simmons* in October 2004, Justice Kennedy signaled his concern about international law when he questioned the prosecutor defending Missouri's law that allowed for the execution of juveniles. Among his questions, he asked, "[L]et us assume that it's an accepted practice in most countries of the world not to execute a juvenile for moral reasons. That has no bearing on whether or not what we're doing is 'unusual'?" The prosecutor, James R. Layton, responded that such practices had no bearing on the U.S. Constitution. But Justice Breyer replied that James Madison and the other founders used foreign documents as sources when they wrote the U.S. Constitution. Justice Ruth Bader Ginsburg then referenced the Declaration of Independence, which contained language about leading the world and showing a "decent respect for the opinions of mankind." Justice Scalia, who believed foreign views had no place in interpreting the plain language of the Constitution, then joked, "What did John Adams think of the French?"[15]

Subsequently, when the Court issued its opinion in *Roper v. Simmons*, the Court voted 5-4 to reverse *Stanford v. Kentucky*, and held it violates the Eighth Amendment to execute offenders who were under eighteen at the time they committed the crime. Justice Kennedy wrote the *Roper* opinion for the Court, stressing that juveniles have diminished culpability because they differ from adults in that they are often impetuous, subject to peer pressure, and constantly changing as they grow up. As in previous cases on similar issues, the Court looked for a "national consensus" against executing juveniles as part of its interpretation of the "evolving standards of decency" of the Court's Eighth Amendment analysis. The majority noted that thirty states prohibited the execution of juveniles: Twelve states did not have capital punishment and eighteen death penalty states banned the execution of juveniles by statute or through court decisions.[16]

As signaled at oral argument, in the written opinion Justice Kennedy also looked outside the nation's borders. He noted that only seven countries besides the United States had executed juveniles in the most recent ten years. He also pointed out that Article 37 of the United Nations Convention of Rights of the Child, ratified by every country except the United States and Somalia, forbids executing individuals under the age of eighteen. He reasoned, "Our determination that the death penalty is disproportionate punishment for offenders under 18 finds confirmation in the stark reality that the United States is the only country in the world that continues to give official sanction to the juvenile death penalty."[17]

In a dissenting opinion, Justice Scalia criticized Justice Kennedy's use of sources from outside the United States. He noted other countries often differ from the United States on issues that include the exclusionary rule and abortion. "To invoke alien law when it agrees with one's own thinking, and ignore it otherwise," he argued, "is not reasoned decision-making, but sophistry."[18]

Many members of the Republican Party agreed with Justice Scalia's criticism of the use of foreign sources. Following the *Roper* decision, more than fifty representatives from Congress sponsored a resolution criticizing the Court's use of other laws. Conservatives argued that Justice Kennedy's use of foreign law created grounds for impeachment, and one called Kennedy "the most dangerous man in America."[19] The critics, however, may not have understood that the Eighth Amendment differs from other parts of the constitution because of its reliance on "evolving standards of decency."

Later, at confirmation hearings for new Supreme Court justices John G. Roberts Jr. and Samuel A. Alito in 2005 and 2006, senators asked the two men about international law. Both future justices revealed that they did not believe the Court should cite international law. But as the United States continued in the twenty-first century, Justice Kennedy's view of the United States as part of a broader world community still had some support, as a majority of the justices joined Justice Kennedy's opinion in *Roper* acknowledging the foreign laws.

The Supreme Court's drastic change on the constitutionality of the execution of prisoners under eighteen and of prisoners with an intellectual disability occurred in a relatively short time span. Although international law had some effect on some of the justices, the main justification for the change came through the legislative process. The changes in states laws affected the Court's interpretation of the Eighth Amendment. Thus, the legislative strategy of trying to limit the death penalty, energized by the failure of the litigation strategy in *McCleskey v. Kemp*, succeeded in those state legislatures that passed laws banning the execution of juveniles and prisoners with an intellectual disability. And further, the success of the legislative strategy eventually paid off in the courts too.

Although in the first decade of the new century the Court reversed earlier opinions on the constitutionality of executing juveniles and defendants with an intellectual disability, the Court has not yet addressed the constitutionality of executing a category of individuals with a significant mental illness. Mental illness remains a mitigating factor, but courts and states have yet to ban executions for some people with mental illness as they did for intellectual disability and youth. Many of the same arguments for banning the executions of juveniles and individuals with an intellectual disability support banning the execution of those with mental illness. Those with mental illness are generally less culpable, and also some are less likely to be deterred by the threat of capital punishment. Additionally, as in the case of intellectual disability, there is a danger that jurors may improperly consider mental illness as an aggravating factor instead of as a mitigating factor.[20]

While capital defense attorneys succeeded in their arguments to get the Supreme Court to interpret the Eighth Amendment to exclude some categories of defendants from capital punishment, death penalty advocates worked to expand the death penalty. After *Roper* and *Atkins*, capital punishment supporters recognized the constitutional importance of legislative action, and in 2008 they made Eighth Amendment arguments to support laws that allowed capital punishment for crimes other than murder.

As discussed in earlier chapters, one of the trends of early American history was a gradual limitation on the number of crimes that could make one eligible for capital punishment. As the number of capital crimes became more and more limited, eventually in 1977 the Supreme Court considered the constitutionality of executing defendants for crimes other than murder. In that case, *Coker v. Georgia*, the Court held that because a sentence of death was "grossly disproportionate and excessive" for the crime of rape of an adult woman, capital punishment for rape violated the Eighth Amendment as a cruel and unusual punishment.[21]

One issue left open in *Coker* was whether or not it violated the Eighth Amendment to sentence a defendant to death for the rape of a child. *Coker* contained some language questioning the constitutionality of a death penalty for any crime where a victim did not die. But the facts of the case involved an adult woman, which limited the Court's holding to that situation and left any implications beyond that as dicta, meaning it was not binding.

Thus, states wrestled with the issue of whether defendants could be executed for child rape where the victim survived. In 1995, for example, Louisiana adopted a child rape statute, and the Louisiana Supreme Court found the statute constitutional in *State v. Wilson*. Other states, including South Carolina, Georgia, Montana, and Oklahoma, followed Louisiana in passing laws that allowed courts to sentence non-homicide defendants to death for sexual assault of minors, although such laws were rarely used.[22]

Then, in 2008 in *Kennedy v. Louisiana,* the Supreme Court addressed the constitutionality of these statutes. The Louisiana statute in the case permitted a jury to sentence a defendant to death for the crime of aggravated rape of a child even where the victim survived. The trial court convicted the defendant of aggravated rape of his eight-year-old stepdaughter, and the jury unanimously voted for death. Therefore, as the case went to the U.S. Supreme Court, the issue became whether there was a consensus against executions for non-homicide crimes so that the "evolving standards of decency" component of the Eighth Amendment prohibits such executions.

As in *Atkins,* the twenty-first century Court ruled in favor of limiting the use of the death penalty. The U.S Supreme Court held that a capital sentence for a person who raped but did not kill a child, and who did not intend to assist another in killing a child, violates the Eighth and Fourteenth Amendments of the U.S. Constitution. The Court explained the Constitution mandates that the death penalty may apply only to a narrow category of the most serious crimes. Here, the Court found a national consensus against the death penalty for child rapists because forty-five states did not execute defendants for child rape. Although Louisiana argued that there was a trend toward allowing such executions, the Court said there had not been a significant shift.

The *Kennedy* Court did not consider the constitutionality of the death penalty for crimes against the State such as treason, terrorism, and drug king activity. But the Court stressed that there should be only a limited use of the death penalty. Because of the high occurrence of child rapes, which occur more often than intentional murders, the Court calculated that if the Constitution allowed executions for child rape, it would result in a dramatic increase in executions. The Court further expressed concern for the victims of child rape, noting defendants might have an extra incentive to kill their rape victims if they would get the same punishment for rape as for murder. Also, the Court explained it would put a heavy burden on child victims to require them to be involved in capital prosecutions where appeals can take many years.[23]

The Court also avoided some issues. As in *Coker,* the *Kennedy* majority did not address the underlying historical connection between race and capital punishment for rape crimes. Legislative attempts to apply the death penalty to crimes besides murder evoked the past southern practice of using broad death penalty statutes that enabled discriminatory application.

Also, in the majority opinion, Justice Kennedy did not mention international law. Writer and legal analyst Jeffrey Toobin suggested Kennedy might have avoided discussing international law because he recognized such citation had caused criticism in the past.[24] But the Court's decision still prompted criticism for other reasons.

Many politicians attacked the result in *Kennedy,* arguing that the Court was being too lenient on child rapists. As in the past, politicians found it easier to take the sound-bite approach to the death penalty instead of delving into the reasoning of the Court. Because the Court decided the case in June of an election year, both presidential candidates criticized the Court's decision as being too protective of child rapists. The future president, Senator Barack Obama, disapproved of the decision, stressing that the "rape of a small child, 6 or 8 years old, is a heinous crime." Obama, however, couched his disapproval of the decision in conditional terms, noting that "if a state makes a decision that under narrow, limited, well-defined circumstances that the death penalty can be pursued," the death penalty would be constitutional.[25]

Commentators gave little attention to another aspect of the majority opinion in *Kennedy* that disclosed an emerging view of the post-*Furman* death penalty. The Court revealed that its rejection of capital punishment for non-murder crimes fit into its ongoing process of defining the Eighth Amendment limits on capital punishment by "the evolving standards of decency that mark the progress of a maturing society." Significantly, Justice Kennedy's majority opinion stressed these standards consistently evolved in a direction to limit, not expand the death penalty. In the opinion—joined by Justices Stevens, Souter, Ginsburg, and Breyer— Kennedy explained that "[c]onfirmed by repeated, consistent rulings of this Court, this principle requires that use of the death penalty be restrained." Thus, the Court concluded that evolving standards required that for crimes against individuals, the death penalty should be reserved "for crimes that take the life of the victim." Thus, the Court indicated the American death penalty would remain limited, continuing the process that began with *Furman* to narrow the use of the death penalty in the United States.[26]

* * *

In the early twenty-first century, the Court has addressed issues besides ones about the constitutional barriers to executing a whole class of defendants. These narrower cases illustrate that many of the justices are troubled by the system that has developed in the decades since the current death penalty system began in the 1970s.

For example, in the early twenty-first century the Court issued some opinions strengthening the application of the ineffective-assistance-of-counsel standard. The standard, which was adopted in 1984 in *Strickland v. Washington*, had made it very difficult for criminal defendants to establish a constitutional violation. But in the new century, in cases such as *Rompilla v. Beard* and *Wiggins v. Smith*, the Court stressed that a defense counsel's failure to prepare adequately for a capital sentencing hearing may constitute constitutional ineffective assistance of counsel if based on inadequate investigation.[27]

While the Supreme Court had limited claims of ineffective assistance of counsel to actions by trial counsel and direct appeal attorneys, some recent decisions reveal the Court's growing concern about errors by later post-conviction attorneys too. In one case, Alabama death row inmate Cory R. Maples had been represented by two lawyers at a major large law firm, but the two associates at the firm who were working on the case during post-conviction proceedings left the firm. After an envelope with a court ruling sent through the mail arrived at the firm, the firm's mailroom returned the letter because nobody had told the court or the mailroom that new lawyers were now on the case. The firm discovered the problem when Maples's mother called the firm upset that the time to appeal had expired. In *Maples v. Thomas*, the Supreme Court stressed the general rule that "when a petitioner's postconviction attorney misses a filing deadline, the petitioner is bound by the oversight."[10] But, in the 7-2 decision, the Court ruled that this case instead involved an attorney abandoning a client without notice, and therefore in that case, "an attorney no longer acts, or fails to act, as the client's representative."[29] Thus, the Court held Maples established the "cause" prong of the requirements for overcoming a procedural default of a habeas corpus claim.

Similarly, in remanding another lawyer error case in 2010's *Holland v. Florida*,[30] the Court expressed concerns about where attorneys completely abandon clients in post-conviction proceedings. In 2012 in *Martinez v. Ryan* the Court stressed the importance of post-conviction defense attorneys. In that case, the Court retreated from language in 1991's *Coleman v. Thompson* and held the ineffectiveness of a post-conviction attorney may be used by a defendant in some jurisdictions as a vehicle to allow federal courts to address claims in habeas corpus proceedings.[31]

Additionally, as the moratorium movement increased the general public's concern about wrongful executions, the modern Supreme Court also displayed concerns about the risk of executing innocent prisoners. Although Justice Scalia noted in *Kansas v. Marsh* that the number of death row exonerations is low compared to the number of people on death row, and that the American people are willing to accept the very small risk of executing an innocent person because of the benefits of the death penalty, some of the Court decisions have shown a concern for potentially innocent capital defendants.[32] For example, in 2011 in *Skinner v. Switzer*,[33] the Court in an opinion by Justice Ginsburg held a convicted state prisoner could seek DNA testing of evidence under 42 U.S.C. Section 1983.

The Court has also considered the impact its procedural rules might have on innocent defendants. In 2006 in *House v. Bell*, the Court held the federal courts should hear Paul G. House's defaulted claims because had the jury heard all of the evidence, which included that another person had confessed to the crime, it was more likely than not that a reasonable juror would not have found House guilty. The Supreme Court remanded, and the federal district court ordered a retrial. In 2008, Tennessee released House after twenty-two years on death row, and in May 2009 the prosecutor dropped all charges against House.[34]

Although a majority of the *McCleskey v. Kemp* Court seemed to remove race from the constitutional calculus, the Court has shown that some race claims may still win for criminal defendants. For example, in June 2005, in *Miller-El v. Dretke*[35] and *Johnson v California*,[36] the Court reasserted the importance of *Batson v. Kentucky*, which held that the exclusion of blacks from juries because of their race denies the jurors and the defendant of equal protection of the laws. A majority of the Court criticized prosecutors for removing competent black jurors from juries in both of those cases, which involved African-American defendants who were charged with crimes against white victims.

Not all decisions by the Supreme Court in the twenty-first century thus far have limited the use of the death penalty, and many of the Court's future decisions likely will broaden its use. Since the decision in *McCleskey v. Zant*, other changes make it more difficult for capital defendants to get courts to review evidence after prosecutors unconstitutionally withheld evidence from the defense. In one of the more recent examples, in 2011 in *Cullen v. Pinholster*, the Supreme Court interpreted 28 U.S.C. Section 2254 to create additional hurdles for capital defendants to have their claims reviewed by federal habeas corpus courts where defense attorneys did not present the evidence in the state courts. In dissent, Justice Sonia Sotomayor explained that the Court's interpretation may prevent defendants with valid *Brady* claims from having their cases reviewed in federal court.[37] Similarly, other decisions have created an extremely high hurdle for capital habeas petitioners claiming they are innocent.

These recent cases will continue to be interpreted by the lower courts, and the Supreme Court will continue to refine the American death penalty procedures with new decisions. Thus, capital prosecutions still continue around the country, and even in states that no longer have the death penalty, the federal government continues to seek death sentences under federal law. Still, many of the nation's judges and justices have shown concerns about the system that has developed in the years since *Furman*. After more than forty years, the Supreme Court continues to recognize problems in the capital punishment system that were highlighted in the 1970s. And it is likely that forty years from now, if the American death penalty still exists, the justices will still be finding problems that have not been repaired in the decades since Warren McCleskey sat in the electric chair.

* * *

Litigation has played a major role in the history of capital punishment, and it continues to do so. The 1960s death penalty abolitionist strategy to end the U.S. death penalty through litigation kept a focus on the courts for decades until Warren McCleskey's case became the final defeat for that approach. While there have been successes outside the courts since McCleskey's execution, a remnant of the legal strategy continues to use the courts to limit the use of the death penalty.

Some may argue that these court victories created a death penalty system that the general public is more likely to tolerate, just as some abolitionists believed that the shift from public to private executions in the late 1800s and early 1900s weakened opposition to capital punishment. They reason that although some Americans might be appalled at executing juveniles or people with an intellectual disability, those same people will accept a death penalty that bans the death penalty for those classes of individuals.

Others, however, respond that no evidence supports the argument that the capital punishment limits increased the punishment's overall popularity. Further, the courtroom strategy that chipped away the edges of the death penalty helped the progress toward abolition. The legal challenges to the death penalty slowed down the use of the death penalty so that executions are far from common. Because executions are so rare, states are more willing to get rid of capital punishment altogether.

Ultimately, litigation attacks played an important role in limiting the American death penalty and exposing its flaws. And for lawyers and courts to have failed to try to respond to the problems with the death penalty would have been unethical and immoral. Attorneys could not let their current clients die for the possibility of ending the death penalty in the future.

And so, today, the *Furman-Gregg-McCleskey* litigation strategy still coexists with other strategies to limit or attack the death penalty. Although abolitionists have little hope the litigation strategy will abolish the death penalty in the immediate future, they can hope the legal limitations on the death penalty will illustrate capital punishment is unnecessary. At the time of Warren McCleskey's 1991 execution, the Supreme Court had held that the death penalty may be applied to juveniles and to those with an intellectual disability. Also, the Court had left open the question of whether the death penalty could apply to defendants who committed crimes other than murder. Since then, the Court has continued to interpret the Eighth Amendment's evolving standards of decency to limit the use of the death penalty. Today, those categories of defendants cannot be executed, and the Court also has expanded its death penalty jurisprudence to restrict the use of life in prison without parole for juvenile defendants.[38] The litigation strategy to abolish the death penalty failed to end the death penalty, but it did save the lives of many defendants and attempted to make the criminal justice system more humane.

Some individual judges, however, are not satisfied with the slow erosion of the death penalty. Like their counterparts on the bench in the 1990s, many respected jurists have raised voices against the death penalty. For example, in 2007, former New Jersey Supreme Court justice Peter G. Verniero wrote an editorial in *The New York Times* explaining he opposed the death penalty because it is ineffective and costly. As the New Jersey State Attorney General, Verniero had enforced the death penalty, and as a member of the state supreme court, he had affirmed death sentences. He explained he followed the law, but he eventually concluded that the irreversible death penalty is not good policy. Further, he reasoned, "[t]he legal process has grown into a complex, lengthy undertaking that consumes enormous energy and resources."[39]

Judges have critiqued the death penalty in recent case opinions. In 2008, the Presiding Justice of the Mississippi Supreme Court, Oliver Diaz, wrote a dissenting opinion in a capital case arguing the death penalty is unconstitutional.[40] In 2009, Judge Boyce F. Martin Jr. of the United States Court of Appeals for the Sixth Circuit wrote a concurring opinion in a capital case where he expressed his concerns about the death penalty. He explained that after thirty years as a judge on the court, he saw how the death penalty is still arbitrary, even as the system becomes more expensive in attempts to try to make it fairer. He argued that "our scarce public resources can be put to better use" than the death penalty, and that, even putting any moral objections aside, the death penalty does not justify its costs.[41] Several years later he reiterated his concerns in his final death penalty case by condemning "the use of the death penalty as an arbitrary, biased, and broken criminal justice tool."[42]

In another example, Ohio Supreme Court justice William O'Neill dissented from an order setting an execution date. Justice O'Neill reasoned that with seventeen states and the District of Columbia no longer using the death penalty, the punishment is becoming unusual and thus violates the Eighth Amendment of the U.S. Constitution and Article I, Section 9 of the Ohio Constitution. While he recognized the death penalty is "the law of the land," he reasoned he could not participate in the death penalty process anymore, concluding, "The time to end this outdated form of punishment in Ohio has arrived."[43]

Not all judges who ruled against the death penalty found a welcome audience. In December 2011, Judge Teresa Hawthorne, a state district judge in Dallas County, held in the case of Roderick Harris that the Texas death penalty statute violated the U.S. Constitution. She reasoned the statute allowed prosecutors to arbitrarily seek death sentences against defendants, one of the concerns expressed at the time the Supreme Court decided *Furman v. Georgia.*[44] Subsequently, another judge ruled that Judge Hawthorne had to recuse herself from another capital case because of her views on the death penalty, and Judge Hawthorne was removed from the Harris case too.[45]

In 2014 in California, a federal judge put a halt to California's death penalty. On July 16, 2014, in *Jones v. Chappell*, U.S. District Court judge Cormac Carney held that California's death penalty violated the Eighth Amendment. Judge Carney concluded that arbitrary factors determine who is executed in California. Additionally, the judge found that under the current system of "inordinate and unpredictable delay," few of the condemned are actually executed, resulting "in a system that serves no penological purpose."[46]

Other judges spoke out against the death penalty in newspaper editorials. In 2009, former federal judge H. Lee Sarokin wrote an editorial about his opposition to the death penalty in the *Huffington Post*. Judge Sarokin, who retired in 1996 after seventeen years as a federal judge, served on the United States District Court for New Jersey and on the United States Court of Appeals for the Third Circuit. In addition to stating his moral opposition to capital punishment, he echoed the concerns raised in McCleskey's case and decried the many variables that determine who is sentenced to death: "Whether or not one receives the death penalty depends upon the discretion of the prosecutor who initiates the proceeding, the competence of counsel who represent the defendant, the race of the victim, the race of the defendant, the make-up of the jury, the attitude of the judge, and the attitude and make-up of the appellate courts that review the verdict."[47]

In March 2011, a California Superior Court judge who served from 1978 to 1993, and who sentenced ten men to death, wrote an editorial in the *Los Angeles Times* explaining why he now wished he had sentenced the prisoners to life in prison instead of to death. Former judge Donald A. McCartin explained that the state could save money by abolishing the death penalty. Further, he reasoned the victims' families would be better off had he not sentenced the murderers to death. Instead of knowing the killer would be spending life in prison, the families have been drawn into years of appeals and retrials waiting for an execution. Thus, he concluded the death penalty has resulted in additional suffering for the victims' families and cost the state "many millions of tax dollars in this meaningless and ultimately fruitless pursuit of death." He looked back on his career and was "angry to have been made a player in a system so inefficient, so expensive and so emotionally costly." In response to Judge McCartin's op-ed, Gil Garcetti, the district attorney of Los Angeles County from 1992 to 2000, replied that from his experience Judge McCartin correctly concluded that the death penalty did not help the victims' families and was too costly when the money could be better spent elsewhere.[48]

After the failed litigation strategy to end the death penalty, these lower court judges had little hope of persuading the U.S. Supreme Court to end capital punishment in America. But they could hope their words would reach voters, governors, and legislators. In 2009, Nebraska's Sarpy County district judge Ronald E. Reagan testified before Nebraska's legislature at a hearing on bills regarding the death penalty. Listeners were surprised when Judge Reagan, who retired in 2005 and who had sentenced one of Nebraska's few condemned men to death, urged legislators to repeal the "state-sanctioned revenge" of the death penalty. Judge Reagan revealed other current judges feel the same way but cannot express their opinions while on the bench.[49]

Thus, the abolitionist strategy used by the lawyers in *Furman v. Georgia, Gregg v. Georgia*, and *McCleskey v. Kemp* saved the lives of capital defendants, changed the law, and significantly affected courts and judges. But after those cases failed to abolish the death penalty, many abolitionists such as Judge Reagan realized that they needed to speak to legislators, governors, politicians, and the general public.

CHAPTER 22

The Early Twenty-First Century Death Penalty in U.S. Politics

McCleskey v. Kemp confirmed that if the death penalty were to be abolished in the United States, successes must come from the political system instead of the judicial system. And, in the early twenty-first century, citizens and politicians began reassessing the value of the death penalty.

LEGISLATIVE RESPONSES TO *MCCLESKEY V. KEMP*

In *McCleskey v. Kemp*, Justice Lewis Powell suggested Warren McCleskey should take his statistical evidence about the role of race in the American death penalty to the "legislative bodies."[1] The legislative process, however, takes time. And McCleskey, who was nearing his execution, could not wait for his state legislators to act.

Still, in the years after that Supreme Court decision in 1987, death penalty critics, governors, and legislators began to recognize that the Supreme Court would not solve all of the problems with the death penalty. Thus, policy makers in recent years wrestled with many important death penalty issues, including the ones raised in McCleskey's case.

In the early twentieth-first century, the issues and arguments that arose in McCleskey's case and during the emergence of the moratorium movement in the 1990s continued to reverberate and take new forms. Several states considered passing a Racial Justice Act that would negate some of the effects of the Supreme Court's ruling in *McCleskey v. Kemp* by allowing capital defendants to prove racial bias in their cases through statistical evidence. David Baldus, who participated in the studies in McCleskey's case, testified before the U.S. Congress in 1991 and in 1994 in support of a federal Racial Justice Act.

The U.S. Congress, however, failed to pass a federal Racial Justice Act. But after Kentucky's legislature failed on two prior occasions to pass a state Racial Justice Act, in 1998 Kentucky became the first state to pass such a law. Kentucky's narrow law permits statistical evidence to be used to argue that a prosecutor has engaged in purposeful discrimination, but the law still requires defendants to meet a high burden and link the evidence to the individual capital defendant in the case.[2] Because the law is narrow, claims based on the law generally have not succeeded. But some have argued that since Kentucky enacted the law, larger cities in the state have been more even-handed in applying the death penalty in black victim and white victim cases.[3]

Subsequently, a little more than twenty years after Justice Powell told McCleskey to take his claims to the legislatures, North Carolina passed the 2009 Racial Justice Act, which was broader than the Kentucky act and resulted from an organized statewide social movement to address racial disparities in the death penalty.[4] The North Carolina law permitted death row defendants to present evidence of a pattern of racial discrimination system-wide or county-wide to argue their death sentences should be reduced to life in prison. Among other factors, appellate courts could consider statistical and other evidence that "[d]eath sentences were sought or imposed significantly more frequently upon persons of one race than upon persons of another race."[5] Under the North Carolina law, prosecutors were allowed to present evidence to rebut inferences of discrimination. But the North Carolina statute required judges to reduce the sentence to life imprisonment without the possibility of parole when race was a "significant factor" in the decision to seek or to impose a death sentence.[6]

The North Carolina Racial Justice Act, however, remained controversial. In April 2011, some members of the N.C. General Assembly sponsored a bill to repeal the law. District attorneys in the state criticized the existing law, arguing the litigation should focus on the merits of individual cases and not require prosecutors to spend time going back through decades of cases to respond to discovery requests regarding statistics. In an *ABA Journal* article, Peg Dorer, the director of the North Carolina Conference of District Attorneys, explained, "We don't think there is a problem of racial bias in the system." In arguing to repeal the law, Republican representative Paul Stam stressed the importance of individual punishment, exclaiming during debate, "Stop using race as a reason not to execute cold-blooded murderers. Race is a red herring."

After a repeal bill went a few rounds in the legislature, the legislators limited and then a year later repealed the North Carolina Racial Justice Act. First, in July 2012, opponents of North Carolina's Racial Justice Act garnered enough votes in the legislature to overcome a governor veto and pass legislation significantly weakening the law. As the Supreme Court did in *McCleskey v. Kemp*, the legislators limited defendants' use of racial statistics. Importantly, the law provided that statistics alone cannot prove race was a significant factor in the conviction or sentence.[7]

Then, in June 2013, both the North Carolina House and the Senate passed a bill that completely repealed the water-downed version of the Racial Justice Act, and North Carolina governor Pat McCrory signed the repeal. After the House passed the repeal, more than one thousand people showed up at a protest organized by the NAACP, and around 300 protesters were arrested.[8]

Although McCleskey's legacy contributed to the political debate surrounding the Racial Justice Acts, the debate also allowed some of the same political posturing as in the past. In a 2010 election for a seat in the North Carolina General Assembly, political groups targeted Democratic incumbent John Snow for his support of the Racial Justice Act, taking a lesson from the Willie Horton ads used to target presidential candidate Michael Dukakis in the 1988 election. In a mass mailing, they featured a photograph of Henry Lee McCollum, an African-American death row inmate convicted of raping and murdering an eleven-year-old girl with three other men. The mailing described the crime in detail and claimed, "Thanks to arrogant State Senator John Snow, McCollum could soon be let off death row." Snow, who otherwise supported the death penalty, lost to his Republican opponent Jim Davis by fewer than 200 votes.[9]

During its brief existence, North Carolina's Racial Justice Act had an impact on the state's death row. In April 2012, Cumberland County Superior Court judge Greg Weeks overturned condemned inmate Marcus Robinson's death sentence on the basis of the Act, sentencing Robinson to life in prison without parole. As in McCleskey's case, Robinson's involved a black defendant and a white victim. The judge based his decision on a study by Michigan State University researchers that found that in 173 capital trials, prosecutors used peremptory challenges to remove blacks from juries twice as often as they were used for whites, even accounting for other variables. Based on the study, Judge Weeks concluded prosecutors intentionally excluded black jurors in the case and that evidence indicated prosecutors were engaging in this practice throughout the state. The judge found the statistical evidence provided "an inference of intentional discrimination."

Subsequently, Judge Weeks reduced the sentences in three other cases for the same reason. In these decisions, the court used statistics to support an inference of discrimination in specific cases, something the Supreme Court denied to McCleskey. The state appealed these cases.[10] Meanwhile, other states continue to consider passing a Racial Justice Act to address the racial disparities still being found in the administration of the American death penalty.[11]

POLITICIANS IN THE TWENTY-FIRST CENTURY

In the early twenty-first century, the politics of the death penalty changed in other ways too. While many politicians in the decades after *Furman* believed that being against the death penalty harmed political careers, this fear has dissipated since the emergence of the moratorium movement. For example, in presidential elections since the 1990s, politicians have not felt the need to be strong advocates for the death penalty. In the 2004 U.S. presidential election, one of the two major parties nominated Senator John F. Kerry, a candidate who was against the death penalty. Kerry became the first anti-death penalty candidate to represent one of the two major parties in the presidential election since then-Vice President George H.W. Bush made an issue of Governor Dukakis's anti-death penalty stance in 1988. But 2004 was not 1988. Senator Kerry's opponent, the pro-death penalty President George W. Bush, did not use Kerry's death penalty position in the campaign. Because of changing attitudes about the death penalty, the former prosecutor's anti-death penalty position did not harm him.

The 2008 and 2012 elections each featured two supporters of the death penalty, but the candidates spent little time on the issue. Despite their stated support for capital punishment, Senator John McCain and Senator Barack Obama had not served as governors and had never enforced an execution. Similarly, in 2012, President Obama ran against Governor Mitt Romney, who had been a governor, but his state of Massachusetts did not have the death penalty. Although President Obama had raised concerns about the possibility of innocent defendants being executed, he supported capital punishment.

As in the past, Republican candidates who already have established strong conservative credentials have the potential to lead on the death penalty issue. In 2010, for example, 2008 Republican primary candidate Mike Huckabee defended signing sixteen death warrants while he was governor of Arkansas, but he also conceded, "I probably could be fine if we didn't have the death penalty."[12]

The death penalty issue still may arise in elections, but it often does not carry the weight it did in the 1970s, 1980s, and early 1990s. For example in the 2012 race for attorney general of the state of Washington, Republican Reagan Dunn ran television ads attacking his opponent, who had helped with the case of a condemned man during a summer internship as a law student. Dunn's ads, however, were unsuccessful and he lost the race, as some commentators speculated Dunn's harsh attacks on someone for helping provide legal representation to an indigent defendant may have hurt Dunn.[13]

In the new century, invigorated by developments out of the moratorium movement, a number of governors raised concerns about capital punishment, either generally or in a specific case. For example, in 2011, Rhode Island governor Lincoln D. Chafee refused to turn a state prisoner over to federal custody where the federal government wanted to seek the death penalty. In an op-ed in the *Providence Journal* defending his position, Governor Chafee proudly cited Rhode Island's long history of opposing capital punishment, going back to when in 1852 it became the second state to abolish the practice. Although the state later had capital punishment for a period, it had not executed anyone since the 1852 ban went into effect. Governor Chafee expressed his concern for the victims in the case, but he stressed he must protect "the sovereignty and laws of the state."[14]

In January 2012, Delaware governor Jack Markell granted clemency to a death row inmate for the first time in that state in recent years. Governor Markell, who was not against the death penalty, granted clemency to Robert A. Gattis and changed his death sentence to one of life in prison without parole. The condemned had been convicted of killing his former girlfriend in 1990 and admitted to the crime, claiming he had become a different person. The Delaware Board of Pardons recommended clemency because of new mitigating evidence about the physical and sexual abuse Gattis experienced as a child.[15]

In some instances in recent years, governors acted unilaterally to stop executions, expressly or implicitly imposing execution moratoriums in their states. Oregon governor John Kitzhaber granted a reprieve to a condemned killer in November 2011 and announced he would do the same for any scheduled execution during the remainder of his term in office. Governor Kitzhaber asked state officials to consider other options besides the death penalty. In making his emotional announcement, Governor Kitzhaber revealed he was haunted by the fact he had allowed Oregon's only two post-*Furman* executions during his previous two terms in office. He further explained that as a licensed physician, he had taken an oath to "do no harm." The governor, however, noted he would not commute the sentences because that decision should ultimately be left up to the voters. The immediate reprieve stopped the execution of forty-nine-year-old Gary Haugen.[16]

In 2013 Colorado governor John Hickenlooper temporarily stopped executions in that state when he granted a reprieve to a death row inmate facing execution, citing the arbitrary nature of capital punishment. Governor Hickenlooper's explanation for the stay aimed at general concerns about the death penalty instead of anything special about the inmate. He reasoned, "Colorado's system of capital punishment is imperfect and inherently inequitable."[17]

Similarly, in February 2014, Governor Jay Inslee instituted a moratorium on executions in Washington state. The governor, who took office in January 2013, explained that convicted murderers are rarely executed, the costs of prosecuting a capital case did not justify the punishment over life in prison, there is no evidence the death penalty deters crime, and the death penalty is not always applied to the worst offenders. He added that it was not applied fairly across the state, noting that death sentences depended on arbitrary factors like a county's budget for prosecuting cases. Although Governor Inslee explained that he was not pardoning the nine men on the state's death row, he asserted that he would issue a reprieve to prevent any executions while he was in office.[18]

Former governors have raised similar concerns about the death penalty. In 1990, former Texas governor Mark White ran for the governor's office with a television commercial showing him walking in front of photos of inmates who had been executed during his term as governor, promising there would be more to come if he were elected. While he was governor from 1983 to 1987, he oversaw the executions of nineteen inmates, and prior to that, as attorney general, he was involved in the first post-*Furman* execution in Texas. But by 2009, White called for Texas to replace the death penalty with life imprisonment without parole. Concerns about innocent defendants being executed affected his change, but he also came to believe the death penalty does not act as a deterrent and, considering the time it takes to execute someone, does not provide swift justice.[19]

As in the 1990s, these statements and unilateral actions by current and former governors had a big impact on the modern death penalty, and they have the potential to set the groundwork for an even larger impact in the future. Meanwhile, additional changes have resulted from governors working with legislators.

LEGISLATIVE CHANGES IN THE TWENTY-FIRST CENTURY

As Justice William Brennan wrote in *McCleskey v. Kemp* about our country being "imprisoned by the past" if we ignore the influence of racism, America's death penalty also remains a prisoner of the past. Were state legislatures and the

U.S. government to begin with a clean slate where the death penalty had no American history, many would not choose to adopt it. In addition to any moral qualms about the punishment, the legislators could weigh the costs and benefits of a capital punishment system without the history that creates a presumption in favor of maintaining the status quo. But we do not write on a clean slate, and the death penalty is embedded in American life and history.

Each state has its own history with the death penalty and clings to that history. Because Michigan has not had a death penalty since 1846, the state likely will remain without a death penalty. Because its neighbor Ohio has had a death penalty for decades, Ohio probably will continue with executions for the foreseeable future. The momentum of the past keeps states on their own paths.

Yet, the past of the death penalty is also a past with problems. So by remaining imprisoned by the past to the death penalty, states also cling to a system with a long history of racism, procedural problems, unfairness, class discrimination, inaccuracies, and risks of executing innocent defendants. Warren McCleskey bore much of the weight of the historical problems with the death penalty.

Sometimes, however, states do break free from the past. In the early twenty-first century, several states re-examined their connection to the death penalty and began a new American period of death penalty abolition.

Despite the national rise in the popularity of the death penalty through the 1980s and early 1990s, some states still operated without capital punishment. But during that time, some abolitionist states returned to the death penalty. In New York, legislators several times passed legislation to re-establish the death penalty in the state, but two-term governor Hugh Carey and three-term New York governor Mario M. Cuomo vetoed the bills each time. In 1994, though, George E. Pataki, who campaigned with the promise to restore the death penalty to New York, defeated Mario Cuomo for governor. During Governor Pataki's inauguration, the audience applauded the loudest for his promise to restore the death penalty. After the inauguration, the New York State Legislature began working on a new death penalty law, and on March 7, 1995, Governor Pataki signed the new death penalty bill into law using two pens that had belonged to police officers who had been killed.[20]

The New York law, however, was not popular with everyone. Several prosecutors, including the District Attorneys of Manhattan, Queens, and the Bronx, raised concerns about the return of the death penalty. In one instance, Governor Pataki removed Bronx District Attorney Robert Johnson from a case after Johnson refused to seek the death penalty.

Soon, the New York law ran into problems in the courts, as the highest court in the state, the New York Court of Appeals, did not affirm one death sentence under the new law. In 2004, in *People v. LaValle*, the Court of Appeals held a portion of the bill violated the state constitution, and executions could not take place until the state legislature fixed the problem. The unconstitutional provision required trial judges to instruct capital juries that if they could not agree unanimously on a sentence of death or life without parole, the judge would impose a sentence with parole eligibility. The Court of Appeals found the instruction had the potential to coerce jurors into voting for the death penalty.

After the *LaValle* decision, the New York State Senate approved a bill to change the unconstitutional deadlock provision. The chairs of three New York General Assembly committees, however, decided to seek input from the public on whether to pass new death penalty legislation. During 2004–2005, Assembly members held three hearings in New York City and two in Albany, listening to 146 witnesses in person plus an additional 24 others in writing. In the end, the Codes Committee voted to reject legislation that would have brought back the death penalty to New York. Assembly Member Helene Weinstein, who was the chair of the Judiciary Committee, noted that the testimony at the hearings had convinced her to change her mind and to no longer support the death penalty.[21]

New York prosecutors in Queens, however, continued to pursue the death penalty under the unconstitutional statute in the case of John B. Taylor, who was involved in a restaurant robbery-murder where he and a another man bound and then shot seven people, killing five of them. After Taylor was sentenced to death, prosecutors argued on appeal that the sentence should stand because the trial judge did not give the unconstitutional deadlock instruction to the jurors. As the media reported on the "Wendy's massacre," once again, an unusual especially egregious murder threatened to reestablish capital punishment in a state. But in 2007 in *People v. Taylor*, the Court of Appeals held that its prior ruling in *LaValle* applied to this one last condemned inmate. Thus, the death penalty could not be imposed in New York until the state legislature rewrote the statute. The decision cleared the state's death row and halted further capital prosecutions in the state courts.[22]

Therefore, only a little more than a decade after Governor Pataki signed the death penalty law, New York emptied its death row and continued on without capital punishment. During the twelve years that New York had the death penalty, only seven defendants were sentenced to death. By the time New York's death row emptied in 2007, there had been no executions. In 2010, New York elected as governor Andrew Cuomo, who opposed the death penalty and had testified against the punishment at one of the legislative hearings on the issue in 2004.[23]

New York's abolition occurred through a unique combination of events. Lawyers succeeded in the courts, not in arguing the death penalty itself was cruel and unusual, but by attacking unfair procedures used to impose the death sentence. The successful argument was part of the strategy of chipping away at the death penalty as opposed to the broad systemic attack in *McCleskey v. Kemp*. But the narrow issue in *LaValle* ultimately resulted in the abolition of the death penalty. Because the legislature had to repair the unconstitutional procedural problem in the statute, the legislature had to reassess its commitment to the death penalty. And once the New York Court of Appeals found the death penalty unconstitutional, enough members of the legislature did not want to try to repair of the statute. Thus, the New York abolition resulted partly from the court-based abolition strategy that peaked with *Furman* and ebbed with *McCleskey v. Kemp*. But the New York death penalty would not have been abolished without the education and legislative focus that became more important after *McCleskey v. Kemp*.

Around the same time as the events in New York, another abolition victory took place in New Jersey. Two decades after McCleskey's case, on December 17, 2007,

New Jersey governor Jon S. Corzine signed a bill abolishing the death penalty in that state, making New Jersey the first state in more than forty years to successfully abolish the death penalty by a vote in the legislature. At the same time, Governor Corzine commuted the sentences of the eight men on New Jersey's death row to life without parole.

Several factors contributed to New Jersey's abolition of the death penalty, including some factors inspired by the work of the lawyers and experts in McCleskey's case. One of the reasons the state abolished the death penalty came from the New Jersey Supreme Court's strict review of death penalty cases. Over the years since New Jersey adopted the death penalty in 1982, the New Jersey Supreme Court overturned nearly 80 percent of all capital cases. As part of the court's review of capital cases, it had interpreted the state constitution to reject the high burden of proof used by the Supreme Court in *McCleskey v. Kemp*, and the court accepted the methods of analysis pioneered by Baldus and his colleagues. Thus, the New Jersey Supreme Court often considered statistical evidence supporting claims of systemic discrimination. Although the court never reversed cases on that ground, lawyers and citizens knew racial discrimination was an ongoing consideration in capital cases. A special master maintained a database monitoring information about race and New Jersey capital cases. Ultimately, despite the most thorough considerations of proportionality and even-handedness by any court in the country, New Jersey discovered it still could not eliminate racial bias from its system, as defendants in white victim cases were more likely to get the death penalty than in cases with black victims.[24]

Other reasons contributed to the end of New Jersey's death penalty, including that it had never become a large part of the state's culture. In deciding whether to seek death sentences in individual cases, prosecutors understood the state supreme court often reversed such sentences, so they invested less in the death penalty's existence. Also, the state funded a strong public defender's office that litigated capital cases thoroughly. So, New Jersey jurors did not often impose the death penalty, and the state's death row was small. Also, during the forty-four years since the state had reinstated capital punishment, New Jersey had not executed anyone.

Additionally, prior actions in the state raised questions about capital punishment. In 2006, out of the moratorium movement, New Jersey's state legislature passed a bill imposing a moratorium on executions and creating a commission to study the death penalty. In 2007, the commission issued a report recommending that the death penalty be abolished and replaced by life in prison without parole. Finally, other factors that contributed to the eventual abolition included a strong grassroots organization against the death penalty and powerful political leaders with strong legislative experience who supported abolition.[25]

A few years after the historical New Jersey abolition, New Mexico followed a similar path. On March 18, 2009, New Mexico governor Bill Richardson signed a bill to replace the death penalty with life in prison without parole. Governor Richardson had long supported the death penalty, but in recent years he questioned the effectiveness of the capital punishment system. In signing the legislature's bill, he noted, "I do not have confidence in the criminal justice system as it currently operates to be the final arbiter when it comes to who lives and who dies for their crime."

The New Mexico abolition culminated from a long-term strategy that had been started more than a decade earlier by a number of anti-death penalty organizations to educate legislators and the public about capital punishment. Part of the education efforts focused on the cost of the death penalty, an issue that became more important as the country went into a recession. Other important factors included advocacy by members of victims' families who were against the death penalty, the adoption of life in prison without parole as a sentencing option, education about exonerated death row inmates, and effective legislators who worked against the death penalty.

Another key factor in the abolition was the work of the New Mexico Coalition to Repeal the Death Penalty, a coalition of 140 organizations working together on lobbying and community outreach. The efforts of these organizers included study groups, petitions, and workshops. Organizations working for abolition included the League of Women Voters, the National Association for the Advancement of Colored People, Amnesty International chapters, the New Mexico Public Health Association, and a number of churches and religious organizations. Also, Murder Victims' Families for Reconciliation created a booklet featuring survivors affected by homicides who wanted the focus shifted from executing murderers to alternatives that help better honor the victims and the victims' families.

The executive director of the New Mexico coalition, Viki Elkey, explained, "The successful abolition effort in New Mexico was the result of over a decade of grassroots work, with advocates from many realms contributing."[26] Thus, the successful abolition of the death penalty occurred through education and advocacy. Although death penalty opponents always did similar work, the moratorium movement that followed *McCleskey v. Kemp* helped them focus their efforts further.

Those opposed to the death penalty succeeded in New Mexico, but the success was not complete. Legislators compromised so that the new law applied only prospectively to crimes committed on or after July 1, 2009. Hence, two men—Robert Fry and Timothy Allen—remained on New Mexico's death row awaiting their execution dates even as Italy lit up the Roman Colosseum in celebration of New Mexico abolishing the death penalty. During the twenty-eight years New Mexico had the death penalty, prosecutors filed capital prosecution notices in 211 cases that ultimately resulted with only fifteen death sentences and one execution during that time.[27]

As discussed in chapter 20, Illinois had played a significant role in the moratorium movement of the 1990s. And after the New York, New Jersey, and New Mexico abolitions, on March 9, 2011, Illinois governor Pat Quinn signed a bill abolishing the death penalty in that state. He also commuted the death sentences of the fifteen Illinois inmates on death row to life in prison. The law, which took effect July 1, 2011, made Illinois the sixteenth state without the death penalty, resulting in the fewest states with capital punishment in more than thirty years.[28]

Illinois governor Quinn explained: "Since our experience has shown that there is no way to design a perfect death penalty system, free from the numerous flaws that can lead to wrongful convictions or discriminatory treatment, I have concluded that the proper course of action is to abolish it." Plus, because maintaining the death penalty costs more than life in prison, Governor Quinn reasoned that "the enormous sums expended by the state in maintaining a death penalty system would be better spent on preventing crime and assisting victims' families in overcoming pain and grief."[29]

In the time since Warren McCleskey entered Georgia's death row, death penalty attitudes in Illinois underwent major changes. In the 1980s and early 1990s, most people in Illinois would think of the killer clown John Wayne Gacy when they thought of the death penalty. But new information about the death penalty revealed underlying systemic problems with the capital punishment system. Some death row inmates turned out to be innocent, and even many of the guilty ones ended up on death row due to luck more than to a logical system. Just as race and arbitrary factors possibly played a role in Warren McCleskey's case, Governor Quinn and the Illinois Legislature recognized that the post-*Furman* death penalty did not solve the problems the Supreme Court recognized in the pre-*Furman* death penalty. And, so, after the earlier moratorium in that state, officials understood that the only way to eliminate those problems was to eliminate the death penalty.

As in the anti-lynching movement and early anti-death penalty movements, where women were among the founders of the American League to Abolish Capital Punishment in the 1920s and were active in creating the National Coalition to Abolish the Death Penalty in 1976,[30] a number of women were leaders in these recent death penalty abolitions. For example, in Illinois, State Representative Karen A. Yarbrough sponsored the House version of the bill to abolish the death penalty. In New Mexico, State Representative Gail Chasey wrote the bill that ended capital punishment in that state.

Around the same time New York, New Jersey, New Mexico, and Illinois eliminated capital punishment, Connecticut also worked toward abolishing the death penalty. In 2010, the Connecticut General Assembly voted to abolish the death penalty but Governor M. Jodi Rell vetoed the bill. The following year, Connecticut again considered abolition legislation under the new governor, Dannel P. Malloy, who announced he would sign such a bill and who was elected by voters who knew the election would lead to abolition.

But as often occurred throughout America's history, a particularly egregious atypical case affected a state's decision on whether to have a death penalty. As Connecticut's legislature considered the new abolition bill, which would have abolished the death penalty for new cases but not old ones, a capital trial began for one of the two men accused of invading the home of Dr. William A. Petit and his family in July 2007. In addition to severely beating Dr. Petit, the two offenders killed his wife and two daughters after sexually assaulting his wife and one of the daughters. As the trial dates approached, Dr. Petit made clear that he wanted the state to execute the two defendants, and he talked to some of the legislators. So, as the Connecticut State Senate prepared to vote on the abolition bill, two critical senators who had previously supported abolishing the death penalty announced they had talked to Dr. Petit and would not vote to repeal the death penalty at that time out of respect for him and the pending trials. The future of Connecticut's death penalty thus waited.[31]

In 2012, though, the Connecticut General Assembly returned to the death penalty issue and became the seventeenth state without capital punishment. This time, the Connecticut House of Representatives voted 86 to 63 to abolish the state's death penalty after the Senate had approved the bill. When Governor Dannel Malloy signed the bill into law on April 25, 2012, he noted that in the last fifty-two years the state had executed only two people, and both of them had voluntarily abandoned their appeals. The state's only post-*Furman* execution occurred in 2005 when Michael Ross gave up his appeals. Under Connecticut's new law, though, the eleven people on death row, including the two men convicted of the Petit murders, remained there because the new law did not repeal the death penalty for those currently on death row.[32]

After Connecticut, Maryland next abolished capital punishment. Similar to Maine's actions in the early 1800s, in the early 2000s Maryland first limited the death penalty and then abolished it. In 2009 Maryland legislators passed a law limiting the use of the death penalty. Under the 2009 law, prosecutors could only seek a death sentence in first degree murder cases with overwhelming proof of guilt. Specifically, the death penalty could apply where DNA or biological evidence linked the defendant to the murder, when the defendant confessed on videotape, or when a video connected the defendant to the murder. By 2012, only five people sat on Maryland's death row.[33]

Then, in March 2013, led by Governor Martin O'Malley, the Maryland Legislature voted to abolish capital punishment in the state, and Governor O'Malley signed the measure into law in May 2013. The bill did not apply retroactively to the five men on Maryland's death row, but the legislation allowed the governor to re-evaluate the individual cases. As the bill became law, Maryland became the eighteenth state without capital punishment and the first one below the Mason-Dixon line. In contrast to the political climate when McCleskey lived on death row, Governor O'Malley signed the bill abolishing capital punishment at the same time he considered running for president.[34]

While death penalty abolitionists worked to eliminate the death penalty in some places, in some other places, those in favor of the death penalty worked to expand or bring back capital punishment. In the book *The Ride*, *Boston Globe* reporter Brian MacQuarrie recounted how Cambridge, Massachusetts, firefighter Bob Curley became a leading advocate for Massachusetts to reinstate capital punishment in the late 1990s. Curley's ten-year-old son had been abducted and murdered in 1996, and Curley lobbied legislators and spoke about the tragedy as a reason for the state to bring back the death penalty. Ultimately, in 1997 the death penalty return failed due to a tie vote in the Massachusetts House of Representatives. Meanwhile, Curley eventually changed his mind about the death penalty and became an advocate against the punishment. Massachusetts changed too. In 2007, the Massachusetts House of Representatives resoundingly defeated another attempt to bring back the death penalty.[35]

In addition to the states that abolished capital punishment in the early twenty-first century, several other states came close to stopping executions during this period. For example, in 2009, Colorado came close to abolishing the death penalty after the Colorado House of Representatives passed a repeal bill but the Colorado Senate failed to pass the bill by one vote. After considering a moratorium on executions, the Nevada Legislature passed a bill calling for a study of the costs of the death penalty, but Nevada governor Brian E. Sandoval vetoed it.[36] Montana considered abolishing the death penalty several times. In early 2013, Arkansas governor Mike Beebe, who ran as a death penalty supporter, announced that he had changed his mind after signing his first death warrant. He explained that if the Arkansas legislators passed an abolition bill, he would sign it.[37] Meanwhile, in May 2013, for the first time in thirty-four years, Nebraska's unicameral legislature had a majority of votes for death penalty abolition, although a filibuster stopped the vote.[38]

New Hampshire has come close to abolishing the death penalty several times in recent decades, sometimes stopped by only one person. The state legislature voted to repeal the death penalty in 2000 but Governor Jeanne Shaheen vetoed the bill. In 2009, the New Hampshire House of Representatives again voted for repeal, but the state senate tabled the bill. In 2014, New Hampshire's governor Maggie Hassan stated she would sign a bill repealing the death penalty. But after the New Hampshire House of Representatives overwhelmingly approved the bill, a tie senate vote of 12-12 kept the bill from passing by one vote.[39]

These near abolitions and the first successful legislative abolitions since *Furman* resulted from the 1990s moratorium movement and the post-*McCleskey v. Kemp* focus on popular opinion and legislatures. Although the good economy may have aided the moratorium movement, the end of the good economy did not end the movement. Toward the end of the first decade of the twenty-first century, the United States faced an economic crisis that continued into the next decade. Not long after the recession started around December 2007, the anti-death penalty movement had some of its biggest successes, including the abolition of the death penalty in New Mexico in 2009 and in Illinois in 2011.

The anti-capital punishment momentum created in the preceding decades contributed to the abolition successes. For example, the 2011 Illinois abolition grew out of Governor Ryan's moratorium. But the twenty-first century abolitions also gained ground in some areas because of the recession. As states suffered through economic shortfalls, one way to save money was to eliminate the death penalty. Thus, the earlier discoveries showing problems with the death penalty gave politicians political justification for eliminating the costly punishment. When Illinois governor Pat Quinn signed the bill abolishing the death penalty in 2011, he made specific reference to the wasted resources of the death penalty.[40]

In the past, economic downturns helped stall death penalty abolition activity, such as during the Great Depression when executions hit record numbers. But in the years after *Gregg,* through the litigation failure of *McCleskey v. Kemp* and throughout the 1990s moratorium movement, death penalty abolitionists educated the public about the high cost of the death penalty. So in the early 2000s, the economic difficulties aided the movement to eliminate the death penalty instead of harming the movement. States facing budget problems considered how much money they might save by eliminating the death penalty. Thus, the economic crisis eventually played a role in states eliminating the death penalty in the early twentieth century.

The recession, however, created some drawbacks for efforts to abolish or reform the death penalty in some states. For example, in May 2011, the Florida Legislature abolished the Commission on Capital Cases, a commission that had been established fifteen years earlier to monitor death penalty post-conviction cases in the state. Part of the commission's role had been to recommend reform to the governor, the legislature, and the state supreme court to address problems with the state's death penalty system. But Florida discontinued the commission to save $400,000 for the state, which since 1973 had exonerated more defendants who had been sentenced to death than any other state.[41]

California continues to reevaluate its commitment to capital punishment, partly because of concerns about the costs of the death penalty and the size of its death row. A federal judge and a law professor completed a 2011 study that considered capital punishment's additional legal and security costs. They found California had spent more than four billion dollars on capital punishment since 1978, translating into more than three hundred million dollars for each of the state's thirteen executions. The study noted that death penalty prosecutions are more complicated than other cases, and thus they cost up to twenty times as much as cases where the harshest potential sentence is life without the possibility of parole. Additionally, the study predicted the state will have spent nine billion dollars by 2030 because it opted for the death penalty in 1978.[42]

These concerns about budgets played a significant role when California voters debated Proposition 34 in 2012, an initiated state statute on the popular ballot. The measure, which was endorsed by the Los Angeles Times, would have replaced the sentence of death with a sentence of life without parole.[43] The measure also was supported by Republican California Supreme Court chief justice Tani Cantil-Sakauye and by former chief justice Ronald George, who as Deputy Attorney General of California in 1971 had successfully argued for the U.S. Supreme Court to uphold the death penalty in McGautha v. California.[44] Other supporters of abolishing California's death penalty included former prosecutor Donald J. Heller, who wrote a 1978 law that expanded California's death penalty, and Ron Briggs, who led that 1978 campaign.[45] The proposition, however, failed when Californians voted in November 2012. But some noted that the close vote of 53-47 percent to retain capital punishment showed a significant change from the 70 percent of people who voted for the death penalty law in 1978.[46]

In California, the anti-death penalty son of former governor Pat Brown returned to the governor's chair in Sacramento starting in January 2011, having previously served as governor 1975-1983. Like his father, Governor Jerry Brown worked to balance his own opposition to capital punishment with the demands of the existing system. In April 2011, Governor Brown opted to save the state money by canceling construction of a new $356-million death row. Governor Brown said the state should not be spending so much on the condemned while it is cutting the budget for social programs and education. Then, following a 2014 U.S. District Court decision finding California's death penalty unconstitutional, Governor Jerry Brown, like his father before him, continued to contemplate what to do about California's massive death penalty system.[47]

Whatever the causes, the decade period starting with 2004 became one of the most successful abolition periods in American history along with the mid-1800s, 1907–1917, and 1957–1965 periods. The abolition in New York started with court decisions as a remnant of the LDF litigation strategy that had its greatest success with *Furman* and its great disappointment with *McCleskey v. Kemp*. But the other abolitions of this recent period came about from legislatures and governors, as during the previous abolition periods. McCleskey's case contributed to those successes by reminding abolitionists about the importance of popular opinion. And his case also reminded governors and legislators that they could not depend on the courts to solve all of the problems with the death penalty.[48]

These twenty-first century abolitions occurred, so far, in six states: in New York (2004), New Jersey (2007), New Mexico (for new cases) (2009), Illinois (2011), Connecticut (for new cases) (2012), and Maryland (for new cases) (2013). Twelve other states that do not have the death penalty from earlier abolitions, with the most recent abolition date in parenthesis, are: Alaska (1957), Hawaii (1957), Iowa (1965), Maine (1887), Massachusetts (1984), Michigan (1846), Minnesota (1911), North Dakota (1973), Rhode Island (1984), Vermont (1964), West Virginia (1965), and Wisconsin (1853). Further, Washington, DC, does not have the death penalty, and the U.S. territories of American Samoa, Guam, Northern Mariana Islands, Puerto Rico, and the U.S. Virgin Islands also do not have capital punishment.

OTHER CHANGES IN THE TWENTY-FIRST CENTURY

In addition to changes in laws, other factors illustrate the dropping popularity of capital punishment in the early twenty-first century. After the number of executions per year grew through the decades after *Gregg*, in the early twenty-first century, the numbers declined. Although constitutional challenges to lethal injection contributed to the decrease in executions, other factors contributed too. After a peak of 98 executions in 1999, executions gradually dropped to around the 40–50 range during the recent abolition period: 2004 (59 executions); 2005 (60 executions); 2006 (53 executions); 2007 (42 executions); 2008 (37 executions); 2009 (52 executions); 2010 (46 executions); 2011 (43 executions); 2012 (43 executions); and 2013 (39). And fewer states were using the death penalty. In 2012, only nine states carried out executions, the fewest number of states in two decades.

Similarly, during 2012, juries sentenced seventy-eight people to death in the United States, the second lowest number since the Supreme Court decided *Gregg v. Georgia* in 1976. By 2013, the size of America's death rows was down to 3,088 prisoners from a peak of 3,593 in the year 2000.[49]

In the context of death penalty history, trends vary across a diverse country. For example, in 2013, the Florida Legislature passed a bill called the "Timely Justice Act" to speed up executions, and Florida governor Rick Scott continued signing death warrants at the highest pace in decades.[50] Similarly, as in the past, death penalty advocates may work to bring back the death penalty in some of the new abolitionist states. Yet, the most recent trend has been toward abolishing the death penalty.

The abolitions in the early twenty-first century are the first to occur since the Supreme Court started regulating capital punishment. One may point to several possible explanations for what prompted the changing attitudes regarding capital punishment after *McCleskey v. Kemp*. First, it could be merely chance that death penalty opponents began obtaining victories outside the courtroom after McCleskey's execution. The popularity and pro-death penalty successes fluctuated throughout United States' history. Several factors contributed to recent changes, and the fact that new scientific developments allowed the use of DNA evidence to prove innocence played a large role. So perhaps the moratorium movement and recent state abolitions are just part of that normal flow of history.

Another possible explanation for the abolitions after McCleskey is the timing in relation to the Court striking down the death penalty in *Furman*. At the time of McCleskey's 1991 execution, the modern post-*Furman* death penalty had been around for fifteen years. In the early years after *Gregg*, people could not fully assess the impact of the changes required by the Supreme Court, and they could hope the new death penalty statutes would give correct and fair results. After more than a decade, though, critics had enough evidence to raise questions about the assessment of the new American capital punishment system. So, the moratorium movement in the 1990s and the abolitions in the early 2000s may have resulted because it took approximately twenty years for the post-*Furman* arguments to take hold.

Although time and chance played some role, an additional reason exists for the historic changes to the death penalty: Warren McCleskey's case taught the lesson that victories against the death penalty also would have to be sought outside the courts. Although the litigation strategy to end the death penalty did not succeed, the efforts behind the failure eventually contributed to success, just as the efforts behind the anti-lynching movement's failure to obtain a federal anti-lynching law contributed to ending the practice of lynching. For example, the Supreme Court ensured that the death penalty would be more expensive to maintain, even as its decisions limiting federal review contributed to fears about executing the innocent. These concerns about cost and innocence that came out of the litigation movement became cornerstones of the moratorium movement and the modern abolition movement. And McCleskey's case formed part of the foundations of this change. Some may dispute the overall importance of his case, but *McCleskey v. Kemp* remains one of the most important Supreme Court cases in American history.

The Supreme Court's decision in *McCleskey v. Kemp* confirmed that the NAACP's strategy that worked so well in school desegregation cases, and seemed to work so well with the death penalty in *Furman v. Georgia*, was not going to end the American death penalty. Because of that failure, death penalty opponents, governors, and legislators knew the abolition litigation strategy had ended. Even if race played a significant role in determining who was executed, the Supreme Court would not stop the death penalty.

McCleskey's case helped change the American death penalty in other ways too. As his case signaled the end of the litigation abolition strategy, it also pointed to a new path. In *McCleskey v. Kemp*, the Supreme Court refused to strike down the death penalty based on sociological and empirical evidence. But the injustices revealed by those studies found some traction outside the courtroom, as the media and others responded to the evidence of racial discrimination in the system. Although the Baldus study did not win in court, the findings found a different kind of success through the years. Besides the fact that the Baldus study is still cited for its findings, other researchers have exposed problems with the American death penalty by building on the work done by Professors Baldus, Woodworth, and Pulaski. This type of objective evidence—ranging from studies about race to studies about geography to DNA evidence—continues to raise concerns among the public and among policymakers.[51]

In a sense, these recent abolitions are a part of Warren McCleskey's continuing imprint on the American death penalty. When McCleskey's death row friend Billy Moore recounted his last conversation with Warren McCleskey, he noted, "We agreed that if there was ever going to be any real fight [to get rid of the death penalty] it must come from the people."[52] Thus, in one of his final conversations hours before his execution, McCleskey unknowingly summed up his role in American history.

CHAPTER 23

Escaping from Imprisonment of the Past

Today's American death penalty is imprisoned by the past, as many states and the federal government retain the punishment as a remnant of our nation's history. Yet, the Supreme Court justices and others who changed their minds about the modern death penalty show a way to escape from that past.

The American death penalty of the early twenty-first century retains much in common with the death penalty from previous centuries and with the laws used to execute Warren McCleskey. But many Americans see the death penalty with a different perspective today than they did while McCleskey lived. These new views arose due to new discoveries and broader access to worldwide critiques through various sources of information in the digital age. Concerns about racial discrimination, costs, wrongful executions and other issues have led several states to abandon the death penalty in recent years. Yet, other states maintain the punishment of death as an option. Considering the country's history, the national inconsistencies on the death penalty issue should not be surprising.

By contrast, a majority of countries around the world do not have the death penalty, and international pressure supporting abolition of capital punishment continues. Several times since 2007 the United Nations passed resolutions calling for a death penalty moratorium. In December 2010, the UN General Assembly reaffirmed its position in favor of a moratorium and recognized a trend toward abolition of the death penalty around the world. In that vote, 109 governments voted in favor of the resolution, continuing the trend of a growing number of countries supporting a moratorium. The United States and forty other countries voted against it, while thirty-five abstained.[1]

One may speculate why many U.S. states and the federal government retain the death penalty while the worldwide trend has been to abandon it, leaving the United States as the only Western industrialized nation with the death penalty. At the time of *Furman* and *Gregg*, this abolition trend spread around much of the world, so many people thought the United States would follow. But because much of the 1970s American abolition movement focused on the courts, legislators revolted against the courts dictating the law for the populace. Thus, state politicians overwhelmingly responded to *Furman* by passing new death penalty laws and making capital punishment even more of a political issue. That political backlash may be one of the reasons America has followed a path of retaining the death penalty.

There are other reasons the United States has bucked the worldwide trend. America, with its high incarceration rate, is generally more punitive toward its criminals than many other countries. Part of the reason for American attitudes toward punishment and the death penalty may relate to American history and attitudes. Of course, a range of factors contribute, and Americans do not all agree with one view. But as a general matter, Americans have a rooted tradition of believing in individual responsibility, going back to the founding of our country through the Western cowboy myth to today. The idea of individual responsibility connects to our ideas of democracy and capitalism, and retribution remains an important part of the country's criminal justice policy.[2] All of these views are complicated by America's legacy of slavery and the role of race, especially when considering the death penalty, a practice tied to a long history in many states.

Still, the United States remains a relatively young country, and minds can change over time. Americans have been trying to figure out a better punishment system since before the first penitentiary in Philadelphia tried to create a system to reform prisoners.

Warren McCleskey's case played a role in changing minds about the death penalty. The case helped expose the connections among race, lynching, and the death penalty. But the case helped change the way death penalty abolitionists battled capital punishment and the way Americans view the death penalty. In the 1960s through the time of *McCleskey v. Kemp*, many abolitionists hoped to abolish the death penalty by judicial decree. But after the Supreme Court ruled against McCleskey, abolitionists had little choice but to sharpen their main focus on the political process. And, at the same time, policy makers also realized the Supreme Court was not going to solve the problems with the death penalty. Although McCleskey lost in the courtrooms, his case helped put the death penalty back on a road to abolition outside the courts.

Abolitionists, of course, all along had been working outside the courts, and one may argue about to what degree, if any, his case led activists to do anything differently. But by chance, by the work of the lawyers and the advocates outside the legal system, and by various factors from the 1990s and the moratorium movement, his case marks a turning point in the history of the American death penalty.

Changes in opinion polls highlight that historical turning point. According to Gallup polls through the years since the 1930s, opposition to the death penalty peaked in 1966 when 47 percent of Americans opposed capital punishment and only 42 percent supported the death penalty. As the death penalty became a major legal issue, popular support for it increased as the Supreme Court threatened to take away the death penalty against public will. In November 1972, less than six months after the Supreme Court held that the American death penalty statutes were unconstitutional in *Furman v. Georgia*, 57 percent of people polled supported the death penalty compared to 32 percent against. As Warren McCleskey sat on death row in the 1970s into the 1990s, support for the death penalty continued to grow up to 80 percent in 1994.

But after McCleskey's case clarified that the courts would not strike down capital punishment and would not eliminate the risk of racial disparities, efforts to educate the public on problems with the death penalty began to pay off. Support for the death penalty continued to be strong, but the support fell below the level of the 1980s and 1990s. By October 2013, a Gallup poll revealed that 60 percent supported the death penalty and 35 percent opposed it, the greatest opposition to the death penalty since 1972 when the Court decided *Furman v. Georgia*. The same poll found that only 52% of Americans believe that the U.S. death penalty is applied fairly.

Further, when respondents are asked to select their preference between the death penalty and the alternative of life imprisonment with no possibility of parole, the population is almost evenly split. One recent poll found that only 49 percent preferred states keep the death penalty and 46 percent chose life in prison.[3] Out of the moratorium movement, and out of education about the death penalty, and out of discoveries of innocent people on death row, significantly more people now oppose the death penalty than they did prior to the post-*McCleskey* moratorium movement.

More dramatically, one sees the effects of changing attitudes in states that have abolished the death penalty in the early twenty-first century. As of 2014, eighteen states and the District of Columbia no longer impose death sentences. By the end of the first decade of the twenty-first century, juries were imposing fewer death sentences than any time since *Furman*.[4]

In the early twenty-first century, as during the death penalty moratorium movement period in the 1990s, a number of former judges and politicians came out against capital punishment, with many of them reversing their position from years ago. Many of these people allowed executions to proceed, so it took some courage for them to admit that their past errors may have contributed to people being executed. As noted earlier, in the 1990s, two members of the *Gregg v. Georgia* plurality—Justice Harry Blackmun and Justice Lewis Powell—confessed they were wrong to have upheld the death penalty. Justice Powell, who wrote the majority opinion in *McCleskey v. Kemp*, revealed that he regretted being the fifth and deciding vote in that case.

Eventually, two decades later, a third member of the *Gregg* plurality concluded that the system they upheld in that case had failed. Justice John Paul Stevens, who, after replacing Justice William O. Douglas voted to uphold the death penalty in *Gregg*, lamented his role in finding the death penalty constitutional. (See Figure 23.1.)

During his last few years on the bench, Justice Stevens wrote about the failures of capital punishment, even though he still followed precedent. In 2008 in *Baze v. Rees*, he voted to uphold Kentucky's lethal injection procedure as constitutional. But while reading Chief Justice John Roberts's draft of the majority opinion and the Chief Justice's reasoning that the Eighth Amendment prohibits needless suffering,

Figure 23.1
Justice John Paul Stevens (Collection of the Supreme Court of the United States)

Stevens had an epiphany. The Court's prior decisions protected defendants from punishments that tried to match the pain suffered by victims. Thus, Stevens concluded, the decisions undermined the retribution rationale for the death penalty, the only remaining possible justification for the punishment. Reflecting on that conclusion, Stevens decided to write a separate concurring opinion explaining why capital punishment is cruel and unusual in violation of the Eighth Amendment.[5]

In his opinion, Justice Stevens pointed to various concerns he had about the current capital punishment system, including the problems raised in Warren McCleskey's case. First, Stevens reasoned that in capital trials, the "death-qualification" process that excludes jurors opposed to capital punishment results in juries that are biased in favor of convictions. Second, he recognized a heightened risk of error in capital cases because of the nature of the disturbing crimes. Third, he lamented that the Court has allowed discriminatory application of the death penalty in decisions as in *McCleskey v. Kemp*. Finally, he wrote that the risk of errors in capital cases, combined with the irrevocable nature of death, creates a great risk of executing innocent defendants.[6]

Justice Stevens concluded that the post-*Furman* death penalty did not solve the problems the Court saw in the pre-*Furman* death penalty. Thus, he made the same assessment about the modern death penalty that Justice Byron White made about the pre-*Furman* death penalty: capital punishment is "'the pointless and needless extinction of life with only marginal contributions'" to society and the state. Such a penalty, then, is "'patently excessive and cruel and unusual punishment violative of the Eighth Amendment.'"[7]

After completing his final term in October 2010, Stevens discussed his qualms about the death penalty system in a National Public Radio interview. He explained that when he voted in the 1976 cases he believed the death penalty would be so narrow that proper procedures would ensure adequate protections to capital defendants. But later decisions—such as ones allowing victim impact statements during sentencing—"load the dice in favor of the prosecution against the defendant." So, after the 1976 capital case decisions, "the court constantly expanded the cases eligible for the death penalty, so that the underlying premise for my vote in those cases has disappeared, in a sense."[8]

Ultimately, three of the justices who voted to uphold the Georgia death penalty law in *Gregg v. Georgia*—Stevens, Powell, and Blackmun—came to conclude that the death penalty had failed. All three referred to McCleskey's case in their announcements. Their conclusions about the problems with the death penalty came through years of seeing it in practice. If those three had voted against the death penalty in 1976, they would have joined Justices Thurgood Marshall and William Brennan for a 5-4 majority in holding the death penalty violates the U.S. Constitution. And nobody would have been executed after that date in Georgia, including Warren McCleskey, and probably not anyone in the country. The history of the American death penalty in this book would have ended with 1976. Similarly, if Powell had changed his mind by the time of *McCleskey v. Kemp*, the American death penalty may have ended in 1987. But the justices' regrets in not striking down Georgia's death penalty did nothing for Warren McCleskey or those affected by the more than a thousand executions that have taken place since 1976.

These five justices do not stand alone with their reservations about the death penalty. As noted earlier, Justice Ruth Bader Ginsburg has stated her preference for a society without capital punishment, and former justice Sandra Day O'Conner expressed some concerns about the capital punishment system. Additionally, Justice Stevens has speculated that Justice Potter Stewart, who voted to uphold the death penalty in *Gregg v. Georgia* but retired only five years later in 1981, would have granted relief to McCleskey after seeing that the post-*Furman* death penalty had failed to cure the arbitrariness and racial discrimination that existed prior to 1972.

Some others who are responsible for the existence of Georgia's death penalty law also changed their minds. While Jimmy Carter was governor of Georgia in 1973, he signed the death penalty law that was used to sentence Warren McCleskey to death. But after decades as a supporter of the death penalty, he followed Justices Blackmun, Powell, and Stevens by changing his mind. In 2000, he called for a moratorium on executions, expressing concern about the executions of "poor, minority, and mentally deficient defendants."[9] In 2012, he wrote an editorial in *The Atlanta Journal-Constitution* arguing "it is time for Georgia and other states to abolish the death penalty." In concluding there are "overwhelming ethical, financial, and religious reasons to abolish the death penalty," he cited racial statistics such as those used in *McCleskey v. Kemp*.[10]

Additionally, the organization that authored the death penalty statute used as a model for laws in Georgia and many states also changed its mind about the death penalty. The Georgia General Assembly and other legislatures based their post-*Furman* capital sentencing statutes on a system devised by the American Law Institute (ALI), an organization of around 4,000 scholars, lawyers, and judges. In 1963, when states were giving jurors complete sentencing discretion, the ALI approved the Model Penal Code, which included a model statute listing aggravating and mitigating factors for jurors to consider in capital sentencing. After *Furman* struck down the death penalty laws in 1972, states turned to the Model Penal Code for their new death penalty laws. The Georgia statute upheld by the Court in *Gregg*, as well as death penalty statutes throughout the country, are based to some extent on the Model Penal Code. Thus, today's capital punishment system was based on the work of scholars and practitioners who had an idea in 1963 about how to make the death penalty less arbitrary: provide jurors with a list of guidelines.

By 2009, though, the scholars and practitioners of the ALI had completely removed the capital punishment provision of the Model Penal Code. The ALI did not take a position on the death penalty in theory. But in withdrawing from efforts to improve the death penalty laws, the organization in effect concluded that the existing model does not work, citing concerns about the administration of the U.S. death penalty. The organization said it was disavowing the structure it had created "in light of the current intractable institutional and structural obstacles to ensuring a minimally adequate system for administering capital punishment."[11]

Like Justices Stevens, Blackmun, and Powell—and like former president Jimmy Carter,—the ALI justified its change partly based on the ongoing connection between race and the death penalty. The ALI cited a report that explained that the evidence of "racial discord" in the United States was "an important explanatory variable" on why the United States maintains capital punishment while other Western countries do not. So, not only did the ALI remove the death penalty provision that formed the basis for the statute used to sentence McCleskey, but part of the reason for doing so was the underlying problems McCleskey's attorneys raised.[12]

Thus, the organization that created the model for the law used to execute McCleskey, the governor who signed the law, a majority of the justices who upheld capital punishment in 1976, and a majority of the justices who upheld McCleskey's death sentence, eventually believed his execution occurred in an unfair system.

Similarly, as discussed in previous chapters, since the 1990s, a large number of politicians, jurists, and others who once supported the death penalty have changed their minds. Those who have changed their hearts argue that the United States must break from its past history with the ultimate punishment.

The post-*McCleskey* and post-litigation-strategy death penalty will continue to face obstacles. History shows that America's love with the death penalty ebbs and flows, as societal changes, wars, economics, high-profile crimes, sympathetic defendants, and other events affect the death penalty's popularity. At the same time, from the gallows to the chair to the chamber to the needle, officials have used various means to execute prisoners. Social movements against the death penalty will continue arguing that it should be abolished because of what the death penalty says about us as a society. Death penalty advocates will respond that American society needs capital punishment.

For now, the death penalty machine grinds on, connected to the past. On September 21, 2011, two decades after McCleskey's execution, Georgia executed another African-American man for killing a white police officer. A jury sentenced Troy Davis to death for killing Mark MacPhail, an off-duty police officer working as a security guard who came to the aid of a homeless man being attacked by Davis, according to witnesses. After his 1989 sentencing, Davis spent time on Georgia's death row with Warren McCleskey. Similar to McCleskey's case, Davis's case went to the Supreme Court, and similar to McCleskey's trial, jurors based his conviction on the eyewitness testimony of others. After Davis's conviction, seven of the nine witnesses against him changed their testimony, and Davis continued to claim innocence. But the Supreme Court applies an extremely high standard for a habeas petitioner who claims innocence. So, Georgia executed Davis in 2011, as people from around the world objected to the execution of someone they thought was innocent.

Some commentators claimed Davis's execution signaled a turning point for the death penalty and would result in its abolition. But these activists ignored the fact that on the same night as Davis's execution, Texas executed Lawrence R. Brewer against little protest. Brewer's crime was particularly heinous, as the white supremacist and two friends were convicted of beating and dragging an African-American man to death. Although some protesters showed up to the Texas execution, unlike Davis's case, Brewer's death brought no international outcry. Brewer's case also led Texas to eliminate its practice of offering last meals to the condemned.[13]

While the Davis case seemed to reveal what is wrong with the American death penalty, the Brewer case seemed to illustrate that the death penalty plays an important role and is racially fair. But even if Brewer's crime appeared to be a perfect fit for the death penalty, the case still showed imperfections in the system. Only two of the three men involved in the crime received the death penalty, and, as one of the rare cases where a state executed a white man for killing a black person, it showed how extreme a case must be for that to happen. Further, while the family of Troy Davis's victim wanted the death penalty, the son and daughter of Brewer's victim wanted Brewer to spend the rest of his life in prison instead of being executed.

On the day Troy Davis and Lawrence Brewer were executed, the different reactions to the two cases highlighted America's conflicted feelings about the death penalty. Emotionally society wants vengeance, but logically many concede that the capital punishment system, like all human endeavors, in imperfect.[14]

There will be more capital defendants in Georgia and in other states. Although Justices Blackmun, Powell, Stevens, Ginsburg, Brennan, and Marshall have reasoned for a way to escape the legacy of capital punishment and its problems, the past maintains its hold on the American death penalty. As shown by the history of capital punishment, reasoned debate about the death penalty has not been the only driving force with the punishment's popularity. Other factors such as individual cases also helped shape that history.

* * *

On a clear autumn day in Marietta in late September 1991, as Warren McCleskey's funeral came to an end, his family closed the services with the recessional music of Walter and Tramaine Hawkins's song "Goin' Up Yonder." [15] In the South, slaves often had used code phrases in their spirituals so the whites would not recognize what they were saying. So, the phrase "going up yonder" appeared in their songs as a code to refer to escaping slavery, the South, and discrimination. At McCleskey's funeral, the gospel song about dying reminded listeners that what one may think is the end is not the end. On that September day as the words to "Goin' Up Yonder" played in Georgia, the funeral attendees could not have known that McCleskey's legacy had not ended. His life would continue to influence American history. (See Figure 23.2.)

In *McCleskey v. Kemp*, when the Supreme Court justices evaluated the constitutionality of Warren McCleskey's death sentence, one aspect of the case was noticeably absent: Warren McCleskey. Understandably, legal analysis principles require the Court to address the abstract constitutional legal issues before it. But Warren McCleskey the person also was relevant to the issues before the Court as much as the web of statistics and the legal precedent.

In dissent, Justice Brennan did attempt to bring the case back to Warren McCleskey by considering a fictional "Warren McCleskey" in his pretrial jail cell asking his lawyer how race might affect the outcome of his case. And, in noting that "we remain imprisoned by the past as long as we deny [racism's] influence on the present," Brennan also addressed the legacy of race in the South and how such information should play a role in the Court's analysis.[16] But the justices need not have created a fictional defendant or looked to general history when it could have seen much of American history in the real Warren McCleskey.

The Court ignored that Warren McCleskey grew up in a racist environment and went to a segregated school where his city did not find him good enough to mingle with white children. Other circumstances punctuated that lesson of inferiority when violence repeatedly intruded into his childhood home.

If the Supreme Court Justices visited McCleskey's hometown of Marietta they would have seen the location where discrimination resulted in the lynching of Leo Frank. The justices would not have needed to drive far from McCleskey's house to

A GIFT *of* DIGNITY

. . . .

HE FOUND JESUS IN A GEORGIA JAIL. HIS DEATH-row friend, Billy Neal Moore, first opened up the good news of the gospel to him. And from then on, he was known as a peacemaker. He intervened when arguments heated toward violence, and he was the one everybody came to when they needed a calming word. Even the prison staff were grateful to him, because they knew their own lives were a lot safer because of the way Warren McCleskey lived.

"His faith meant everything in life," says Murphy Davis, Georgia director of the Southern Prison Ministry and a member of the Open Door Community in Atlanta, who knew McCleskey for 10 years while he was on death row. "He came out of a life in chaos and ordered everything around his commitment to faith."

THE STORY OF WARREN MCCLESKEY

That chaos included a mother who sold bootleg corn liquor to help support her seven children, and an abusing stepfather who operated an illegal gambling casino in their home in the "Skid Row" area of Marietta, Georgia. In 1963—a year before Warren graduated from high school—his mother shot his stepfather; the killing was ruled an act of self-defense.

Fifteen years later, on the morning of May 13, 1978, Warren McCleskey, Ben Wright Jr., Bernard Dupree, and David Burney robbed the Dixie Furniture Store in Atlanta. Atlanta police officer Frank Schlatt responded to a silent alarm. Evidence suggests that two bullets from the gun of Ben Wright killed Schlatt.

Wright left behind a leather jacket with a laundry ticket stapled inside one sleeve, which led to his arrest. Wright's girlfriend told police the names of the other three men. McCleskey and Burney both confessed to robbing the furniture store but denied killing Schlatt. Wright, assuming from his arrest that the others had told on him, devised statements against his three accomplices and told police that Warren McCleskey was the "triggerman." Offie Evans, a prisoner in the cell next to McCleskey in the Fulton County Jail, testified that McCleskey had confessed to him that he killed Schlatt.

David Burney and Bernard Dupree are serving life prison sentences. Ben Wright was released from prison in 1987; he committed several more crimes and was subsequently sentenced to life plus 20 years. Warren McCleskey was sentenced to death on October 12, 1978.

. . . .
BY JOYCE HOLLYDAY

Figure 23.2
Organizations followed the story of Warren McCleskey (*Sojourners* magazine, www.sojo.net; photo by Marlene Karas)

see sites of other past lynchings. Along the way, they would have seen the lingering presence of the Civil War and the Ku Klux Klan, from Kennesaw Mountain to Stone Mountain.

In their Washington courthouse, the majority of the Supreme Court justices focused on Georgia's sentencing standards to find that McCleskey's trial was fair. But the Court overlooked that many of the jurors likely grew up in segregated schools just like McCleskey. The Court ignored the Confederate battle flag incorporated in the Georgia state flag hanging in the courthouse during McCleskey's trial for killing a white police officer. The Court assumed that race affected one's odds of getting the death penalty, but five white justices who made up a majority of the Court concluded those risks were acceptable under the Constitution. Had the Court dug deeper, it also might have connected the racial disparities to the way socioeconomic factors and geography affect capital sentencing.

Several years after *McCleskey v. Kemp*, the Court revisited McCleskey's case when his lawyers petitioned the Court again with new evidence about a key witness's bias. But the justices, who surprised McCleskey's lawyers by changing the procedural requirements for this case, did not address the merits of the claim. And by that time, they also did not know that on death row McCleskey had become a model prisoner who helped others and worked to change his life. Finally, although Justice Blackmun and some of the other justices may have read about McCleskey's trips to the electric chair on his final night, they did not make the connection between the electric chair and the legacy of burning and maiming African Americans in the South.

The Court's opinion in *McCleskey v. Kemp* also contained little discussion of Officer Frank Schlatt. One of the many unfortunate side effects of the death penalty is that the crime victims and their families are often lost in the story. Media attention does cover the victims and their families through the trial. But by the time an execution comes around, the media focus on the defendant and the litigation surrounding the execution. One lesson from McCleskey's case is that the courts are not going to resolve the problems with the death penalty or find a way to better help victims and their families. Ultimately, the responsibility for getting rid of an unfair death penalty, preventing crime, and providing aid to the victims' families falls on the people, legislatures, and governors.

There are many other stories surrounding the case that cannot fit into one book. Other people, such as the employees of the Dixie Furniture Company and the jurors, were affected by the case, while lawyers and judges throughout the system worked long hours in what they all saw as a pursuit of justice. The execution affected the prison workers and other prisoners, just as McCleskey's friend Billy Moore remains haunted by his time on death row and the execution of his friend.

While Officer Schlatt was a hero who died in the line of duty trying to help others, the term "hero" does not apply to Warren McCleskey, and the purpose of this book is not to make him into one. But Warren McCleskey's story is an American story of childhood violence turned into adult violence, of a boy and man who experienced racial bias, and of a wayward life seeking redemption. As such, to understand the broad range of issues in his case one needs to understand the human being.

The issues in his case haunted many in society as well as those directly involved in the case. A majority of the Supreme Court justices who decided McCleskey's case came to believe he should not have been executed, and several justices regretted their key votes that launched the modern American death penalty in 1976. Similarly, some of the jurors in McCleskey's case later regretted their vote condemning him to death. Others changed their minds too, such as the governor who signed the law that condemned McCleskey and the Georgia court that eventually acknowledged that Warren McCleskey's electric chair execution was cruel and unusual.

But these changed minds came too late for Warren McCleskey. His case *McCleskey v. Kemp* remains a striking reminder that although the Court can play a role in these issues, ultimately the American people are left to address and resolve these problems. McCleskey's legacy teaches this lesson.

When Americans seek guidance on what to do about these complicated issues, a good starting point is to see what one may learn from a man who grew up in a troubled, violent, abusive, segregated environment to become a troubled and violent person but who ultimately worked to discover some redeeming qualities within himself. American society could do worse than learning some of the same lessons Warren McCleskey learned. Out of its own similar past of violence, segregation, discrimination, and mistakes, America continues to seek the peace Warren McCleskey struggled to find on death row as an escape from the imprisonment of his own past.

PART H

Epilogue

Warren McCleskey's Case and the American Death Penalty Today

People directly touched by Warren McCleskey's case and crimes have gone in various directions, while the American death penalty continues. Warren McCleskey's case, the death penalty, the criminal justice system, and new studies inform us about today's America.

Warren McCleskey's case lives on in the form of the modern American death penalty and a complicated America imprisoned by the past. More directly, the case personally affected those touched by the litigation and the crime. In the new century, the trial and appeals from the Dixie Furniture Company robbery and the murder of Officer Schlatt still have ramifications. Those who loved Officer Schlatt and Warren McCleskey are still without their deceased loved ones. Two daughters grew up without their fathers because of what happened on May 13, 1978.

Early in the twenty-first century, Georgia released from prison the three men who participated in the Dixie Furniture Company robbery with Warren McCleskey. In 2005, the state released on parole Bernard Depree, who had served nearly thirty years in prison. Several years later in March 2011, the state released on parole another one of the robbers, David Burney. Burney and Depree served sentences for both armed robbery and the murder connected to the robbery. Ben Wright, the mastermind behind the robbery who testified against McCleskey and was sentenced only for armed robbery, was released from prison much earlier, in September 1988. Within a few years, however, a Georgia court convicted him of another armed robbery. For the new charge, Wright served more time in prison until Georgia paroled him in June 2011 when he was around sixty-nine years old.[1]

By contrast, one of the police officers involved in McCleskey's case now sits in prison for murder. Officer Sidney Dorsey, who investigated one of McCleskey's codefendants, testified in the case that he did not ask anyone to move the informant Offie Evans to a cell near McCleskey.[2] Officer Dorsey went on to become sheriff of DeKalb County in Georgia, but later he was convicted of ordering the December

2000 murder of a man who had defeated him in a runoff election for the sheriff's office. Dorsey reportedly feared the new sheriff would investigate the corruption in his office. Prosecutors did not seek the death penalty against Dorsey, who is now serving a life sentence.[3]

The attorneys and judges involved in McCleskey's case through the years have gone on to other cases and other careers. For example, Mary Beth Westmoreland, who argued both *McCleskey v. Zant* and *McCleskey v. Kemp* for the state of Georgia before the U.S. Supreme Court, went on to serve as the Deputy Georgia Attorney General and Director of the Criminal Justice Division. Jack Boger, who argued those cases for McCleskey as Director of the NAACP Legal Defense and Education Fund Inc.'s Capital Punishment Project and Poverty and Justice Program, went on to become Dean of the University of North Carolina School of Law.

Additional attorneys, investigators, police officers, and others who worked on the case have had distinguished careers too. U.S. District Court Judge J. Owen Forrester, who rejected the findings of the Baldus study but several times stayed McCleskey's execution, continued to serve on the bench and took senior status in 2004. Robert Stroup, who began representing McCleskey after his trial and continued until McCleskey's death, became a trial judge in Atlanta for several years and later was Director of the Economic Justice Group at the NAACP Legal Defense Fund. He now is a partner at Levy Rater, P.C. in New York City, where his practice focuses on employment and civil rights issues.

The trial attorneys also had successful careers. McCleskey's trial attorney John Turner went to work as an assistant district attorney in Fulton County for sixteen years starting in 1981 and then returned to private practice in 1997. As a military judge in the Georgia National Guard, he also served in Operations Desert Shield and Desert Storm for several months in 1990–1991. Russell Parker, the lead prosecutor at the trial, continued working with the Fulton County District Attorney's Office. Thomas W. Thrash Jr., who worked on the trial with Parker as a young assistant district attorney, went on to be a law professor at Georgia State University and then a United States District Court judge for the Northern District of Georgia.

Two attorneys connected to McCleskey's case later ran for governor. Michael J. Bowers, who was Georgia's Attorney General when the state executed McCleskey, left his office after sixteen years of service in 1997 for an unsuccessful campaign for the Georgia Republican gubernatorial nomination. He became a partner at the Atlanta office of the law firm Balch & Bingham where he does civil litigation work. Another attorney connected with the case did become a governor and make history. Deval Patrick, who as a young staff attorney for the NAACP Legal Defense Fund helped prepare McCleskey's Supreme Court brief in *McCleskey v. Kemp,* in 2007 became the first African-American governor of Massachusetts and the second elected African-American governor of any state.[4]

Meanwhile, Warren McCleskey's death row friend Billy Moore was paroled from prison six weeks after McCleskey's execution. Moore had helped McCleskey find his faith, and the two men worked together to make Georgia's death row a more humane place. Today, Billy Moore travels around the world talking about his faith in redemption and his opposition to the death penalty.[5]

Only one Supreme Court justice who decided McCleskey's landmark case on race and the death penalty remains on the Court as of 2014. In 2010, Justice John Paul Stevens became the last of the four dissenters in *McCleskey v. Kemp* to retire, while Justice Antonin Scalia remained on the Court to be the last from the majority of the 1987 *McCleskey v. Kemp* Court.

The *McCleskey v. Kemp* justices who have passed away include Justice F. Powell, Jr., who wrote the decision and later changed his mind too late to save Warren McCleskey; Chief Justice William Rehnquist, who assigned the majority opinion to Powell; Justice Harry Blackmun, who was so affected by McCleskey's execution that he later began voting against every execution; Justice William J. Brennan, Jr., who wrote the moving dissent; and Justice Thurgood Marshall, who brought his capital defense work and experience with lynching to the Court. Justice Anthony Kennedy is the only other justice besides Scalia who took part in the 1991 *McCleskey v. Zant* decision who remains on the Court.

The NAACP Legal Defense Fund, which provided legal representation to Warren McCleskey and helped lead the fight against the death penalty for decades, continues to work on racial justice claims in the courts. In 1998, though, its death penalty project was renamed "the criminal justice practice" as it broadened its focus to include ending racial discrimination throughout the criminal justice system.

LDF could redirect its focus because other organizations formed to specialize in capital defense work. For example, in the 1980s and 1990s, federal and state governments helped with the load of post-conviction capital representation by funding twenty death penalty resource centers across the country. These legal resource centers effectively helped provide quality representation to capital defendants, but in 1996 the federal government stopped funding them. Some of the organizations continue as smaller nonprofit organizations and a number of attorneys work long hours on capital cases pro bono. Additionally, after *Gregg v. Georgia* and *McCleskey v. Kemp*, many organizations found some success by shifting some resources from appeals and post-conviction to increasing the quality of representation at capital trials. But death penalty defense remains underfunded in many states, and there is still a need for qualified capital defense attorneys.[6]

Regarding the authors of the statistical study that became the focus of *McCleskey v. Kemp*, George Woodworth is a Professor Emeritus at the University of Iowa, but the other two authors have passed away. Charles Pulaski passed away in June 2012 in Phoenix, Arizona. In June 2011, David Baldus passed away in Iowa City at the age of seventy-five. After Baldus's passing, Tony Amsterdam, the architect behind much of the national death penalty litigation, who is now a professor at New York University School of Law, told the *New York Times*, "Dave had a unique genius for digging into masses of messy factual information and discovering crucial human forces at work behind the purportedly impersonal administration of criminal law."[7]

There have been some changes in the key locations of this book. Today, McCleskey's hometown of Marietta is an affluent city described by one tour book as "Atlanta's grandest suburb." Country singer Travis Tritt was born in Marietta, and Alton Brown, who hosted *Good Eats* and other cooking shows, lives there.

Government dollars and the aerospace industry fuel the local economy, as Lockheed Martin Aeronautics manufactures jets in the area.[8]

Marietta continues to prosper, while trying to recognize its past with museums and Civil War cemeteries. In 2006, the National City League named Marietta an All-American City and one of the ten best communities in the United States. The city's population today nears 70,000. And, while the Cobb County African-American population declined from 30 percent in 1900 to only 4 percent around the time McCleskey went to death row, the migration reversed by the end of the century. The 2000 census showed the African-American population of Cobb County grew to 19 percent.[9]

Marietta hosts a *Gone with the Wind* Museum based on the book and the movie that depict General Sherman's march on the Atlanta area. The modest museum opened in 2003, and its website invites one to step back in time to "The rustle of petticoats. The smell of gunpowder. Cotton fields and plantations." Next to the *Gone with the Wind* Museum sits the Marietta Museum of History. The well-kept museum features interesting exhibits ranging from housewares to instruments of war. Museum administrators humorously dedicate the men's bathroom to one man, General Sherman. The bathroom wall features a mural of Sherman, and photos of the general who destroyed the town appear above each urinal.[10]

In Marietta, the effects of the Leo Frank lynching never disappeared. In recent years, the city hosted a play about the lynching. Historical markers indicate where a group of men from Marietta lynched Frank, but none of the lynchers would recognize the spot. In 2008, the Georgia Historical Society—with the Jewish American Society for Historic Preservation, Congregation Kol Emeth, and the Anti-Defamation League—erected a historical marker at the site of the lynching. The marker sits under a tree on the sidewalk of a busy suburban multi-lane intersection where you can smell the grease from the nearby fast-food restaurants. The location does not see many pedestrians, and few driving by the area probably notice the sign unless they happen to be visiting the office parking lot nearby. Before the Georgia Historical Society erected the historical marker, Jewish organizations in 1995 and 2005 placed small plaques on the side of an office building near the lynching spot.

In the early twenty-first century, many Marietta citizens reacted angrily when the local newspaper, the *Marietta Daily Journal*, published a letter advocating the community make a public apology for the Frank lynching. Also, in recent years locals argued about whether or not researchers should publish the names of those involved in the lynching, as many of the descendants of the lynchers still live in the community.[11]

The statue of U.S. senator Thomas E. Watson, whose editorials stirred the hate that led to Frank's lynching and to the resurrection of the Ku Klux Klan, still stands on the grounds of the Georgia State Capitol in Atlanta with the words, "A champion of right who never faltered in the cause." Watson, who was a publisher at the time of the Frank lynching, helped provoke the Marietta vigilantes by calling for citizens to take action after the governor commuted Frank's sentence. The statue continues to be a subject of controversy because of Watson's role in the Frank lynching and Watson's racism and anti-Semitism. In August 2000, an op-ed in the *Atlanta*

Journal-Constitution argued that the twelve-foot-high statue of Watson should be removed from the grounds of the Capitol. Some citizens continue to call for its removal. (See Figure Epilogue.1.)

The Marietta teenager whom Frank was accused of killing is also remembered. In April 2013 on the one-hundredth anniversary of Mary Phagan's murder, people came from across the country to visit her grave in the Marietta City Cemetery.

Figure Epilogue.1
Statue of Thomas E. Watson at the Georgia State Capitol (photo by J.L.K.)

Those who came to the grave included lawyers and students interested in the historical significance of the Leo Frank lynching. Other visitors included some former members of the Ku Klux Klan. One eighty-year-old Marietta resident explained how the Klan held power in Marietta up through the 1980s, when as the Grand Cyclops of the organization he led a parade through the town square. The former Klansman told the reporter he blamed "the Jews" for stirring up sympathy for Frank.[12]

Marietta, Atlanta, and Georgia continue to recognize the past in various ways. In 2012, Marietta erected a historical marker at the site of the former all-black Lemon Street High School, which was where McCleskey attended school.[13] The Fulton County Superior Court in Atlanta, where McCleskey was tried, now sits on the corner of a street named after Martin Luther King Jr. The city where Dr. King was born also honors the man with The Martin Luther King Jr. Center for Nonviolent Social Change. Georgia celebrates Martin Luther King Day every January, while also recognizing Robert E. Lee's Birthday that month and Confederate Memorial Day in April. In Atlanta, other connections to the past remain too, but the crime scene's furniture store named after Dixie is long gone.

Officials have taken similar actions to address the past across the United States. For example, in 2005, the United States Senate passed a resolution apologizing for its failure to pass federal anti-lynching legislation in the early twentieth century.[14]

As is true around the country, Georgia still struggles with race and related issues. In 2001, Georgia removed the Confederate battle flag from the state flag that hung in the courthouse when McCleskey was sentenced to death and that flew over the prison where he was executed. The flag that flies over Georgia today no longer incorporates the controversial Confederate battle flag. Instead, the redesigned flag is based upon the first official Confederate national flag, made up of stars on a field of blue in the corner with two red bars and one white bar. The Confederate battle flag, however, caused some controversy in 2014 when Georgia continued to include it in a redesign of a special Sons of Confederate Veterans license plate.[15]

Warren McCleskey's hometown and his state are microcosms of America. Marietta's and Georgia's past reflects America's history of Native American mistreatment, racism, slavery, racial violence, lynching, and discrimination. The history of Marietta and Georgia illustrates good things about America too, including the struggle to come to terms with past national legacies. The NAACP's Cobb County branch hosts an annual Juneteenth celebration to recognize the date the last slaves in America were freed. The Georgia Chapter of the Trail of Tears Association works to develop the Trail of Tears National Historic Trail to educate people about the past treatment of Georgia's Native Americans. Like Leo Frank's lynching, these and other past events are recalled and remembered and discussed in Marietta and Georgia.

* * *

Yet, the town, the state, and the nation have yet to confront the legacy of the evidence presented in Warren McCleskey's case. These remnants of history linger on in the nation's death penalty, despite other attempts to rectify past injustices. For example, an August 2010 report by the Equal Justice Initiative entitled *Illegal Racial Discrimination in Jury Selection: A Continuing Legacy*, found racial discrimination in jury selection in the eight southern states it examined, including Georgia. The study found some prosecutors used a number of improper reasons to exclude African Americans from juries, noting in some situations prosecutors had been trained in how to exclude potential jurors based on race. For example, in 1996, a training video made for Philadelphia district attorneys taught prosecutors how to exclude blacks from juries.[16]

Despite the Court's rejection of statistical evidence in McCleskey's case, other experts continue to work on studies similar to the Baldus study. Within a few years of *McCleskey v. Kemp*, the United States General Accounting Office (GAO) submitted a report to the Senate and House Committees of the Judiciary. The report synthesized twenty-eight studies that showed "a pattern of evidence indicating racial disparities in the charging, sentencing, and imposition of the death penalty after the *Furman* decision." The GAO report noted that "[i]n 82 percent of the studies, race of victim was found to influence the likelihood of being charged with capital murder or receiving the death penalty, i.e., those who murdered whites were found to be more likely to be sentenced to death than those who murdered blacks." The GAO found the disparity based on the race of the victim existed across different kinds of studies and was consistent through other states across the country.[17]

Since 1976, of all of those executed, approximately 80 percent of their victims have been white.[18] After the Supreme Court decided *McCleskey v. Kemp*, numerous studies have confirmed that the race of a victim continues to play a significant role in distinguishing who is sentenced to death and who is sentenced to life in prison. Studies have found racial disparities in capital sentencing in a wide range of jurisdictions that include California, Colorado, Connecticut, Florida, Delaware, Illinois, Kentucky, Maryland, Missouri, Nebraska, New Jersey, New Mexico, North Carolina, South Carolina, Philadelphia, and the federal death penalty system.[19]

Other studies have found that at least in some jurisdictions the race of the defendant affects capital sentencing too. In 2002, the Defender Association of Philadelphia in *Commonwealth v. Arrington* submitted a study of 338 cases in Philadelphia County that found that the risk of a death sentence for a black defendant was twice as high as it is for a nonblack defendant.[20] A study of death sentences in Harris County, Texas, during the time from the 1970s through the early 2000s found that statistically, for every 100 black capital defendants, five of them would be sentenced to death because of race.[21] A study published in 2006 concluded that judges and jurors found defendants more "death worthy" if they have physical features that are stereotypically associated with being black.[22] Similarly, a 2014 study of Washington state cases from 1981 through 2012 found "that juries were three times more likely to impose a sentence of death when the defendant was black than in cases involving similarly situated white defendants."[23]

Similarly, in a 2011 study, a group of law and statistics professors that included David Baldus discovered the use of the U.S. military death penalty resulted in a significant racial imbalance. The study concluded minorities were twice as likely to be sentenced to death as white defendants in the military court system. As in many of the studies of the civilian court system, the military study did not allege the system consciously and knowingly discriminated, but that actors within the system were unconsciously influenced by the race of both the victims and the defendants.[24]

Black defendants charged with killing white victims are more likely to receive the death penalty than any other race combination. For example, a 2003 study by Professors Raymond Paternoster and Robert Brame examined 1,130 death-eligible cases in Maryland from 1978 to 1999. After controlling for numerous factors that affect culpability, they found black defendants charged with killing white victims were 4.1 times more likely to receive a death sentence than other defendants with similar nonracial characteristics.[25]

Through the years, defense attorneys in state courts have used new studies about race to argue that the death penalty is unconstitutional. Generally, those arguments have been unsuccessful. Some courts have interpreted their state constitutions to follow *McCleskey v. Kemp*'s reasoning that statistically based claims of systemic discrimination cannot be a basis for relief. Other courts have accepted such evidence as relevant but still rejected the claims because the studies were not conclusive enough. As discussed in chapter 22, one exception where a state court did seriously evaluate racial discrimination in capital sentencing was the New Jersey Supreme Court. Until the state abolished the death penalty in 2007, the New Jersey Supreme Court maintained an empirical database of death-eligible cases and interpreted the New Jersey Constitution to address claims of systemic discrimination that were based on statistical evidence.[26]

The statistical studies do not prove that people on juries plan to discriminate, although that may happen in some cases. The studies show the pervasiveness of racism that lies undetected under the surface. People who would never think of intentionally discriminating and who would never think of themselves as racist still have subconscious biases that may affect the outcome of cases. Other studies demonstrate that people relate to other people who are similar to themselves when they think about death, so in capital cases white jurors may be more likely to relate to white victims.[27]

Supreme Court decisions have done little to limit the racial disparities, and some cases have made them even more likely to occur. After *McCleskey v. Kemp*, in *Payne v. Tennessee* the Supreme Court allowed information about the victims to play a broader role in capital sentencing, paving the way for jurors to use the characteristics of victims even more as a sentencing factor.[28]

During the modern death penalty era, American incarceration has grown overall. Since 1972, when the U.S. Supreme Court considered the death penalty in *Furman v. Georgia*, the number of incarcerated inmates in the country has grown by 600 percent. Regardless of what happens with the death penalty, the country will continue to grapple with problems created by the imprisonment of more than 2.2 million people. The number of inmates serving life and life-without-parole sentences also has grown. More than 140,000 individuals are serving life sentences, and a little less than one-third of those prisoners are sentenced to life without parole. As in the death penalty area, the racial statistics are disturbing. Two-thirds of people with life sentences and 77 percent of juveniles sentenced to life are people of color.[29]

The racial injustices raised by McCleskey's lawyers similarly exist for other sentences throughout the criminal justice system. Minorities are more likely to go to prison than whites for drug crimes even though whites have higher rates of drug use. More than 40 percent of those held as prisoners in the United States are black, even though the percentage of blacks in the general population is around 12 percent. Professor Michelle Alexander, who as a clerk for Justice Blackmun helped write Blackmun's dissent in Callins v. Collins, discussed this disparity in her book The New Jim Crow: Mass Incarceration in the Age of Colorblindness. She and others have noted that "more African Americans are under correctional control today—in prisons or jail, on probation or parole—than were enslaved in 1850."[30] Professor Alexander concludes that the country's policy of mass incarceration has merely redesigned racial discrimination and created a subordinate caste of people largely defined by race.[31]

Many courtrooms in the South today still look as they did in the 1950s and in earlier years with white lawyers, white judges, white clerks, white court reporters, and white jurors. And then, as Georgia attorney Steve Bright has noted, "[W]hen the defendants are brought in—when a group of African American men all handcuffed together wearing orange jumpsuits are brought into the courtroom—it looks like a slave ship has docked outside the courthouse."[32] These examples show why a majority of the justices in McCleskey v. Kemp feared that giving constitutional weight to the Baldus study would force them to address the racial disparities throughout the criminal justice system.

In Georgia—the setting for the landmark Supreme Court capital cases of Furman v. Georgia, Gregg v. Georgia, and McCleskey v. Kemp—there continues to be arbitrariness and discrimination decades after those cases wrestled with those problems. A few years after McCleskey's execution, the Georgia Supreme Court in February 1993 established the Commission on Racial and Ethnic Bias in the Court System. The court charged the commission with several tasks, including studying bias in the criminal justice system. After study, hearings, forums, interviews, and other investigation, the commission released a report in 1995 entitled Let Justice Be Done: Equally, Fairly, and Impartially. The report found "there are still areas within the state where members of minorities, whether racial or ethnic, do not receive equal treatment from the legal system."[33] The report made various recommendations, and the Georgia Supreme Court established the "Commission on Equality," which was later renamed the "Georgia Commission on Access and Fairness in the Courts," to work on implementing the recommendations.

Then, in 2006, the American Bar Association evaluated the commission's progress, concluding that the number of recommendations that Georgia effectively implemented was "questionable." The ABA report chastised the state, noting that "it appears that the State of Georgia needs to reexamine the impact of racial discrimination in the criminal justice system, thoroughly investigate the impact of racial discrimination in capital sentencing, and develop new strategies to eliminate racial discrimination."[34]

A year later, in 2007, the *Atlanta Journal-Constitution* featured a four-part series investigating 2,328 murder convictions in Georgia between January 1, 1995, and December 31, 2004. The newspaper found that the systemic problems that troubled some of the *McCleskey v. Kemp* Supreme Court justices still existed. Although the post-*Furman* statutes promised that the death penalty would be narrowed, 56 percent of all murder convictions were still eligible for the death penalty, thus still allowing prosecutors discretion in a large number of cases. The newspaper revealed that across the state, prosecutors were twice as likely to pursue a death sentence in cases where the victim was white than in cases where the victim was black. Further, in cases involving murder during an armed robbery, prosecutors were six times more likely to seek the death penalty in cases involving white victims than those involving black victims.

The *Atlanta Journal-Constitution* found arbitrariness in other areas besides race too. The newspaper discovered that the location of the murder within the state also affected the result of who received the death penalty. Further, the paper considered the 132 murders that were the worst 10 percent of potential death penalty cases and found that only twenty-nine of the defendants in that group received the death penalty. Instead of the most culpable crimes getting the death penalty, death sentences are determined by factors such as whether or not the defendant pleaded guilty, whether a prosecutor was already overloaded with work, and the strength of the evidence. Similarly, a recent study by the Capital Jury Project revealed that the racial makeup of a jury constitutes a significant factor in whether or not a defendant is sentenced to death.[35] The worst-of-the worst still do not typically get the death penalty; the punishment applies to the unluckiest of the worst and the unluckiest of the unlucky.

Similarly, national studies also establish that arbitrary factors such as the location of the crime significantly affect whether or not a capital defendant gets the death penalty.[36] Not only does it matter whether or not the crime took place in a state that has the death penalty, but the use of the punishment even varies within death penalty jurisdictions. For example, Justice Stephen Breyer noted in *Ring v. Arizona* that only 3 percent of counties in the United States have imposed 50 percent of American death sentences since 1972. Further, since *Furman*, more than two-thirds of counties in the United States have never sentenced a defendant to death, and during a recent five-year period of 2004–2009, executions only came from 1 percent of U.S. counties.

Recalling the past, scholars have noted that in many places lynchings also were clustered in specific counties.[37] Death penalty advocates, however, are correct to point out that the death penalty of today differs in many ways from the early American death penalty. Executions are no longer done in public. Lynching is no longer a common practice, and modern society would not accept execution methods such as burning or hanging in chains. Mandatory death sentences are gone, and capital punishment is used for fewer crimes than during the early years of the United States. The United States has traveled a long road from its first president who had, not wooden teeth, but slaves' teeth, to electing a black president.

But the past is still present.[38] McCleskey's case and the Baldus study showed that the modern death penalty remains imprisoned by the past, and more recent studies confirm that race still plays a role in capital sentencing, as do other arbitrary factors, such as the location of the trial. None of the justices who decided *McCleskey v. Kemp* attempted to argue that race does not play a role in the capital sentencing process, and not one justice has denied the role of race in the American death penalty since McCleskey's execution.[39] Similarly, other new cases continue to highlight the connection, such as that of Duane Buck, whose Texas jury sentenced him to death after a psychologist told them that Buck was more likely to commit future acts of violence because he was black.

Were members of society to sit down together with their collective knowledge and begin from scratch to create a criminal justice system, they would not design America's system of capital punishment. Still, many states and the federal government continue to build on the death penalty system of the past, striving for a fairer system with equitable procedures, unbiased jurors, impartial judges, honorable prosecutors, and quality defense attorneys that ensure accuracy. They strive to build a system that does not allow racial or other improper bias and does not convict the innocent.[40] At the same time, these jurisdictions tinker with the ways they take the lives of prisoners, and courts and legislatures keep tweaking the post-conviction review procedures.

While some states recognize that capital punishment in the present is not worth the costs, many others continue using stopgap measures to try to repair a punishment system locked in the past. Similar struggles have persisted since the Jamestown settlers conducted the first American execution in 1608, yet the system of taking the lives of prisoners still remains flawed and arbitrary. Four hundred years later, the world waits to see how much longer America will remain imprisoned by the past.

END NOTES

INTRODUCTION
1. Although there are other countries located on the North American and South American continents, this book uses the term "America" throughout in its common United States' usage that focuses on the land that became the United States. Because the book encompasses history before the formation of the United States and to avoid awkward phrasing, the book uses the simplified term.
2. McCleskey v. Kemp, 481 U.S. 279, 344 (1987) (Brennan, J., dissenting).

PROLOGUE: AMERICA'S MARIETTA
1. Rebecca Nash Paden and Joe McTyre, *175 Facts about Marietta, Georgia* (Georgia: City of Marietta, GA, 2009) 1; Sarah Blackwell Gober Temple, *The First Hundred Years: A Short History of Cobb County, in Georgia* (Georgia: Cobb Landmarks and Historical Society, Inc. 1997) 86.
2. Patrice Shelton Lassiter, *Kennesaw & Marietta, Generations of Black Life in Georgia* (Great Britain: Arcadia Publishing 1999) 11.
3. Temple, *The First Hundred Years* 270.
4. James McPherson, *Battle Cry of Freedom* (New York: Oxford University Press, 1988) 749–750; Paden and McTyre, *175 Facts about Marietta, Georgia* 15; Temple, *The First Hundred Years* 356. One of the Union soldiers, who lost a leg during the Battle of Kennesaw Mountain, was Abraham Hoch Landis. Although the spelling got mangled, he later named his son Kenesaw Mountain Landis after the battle. Judge Kenesaw Mountain Landis would do much as a jurist and as the first commissioner of baseball. But he also will always be remembered for presiding over a baseball era that kept black players out of baseball.
5. Temple, *The First Hundred Years* 387–413, 439.
6. The Marietta Confederate Cemetery was established in 1863 and is located on 381 Powder Springs Street. City of Marietta Web page: City Cemeteries, 8 June 2010, http://www.mariettaga.gov/departments/parks_rec/cemeteries.aspx#3.
7. *Marietta*, The New Georgia Encyclopedia Website, 8 June 2010, http://www.georgiaencyclopedia.org/nge/Article.jsp?id=h-765,
8. *City Cemeteries*, City of Marietta Web page, 8 June 2010, http://www.mariettaga.gov/departments/parks_rec/cemeteries.aspx#3.
9. W.E.B. Du Bois, *The Souls of Black Folk* (New York: 1903; repr. New York: New American Library, 1982) 141.
10. Thomas Allan Scott, *Cobb County, Georgia and the Origins of the Suburban South: A Twentieth-Century History* (Marietta, Georgia: Cobb Landmarks and Historical Society, Inc., 2003) 1–2, xv. Scott notes that Cobb County's African-American population in 1980 was 4 percent.
11. Steve Oney, *And the Dead Shall Rise* (New York: Vintage Books, 2004) 562; Nancy MacLean, "Gender, Sexuality, and the Politics of Lynching: The Leo Frank Case Revisited," in *Under Sentence of Death: Lynching in the South*, ed. W. Fitzhugh

Brundage (Chapel Hill & London: University of North Carolina Press, 1997) 158–188; *Marietta's Shame: The Lynching of Leo Frank*, Cobb Online Website, 8 June 2010, http://www.atlantanation.com/leofrank.html.

12. Oney, *And the Dead Shall Rise* 560–572.

13. Oney, *And the Dead Shall Rise* 567.

14. Oney, *And the Dead Shall Rise* 570–571; 576–578; 619–621. The future congressman was John Wood, whose role in the lynching is somewhat unclear. He helped Judge Morris take Frank's body from Marietta to Atlanta, but beyond that his involvement is unknown.

15. Oney, *And the Dead Shall Rise* 604–607.

16. Jonathan L. Entin, "Using Great Cases to Think About the Criminal Justice System," 89 *Journal of Criminal Law & Criminology* (1999): 1141, 1154. Before Frank's death, the Supreme Court denied habeas corpus relief by applying a standard that gave great deference to the state courts, much as the Court would do later in one of McCleskey's cases. Frank v. Mangum, 237 U.S. 309 (1915). "Although the Court rejected Frank's claim, his case is widely viewed as a habeas landmark because the justices unanimously agreed that mob domination could support habeas relief in some circumstances." Jonathan Entin, "Why the Billy Mitchell Case Still Matters," 80 *Journal of Air Law and Commerce* (2005): 578 n.3; Oney, *And the Dead Shall Rise* 644–649; Eric M. Freedman, "Leo Frank Lives: Untangling the Historical Roots of Meaningful Federal Habeas Corpus Review of State Convictions," 51 *Alabama Law Review* (2000): 1467, 1533–1534.

17. The United States ratified the Twenty-Fourth Amendment to the U.S. Constitution in January 1964 without Georgia's approval. Similarly, after the Thirteenth Amendment abolishing slavery was ratified, some Southern states were slow in voting for the amendment, perhaps because such votes were unnecessary after the amendment passed. Mississippi became the last state to vote to ratify the Thirteenth Amendment in 1995, although due to a clerical error the vote was not official until 2013 when after watching the 2012 film *Lincoln*, a viewer researched the issue. Adam Clark Estes, "Thanks to 'Lincoln,' Mississippi Has Finally Definitely Ratified the Thirteenth Amendment," *The Atlantic Wire*, 28 Feb. 2013, http://news.yahoo.com/thanks-lincoln-mississippi-finally-definitel y-ratified-thirteenth-amendment-024920825.html.

18. Coleman v. Miller, 117 F.3d 527, 528 (11th Cir. 1997).

19. *Coleman v. Miller*, 117 F.3d 527 at 528. Eventually, in 2001, Georgia removed the Confederate battle flag from the state flag. The current flag adopted in 2003 is based upon the original official Confederate national flag, often called the "Stars and Bars," made up of stars on a field of blue in the corner with a white bar between two red bars.

20. John F. Kennedy, "Radio and Television Report to the American People on Civil Rights" 11 June 1963, *The American Presidency Project*, (last visited 9 June 2012), http://www.presidency.ucsb.edu/ws/index.php?pid=9271&st=&st1=.

21. Martin Luther King Jr., "Letter from Birmingham Jail" 16 April 1963, African Studies Center—University of Pennsylvania. Ali B. Ali-Dinar, PhD, n.d., http:// www.africa.upenn.edu/Articles_Gen/Letter_Birmingham.html.

CHAPTER 1: A DEATH IN DIXIE

1. Joyce Hollyday, "A Gift of Dignity", *Sojourners Magazine* (January 1992): 24; Warren McCleskey, Letter to Sister Reginald, 12 May 1982; Paul Cadenhead, Esq., et al., Documentation Submitted in Support of Application of Warren McCleskey for a 90-Day Stay of Execution and for Commutation of his Sentence of Death, 1991, 7 [on file with author]. McCleskey's letter states his birthday as 1948 but other documents indicate it was 1946.

2. "As a result of the great migration to northern industrial centers, Cobb County's African American population dropped from 30 percent in 1900 to 4 percent in

1980." *Marietta,* The New Georgia Encyclopedia Website, 10 July 2010, http://www.georgiaencyclopedia.org/nge/Article.jsp?id=h-765.

3. Mark Curriden, "Ready to Die, But Insisting He's Innocent," *The Atlanta Constitution* (21 Sept. 1991): A01.

4. Laura Magzis, PhD, Report, 8 July 1987 [on file with author].

5. Magzis, Report.

6. Edward Lazarus, "Mortal Combat: How the Death Penalty Polarized the Supreme Court," *Washington Monthly* (1 June 1998): 32 at *7–8.

7. Robert Stroup, Telephone Interview, 31 July 2012; Hollyday, "A Gift of Dignity" 24; Magzis, Report.

8. Brown v. Board of Education, 349 U.S. 294, 299 (1955) (*"Brown II"*).

9. Scott, *Cobb County, Georgia and the Origins of the Suburban South,* 281–285.

10. Robert H. Stroup, "The Political, Legal, and Social Context of the McCleskey Habeas Litigation," 39 *Columbia Human Rights Law Review* (2007): 74, 79; *Marietta,* The New Georgia Encyclopedia Website, 8 June 2010, http://www.georgiaencyclopedia.org/nge/Article.jsp?id=h-765.

11. Vicke L. Martin, "Who Killed Frank Schlatt?," *Atlanta Voice (Georgia)* (21 Oct. 1978): 1; Magzis, Report.

12. Curriden, "Ready to Die" A01; Certificate of Death for John H. Brown 3 Dec. 1963 (Marietta, Georgia). One report claims that McCleskey was married and not living at home at the time his stepfather was killed, but McCleskey's sister Betty Myers confirmed he was in high school. Magzis, Report; Betty Myers, Affidavit, May, 18, 1987; Mark Curriden, "I Deeply Regret a Life Was Taken," *The Atlanta Journal Constitution* (21 Sept. 1991): A/12.

13. Hollyday, "A Gift of Dignity" 24.

14. Betty Myers, Affidavit 18 May 1987.

15. Paden and McTyre, *175 Facts about Marietta, Georgia* 52–53; Felecca Wilson Taylor, Interview by Jessica Renee Drysdale, Kennesaw State University Oral History Project, *Cobb NAACP/Civil Rights Series,* No. 2, 25 Sept. 2009, http://archon.kennesaw.edu/?p=digitallibrary/digitalcontent&id=5.

16. Curriden, "Ready to Die" A01; "Mortal Combat: How the Death Penalty Polarized the Supreme Court," *Washington Monthly* (1 June 1998): 32 at *7; Martin, "Who Killed Frank Schlatt?" 1; McCleskey, Letter to Sister Reginald. At one point, McCleskey worked for a major employer in Marietta: Lockheed. Mark Curriden, "McCleskey Put to Death after Hours of Delays, Final Apology," *Atlanta Journal and Constitution* (26 Sept. 1991): D3.

17. Curriden, "Ready to Die," A01; Trial Transcript, *Georgia v. Warren McCleskey,* Superior Court of Fulton County, GA, Commencing 9 Oct. 1978, Crim. Action No. A-40553, 846 (Warren McCleskey); John H. Dean, "Letter to the Editor," *Atlanta Constitution* (4 Oct. 1991): A/10.

18. Offie Evans Statement to Atlanta Police, 1 Aug. 1978; Magzis, Report.

19. Trial Transcript, *Georgia v. Warren McCleskey,* Superior Court of Fulton County, GA, Commencing 9 Oct. 1978, Crim. Action No. A-40553, 808–809 (Warren McCleskey).

20. Records of David Burney, Bernard Depree, Mary Jenkins, Warren McCleskey, and Ben Wright, I.D. Unit of Bureau of Police Services, Atlanta, GA (court file).

21. Report of Dr. Lloyd T. Baccus, M.D., Dir. Inpatient Psychiatry, Psychology and Law Services, 2, Sept. 1978. In this report prepared for Depree's trial in the Dixie Furniture Store case, Dr. Lloyd T. Baccus explained that Depree never knew his mother or father because both died while Depree was very young. The report states that Depree was raised in an "orphanage" in Letchworth Village until he was eight, and then he lived at "Willowbrook" before going to prison at the age of seventeen. Dr. Baccus noted that Depree had been incarcerated numerous times since he was fourteen, and he diagnosed Depree with antisocial personality disorder. The doctor did not explain that Letchworth Village, where Depree was raised, was a mental

institution, and "Willowbrook," or Willlowbrook State School, was an institution for children with intellectual disabilities.

22. Trial Transcript, *Georgia v. Warren McCleskey*, Superior Court of Fulton County, GA Commencing 9 Oct. 1978, Crim. Action No. A-40553, 665–666 (Ben Wright).

23. Transcript of Testimony of Mary Dorsey Jenkins before the Grand Jury of Fulton County, on Tuesday, 13 June 1978, *State v. David Burney, Jr., Bernard Depree, Warren McCleskey, Ben Wright, Jr.*, No. A-40553.

24. Trial Transcript, *Georgia v. Warren McCleskey*, Superior Court of Fulton County, GA Commencing 9 Oct. 1978, Crim. Action No. A-40553, 648–649 (Testimony of Ben Wright).

25. Trial Transcript, *Georgia v. Warren McCleskey*, Superior Court of Fulton County, GA Commencing 9 Oct. 1978, Crim. Action No. A-40553, 270–304, 651–652.

26. McCleskey v. State, 263 S.E.2d 146 (Ga. 1980); Edward Lazarus, *Closed Chambers* (New York: Random House 1998): 170. Many years later, the owner of the Dixie Furniture Co., James William "Billy" Dukes Jr. told a reporter that he lost $4,100 in the robbery. Bill Robinson, "Robbery Victim: McCleskey Was 'Guilty as Sin,'" *The Atlanta Journal* (25 Sept. 1991): A/6.

27. Trial Transcript, *Georgia v. Warren McCleskey*, Superior Court of Fulton County, GA Commencing 9 Oct. 1978, Crim. Action No. A-40553, 270–298.

28. McCleskey v. State, 263 S.E.2d 146 (Ga. 1980); Hollyday, "A Gift of Dignity" 24; Martin, "Who Killed Frank Schlatt?" 1.

29. Trial Transcript, *Georgia v. Warren McCleskey*, Superior Court of Fulton County, GA Commencing 9 Oct. 1978, Crim. Action No. A-40553, 329–333.

30. Trial Transcript, *Georgia v. Warren McCleskey*, Superior Court of Fulton County, GA Commencing 9 Oct. 1978, Crim. Action No. A-40553, 663–665 (Ben Wright).

31. *City of Atlanta Officer Memorial Page*, 4 Apr. 2011, http://www.atlantapd.org/index. asp?nav=Memorial&Task=Details&ID=57; Lewis Grizzard, "Frank Schlatt: Don't Forget," *The Covington News* [Newton Co. Georgia], 26 May 2010, (last visited 5 June 2011), http://www.covnews.com/news/article/12558/; Peter Applebome, "Georgia Inmate Is Executed after 'Chaotic' Legal Move" *New York Times*, 26 Sept. 1991, (last visited 15 July 2011), http://www.nytimes.com/1991/09/26/us/georgia-inmate-is-executed-after-chaotic-legal-move.html.

32. Trial Transcript, *Georgia v. Warren McCleskey*, Superior Court of Fulton County, GA Commencing 9 Oct. 1978, Crim. Action No. A-40553, 349–355, 635, 793–794.

33. Martin, "Who Killed Frank Schlatt?" 1; Trial Transcript, *Georgia v. Warren McCleskey*, Superior Court of Fulton County, GA Commencing 9 Oct. 1978, Crim. Action No. A-40553, 794 (Margene Turner).

34. Edward Lazarus, *Closed Chambers* (New York: Random House, 1998) 170.

35. Trial Transcript, *Georgia v. Warren McCleskey*, Superior Court of Fulton County, GA Commencing 9 Oct. 1978, Crim. Action No. A-40553, 359–419; Hollyday, "A Gift of Dignity" 24; Lazarus, *Closed Chambers* 173.

36. David Laurence Faigman, *Laboratory of Justice: The Supreme Court's 200-Year Struggle to Integrate* (New York: Times Books 2004), 256; David G. Stout, "The Lawyers of Death Row," *New York Times Magazine* (14 Feb. 1988): 5, (last visited 11 July 2011), http://www.nytimes.com/1988/02/14/magazine/the-lawyers-of-death-row. html?src=pm.

37. Lazarus, *Closed Chambers* 172.

38. Faigman, *Laboratory of Justice* 256; Stroup, "The Political, Legal, and Social Context of the McCleskey Habeas Litigation" 78–79; Transcript of State Habeas Hearing, *McCleskey v. State* (Superior Court of Butts County, Georgia 16 Feb. 1981).

39. Memorandum from Justice Lewis F. Powell Jr. to Conference of 16 Oct. 1986, 1, McCleskey v. Kemp Case File, No. 811-6811, Basic File, *Justice Lewis F. Powell Jr. Archives*, Washington and Lee University, Lexington, VA, 100, (last visited 28 June 2012), http://law.wlu.edu/deptimages/powell%20archives/McCleskeyKempBasic. pdf (quoting John Turner at state habeas hearing); Lazarus, *Closed Chambers* 172.

CHAPTER 2: THE TRIAL OF WARREN McCLESKEY

1. Trial Transcript, *Georgia v. Warren McCleskey*, Superior Court of Fulton County, GA, Commencing 9 Oct. 1978, Criminal Action No. A-40553, 63–160; Lazarus, *Closed Chambers* 176; Stroup, "The Political, Legal, and Social Context of the McCleskey Habeas Litigation" 80.
2. Trial Transcript, *Georgia v. Warren McCleskey*, Superior Court of Fulton County, GA, Commencing 9 Oct. 9 1978, Criminal Action No. A-40553, 270–298, 305–307.
3. McCleskey v. Kemp, 481 U.S. 279, 283–284 (1987); Martin, "Who Killed Frank Schlatt?" 1.
4. Trial Transcript, *Georgia v. Warren McCleskey*, Superior Court of Fulton County, GA Commencing 9 Oct. 1978, Crim. Action No. A-40553, 647–680.
5. Brief for Petitioner, McCleskey v. Zant, 1990 WL 508085 (U.S. 30 July 1990), at 12.
6. Trial Transcript, *Georgia v. Warren McCleskey*, Superior Court of Fulton County, GA, Commencing Oct. 9, 1978, Crim. Action No. A-40553, 716–718 (Ben Wright).
7. Brief for Petitioner, McCleskey v. Zant, 1990 WL 508085 (U.S. 30 July 1990), at 11.
8. Trial Transcript, *Georgia v. Warren McCleskey*, Superior Court of Fulton County, GA, Commencing 9 Oct 1978, Crim. Action No. A-40553, 825–848.
9. Trial Transcript, *Georgia v. Warren McCleskey*, Superior Court of Fulton County, GA, Commencing 9 Oct 1978, Crim. Action No. A-40553, 832.
10. Trial Transcript, *Georgia v. Warren McCleskey*, Superior Court of Fulton County, GA, Commencing 9 Oct. 1978, Crim. Action No. A-40553, 870–871.
11. Brief for Petitioner, McCleskey v. Zant, 1990 WL 508085 (U.S. 30 July 1990), at 8.
12. After the trial, defense attorneys discovered that Evans had told police that McCleskey told him that Mary Jenkins helped with the robbery by acting as a lookout. Offie Evans Statement to Atlanta, GA Police, 1 Aug. 1978 (court record).
13. McCleskey v. Zant, 580 F. Supp. 338, 382 (N.D. Ga. 1984).
14. *McCleskey v. Zant*, 580 F. Supp. at 382 (quoting Trial Transcript, *Georgia v. Warren McCleskey*, Superior Court of Fulton County, GA, Commencing 9 Oct. 1978, Crim. Action No. A-40553, 974–975).
15. Trial Transcript, *Georgia v. Warren McCleskey*, Superior Court of Fulton County, GA, Commencing 9 Oct. 1978, Crim. Action No. A-40553, 907–940.
16. Georgia Code Ann. Sec. 26-1902 (1978); *McCleskey v. Zant*, 580 F. Supp. at 385–386.
17. *McCleskey v. Zant*, 580 F. Supp. at 383; McCleskey v. Kemp, 481 U.S. 279, 283–284 (1987).
18. Jill Darmer, Affidavit, 12 May 1987, 2–3; Robert F. Burnette, Affidavit, 9 May 1987, 2–3. For a discussion of the evidence about Offie Evans's possible motive to lie, see chapter 3.
19. *McCleskey v. Zant*, 580 F. Supp. at 388.
20. Thurgood Marshall, "Remarks on the Death Penalty Made at the Judicial Conference of the Second Circuit," 86 *Columbia Law Review* (1986): 1–3. See also chapters 8 and 14.
21. *McCleskey v. Zant*, 580 F. Supp. at 402; Stroup, "The Political, Legal, and Social Context of the McCleskey Habeas Litigation" 78–79.
22. Trial Transcript, *Georgia v. Warren McCleskey*, Superior Court of Fulton County, GA, Commencing 9 Oct. 1978, Crim. Action No. A-40553, 1021–1025. In Turner's opening remarks about "the discriminatory application of the death penalty," he unknowingly foreshadowed a major issue that McCleskey would take to the Supreme Court. See chapters 12 and 13.
23. Burnette, Affidavit, 2.
24. Cadenhead et al., Documentation Submitted in Support of Application of Warren McCleskey for a 90-Day Stay of Execution and for Commutation of His Sentence of Death, 1991, 7; Faigman, *Laboratory of Justice* 256.
25. Order of Judge Sam Phillips McKenzie, *Georgia v. Warren McCleskey*, Superior Court of Fulton County, 13 Oct. 1978, Crim. Action, No. A-40553; Extraordinary Motion for New Trial, *Georgia v. Warren McCleskey*, Crim. Action, No. A-40553.

26. Michael Mears, *The Death Penalty in Georgia: A Modern History 1970–2000* (Atlanta: Georgia Indigent Defense Division of Professional Education) 127–128; Lazarus, *Closed Chambers* 181.
27. Martin, "Who Killed Frank Schlatt?" 1.
28. Arthur Koestler, *Dialogue with Death* (Chicago: University of Chicago Press 2011) 205.

CHAPTER 3: OFFIE EVANS AND *McCLESKEY v. ZANT*

1. McCleskey v. State, 263 S.E.2d 146 (Ga. 1980).
2. Trial Transcript of Resentencing, *Georgia v. Warren McCleskey*, Superior Court of Fulton County, 19 Dec. 1980, Crim. Action, No. A-40553; Extraordinary Motion for New Trial, *Georgia v. Warren McCleskey*, Superior Court of Fulton County, 19 Dec. 1980, Crim. Action, No. A-40553; Letter to Hon. Judge Sam McKenzie from Robert Stroup, Extraordinary Motion for New Trial, *Georgia v. Warren McCleskey*, Superior Court of Fulton County, 19 Dec. 1980, Crim. Action No. A-40553.
3. Source for most facts are from McCleskey v. Zant, 499 U.S. 467, 470–471 (1991).
4. Trial Transcript, *Georgia v. Warren McCleskey*, Superior Court of Fulton County, GA Commencing 9 Oct. 1978, Crim. Action No. A-40553, 647–680.
5. Trial Transcript, *Georgia v. Warren McCleskey*, Superior Court of Fulton County, GA, Commencing 9 Oct. 1978, Crim. Action No. A-40553, 875–876. Evans went back and forth between agreeing he was "good friends" with Wright to saying they just hung out together a lot but were not friends.
6. Brady v. Maryland, 373 U.S. 83 (1963).
7. *McCleskey v. State*, 263 S.E.2d at 150.
8. *See* Giglio v. United States, 405 U.S. 150 (1972).
9. Trial Transcript, *Georgia v. Warren McCleskey*, Superior Court of Fulton County, GA, Commencing 9 Oct. 1978, Crim. Action No. A-40553, 868–869.
10. Trial Transcript, *Georgia v. Warren McCleskey*, Superior Court of Fulton County, GA, Commencing 9 Oct. 1978, Crim. Action No. A-40553, 872–873.
11. Giglio v. United States, 405 U.S. 150 (1971) (holding that a prosecutor's failure to disclose a promise of leniency to a testifying co-conspirator violated prosecutor's duty to present all material evidence to a jury and violates due process).
12. McCleskey v. Kemp, 753 F.2d 877, 883 (11th Cir. 1985).
13. McCleskey v. Zant, 580 F. Supp. 338, 383 (N.D. Georgia 1984). At the same time, Judge Forrester noted that he believed the information in Evans's written statement. *McCleskey v. Zant*, 499 U.S. at 502 (quoting hearing transcript). In the same opinion, Judge Forrester also rejected McCleskey's race claim that is discussed later in this book in Chapter 12.
14. Darmer, Affidavit, 2–3; Burnette, Affidavit, 2–3; Peter Applebome, "Inmate Whose Appeals Shook System Faces Execution," *New York Times*, 24 Sept. 1991, (last visited 12 June 2013), http://www.nytimes.com/1991/09/24/us/inmate-whose-appeals-shook-system-faces-execution.html.
15. McCleskey v. Zant, 753 F.2d 877, 882–885 (11th Cir. 1985).
16. Murphy Davis, "Warren McCleskey: A Faith Refined," *Hospitality* [newspaper of The Open Door Community, Atlanta, GA] (Jan. 1992): 3.
17. Massiah v. United States, 377 U.S. 201 (1964).
18. McCleskey v. Zant, 890 F.2d 342, 345 (11th Cir. 1989).
19. *McCleskey v. Zant*, 499 U.S. at 474, 526.
20. Offie Evans Statement to Atlanta, GA Police, Aug. 1, 1978, 5 (court record); Trial Transcript, *Georgia v. Warren McCleskey*, Superior Court of Fulton County, GA, Commencing Oct. 9, 1978, Crim. Action No. A-40553, 635. Although attorneys focused on the statement's revelation about the connection between Evans and the police, the statement also revealed that Evans claimed McCleskey reported that Mary Jenkins acted as a lookout during the robbery. The prosecution used Jenkins as one of the witnesses against McCleskey at his trial, but the jurors may have incorrectly believed that Jenkins, like Evans, was an impartial witness against

McCleskey. Because McCleskey's attorney did not have the statement from Evans, he could not cross-examine her more about her role in the crime. Jurors did know, however, that she was in a serious relationship with suspect Ben Wright, and Evans did testify at trial that Jenkins put makeup on McCleskey on the day of the robbery to help disguise him. They also knew a police officer told Jenkins that Dixie Furniture Company would likely give her a $1,000 reward for her testimony against McCleskey.

21. Gayle White, "Jailer Testifies He Can't Recall Who Sought Informant in Cell Adjacent to McCleskey," *The Atlanta Constitution* (11 Aug. 1987): A/34.
22. Robert Stroup, Telephone Interview, 31 July 2012.
23. McCleskey v. Zant, 499 U.S. 467, 475 (1991).
24. *McCleskey v. Zant*, 890 F.2d at 353.
25. McCleskey v. Zant, 496 U.S. 904 (1990) (granting petition for writ of certiorari).
26. Oral Argument in *McCleskey v. Zant*, No. 89-2024, U.S. Supreme Court, 16 Apr. 1991, http://www.oyez.org/cases/1990-1999/1990/1990_89_7024/. In addition to Boger, other attorneys who signed onto McCleskey's brief before the Supreme Court in *McCleskey v. Zant* were Julius L. Chambers, III; Richard H. Burr, III; George H. Kendall, Anthony G. Amsterdam, and Robert H. Stroup. For Georgia, Westmoreland was joined on the state's brief by Attorney General Michael J. Bowers, William B. Hill Jr., and Susan V. Boleyn.
27. Frank v. Magnum, 237 U.S. 309 (1915). Because a majority of the Court found Georgia gave Frank the "corrective process" of an appeal, the Court denied habeas corpus relief to Frank. For more on Leo Frank, see the Prologue.
28. Harris v. Nelson, 394 U.S. 286 (1969).
29. *McCleskey v. Zant*, 499 U.S. at 467.
30. *McCleskey v. Zant*, 499 U.S. at 492–493.
31. Additionally, the Court found there was no miscarriage of justice in McCleskey's case because even if his *Massiah* claim were a winning one, it did not mean he was innocent of the crime. In fact, the district court had found reliable Evans's statement that McCleskey confessed. A successful *Massiah* claim would only mean McCleskey's Sixth Amendment rights were violated, not that he was innocent. *McCleskey v. Zant*, 499 U.S. at 502.
32. Trial Transcript, *Georgia v. Warren McCleskey*, Superior Court of Fulton County, GA, Commencing 9 Oct. 1978, Crim. Action No. A-40553, 868–869.
33. *McCleskey v. Zant*, 499 U.S. at 526 (Marshall, J., dissenting).
34. *McCleskey v. Zant*, 499 U.S. at 527–528.
35. Papers of Thurgood Marshall, Library of Congress, Manuscripts Division, Container 538, Folder 5; Michael Mello, "Ivon Stanley and James Adams' America: Vectors of Racism in Capital Punishment," 43 *Criminal Law Bulletin* (Fall 2007): 699.
36. Editorial, "Supreme Court v. the Great Writ," *The Atlanta Constitution* [Georgia] (19 April 1991): A12.
37. Mark Curriden, "After McCleskey, Some Expect Leap in Ga. Executions," *Atlanta Journal and Constitution* (26 Sept. 1991): D3.
38. Letter from Warren McCleskey to George Wirth, 27 April 1991.

CHAPTER 4: THE FIRST LIMITS

1. James B. Christoph, *Capital Punishment and British Politics: The British Movement to Abolish the Death Penalty, 1945–57* (Chicago: University of Chicago Press, 1962) 175.
2. David V. Baker, "American Indian Executions in Historical Context" *Criminal Justice Studies* 20 (2007): 317–318; Edward Adamson Hoebel, *The Law of Primitive Man* (Cambridge, MA: Harvard University Press, 1954).
3. "Captain George Kendall: Mutineer or Intelligencer?" *The Virginia Magazine of History and Biography* 70(3) (July 1962): 297–313; *A Punishment in Search of a Crime: Americans Speak Out against the Death Penalty*, (ed. Ian Gray and Moira Gray) (New York: Avon Books, 1989) 48. Some sources state the blacksmith's name as "William Reed."

4. Frederick Drimmer, *Until You Are Dead: The Book of Executions in America* (New York: Carol Publishing Group, 1990) 137–138.
5. Baker, "American Indian Executions in Historical Context" 315–373; D. Hearn, *Legal Executions in New England: A Comprehensive Reference, 1623–1960* (Jefferson, NC: McFarland 1999).
6. Watt Espy, "Executions in the U.S. 1608–1987: The Espy File Executions by State," 2 Feb. 2013, http://www.deathpenaltyinfo.org/documents/ESPYstate.pdf.
7. Office of Planning and Analysis of Georgia Department of Corrections, *A History of the Death Penalty in Georgia*, Jan. 2010, 2, http://www.dcor.state.ga.us/pdf/TheDeathPenaltyinGeorgia.pdf.
8. Furman v. Georgia, 408 U.S. 238, 340–341 (Marshall, J., concurring).
9. Deborah L. Heller, "Death Becomes the State: The Death Penalty in New York—Past, Present, and Future," 28 *Pace Law Review* (2005): 589, 590.
10. *Capital Punishment in the United States: A Documentary History* (ed. Bryan Vila and Cynthia Morris) (Westport, CT: Greenwood Publishing Group, 1997) xxv.
11. Woodson v. North Carolina, 428 U.S. 280, 289 (1976); *Furman v. Georgia*, 408 U.S. at 340–341.
12. Donald D. Hook and Lothar Kahn, *Death in the Balance: The Debate over Capital Punishment* (Lexington, MA: Lexington Books, 1989) 23; James Avery Joyce, *The Right to Life: A World View of Capital Punishment* (London: Victor Gollancz Ltd., 1962) 156.
13. *Capital Punishment in the United States* 25; Benjamin Rush, *An Enquiry into the Effects of Public Punishments upon Criminals and upon Society* (Philadelphia: Joseph James, 1787); Benjamin Rush, "On Punishing Murder by Death," in *The Selected Writings of Benjamin Rush* (New York: Philosophical Library, 1947) 52; John D. Bessler, *Cruel & Unusual* (Boston: Northeastern University Press, 2012) 54, 111.
14. Bessler, *Cruel & Unusual* 51–53, 54.
15. Louis P. Masur, *Rites of Execution: Capital Punishment and the Transformation of American Culture, 1776–1865* (New York: Oxford University Press, 1989) 62.
16. *Furman v. Georgia*, 408 U.S. at 340–341.
17. Masur, *Rites of Execution* 72–73.
18. Nicholas N. Kittrie, Elyce H. Zenoff, and Vincent A. Eng, *Sentencing, Sanctions, and Corrections* (New York: Foundation Press 2002) (2d ed.) 860–861.
19. Bessler, *Cruel & Unusual* 152–153.
20. Stuart Banner, *The Death Penalty: An American History* (Cambridge, MA: Harvard University Press, 2002) 32–33; Masur, *Rites of Execution* 28.
21. Bessler, *Cruel & Unusual* 115, 121–123; Jeffrey L. Kirchmeier, "Let's Make a Deal: Waiving the Eighth Amendment by Selecting a Cruel and Unusual Punishment," 32 *Connecticut Law Review* (2000): 618–619.
22. U.S. Constitution, amend. V.
23. Bessler, *Cruel & Unusual* 127. During the Revolutionary War, Washington wrote, "I always hear of capital executions with concern, and regret that there should occur so many instances in which they are necessary." Ibid., 132.
24. Act of April 30, 1790, ch. 9, §§ 1, 3, 8–10, 14, 23, 1 Stat. 112–119 ("1790 Crime Bill"); Eric A. Tirschwell and Theodore Hertzberg, "Politics and Prosecution: A Historical Perspective on Shifting Federal Standards for Pursuing the Death Penalty in Non-Death Penalty States," 12 *University of Pennsylvania Journal of Constitutional Law* (2009): 57, 67.
25. Caleb Crain, "Unfortunate Events: What Was the War of 1812 Even About?" *The New Yorker* (22 Oct. 2012): 77–80, 80.
26. Baze v. Rees, 553 U.S. 35, 94 (2008) (Thomas, J., dissenting).
27. Robert Jay Lifton and Greg Mitchell, *Who Owns Death?: Capital Punishment, The American Conscience, and the End of Executions* (New York: William Morrow & Co., 2000) 26.
28. Bessler, *Cruel & Unusual* 270.

29. Christopher Q. Cutler, "Nothing Less than the Dignity of Man: Evolving Standards, Botched Executions and Utah's Controversial Use of the Firing Squad" 50 *Cleveland State Law Review* (2003): 335, 340–341.
30. David Brion Davis, "The Movement to Abolish Capital Punishment in America, 1787–1861," 63 *American Historical Revew* (1957): 23, 33.
31. Masur, *Rites of Execution* 157.
32. David G. Chardavoyne, *A Hanging in Detroit: Stephen Gifford Simmons and the Last Execution under Michigan Law* (Detroit: Wayne State University Press, 2003) 150–152.
33. David Greenberg, "The Unkillable Death Penalty," *Slate Magazine* (2 June 2000) (Lexis); *The Death Penalty in America: Current Controversies* (ed. Hugo Adam Bedau) (New York: Oxford University Press, 1997) 8; Louis Filler, "Movements to Abolish the Death Penalty in the United States," in *Capital Punishment* (ed. Thorsten Sellin) (New York: J & J Harper 1969) 113; Masur, *Rites of Execution* 158–159; John F. Galliher et al., *America without the Death Penalty: States Leading the Way* (Boston: Northeastern University Press, 2002) 36. Because Rhode Island eventually brought back the death penalty, and because Michigan's 1846 law kept the death penalty for treason, Wisconsin today may claim to be the first state to completely permanently abolish capital punishment.
34. William S. McFeely, *Frederick Douglass* (New York: W.W. Norton & Co., 1991) 189; Masur, *Rites of Execution* 117; Deborah Denno, "Is Electrocution an Unconstitutional Method of Execution? The Engineering of Death over the Century" 35 *William & Mary Law Review* (1994): 551, 563.
35. Rob Zaleski, "State Culture Mapped Out," *Capital Times* [Madison, Wisconsin] (7 Nov. 1996): 1E; Judge James H. Lincoln, "The Everlasting Controversy: Michigan and the Death Penalty," 33 *Wayne Law Review* (1987): 1765, 1772–1775. One scholar has challenged the accuracy of the account of the mob and questioned whether the Simmons execution really had much effect on the Michigan abolition. Chardavoyne, *A Hanging in Detroit* 136–139.
36. Tirschwell & Hertzberg, "Politics and Prosecution" 57, 67; Nell Battle Lewis, ed., "Capital Punishment in North Carolina: Special Bulletin Number 10" (Raleigh, NC: The N.C. State Board of Charities and Public Welfare, 1929) 13–14; Denno, "Is Electrocution an Unconstitutional Method of Execution?" 564.
37. Campbell v. Wood, 1994 U.S. App. LEXIS 1991 n.16 at *34 (9th Cir. 1994) (quoting Letter of 13 Dec. 1849, in *Letters of Charles Dickens* 200 (New York: Macmillan and Co., 1903)).
38. Masur, *Rites of Execution* 109.

CHAPTER 5: WARS AND DEATH PENALTY ABOLITION
1. Dred Scott v. Sandford, 60 U.S. 393 (1857).
2. John W. Cromwell, "The Aftermath of Nat Turner's Insurrection," 5 *The Journal of Negro History* (Apr. 1920): 214, 216, 218. Some accounts differ in the number of slaves and free blacks who were executed, but a number of reliable accounts from the time state that Virginia executed seventeen slaves and three free blacks prior to capturing Turner.
3. Masur, *Rites of Execution* 160.
4. Robert I. Alotta, *Civil War Justice: Union Army Executions under Lincoln* (Shippensburg, PA: White Mane Publishing, 1989) ix, 187–188.
5. Michael Burlingame, *Abraham Lincoln: A Life*, Vol. 1 (Baltimore: Johns Hopkins University Press, 2008) 342.
6. Drimmer, *Until You Are Dead* 120–125; Galliher et al., *America without the Death Penalty* 80. In the next century, Harry A. Blackmun served as general counsel for the Mayo Clinic before playing an important role in death penalty history as a U.S. Supreme Court justice.
7. Elizabeth Steger Trindal, *Mary Surratt: An American Tragedy* (Gretna, LA: Pelican Publishing Company, 1996); Lionel Van Deerlin, "History Casts Doubts on

Tribunals," *San Diego Union-Tribune* (Nov. 21, 2001): B7 (stating that "nowhere does one find clinching evidence of Mrs. Surratt's involvement" in the conspiracy).

8. Drimmer, *Until You Are Dead*, 129.
9. U.S. Constitution, amend. XIV.
10. Galliher et al., *America without the Death Penalty* 170–171.
11. Galliher et al., *America without the Death Penalty* 59–60, 75.
12. Cutler, "Nothing Less than the Dignity of Man" 340–341, 348.
13. Mark Curriden, "Congress Passes First Major Law Restricting Immigration," *ABA Journal* (May 2013): 72.
14. James W. Marquart, Sheldon Ekland-Olson, and Johnathan R. Sorensen, *The Rope, the Chair & the Needle* (Austin: University of Texas Press, 1994) 13.
15. Baze v. Rees, 553 U.S. at 42. For more on the electric chair and other methods of execution, see chapters 15 and 16.
16. Stuart Banner, "Race and the Death Penalty in Historical Perspective," in *From Lynch Mobs to the Killing State* (ed. Charles J. Ogletree Jr. and Austin Sarat) (New York: New York University Press, 2006) 100, 111.
17. Jeffrey Abramson, *We the Jury* (Cambridge, MA: Harvard University Press, 1994) 217; William J. Bowers, et al., *Legal Homicide: Death as Punishment in America, 1864–1982*, (Boston: Northeastern University Press, 1984) 10; Campbell v. Wood, 1994 U.S. App. LEXIS 1991 n. 16 at *34 (9th Cir. 1994) (quoting Letter of 13 Dec. 1849, in *Letters of Charles Dickens* 200). For more about mandatory and discretionary capital sentences, see chapters 7 and 8.
18. Czolgosz's execution is the last presidential assassin execution to date because President John F. Kennedy's assassin was killed before trial. Another man, however, was executed after attempting to assassinate President Franklin D. Roosevelt, and another man who attempted to kill President Harry S. Truman was sentenced to death but Truman commuted the man's sentence to imprisonment.
19. John F. Galliher, Gregory Ray, and Brent Cook, "Abolition and Reinstatement of Capital Punishment during the Progressive Era and Early 20th Century," 83 *Journal of Criminal Law and Criminology* (Fall 1992): 538, 545; Herbert H, Haines, *Against Capital Punishment: The Anti-Death Penalty Movement in America, 1972–1994*. (New York: Oxford University Press, 1996) 10; Galliher et al., *America without the Death Penalty* 100.
20. Galliher et al., "Abolition and Reinstatement" 545–546.
21. James Avery Joyce, *The Right to Life: A World View of Capital Punishment* (London: Victor Gollancz Ltd., 1962) 150.
22. George W.P. Hunt, "Message of Governor George W.P. Hunt to the First Legislature of Arizona," *The Arizona Republican* [Phoenix] (12 Sept. 1912): 4.
23. Crane McClennen, "Capital Punishment in Arizona," *Arizona Attorney* (Oct. 1992): 18.
24. Galliher et al. "Abolition and Reinstatement" 538, 561–562, 564–565.
25. Drimmer, *Until You Are Dead* 132.
26. Michael L. Radelet, Hugo Adam Bedau, and Constance E. Putnam, *In Spite of Innocence* (Boston: Northeastern University Press, 1992) 314.
27. Steven Greenhouse, "Examining a Labor Hero's Death," *New York Times*, 26 Aug. 2011, (last visited 9 June 2012), http://www.nytimes.com/2011/08/27/us/27hill.html?_r=2&scp=1&sq=Joe%20Hill&st=cse. The prosecution argued Hill had been wounded by a gunshot during the murders, but a 2011 book by William M. Adler, *The Man Who Never Died*, argued Hill was innocent. Adler presented evidence that included a long-forgotten letter from Hill's girlfriend that disclosed that Hill had been shot by her spurned lover. William M. Adler, *The Man Who Never Died* (New York: Bloomsbury USA, 2012).
28. Louis Filler, "Movements to Abolish the Death Penalty in the United States," in *Capital Punishment* (ed. Thorsten Sellin) (New York: J & J Harper, 1969) 118–119.
29. Bedau, *The Death Penalty in America: Current Controversies* 8.

30. Galliher "Abolition and Reinstatement of Capital Punishment during the Progressive Era and Early 20th Century" 538, 574–576; Bowers et al., *Legal Homicide*, 9–10.

31. Bedau, *The Death Penalty in America: Current Controversies* 9–13.

32. *Attorney for the Damned: Clarence Darrow in the Courtroom* (ed. Arthur Weinberg) (Chicago: University of Chicago Press, 1989) 19, 87.

33. Hook and Kahn, *Death in the Balance* 5–7.

34. Filler, "Movements to Abolish the Death Penalty in the United States" 118–119.

35. Felix Frankfurter, *The Case of Sacco and Vanzetti: A Critical Analysis for Lawyers and Laymen* (New York: Little, Brown & Co., 1962) 3–8, 97–98; Louis B. Schwartz, "Book Review of David Felix, *Protest: Sacco-Vanzetti and the Intellectuals*," 114 *University of Pennsylvania Law Review* (1966): 1260.

36. *The Letters of Sacco and Vanzetti* (ed. Marion Denmon Frankfurter and Gardner Jackson) (Boston: E.P. Dutton & Company, 1960) 363. Sacco was born in Italy with the name Ferdinando Sacco.

37. Stephen Landsman, "Legal History: History's Stories," 93 *Michigan Law Review* (1995): 1739, 1759–1760.

38. Haines, *Against Capital Punishment* 10–11. Also, the execution of Sacco and Vanzetti led to the creation of the Massachusetts Council against the Death Penalty. Alan Rogers, "'Success—at Long Last': The Abolition of the Death Penalty in Massachusetts, 1928–1984," 22 *Boston College Third World Law Journal* (2002): 281.

39. Ralph Blumenthal, "A Man Who Knew about the Electric Chair," *New York Times*, 6 Nov. 2011, http://cityroom.blogs.nytimes.com/2011/11/06/a-man-who-knew-about-the-electric-chair/.

40. Korematsu v. United States, 323 U.S. 214 (1944).

41. Ken Driggs, "A Current of Electricity in Intensity to Cause Immediate Death: A Pre-*Furman* History of Florida's Electric Chair," 22 *Stetson Law Review* (1993): 1197–1198.

42. Robert R. Bryan, "The Execution of the Innocent: The Tragedy of the Hauptmann-Lindbergh and Bigelow Cases," 18 *New York Review of Law and Social Change* (1991): 831, 837; Edward Kosner, "An Infamous Crime Revisited," *Wall Street Journal*, 14 June 2012, http://online.wsj.com/article/SB10001424052702303822204577466420187730062.html.

43. John G. Leyden, "Death in the Hot Seat: A Century of Electrocutions," *The Washington Post* (5 Aug. 1990): D5.

44. Edmund Pearson, "A Reporter at Large: Hauptmann and Circumstantial Evidence," *The New Yorker* (9 Mar. 1935): 37–48; John F. Keenan, "The Lindbergh Kidnapping Revisited," 84 *Michigan Law Review* (1986): 819, 822; Anthony R. Tempesta, "Book Review of Jim Fisher's *The Lindbergh Case*," 147 *Milwaukee Law Review* (1995): 293. Others have argued, however, that the ladder evidence was weak and possibly fraudulent. Radelet et al., *In Spite of Innocence* 100–101; Bryan, "The Execution of the Innocent" 831.

45. In the 2012 book *Cemetery John*, author Robert Zorn argued a deli worker in the Bronx named John Knoll was the mastermind behind the kidnapping while Hauptmann was an accomplice. Robert Zorn, *Cemetery John: The Undiscovered Mastermind behind the Lindbergh Kidnapping* (New York: The Overlook Press, 2012).

46. Marquart et al. *The Rope, the Chair & the Needle* 33.

47. Ian Katz, "Pictures at an Execution," *The Guardian* (26 July 1996): T2; Banner, "Race and the Death Penalty in Historical Perspective" 106.

48. Tirschwell and Hertzberg, "Politics and Prosecution" 57, 70–72.

49. In January 2011, outgoing Colorado governor Bill Ritter, a former prosecutor, granted a pardon to Arridy. Kirk Mitchell, "Gov. Bill Ritter Issues 29 Pardons, Commutations," *The Denver Post*, 8 Jan. 2011, http://www.denverpost.com/search/ci_17040359.

50. Rob Warden, "Reflections on Capital Punishment," 4 *Northwestern Journal of Law and Social Policy* (2009): 329, 354; Louisiana *ex rel.* Francis v. Resweber, 329 U.S. 459 (1947).
51. Jeffrey H. Bowman, "Slow Dance on the Killing Field," *Arizona Attorney* (July 1996): 21–34, 24, 28.
52. Driggs, "A Current of Elecricity Sufficient in Intensity to Cause Immediate Death" 1170, 1191.
53. Marquart et al. *The Rope, the Chair & the Needle* 35.
54. Galliher et al., "Abolition and Reinstatement" 572–573.
55. Michael Radelet, "The Role of the Innocence Argument in Contemporary Death Penalty Debates," 41 *Texas Tech Law Review* (2008): 199, 205.
56. Shigemitsu Dando, "Toward the Abolition of the Death Penalty," 72 *Indiana Law Journal* (1996): 7, 8.
57. Haley v. Ohio, 332 U.S. 596, 602 (1948) (Frankfurter, J., concurring).
58. Linda Greenhouse, *Becoming Justice Blackmun* (New York: Times Books, 2005): 162. When Justice Blackmun was considering *Furman v. Georgia* and other death penalty cases, he retyped the above passage from Justice Frankfurter's opinion in *Haley v. Ohio*. Justice Blackmun titled the page "Re: Capital Punishment" and put his initials under the passage, apparently as an endorsement of Justice Frankfurter's views. Ibid.

CHAPTER 6: A TIME OF CHANGE

1. Frank Newport, "In U.S., Support for Death Penalty Falls to 39-Year Low," *Gallup Website*, 13 Oct. 2011, http://www.gallup.com/poll/150089/support-de ath-penalty-falls-year-low.aspx.
2. Norman Redlich, "Fighting the Death Penalty: A Thirty-Five Year Perspective," 54 *Albany Law Review* (1989–1990): 617, 617–618.
3. Allen Pusey, "Truman Escapes Assassination," *ABA Journal* (Nov. 2012): 72.
4. Sheila M. Brennan, "Popular Images of American Women in the 1950s and Their Impact on Ethel Rosenberg's Trial and Conviction," 14 *Women's Rights Law Reporter* (1992): 43, 45–46; Atossa M. Alavi, "The Government against Two: Ethel and Julius Rosenberg's Trial," 53 *Case Western Reserve Law Review* (2003): 1057, 1065; Bernard Ryan Jr., "Trials of Julius and Ethel Rosenberg and Morton Sobell: 1951," in *American Trials of the 20th Century* (ed. Edward W. Knappmann) (Detroit: Visible Ink Press, 1995) 232; John Wexley, *The Judgment of Julius and Ethel Rosenberg* (New York: Ballantine Books, 1977) 536. Recently released government files in the United States and the former Soviet Union revealed Julius Rosenberg was a spy, and some commentators argue that the records indicated it is likely Ethel Rosenberg supported her husband's activities. Alavi, "The Government against Two" 1089; Michael E. Parrish, "Revisited: The Rosenberg 'Atom Spy' Case," 68 *University of Missouri-Kansas City Law Review* (2000): 601.
5. James McEnteer, *Deep in the Heart: The Texas Tendency in American Politics* (Westport, CT: Praeger Publishers, 2004) 87. The Texas Legislature instead made the penalty for communists a sentence of twenty years in prison and a fine of $20,000. Ibid., 88.
6. Lifton and Mitchell, *Who Owns Death?* 38.
7. Scott Christianson, *The Last Gasp: The Rise and Fall of the American Gas Chamber* (Berkeley: University of California Press, 2010) 181; Helen Prejean, *The Death of Innocents: An Eyewitness Account of Wrongful Executions* (London: Canterbury Press Norwich, 2006) 235.
8. Albert Camus, "Reflections on the Guillotine," *Resistance, Rebellion, and Death* (New York: Alfred A. Knoff, 1961) 211–212. Sources vary about who actually made the call to the prison, but all agree that the call with the news of the temporary reprieve arrived too late.
9. Alan Bisbort, *When You Read This, They Will Have Killed Me* (New York: Carroll & Graf Publishers, 2006) 376.

10. Bisbort, *When You Read This, They Will Have Killed Me* 364.
11. Drimmer, *Until You Are Dead* 64–67.
12. Bisbort, *When You Read This, They Will Have Killed Me* 303–313; Theodore Hamm, *Rebel and a Cause* (Berkeley: University of California Press, 2001) 144–145.
13. Redlich, "Fighting the Death Penalty" 620 (noting the early division among civil rights leaders on the death penalty issue).
14. Martin Luther King Jr., "Advice for Living," Nov. 1957, in *The Martin Luther King, Jr. Papers Project*, http://mlk-kpp01.stanford.edu/primarydocuments/Vol4/Nov-1957_AdviceForLiving.pdf; Martin Luther King Jr., "Letter to G.W. Sanders," 15 June 1959, in *The Martin Luther King, Jr. Papers Project,* http://mlk-kpp01.stanford.edu/primarydocuments/Vol5/15June1959_ToG.W.Sanders.pdf
15. Herbert H. Haines, *Against Capital Punishment: The Anti-Death Penalty Movement in America, 1972–1994* (New York: Oxford University Press, 1996).
16. Phil Ochs, "Iron Lady," from *I Ain't Marching Anymore* (Rhino/Elektra 2006).
17. Johnny Cash, *At Folsom Prison* (Columbia 1968); Johnny Cash, *At San Quentin* (Columbia 1969).
18. Robert Wise, Director, *I Want to Live!*, 1958.
19. Thorsten Sellin, "Executions in the United States," in *Capital Punishment* (ed. Thorsten Sellin) (New York: J & J Harper, 1969) 32–33.
20. "National Affairs: Capital Punishment: A Fading Practice," *Time Magazine*, 21 Mar. 1960, http://www.time.com/time/magazine/article/0,9171,894775-1,00.html.
21. Bowers, *Legal Homicide* 10; Galliher, *America without the Death Penalty* 167.
22. Michigan Const., art IV, sec. 46.
23. Redlich, "Fighting the Death Penalty" 621; Heller, "Death Becomes the State" 589, 590.
24. Code of Ga. Ann. Sec. 26-8117; Hugh Adam Bedau, "The Death Penalty in America: Yesterday and Today," 95 *Dickenson Law Review* (Summer 1991): 759–772, 764.
25. Banner, *The Death Penalty* 244; Galliher, *America without the Death Penalty* 177.
26. *See* Hugo Adam Bedau, *Death Is Different: Studies in the Morality, Law, and Politics of Capital Punishment* (Boston: Northeastern University Press, 1987) 157–163. Freeman's lover, Gertrude Jackson, had received a prison sentence for her role in killing her children while Freeman received a death sentence. But after Oregon voters abolished the death penalty, the state's governor commuted Freeman's sentence to imprisonment, and Freeman eventually was paroled in 1983 and changed her name to Wilma Lin Rhule. Eventually, Freeman returned to prison, and she passed away in 2003.
27. Banner, *The Death Penalty* 240–241.
28. Banner, *The Death Penalty* 241.
29. Redlich, "Fighting the Death Penalty" 617.
30. Witherspoon v. Illinois, 391 U.S. 510, 520 (1968); Lazarus, *Closed Chambers* 98. In *Witherspoon*, the Court reversed a death sentence because the trial judge had excluded jurors with concerns about the use of the death penalty
31. Until his death in 1997, Speaker, who was a Republican later appointed by President Richard Nixon to direct the legal services program, remained an opponent of capital punishment and believed his act in dismantling the chair was his highest accomplishment. Robert McG. Thomas Jr., "Fred Speaker, 66, a Crusader against Capital Punishment," *New York Times* (16 Sept. 1996): B9, http://www.nytimes.com/1996/09/16/us/fred-speaker-66-a-crusader-against-capital-punishment.html.
32. Bedau, *The Death Penalty in America: Current Controversies*, 13; Bowers, *Legal Homicide* 10; Galliher, *America without the Death Penalty*, 194.
33. "National Affairs: Capital Punishment: A Fading Practice."
34. Wilkerson v. Utah, 99 U.S. 130 (1879). Evan J. Mandery, *A Wild Justice: The Death and Resurrection of Capital Punishment in America* (New York: W.W. Norton, 2013) 15. For further discussion of *Wilkerson*, see Chapter 16.
35. Trop v. Dulles, 356 U.S. 86, 101 (1958).

36. Banner, *The Death Penalty* 248–249; William J. Brennan Jr., "Constitutional Adjudication and the Death Penalty: A View from the Court," 100 *Harvard Law Review* (1986): 313, 315.
37. Rudolph v. Alabama, 375 U.S. 889 (1963) (Goldberg, J., dissenting from denial of petition for writ of certiorari). The opinion also included a dissent from *Snider v. Cunningham*, 375 U.S. 889 (1963), a capital rape case from Virginia. Although Frank Lee Rudolph and Frank Jimmy Snider Jr. were unsuccessful before the United States Supreme Court, they each avoided execution. Watt Espy, *Executions in the U.S. 1608-2002: The ESPY File*, 26 July 2014, <http://deathpenaltyinfo.org/executions-us-1608-2002-espy-file>.
38. Arthur J. Goldberg, "Memorandum to the Conference re: Capital Punishment," 27 *Southern Texas Law Review* (1985): 493, 505.
39. Mandery, *A Wild Justice* 25–28.
40. *Rudolph v. Alabama*, 375 U.S. at 889 (Goldberg, J., dissenting from denial of petition for writ of certiorari).
41. Mandery, *A Wild Justice* 25–28.
42. Randall W. Bland, *Justice Thurgood Marshall: Crusader for Liberalism* (Bethesda, MD: Academic Press 2001) 30–31.
43. Gilbert King, *Devil in the Grove* (New York: HarperCollins, 2012) 70.
44. Bowers, *Legal Homicide* 17; Banner, *The Death Penalty* 247.
45. Banner, *The Death Penalty* 252.
46. Bowers, *Legal Homicide* 16–17; Lazarus, *Closed Chambers* 96.
47. Anthony G. Amsterdam, "Selling a Quick Fix for Boot Hill: The Myth of Justice Delayed in Death Cases," in *The Killing State: Capital Punishment in Law, Politics, and Culture* (ed. Austin Sarat) (New York: Oxford University Press, 1999) 148–183, 149.
48. Mandery, *A Wild Justice* 60–62.
49. Haines, *Against Capital Punishment* 44.
50. Hamm, *Rebel and a Cause* 152–155.
51. Hamm, *Rebel and a Cause* 154; Brennan, "Constitutional Adjudication and the Death Penalty" 313, 315.
52. Banner, *The Death Penalty* 251.
53. U.S. Constitution, amend. XIV; Norman Redlich, "'Out Damned Spot; Out, I Say.' The Persistence of Race in American Law," 25 *Vermont Law Review* (2001): 475, 483–484.
54. U.S. Constitution, amend. VIII.
55. Sandra Babcock, "Human Rights Advocacy in United States Capital Cases," *Bringing Human Rights Home Vol. 3* (ed. Cynthia Soohoo, Catherine Albisa, and Martha F. Davis) (Westport, CT: Praeger Publishers, 2008) 95.
56. Bedau, *The Death Penalty in America: Current Controversies* 8.
57. Banner, *The Death Penalty* 252–253.
58. Declaration of Lawrence Wilson, former Associate Warden of Custody at Folsom Prison and former Warden at San Quentin, 14 Apr. 1992, 2–4.
59. Hamm, *Rebel and a Cause* 149–150, 160. Because later that year Governor Ronald Reagan commuted another death row inmate's sentence and because of the subsequent court decisions on capital punishment, Williams's execution was the only one during Reagan's eight years as governor of California.
60. Drimmer, *Until You Are Dead* 244–245.
61. Donald M. Roper, *Goldberg, Arthur Joseph*, in *The Oxford Companion to the Supreme Court of the United States* (ed. Kermit L. Hall) (New York: Oxford University Press, 1992) 341.

CHAPTER 7: INTO THE COURTHOUSE

1. Lazarus, *Closed Chambers* 98.
2. Winthrop Rockefeller, "Executive Clemency and the Death Penalty," 21 *Catholic University Law Review* (1971): 94, 102; James Acker and Charles S. Lanier, "May

God—Or the Governor—Have Mercy: Executive Clemency and Executions in Modern Death-Penalty Systems," 36 *Criminal Law Bulletin* (2000): 200, 210 n.52.
3. David C. Baldus, George G. Woodworth, and Charles A. Pulaski Jr., *Equal Justice and the Death Penalty* (Boston: Northeastern University Press, 1990) 7.
4. Bob Woodward and Scott Armstrong, *The Brethren: Inside the Supreme Court* (New York: Simon & Schuster, 1979) 207.
5. McGautha v. California, 398 U.S. 935 (1970) (granting petition for writ of certiorari); Crampton v. Ohio, 398 U.S. 936 (1970) (granting petition for writ of certiorari).
6. McGautha v. California, 402 U.S. 183, 204 (1971).
7. John Paul Stevens, *Five Chiefs* (New York: Little, Brown and Company, 2011) 144.
8. People v. Anderson, 493 P.2d 880 (Cal. 1972); Brennan, "Constitutional Adjudication and the Death Penalty" 313, 314.
9. Brennan, "Constitutional Adjudication and the Death Penalty" 320–321.
10. Woodward and Armstrong, *The Brethren* 207.
11. Mandery, *A Wild Justice* 128.
12. Mears, *The Death Penalty in Georgia* 3–6.
13. Mandery, *A Wild Justice* 135–165.
14. Furman v. Georgia, 408 U.S. 238 (1972).
15. Woodward and Armstrong, *The Brethren* 220.
16. *Furman v. Georgia*, 408 U.S. at 364 (Marshall, J., concurring).
17. *Furman v. Georgia*, 408 U.S. at 305–306 (Brennan, J., concurring), 358–360 (Marshall, J., concurring). As a U.S. Court of Appeals judge, Marshall joined the unanimous majority denying relief in *United States v. Jackson*, 309 F.2d 573 (2d Cir. 1962), where Nathan Jackson argued his New York trial was unfair because of the introduction of certain evidence.
18. *Furman v. Georgia*, 408 U.S. at 242, 256, 257 (Douglas, J., concurring).
19. David M. Oshinsky, *Capital Punishment on Trial* (Lawrence: University Press of Kansas, 2010) 2.
20. *Furman v. Georgia*, 408 U.S. at 309–310 (Stewart, J., concurring).
21. *Furman v. Georgia*, 408 U.S. at 313 (White, J., concurring).
22. Woodward and Armstrong, *The Brethren* 209–214.
23. Franklin E. Zimring and Gordon Hawkins, *Capital Punishment and the American Agenda* (Cambridge: Cambridge University Press, 1989) 37; Mears, *The Death Penalty in Georgia* 16–17; Stephen B. Bright, "Discrimination, Death, and Denial," in *From Lynch Mobs to the Killing State* (ed. Charles J. Ogletree Jr. and Austin Sarat) (New York: New York University Press, 2006) 216.
24. Oshinsky, *Capital Punishment on Trial* 122–125.
25. M. Watt Espy and John Ortiz Smykla, "Executions in the United States: 1608–1987," *The Espy File*, 1987, http://www.deathpenaltyinfo.org/executions-us-1608-2002-espy-file.

CHAPTER 8: A NEW ERA
1. Greenburg, "The Unkillable Death Penalty".
2. Woodward and Armstrong, *The Brethren* 218; Joel Jacobsen, "Remembered Justice: The Background, Early Career and Judicial Appointments of Justice Potter Stewart," 35 *Akron Law Review* (2002): 227, 232–238.
3. Wallace personally opposed the death penalty, but in public supported it as part of his law-and-order platform. He also signed into law new death penalty statutes while governor of Alabama. Mandery, *A Wild Justice* 250.
4. Hamm, *Rebel and a Cause* 144–152.
5. Hamm, *Rebel and a Cause* 148–151, 160.
6. Hamm, *Rebel and a Cause* 154.
7. Nathan Heller, "What She Said," *The New Yorker* (24 Oct. 2011): 74–80, 78.
8. Redlich, "Fighting the Death Penalty" 621.
9. Roe v. Wade, 410 U.S. 113 (1973).

10. Jill Lepore, "Birthright," *The New Yorker* (14 Nov. 2011): 44–55, 52.
11. Lepore, "Birthright" 52.
12. Hamm, *Rebel and a Cause* 159; Oshinsky, *Capital Punishment on Trial* 84; Bedau, *Death Is Different* 155. Ten months earlier, the California Supreme Court had struck down that state's death penalty statute.
13. Michael Meltsner, *Cruel and Unusual* (New York: Random House, 1973) 290.
14. Mears, *The Death Penalty in Georgia* 26–27.
15. Mears, *The Death Penalty in Georgia* 3, 19.
16. Mears, *The Death Penalty in Georgia* 33, 30–40.
17. Mears, *The Death Penalty in Georgia* 30–31.
18. Mears, *The Death Penalty in Georgia* 3, 19, 40; Akins v. State, 202 S.E.2d 62 (Ga. 1973); Massey v. State, 195 S.E.2d 28 (Ga. 1972).
19. Banner, *The Death Penalty* 268.
20. Banner, *The Death Penalty* 270; Lazarus, *Closed Chambers* 113
21. McClennen, "Capital Punishment in Arizona" 18.
22. Bowers, *Legal Homicide* 174; Haines, *Against Capital Punishment* 45–46.
23. Fowler v. North Carolina, 428 U.S. 904 (1976).
24. Haines, *Against Capital Punishment* 51.
25. Woodward and Armstrong, *The Brethren* 431.
26. Gregg v. State, 210 S.E.2d 659 (Ga. 1974).
27. Oshinsky, *Capital Punishment on Trial* 67–69; Woodward & Armstrong, *The Brethren* 434.
28. Woodward and Armstrong, *The Brethren* 433.
29. *Gregg v. State*, 428 U.S. at 173 (quoting Trop v. Dulles, 356 U.S. 86, 101 (1958)).
30. Gregg v. Georgia, 428 U.S. 153, 169 (1976); Jurek v. Texas, 428 U.S. 262 (1976); Proffitt v. Florida, 428 U.S. 242 (1976).
31. Georgia Code Ann. Sec. 17-10-30 (1976).
32. Texas Code Crim. Proc. Art. 37.071(2)(b) (1976).
33. *Gregg v. Georgia*, 428 U.S. at 196–198.
34. *Gregg v. State*, 428 U.S. at 199.
35. Woodson v. North Carolina, 428 U.S. 280 (1976); Roberts v. Louisiana, 428 U.S. 325 (1976).
36. *Woodson v. North Carolina*, 428 U.S. at 304.
37. *Woodson v. North Carolina*, 428 U.S. at 293.
38. Lockett v. Ohio, 438 U.S. 586, 604–606 (1978) (holding the Eighth and Fourteenth Amendments require individualized consideration of mitigating factors); Godfrey v. Georgia, 446 U.S. 420, 427–428 (1980) (holding aggravating factors must provide meaningful guidance to a sentencing jury).
39. Beck v. Alabama, 447 U.S. 625, 637 (1980) (Stevens, J., plurality opinion).
40. Lewis v. Jeffers, 497 U.S. 764, 774 (1990); McCleskey v. Kemp, 497 U.S. 764, 774 (1990).
41. Mandery, *A Wild Justice* 408–409.
42. Jacobsen, "Remembered Justice" 248.
43. Woodward and Armstrong, *The Brethren* 434.
44. Woodward and Armstrong, *The Brethren* 441.
45. Woodward and Armstrong, *The Brethren* 433.
46. Woodward and Armstrong, *The Brethren* 441; Mandery, *A Wild Justice* 423.
47. Oshinsky, *Capital Punishment on Trial* 72–73; Mears, *The Death Penalty in Georgia* 96–97. Gregg and McCorquodale earlier had prompted an argument among the Supreme Court justices in 1976 when the Court was deciding which Georgia case to review. A majority of the justices opted for Gregg's case because the aggravated nature of McCorquodale's rape-torture-murder crime distracted from the legal issue. Mandery, *A Wild Justice* 344–353.
48. Woodward and Armstrong, *The Brethren* 442.

CHAPTER 9: STARTING OVER: EXECUTIONS RESUME IN THE 1970S AND 1980S

1. Bedau, *The Death Penalty in America: Current Controversies* 17; Edmund (Pat) Brown, *Public Justice, Private Mercy* (New York: Weidenfeld & Nicolson, 1989) 139.
2. Haines, *Against Capital Punishment* 45.
3. Bedau, *The Death Penalty in America: Current Controversies* 16.
4. Haines, *Against Capital Punishment* 45; Robert M. Bohm, "American Death Penalty Opinion: Past, Present, and Future," in *America's Experiment with Capital Punishment* 28–29 (ed. James R. Acker, Robert M. Bohm, and Charles S. Lanier) *America's Experiment with Capital Punishment* (Durham, NC: Carolina Academic Press, 2003).
5. Sheri Lynn Johnson, John H. Blume, Theodore Eisenberg, Valerie P. Hans, and Martin T. Wells, "The Delaware Death Penalty: An Empirical Study," 97 *Iowa Law Review* (2012): 1925, 1930.
6. Lockett v. Ohio, 438 U.S. 586, 604 (1978). For further discussion of mitigating circumstances in capital cases, see chapter 14.
7. Godfrey v. Georgia, 446 U.S. 420, 428 (1980) (citations omitted).
8. *Capital Punishment in the United States: A Documentary History* 175 (ed. Bryan Vila and Cynthia Morris) (Westport, CT: Greenwood Publishing, 1997) [hereinafter "*Documentary History*"]; Gilmore v. Utah, 429 U.S. 1012 (1976).
9. Mikal Gilmore, *Shot in the Heart* (New York: Doubleday, 1993) 350–351; Norman Mailer, *Executioner's Song* (New York: Little Brown & Co., 1979); Katherine Ramsland, "Gary Gilmore," *TruTV Crime Library*, (last visited 26 July 2014), http://www.trutv.com/library/crime/notorious_murders/mass/gilmore/index_1.html.
10. Acker and Lanier, "May God—or the Governor—Have Mercy" 229 n.152.
11. See chapter 16 for more on lethal injection.
12. William Carlsen, "Support for Death Penalty—Sometimes," *San Francisco Chronicle* (28 March 1990): A9.
13. Hook and Kahn, *Death in the Balance* 27; Daniel Gerould, *Guillotine: Its Legend and Lore* (New York: Blast Books, 1992) 6.
14. Mello, "Ivon Stanley and James Adams' America" 667. Kendall later represented President Bill Clinton in the Senate against articles of impeachment.
15. Oshinsky, *Capital Punishment on Trial* 85.
16. Bill Curry, "Convicted Murderer Executed by Florida; Three Surges of Electricity, Convicted Killer Is Executed," *Washington Post* (26 May 1979): A1; George L. Thurston III, "Probers Say Spenkelink Was Denied His Rights before Being Executed," *Washington Post* (21 Sept. 1979): A9. Later, a governor's report criticized the prison superintendent because Spenkelink's mother and the other female visitors had to go through vaginal and rectal body searches before the visits.
17. Oshinsky, *Capital Punishment on Trial* 87.
18. Bill Curry, "Bishop Granted His Wish: Death without Delay," *Washington Post* (23 Oct. 1979): A3.
19. Oshinsky, *Capital Punishment on Trial* 83; Amsterdam, "Selling a Quick Fix for Boot Hill" 150.
20. Amsterdam, "Selling a Quick Fix for Boot Hill" 150–151.
21. Drimmer, *Until You Are Dead* 71–75; United Press International, "Charlie Brooks: First Execution by Injection, *Baltimore Afro-American* (14 Dec. 1982): 6. Woodie Loudres, who is sometimes referred to as "Woody," served eleven years for the murder and was released on parole in 1989.
22. State v. Quinn, 623 P.2d 630 (Or. 1981); Hook and Kahn, *Death in the Balance* 26; Bedau, *Death Is Different*, 156. Oregon is the only state that has twice voted to abolish the death penalty. It abolished the death penalty by a small margin on an initiative measure in 1914 and by a large majority on a referendum in 1964. Bedau, *Death Is Different*, 155–156.
23. District Attorney for the Suffolk District v. Watson, 411 N.E.2d 1274 (Mass. 1980); Barbara Stewart, "Life and Death. It's a Living," *New York Times* (5 May 1996): 13NJ-4.

24. Aaron Scherzer, "The Abolition of the Death Penalty in New Jersey and Its Impact on Our Nation's 'Evolving Standards of Decency,'" 15 *Michigan Journal of Race and the Law* (2009): 223, 230.
25. Barefoot v. Estelle, 463 U.S. 880 (1983); Anthony G. Amsterdam, "*In Favorem Mortis*: The Supreme Court and Capital Punishment," 14 *Human Rights* (Winter 1987): 50–55.
26. Mears, *The Death Penalty in Georgia* 86–96, 144–146. Machetti was released from prison on parole in 2010. Jeannie Kerns, "After 35 Years in Prison, One Time Death Row Inmate Rebecca Machetti Released," *The Guardian*, 3 July 2010, http://www.examiner.com/article/after-35-years-prison-one-time-death-row-inmate-rebecca-machetti-released.
27. Mello, "Ivon Stanley and James Adams' America" 690–691. Fore more on the race claim, see chapters 12 and 13.
28. Brad Hahn, "Executions Hit 38-Year High in '95; Numbers Likely to Rise if Appeals Are Limited," *Chicago Tribune* (5 Dec. 1996): 18.
29. State v. Anthony, 398 A.2d 1157 (R.I. 1979); State v. Cline, 397 A.2d 1309 (R.I. 1979).
30. Billy Neal Moore, *I Shall Not Die* (Bloomington, IN: AuthorHouse, 2005) 6–8, 51–53, 70, 84–85. The Georgia Board of Pardons and Paroles commuted Moore's sentence on August 21, 1990, just twenty hours before another execution date. Then, on November 8, 1991, the state released Moore.
31. David Rose, "Dead Man Stalking," *The Observer* (21 Apr. 1996): 8.
32. Drimmer, *Until You Are Dead* 85–86.
33. Acker and Lanier, "May God—or the Governor—Have Mercy" 202 n.12. In the "Afterword" to Velma Barfield's account of her life in the book *Woman on Death Row*, Ruth Bell Graham, the daughter of Reverend Billy Graham, revealed Barfield wrote letters before her death to the families of her victims expressing her remorse. After Barfield's execution, Graham arranged by telephone with the families to meet. But when she drove to their houses, they elected not to see her. Ruth Bell Graham, "Afterward," in Velma Barfield, *Woman on Death Row* (Nashville: Oliver-Nelson Books, 1985) 171–172.
34. Maura Dolan, "Rose Bird's Quest for Obscurity," *Los Angeles Times* (15 Nov. 1995): A1; Adam Pertman, "Judge's Obscurity after Vote a 'Tragedy,'" *Boston Globe* (19 May 1996): 2; Hamm, *Rebel and a Cause* 164. Former governor Pat Brown's anti-death penalty son, Jerry Brown, was elected governor of California after Governor Reagan did not run for a third term, and the new governor Brown tried to battle against legislative expansion of the death penalty. Hamm, *Rebel and a Cause* 163–164.
35. Statement by Governor Toney Anaya on Crime and Capital Punishment; Santa Fe, New Mexico, 26 Nov. 1986.
36. "Md. Woman's Death Term Commuted," *Washington Post* (21 Jan. 1987): B7.
37. Atkins v. Virginia, 536 U.S. 304, 313–314, n.5 (2002).
38. "1,788 Await Death; 68 Have Been Executed since '72," *The Phoenix Gazette* (7 Feb. 1987): A-6.
39. "Executions by Year," Death Penalty Information Center, 8 June 2012, http://www.deathpenaltyinfo.org/executions-year.

CHAPTER 10: LYNCHING AND RACE IN AMERICA

1. "Clara Garrett Jenkins, Interview by Erin Sandlin," Kennesaw State University Oral History Project, Cobb NAACP/Civil rights Series, No. 33, 19 Oct. 2009, http://archon.kennesaw.edu/index.php?p=digitallibrary/digitalcontent&id=36&q=menaboni.
2. Scott, *Cobb County, Georgia and the Origins of the Suburban South* 26–28; McPherson, *Battle Cry of Freedom* 749–750; Paden and McTyre, *175 Facts about Marietta, Georgia* 28.
3. Scott, *Cobb County, Georgia and the Origins of the Suburban South* 28–30.

4. David Rose, "The One Empty Seat in Atlanta," *The Observer* (14 July 1996). 3; "Lynching This Morning in Columbus," *The Butler Herald* (13 Aug. 1912): 5. Some sources list T.Z. McElhenny's age as fourteen, while a contemporary source lists his age as seventeen.
5. Scott, *Cobb County, Georgia and the Origins of the Suburban South* 28.
6. Galliher, *America without the Death Penalty* 85–86, 101.
7. According to some reports, members of the mob raped Laura Nelson before she was lynched. Rob Collins, "A Century Later, the Photograph of an Oklahoma Lynching Still Resonates," *Oklahoma Gazette* (Oklahoma City), 24 May 2011, http://www.okgazette.com/oklahoma/print-article-11750-print.html.
8. Timothy V. Kaufman-Osborn, "Capital Punishment as Legal Lynching?" in *From Lynch Mobs to the Killing State: Race and the Death Penalty in America* (ed. Charles J. Ogletree Jr. and Austin Sarat) (New York: New York University Press, 2006) 46.
9. Kaufman-Osborn, "Capital Punishment as Legal Lynching?" 46.
10. William Bradford Huie, "The Shocking Story of Approved Killing in Mississippi," *Look*, 24 Jan. 1956, http://www.pbs.org/wgbh/amex/till/sfeature/sf_look_confession.html.
11. Walter C. Jones, "Federal Official Rebuts Claims; Justice Spokeswoman Stands Up to Challenge on Lynching Cases," *The Florida Times-Union* (23 July 2011): B-3.
12. King, *Devil in the Grove* 101–105.
13. Similarly, the NAACP defined a "lynching" as an illegal killing that is done by at least three people who claim to serve justice or tradition. King, *Devil in the Grove* 86.
14. Abraham Lincoln, *On the Perpetuation of Our Political Institutions,* Teaching American History. 27 Jan. 1838, http://teachingamericanhistory.org/library/document/the-perpetuation-of-our-political-institutions/.
15. David Garland, "Penal Excess and Surplus Meaning: Public Torture Lynchings in Twentieth-Century America," 39 *Law & Sociology Review* (2005): 793, 799.
16. Ralph Ginzburg, *100 Years of Lynching* (Baltimore: Black Classic Press, 1988) 168 (quoting "Whites in Georgia Display Parts of Negroes' Bodies," *Chicago Defender* (17 Feb. 1923)).
17. Garland, "Penal Excess and Surplus Meaning" 815.
18. Kaufman-Osborn, "Capital Punishment as Legal Lynching?" 27; W. Fitzhugh Brundage, *Lynching in the New South: Georgia and Virginia, 1880–1930* (Urbana and Chicago: University of Illinois Press, 1993).
19. Richard Delgado, "The Law of the Noose: A History of Latino Lynching," 44 *Harvard Civil Rights—Civil Liberties Law Review* (2009): 298–301.
20. Baker, "American Indian Executions in Historical Context" 321.
21. Franklin Zimring, *The Contradictions of American Capital Punishment* (New York: Oxford University Press, 2003) 90–92; Charles J. Ogletree Jr., "Making Race Matter in Death Matters," in *From Lynch Mobs to the Killing State* (ed. Charles J. Ogletree Jr. and Austin Sarat) (New York: New York University Press, 2006) 57–59.
22. Marquart et al., *The Rope, the Chair & the Needle* 5–7; Zimring, *The Contradictions of American Capital Punishment* 90–92.
23. Robert L. Zangrando, *The NAACP Crusade against Lynching, 1909–1950,* (Philadelphia: Temple University Press, 1980) 4; George C. Wright, *Racial Violence in Kentucky 1865–1940: Lynchings, Mob Rule, and "Legal Lynchings"* (Baton Rouge: Louisiana State University Press, 1990) 100–101.
24. Brundage, *Lynching in the New South* 103.
25. David Garland, *Peculiar Institution: America's Death Penalty in an Age of Abolition* (Cambridge, MA: Belknap Press, 2012) 38.
26. Brundage, *Lynching in the New South* 54.
27. Garland, "Penal Excess and Surplus Meaning" 818–819.
28. Charles J. Ogletree, Jr., "Black Man's Burden: Race and the Death Penalty in America," 81 *Oregon Law Review* (2002): 15.

29. Donald Bogle, *Toms, Coons, Mulattoes, Mammies, & Bucks* (New York: The Continuum International Publishing Group, 2004) 362.
30. Mary Jane Brown, *Eradicating This Evil: Women in the American-Anti-Lynching Movement 1892–1940* (New York: Routledge, 2000) 3–6.
31. Banner, "Race and the Death Penalty in Historical Perspective" 107.
32. Jacquelyn Dowd Hall, *Revolt against Chivalry: Jessie Daniel Ames and the Women's Campaign against Lynching* (New York: Columbia University Press, 1993) 131–136.
33. Patricia A. Schechter, "Unsettled Business: Ida B. Wells against Lynching, or, How Antilynching Got Its Gender," in *Under Sentence of Death: Lynching in the South* (ed. W. Fitzhugh Brundage) (Chapel Hill & London: University of North Carolina Press, 1997) 292, 292–300.
34. Brown, *Eradicating This Evil* 171–209; Hall, *Revolt against Chivalry.*
35. Brundage, *Lynching in the New South* 215–225, 225, 234–240.
36. Banner, "Race and the Death Penalty in Historical Perspective" 107. Three lynchings occurred in 1939 and five in 1940 as "double-digit numbers disappeared altogether from the statistics."
37. Zangrando, *The NAACP Crusade against Lynching.*
38. W. Fitzhugh Brundage, "Introduction," in *Under Sentence of Death: Lynching in the South* (ed. W. Fitzhugh Brundage) (Chapel Hill & London: University of North Carolina Press, 1997) 15.
39. Brown, *Eradicating This Evil* 321–322.
40. Brundage, *Lynching in the New South* 249–252, 251. The economist was Gavin Wright.
41. Kaufman-Osborn, "Capital Punishment as Legal Lynching?" 37–38.
42. Bright, "Discrimination, Death, and Denial" 215.
43. William S. McFeely, "A Legacy of Slavery and Lynching: The Death Penalty as a Tool of Social Control," *Champion* (Nov. 1997): 30.
44. Brundage, *Lynching in the New South* 215.
45. Ta-Nehisi Coates, "Fear of a Black President," *The Atlantic* (Sept. 2012): 82 (quoting William F. Buckley), http://www.theatlantic.com/magazine/archive/2012/09/fear-o f-a-black-president/309064/.

CHAPTER 11: RACE AND THE COURTS

1. Hendrik Hertzberg, "Over There," *The New Yorker* (1 Aug. 2011): 62.
2. McCleskey v. Kemp, 481 U.S. 279, 329 (1987) (Brennan, J., dissenting).
3. Bright, "Discrimination, Death, and Denial" 214.
4. Stuart Banner, "Traces of Slavery," in *From Lynch Mobs to the Killing State: Race and the Death Penalty in America* 98 (ed. Charles J. Ogletree, Jr. and Austin Sarat) (New York: New York University Press, 2006).
5. Banner, "Traces of Slavery" 99 (citing George M. Stroud, *A Sketch of the Laws Relating to Slavery in the Several States of the United States of America,* 2d ed. (Philadelphia: Henry Longstreth, 1856) 75–87.
6. Banner, "Race and the Death Penalty in Historical Perspective" 98–99.
7. Dred Scott v. Sandford, 60 U.S. 393, 407 (1857).
8. Victor Streib, "Death Penalty for Female Offenders," 58 *University of Cincinnati Law Review* (1990): 845; Melton A. Mclaurin, *Celia, A Slave* (Athens: University of Georgia Press, 1991); Randall Coyne and Lyn Entzeroth: *Capital Punishment and the Judicial Process* (Durham, NC: Carolina Academic Press, 2012).
9. Banner, "Race and the Death Penalty in Historical Perspective," in *From Lynch Mobs to the Killing State* (ed. Charles J. Ogletree Jr. and Austin Sarat) (New York: New York University Press, 2006) 100, 111.
10. Ada Cooper, "Editorial," *The Christian Recorder* [Philadelphia] 28 Sept. 1899 [from Accessible Archives: http://www.accessible.com/accessible/preLog].
11. Banner, "Race and the Death Penalty in Historical Perspective" 101, 107.

12. Andrew E. Taslitz and Carol Steiker, "Introduction to the Symposium: The Jena Six, the Prosecutorial Conscience, and the Dead Hand of History," 44 *Harvard Civil Rights—Civil Liberties Law Review* (2009): 275.

13. The tie, along with another prosecutor's Grim Reaper tie was explained as a joke, but the racial aspect of the noose resonated for some who noted the Louisiana Parish where the prosecutor wore a noose tie was the same area that had elected a former Ku Klux Klan leader, David Duke, as a state representative the same year *McCleskey v. Kemp* was decided in 1987. Jeffrey Gettleman, "Prosecutors' Morbid Neckties Stir Criticism," *New York Times*, 5 Jan. 2003, http://www.nytimes.com/2003/01/05/us/prosecutors-morbid-neckties-stir-criticism.html.

14. Andrews v. Shulsen, 485 U.S. 919, 922 (1988) (Marshall, J., dissenting from denial of petition for writ of certiorari); Dirk Johnson, "Utah Execution Hinges on Issue of Racial Bias," *New York Times,* 19 July 1992, http://www.nytimes.com/1992/07/19/us/utah-execution-hinges-on-issue-of-racial-bias.html; Glen Warchol, "Hi-Fi Torture Victim Dies 28 Years Later," *The Salt Lake Tribune,* 15 July 2002, http://www.freerepublic.com/focus/f-news/716825/posts.

15. Stuart Taylor Jr., "Glimpses of the Least Pretentious of Men," *Legal Times* (8 Feb. 1993): 36. According to other sources, Marshall reported that Roosevelt, who was not happy with his wife's involvement with the NAACP, instead told Biddle, "I warned you not to call me again about any of Eleanor's niggers. Call me one more time and you are fired." King, *Devil in the Grove* 30–31.

16. Kaufman-Osborn, "Capital Punishment as Legal Lynching?" 35, 33–36; Zangrando, *The NAACP Crusade against Lynching* 14.

17. Brown, *Eradicating This Evil* 4.

18. Zimring and Hawkins, *Capital Punishment and the American Agenda* 89.

19. The number of lynchings in each of these states during 1882–1968 are Mississippi (581), Georgia (531), Texas (493), Louisiana (391), Alabama (347), Arkansas (284), Florida (282), Tennessee (251), Kentucky (205), South Carolina (160), Missouri (122) and Oklahoma (122), North Carolina (101), and Virginia (100). Zangrando, *The NAACP Crusade against Lynching* 5.

20. "Number of Executions by State and Region since 1976," *Death Penalty Information Center*, 27 July 2013, http://www.deathpenaltyinfo.org/number-executions-state-and-region-1976.

21. Marquart et al., *The Rope, the Chair & the Needle* 17; Banner, *The Death Penalty* 278–279.

22. Banner, *The Death Penalty* 278–279; Bright, "Discrimination, Death and Denial" 433; David C. Baldus and George Woodworth, "Race Discrimination and the Legitimacy of Capital Punishment: Reflections on the Interaction of Fact and Perception," 53 *DePaul L. Rev.* (2004): 1411, 1416–1417; M.E. Wolfgang, "Racial Discrimination in the Death Sentence for Rape," in *Executions in America* (W. Bowers ed.) (New York: Lexington Books, 1974) 110–120.

23. Ronald J. Tabak, "The Continuing Role of Race in Capital Cases, Notwithstanding President Obama's Election," 37 *Northern Kentucky Law Review* (2010): 243, 250–271.

24. W. Fitzhugh Brundage, "Introduction" 8.

25. Benjamin M. Friedman, *The Moral Consequences of Economic Growth* (New York: Alfred A. Knopf, 2005).

26. Zangrando, *The NAACP Crusade against Lynching* 15–19. When the NAACP's efforts to obtain a federal law against lynching failed in 1922, the organization de-emphasized the federal goal and concentrated on state reforms. Claudine L. Ferrell, *Nightmare and Dream: Anti-lynching in Congress 1917–1922* (New York: Taylor & Francis, 1986) 301.

27. Brundage, *Lynching in the New South* 255–259.

28. Marquart et al. *The Rope, the Chair & the Needle* 2.

29. Dan T. Carter, *Scottsboro: A Tragedy of the American South* (Baton Rouge: Louisiana State University Press, 1979) 3–6, 7–10, 48–49.
30. Powell v. Alabama, 287 U.S. 45 (1932) (holding that states must provide counsel in capital cases where the defendants are incapable of representing themselves).
31. King, *Devil in the Grove* 7–20.
32. John Paul Stevens, "On the Death Sentence," *New York Review of Books*, 23 Dec. 2010 (review of David Garland, *Peculiar Institution: America's Death Penalty in an Age of Abolition* (Cambridge, MA: Harvard University Press, 2010)), http://www.nybooks.com/articles/archives/2010/dec/23/death-sentence/.

CHAPTER 12: WARREN McCLESKEY AND THE BALDUS STUDY

1. Scott, *Cobb County, Georgia and the Origins of the Suburban South* 253–254.
2. Reece v. Georgia, 350 U.S. 85 (1955).
3. Scott, *Cobb County, Georgia and the Origins of the Suburban South* 259–260.
4. Barrett Prettyman, Jr., *Death and the Supreme Court* (New York: Harcourt, Brace & World, Inc., 1961) 258–294.
5. Scott, *Cobb County, Georgia and the Origins of the Suburban South* 249–262.
6. Bright, "Discrimination, Death, and Denial" 220–230.
7. Maxwell v. Bishop, 398 F.2d 138 (8th Cir. 1968), *vacated* 398 U.S. 262 (1970); Marvin E. Wolfgang and Marc Riedel, "Race Judicial Discretion, and the Death Penalty," 407 *American Academy of Political and Social Science* (1973): 119, 127; Samuel R. Gross, "David Baldus and the Legacy of *McCleskey v. Kemp*," 91 *Iowa Law Review* (2012): 1906. Eventually, Arkansas governor Winthrop Rockefeller commuted William Maxwell's death sentence when he commuted the sentences of everyone on the state's death row.
8. Oshinsky, *Capital Punishment on Trial* 91.
9. William J. Bowers and Glenn L. Pierce, "Arbitrariness and Discrimination under Post-*Furman* Capital Statutes," 26 *Crime & Delinquency* (1980): 563; Smith v. Balkcom, 671 F.2d 858 (5th Cir. 1982).
10. Gross, "David Baldus and the Legacy of *McCleskey v. Kemp*" 1905, 1912–1913; William J. Bowers, "A Tribute to David Baldus, a Determined and Relentless Champion of Doing Justice," 97 *Iowa Law Review* (2012): 1890. Unlike the later Charging and Sentencing Study, the earlier Procedural Reform Study did not include data on the strength of evidence of the defendant's guilt and did not evaluate charging and plea bargaining.
11. Scott W. Howe, "Race, Death and Disproportionality," 37 *Northern Kentucky Law Review* (2010): 213, 225.
12. Baldus et al., *Equal Justice and the Death Penalty* 384. The researchers found the 4.3 odds multiplier by using multivariate regression analysis, finding that the 4.3 odds multiplier was significant at the .005 level. Ibid., 316.
13. One may reach the same result using the probabilities and the equation: $(PW/(1-PW)) = (4.3(PB/(1-PB)))$, where "PW is the probability that a guilty defendant would be sentenced to death if the victim were white, and … PB [is] the probability that the defendant would receive the death sentence if the victim were black." Arnold Barnett, "How Numbers Can Trick You," *Technology Review* (Oct. 1994): 42–43.
14. The 4.3 odds multiplier is symmetric because a 4.3 increase in the odds of a death sentence also means there is a 4.3-fold decrease in the odds of a life sentence. So, even in the aggravated example, the 4 percent increase in risk of a death penalty due to the race of the victim is important. If one looks at it another way, a person in the reference group with a 95 percent probability of getting the death penalty would have a 5 percent probability of getting a life sentence. By comparison, a defendant with a similar crime who kills a nonwhite victim will only have a 1 percent probability of getting a life sentence.
15. Baldus et al., *Equal Justice and the Death Penalty* 321; George Woodworth, Email Interview, 25 June 2013.
16. Baldus et al., *Equal Justice and the Death Penalty* 384.

17. Baldus et al., *Equal Justice and the Death Penalty* 286–287.
18. David C. Baldus, George G. Woodworth, and Charles A. Pulaski Jr., "Law and Statistics in Conflict: Reflections on McCleskey v. Kemp" (1991), in Coyne and Entzeroth, *Capital Punishment and the Judicial Process* 206.
19. Baldus et al., "Law and Statistics in Conflict" 287.
20. Howard Ball, "Thurgood Marshall's Forlorn Battle against Racial Discrimination in the Administration of the Death Penalty: The McCleskey Cases, 1987, 1991," 27 *Mississippi College Law Review* (2007–2008): 335, 344–345 (quoting Federal Trial Transcript at 41–46, McCleskey v. Zant, 580 F. Supp. 338 (N.D. Ga. 1984)).
21. Georgia v. McCollum, 505 U.S. 42, 68 (1992) (O'Connor, J., dissenting).
22. During a televised interview promoting his 2010 memoir, former president George W. Bush stated the lowest point of his presidency was when Kanye West, during a 2005 telethon to aid victims of Hurricane Katrina, claimed, "George Bush doesn't care about black people." David Samuels, "American Mozart," *Atlantic Monthly* (May 2012): 72, 75.
23. When the Supreme Court restated the findings of the Baldus study, the Court correctly understood the general conclusions, but like a number of other lawyers, judges, and reporters before and since, the Court incorrectly stated some of the numerical conclusions, confusing the difference between probabilities and odds. In the majority opinion, Justice Powell incorrectly summarized that "defendants charged with killing white victims were 4.3 times as likely to receive a death sentence as defendants charged with killing blacks" and black defendants were "1.1 times as likely to receive a death sentence as other defendants." McCleskey v. Kemp, 481 U.S. 279, 287 (1987). Recognizing the confusion that perplexed lawyers and judges, Baldus and his colleagues noted wryly in their book: "Since it appears that lawyers instinctively equate odds and probabilities, we believe it would be preferable to express the multiplier in terms of probabilities rather than odds." Baldus et al., *Equal Justice and the Death Penalty*, 384
24. Criminal Justice Legal Foundation Website, (last visited 29 Jan. 2013), http://www.cjlf.org/about/about.htm.
25. Some critics of the Baldus study have jumped on this misstatement by the Court to argue that the racial effects were overstated in the case by the lawyers and the justices. Kent Scheidegger, "Rebutting the Myths about Race and the Death Penalty," 10 *Ohio State Journal of Criminal Law* (2012): 147, 155, 157, 164–165.
26. Scheidegger, "Rebutting the Myths about Race and the Death Penalty" 155, 157, 164–165; Barnett, "How Numbers Can Trick You" 42–43; Arnold Barnett, "How Numbers Are Tricking You," (last visited 27 July 2014), http://reocities.com/CapitolHill/4834/barnett.htm. In 1987, Scheidegger acknowledged that the influence of race was inevitable: "Racism is a cancer that infects all aspects of government, including the criminal justice system." Kent S. Scheidegger, "Capital Punishment in 1987: The Puzzle Nears Completion," 15 *Western State University Law Review* (1987): 95, 124.
27. Anthony G. Amsterdam, "Opening Remarks: Race and the Death Penalty before and after *McCleskey*," 39 *Columbia Human Rights Law Review* (2007): 46.
28. Theodore Eisenberg, "Death Sentence Rates and County Demographics: An Empirical Study," 90 *Cornell Law Review* (2005): 347, 370 (noting that sentencing rates suggest that "minority community skepticism about the justness of the death penalty is a contributing factor to low death sentence rates in black defendant-black victim cases").
29. William J. Bowers et al., "Death Sentencing in Black and White: An Empirical Analysis of the Role of Jurors' Race and Jury Racial Composition," 3 *University of Pennsylvania Journal of Constitutional Law* (2001): 171.
30. Bright, "Discrimination, Death, and Denial" 220–230; Mona Lynch and Craig Haney, "Looking across the Emphatic Divide: Racialized Decision Making on the Capital Jury," 2011 *Michigan State Law Review* (2011): 573–607.

31. Baldus and Woodworth, "Race Discrimination and the Legitimacy of Capital Punishment" 1453.
32. Robert Stroup, Telephone Interview, 31 July 2012.
33. Oshinsky, *Capital Punishment on Trial* 95; Dennis D. Dorin, "Far Right of the Mainstream: Racism, Rights, and Remedies from the Perspective of Justice Antonin Scalia's *McCleskey* Memorandum," 45 *Mercer Law Review* (1994): 1035, 1048.
34. Spencer v. Zant, 715 F.2d 1562, 1579 (11th Cir. 1983). James Lee Spencer's death sentence was later overturned based on his intellectual disability. Billy Mitchell was executed in Georgia's electric chair on September 2, 1987. Willie Ross, who like McCleskey was convicted of killing a white police officer, later won a new trial because blacks and women were excluded from his jury. Associated Press, "Willie Ross Will Get New Trial or Freedom," AP News Archive, 26 May 1988, http://www.apnewsarchive.com/1988/14-Years-After-Conviction-Willie-Ross-Will-Get-New-Trial-Or-Freedom/id-57baf0fb54f12a9e29d6a87ba98c1b1a.
35. *McCleskey v. Zant*, 580 F. Supp. at 350.
36. Thomas J. Keith, "Jarndyce v. Jarndyce Drones On: A History of the Racial Justice Act," *North Carolina State Bar Journal* (Fall 2012): 10–21, 11–12. For a more detailed explanation of Dr. Katz's analysis, see Joseph L. Katz, PhD, *Warren McCleskey v. Ralph Kemp: Is the Death Penalty in Georgia Racially Biased?*, June 1991, http://www.ourpaws.info/cramer/death/katz.htm.
37. *McCleskey v. Zant*, 580 F. Supp. at 360–361, 367, 379.
38. McCleskey v. Kemp, 753 F.2d 877 (11th Cir. 1985).
39. *McCleskey v. Kemp*, 753 F.2d at 906 (Vance, J., concurring).
40. Mello, "Ivon Stanley and James Adams' America" 654–655.
41. Dorin, "Far Right of the Mainstream"1062.
42. Certiorari Petition Vote, 26 June 1986, McCleskey v. Kemp Case File, No. 811–6811, Basic File, *Justice Lewis F. Powell Jr. Archives*, Washington and Lee University, Lexington, VA (last visited 28 June 2012), http://law.wlu.edu/deptimages/powell%20archives/McCleskeyKempBasic.pdf; Scott E. Sunby, "The Loss of Constitutional Faith: *McCleskey v. Kemp* and the Dark Side of Procedure," 10 *Ohio State Journal of Criminal Law* (2012): 11–12; McCleskey v. Kemp, 478 U.S. 1019 (1986).
43. John Charles ("Jack") Boger, Telephone Interview, 20 Aug. 2012.
44. Furman v. Georgia, 408 U.S. 238, 256 (1972) (Douglas, J., concurring).
45. Scott W. Howe, "Race, Death and Disproportionality," 37 *Northern Kentucky Law Review* (2010): 213, 225.
46. Darden v. Wainwright, 477 U.S. 168 (1986).
47. Stroup, "The Political, Legal, and Social Context of the McCleskey Habeas Litigation" 93.
48. Baldus and Woodworth, "Race Discrimination and the Legitimacy of Capital Punishment" 1438.
49. Debra Cassens Moss, "The Statistics of Death," 1 *ABA Journal* (Jan. 1987): 54–55.

CHAPTER 13: THE SUPREME COURT AND *McCLESKEY v. KEMP*

1. Dorin, "Far Right of the Mainstream" 1056. Joining Ms. Westmoreland on the brief were Georgia Attorney General Michael J. Bowers, Marion O. Gordon (First Attorney General), and William B. Hill Jr. (Senior Assistant Attorney General).
2. Dorin, "Far Right of the Mainstream" 1056–1057. The other attorneys who worked on the briefs for McCleskey included Julius L. Chambers, James M. Nabrit III, Vivian Berger, Robert H. Stroup, Timothy K. Ford, Anthony G. Amsterdam, and Deval Patrick.
3. Justice Lewis F. Powell Jr. Notes of 17 Oct. 1986, 1–3, McCleskey v. Kemp Case File, No. 811-6811, Basic File, *Justice Lewis F. Powell Jr. Archives*, Washington and Lee University, Lexington, VA (last visited 29 June 2013), http://law.wlu.edu/deptimages/powell%20archives/McCleskeyKempBasic.pdf.
4. Furman v. Georgia, 408 U.S. 238, 449, 450 (1972) (Powell, J., dissenting).

5. Stephens v. Kemp, 464 U.S. 1027, 1030 n.2 (1983) (Powell, J., dissenting from granting a stay of execution).
6. Stephens v. Kemp, 721 F.2d 1300 (11th Cir. 1983); Stephens v. Kemp, 722 F.2d 627 (11th Cir. 1983).
7. Memorandum to Leslie from Justice Lewis F. Powell Jr. of 16 Sept. 1986, 1, McCleskey v. Kemp Case File, No. 811-6811, Basic File, *Justice Lewis F. Powell Jr. Archives*, Washington and Lee University, Lexington, VA (last visited 28 June 2012), http://law.wlu.edu/deptimages/powell%20archives/McCleskeyKempBasic.pdf; Lazarus, *Closed Chambers* 201.
8. Bench Memorandum from Leslie to Justice Lewis F. Powell Jr. of 1 Oct. 1986, 8 n.1, McCleskey v. Kemp Case File, No. 811-6811, Basic File, *Justice Lewis F. Powell Jr. Archives*, Washington and Lee University, Lexington, VA (last visited 28 June 2012), http://law.wlu.edu/deptimages/powell%20archives/McCleskeyKempBasic.pdf; Lazarus, *Closed Chambers* 201. As of 2014, Leslie Gielow Jacobs is a professor of law and Director of the Capital Center for Public Law & Policy at Pacific McGeorge School of Law.
9. A 2001 study by the Capital Jury Project found that sentencing jurors—consciously or subconsciously—factor in the race of the defendant in assessing the defendant's character for sentencing purposes. Bowers et al., "Death Sentencing in Black and White" 171.
10. Memorandum from Leslie to Justice Lewis F. Powell Jr. of 14 Oct. 1986, 4, McCleskey v. Kemp Case File, No. 811-6811, Basic File, *Justice Lewis F. Powell Jr. Archives*, Washington and Lee University, Lexington, VA (last visited 28 June 2012), http://law.wlu.edu/deptimages/powell%20archives/McCleskeyKempBasic.pdf; Dorin, "Far Right of the Mainstream" 1059–1060; Lazarus, *Closed Chambers* 205.
11. Note from Justice Sandra Day O'Connor to Justice Lewis F. Powell of 13 Nov. 1986, 1, McCleskey v. Kemp Case File, No. 811-6811, Basic File, *Justice Lewis F. Powell Jr. Archives*, Washington and Lee University, Lexington, VA (last visited 28 June 2012), http://law.wlu.edu/deptimages/powell%20archives/McCleskeyKempBasic.pdf.
12. Note from Justice William Brennan to Justice Lewis F. Powell Jr. of 14 Nov. 1986, 1, McCleskey v. Kemp Case File, No. 811-6811, Basic File, *Justice Lewis F. Powell Jr. Archives*, Washington and Lee University, Lexington, VA (last visited 28 June 2012), http://law.wlu.edu/deptimages/powell%20archives/McCleskeyKempBasic.pdf; Dorin, "Far Right of the Mainstream" 1059–1060.
13. Memorandum to the Conference from Justice Antonin Scalia of 6 Jan. 1987, 1, McCleskey v. Kemp Case File, No. 811-6811, Basic File, *Justice Lewis F. Powell Archives* (last visited 28 June 2012), http://law.wlu.edu/deptimages/powell%20archives/McCleskeyKempBasic.pdf.
14. McCleskey v. Kemp, 481 U.S. 279, 282–283 (1987). Although the Supreme Court accepted the Baldus findings for its legal analysis, I provide some of the critiques and conclusions of the Baldus study here for some background on the complex analysis that faced the Court. A more detailed analysis is beyond the scope of this book, but for more information, see Baldus et al. *Equal Justice and the Death Penalty*.
15. McCleskey v. Kemp, 481 U.S. 279, 289 n. 7 (1987); Bench Memorandum from Leslie to Justice Lewis F. Powell Jr. of 1 Oct. 1986, 5–8, McCleskey v. Kemp Case File, No. 811-6811, Basic File, *Justice Lewis F. Powell Jr. Archives*, Washington and Lee University, Lexington, VA (last visited 28 June 2012), http://law.wlu.edu/deptimages/powell%20archives/McCleskeyKempBasic.pdf.
16. *McCleskey v. Kemp*, 481 U.S. at 291 n.7.
17. *McCleskey v. Kemp*, 481 U.S. at 292 n.8. During earlier consideration of the case, Justice Powell and Justice O'Connor questioned whether McCleskey had standing to assert an Equal Protection claim based on the race of the victim. Sunby, "The Loss of Constitutional Faith: *McCleskey v. Kemp* and the Dark Side of Procedure" 18-19.
18. *McCleskey v. Kemp*, 481 U.S. at 305–308; Baldus and Woodworth, "Race Discrimination and the Legitimacy of Capital Punishment" 1442–1443.

19. *McCleskey v. Kemp*, 481 U.S. at 308–314.
20. *McCleskey v. Kemp*, 481 U.S. at 314–320. Although Justice Powell's majority opinion expressed these fears about how a ruling for McCleskey might affect all criminal cases, when he worked on the opinion he had considered that an Eighth Amendment ruling might be limited to capital cases. Memorandum from Leslie to Justice Lewis F. Powell Jr. of 14 Oct. 1986, 1, McCleskey v. Kemp Case File, No. 811–6811, Basic File, *Justice Lewis F. Powell Jr. Archives*, Washington and Lee University, Lexington, VA (last visited 28 June 2012), http://law.wlu.edu/deptimages/powell%20archives/McCleskeyKempBasic.pdf.
21. *McCleskey v. Kemp*, 481 U.S. at 320.
22. David C. Baldus et al, "*McCleskey v. Kemp* (1987): Denial, Avoidance, and the Legitimization of Racial Discrimination in the Administration of the Death Penalty," in *Death Penalty Stories* (ed. John H. Blume and Jordan M. Steiker) (New York: Foundation Press 2009) 236.
23. *McCleskey v. Kemp*, 481 U.S. at 321 (Brennan, J., dissenting).
24. *McCleskey v. Kemp*, 481 U.S. at 334 (Brennan, J., dissenting).
25. *McCleskey v. Kemp*, 481 U.S. at 322–329, 335–344.
26. *McCleskey v. Kemp*, 481 U.S. at 343.
27. Note from Justice Lewis F. Powell Jr. to Chief Justice William Rehnquist of 31 March 1987, 1, McCleskey v. Kemp Case File, No. 811-6811, Basic File, *Justice Lewis F. Powell Jr. Archives*, Washington and Lee University, Lexington, VA (last visited 28 June 2012), http://law.wlu.edu/deptimages/powell%20archives/McCleskeyKempBasic.pdf ("I have heard nothing from Harry.")
28. *McCleskey v. Kemp*, 481 U.S. at 351–364 (Blackmun, J., dissenting).
29. Jeffrey Rosen, *The Supreme Court: The Personalities and Rivalries That Defined America* (New York: Holt Paperbacks, 2007) 13–14.
30. *McCleskey v. Kemp*, 481 U.S. at 367.
31. Bench Memorandum from Leslie to Justice Lewis F. Powell Jr. of 1 Oct. 1986, 21, McCleskey v. Kemp Case File, No. 811-6811, Basic File, *Justice Lewis F. Powell Jr. Archives*, Washington and Lee University, Lexington, VA (last visited 28 June 2012), http://law.wlu.edu/deptimages/powell%20archives/McCleskeyKempBasic.pdf.
32. Baldus et al. *Equal Justice and the Death Penalty* 3; Biko Agozino, "How Scientific Is Criminal Justice?: A Methodological Critique of Research on *McCleskey v. Kemp* and Other Capital Cases," 17 *National Black Law Journal* (2003): 84, 92.
33. Moss, "The Statistics of Death" 51, 55.
34. Dorin, "Far Right of the Mainstream" 1084–1085.
35. James S. Liebman, "Slow Dancing with Death: The Supreme Court and Capital Punishment, 1963–2006," 107 *Columbia Law Review* (2007): 85.
36. Memorandum to Leslie from Justice Lewis F. Powell Jr. of 16 Sept. 1986, McCleskey v. Kemp Case File, No. 811-6811, 6, *Justice Lewis F. Powell Jr. Archives*, Washington and Lee University, Lexington, VA (last visited 28 June 2012), http://law.wlu.edu/deptimages/powell%20archives/McCleskeyKempBasic.pdf; Robert Stroup, Telephone Interview, 31 July 2012.
37. John Paul Stevens, "On the Death Sentence." During Stewart's Senate confirmation hearings in April 1959, when facing hostile questioning about *Brown v. Board of Education*, Stewart stated, "I would not like for you to vote for me on the assumption that I am dedicated to the cause of overturning that decision, because I'm not." Every senator in Virginia, North Carolina, South Carolina, Georgia, Alabama, Mississippi, Louisiana, and Arkansas voted against Stewart's confirmation. Although one Florida senator voted for Stewart, that senator said that he regretted the vote the next day. Every other senator voted for Stewart, and he was confirmed. Jacobsen, "Remembered Justice" 249–250.
38. Haines, *Against Capital Punishment* 76.
39. Richard Lacayo, Anne Constable and Daniel S. Levy, "Clearing a Path to the Chair," *Time Magazine*, 4 May 1987, http://www.time.com/time/magazine/article/0,9171,964240-1,00.html.

40. Anthony Lewis, "Bowing to Racism," *New York Times* (28 Apr. 1987): A31, Coyne and Entzeroth, *Capital Punishment and the Judicial Process* 222.
41. Oshinsky, *Capital Punishment on Trial* 107.
42. Adam Liptak, "New Look at Death Sentences and Race," *New York Times*, 29 April 2008, http://www.nytimes.com/2008/04/29/us/29bar.html.
43. Randall L. Kennedy, "*McCleskey v. Kemp*: Race, Capital Punishment, and the Supreme Court," 101 *Harvard Law Review* (1988): 1388, 1389.
44. Stout, "The Lawyers of Death Row" 5.
45. Sandra L. Simpson, "Everyone Else Is Doing It, Why Can't We? A New Look at the Use of Statistical Data in Death Penalty Cases," 12 *Journal of Gender, Race & Justice* (Spring 2009): 509.
46. Dobbs v. Zant, 963 F.2d 1403 (11th Cir. 1991), *rev'd on other grounds*, Dobbs v. Zant, 506 U.S. 357 (1993).
47. Liebman, "Slow Dancing with Death" 84.
48. Terry Carter, "Lady of the Last Chance: Lawyer Makes Her Mark Getting Convicts Off Death Row," ABA Journal, 1 Aug. 2012, http://www.abajournal.com/magazine/article/lady_of_the_last_chance/.
49. Dorin, "Far Right of the Mainstream" 1057–1059; Henry J. Reske, "Behind the Scenes," *ABA Journal* (Aug. 1993): 28; John Charles ("Jack") Boger, Telephone Interview, 20 Aug. 2012.
50. Order by Judge Joel J. Pryor, Chief Judge Superior Court of Atlanta (GA) Judicial Circuit, 25 June 1987.
51. For further discussion of these developments in Warren McCleskey's case, see chapter 3.
52. Hollyday, "A Gift of Dignity" 24. Ben Wright was sentenced to prison and released in 1987, but after his release "he committed several more crimes and was subsequently sentenced to life plus 20 years." Ibid.
53. Letter from Warren McCleskey to Rev. George Wirth, 29 Dec. 1990.

CHAPTER 14: MITIGATION AND REFORM

1. C.S. Lovett, *Dealing with the Devil* (Baldwin Park, CA: Personal Christianity, 1967).
2. Warren McCleskey, Letter to Sister Reginald, 7 July 1982.
3. Murphy Davis, Telephone Interview, 13 May 2011. Years after McCleskey's death, when Reverend Davis was diagnosed with cancer, she found inspiration in the way McCleskey had turned his life around. "He moved toward a peace and serenity I have never seen in another human being." John Blake, "Murphy's Law: Death Row Activist Keeps the Faith in Her Battle with Rare Cancer," *Atlanta Journal-Constitution* (14 Apr. 1996): M3.
4. Billy Moore, "In Memory of Warren McCleskey," 25 Sept. 1991 (on file with author); William "Billy" Neal Moore, Telephone Interview, 5 July 2011.
5. Lockett v. Ohio, 438 U.S. 586, 604 (1978).
6. Williams v. Taylor, 529 U.S. 362, 395 (2000). Another case that documents mitigating facts is *Hardwick v. Crosby*, 320 F.3d 1127, 1162–1182 (11th Cir. 2003) (noting mitigating evidence including a physically and emotionally abusive father who beat the defendant, routinely exposed himself and urinated on the floor in front of the children, and gave drugs and alcohol to the defendant when he was a child).
7. Darmer, Affidavit, 2; Burnette, Affidavit, 2.
8. Marvin Henberg, *Retribution: Evil for Evil in Ethics, Law, and Literature* (Philadelphia: Temple University Press, 1990) 191.
9. Jeremy Bentham, *An Introduction to the Principles of Morals and Legislation* 83–84 (ed. John Bowring) (Edinburgh: William Tait, 1843).
10. Cesare Beccaria, *Of Crimes and Punishments* (New York: Marsilio Publishers Corporation, 1996) 14.
11. Albert W. Alschuler, "The Changing Purposes of Criminal Punishment: A Retrospective on the Past Century and Some Thoughts about the Next," 70 *University*

of Chicago Law Review (2003): 1, 6, 9, 11; Paul H. Robinson and John M. Darley, "The Utility of Desert," 91 *Northwestern University Law Review* (1997): 453, 456.

12. Alschuler, *The Changing Purposes of Criminal Punishment* 15.
13. Immanuel Kant, *The Science of Right* (W. Hastie trans.), *reprinted in Great Books of the Western World*: Kant (ed. Robert M. Hutchins) (Chicago: Encyclopedia Britannica, 1952) 397, 447.
14. Henberg, *Retribution* 159–160 (quoting Immanuel Kant, *The Metaphysical Elements of Justice* 102 (John Ladd trans.) (Indianapolis: Bobbs-Merrill Pub., 1965)).
15. 504 U.S. 719, 739 (1992) (Scalia, J., dissenting); Ibid., 752 n.6 (quoting Immanuel Kant, *The Philosophy of Law* 198 (W. Hastie trans.) (Clifton, NJ: Augustus M. Kelley Publishers, 1974) (1887)).
16. James Q. Whitman, *Harsh Justice: Criminal Punishment and the Widening Divide between America and Europe* (New York: Oxford University Press, 2003) 23–24.
17. Whitman, *Harsh Justice* 55, 56–58.
18. For some examples of the role of politics in death penalty decisions, see chapters 6, 8, and 17.
19. G. Ben Cohen, "McCleskey's Omission: The Racial Geography of Retribution," 10 *Ohio State Journal of Criminal Law* (2012): 97–98.
20. Furman v. Georgia, 408 U.S. 238, 345, 354 (1971) (Marshall, J., concurring). Ibid., 394–395 (Burger, C.J., dissenting); ibid., 452–454 (Powell, J., dissenting); Powell v. Texas, 392 U.S. 514, 531, 535–536 (1968) (plurality opinion).
21. Gregg v. Georgia, 428 U.S. 153, 183 (1976) (quoting Williams v. New York, 337 U.S. 241, 248 (1949)).
22. *Gregg v. Georgia*, 428 U.S. at 183.
23. *Gregg v. Georgia*, 428 U.S. at 236–240.
24. Clint Williams, "Paths Paved in Violence: Consequences of Abuse Evident on Death Row," *Arizona Republic* (Phoenix) (21 Nov. 1993): A25.
25. Eddings v. Oklahoma, 455 U.S. 104, 115 n.11 (1982) (quoting *Twentieth Century Fund Task Force on Sentencing Policy toward Young Offenders, Confronting Youth Crime* 7 (1978)).
26. *Eddings v. Oklahoma*, 455 U.S. at 116; Hitchcock v. Dugger, 481 U.S. 393, 397 (1987) (holding that it was mitigating that "petitioner had been one of seven children in a poor family that earned its living by picking cotton; that his father had died of cancer; and that petitioner had been a fond and affectionate uncle.").
27. Beverly Lowry, "The Good Bad Girl," *The New Yorker* (9 Feb. 1998): 60–69; Joseph Geringer, "Karla Faye Tucker: Texas' Controversial Murdress," *truTV Crime Library*, (last visited 25 July 2014), http://www.trutv.com/library/crime/notorious_ murders/women/tucker/1.html; Sam Howe Verhovek, "Karla Tucker Is Now Gone, but Several Debates Linger," *New York Times*, 5 Feb. 1998, http://www.nytimes. com/1998/02/05/us/karla-tucker-is-now-gone-but-several-debates-linger. html?ref=karlafayetucker.
28. Later, conservative writer Tucker Carlson recounted a conversation he had with Governor Bush where Governor Bush had mocked Karla Faye Tucker's appearance on the *Larry King Live* TV show. Timothy Noah, "Bush's Tookie: Remembering Bush's Worst Public Moment," *Slate Magazine*, 2 Dec. 2005, http://www.slate.com/ id/2131451/.
29. Evans v. Muncy, 498 U.S. 927, 927, 930 (1990) (Marshall, J., dissenting); Stuart Taylor, "We Will Kill You Anyway," *The American Lawyer* (Dec. 1990): 55–56, http:// stuarttaylorjr.com/content/we-will-kill-you-anyway.
30. Taylor, "We Will Kill You Anyway" 55–56.
31. The injustice in Evans's case caused Shapiro to cease practicing law for a few years, but he eventually returned to law practice, and he later represented John Allen Muhammad, who was convicted and executed for sniper killings around Washington, DC. The Evans case continued to haunt Shapiro, and fourteen years after Evans's execution, Shapiro still had a portrait of Evans on the wall in his law office and the file from the case still sat next to his desk. Josh White, "Sniper Trial

Took Toll on Attorneys, Muhammad's Lawyers Shoulder Own Stress, Depression and Guilt," *Washington Post* (21 Mar. 2004): C01.

32. Joe Jackson and William F. Burke Jr., *Dead Run: The Shocking Story of Dennis Stockton and Life on Death Row in America* (New York: Walker & Company, 2000) 196; David A. Kaplan and Bob Cohn, "Pardon Me, Governor Wilder," *Newsweek* (3 Mar. 1991): 56. Evans's case also had some other unlucky breaks that led to his death sentence, such as the revelation the prosecutor used improper evidence at his first sentencing hearing, and had the error been discovered earlier, the law would have resulted in a life sentence for Evans. Taylor, "We Will Kill You Anyway."

33. Erwin James, "Dead Man' Talking," *The Guardian*, 23 Apr. 2008, http://www.guardian.co.uk/society/2008/apr/23/prisonsandprobation. In another rare commutation, in April 2012, the Georgia Board of Pardons and Paroles commuted the death sentence of Daniel Greene to life without parole. The African-American Greene had been sentenced to death for the fatal stabbing of a man who walked in on him while he was robbing a convenience store clerk. The Board commuted Greene's sentence after hearing testimony about how Greene had been a model inmate on death row. Jim Mustian, "Georgia Pardons Board Spares Condemned Killer Daniel Greene," *Ledger-Enquirer* (Columbus, Georgia), 20 Apr. 2012, http://www.ledger-enquirer.com/2012/04/20/2019904/georgia-pardons-board-spares-condemned.html.

34. Michael Albanese, "From Warren McCleskey to Troy Davis, History Repeats," *Huffington Post*, 23 Sept. 2011, http://www.huffingtonpost.com/michael-albanese/post_2398_b_958515.html.

35. Paul Cadenhead, Esq. et al., Documentation Submitted in Support of Application of Warren McCleskey for a 90-Day Stay of Execution and for Commutation of His Sentence of Death, 1991, 10 (Warren McCleskey court files).

36. Stroup, "The Political, Legal, and Social Context of the McCleskey Habeas Litigation" 86 n.61; Memorandum of Cheyenne Puckett, Performance Recording Sheet (Mar. 1988); Performance Recording Sheet (Apr. 1991).

37. Rev. Murphy Davis, Telephone Interview, 13 May 2011.

CHAPTER 15: WARREN McCLESKEY AND THE ELECTRIC CHAIR

1. Baze v. Rees, 553 U.S. 35, 42 (2008).
2. For information about Westinghouse, Edison, and Kemmler's execution, see Richard Moran, *Executioner's Current* (New York: Alfred A. Knopf, 2002).
3. Glass v. Louisiana, 471 U.S. 1080 (1985) (Brennan, J., dissenting); Denno, "Is Electrocution an Unconstitutional Method of Execution?" 551.
4. In re Kemmler, 136 U.S. 436, 447 (1890).
5. *Kemmler*, 136 U.S. at 447.
6. Marquart et al., *The Rope, the Chair & the Needle* 14.
7. Moran, *Executioner's Current* 14–25.
8. Denno, "Is Electrocution an Unconstitutional Method of Execution?" 603.
9. Leyden, "Death in the Hot Seat" D5.
10. *Kemmler*, 136 U.S. 436 (1890); *Glass v. Louisiana*, 471 U.S. 1080 (Brennan, J., dissenting).
11. Moran, *Executioner's Current* 102.
12. Mears, *The Death Penalty in Georgia* 79.
13. *Baze v. Rees*, 553 U.S. at 42; Marquart et al., *The Rope, the Chair & the Needle* 14.
14. Louisiana ex rel. Francis v. Resweber, 329 U.S. 459, 462 (1947).
15. Jacob Weisberg, "This Is Your Death," *The New Republic* (1 July 1991): 24.
16. Don Schanche Jr. "Georgia's Electric Chair Has Grim History," *Knight Ridder/Tribune News Service*, 8 Oct. 2001, http://www.accessmylibrary.com/coms2/summary_0286-6782784_ITM.
17. Kaufman-Osborn, "Capital Punishment as Legal Lynching?" 40–41.
18. Moran, *Executioner's Current* 221.
19. Weisberg, "This Is Your Death" 24–25.

20. Ginzburg, *100 Years of Lynching* 140 (quoting "Letter from Texas Reveals Lynching's Ironic Facts," *New York Negro World*, 22 Aug. 1920).
21. Ed Loring, "Warren and the Warden," *Hospitality* (newspaper of The Open Door Community, Atlanta, GA) (Jan. 1992): 4.
22. Order by Judge William W. Daniel, Chief Judge Superior Court of Atlanta (GA) Judicial Circuit, Sept. 9, 1991. Different news sources list McCleskey's age as anywhere between forty-four and forty-six, but official records indicate he was forty-five.
23. Curriden, "I Deeply Regret a Life Was Taken" A/12.
24. Curriden, "Ready to Die" A/1.
25. Applebome, "Inmate Whose Appeals Shook System Faces Execution" (article incorrectly spells Rev. Wirth's name as "Worth").
26. Curriden, "Ready to Die" A/1.
27. Letter from Mike Berryhill to Georgia Board of Pardons and Parole, 1 June 1991; Letter from Sen. Paul Wellstone to Wayne Snow Jr., Chairman of State Board of Pardons and Paroles, 27 June 1991.
28. Robinson, "Robbery Victim" A/6.
29. Applebome, "Inmate Whose Appeals Shook System Faces Execution"; Applebome, "Georgia Inmate Is Executed after 'Chaotic' Legal Move."
30. Mark Curriden, "Clemency Denied for McCleskey: Execution Set Tonight for Police Killing," *The Atlanta Journal* (24 Sept. 1991): A/1.
31. Curriden, "Clemency Denied for McCleskey" A/1.
32. Reverend Murphy Davis, Telephone Interview, 13 May 2011.
33. Lyle V. Harris and Mark Curriden, "McCleskey Is Executed for '78 Killing," *Atlanta Constitution* (25 Sept. 1991): A/1.
34. Weisberg, "This Is Your Death" 24–25; Georgia Bureau of Investigation Division of Forensic Sciences, "Autopsy or Report of Examination of Body: Warren McCleskey," Case No. B91-4487, 25 Sept. 1991.
35. "Warren McCleskey's Last Will and Testament," Jackson State Prison, Georgia: 24 Sept. 1991, 3:45 pm. A recording of his final statement in his cell is available at http://soundportraits.org/on-air/execution_tapes/complete_audio.php.
36. Curriden, "McCleskey Put to Death after Hours of Delays" D3.
37. Susan Laccetti, "McCleskey's Letters Showed 'a Deep Faith,' " *The Atlanta Journal* (25 Sept. 1991): A/6.
38. Moore eventually was released from prison, as discussed in Chapter 14.
39. William Neal Moore, "Remembering Warren," *Hospitality* (newspaper of The Open Door Community, Atlanta, GA) (Jan. 1992): 5, 11.
40. McCleskey v. Bowers, 501 U.S. 1281 (1991) (Marshall, J., dissenting).
41. Curriden, "McCleskey Put to Death after Hours of Delays" D3; Harris and Curriden, "McCleskey Is Executed" A/1; Ronda Cook and Jeanne Cummings, "Pace of Execution Bothers Miller," *Atlanta Constitution* (27 Sept. 1991): C/4.
42. Curriden, "McCleskey Put to Death after Hours of Delays" D3; Applebome, "Georgia Inmate Is Executed after 'Chaotic' Legal Move."
43. McCleskey v. Bowers, 501 U.S. 1281 (Marshall, J., dissenting from denial of application for stay of execution); King, *Devil in the Grove* 123 ("For [Marshall] the Supreme Court was as level a playing field as you'd find in the land: that was the courtroom he wanted to fight in.").
44. Soon after replacing Marshall on the Court, Justice Thomas referenced the evidence of racism in McCleskey's case to advocate for allowing states to limit the mitigating evidence that capital defendants may present at their sentencing hearings. Graham v. Collins, 506 U.S. 461, 493 (1993) (Thomas, J., concurring).
45. Mears, *The Death Penalty in Georgia* 135; Curriden, "McCleskey Put to Death after Hours of Delays" D3.
46. Moore, "Remembering Warren" 11.
47. John Charles ("Jack") Boger, Telephone Interview, 21 Aug. 2012. In 1998, criminal defense lawyer Michael Mears subpoenaed the audio tapes of twenty-two Georgia

executions as part of a lawsuit challenging the state's use of the electric chair. The recordings, available online, include Warren McCleskey's execution, where one may hear the audio cut out during McCleskey's final statement, available at http://soundportraits.org/on-air/execution_tapes/complete_audio.php.

48. Mears, *The Death Penalty in Georgia* 80–81.
49. Curriden, "McCleskey Put to Death after Hours of Delays" D3; Mears, *The Death Penalty in Georgia* 82–83.
50. Denno, "Is Electrocution an Unconstitutional Method of Execution?" 637–643; Weisberg, "This Is Your Death" 24; *Glass v. Louisiana*, 471 U.S. 1080 (Brennan, J., dissenting).
51. Curriden, "McCleskey Put to Death after Hours of Delays" D3; Applebome, "Georgia Inmate Is Executed after 'Chaotic' Legal Move."
52. Moore, "Remembering Warren" 11.
53. "Death Penalty Supporters, One a Ku Klux Klan Member, Advocating Capital Punishment, outside the Georgia Diagnostic and Classification State Prison, Jackson, Georgia, September 24, 1991," Georgia State University Library Digital Archive, (last visited 25 July 2014), http://digitalcollections.library.gsu.edu/cdm/singleitem/collection/ajc/id/2831/rec/2.
54. Ed Weir, "A Time to Weep," *Hospitality* (newspaper of The Open Door Community, Atlanta, GA) (Jan. 1992): 8.
55. Applebome, "Georgia Inmate Is Executed after 'Chaotic' Legal Move."
56. "Warren McCleskey Is Dead," *New York Times*, 29 Sept. 1991, http://www.nytimes.com/1991/09/29/opinion/warren-mccleskey-is-dead.html.
57. Applebome, "Georgia Inmate Is Executed after 'Chaotic' Legal Move."
58. Bill Montgomery, "Both Sides of Debate Agree: Executions Aren't Pleasant," *Atlanta Journal and Constitution* (26 Sept. 1991): D3.
59. Bill Montgomery, "McCleskey-Case Informant Freed on Execution Eve," *Atlanta Journal and Constitution* (28 Sept. 1991): B/3.
60. Cook and Cummings, "Pace of Execution Bothers Miller" C/4.
61. Martha Dragich, "Revelations from the Blackmun Papers on the Development of Death Penalty Law," 70 *Missouri Law Review* (2005): 1183, 1195.
62. "The Celebration of the Home Going of Warren McCleskey," *Hanley Shelton Funeral Home*, 28 Sept. 1991 (funeral pamphlet).
63. Michelle Piscopo, "*Provenzano v. Moore & Bryan v. Moore*: How These Two Challenges Finally Forced the Florida Legislature to Pull the Plug on Old Sparky," 10 *Temple Political & Civil Rights Law Review* (2000): 245, 253–254. Alabama executed Robert L. Tarver in the electric chair in April 2000.
64. Dawson v. State, 554 S.E.2d 137, 143–144 (Ga. 2001).
65. *Dawson v. State*, 554 S.E.2d at 140.
66. *Dawson v. State*, 554 S.E.2d at 143.
67. State v. Mata, 745 N.W.2d 229 (Neb. 2008).
68. Warden, "Reflections on Capital Punishment" 355.
69. Mark Berman, "Tennessee Has Long Had the Electric Chair, But Now It's Going to Be Available for More Executions," *Washington Post*, 23 May 2014, http://www.washingtonpost.com/news/post-nation/wp/2014/05/23/tennessee-has-long-had-the-electric-chair-but-now-its-going-to-be-available-for-more-executions/.
70. Frank Green, "Va. Man Who Killed Two Inmates Is Executed," *Richmond Times-Dispatch*, 16 Jan. 2013, (last visited 25 July 2014), http://www.timesdispatch.com/news/latest-news/convicted-killer-robert-charles-gleason-jr-dies-in-electric-chair/article_533cc100-6029-11e2-9393-0019bb30f31a.html; Associated Press, "Inmate-Chosen Electric Chair Execution Looms," *CBS News*, 16 Jan. 2013, (last visited 1 Aug. 2014), http://www.cbsnews.com/8301-201_162-57564227/inmate-chosen-electric-chair-execution-looms/. Some states have alternative methods of execution in case lethal injection is found unconstitutional or they may give the option of the old execution method to prisoners sentenced before the adoption of lethal injection.

71. "Authorized Methods of Execution," *Death Penalty Information Center*, 5 Aug. 2014, http://www.deathpenaltyinfo.org/methods-execution#wa.
72. Moran, *Executioner's Current* 228.
73. Associated Press, "Georgia Court Blocks Electric Chair Use," 5 Oct. 2001, (last visited 2 Feb. 2012), http://www.commondreams.org/headlines01/1005-03.htm.
74. Schanche, "Georgia's Electric Chair Has Grim History."

CHAPTER 16: OTHER AMERICAN EXECUTION METHODS

1. Espy and Smykla, "Executions in the United States: 1608–1987"; Banner, "Race and the Death Penalty in Historical Perspective."
2. Espy and Smykla, "Executions in the United States: 1608–1987"; Banner, "Race and the Death Penalty in Historical Perspective" 103, 105.
3. Bessler, *Cruel & Unusual* 270–271.
4. Baze v. Rees, 553 U.S. 35, 48 (2008).
5. Wilkerson v. Utah, 99 U.S. 130, 135–136 (1879).
6. Banner, *The Death Penalty* 48.
7. *Baze v, Rees*, 553 U.S. at 95–96 (Thomas, J., dissenting).
8. *Baze v. Rees*, 553 U.S. at 41–42.
9. Office of Planning and Analysis of Georgia Department of Corrections, *A History of the Death Penalty in Georgia* 2.
10. McClennen, "Capital Punishment in Arizona" 18.
11. Weisberg, "This Is Your Death" 24.
12. Deborah W. Denno, "Getting to Death: Are Executions Constitutional?," 82 *Iowa Law Review* (1997): 319, 365 n.277.
13. Pamela S. Nagy, "Hang by the Neck until Dead: The Resurgence of Cruel and Unusual Punishment in the 1990s," 26 *Pace Law Journal* (1994): 85; Campbell v. Wood, 18 F.3d 662 (9th Cir. 1994).
14. Associated Press, "Killer of 2 Is Hanged in Delaware as Kin of Victims Watch," *New York Times*, 26 Jan. 1996, http://www.nytimes.com/1996/01/26/us/killer-of-2-is-hanged-in-delaware-as-kin-of-victims-watch.html.
15. Revised Code of Washington 10.95.180 (2014).
16. *Campbell v. Wood*, 18 F.3d at 701.
17. Wilkerson v. Utah, 99 U.S. 130, 134 (1879). Although *Wilkerson* is often cited for the proposition that the firing squad does not violate the Eighth Amendment, the Supreme Court's discussion on that issue was dicta and based on what is now an outdated interpretation of the amendment.
18. Cutler, "Nothing Less than the Dignity of Man" 337, 348.
19. Peter N. Walker, *Punishment: An Illustrated History* (New York: ARCO Publishing Company, 1973) 134; Cutler, "Nothing Less than the Dignity of Man" 337, 356.
20. Weisberg, "This Is Your Death" 24.
21. Deborah W. Denno, "When Legislatures Delegate Death: The Troubling Paradox behind State Uses of Electrocution and Lethal Injection and What It Says about Us," 63 *Ohio State Law Journal* (2002): 63, 82–83.
22. Christianson, *The Last Gasp* 60–64.
23. Stephen Trombley, *The Execution Protocol: Inside America's Capital Punishment Industry* (New York: Crown Publishers, 1992) 12–13.
24. Kristina E. Beard, Comment, "Five under the Eighth: Methodology Review and the Cruel and Unusual Punishments Clause," 51 *University of Miami Law Review* (1997): 445, 463.
25. Christianson, *The Last Gasp* 69–75; Drimmer, *Until You Are Dead* 56.
26. Associated Press, "Humane Death by Gas Has History of Doubters," *Los Angeles Times* (20 Apr. 1992): A19.
27. Christianson, *The Last Gasp* 189.
28. Gomez v. United States District Court, 503 U.S. 653 (1992) (Stevens, J., dissenting); Trombley, *The Execution Protocol* 13.

29. Christianson, *The Last Gasp* 223.
30. Fierro v. Gomez, 865 F. Supp. 1387 (N.D. Cal. 1994); Fierro v. Gomez, 77 F.3d 301 (9th Cir. 1996), *vacated on other grounds,* Gomez v. Fierro, 519 U.S. 918 (1996) (remanding for reconsideration in light of new lethal injection statute).
31. Denno, "Is Electrocution an Unconstitutional Method of Execution?" 551; Trombley, *The Execution Protocol* 72.
32. Christianson, *The Last Gasp* 203–204.
33. *Baze v. Rees,* 553 U.S. at 42; Deborah Denno, "The Lethal Injection Quandary: How Medicine Has Dismantled the Death Penalty," 76 *Fordham Law Review* (2007): 49, 65–66.
34. *Baze v. Rees,* 553 U.S. at 75 (Stevens, J., concurring).
35. Denno, "When Legislatures Delegate Death" 82.
36. Marquart et al., *The Rope, the Chair & the Needle* 132–133; Chaney v. Heckler, 718 F.2d 1174 (D.C. 1983), *reversed by* Heckler v. Chaney, 470 U.S. 821 (1984).
37. "Physician Participation in Capital Punishment," *JAMA (Journal of the American Medical Association)* 1993: 365–382.
38. Andrew Welsh-Huggins, "Ohio Executes Inmate with New Death Penalty Drug," *Huffington Post,* 10 Mar. 2011, http://www.huffingtonpost.com/huff-wires/20110310/us-ohio-execution/. In 2014, the Ohio Supreme Court agreed to hear Romell Broom's constitutional challenge to his second execution.
39. Warden, "Reflections on Capital Punishment" *106; Michael Radelet, "Post-*Furman* Botched Executions," *LIFElines* (1991): 7.
40. Kevin Fagan, "'This Was Not a Man Who Went Meekly': An Eyewitness Account of Stanley Tookie Williams' Execution," *San Francisco Chronicle,* 13 Dec. 2005. http://www.sfgate.com/news/article/This-was-not-a-man-who-went-meekly-An-2588939.php.
41. Warden, "Reflections on Capital Punishment" *115–117, 118.
42. Denno, "The Lethal Injection Quandary" 56; Deborah Denno, E-mail interview, 10 June 2013.
43. Denno, "The Lethal Injection Quandary" 116.
44. *Baze v. Rees,* 553 U.S. at 42.
45. *Baze v, Rees,* 553 U.S. at 42. The brand name sometimes used for sodium thiopental is Pentothal, while the brand name used for pancuronium bromide is Pavulon.
46. *Baze v. Rees,* 553 U.S. at 72–73 (Stevens, J., concurring).
47. *Baze v. Rees,* 553 U.S. at 50.
48. *Baze v. Rees,* 553 U.S. at 52.
49. Unlike the dissenters, Justice Stevens concurred in the plurality's result finding that under current precedent the petitioners did not establish an Eighth Amendment violation. But in another way, he went further than the dissent. As discussed in chapter 23, Stevens devoted a substantial portion of his opinion explaining why he now believed the death penalty itself is a cruel and unusual punishment. *Baze v. Rees,* 553 U.S. at 86 (Stevens, J., concurring) (quoting Furman v. Georgia, 408 U.S. 238, 312 (1972) (White, J., concurring).
50. Brett Barrouquere, "Court Upholds Temporary Ban on Executions," *Kentucky Post,* 25 Mar. 2011, http://www.kypost.com/dpp/news/state/Kentucky-Executions_02100031.
51. Rob Stein, "Ohio Executes Inmate Using Single Drug," *Washington Post,* 10 Mar. 2011, http://www.washingtonpost.com/wp-dyn/content/article/2011/03/10/AR2011031000737.html?hpid=topnews.
52. Stein, "Ohio Executes Inmate Using Single Drug."
53. Associated Press, "Shortage Forces Texas to Switch Execution Drug," *National Public Radio,* 16 Mar. 2011, available at http://www.npr.org/templates/story/story.php?storyId=134591261.
54. Stein, "Ohio Executes Inmate Using Single Drug."
55. Associated Press, "Oklahoma Governor Signs Lethal Injection Legislation," *Tulsa World,* 18 Apr. 2011.

56. Associated Press, Shortage Forces Texas to Switch Execution Drug.
57. Greg Bluestein, "Ga. Execution Is Fodder for Challenges to New Drug," *Chattanooga Times Free Press* [Tennessee], 28 June 2011, http://www.timesfreepress.com/news/2011/jun/29/georgia-execution-fodder-challenges-new-drug/.
58. Stein, "Ohio Executes Inmate Using Single Drug." Although Baston's attorneys argued that the victim's family opposed the execution and pointed to mitigating evidence about Baston's traumatic childhood and being abandoned as a child, Ohio governor John Kasich denied clemency.
59. Welsh-Huggins, "Ohio Executes Inmate with New Death Penalty Drug."
60. Ed Pikington, "Georgia Rushes through Executions before Lethal Injection Drugs Expire," *The Guardian* (UK), 21 Feb. 2013, http://www.guardian.co.uk/world/2013/feb/21/georgia-executions-lethal-injection-drug-pentobarbital.
61. Jeannie Nuss, "Arkansas Turns to Different Lethal Injection Drug," *Associated Press*, 20 Apr. 2013, http://abcnews.go.com/US/wireStory/arkansas-turns-lethal-injection-drug-19001808#.UXmtDKLU-86.
62. Erica Goode, "After a Prolonged Execution in Ohio, Questions Over 'Cruel and Unusual,'" *New York Times*, 17 Jan. 2014, http://www.nytimes.com/2014/01/18/us/prolonged-execution-prompts-debate-over-death-penalty-methods.html.
63. Prior to the execution, Lockett's attorneys unsuccessfully tried to stop the execution and to force the state to give them information about the source of the drugs. The Oklahoma Supreme Court stayed the execution at one point before lifting the stay. Paige Williams, "Witness to a Botched Execution," *New Yorker*, 30 April 2014, http://www.newyorker.com/news/news-desk/witnesses-to-a-botched-execution; Josh Sanburn, "Report: Executioner Errors Led to Botched Lethal Injection," *Time Magazine*, 13 June 2014, http://time.com/2871154/clayton-lockett-botched-execution-due-to-iv-problems/. An investigation into the events surrounding Clayton Lockett's execution continues as this book goes to publication.
64. Fernanda Santos and John Schwartz, "A Prolonged Execution in Arizona Leads to a Temporary Halt," *New York Times*, 24 July 2014, http://www.nytimes.com/2014/07/25/us/a-prolonged-execution-in-arizona-leads-to-a-temporary-halt.html. After Wood's execution, the Arizona attorney general announced that the state would temporarily halt all executions.
65. "Death Sentences and Executions in 2010," *Amnesty International* 2011, Amnesty International (London), 6, http://www.amnesty.org/en/library/info/ACT50/001/2011/en.
66. Justin Jouvenal, "Ex-Virginia Executioner Becomes Opponent of Death Penalty," *Washington Post*, 10 Feb. 2013, http://www.washingtonpost.com/local/ex-virginia-executioner-becomes-opponent-of-death-penalty/2013/02/10/9e741124-5e89-11e2-9940-6fc488f3fecd_story.html.
67. "Capital Punishment in Britain: The Hangman's Story," *The Independent* (UK), 7 Apr. 2006, http://www.independent.co.uk/news/uk/crime/capital-punishment-in-britain-the-hangmans-story-473138.html.

CHAPTER 17: THE UNSTOPPABLE DEATH PENALTY AFTER *McCLESKEY*

1. Stout, "The Lawyers of Death Row".
2. Carol S. Steiker and Jordan M. Steiker, "Sober Second Thoughts: Reflections on Two Decades of Constitutional Regulation of Capital Punishment," 109 *Harvard Law Review* (1995): 355, 438.
3. Baldus and Woodworth, "Race Discrimination and the Legitimacy of Capital Punishment" 1438.
4. Scheidegger, "Capital Punishment in 1987" 125, 126.
5. Anna Stolley Persky, "Numbers Tell the Tale: North Carolina's Death Row Inmates Let Statistics Back Up Bias Claims," *ABA Journal* (May 2011): 18.

6. Jeffrey L. Kirchmeier, "Aggravating and Mitigating Factors: The Paradox of Today's Arbitrary and Mandatory Capital Punishment Scheme," 6 *William and Mary Bill of Rights Journal* (1998): 345, 397–399.
7. Pub. L. No. 100-690 (1988); Pub. L. No. 103-322 (1994); Jan Hoffman, "As State after State Resumes Executions, U.S. Death-Penalty Law Is Still in Limbo," *New York Times*, 10 July 1992, http://www.nytimes.com/1992/07/10/news/as-state-after-state-resumes-executions-us-death-penalty-law-is-still-in-limbo.html?pagewanted=all&src=pm.
8. Tirschwell and Hertzberg, "Politics and Prosecution" 57, 75–77; Lord Windlesham, *Politics, Punishment, and Populism* (New York: Oxford University Press 1998) 86–90.
9. Wainwright v. Sykes, 433 U.S. 72 (1977); Rose v. Lundy, 455 U.S. 509 (1982); Teague v. Lane, 489 U.S. 288 (1989); Coleman v. Thompson, 501 U.S. 722 (1991); *McCleskey v. Zant*, 499 U.S. 467, 467 (1991).
10. Kirchmeier, "Aggravating and Mitigating Factors" 434; *Teague v. Lane*, 489 U.S. 288; *Wainwright v. Sykes*, 433 U.S. 72.
11. Amsterdam, "Selling A Quick Fix for Boot Hill" 157.
12. Antiterrorism and Effective Death Penalty Act of 1996, Pub. L. No. 104-132, 110 Stat. 1214.
13. Amnesty International, "The Death Penalty in Georgia: Racist, Arbitrary and Unfair," AMR 51/025/1996, 1 June 1996, (last visited 8 June 2010), http://asiapacific.amnesty.org/library/Index/ENGAMR510251996?open&of=ENG-2M4.
14. Bedau, *The Death Penalty in America* 18.
15. "State by State Database," *Death Penalty Information Center*, 8 June 2012, http://www.deathpenaltyinfo.org/state_by_state.
16. "Oklahoma Killer Is Put to Death," *New York Times* (11 Sept. 1990): A15.
17. George McEvoy, "Too Bad Most Last Meals Aren't Well Done," *The Palm Beach Post* (10 April 1995): 13A.
18. "Killers in Arkansas, Texas Executed by Lethal Injection," *New York Times* (26 June 1990): A2.
19. Bill Miller, "The Execution of a Disabled Killer Rekindles the Debate on Capital Punishment," *The Washington Post*, 2 Feb. 1993: Z10.
20. Brian Wice, "Capital Punishment, Texas Style," *Texas Bar Journal* (Apr. 1992): 386–389, 388.
21. Michael Mello, "On Metaphors, Mirrors, and Murders: Theodore Bundy and the Rule of Law," 18 *New York University Review of Law & Social Change* (1990/1991): 887, 901.
22. Mello, "On Metaphors, Mirrors, and Murders" 918–935.
23. Howard Chua-Eoan, "The Top 25 Crimes of the Century," *Time Magazine*, 8 June 2010, http://www.time.com/time/2007/crimes/14.html.
24. Mello, "On Metaphors, Mirrors, and Murders" 917.
25. David Von Drehle, *Among the Lowest of the Dead* (New York: Times Books, 1995) 388–389, 394, 401.
26. "John Wayne Gacy," *Chicago Tribune* Website, 2 Feb. 2012, http://www.chicagotribune.com/topic/crime-law-justice/crimes/murder/john-wayne-gacy-PEHST002275.topic.
27. "Ad Features Bundy," *Advertising Age* (12 Mar. 1990): 23; Mello, "On Metaphors, Mirrors, and Murders" 892 n.15.
28. "Executions by Year," *Death Penalty Information Center*, 9 June 2012, http://www.deathpenaltyinfo.org/executions-year.
29. John Seabrook, "Don't Shoot," *The New Yorker* (22 June 2009): 36.
30. Dolan, "Rose Bird's Quest for Obscurity" A1; Pertman, "Judge's Obscurity after Vote a 'Tragedy'" 2.
31. John Gibeaut, "Taking Aim," *American Bar Association Journal* (Nov. 1996): 50, 51. Similarly, in 1994, Texans voted Judge Charles Campbell, a conservative former prosecutor, off the Court of Criminal Appeals and elected an obscure lawyer with ethics problems who promised to uphold more death sentences. *See* Stuart Taylor Jr.,

"The Politics of Hanging Judges," *Legal Times* (30 Oct. 1995): 25; Stephen B. Bright and Patrick J. Keenan, "Judges and the Politics of Death: Deciding between the Bill of Rights and the Next Election in Capital Cases," 75 *Boston University Law Review* (1995): 759.

32. Bedau, *The Death Penalty in America* 18.
33. Jane Mayer, "Attack Dog," *The New Yorker* (13 and 20 Feb. 2012): 42 (article starts on 40). Some commentators also criticized Governor Dukakis's ability to handle a question about his opposition to the death penalty during the presidential debates.
34. Marshall Frady, "Death in Arkansas," *The New Yorker* (22 Feb. 1993): 105–133.
35. Haines, *Against Capital Punishment* 100.
36. Paul Haven, "Doubts Arise on Death Penalty," *Boston Globe* (31 May 1999): A4.
37. State v. Grannis, 900 P.2d 1, 6 (Ariz. 1995); Rene Ramo, "Ex-convict Works to Rebuild Life after Spending Years on Death Row," *Denver Post* (22 May 1998): A-32.
38. Haines, *Against Capital Punishment* 59–69, 149.
39. Mark Gillespie, "Public Opinion Supports the Death Penalty," *Gallup News Service*, 24 Feb. 1999, http://www.gallup.com/poll/releases.
40. Greg Lucas, "Poll Takes Snapshot of Californians' Views," *San Francisco Chronicle*, (14 Jan. 2000): A20; Kathy Walt, "Death Penalty Support Plunges to 30-Year Low," *Houston Chronicle* (15 Mar. 1998): A1 (noting that opposition to the death penalty grew from 7 percent in 1994 to 26 percent in 1998). Another study found a 20 percent drop in support for the death penalty among California residents between 1990 and 2000. Henry Weinstein, "Support for Death Penalty Drops Sharply in State," *Los Angeles Times* (2 Nov. 2000): A1.

CHAPTER 18: NEW ABOLITIONIST VOICES IN THE 1990S

1. McCleskey v. Kemp, 481 U.S. 279, 319 (1987).
2. Haines, *Against Capital Punishment* 78 (quoting David Bruck).
3. Richard H. Burr, III, "Representing the Client on Death Row: The Politics of Advocacy," 59 *University of Missouri-Kansas City Law Review* (1990): 1–16. At the time of his September 13, 1990 address, Burr was Director of the Capital Punishment Project of the NAACP Legal Defense and Education Fund. Burr was one of the attorneys who helped with the Supreme Court brief in *McCleskey v. Zant*. See chapter 3.
4. Helen Prejean, C.S.J., *Dead Man Walking: An Eyewitness Account of the Death Penalty in the United States* (New York: Random House, 1993); Lawrence Van Gelder, "Footlights," *New York Times* (12 Mar. 1998): E1.
5. Jan Breslaver, "A Troupe Intent on Creating American Operas and a Pair Unafraid of a Topical Subject Team for 'Dead Man Walking,'" *Los Angeles Times*, 1 Oct. 2000. The show was commissioned by the San Francisco Opera.
6. Prejean, *Dead Man Walking* 48–49.
7. Beccaria, *Of Crimes and Punishments*.
8. Beccaria, *Of Crimes and Punishments* 52–61; Marvin E. Wolfgang, "Introduction," in Beccaria, *Of Crimes and Punishments*.
9. *The Death Penalty: Abolition in Europe* (Strasbourg, France: Council of Europe Publishing, 1999) 106.
10. Camus, "Reflections on the Guillotine" 175.
11. David Herbert Donald, *Lincoln* (New York: Simon & Schuster, 1995) 542.
12. Craig Pittman, "'Dead Man Walking' Brings Nun's Crusade to Screen," *Star Tribune* (Minneapolis) (19 Jan. 1996): E1.
13. Austin Sarat, "The Cultural Life of Capital Punishment: Responsibility and Representation in *Dead Man Walking* and *Last Dance*," in *The Killing State: Capital Punishment in Law, Politics, and Culture* (ed. Austin Sarat) (New York: Oxford University Press, 1999) 248.
14. Greenhouse, *Becoming Justice Blackmun* 177–179.
15. Sawyer v. Whitley, 505 U.S. 333, 351 (1992) (Blackmun, J., concurring)
16. Herrera v. Collins, 506 U.S. 390, 446 (1993).
17. Dragich, "Revelations from the Blackmun Papers" 1183, 1195.

18. Greenhouse, *Becoming Justice Blackmun* 177–179.
19. Callins v. Collins, 510 U.S. 1141, 1145 (1994) (Blackmun, J., dissenting from denial of petition for writ of certiorari).
20. *Callins v. Collins*, 510 U.S. at 1148–1159, 1153.
21. *Callins v. Collins*, 510 U.S. at 1152–1153, 1156, 1157–1158.
22. *Callins v. Collins*, 510 U.S. at 1159.
23. *Callins v, Collins*, 510 U.S. at 1153.
24. "Interview with Justice Harry A. Blackmun by Harold Hongju Koh," Washington, DC (9 Sept. 1994): 41 (Justice Blackmun did not reveal the name of the justice), Library of Congress Website, 25 June 2012, http://lcweb2.loc.gov/diglib/blackmun-public/page.html?page=25&size=640&SERIESID=D09&FOLDERID=D0901; Greenhouse, *Becoming Justice Blackmun* 179–181.
25. *Callins v, Collins*, 510 U.S. at 1145.
26. John C. Jeffries Jr., *Justice Lewis F. Powell, Jr.: A Biography* (New York: Fordham University Press, 1994) 451; John C. Jeffries Jr., "A Change of Mind That Came Too Late," *New York Times* (23 June 1994): A23.
27. Woodward and Armstrong, *The Brethren* 13–18, 97; David Von Drehle, "Retired Justice Changes Stand on Death Penalty," *Washington Post* (10 June 1994): A1.
28. Lazarus, *Closed Chambers* 104
29. Austin Sarat, "ABA's Proposed Moratorium: Recapturing the Spirit of *Furman*: The American Bar Association and the New Abolitionist Politics," 61 *Law and Contemporary Problems* (1998): 5, 12–13.
30. Anne Gearan, "Ginsburg Backs Ending Death Penalty," *AP Online* 10 Apr. 2001, 2001 WL 18926396.
31. Bob Egelko, "Justice Ginsburg Discusses Equality, Death Penalty," *San Francisco Chronicle*, 16 Sept. 2011, http://www.sfgate.com/cgi-bin/article.cgi?f=/c/a/2011/09/15/BAHD1L5CNN.DTL&tsp=1.
32. Associated Press, "O'Connor Questions Death Penalty," *New York Times* (4 July 2001): A9.
33. Rosen, *The Supreme Court* 14–17.
34. Peter Wallsten, "Chief Justice Criticizes Death Penalty," *Stuart News/Port St. Lucie News* (Florida) (2 Jan. 1998): A1; Lesley Clark and Phil Long, "Florida's Former Chief Justice Seeks to Bar Executions," *The Record* (Bergen County, New Jersey) (24 Oct. 1999): A7; Jacqueline Soteropoulos, "Ex-state Justice: Innocent Executed," *Tampa Tribune* (Florida), (12 Feb. 2000): 1. Chief Justice Kogan began speaking out against the death penalty after he dissented from a ruling upholding the use of the electric chair. Jones v. State, 701 So. 2d 76, 81 (Fla. 1997) (Kogan, J., dissenting).
35. Bruce Mulkey, "Time for a Moratorium on Death Penalty?," *Asheville Citizen-Times* (North Carolina) (8 July 2000): A6.
36. Frank Green, "Bipartisan Group Targets Wrongful Death Sentences," *Richmond Times Dispatch* (Virginia) (12 May 2000): A-3; Anthony Spangler, "Judge Expresses Concerns about Fairness of Death Penalty," *Fort Worth Star-Telegram* (24 July 2001: 4).
37. Joe Hallett, "Death Penalty Isn't Effective, Law's Co-author Now Believes," *Columbus Dispatch* (18 Feb. 1999): 01A. Justice Pfeifer's announcement came days before Ohio's first execution since *Furman*.
38. T.C. Brown, "Repeal Death Penalty, Original Sponsor Urges," *Cleveland Plain Dealer* (19 Feb. 1999): 1A.
39. Paul E. Pfeifer, "Retire Ohio's Death Penalty," *Cleveland Plain Dealer*, 26 Jan. 2011, http://www.cleveland.com/opinion/index.ssf/2011/01/retire_ohios_death_penalty_pau.html.
40. Karl Turner, "Judge Orders Killer's Death, Decries Death Penalty," *Plain Dealer* (Cleveland) (17 Nov. 2000): 1A.
41. Jerry Staletovich, "Justice Raising Voice to Bury Death Penalty," *Palm Beach Post* (Florida) (19 Jan. 1998): 1A.
42. Pamela Manson, "New Chief Justice Hopes to Eliminate 'Unhealthy' Tension," *Arizona Republic* (Phoenix) (15 Dec. 1996): B1.

43. People v. Bull, 705 N.E.2d 824, 846–848 (Ill. 1999) (Harrison, J., dissenting); People v. Enis, No. 86636, 2000 WL 1728576 (Ill. Nov. 22, 2000) (Harrison, C.J., dissenting).
44. R.G. Dunlop, "Kentucky's Troubled Death-Penalty System Lets Cases Languish for Decades," *Louisville Courier-Journal.com*, 7 Nov. 2009, http://www.courier-journal. com/article/20091107/NEWS01/911080316/.
45. State v. Timmendequas, No. A-109, 2001 N.J. LEXIS 24 (N.J. 1 Feb. 2001) (Long, J., dissenting); State v. Feaster, 757 A.2d 266, 295–296 (N.J. 2000) (Long, J., dissenting).
46. Singleton v. Norris, 108 F.3d 872, 874 (8th Cir. 1997) (Heaney, J., concurring).
47. *Singleton v. Norris*, 108 F.3d at 876.
48. Judge Michael Ponsor, "Life, Death and Uncertainty," *Boston Globe* (8 July 2001): D2.
49. Terry Tang, "We Delude Ourselves about Barbarity of Death Penalty," *Seattle Times* (5 Apr. 1995): B4; Alex Kozinski and Sean Gallagher, "Death: The Ultimate Run-On Sentence," 46 *Case Western Reserve Law Review* (1995): 1.
50. Lifton and Mitchell, *Who Owns Death?* 159–160.
51. Sue Lindsay, "Judge Resigns over Death Penalty Law: Heydt, on Panel Picked to Rule in 1997 Slaying, Says System Is Flawed, Statute 'Unworkable,'" *Denver Rocky Mountain News* (13 Apr. 1999): 19A.
52. Jim Simon et al., "Utter Quitting Supreme Court—Justice Says He Can't Be Party to State's Capital Punishment," *Seattle Times* (29 Mar. 1995): A1; Patti Epler, "Utter Quits Supreme Court in Protest of Death Penalty," *News Tribune* (Tacoma, Washington) (30 Mar. 1995): A1; Robert F. Utter, "Washington State Must Abandon the Death Penalty," *Seattle Times*, 11 Mar. 2009, http://seattletimes.com/html/ opinion/2008843232_opinb12utter.html.
53. Haines, *Against Capital Punishment* 158.
54. Sam D. Millsap Jr., "Your Turn: Until the System Is Fixed, Executions Must Stop," *Express-News* (San Antonio) (29 June 2000): 5B.
55. Associated Press, "Ohio Catholic Bishops Support State Supreme Court Justice's Call to End Use of Death Penalty," *Los Angeles Times*, 5 Feb. 2011, http://www.latimes. com/news/nationworld/nation/wire/sns-ap-us-death-penalty-ohio,0,7231235. story.
56. George F. Will, "Innocent on Death Row," *Washington Post* (6 Apr. 2000): A23; Bill O'Reilly, "Commentary: Worse than the Death Penalty," *2000 APBnews.com Online*, 8 June 2000; Evan Thomas, "Life of O'Reilly," *Newsweek* (12 Feb. 2001): 29; Brooke A. Masters, "Pat Robertson Urges Moratorium on U.S. Executions," *Washington Post* (8 Apr. 2000): A1; "Robertson Backs Moratorium: Says Death Penalty Used Unfairly," *Chicago Tribune* (8 Apr. 2000): N12.
57. Thomas W. Waldron, "Rawlings, Schmoke Call for a Moratorium on State Executions; Noting 'Uncertainties,' They Appeal to Glendening," *Baltimore Sun* (18 May 2000): 2B.
58. Craig Timberg, "A Death Penalty Change of Heart; Va. Lawmakers to Weigh Legislation to Stop, Stall or Study the System," *Washington Post* (28 Jan. 2001): C1; "National Briefs: N.H. House Deals Blow to Death Penalty," *New Orleans Times-Picayune* (11 Mar. 2000): A9.
59. Daniel Wise, "Prosecutors Want Death Penalty; Qualms Voiced about Costs, Time, Training of Lawyers," *New York Law Journal* (3 Mar. 1995): 1.
60. Lifton and Mitchell, *Who Owns Death?* 119; Wise, "Prosecutors Want Death Penalty" 1.
61. Ted Sickinger, "Coalition Opposes Executions," *Kansas City Star* (14 Feb. 2000): B1; Brooke A. Masters, "Reforms in System of Capital Punishment Are Urged; An Unusual Coalition Joins the Debate over 'Many Problems' in Meting Out the Death Penalty," *Washington Post* (12 May 2000): A31.
62. David Rosenfeld, "Ex-member of Clemency Board Alters Death View," *Mesa Tribune* (29 Oct. 2000): A5.
63. Ed Timms, "Terrell Unit Is Renamed," *Dallas Morning News* (21 July 2001): 32A.

64. John Harwood, "Bush May Be Hurt by Handling of Death Penalty Issue," *Wall Street Journal* (21 Mar. 2000): A28.

65. Ioannes Paulus PP. II, *Evangelium Vitae*, 25 Mar. 1995, http://www.vatican.va/holy_father/john_paul_ii/encyclicals/documents/hf_jp-ii_enc_25031995_evangelium-vitae_en.html.

66. Hugh Aynesworth, "Spotlight Expected at Texas Execution," *Washington Times*, 7 May 2000; Robert Hilburn, "Beyond Artistry: Steve Earle's Inspirational Comeback from the Lost Years of Drug Addiction Yields a Rare Musical Intimacy and a Poetic Legacy," *Los Angeles Times* (5 Aug. 2000): F1; Nadine Brozan, "Chronicle," *New York Times* (22 Aug. 1994): B4; Fred Shuster, "Musicians Join Voices against Death Penalty," *Daily News of Los Angeles* (25 Mar. 1998): L5; Scott Martelle, "The Faithful Report for Duty to the Boss," *Los Angeles Times* (22 May 2000): B3.

67. Steve Earle, "Billy Austin," *The Hard Way*, MCA, 1990, CD.

68. Bob Piazza, "Opposing the Death Penalty; Relatives of Victims Join Call for Moratorium," *Richmond Times Dispatch* (Virginia) (30 Apr. 2000): B-6.

69. Lifton and Mitchell, *Who Owns Death?* 210.

70. Haines, *Against Capital Punishment* 110.

71. Susan L. Pena, "A Cantata of Redemption: Warren McCleskey's Final Statement Set to Music," *Sojourners Magazine* (May–June 1995): 61.

72. Lifton and Mitchell, *Who Owns Death?* 60. Florida state senator Ginny Brown-Waite witnessed the execution of Alvin "Tiny" Davis, where the inmate screamed and blots of blood appeared on his shirt. She thought the bloodstain resembled a cross and meant either that Mr. Davis had made his peace with God or that God blessed Florida's execution policy. Lifton and Mitchell, *Who Owns Death?* 59–60.

73. Ronald J. Tabak, "Finality without Fairness: Why We Are Moving Towards Moratoria on Executions, and the Potential Abolition of Capital Punishment," 33 *University of Connecticut Law Review* (2001): 750–752.

CHAPTER 19: INNOCENCE AND THE AMERICAN DEATH PENALTY

1. Sandra Day O'Connor, "Thurgood Marshall: The Influence of a Raconteur," 44 *Stanford Law Review* (1992): 1217, 1218. Although Justice O'Connor does not specifically mention McCleskey's case in recounting Justice Marshall's tale, she wrote that he told the story "during the time the Court was considering a case in which an African American defendant challenged his death sentence as racially biased."

2. Pearson, "A Reporter at Large" 41.

3. Hamm, *Rebel and a Cause* 16, 20, 29; Carol S. Steiker and Jordan M. Steiker, "The Seduction of Innocence: The Attraction and Limitations of the Focus on Innocence in Capital Punishment Law and Advocacy," 95 *Journal of Criminal Law and Criminology* (2005): 587, 590–593.

4. Haines, *Against Capital Punishment* 44, 87.

5. Radelet et al., *In Spite of Innocence* 98–99; Haines, *Against Capital Punishment* 208 n.31; Robert H. Montgomery, *Sacco-Vanzetti: The Murder and the Myth* (New York: Devin-Adair Co., 1960) 347.

6. Fifty years after their execution, Massachusetts governor Michael Dukakis proclaimed August 23, 1977, to be "Nicola Sacco and Bartolomeo Vanzetti Memorial Day" and declared "that [all] stigma and disgrace should be…removed…from the names of their families." Russell Aiuto, "The Legacy of Sacco & Vanzetti," ch. 8, 6 Oct. 2010, http://www.crimelibrary.com/notorious_murders/not_guilty/sacco/8.html.

7. Alavi, "The Government against Two" 1089; Parrish, "Revisited: The Rosenberg 'Atom Spy' Case" 601 (noting that evidence indicating that Julius spied for the Soviet Union has been found to be "overwhelming," while Ethel's involvement was "marginal").

8. Years later, his case was cited as Great Britain abolished capital punishment. Additionally, Bentley's story was made into a movie called *Let Him Have It*, and in 1998, Bentley received a conditional posthumous pardon. Christoph, *Capital*

Punishment and British Politics 98–100; Vivian Rakoff, "The Death Penalty and Youth," *Family Practice News* (15 May 2005): 10, http://www.familypracticenews.com/index.php?id=2934&type=98&tx_ttnews[tt_news]=43084&cHash=da03e20e36.

9. Hugo Adam Bedau and Michael L. Radelet, "Miscarriages of Justice in Potentially Capital Cases," 40 *Stanford Law Review* (1987): 21; Michael L. Radelet and Hugo Adam Bedau, "The Execution of the Innocent," in *America's Experiment with Capital Punishment: Reflections of the Past, Present, and Future of the Ultimate Penal Sanction* (ed, James R. Acker et al.) (Durham, NC: Carolina Academy Press, 2003) 325–346, 341.

10. Radelet et al., *In Spite of Innocence* 271; Haines, *Against Capital Punishment* 88. James Adams, who was executed on May 10, 1984, is listed as the only post-1976 wrongful execution at the time of the book's publication.

11. "The Innocence List" *Death Penalty Information Center*, last visited 25 July 2014, http://www.deathpenaltyinfo.org/innocence-list-those-freed-death-row ; "Executions: Dead Man Walking Out," *Economist* (10 June 2000): 21. Because of the difficulties in actually proving someone is completely innocent, some have criticized the inclusion of some inmates on the lists of the exonerated.

12. Samuel R. Gross, Barbara O'Brien, Chen Hu, and Edward H. Kennedy, "Rate of False Conviction of Criminal Defendants Who are Sentenced to Death," *PNAS Early Edition*, 25 March 2014, http://www.pnas.org/content/early/2014/04/23/1306417111.full.pdf+html; Douglas A. Blackmon, "Louisiana Death-Row Inmate Damon Thibodeaux Exonerated with DNA Evidence," *The Washington Post*, 28 Sept. 2012, http://www.washingtonpost.com/national/louisiana-death-row-inmate-damon-thibodeaux-is-exonerated-with-dna-evidence/2012/09/28/26e30012-0997-11e2-afff-d6c7f20a83bf_story.html.

13. Carl M. Cannon, "The Problem with the Chair: A Conservative Case against Capital Punishment," *National Review* (19 June 2000): 28, 30.

14. Jeff Jacoby, "Supporters of Capital Punishment Can Cheer Gov. Ryan's Decision," *Boston Globe* (28 Feb. 2000): A15; Warden, "Reflections on Capital Punishment" 338.

15. "Executions: Dead Man Walking Out" 21. The lawyers published a book about their work. Jim Dwyer, Peter Neufeld, and Barry Scheck, *Actual Innocence* (New York: Signet, 2001).

16. Jackie Hallifax, "Dead Inmate Cleared by DNA Tests," *Washington Post*, 15 December 2000; Jonathan Alter and Mark Miller, "A Life or Death Gamble," *Newsweek* (29 May 2000): 22; Christina Nuckols, "Gilmore Signs Bill Opening DNA Window," *Virginian-Pilot* (Norfolk, Virginia) (3 May 2001): A1; House v. Bell, 547 U.S. 518 (2006).

17. Blackmon, "Louisiana Death-Row Inmate Damon Thibodeaux Exonerated with DNA Evidence."

18. Brandon L. Garrett, "After Osama bin Laden's Death, Imagining a World without DNA Evidence," *Washington Post*, 13 May 2011, http://www.washingtonpost.com/opinions/after-osama-bin-ladens-death-imagining-a-world-without-dna-evidence/2011/05/03/AFD90W2G_story.html.

19. John C. Tucker, *May God Have Mercy: A True Story of Crime and Punishment* (New York: W.W. Norton & Company, 1997) 110–116; James Dao, "DNA Ties Man Executed in '92 to the Murder He Denied," *New York Times* (13 Jan. 2006): A14.

20. Coleman v. Thompson, 501 U.S. 722, 727, 729, 735–757 (1991). Although the Court's opinion recounts that the notice of appeal was filed three days too late, the Court incorrectly included weekend days in its count, and a more accurate statement is that it was filed one day too late. Jeffrey L. Kirchmeier, "Dead Innocent: The Death Penalty Abolitionist Search for a Wrongful Execution," 42 *Tulsa Law Review* (2006): 416 n.100.

21. Tucker, *May God Have Mercy* 246–251, 273–274, 276–277; 289; *Time Magazine*, Cover, 18 May 1992, (last visited Jan. 24, 2007), http://www.time.com/time/covers/0,16641,1101920518,00.html.

22. Howard Witt, "Texas Urged to Probe Claims of Wrongful Executions," *Chicago Tribune* (7 July 2006): 6; James S. Liebman et al., "Los Tocayos Carlos," 43 *Columbia Human Rights Law Review* (2012): 711.
23. James S. Liebman and the Columbia DeLuna Project, *The Wrong Carlos: Anatomy of a Wrongful Conviction* (New York: Columbia University Press, 2014).
24. Peter Gilbert and Steve James, Directors, *At the Death House Door*, 2008.
25. Lise Olsen, "The Cantu Case: Death and Doubt," *Houston Chronicle*, 24 July 2006, http://www.chron.com/disp/story.mpl/metropolitan/3472872.html; Lise Olsen and Maro Robbins, "Lawyers Join Chorus for an Outside Cantu Review," *Houston Chronicle* (25 July 2006): A1; Lise Olsen and Maro Robbins, "Tapes Spur Calls for DA to Relinquish Cantu Case," *San Antonio Express-News*, 24 July 2006, http://www.mysanantonio.com/news/crime/stories/MYSA072506.1A.CantuFollo.14c6778.html (listing other articles in the series). An added twist to Cantu's case is that he was seventeen when he was charged with the capital murder for the shooting of a man during an attempted robbery. Because of Cantu's young age, under the Supreme Court's decision in *Roper v. Simmons* decided after his execution, Cantu could not be executed today. Roper v. Simmons, 543 U.S. 551, 578–579 (2005).
26. Samuel R. Gross and Josiah Thompson, *NAACP Legal Defense and Educational Fund Report on Larry Griffin*, 24 Jan. 2007, http://www.truthinjustice.org/griffin-report.htm.
27. *Report of the Circuit Attorney on the Murder of Quintin Moss and Conviction of Larry Griffin* (12 July 2007): 13–14, http://www.deathpenaltyinfo.org/finalreport_execsum.pdf.
28. Jonathan Alter, "A Reckoning on Death Row," *Newsweek* (3 July 2000): 31; Pittman, "'Dead Man Walking' Brings Nun's Crusade to Screen" E1.
29. Dave Mann, "DNA Tests Undermine Evidence in Texas Execution," *Texas Observer*, 11 Nov. 2010, http://www.texasobserver.org/cover-story/texas-observer-exclusive-dna-tests-undermine-evidence-in-texas-execution.
30. Maurice Possley, "Man Executed on Disproven Evidence, Experts Say," *Chicago Tribune*, 2 May 2006, http://www.chicagotribune.com/news/local/chi-060502willingham,0,7161822.story; Rob Warden, "Uncertainty Principle Is Wrong Theory for the Death Penalty," *Chicago Sun-Times* (21 Jan. 2006): 18; Maurice Possley, "Fresh Doubts Over a Texas Execution," *Washington Post*, 3 Aug. 2014, http://www.washingtonpost.com/sf/national/2014/08/03/fresh-doubts-over-a-texas-execution/.
31. Aziza Musa, "Board Approves Report on Willingham," *The Texas Tribune*, 15 Apr. 2011, http://www.texastribune.org/texas-dept-criminal-justice/cameron-todd-willingham/board-approves-report-on-willingham-/; Tim Easton, "AG Says Forensic Science Commission Can't Consider Willingham Case, Others before Sept. 2005," *Austin American-Statesman*, 29 July 2011, http://www.statesman.com/blogs/content/shared-gen/blogs/austin/politics/entries/2011/07/29/ag_says_forensic_science_commi.html.
32. Prejean, *The Death of Innocents*.
33. James S. Liebman, "The New Death Penalty Debate: What's DNA Got to Do with It?," 33 *Columbia Human Rights Law Review* (2002): 527, 553.
34. James S. Liebman and Lawrence C. Marshall, "Less Is Better: Justice Stevens and the Narrowed Death Penalty," 74 *Fordham Law Review* (2006): 1607, 1651 n.192.
35. Kansas v. Marsh, 548 U.S. 163, 209–210 (2006) (Souter, J., dissenting) (citing Gregg v, Georgia, 428 U.S. 153, 188 (1976).
36. *Kansas v. Marsh*, 548 U.S. at 190, 193–194.
37. *Kansas v. Marsh*, 548 U.S. at 198–199.
38. Cannon, "The Problem with the Chair" 29.
39. Liz Halloran, "Pulling Back from the Brink," *U.S. News & World Report* (8 May 2006): 36.

CHAPTER 20: A MORATORIUM MOVEMENT EMERGES IN THE 1990S

1. *A Gathering Momentum: Continuing Impacts of the American Bar Association Call for a Moratorium on Executions* (American Bar Association Section of Individual Rights and Responsibilities, 2000) 1; *ABA, Report with Recommendations* No. 107, 3 Feb. 1997, http://www.abanet.org/irr/rec107.html.

2. Leslie A. Harris, Chair, Section of Individual Rights and Responsibilities, ABA Report with Recommendation No. 107 (Feb. 1997): 3, 13–14, http://www.americanbar.org/content/dam/aba/migrated/legalservices/downloads/sclaid/20110325_aba_107.authcheckdam.pdf.

3. Harris, Report, 8; Young v. Kemp, No. 85-98-2-MAC (M.D. Ga. 1985); Frey v. Fulcomer, 974 F.2d 348 (3d Cir. 1992) (defense counsel relied upon statute that had been declared unconstitutional); Romero v. Lynaugh, 884 F.2d 871 (5th Cir. 1989) (defense counsel made a four-sentence closing argument saying the jury could do what it wanted to do); Smith v. State, 581 So. 2d 497 (Ala. Crim. App. 1990) (defense counsel asked for extra time during trial to read the state's death penalty statute for the first time).

4. Harris, Report, 11–15.

5. Austin Sarat, "ABA's Proposed Moratorium: Recapturing the Spirit of *Furman*: The American Bar Association and the New Abolitionist Politics," 61 *Law and Contemporary Problems* (1998): 5, 9.

6. Tabak, "Finality without Fairness" 744–745; James Podgers, "A Break for Executions: New ABA President Calls for Push on Death Penalty Moratorium," *ABA Journal* (Sept. 2000): 99.

7. Sarat, "ABA's Proposed Moratorium" 27–28.

8. *A Gathering Momentum* 2–3.

9. Robynn Tysver, "Execution Suspension Approved; Senators Hand Johanns Life-and-Death Decision," *Omaha World-Herald* (Nebraska) (20 May 1999): 1; Henry Weinstein, "Nebraska Governor Vetoes Moratorium on Executions Legislation," *Los Angeles Times* (27 May 1999): A4.

10. *A Gathering Momentum* 5.

11. Judith Graham, "Study: Nebraska Is Fair in Giving Death Penalty," *Chicago Tribune* (2 Aug. 2001): N11.

12. Robynn Tysver, "Death Penalty Report Author Fires Back," *Omaha World-Herald* (8 Aug. 2001): 1.

13. "Executions: Dead Man Walking Out" 21; Weinstein, "Nebraska Governor Vetoes Moratorium on Executions Legislation" A4.

14. Ken Armstrong and Steve Mills, "Ryan 'Until I Can Be Sure'; Illinois Is First State to Suspend Death Penalty," *Chicago Tribune* (1 Feb. 2000): 1; Bedau, *Death Is Different*, 129–130.

15. Harwood, "Bush May Be Hurt by Handling of Death-Penalty Issue" A28; James Coates, "A Governor's Fit of Conscience over an Unconscionable Crime," *Chicago Tribune* (7 Dec. 1986): 3; Mary Beth Lane, "Celeste Commutes Eight Death Sentences," *Plain Dealer* (Cleveland) (11 Jan. 1991): 1-A.

16. Richard Carelli, "Lawyers See Shift against Death Penalty: ABA Takes No Position, but Wants to Ensure Safeguards and Legal Support for Defendants," *Star-Ledger* (Newark, NJ) (13 Feb. 2000): 43.

17. Ed Vogel, "Assembly Committee Rejects Two-Year Suspension of Death Penalty," *Las Vegas Review-Journal* (17 May 2001): 1A.

18. Frank Green, "Executions Moratorium Urged," *Richmond Times-Dispatch* (Virginia), (2 Feb. 2000): B4; *A Gathering Momentum*, 24.

19. Henry Weinstein, "Death Penalty Moratorium Attracting Unlikely Adherents," *Los Angeles Times* (17 Oct. 2000): A5; Rebecca Schwartzman, "ABA Conference Brings Scrutiny to Ga.'s Capital Procedures," *Fulton County Daily Report* (Georgia) (17 Oct. 2000); William Claiborne, "Philadelphia City Council Backs Halt to Executions," *Washington Post* (11 Feb. 2000): A02.

20. David Baldus, George Woodworth, and Catherine M. Grosso, "Race and Proportionality since *McCleskey v. Kemp (1987)*: Different Actors with Mixed Strategies of Denial and Avoidance," 39 *Columbia Human Rights Law Review* (2007): 159–162.
21. Michael Graczyk, "5 States Consider Ban on Executions," *The Gazette* (1 Feb. 2000): A6; Editorial, "The New Death Penalty Politics," *New York Times* (7 June 2000): A30.
22. David Protess, "Two Volunteers for Execution, Two Governors Who Would Not Let Them Die," *Huffington Post*, 28 Nov. 2011, http://www.huffingtonpost.com/david-protess/kitzhaber-death-penalty-moratorium-oregon_b_1113616.html. Governor Ryan later faced his own legal problems and went to prison for several years.
23. Bruce Tomaso and Christy Hoppe, "Tucker Execution Case Expected to Have a Lasting Legacy," *Dallas Morning News* (5 Feb. 1998): 12A (quoting a spokesperson for Amnesty International).
24. Larry Witham, "Faiths Vary Widely on Execution," *Washington Times* (7 Feb. 1998): B8; David Gibson, "Religions Rethinking the Death Penalty," *Record* (Bergen County, NJ) (8 Aug. 1999): A01.
25. Ogletree, "Black Man's Burden" 22.
26. "Editorial: Even in This Case," *Washington Post* (12 May 2001): A24.
27. The Death Penalty Information Center reports are available at http://www.deathpenaltyinfo.org/rpts.html.
28. James S. Liebman, Jeffrey Fagan, and Valerie West, "A Broken System: Error Rates in Capital Cases, 1973–1995," 12 June 2000, http://www2.law.columbia.edu/instructionalservices/liebman/.
29. Texas Civil Rights Project, "The Death Penalty in Texas: Due Process and Equal Justice . . . or Rush to Execution?," Sept. 2000, http://www.texascivilrightsproject.org/wp-content/uploads/2009/01/2000-the-death-penalty-in-texas.pdf.
30. Georg Rusche and Otto Kirchheimer, *Punishment and Social Structure* (New York: Columbia University Press, 1939); "Violence on Rise despite Dip in Crime Rate," *Ottawa Sun* (20 July 2001): 7; Harwood, "Bush May Be Hurt by Handling of Death-Penalty Issues" A28; Simmons v. South Carolina, 512 U.S. 154 (1994).
31. "Executions: Dead Man Walking Out" 21; Eric Zorn, "Prosecutors Deaf to Outcry against Death Penalty," *Chicago Tribune* (7 Mar. 2000): 1. By 2013, forty-nine states had a sentencing option of life in prison without parole, with the only exception being Alaska, which is not a death penalty state.
32. State v. T. Makwanyane and M Mchunu, No. CCT/3/94 (Constitutional Court of the Republic of South Africa 6 June 1995).
33. William A. Schabas, *The Abolition of the Death Penalty in International Law* (2d ed.) (Cambridge: Cambridge University Press, 1997) 2. Countries that still have death penalty laws on the books but have not executed anyone for ten years or more are considered to have abolished the death penalty de facto, as opposed to countries that no longer have death penalty laws at all, abolishing the punishment de jure. Ibid., 295 n.3. The trend of countries changing their law to abolish the death penalty is of relatively recent origin, dating from the adoption of the *Universal Declaration of Human Rights* on December 10, 1948.
34. Bruce Shapiro, "Dead Reckoning: A World Effort to Force an End to the U.S. Death Penalty Is Gaining Strength," *The Nation* (6 Aug. 2001): 14.
35. Schabas, *The Abolition of the Death Penalty in International Law* 307.
36. T.R. Reid, "Many Europeans See Bush as Executioner Extraordinaire," *Washington Post* (17 Dec. 2000): A36; Felix Rohatyn, "The Shadow over America," *Newsweek* (29 May 2000): 27; Daniel Tarschys, "Preface," in *The Death Penalty. Abolition in Europe* (Strasbourg, France: Council of Europe Publishing, 1999) 7. The Council of Europe is an organization of governments that aims, among other things, to protect human rights. *The Council of Europe in Brief*, (last visited 25 July 2014), http://www.coe.int/en/web/about-us/who-we-are.

37. Jerome Socolovsly, "Germany Opposes U.S. Death Penalty," *AP Online*, 2000 WL 29040420, 13 Nov. 2000. The lawsuit arose because of U.S. authorities' failures to notify foreign detainees of consular rights as required by the 1963 Vienna Convention on Consular Relations.

38. Anjali Sachdeva, "French Leader Says U.S. Should Abolish Death Penalty," *Pittsburgh Post-Gazette* (29 Aug. 2000): D-6; Rohatyn, "The Shadow over America" 27.

39. Shapiro, "Dead Reckoning" 14.

40. Toni M. Fine, "Moratorium 2000: An International Dialogue toward a Ban on Capital Punishment," 30 *Columbia Human Rights Law Review* (1999): 421, 427; Tribune News Services, "Rome Honors Ryan's Execution Moratorium," *Chicago Tribune* (2 Feb. 2000): 12.

41. Minister of Justice v. Burns, No. 26129, 2001 S.C.C. 7, 2001 Can. Sup. Ct. LEXIS 9 (Canada, 15 Feb. 2001); Shapiro, "Dead Reckoning" 14. Another example of where outside pressure had a direct effect was when Pope John Paul II visited St. Louis and asked Missouri governor Mel Carnahan to spare the life of triple murderer Darrell Mease, who was scheduled to be executed in January 1999. Governor Carnahan had denied clemency in twenty-six previous executions, but he granted the pope's request and commuted Mease's sentence to life imprisonment without the possibility of parole. In the pope's absence, Governor Carnahan went back to denying clemency for other condemned. Acker and Lanier, "May God—Or the Governor—Have Mercy" 201.

42. Shapiro, "Dead Reckoning," 14; Amnesty International, *Death Sentences and Executions in 2010* (London: Amnesty International 2011) 7, http://www.amnesty. org/en/library/info/ACT50/001/2011/en.

43. Amnesty International, *Death Sentences and Executions in 2013* (London: Amnesty International 2014) 7, http://www.amnestyusa.org/sites/default/files/ act500012014en.pdf. In 2013, the United States was the only country in the Americas to carry out executions, and 173 of the 193 states that are members of the United Nations did not have any executions in 2013. There were, however, at least 778 executions worldwide, not counting thousands more in China, where the country keeps its executions secret. During the year, at least 1,925 people worldwide were known to be sentencd to death. Ibid., 6–8.

44. Alter, "A Reckoning on Death Row" 31; Stephen B. Bright, "Death by Lottery— Procedural Bar of Constitutional Claims in Capital Cases due to Inadequate Representation of Indigent Defendants," 92 *West Virginia Law Review* (1990): 679; Jeffrey L. Kirchmeier, "Drinks, Drugs, and Drowsiness: The Constitutional Right to Effective Assistance of Counsel and the Strickland Prejudice Requirement," 75 *Nebraska Law Review* (1996): 425.

45. David Cole, "It's Time the Law Stopped Executing the Mentally Retarded," *Legal Times* (19 May 1997): 27; "Jeb Bush Signs Bill Barring Executing the Retarded," *New York Times* (13 June 2001): A30; Tim Hoover, "Missouri to Stop Executing Retarded," *Kansas City Star* (3 July 2001): B1; Stan Swofford, "State Law Could Affect McCarver Case," *News & Record* (Greensboro, NC) (7 Aug. 2001): B3.

CHAPTER 21: THE EARLY TWENTY-FIRST CENTURY DEATH PENALTY IN THE COURTS

1. Rudolph v. Alabama, 375 U.S. 889 (1963) (Goldberg, J., dissenting from denial of petition for writ of certiorari).

2. Babcock, "Human Rights Advocacy" 96; Coker v. Georgia, 433 U.S. 584, 596 n.10 (1977); Enmund v. Florida, 458 U.S. 782 (1982).

3. Babcock, "Human Rights Advocacy" 96–97.

4. Thompson v. Oklahoma, 487 U.S. 815 (1988).

5. Stanford v. Kentucky, 492 U.S. 361, 370 n.1 (1989) (emphasis in original).

6. For thirteen years after *Stanford*, only Justices Breyer and Stevens occasionally cited international law, and those appeared in opinions regarding certiorari

denials. Knight v. Florida, 528 U.S. 990 (1999) (Breyer, J., dissenting from denial of certiorari); Lackey v. Texas, 514 U.S. 1045 (1995) (Stevens, J., respecting denial of certiorari). Babcock, "Human Rights Advocacy" 98.

7. Breard v. Greene, 523 U.S. 371 (1998). The Court's decision *Medellin v. Texas*, 552 U.S. 491 (2008), however, made international law more difficult to enforce in U.S. courts.

8. Knight v. Florida, 528 U.S. 990, 120 S. Ct. 459 (1999) (Breyer, J., dissenting from denial of certiorari). Justice Breyer looked to decisions from the high courts in India and Zimbabwe, the Privy Council in Jamaica, and the European Court of Human Rights. Justice Breyer dissented from a denial of a petition for a stay on similar grounds in a case where a condemned prisoner had been sentenced to death more than thirty-three years earlier. Valle v. Florida, 132 S. Ct. 1 (2011) (Breyer, J., dissenting from denial of stay).

9. Jeffrey Toobin, *The Nine: Inside the Secret World of the Supreme Court* (New York: First Anchor Books, 2008) 212–217.

10. Penry v. Lynaugh, 492 U.S. 302 (1989). Although many of the Supreme Court opinions and most current state statutes use the term "mental retardation," the term is being replaced with "intellectual disability." So, this book uses the phrase "intellectual disability" in most places, but the Court's actual language in death penalty opinions prior to 2014 uses the term "mental retardation."

11. Atkins v. Virginia, 536 U.S. 304 (2002).

12. "State-by-State Strategy Propelled Atkins to Success, Ellis Says," *University of Virginia School of Law Website*, 3 Mar. 2005, (last visited 25 June 2013), http://www.law.virginia.edu/html/news/2005_spr/atkins.htm.

13. Stripling v. State, 711 S.E.2d 685 (Ga. 2011); Hill v. Humphrey, 662 F.2d 1335 (11th Cir. 2011).

14. Hall v. Florida, 134 S. Ct. 1986, 2001 (2014).

15. Toobin, *The Nine* 227–229.

16. Roper v. Simmons, 543 U.S. 551 (2005).

17. *Roper v. Simmons*, 543 U.S. at 575.

18. *Roper v. Simmons*, 543 U.S. at 627 (Scalia, J., dissenting).

19. Toobin, *The Nine* 231–232.

20. Some argue it may be more difficult to assess degrees of mental illness than it is to assess age or intellectual disability. But organizations that favor such a ban, such as the American Bar Association, clarify they do not seek a ban that would apply broadly to all mental illnesses. The ABA embraces a ban on executing those with severe mental disorders or disabilities that "significantly impaired" their rational judgment or ability to appreciate the wrongfulness of their conduct. The American Psychiatric Association, the National Alliance on Mental Illness, and the American Psychological Association have adopted the same conclusions. Ronald J. Tabak, "Executing People with Mental Disabilities: How We Can Mitigate an Aggravating Situation," 25 *Saint Louis University Public Law Review* (2006): 283, 305.

21. *Coker v. Georgia*, 433 U.S. at 587. In the Court's opinion in *Coker*, the justices did not address the racial aspect underlying the case that the overwhelming number of people who had been executed for rape had been black men, leaving any statistical race claims to later be addressed in *McCleskey v. Kemp*.

22. State v. Wilson, 685 So. 2d 1063, 1073 (La. 1996); Jeffrey L. Kirchmeier, "Casting a Wider Net: Another Decade of Legislative Expansion of the Death Penalty in the United States," 34 *Pepperdine Law Review* (2006): 1, 17 n.89.

23. Kennedy v. Louisiana, 554 U.S. 407 (2008).

24. Toobin, *The Nine* 402–403.

25. Jim Geraghty, "What Does Obama Think of *Kennedy v. Louisiana*?," *National Review Online*, 25 June 2008, http://www.nationalreview.com/campaign-spot/9402/what-does-obama-think-i-kennedy-vs-louisiana-i-updated.

26. *Kennedy v. Louisiana*, 554 U.S. at 411.

27. Strickland v. Washington, 466 U.S. 668 (1984); Wiggins v. Smith, 539 U.S. 510 (2003); Rompilla v. Beard, 545 U.S. 374 (2005).
28. Maples v. Thomas, 132 S. Ct. 912, 922 (2012).
29. Maples v. Thomas, 132 S. Ct. at 922–923.
30. Holland v. Florida, 130 S. Ct. 2549 (2010).
31. Martinez v. Ryan, 132 S. Ct. 1309 (2012); Coleman v. Thompson, 501 U.S. 722 (1991).
32. Kansas v. Marsh, 548 U.S. 163 (2006) (Scalia, J., concurring).
33. Skinner v. Switzer, 131 S. Ct. 1289 (2011).
34. House v. Bell, 547 U.S. 518 (2006); Bill Mears, "Man Who Spent 22 Years on Death Row Is Cleared," *CNN*, 12 May 2009, http://www.cnn.com/2009/CRIME/05/12/death.row.exoneration/. House suffers from multiple sclerosis.
35. Miller-El v. Dretke, 545 U.S. 231 (2005).
36. Johnson v. California, 545 U.S. 162 (2005).
37. Cullen v. Pinholster, 131 S. Ct. 1388, 1416–1419 (2011) (Sotomayor, J., dissenting).
38. Miller v. Alabama, 132 S. Ct. 2455 (2012).
39. Peter G. Verniero, "Appealed to Death," *New York Times*, 14 Jan. 2007, http://www.nytimes.com/2007/01/14/opinion/nyregionopinions/14NJverniero.html.
40. Doss v. Mississippi, No. 2007-CA-00429-SCT, 2008 WL 5174209 (Miss. Dec. 11, 2008), opinion withdrawn on grant of rehearing.
41. Wiles v. Bagley, 561 F.3d 636, 642 (6th Cir. 2009).
42. Nichols v. Heidle, No. 06-6495, 2013 WL 3821537 (6th Cir. 26 July 2013) (Martin, Boyce F., Jr., concurring).
43. State v. Wogenstahl, No. 1995-0042, slip op. at 3 (Ohio, Jan. 25, 2013) (O'Neill, J., dissenting).
44. Jennifer Emily, "Dallas Criminal Courts Judge Rules Death Penalty Unconstitutional," *Dallas Morning News*, 24 Dec. 2011, http://www.dallasnews.com/news/crime/headlines/20111224-dallas-criminal-courts-judge-rules-death-penalty-unconstitutional.ece.
45. In May 2012, Roderick Harris was sentenced to death. Anna Merlan, "Dallas County Judge Who Ruled Death Penalty Unconstitutional Is Forced to Recuse Herself," *Dallas Observer Blogs*, 3 Jan. 2012, http://blogs.dallasobserver.com/unfairpark/2012/01/judge_who_declared_death_penal.php; Anna Merlan, "Teresa Hawthorne: The Decider," Dallas Observer Blogs, 24 June 2012, http://blogs.dallasobserver.com/unfairpark/2012/06/judge_teresa_hawthorne_people.php.
46. Jones v. Chappell, No. CV 09-02158, 2014 WL 3567365 (C.D. Calif. 16 July 2014).
47. Judge H. Lee Sarokin, "Does a Botched Execution Constitute Double Jeopardy?," *Huffington Post*, 5 Oct. 2009, http://www.huffingtonpost.com/judge-h-lee-sarokin/does-a-botched-execution_b_309751.html.
48. Donald A. McCartin, "Second Thoughts of a 'Hanging Judge,'" *Los Angeles Times*, 25 Mar. 2011, http://www.latimes.com/news/opinion/commentary/la-oe-mccartin-death-penalty-20110325,0,2340912.story; Gil Garcetti, "California's Death Penalty Doesn't Serve Justice," *Los Angeles Times*, 25 Mar. 2011. Judge McCartin also discussed his concerns with the death penalty three years earlier. Gordon Dillow, "Judge McCartin Turns against Death Penalty," *Orange County (CA) Register*, 2 Mar. 2008, 2008 WLNR 4174545.
49. P. Hammel, "Judge Put Execution Views Aside," *Omaha World-Herald*, 2 Feb. 2009, 2009 WLNR 1933917.

CHAPTER 22: THE EARLY TWENTY-FIRST CENTURY DEATH PENALTY IN U.S. POLITICS

1. McCleskey v. Kemp, 481 U.S. 279, 319 (1987). Professor Scott Sunby has argued that Justice Powell's opinion made it more difficult to get legislatures to address the racial disparity found in the Baldus study because legislators believed that the Supreme Court had proclaimed that the system works. Sunby, "The Loss of Constitutional Faith" 34.

2. Kan. Stat. Ann. Sec. 532.300 (1998).
3. Baldus et al. "Race and Proportionality since *McCleskey v. Kemp*" 147.
4. Barbara O'Brien and Catherine M. Grosso, "Confronting Race: How a Confluence of Social Movements Convinced North Carolina to Go Where the McCleskey Court Wouldn't," 2011 *Michigan State Law Review* (2011): 463–504.
5. N.C. Gen. Stat. Sec. 15A-2011(b) (2009);
6. N.C. Gen. Stat. Sec. 15A-2010 (2009); Persky, "Numbers Tell the Tale" 19.
7. Gary Robertson, "Veto Override Scuttles N.C. Racial Justice Act," *The Charlotte Post*, 3 July 2012, http://www.thecharlottepost.com/index.php?src=news&srctype=detail &category=News&refno=4765.
8. Persky, "Numbers Tell the Tale" 18–19; Jessica Kim, "North Carolina Lawmakers Nearly Repeal 'Racial Justice Act,' *Talking Points Memo*, 17 June 2011, http://tpmdc. talkingpointsmemo.com/2011/06/north-carolina-lawmakers-challenge-law-that-attempts-to-restore-racial-justice-to-death-penalty.php; Kim Severson, "North Carolina Repeals Law Allowing Racial Bias Claim in Death Penalty Challenges," *New York Times*, 5 June 2013, http://www.nytimes.com/2013/06/06/ us/racial-justice-act-repealed-in-north-carolina.html.
9. Jane Mayer, "State for Sale," *The New Yorker* (10 Oct. 2011): 90.
10. James Eng, "Judge Rules Race Tainted North Carolina Death Penalty Case," *MSNBC.com*, 20 Apr. 2012, http://usnews.msnbc.msn.com/_news/2012/04/20/ 11307519-judge-rules-race-tainted-north-carolina-death-penalty-case-inmate-marcus-robinson-spared-from-death-row.
11. Andrew Welsh-Huggins, "Analysis: Divisions Mark Ohio Death Penalty Panel," *Akron Beacon Journal Online*, 15 July 2013, http://www.ohio.com/news/ analysis-divisions-mark-ohio-death-penalty-panel-1.413322.
12. Ariel Levy, "Prodigal Son," *The New Yorker* (28 June 2010): 53.
13. Brad Shannon, "GOP's Dunn Concedes to Bob Ferguson in AG Race," *The Olympian*, 8 Nov. 2012, http://www.theolympian.com/2012/11/08/2312527/ gops-dunn-concedes-to-bob-ferguson.html.
14. Lincoln D. Chafee, "My Pleau Stand Affirms Core R.I. Values," *Providence Journal*, 24 Aug. 2011, http://www.projo.com/opinion/contributors/content/ CT_chafee_08-24-11_63PRJF6_v11.53bcc.html.
15. MSNBC.com News Service, "Del Governor Spares Murderer Facing Execution," *MSNBC.com*, 17 Jan. 2012, http://www.msnbc.msn.com/id/46026790/ns/ us_news-crime_and_courts/#.TxYBJYHsbPo.
16. Jonathan J. Cooper, "Ore. Governor Bans Death Penalty for Rest of Term," *The Seattle Times*, 24 Nov. 2011, http://seattletimes.nwsource.com/text/2016834596. html. Haugen's attorney revealed that because Haugen had waived his appeals in a desire to be executed, the condemned man would not be happy with the reprieve stopping his execution.
17. Scherzer, "The Abolition of the Death Penalty in New Jersey" 254–256; Karen Augéand Lynn Bartels, "Nathan Dunlap Granted Temporary Reprieve by Colorado Gov. Hickenlooper," *The Denver Post*, 22 May 2013, http://www.denverpost.com/ breakingnews/ci_23299865/nathan-dunlap-temporary-reprieve-from-governor.
18. Jay Inslee, "Governor Inslee's Remarks Announcing a Capital Punishment Moratorium," 11 Feb. 2014, http://governor.wa.gov/news/speeches/20140211_ death_penalty_moratorium.pdf.
19. R.G. Ratcliffe, "Review Death Penalty Law, Ex-Governor Urges," *Houston Chronicle*, 18 Oct. 2009, http://www.chron.com/disp/story.mpl/metropolitan/6673921.html.
20. Banner, *The Death Penalty* 276–277; Amanda Marzullo, "Last Man Out: *People v. Taylor* and Its Precursors in New York Death Penalty Jurisprudence," 11 *University of Pennsylvania Journal of Law and Social Change* (2007–2008): 271, 271–272.
21. James R. Acker, "Be Careful What You Ask For: Lessons from New York's Recent Experience with Capital Punishment," 32 *Vermont Law Review* (2008): 683, 683–688; Thomas H. Koenig and Michael L. Rustad, "Book Review: Deciding

Whether the Death Penalty Should Be Abolished," 44 *Suffolk University Law Review* (2011): 208.

22. People v. LaValle, 817 N.E.2d 341 (N.Y. 2004); People v. Taylor, 878 N.E.2d 969 (N.Y. 2007).

23. Acker, "Be Careful What You Ask For" 683–688. Andrew Cuomo is the son of former New York governor Mario Cuomo, who also opposed capital punishment and had vetoed attempts to revive the death penalty in New York.

24. State v. Marshall, 613 A.2d 1059 (N.J. 1992); Baldus et al. "Race and Proportionality since *McCleskey v. Kemp* (1987)" 164–175. One of the reasons the New Jersey Supreme Court could act as it did without political pressures was because, unlike justices in many other states, New Jersey Supreme Court justices are tenured until the age of seventy and do not have to regularly seek election.

25. Scherzer, "The Abolition of the Death Penalty in New Jersey," 224–227, 248–249.

26. Angelyn C. Frazier, "Taking Death Off the Table in the Land of Enchantment," *Champion* (June 2009): 42.

27. Richard C. Dieter, *Struck by Lightning: The Continuing Arbitrariness of the Death Penalty Thirty-Five Years after Its Re-instatement in 1976* (Report of the Death Penalty Information Center), July 2011, http://www.deathpenaltyinfo.org/documents/StruckByLightning.pdf.

28. "Illinois Governor Signs Bill Ending Death Penalty, Marking the Fewest States with Capital Punishment since 1978," *Death Penalty Information Center Press Release*, 9 Mar. 2011, http://www.deathpenaltyinfo.org/documents/ILRepealPR.pdf.

29. "Statement from Governor Pat Quinn," *Illinois Government New Network*, 9 Mar. 2011, http://www.illinois.gov/PressReleases/ShowPressRelease.cfm?SubjectID=2&RecNum=9265.

30. Margaret Summers, *The Death Penalty Gender Gap, Womensenews.org*, 21 Apr. 2011, http://www.womensenews.org/story/crime-policylegislation/110424/the-death-penalty-gender-gap.

31. Mark Pazniokas, "At Petit's Request, Two Senators Stop Repeal of Death Penalty," *Connecticut Mirror*, 11 May 2011. Senator Edith G. Prague and Senator Andrew Maynard both announced that after talking to Dr. Petit they would not vote for abolition during the current session.

32. Governor Malloy noted he first opposed capital punishment when he worked as a prosecutor. Ebong Udomoa, "Connecticut Abolishes Death Penalty," *Chicago Tribune*, 25 Apr. 2012, http://www.chicagotribune.com/news/sns-rt-us-usa-deathpenalty-connecticutbre83o1cm-20120425,0,5387703.story.

33. Editorial Board, "Maryland's Broken Death Penalty," *Washington Post*, 6 Mar. 2012, http://www.washingtonpost.com/opinions/marylands-broken-de ath-penalty/2012/03/06/gIQA7tMhvR_story.html.

34. Erin Cox, "Martin O'Malley Running for President? Maryland Governor Says He Will Consider White House Run Now That General Assembly Session Is Over," *Baltimore Sun*, 11 Apr. 2013, http://www.huffingtonpost.com/2013/04/11/martin-omalley-running-for-president_n_3059043.html.

35. Brian MacQuarrie, *The Ride: A Shocking Murder and a Bereaved Father's Journey from Rage to Redemption* (Cambridge, MA: Da Capo Press, 2009).

36. Cy Ryan, "Governor Vetoes Bill Calling for Study of Death Penalty Costs," *Las Vegas Sun News*, 9 June 2011, http://www.lasvegassun.com/news/2011/jun/09/governor-vetoes-bill-calling-study-death-penalty-c/.

37. Michael Stratford, "Ark. Governor Reverses Course on Death Penalty," *San Francisco Chronicle*, 21 Jan. 2013, http://www.sfgate.com/default/article/Ark-governor-reverses-course-on-death-penalty-4199466.php.

38. Kevin O'Hanlon, "Bill Abolishing the Death Penalty Could Be in Peril," *Lincoln Journal Star*, 13 May 2012, http://journalstar.com/legislature/bill-abolishing-the-death-penalty-could-be-in-peril/article_f8a967f5-f239-5486-aebf-93466fdfd369.html. Unlike other states, Nebraska's legislature is unicameral with one chamber.

39. Katharine Q. Seelye, "Measure to Repeal Death Penalty Fails by a Single Vote in New Hampshire Senate," *New York Times*, 17 Apr. 2014, http://www.nytimes.com/2014/04/18/us/in-new-hampshire-measure-to-repeal-death-penalty-fails-by-a-single-vote.html.
40. "Statement from Governor Pat Quinn."
41. Raoul G. Cantero and Mark R. Schlakman, "Florida Death Penalty Law Overdue for Review," *The Gainesville Sun* (Florida), 29 May 2011, http://www.gainesville.com/article/20110528/OPINION/110529512/.
42. Carol J. Williams, "Death Penalty Costs California $184 Million a Year, Study Says," *Los Angeles Times*, 20 June 2011, http://www.latimes.com/news/local/la-me-adv-death-penalty-costs-20110620,0,3505671.story.
43. "Recapping the Times' Election Endorsements," *Los Angeles Times*, 4 Nov. 2012, http://www.latimes.com/news/opinion/endorsements/la-ed-end-recap-20121104,0,5024503.story.
44. Mandery, *A Wild Justice* 98–99.
45. Adam Nagourney, "Seeking an End to an Execution Law They Once Championed," *New York Times*, 6 Apr. 2012, http://www.nytimes.com/2012/04/07/us/fighting-to-repeal-california-execution-law-they-championed.html.
46. Howard Minz, "Defeat of Proposition 34: California's Death Penalty Battle Will Continue," *The Herald* (Monterey County), 8 Nov. 2012, http://www.montereyherald.com/politics-local/ci_21951068/defeat-proposition-34-californias-death-penalty-battle-will.
47. Jack Dolan and Carol J. Williams, "Jerry Brown Cancels Plan for $356-Million Death Row," *Los Angeles Times*, 29 Apr. 2011, http://www.latimes.com/news/local/la-me-death-row-20110429,0,1177207.story. Similarly, in 2014, Governor Brown had to decide whether or not the state would appeal a decision by a federal court judge finding the state's death penalty unconstitutional. Jones v. Chappell, No. CV 09-02158, 2014 WL 3567365 (C.D. Calif. 16 July 2014).
48. During the most recent abolition period, Tennessee imposed a moratorium on executions for a short time in 2007 to re-examine its lethal injection procedures.
49. "Executions by Year since 1976," *Death Penalty Information Center*, 8 August 2014, http://www.deathpenaltyinfo.org/executions-year; "Size of Death Row by Year," *Death Penalty Information Center*, 8 August 2014, http://www.deathpenaltyinfo.org/death-row-inmates-state-and-size-death-row-year#year.
50. Steve Bousquet, "Gov. Rick Scott Speeding Up Florida Inmate Execution Process," *Tampa Bay Times*, 19 May 2013, http://www.tampabay.com/news/courts/criminal/gov-rick-scott-speeding-up-execution-process/2121883.
51. For a further discussion of some of these recent studies, see the Epilogue.
52. Moore, "Remembering Warren" 11.

CHAPTER 23: ESCAPING FROM IMPRISONMENT OF THE PAST

1. "New Resolution Approved by the U.N.: The Pro Moratorium Front Grows," *Hands Off Cain* Website, 22 Dec. 2010, http://www.handsoffcain.info/news/index.php?iddocumento=13317774; Dunstan Prial, "UN Receives Anti-execution Petition," *AP Online*, 2000 WL 30834462, 18 Dec. 2000; Amnesty International, *Death Sentences and Executions in 2010* (London: Amnesty International, 2011) 7, http://www.amnesty.org/en/library/info/ACT50/001/2011/en. For more on international opposition to the death penalty, see chapter 20.
2. For some recent books discussing differences between other countries and the United States, and how those differences may contribute to the U.S. retention of capital punishment, see Whitman, *Harsh Justice*; Zimring, *The Contradictions of American Capital Punishment*, and Garland, *Peculiar Institution*.
3. Jeffrey M. Jones, "U.S. Death Penalty Support Lowest in More than 40 Years," *Gallup Politics*, 29 Oct. 2013, (last visited 25 July 2014), http://www.gallup.com/poll/165626/death-penalty-support-lowest-years.aspx; Jeff Jones and Lydia

Saad, "Gallup Poll Social Series: Crime," *Gallup News Service Report*, 6–9 Oct. 2011; Newport, "In U.S., Support for Death Penalty Falls to 39-Year Low; Frank Newport, "In U.S., 64% Support Death Penalty in Cases of Murder," *Gallup Politics* Website, 8 Nov. 2010, (last visited 20 June 2013), http://www.gallup.com/poll/144284/ Support-Death-Penalty-Cases-Murder.aspx.

4. Ronald J. Tabak, "Capital Punishment," in *The State of Criminal Justice 2012* (American Bar Association Criminal Justice Section, 2012) 317.

5. Stevens, *Five Justices* 218.

6. Baze v. Rees, 553 U.S. 35, 83–86 (2008) (Stevens, J., concurring).

7. *Baze v. Rees*, 553 U.S. at 86 (Stevens, J., concurring).

8. Nina Totenberg, "Justice Stevens: An Open Mind on a Changed Court," *NPR*, 4 Oct. 2010, http://www.npr.org/templates/story/story.php?storyId=130198344. The written article leaves out "in those cases" in the first quoted sentence, but they appear in the audio interview at the website. Additionally, in his book *Five Justices*, Justice Stevens noted that he regretted his vote in *Jurek v. Texas*, the 1976 case upholding Texas's death penalty statute, stating that he should have grouped it with the mandatory death penalty statutes. Stevens, *Five Justices* 215–216. Finally, in another post-retirement book by Justice Stevens, *Six Amendments: How and Why We Should Change the Constitution*, he explained how the Eighth Amendment might be amended to clarify that the death penalty is a "cruel and unusual punishment": "Excessive bail shall not be required, nor excessive fines imposed, nor cruel and unusual punishments such as the death penalty inflicted." John Paul Stevens, *Six Amendments: How and Why We Should Change the Constitution* (New York: Little Brown and Company, 2014) 123.

9. Weinstein, "Death Penalty Moratorium Attracting Unlikely Adherents" A5.

10. Jimmy Carter, "Show Death Penalty the Door," *The Atlanta Journal-Constitution*, 25 Apr. 2012, http://www.ajc.com/news/news/opinion/show-death-penalty-the-door/ nQTLS/.

11. American Law Institute, *Report of the Council to the Membership of the American Law Institute on the Matter of the Death Penalty* (19 May 2009): 7, http://www.ali.org/doc/ Capital%20Punishment_web.pdf; Franklin F. Zimring, "Pulling the Plug on Capital Punishment," *National Law Journal*, 7 Dec. 2009, http://www.deathpenaltyinfo.org/ legal-scholar-calls-withdrawal-model-penal-code-quiet-blockbuster.

12. Carol S. Steiker and Jordan M. Steiker, "Report to the ALI concerning Capital Punishment," in The American Law Institute, *Report of the Council to the Membership of the American Law Institute on the Matter of the Death Penalty*, Annex. B (15 Apr. 2009): 28–20.

13. Kirk Johnson, "Dish by Dish, Art of Last Meals," *New York Times*, 25 Jan. 2013, http://www.nytimes.com/2013/01/26/arts/design/the-last-supper-by- julie-green-at-arts-center-in-oregon.html. Texas officials were upset that Brewer ordered a large last meal and then did not eat it. Thus, they stopped offering last meals after his case.

14. Tom Watkins, "Religious Leaders Seek Clemency for Georgia Man on Death Row," *CNN*, May 5, 2011, http://articles.cnn.com/2011-05-05/justice/georgia. execution_1_religious-leaders-innocence-claim-martina-correia; Karen Brooks, "Victim's Son Objects as Texas Sets Execution in Hate Crime Death," *Huffington Post*, 21 Sept. 2011, http://www.huffingtonpost.com/2011/09/21/victims-son-objects- as-t_n_973654.html.

15. "The Celebration of the Home Going of Warren McCleskey."

16. McCleskey v. Kemp, 481 U.S. 279, 344 (1987) (Brennan, J., dissenting).

EPILOGUE: WARREN McCLESKEY'S CASE AND THE AMERICAN DEATH PENALTY TODAY

1. Georgia Department of Corrections Website, available through search at http:// www.dcor.state.ga.us/GDC/OffenderQuery/jsp/OffQryRedirector.jsp

2. Depree v. Thomas, 946 F.2d 784 (11th Cir. 1991).
3. John J. Goldman, "Ex-Sheriff Given Life Term for Murder of Rival," *Los Angeles Times*, 16 Aug. 2002, http://articles.latimes.com/2002/aug/16/nation/na-sheriff16.
4. Both during Patrick's 2007 inauguration and, after his re-election, during his 2011 inauguration, Patrick gave a nod to America's past. He took the oath of office both times on the Mendi Bible, which African captives who were freed in the 1841 Amistad Supreme Court case gave to their lawyer, John Quincy Adams. Michael Hirsley, "Legal Challenge an Indictment of Capital Punishment in U.S.," *Chicago Tribune*, 13 July 1986, http://articles.chicagotribune.com/1986-07-13/news/8602190518_1_death-penalty-law-professor-david-baldus-sentences/2; Associated Press, "Massachusetts Gov. Deval Patrick's 2nd Inaugural Ceremonies Begin with Prayer Service," *The Republican* (Massachusetts), 6 Jan. 2011 (last visited 20 Jan. 2011), http://www.masslive.com/news/index.ssf/2011/01/massachusetts_gov_deval_patric_43.html.
5. William "Billy" Neal Moore, Telephone Interview, 5 July 2011; Shelia M. Poole, "Forgiven," *The Atlanta Journal-Constitution*, 30 Mar. 2013, http://www.myajc.com/news/news/forgiven/nW6tj/.
6. Carter, "Lady of the Last Chance."
7. Adam Liptak, "David Baldus, 75, Dies; Studied Race and the Law," *New York Times*, 14 June 2011, http://www.nytimes.com/2011/06/15/us/15baldus.html.
8. Kap Stann, *Moon Handbooks: Georgia* (Emeryville, CA: Avalon Travel Publishing, 2008) 81. Cobb County, where Marietta is located, has adopted some controversial laws, as has Georgia. Kennesaw passed a law requiring every household to own a firearm, and in 2003 its city council passed a resolution to recognize God "as the foundation of our national heritage." Also, in 2011, the Georgia legislature passed a tough immigration bill, imposing requirements on business hiring and giving police more powers to investigate an individual's immigration status. But not all Georgians were supportive of the new law, and many protested against it. Jeremy Redmon, "Georgia Lawmakers Pass Illegal Immigration Crackdown," *Atlanta Journal-Constitution*, 14 April 2011, http://www.ajc.com/news/georgia-lawmakers-pass-illegal-909988.html; Jeremy Redmon and Craig Schneider, "Georgians React to Judge's Decision to Halt Parts of Anti-Illegal Immigration Law," *Atlanta Journal-Constitution*, 28 June 2011, http://www.ajc.com/news/georgia-politics-elections/georgians-react-to-judges-991342.html.
9. Paden and McTyre, *175 Facts about Marietta, Georgia* 69–71; Scott, *Cobb County, Georgia and the Origins of the Suburban South* xv.
10. Gone with the Wind Museum Website, 28 June 2010, http://www.mariettaga.gov/gwtw/; author's visit to museum 16 May 2011.
11. Jane Gross, "Georgia Town Is Still Divided over the 1915 Lynching of a Jew," *New York Times*, 26 Aug. 2000 (last visited 8 June 2010), http://www.nytimes.com/2000/08/26/us/georgia-town-is-still-divided-over-the-1915-lynching-of-a-jew.html. Some remember Leo Frank in ignorance, as in one instance where a local resident threatened a Jewish person with the taunt, "Remember what happened to Leo Frank."
12. Leo Hohmann, "A Pilgrimage for 'Little Mary,'" *Marietta Daily Journal*, 28 Apr. 2013, http://www.mdjonline.com/view/full_story/22388225/article-A-pilgrimage-for-%E2%80%98little-Mary%E2%80%99-.
13. Officials encountered some debate about the language on the historical marker, ultimately conceding to alum of the school who requested that in the interest of historical accuracy, the marker refer to "Negro students" instead of "African-American students." Noreen Cochran, "Marker Honors Lemon Street High School," *Marietta Daily Journal* [Georgia] (26 Oct. 2012), http://mdjonline.com/bookmark/20618095-Marker-honors-Lemon-Street-High-School.
14. Avis Thomas-Lester, "A Senate Apology for History on Lynching," *Washington Post*, 14 June 2005, http://www.washingtonpost.com/wp-dyn/content/article/2005/06/13/AR2005061301720.html.

15. Josh Sanburn, "Designer of Georgia's Confederate License Plate Doesn't Understand Why People Are Upset," *Time Magazine*, 20 Feb. 2014, http://nation.time.com/2014/02/20/confederate-flag-georgia-license-plate/.

16. Equal Justice Initiative, *Illegal Racial Discrimination in Jury Selection: A Continuing Legacy* (Montgomery, AL: EJI, Aug. 2010) 4, http://eji.org/eji/files/EJI%20Race%20and%20Jury%20Report.pdf.

17. United States General Accounting Office Report to Senate and House Committees on the Judiciary, *Death Penalty Sentencing: Research Indicates Pattern of Racial Disparities* (Feb. 1990): 5.

18. Charles J. Ogletree Jr. and Austin Sarat, "Introduction," in *From Lynch Mobs to the Killing State* 2.

19. Simpson, "Everyone Else Is Doing It" 509, 541; Scott Phillips, "Racial Disparities in the Capital of Capital Punishment," 45 *Houston Law Review* (2008): 807, 808–810; Stephen B. Bright, "The Failure to Achieve Fairness: Race and Poverty Continue to Influence Who Dies," 11 *University of Pennsylvania Journal of Constitutional Law* (2008): 23; Sheri Lynn Johnson et al., "The Delaware Death Penalty: An Empirical Study," 97 *Iowa Law Review* (2012): 1925, 1940; Cohen, "McCleskey's Omission" 74–76; Roger Hood, *The Death Penalty: A World-Wide Perspective* (2d ed.) (Oxford: Clarendon Press, 1996) 169; Dr. Matthew Robinson, "The Death Penalty in North Carolina," 1 Mar. 2011 (citing working paper by M. Radelet and G. Pierce, "Race and Death Sentencing in North Carolina 1980–2007"), http://pscj.appstate.edu/ncdeathpenalty/; Michael L. Radelet and Glenn L. Pierce, "The Role of Victim's Race and Geography on Death Sentencing," in *From Lynch Mobs to the Killing State* (ed. Charles J. Ogletree Jr. and Austin Sarat) (New York: New York University Press, 2006) 143; John J. Donohue III, "An Empirical Evaluation of the Connecticut Death Penalty System Since 1973: Are There Unlawful Racial, Gender, and Geographic Disparities?," 11 *Journal of Empirical Legal Studies* (December 2014): n.p.

20. Baldus et al., "Race and Proportionality since *McCleskey v. Kemp* (1987).

21. Liptak, "New Look at Death Sentences and Race."

22. Jennifer L. Eberhardt, Paul G. Davies, Valerie J. Purdie-Vaughns, and Sheri Lynn Johnson, "Looking Deathworthy: Perceived Stereotypicality of Black Defendants Predicts Capital-Sentencing Outcomes," 17(5) *Psychological Science* (May 2006): 383–386.

23. Katherine Beckett and Heather Evans, "The Role of Race in Washington State Capital Sentencing, 1981-2012," 27 Jan. 2014 (last visited 25 July 2014), http://www.deathpenaltyinfo.org/documents/WashRaceStudy2014.pdf.

24. Marisa Taylor, "Study: Racial Disparities Taint Military's Use of Death Penalty," *The Kansas City Star*, 28 Aug. 2011, http://www.kansascity.com/2011/08/28/3104989/study-racial-disparities-taint.html.

25. Baldus et al. "Race and Proportionality since *McCleskey v. Kemp* (1987)" 151–152; Raymond Paternoster, Robert Brame, Sarah Bacon & Andrew Ditchfield, "Justice by Geography and Race: The Administration of the Death Penalty in Maryland, 1978–1999," 4 *University of Maryland Law Journal of Race, Religion, Gender and Class* (2004): 1, 45–51.

26. Baldus et al., "Race and Proportionality since *McCleskey v. Kemp* (1987)" 151–152.

27. "Study: White and Black Children Biased toward Lighter Skin," *CNN U.S.*, 13 May 2010, http://articles.cnn.com/2010-05-13/us/doll.study_1_black-children-pilot-study-white-doll?_s=PM:US; Jeffrey L. Kirchmeier, "Our Existential Death Penalty: Judges, Jurors, and Terror Management," 32 *Law & Psychology Review* (2008): 55.

28. Payne v. Tennessee, 501 U.S. 808 (1991).

29. Ashley Nellis and Ryan S. King, *No Exit: The Expanding Use of Life Sentences in America* (Washington, DC: The Sentencing Project, July 2009) 1, 3.

30. Michelle Alexander, *The New Jim Crow: Mass Incarceration in the Age of Colorblindness* (New York: The New Press, 2010) 175; Adam Gopnik, "The Caging of America," *The New Yorker* (30 Jan. 2012): 72–77, 73.
31. Alexander, *The New Jim Crow* 175; Greenhouse, *Becoming Justice Blackmun* 177; Jeffrey Fagan, "Symposium on Pursuing Racial Fairness in Criminal Justice: Twenty Years after *McCleskey v. Kemp*," 39 *Columbia Human Rights Law Review* (2008): 5.
32. Stephen B. Bright, "The Death Penalty and the Society We Want," 6 *Pierce Law Review* (2008): 369, 382.
33. Georgia Supreme Court Commission on Racial and Ethnic Bias in the Court System, "Let Justice Be Done: Equally, Fairly, and Impartially," 12 *Georgia State University Law Review* (1996): 687, 695.
34. American Bar Association, *Evaluating Fairness and Accuracy in State Death Penalty Systems: The Georgia Death Penalty Assessment Report* 285 (2006).
35. Ogletree, "Black Man's Burden" 31–32; Bill Rankin, Heather Vogell, Sonji Jacobs, and Megan Clarke, "A Matter of Life or Death," *Atlanta Journal-Constitution*, 22–25 Sept. 2007 (four-part series), http://www.ajc.com/metro/content/metro/stories/deathpenalty/dayone/dpdayone1.html.
36. Jennifer Adger and Christopher Weiss, "Why Place Matters: Exploring County-Level Variations in Death Sentencing in Alabama," 2011 *Michigan State Law Review* (2011): 659.
37. Ring v. Arizona, 536 U.S. 584, 617 (2002) (Breyer, J., concurring). Cohen, "McCleskey's Omission" 81–89.
38. These problems, of course, still exist outside the criminal justice system too. For example, in 2013, high school students in Wilcox County in Georgia had to take a stand to have their first racially integrated prom. Mark Hanrahan, "Ga. High School Students Set Up First Integrated Prom," *The Huffington Post*, 4 Apr. 2013, http://www.huffingtonpost.com/2013/04/04/segregated-prom-wilcox-county-ga-high-school_n_3013733.html.
39. Samuel R. Gross, "David Baldus and the Legacy of *McCleskey v. Kemp*," 91 *Iowa Law Review* (2012): 1920–1924.
40. Bright, "The Death Penalty and the Society We Want" 372; American Bar Association Standing Committee on Legal Aid and Indigent Defendants, *Gideon's Broken Promise: America's Continuing Quest for Equal Justice* (2004).

BIBLIOGRAPHY

"A Gathering Momentum: Continuing Impacts of the American Bar Association Call for a Moratorium on Executions." *American Bar Association Section of Individual Rights and Responsibilities* 2000.

"Ad Features Bundy." *Advertising Age* 12 March 1990: 23.

Abramson, Jeffrey. *We the Jury*. Cambridge, MA: Harvard University, 1993.

Acker, James and Charles S. Lanier. "May God—Or the Governor—Have Mercy: Executive Clemency and Executions in Modern Death-Penalty Systems." *Criminal Law Bulletin* 36 (2000): 107–152.

Acker, James R. "Be Careful What You Ask For: Lessons from New York's Recent Experience with Capital Punishment." *Vermont Law Review* 32 (2008): 683–763.

Adger, Jennifer and Christopher Weiss. "Why Place Matters: Exploring County-Level Variations in Death Sentencing in Alabama." *Michigan State Law Review* 2011 (2011): 659–704.

Adler, William M. *The Man Who Never Died*. New York: Bloomsbury USA, 2012.

Agozino, Biko. "How Scientific Is Criminal Justice?: A Methodological Crtiique of Research on *McCleksey v. Kemp* and Other Capital Cases." *National Black Law Journal* 17 (2003): 84–97.

Aiuto, Russell. "The Legacy of Sacco and Vanzetti." Crime Library, n.d., http://www.crimelibrary.com/notorious_murders/not_guilty/sacco/8.html.

Alavi, Atossa M. "The Government against Two: Ethel and Julius Rosenberg's Trial." *Case Western Law Review* 53 (2003): 1057–1090.

Albanese, Michael. "From Warren McCleskey to Troy Davis, History Repeats." *Huffington Post*. 23 September 2011, http://www.huffingtonpost.com/michael-albanese/post_2398_b_958515.html.

Alexander, Michelle. *The New Jim Crow: Mass Incarceration in the Age of Colorblindness*. New York: The New Press, 2010.

Alotta, Robert I. *Civil War Justice: Union Army Executions under Lincoln*. Shippensburg, PA: White Mane, 1989.

Alschuler, Albert W. "The Changing Purposes of Criminal Punishment: A Retrospective on the Past Century and Some Thoughts about the Next." *University of Chicago Law Review* 70 (2003): 1–22.

Alter, Jonathan and Mark Miller. "A Life or Death Gamble." *Newsweek* 29 May 2000: 22–28.

American Bar Association Standing Committee on Legal Aid and Indigent Defendants. *Gideon's Broken Promise: America's Continuing Quest for Equal Justice* December 2004, (last visited 1 July 2013), http://www.americanbar.org/content/dam/aba/administrative/legal_aid_indigent_defendants/ls_sclaid_def_bp_right_to_counsel_in_criminal_proceedings.authcheckdam.pdf.

American Bar Association. *Evaluating Fairness and Accuracy in State Death Penalty Systems: The Georgia Death Penalty Assessment Report* 2006, http://www.americanbar.org/content/dam/aba/migrated/moratorium/assessmentproject/georgia/report.authcheckdam.pdf.

American Law Institute. *Report of the Council to the Membership of the American Law Institute on the Matter of the Death Penalty* 19 May 2009, (last visited 1 July 2013), http://www.ali.org/doc/Capital%20Punishment_web.pdf.

Amnesty International. "Death Sentences and Executions in 2013." London: Amnesty International, 2014, http://www.amnestyusa.org/sites/default/files/act500012014en.pdf.

Amnesty International. "Death Sentences and Executions in 2010." London: Amnesty International, 2011, http://www.amnesty.org/en/library/info/ACT50/001/2011/en.

Amnesty International. "The Death Penalty in Georgia: Racist, Arbitrary and Unfair." *AMR 51/025/1996.* 1 June 1996, (last visited 8 June 2010), http://asiapacific.amnesty.org/library/Index/ENGAMR510251996?open&of=ENG-2M4.

Amsterdam, Anthony G. "*In Favorem Mortis:* The Supreme Court and Capital Punishment." *Human Rights* (Winter 1987): 14–18.

Amsterdam, Anthony G. "Opening Remarks: Race and the Death Penalty before and after *McCleskey.*" *Columbia Human Rights Law Review* 39 (2007): 35–58.

Amsterdam, Anthony G. "Selling a Quick Fix for Boot Hill: The Myth of Justice Delayed in Death Cases." In *The Killing State: Capital Punishment in Law, Politics and Culture.* Austin Sarat ed. New York: Oxford University, 1999.

Anaya, Governor Toney. "Statement by Governor Toney Anaya on Crime and Capital Punishment." 26 November 1986.

Applebome, Peter. "Georgia Inmate Is Executed after 'Chaotic' Legal Move." *New York Times* 26 September 1991, (last visited 15 July 2011), http://www.nytimes.com/1991/09/26/us/georgia-inmate-is-executed-after-chaotic-legal-move.html.

Applebome, Peter. "Inmate Whose Appeals Shook System Faces Execution." *New York Times* 24 September 1991: A5.

Armstrong, Ken and Steve Mills. "Ryan 'Until I Can Be Sure'; Illinois Is First State to Suspend Death Penalty." *Chicago Tribune* 1 February 2000, 3.

Associated Press. "5 States Consider Ban on Executions." *The Gazette* 1 February 2000, A6.

Associated Press. "Georgia Court Blocks Electric Chair Use." 5 October 2001, 2 February 2012, http://www.commondreams.org/headlines01/1005-03.htm.

Associated Press. "Humane Death by Gas Has History of Doubters." *Los Angeles Times* 20 April 1992, A19.

Associated Press. "Inmate-Chosen Electric Chair Execution Looms." CBS News 16 January 2013, (last visited 30 January 2013), http://www.cbsnews.com/8301-201_162-57564227/inmate-chosen-electric-chair-execution-looms/.

Associated Press. "Killer of Two Is Hanged in Delaware as Kin of Victims Watch." *New York Times* 26 January 1996, http://www.nytimes.com/1996/01/26/us/killer-of-2-is-hanged-in-delaware-as-kin-of-victims-watch.html.

Associated Press. "Massachusetts Gov. Deval Patrick's 2nd Inaugural Ceremonies Begin with Prayer Service." *The Republican* (Massachusetts) 6 January 2011, http://www.masslive.com/news/index.ssf/2011/01/massachusetts_gov_deval_patric_43.html.

Associated Press. "O'Connor Questions Death Penalty." *New York Times* 4 July 2001: A9.

Associated Press. "Oklahoma Governor Signs Lethal Injection Legislation." *Tulsa World* 18 April 2011, http://www.tulsaworld.com/article.aspx/Oklahoma_governor_signs_lethal_injection_legislation/20110418_336_0_oklaho875935.

Associated Press. "Ohio Catholic Bishops Support State Supreme Court Justice's Call to End Use of Death Penalty." *Los Angeles Times* 5 February 2011, http://www.latimes.com/news/nationworld/nation/wire/sns-ap-us-death-penalty-ohio,0,7231235.story.

Associated Press, "1,788 Await Death: 68 Have Been Executed since '72." *Phoenix Gazette* 7 February 1987: A-6.

Associated Press. "Robertson Backs Moratorium: Says Death Penalty Used Unfairly." *Chicago Tribune* 8 April 2000: N12.

Associated Press. "Willie Ross Will Get New Trial or Freedom." AP News Archive. 26 May 1988, http://www.apnewsarchive.com/1988/14-Ye ars-After-Conviction-Willie-Ross-Will-Get-New-Trial-Or-Freedom/ id-57baf0fb54f12a9e29d6a87ba98c1b1a.

At the Death House Door. Dir. Peter Gilbert and Steve James. IFC, 2008.

Atler, Jonathan. "A Reckoning on Death Row." *Newsweek* 3 July 2000, http://www. highbeam.com/doc/1G1-63042466.html.

"Authorized Methods of Execution." *Death Penalty Information Center.* 6 May 2011, http://www.deathpenaltyinfo.org/methods-execution#wa.

Aynesworth, Hugh. "Spotlight Expected at Texas Execution." *Washington Times* 7 May 2000.

Babcock, Sandra. "Human Rights Advocacy in United States Capital Cases." *Bringing Human Rights Home Vol. 3.* Cynthia Soohoo, Catherine Albisa, and Martha F. Davis, eds. Westport, CT: Praeger, 2008.

Baker, David V. "American Indian Executions in Historical Context." *Criminal Justice Studies* 20 (2007): 315–373.

Baldus, David C. and George Woodworth. "Race Discrimination and the Legitimacy of Capital Punishment: Reflections on the Interaction of Fact and Perception." *DePaul Law Review* 53 (2004): 1411–1495.

Baldus, David C., George G. Woodworth, and Charles A. Pulaski, Jr. *Equal Justice and the Death Penalty.* Boston: Northeastern University Press, 1990.

Baldus, David C., George G. Woodworth, and Charles A. Pulaski, Jr. "Law and Statistics in Conflict: Reflections on *McCleskey v. Kemp.*" In *Capital Punishment and the Judicial Process.* Randall Coyne and Lyn Entzeroth eds. Durham, NC: Carolina Academic, 2012.

Baldus, David C. et al. "*McCleskey v. Kemp* (1987): Denial, Avoidance and the Legitimization of Racial Discrimination in the Administration of the Death Penalty." In *Death Penalty Stories.* John H. Blume and Jordan M. Steiker eds. New York: Foundation, 2009.

Baldus, David, George Woodworth, and Catherine M. Grosso, "Race and Proportionality since *McCleskey v. Kemp* (1987): Different Actors with Mixed Strategies of Denial and Avoidance." *Columbia Human Rights Law Review* 39 (2007): 143–177.

Ball, Howard. "Thurgood Marshall's Forlorn Battle against Racial Discrimination in the Administration of the Death Penalty: The McCleskey Cases, 1987, 1991." *Mississippi College Law Review* 27 (2008): 335–371.

Banner, Stuart. *The Death Penalty: An American History.* Cambridge, MA: Harvard University Press, 2002.

Banner, Stuart. "Race and the Death Penalty in Historical Perspective." *From Lynch Mobs to the Killing State.* Charles J. Ogletree Jr. and Austin Sarat eds. New York: New York University Press, 2006.

Banner, Stuart. "Traces of Slavery." *From Lynch Mobs to the Killing State: Race and the Death Penalty in America.* Charles J. Ogletree Jr. and Austin Sarat eds. New York: New York University Press, 2006.

Barbour, Phillip L. "Captain George Kendall: Mutineer or Intelligencer?" *Virginia Magazine of History and Biography* 70 No. 3 (1962): 297:313.

Barnett, Arnold. "How Numbers Can Trick You." *Technology Review* October 1994: 38–46.

Barrouquere. "Court Upholds Temporary Ban on Executions." *Kentucky Post* 25 March 2011, http://www.kypost.com/dpp/news/state/ Kentucky-Executions_02100031.

Bartels, Karen Augéand Lynn. "Nathan Dunlap Granted Temporary Reprieve by Colorado Gov. Hickenlooper." *Denver Post* 22 May 2013,

http://www.denverpost.com/breakingnews/ci_23299865/
nathan-dunlap-temporary-reprieve-from-governor.

Beckett, Katherine and Heather Evans, "The Role of Race in Washington State Capital Sentencing, 1981-2012." 27 Jan. 2014, (last visited 25 July 2014), http://www. deathpenaltyinfo.org/documents/WashRaceStudy2014.pdf.

Beard, Kristina E. "Five under the Eighth: Methodology Review and the Cruel and Unusual Punishments Clause." *University of Miami Law Review* 51 (1997): 445–480.

Beccaria, Cesare. *Of Crimes and Punishments*. New York: Marsilio Publishers, 1996.

Bedau, Hugh Adam. "The Death Penalty in America. Yesterday and Today." *Dickenson Law Review* 95 (1991): 749–772.

Bedau, Hugh Adam. *Death Is Different: Studies in the Morality, Law and Politics of Capital Punishment*. Boston: Northeastern University Press, 1987.

Bedau, Hugo Adam (ed.). *The Death Penalty in America: Current Controversies*. New York: Oxford University Press, 1997.

Bentham, Jeremy. *An Introduction to the Principles of Morals and Legislation*. John Bowring ed. Edinburgh: William Tait, 1843.

Berman, Mark. "Tennesse Has Long Had the Electric Chair, But Now It's Going to Be Available for More Executions." *Washington Post* 23 May 2014, <http://www.washingtonpost.com/news/post-nation/wp/2014/05/23/ tennessee-has-long-had-the-electric-chair-but-now-its-going-to- be-available-for-more-executions/>

Berryhill, Mike. Letter to Georgia Board of Pardons and Parole. 1 June 1991.

Bessler John D. *Cruel and Unusual*. Boston: Northeastern University Press, 2012.

Bisbort, Alan. *When You Read This, They Will Have Killed Me*. New York: Carroll and Graf, 2006.

Blackmon, Douglas A. "Louisiana Death-Row Inmate Damon Thibodeaux Exonerated with DNA Evidence." *Washington Post* 28 September 2012, http://www. washingtonpost.com/national/louisiana-death-row-inmate-damon-thibode aux-is-exonerated-with-dna-evidence/2012/09/28/26e30012-0997- 11e2-afff-d6c7f20a83bf_story.html.

Blake, John. "Murphy's Law: Death Row Activist Keeps the Faith in Her Battle with Rare Cancer." *Atlanta Journal-Constitution* 14 April 1996: M3.

Bland, Randall W. *Justice Thurgood Marshall: Crusader for Liberalism*. Bethesda, MD: Academica Press, 2001.

Bluestein, Greg. "Georgia Execution Is Fodder for Challenges to New Drug." *Chattanooga Times Free Press* (Tennessee) 28 June 2011, http://www.timesfreepress.com/news/2011/jun/29/ georgia-execution-fodder-challenges-new-drug/.

Blumenthal, Ralph "A Man Who Knew about the Electric Chair." *New York Times*: City Room. 6 November 2011, http://cityroom.blogs.nytimes.com/2011/11/0 6/a-man-who-knew-about-the-electric-chair/#.

Boger, John Charles. Telephone Interview. 20 August 2012.

Bogle, Donald. *Toms, Coons, Mulattoes, Mammies and Bucks*. New York: The Continuum International Publishing Group, 2004.

Bohm, Robert M. "American Death Penalty Opinion: Past, Present and Future." *American's Experiment with Capital Punishment*. James R. Acker, Robert M. Bohm, and Charles S. Lanier eds. Durham, NC: Carolina Academic, 2003.

Bosco, Antoinette. *Choosing Mercy: A Mother of Murder Victims Pleads to End the Death Penalty*. Maryknoll, NY: Orbis Books, 2001.

Bousquet, Steve. "Gov. Rick Scott Speeding up Florida Inmate Execution Process." *Tampa Bay Times* 19 May 2013, http://www.tampabay.com/news/courts/ criminal/gov-rick-scott-speeding-up-execution-process/2121883.

Bowers, William J. "A Tribute to David Baldus, a Determined and Relentless Champion of Doing Justice." *Iowa Law Review* 97 (2012): 1879–1904.

Bowers, William J. and Glenn L. Pierce. "Arbitrariness and Discrimination under Post-*Furman* Capital Statutes." *Crime & Delinquency* 26 (1980): 563–632.

Bowers, William J. et al. *Legal Homicide: Death as Punishment in America, 1864–1982.* Boston: Northeastern University Press, 1984.

Bowers, William J. et al. "Death Sentencing in Black and White: An Empirical Analysis of the Role of Jurors' Race and Jury Racial Composition." *University of Pennsylvania Journal of Constitutional Law* 3 (2001): 171–274.

Bowman, Jeffrey H. "Slow Dance on the Killing Field." *Arizona Attorney* July 1996: 20.

Brennan, Jr., William J. "Constitutional Adjudication and the Death Penalty: A View from the Court." *Harvard Law Review* 100 (1986): 313–331.

Brennan, Sheila M. "Popular Images of American Women in the 1950s and Their Impact on Ethel Rosenberg's Trial and Conviction." *Women's Rights Law Reporter* 14 (1992): 43–63.

Breslaver, January "A Troupe Intent on Creating American Operas and a Pair Unafraid of a Topical Subject Team for 'Dead Man Walking.'" *Los Angeles Times* 1 October 2000.

Bright, Stephen B. "The Death Penalty and the Society We Want." *Pierce Law Review* 6 (2008): 369–385.

Bright, Stephen B. "Death by Lottery—Procedural Bar of Constitutional Claims in Capital Cases due to Inadequate Representation of Indigent Defendants." *West Virginia Law Review* 92 (1990): 679–697.

Bright, Stephen B. "Discrimination, Death and Denial." *From Lynch Mobs to the Killing State.* Charles J. Ogletree Jr. and Austin Sarat eds. New York: New York University Press, 2006.

Bright, Stephen B. "The Failure to Achieve Fairness: Race and Poverty Continue to Influence Who Dies." *University of Pennsylvania Journal of Constitutional Law* 11 (December 2008): 23–38.

Bright, Stephen B. and Patrick J. Keenan. "Judges and the Politics of Death: Deciding between the Bill of Rights and the Next Election in Capital Cases." *Boston University Law Review* 75 (1995): 759–835.

Brooks, Karen. "Victim's Son Objects as Texas Sets Execution in Hate Crime Death." *Huffington Post* 21 September 2011, http://www.huffingtonpost.com/2011/09/21/victims-son-objects-as-t_n_973654.html.

Brown, Mary Jane. *Eradicating This Evil: Women in the American-Anti-Lynching Movement 1892–1940.* New York: Routledge, 2000.

Brown, T.C. "Repeal Death Penalty, Original Sponsor Urges." *Cleveland Plain Dealer* 19 February 1999: 1A.

Brozan, Nadine. "Chronicle." *New York Times* 22 August 1994: B4.

Brundage, W. Fitzhugh. "Introduction." In *Under Sentence of Death: Lynching in the South.* W. Fitzhugh Brundage ed. Chapel Hill & London: University of North Carolina, 1997.

Brundage, W. Fitzhugh. *Lynching in the New South: Georgia and Virginia, 1880–1930.* Urbana and Chicago: University of Illinois, 1993.

Bryan, Robert R. "The Execution of the Innocent: The Tragedy of the Hauptmann-Lindbergh and Bigelow Cases." *New York Review of Law and Social Change.* 18 (1991): 831–873.

Burlingame, Michael. *Abraham Lincoln: A Life,* Vol. 1. Baltimore, MD: Johns Hopkins University Press, 2008.

Burnette, Robert F., *Affidavit of Robert F. Burnette,* 9 May 1987 [on file with author].

Burr, Richard H., III. "Representing the Client on Death Row: The Politics of Advocacy." University of Missouri-Kansas City Law Review 59 (1990): 1–16.

Cadenhead, Paul et al. *Documentation Submitted in Support of Application of Warren McCleskey for a 90 Day Stay of Execution and for Commutation of His Sentence of Death.* 1991. [on file with author]

Camus, Albert. *Resistance, Rebellion, and Death.* New York: Alfred A. Knoff, 1961.

Cannon, Carl M. "The Problem with the Chair: A Conservative Case against Capital Punishment." *National Review* 19 June 2000: 28–32.

Cantero, Raoul G. and Mark R. Schlakman. "Florida Death Penalty Law Overdue for Review." *The Gainseville Sun* (Florida) 29 May 2011, http://www.gainesville.com/article/20110528/OPINION/110529512/.

"Capital Punishment in Britain: The Hangman's Story." *The Independent* 7 April 2006, http://www.independent.co.uk/news/uk/crime/capital-punishment-in-britain-the-hangmans-story-473138.html.

Carelli, Richard. "Lawyers See Shift against Death Penalty: ABA Takes No Position, But Wants to Ensure Safeguards and Legal Support for Defendants." *Star-Ledger* 13 February 2000: 43.

Carlsen, William. "Support for Death Penalty—Sometimes." *San Francisco Chronicle* 28 March 1990: A9.

Carter, Dan T. *Scottsboro: A Tragedy of the American South.* Baton Rouge: Louisiana State University Press, 1979.

Carter, Jimmy. "Show Death Penalty the Door." *The Atlanta Journal-Constitution* 25 April 2012, http://www.ajc.com/news/news/opinion/show-death-penalty-the-door/nQTLS/.

Carter, Terry. "Lady of the Last Chance: Lawyer Makes Her Mark Getting Convicts off Death Row." *ABA Journal* 1 August 2012, http://www.abajournal.com/magazine/article/lady_of_the_last_chance/.

"The Celebration of the Home Going of Warren McCleskey." *Hanley Shelton Funeral Home.* 28 September 1991 [funeral pamphlet].

Certiorari Petition Vote, 26 June 1986, McCleskey v. Kemp Case File, No. 811-6811, Basic File. Justice Lewis F. Powell, Jr. Archives. n.p., n.d., (last visited 28 June 2012), http://law.wlu.edu/deptimages/powell%20archives/McCleskeyKempBasic.pdf.

Chafee, Lincoln D. "My Pleau Stand Affirms Core R.I. Values." *Providence Journal* 24 August 2011, http://www.projo.com/opinion/contributors/content/CT_chafee_08-24-11_63PRJF6_v11.53bcc.html.

Chardavoyne, David G. *A Hanging in Detroit: Stephen Gifford Simmons and the Last Execution under Michigan Law.* Detroit: Wayne State University Press, 2003.

Christianson, Scott. *The Last Gap: The Rise and Fall of the American Gas Chamber.* Berkeley: University of California, 2010.

Christoph, James B. *Capital Punishment and British Politics.* London: Allen and Uwin, 1962.

Chua-Eoan, Howard. "The Top 25 Crimes of the Century." *Time Magazine* 8 June 2010, http://www.time.com/time/2007/crimes/14.html.

Claiborne, William. "Philadelphia City Council Backs Halt to Executions." *Washington Post* 11 February 2000: A02.

Clark, Lesley and Phil Long. "Florida's Former Chief Justice Seeks to Bar Executions." *The Record* (Bergen County, New Jersey) 24 October 1999: A7.

Clarke, Oscar W. et al. "Physician Participation in Capital Punishment." *Journal of the American Medical Association* 1993: 333–352.

Coates, James. "A Governor's Fit of Conscience Over an Unconscionable Crime." *Chicago Tribune* 7 December 1986: 7.

Coates, Ta-Nehisi. "Fear of a Black President." *Atlantic* September 2012: 76–90.

Cochran, Noreen. "Marker Honors Lemon Street High School." *Marietta Daily Journal* (Georgia) 26 October 2012, <http://mdjonline.com/bookmark/20618095-Marker-honors-Lemon-Street-High-School>.

Cohen, G. Ben. "McCleskey's Omission: The Racial Geography of Retribution." *Ohio State Journal of Criminal Law* 10 (2012): 65–101.

Cole, David. "It's Time the Law Stopped Executing the Mentally Retarded." *Legal Times* 19 May 1997, 27.

Collins, Rob. "A Century Later, the Photograph of an Oklahoma Lynching Still Resonates." *Oklahoma Gazette* 24 May 2011, http://www.okgazette.com/oklahoma/print-article-11750-print.html.

Cook, Ronda and Jeanne Cummings. "Pace of Execution Bothers Miller." *Atlanta Constitution* 27 September 1991: C4.

Cooper, Ada. "Editorial." *Christian Recorder* 28 September 1899, http://www. accessible.com/accessible/preLog.

Cooper, Jonathan J. "Ore. Governor Bans Death Penalty for Rest of Term." *Seattle Times* 24 November 2011, http://seattletimes.nwsource.com/text/2016834596.html.

Cox, Erin. "Martin O'Malley Running for President? Maryland Governor Says He Will Consider White House Run Now That General Assembly Session Is Over." *Baltimore Sun* 11 April 2013, http://www.huffingtonpost.com/2013/04/11/ martin-omalley-running-for-president_n_3059043.html.

Coyne, Randall and Lyn Entzeroth. *Capital Punishment and the Judicial Process.* Durham, NC: Carolina Academic, 2012.

Crain, Craig. "Unfortunate Events: What Was the War of 1812 Even About?" *New Yorker* 22 October 2012: 77–80.

"Criminal Justice Legal Foundation." n.p, n.d., (last visited 29 January 2013), http:// www.cjlf.org/about/about.htm.

Cromwell, John W. "The Aftermath of Nat Turner's Insurrection." *Journal of Negro History* 5 April 1920: 208–234.

Curriden, Mark. "After *McCleskey*, Some Expect Leap in Ga. Executions." *Atlanta Journal-Constitution* 26 September 1991: D3.

Curriden, Mark. "Clemency Denied for McCleskey: Execution Set Tonight for Police Killing." *Atlanta Journal* 24 September 1991: A1.

Curriden, Mark. "Congress Passes First Major Law Restricting Immigration," *ABA Journal,* May 2013: 72.

Curriden, Mark. "I Deeply Regret That a Life Was Taken." *Atlanta Journal-Constitution* 21 September 1991: A12

Curriden, Mark. "McCleskey Put to Death after Hours of Delays, Final Apology." *Atlanta Journal-Constitution* 26 September 1991: D3.

Curriden, Mark. "Ready to Die, but Insisting He's Innocent." *Atlanta Constitution* 21 September 1991: A01

Curry, Bill. "Convicted Murderer Executed by Florida: Three Surges of Electricity, Convicted Killer Is Executed." *Washington Post* 26 May 1979: sec. A.

Curry, Bill. "Bishop Granted His Wish: Death without Delay." *Washington Post* 23 October 1979: A1.

Cutler, Christopher Q. "Nothing Less than the Dignity of Man: Evolving Standards, Botched Executions and Utah's Controversial Use of the Firing Squad." *Cleveland State Law Review* 50 (2003), 335–424.

Dando, Shigemitsu. "Toward the Abolition of the Death Penalty." *Indiana Law Journal* 72 (1996): 7–19.

Dao, James. "DNA Ties Man Executed in '92 to the Murder He Denied." *New York Times* 13 January 2006: A14.

Darmer, Jill, *Affidavit of Jill Darmer,* 12 May 1987 [on file with author].

Davis, David Brion. "The Movement to Abolish Capital Punishment in America, 1787–1861." *American Historical Review* 63 (1957): 23–46.

Davis, Murphy. "Warren McCleskey: A Faith Refined." *Hospitality* January 1992: 3.

Davis, Murphy. Telephone Interview. 13 May 2011.

"The Death Penalty in Texas: Due Process and Equal Justice…or Rush to Execution?" Texas Civil Rights Project. September 2000, http://www.texascivilrightsproject. org/wp-content/uploads/2009/01/2000-the-death-penalty-in-texas.pdf.

The Death Penalty: Abolition in Europe. Strasbourg, France: Council of Europe Publishing, May 1999.

Delgado, Richard. "The Law of the Noose: A History of Latino Lynching." *Harvard Civil Rights—Civil Liberties Law Review* 44 (2009): 297–312.

Denno, Deborah W. "Getting to Death: Are Executions Constitutional?" *Iowa Law Review* 82 (1997): 319–464.

Denno, Deborah. "Is Electrocution an Unconstitutional Method of Execution? The Engineering of Death over the Century." *William and Mary Law Review* 35 (1994): 551–692.

Denno, Deborah W. "The Lethal Injection Quandary: How Medicine Has Dismantled the Death Penalty." *Fordham Law Review* 76 (2007): 49–124.

Denno, Deborah W. "When Legislatures Delegate Death: The Troubling Paradox behind State Uses of Electrocution and Lethal Injection and What It Says about Us." *Ohio State Law Journal* 63 (2002): 63–128.

Denno, Rob Zaleski. "State Culture Mapped Out." *Capital Times* 7 November 1996: 1E.

Dieter, Richard C. "Struck by Lightning: The Continuing Arbitrariness of the Death Penalty Thirty-Five Years after Its Re-Instatement in 1976." *Report of the Death Penalty Information Center* July 2011, http://www.deathpenaltyinfo.org/documents/StruckByLightning.pdf.

Dillow, Gordon. "Judge McCartin Turns against Death Penalty." *Orange County* (California) *Register* 2 March 2008.

Dolan, Jack and Carol J. Williams. "Jerry Brown Cancels Plan for $356-million Death Row." *Los Angeles Times* 29 April 2011, http://www.latimes.com/news/local/la-me-death-row-20110429,0,1177207.story.

Dolan, Maura. "Rose Bird's Quest for Obscurity." *Los Angeles Times* 15 November 1995: A1.

Donald, David Herbert. *Lincoln.* New York: Simon & Schuster, 1995.

Donohue, John J. III. "An Empirical Evaluation of the Connecticut Death Penalty System Since 1973: Are There Unlawful Racial, Gender, and Geographic Disparities?" *Journal of Empirical Legal Studies* 11 (December 2014) (forthcoming): n.p.

Dorin, Dennis D. "Far Right of the Mainstream: Racism, Rights and Remedies from the Perspective of Justice Antonin Scalia's McCleskey Memorandum." *Mercer Law Review* 45 (1994): 1035–1088.

Dow, David R. "Death Penalty, Still Racist and Arbitrary." *New York Times* 8 July 2011, http://www.nytimes.com/2011/07/09/opinion/09dow.html

Dragich, Martha. "Revelations from the Blackmun Papers on the Development of Death Penalty Law." *Missouri Law Review* 70 (2005): 1183–1198.

Driggs, Ken. "A Current of Electricity in Intensity to Cause Immediate Death: A Pre-*Furman* History of Florida's Electric Chair." *Stetson Law Review* 22 (1993): 1169–1211.

Drimmer, Frederick. *Until You Are Dead: The Book of Executions in America.* New York: Carol Publishing Group, 1990.

Drysdale, Jessica Renee. Interview with Felecca Wilson Taylor. Kennesaw State University Oral History Project. 25 September 2009, http://archon.kennesaw.edu/?p=digitallibrary/digitalcontent&id=5.

Du Bois, W.E.B. *The Souls of Black Folk.* New York: New American Library, 1982.

Dunlop, R.G. "Kentucky's Troubled Death-Penalty System Lets Cases Languish for Decades." *Louisville Courier-Journal* (2009), http://www.courier-journal.com/article/20091107/NEWS01/911080316/.

Earle, Steve. "Billy Austin." *The Hard Way.* MCA, 1990. CD.

Eason, Tim. "AG Says Forensic Science Commission Can't Consider Willingham Case, Others before September 2005." *Austin American-Statesman* 29 July 2011, http://www.statesman.com/blogs/content/shared-gen/blogs/austin/politics/entries/2011/07/29/ag_says_forensic_science_commi.html.

Eberhardt, Jennifer L., Paul G. Davies, Valerie J. Purdie-Vaughns, and Sheri Lynn Johnson. "Looking Deathworthy: Perceived Stereotypicality of Black Defendants Predicts Capital-Sentencing Outcomes." *Psychological Science* 17 (2006): 383–386.

Editorial Board. "Maryland's Broken Death Penalty." *Washington Post* 6 March 2012, http://www.washingtonpost.com/opinions/marylands-broken-death-penalty/2012/03/06/gIQA7tMhvR_story.html.

Editorial. "Supreme Court v. the Great Writ." *Atlanta Constitution* 19 April 1991: A12.

Editorial. "Even in This Case." *Washington Post* 12 May 2001: A24.

Editorial. "The New Death Penalty Politics." *New York Times* 7 June 2000: A30.

Egelko, Bob. "Justice Ginsburg Discusses Equality, Death Penalty." *San Francisco Chronicle* 16 September 2011, http://www.sfgate.com/cgi-bin/article.cgi?f=/c/a/2011/09/15/BAHD1L5CNN.DTL&tsp=1.

Eisenberg, Theodore. "Death Sentence Rates and County Demographics: An Empirical Study." *Cornell Law Review* 90 (2005): 347–370.

Emily, Jennifer. "Dallas Criminal Courts Judge Rules Death Penalty Unconstitutional." *Dallas Morning News* 24 December 2011, http://www.dallasnews.com/news/crime/headlines/20111224-dallas-criminal-courts-judge-rules-death-penalty-unconstitutional.ece.

Eng, James. "Judge Rules Race Tainted North Carolina Death Penalty Case." *MSNBC.com* 20 April 2012, http://usnews.msnbc.msn.com/_news/2012/04/20/11307519-judge-rules-race-tainted-north-carolina-death-penalty-case-inmate-marcus-robinson-spared-from-death-row.

Entin, Jonathan L. "Using Great Cases to Think about the Criminal Justice System." *Journal of Criminal Law and Criminology* 89 (1999): 1141–1156.

Entin, Jonathan L. "Why the Billy Mitchell Case Still Matters." *Journal of Air Law and Commerce* 70 (2005): 577–606.

Epler, Patti. "Utter Quits Supreme Court in Protest of Death Penalty." *News Tribune* (Tacoma, Washington) 30 March 1995: A1.

Equal Justice Initiative. *Illegal Racial Discrimination in Jury Selection: A Continuing Legacy* August 2010, http://eji.org/eji/files/EJI%20Race%20and%20Jury%20Report.pdf.

Espy, Watt, and John Ortiz Smykla. "Executions in the U.S. 1608–1987: The Espy File Executions by State." *The Death Penalty Information Center*, (last visited 2 February 2013), http://www.deathpenaltyinfo.org/documents/ESPYstate.pdf.

Estes, Adam Clark. "Thanks to 'Lincoln,' Mississippi Has Finally Definitely Ratified the Thirteenth Amendment." *The Atlantic Wire* 18 February 2013, (last visited 28 February 2013), http://news.yahoo.com/thanks-lincoln-mississippi-finally-definitely-ratified-thirteenth-amendment-024920825.html.

"Executions by Year." *Death Penalty Information Center* (last visited 8 June 2014), http://www.deathpenaltyinfo.org/executions-year.

"Executions: Dead Man Walking Out." *Economist* 10 June 2000, 21–33.

Extraordinary Motion for New Trial, Georgia v. McCleskey. No. A-40553 (Superior Court of Fulton County, GA. October 13, 1978).

Fagan, Jeffrey. "Symposium on Pursuing Racial Fairness in Criminal Justice: Twenty Years after *McCleskey v. Kemp.*" *Columbia Human Rights Law Review* 39 (2008): 1–33.

Fagan, Kevin. "'This Was Not a Man Who Went Meekly': An Eyewitness Account of Stanley Tookie Williams' Execution." *San Francisco Chronicle* 13 December 2005, http://www.sfgate.com/news/article/This-was-not-a-man-who-went-meekly-An-2588939.php.

Faigman, David Laurence. *Laboratory of Justice: The Supreme Court's 200-Year Struggle to Integrate.* New York: Times Books, 2004.

Ferrell, Claudine L. *Nightmare and Dream; Antilynching in Congress 1917–1922.* New York: Taylor & Francis, Inc., 1986.

Filler, Louis. "Movements to Abolish the Death Penalty in the United States." In *Capital Punishment.* Thorsten Sellin ed. New York: J&J Harper, 1969.

Fine, Toni M. "Moratorium 2000: An International Dialogue toward a Ban on Capital Punishment." *Columbia Human Rights Law Review* 30 (1999): 421–438.

Frady, Marshall. "Death in Arkansas." *New Yorker* 22 February 1993: 105–133.

Frankfurter, Felix. *The Case of Sacco and Vanzetti: A Critical Analysis for Lawyers and Laymen.* New York: Little, Brown and Company, 1962.

Frankfurter, Marion D. and Gardner Jackson (eds.). *The Letters of Sacco and Vanzetti.* Boston: E.P. Dutton and Co., 1960.

Frazier, Angelyn C. "Taking Death off the Table in the Land of Enchantment."
    Champion June 2009: 42.
Freedman, Eric. M. "Leo Frank Lives: Untangling the Historical Roots of Meaningful
    Federal Habeas Corpus Review of State Convictions." *Alabama Law Review* 51
    2000: 1467–1540.
Friedman, Benjamin M. *The Moral Consequences of Economic Growth*. New York: Alred
    A. Knopf, 2005.
Galliher, John F. et al. *America without the Death Penalty: States Leading the Way*.
    Boston: Northeastern University Press, 2002.
Galliher, John F., Gregory Ray, and Brent Cook. "Abolition and Reinstatement of
    Capital Punishment during the Progressive Era and Early 20th Century."
    Journal of Criminal Law and Criminology 83 (1992): 538–572.
Garcetti, Gil. "California's Death Penalty Doesn't Serve Justice." *Los Angeles Times* 25
    March 2011, Opinion.
Garland, David. *Peculiar Institution: America's Death Penalty in an Age of Abolition*.
    Cambridge, MA: Belknap Press, 2012.
Garland, David. "Penal Excess and Surplus Meaning: Public Torture Lynchings in
    Twentieth-Century America." *Law and Sociology Review* 39 (2005): 793–833.
Garrett, Brandon L. "After Osama bin Laden's Death, Imagining a World without
    DNA Evidence." *Washington Post* 13 May 2011, http://www.washingtonpost.
    com/opinions/after-osama-bin-ladens-death-imagining-a-world-without-dna-
    evidence/2011/05/03/AFD90W2G_story.html.
Gearan, Anne. "Ginsburg Backs Ending Death Penalty." *AP Online* 10 April 2001.
Georgia Bureau of Investigation Division of Forensic Sciences. "Autopsy or Report of
    Examination of Body: Warren McCleskey." Case No. B91-4487, 25 September
    1991.
Georgia Department of Corrections Website, http://www.dcor.state.ga.us/GDC/
    OffenderQuery/jsp/OffQryRedirector.jsp.
Georgia Supreme Court Commission on Racial and Ethnic Bias in the Court System.
    "Let Justice Be Done: Equally, Fairly, and Impartially." *Georgia State University
    Law Review* 12 (1996): 687–843.
Geringer, Joseph. "Karla Faye Tucker: Texas' Controversial Murdress." *truTV Crime
    Library*. (last visited 25 July 2014), http://www.trutv.com/library/crime/
    notorious_murders/women/tucker/1.html.
Gerould, Daniel. *Guillotine: Its Legend and Lore*. New York: Blast Books, 1992.
Gettleman, Jeffrey. "Prosecutors' Morbid Neckties Stir Criticism." *New York
    Times* 5 January 2003, http://www.nytimes.com/2003/01/05/us/
    prosecutors-morbid-neckties-stir-criticism.html.
Gibeaut, John. "Taking Aim," *A.B.A. Journal* November 1996: 50–55.
Gibson, David. "Religions Rethinking the Death Penalty." *Record* 8 August 1999: A01.
Gillespie, Mark. "Public Opinion Supports the Death Penalty." *Gallup News Service* 24
    February 1999, http://www.gallup.com/poll/releases.
Gilmore, Mikal. *Shot in the Heart*. New York: Doubleday, 1993.
Ginzburg, Ralph. *100 Years of Lynching*. Baltimore: Black Classic, 1988.
Goldman, John J. "Ex-sheriff Given Life Term for Murder of Rival." *Los Angeles Times*
    16 August 2002, http://articles.latimes.com/2002/aug/16/nation/na-sheriff16.
"Gone with the Wind Museum: Scarlett on the Square." Gone with the Wind Museum
    Website, n.d., (last visited 28 June 2010), http://www.mariettaga.gov/gwtw/.
Goode, Erica. "After a Prolonged Execution in Ohio, Questions Over 'Cruel
    and Unusual.'" *New York Times* 17 January 2014, <http://www.nytimes.
    com/2014/01/18/us/prolonged-execution-prompts-debate-over-death-
    penalty-methods.html>.
Gopnik, Adam. "The Caging of America." *New Yorker* 30 January 2012: 72–77.
Graham, Judith. "Study: Nebraska Is Fair in Giving Death Penalty." *Chicago Tribune*
    2 August 2001: N11.

Graham, Ruth Bell. "Afterward." *Woman on Death Row.* Velma Barfield ed. Nashville: Oliver-Nelson, 1985.

Graczyk, Michael. "Shortage Forces Texas to Switch Execution Drug." *National Public Radio* 16 March 2011, http://www.npr.org/templates/story/story. php?storyId=134591261.

Gray, Ian and Moira Gray (eds.). *A Punishment in Search of a Crime: Americans Speak Out against the Death Penalty.* New York: Avon Books, 1989.

Green, Frank. "Bipartisan Group Targets Wrongful Death Sentences." *Richmond Times Dispatch* (Virginia) 12 May 2000: A-3.

Green, Frank. "Executions Moratorium Urged." *Richmond Times-Dispatch* 2 February 2000: B4.

Green, Frank. "Va. Man Who Killed Two Inmates Is Executed." *Richmond Times-Dispatch* 16 January 2013, (last visited 30 January 2013), http://www. timesdispatch.com/news/latest-news/convicted-killer-robert-charles-gleason-jr-dies-in-electric-chair/article_533cc100-6029-11e2-9393-0019bb30f31a. html.

Greenberg, David. "The Unkillable Death Penalty." *Slate Magazine* 2 June 2000, http://www.slate.com/articles/news_and_politics/history_lesson/2000/06/ the_unkillable_death_penalty.html.

Greenhouse, Linda. *Becoming Justice Blackmun.* New York: Times Books, 2005.

Greenhouse, Steven. "Examining a Labor Hero's Death." *New York Times* 26 August 2011, (last visited 9 June 2012), http://www.nytimes.com/2011/08/27/ us/27hill.html?_r=2&scp=1&sq=Joe%20Hill&st=cse.

Grizzard, Lewis, "Frank Schlatt: Don't Forget." *Covington News* 26 May 2010, (last visited 5 June 2011), http://www.covnews.com/archives/12558/.

Gross, Jane. "Georgia Town Is Still Divided over the 1915 Lynching of a Jew." *New York Times* 26 August 2000, (last visited 8 June 2010), http://www. nytimes.com/2000/08/26/us/georgia-town-is-still-divided-over-the-1915-lynching-of-a-jew.html.

Gross, Samuel R. "David Baldus and the Legacy of *McCleskey v. Kemp.*" *Iowa Law Review* 91 (2012): 1905–1924.

Gross, Samuel R. and Barbara O'Brien, Chen Hu, and Edward H. Kennedy. "Rate of False Conviction of Criminal Defendants Who Are Sentenced to Death." *PNAS Early Edition.* 25 March 2014, <http://www.pnas.org/content/ early/2014/04/23/1306417111.full.pdf+html>.

Gross, Samuel R. and Josiah Thompson. "NAACP Legal Defense and Educational Fund Report on Larry Griffin." *Truth in Justice.* 24 January 2007, http://www. truthinjustice.org/griffin-report.htm.

Hahn, Brad. "Executions Hit 38-Year High in '95: Numbers Likely to Rise if Appeals Are Limited." *Chicago Tribune* 5 December 1996: 18.

Haines, Herbert H. *Against Capital Punishment: The Anti-death Penalty Movement in America, 1972–1994.* New York: Oxford University Press, 1996.

Hall, Jacquelyn Dowd. *Revolt against Chivalry: Jesse Daniel Ames and the Women's Campaign against Lynching.* New York: Columbia University Press, 1993.

Hallett, Joe. "Death Penalty Isn't Effective, Law's Co-Author Now Believes." *Columbus Dispatch* 18 February 1999: 01A.

Hallifax, Jackie. "Dead Inmate Cleared by DNA Tests." *Washington Post* 15 December 2000: A16

Halloran, Liz. "Pulling Back from the Brink." *U.S. News and World Report* 30 April, 2006, (last visited 8 May 2006), http://www.usnews.com/usnews/news/ articles/060508/8death.htm.

Hamm, Theodore. *Rebel and a Cause.* Berkeley: University of California Press, 2001.

Hammel, P. "Judge Put Execution Views Aside." *Omaha World-Herald* 2 February 2009.

Hanrahan, Mark. "Ga. High School Students Set Up First Integrated Prom." *Huffington Post* 4 April 2013, http://www.huffingtonpost.com/2013/04/04/ segregated-prom-wilcox-county-ga-high-school_n_3013733.html.

Harris, Leslie A. "Section of Individual Rights and Responsibilities, Report with Recommendation." *ABA* No. 107 (February 1997), http://www.americanbar. org/content/dam/aba/migrated/legalservices/downloads/sclaid/20110325_ aba_107.authcheckdam.pdf.

Harris, Lyle V. and Mark Curriden. "McCleskey Is Executed for '78 Killing." *Atlanta Constitution* 25 September 1991: A1.

Harwood, John. "Bush May Be Hurt by Handling of Death-Penalty Issue." *Wall Street Journal* 21 March 2000: A28.

Haven, Paul. "Doubts Arise on Death Penalty." *Boston Globe* 31 May 1999: A4.

Hearn, Daniel. *Legal Executions in New England.* Jefferson, NC: MacFarland, 1999.

Heller, Deborah L. "Death Becomes the State: The Death Penalty in New York—Past, Present and Future." *Pace Law Review* 28 (2008): 589–615.

Heller, Nathan. "What She Said." *New Yorker* 24 October 2011: 74–80.

Henberg, Marvin. *Retribution: Evil for Evil in Ethics, Law and Literature.* Philadelphia: Temple University Press, 1990.

Hertzberg, Hendrik. "Over There." *New Yorker* 1 August 2011.

"High Court Halts Duane Buck's Texas Execution." *CBS News* 15 September 2011, http://www.cbsnews.com/stories/2011/09/15/national/main20107049.shtml.

Hilburn, Robert. "Beyond Artistry: Steve Earle's Inspirational Comeback from the Lost Years of Drug Addiction Yields a Rare Musical Intimacy and a Poetic Legacy." *Los Angeles Times* 5 August 2000: F1.

Hirsley, Michael. "Legal Challenge an Indictment of Capital Punishment in U.S." *Chicago Tribune* 13 July 1986, http://articles.chicagotribune.com/1986-07-13/ news/8602190518_1_death-penalty-law-professor-david-baldus-sentences/2.

Hoebel, Edward Adamson. *The Law of Primitive Man.* Cambridge, MA: Harvard University Press, 1954.

Hoffman, January "As State after State Resumes Executions, U.S. Death-Penalty Law Is Still in Limbo." *New York Times* 10 July 1992, http://www.nytimes. com/1992/07/10/news/as-state-after-state-resumes-executions-us- death-penalty-law-is-still-in-limbo.html?pagewanted=all&src=pm.

Hohmann, Leo. "A Pilgrimage for 'Little Mary.'" *Marietta Daily Journal* 28 April 2013, <http://www.mdjonline.com/view/full_story/22388225/ article-A-pilgrimage-for-%E2%80%98little-Mary%E2%80%99->.

Hollyday, Joyce. "A Gift of Dignity." *Sojourners Magazine* 24 January 1992: 24–26.

Holzer, Harold. "An Inescapable Conflict." *ABA Journal* 97 (April 2011), http://www. abajournal.com/magazine/article/civil_war_ended_ slavery_an_inescapable_ conflict/

Hood, Roger. *The Death Penalty: A World-Wide Perspective.* Oxford: Clarendon Press, 1996.

Hook, Donald. D. and Lothar Kahn. *Death in the Balance: The Debate over Capital Punishment.* Lexington, MA: Lexington Books, 1989.

Hoover, Tim. "Missouri to Stop Executing Retarded." *Kansas City Star* 3 July 2001: B1.

Howe, Scott W. "Race, Death and Disproportionality." *Northern Kentucky Law Review* 37 (2010): 213–241.

Huie, William Bradford. "The Shocking Story of Approved Killing Mississippi." *Look* 24 January 1956, http://www.pbs.org/wgbh/amex/till/sfeature/sf_look_ confession.html.

Hunt, Governor George W.P. "Message of Governor George W.P. Hunt to the First Legislature of Arizona." *Phoenix Arizona Republican* 12 September 1993: 3.

Ifill, Gwen. "Md. Woman's Death Term Commuted." *Washington Post* 21 January 1987: B7.

"Illinois Governor Signs Bill Ending Death Penalty, Marking the Fewest States with Capital Punishment since 1978." *Death Penalty Information Center* 9 March 2011, http://www.deathpenaltyinfo.org/documents/ILRepealPR.pdf.

"The Innocence List." *Death Penalty Information Center*, (last visited 25 July 2014), http://www.deathpenaltyinfo.org/innocence-list-those-freed-death-row.

Inslee, Jay. "Governor Inslee's Remarks Announcing a Capital Punishment Moratorium." 11 February 2014, <http://governor.wa.gov/news/speeches/20140211_death_penalty_moratorium.pdf>

"Interview with Justice Harry A. Blackmun by Harold Hongju Koh." *Library of Congress* 9 September 1994, http://lcweb2.loc.gov/diglib/blackmun-public/page.html?page=25&size=640&SERIESID=D09&FOLDERID=D0901.

Jackson, Joe and William F. Burke Jr. *Dead Run: The Shocking Story of Dennis Stockton and Life and Death Row in America*. New York: Walker & Company, 2000.

Jacobs, Leslie Gielow "Bench Memorandum from Leslie to Justice Lewis F. Powell, Jr. of 1 October 1986, McCleskey v. Kemp Case File, No. 811-6811, Basic File." *Justice Lewis F. Powell Jr. Archives, Washington and Lee University, Lexington, VA.* n.d., (last visited 28 June 2012), http://law.wlu.edu/deptimages/powell%20archives/McCleskeyKempBasic.pdf.

Jacobs, Leslie Gielow. "Memorandum from Leslie to Justice Lewis F. Powell, Jr. of 14 October 1986. McCleskey v. Kemp, Case File No. 811-6811." *Justice Lewis F. Powell, Jr. Archives*. n.p., n.d., (last visited 28 June 2012), http://law.wlu.edu/deptimages/powell%20archives/McCleskeyKempBasic.pdf.

Jacobsen, Joel. "Remembered Justice: The Background, Early Career and Judicial Appointments of Justice Potter Stewart." *Akron Law Review* 35 (2002): 227–250.

Jacoby, Jeff. "Supporters of Capital Punishment Can Cheer Gov. Ryan's Decision." *Boston Globe* 28 February 2000: A15.

James, Erwin. "Dead Man Talking." *Guardian* 23 April 2008, http://www.guardian.co.uk/society/2008/apr/23/prisonsandprobation.

"Jeb Bush Signs Bill Barring Executing the Retarded." *New York Times* 13 June 2001: A30.

Jeffries, John C. "A Change of Mind That Came Too Late." *New York Review of Books* 23 December 2010: A23.

Jeffries, John C. *Justice Lewis Powell, Jr.: A Biography*. New York: Fordham University Press, 1994.

"John Wayne Gacy." *Chicago Tribune* 2 February 2012, http://www.chicagotribune.com/topic/crime-law-justice/crimes/murder/john-wayne-gacy-PEHST002275.topic.

Johnson, Dirk. "Utah Execution Hinges on Issue of Racial Bias." *New York Times* 19 July 1992: sec. 1, http://www.nytimes.com/1992/07/19/us/utah-execution-hinges-on-issue-of-racial-bias.html.

Johnson, Kirk. "Dish by Dish, Art of Last Meals." *New York Times* 25 January 2013, http://www.nytimes.com/2013/01/26/arts/design/the-last-supper-by-julie-green-at-arts-center-in-oregon.html>

Johnson, Sheri Lynn, John H. Blume, Theodore Eisenberg, Valerie P. Hans, and Martin T. Wells. "The Delaware Death Penalty: An Empirical Study." *Iowa Law Review* 97 (2012): 1925–1964.

Jones, Jeffrey. "U.S. Death Penalty Support Lowest in More than 40 Years." *Gallup Politics* 29 October 2013, (last visited 25 July 2014), <http://www.gallup.com/poll/165626/death-penalty-support-lowest-years.aspx>.

Jones, Jeff and Lydia Saad. "Gallup Poll Social Series: Crime." *Gallup News Service Report* 9 October 2011, http://s3.amazonaws.com/zanran_storage/www.gallup.com/ContentPages/2532685075.pdf.

Jones, Walter C. "Gederal Official Rebuts Claims; Justice Spokewoman Stands Up to Challenge on Lynching Case." *Florida Times-Union*. 23 July 2011: B-3.

Jouvenal, Justin. "Ex-Virginia Executioner Becomes Opponent of Death Penalty." *Washington Post* 10 February 2013, http://www.washingtonpost.com/local/ex-virginia-executioner-becomes-opponent-of-death-penalty/2013/02/10/9e741124-5e89-11e2-9940-6fc488f3fecd_story.html.

Joyce, James Avery. *The Right to Life: A World View of Capital Punishment.* London: Victor Gollancz, 1962.

Judges, Donald P. "Scared to Death: Capital Punishment as Authoritarian Terror Management." *University of California Davis Law Review* 33 (1999): 155–248.

Kant, Immanuel. "The Science of Right." William Hastie, trans. *Great Books of the Western World.* Robert M. Hutchins ed. Chicago: Encyclopedia Britannica, 1952.

Kaplan, David A. and Bob Cohn. "Pardon Me, Governor Wilde." *Newsweek* 3 March 1991: 56.

Katz, Ian. "Pictures at an Execution." *Guardian* 26 July 1996: T2.

Katz, Joseph L. "*Warren McCleskey v. Ralph Kemp*: Is the Death Penalty in Georgia Racially Biased?" June 1991, http://www.ourpaws.info/cramer/death/katz.htm.

Kaufman-Osborn, Timothy V. "Capital Punishment as Legal Lynching." In *From Lynch Mobs to the Killing State: Race and the Death Penalty in America.* Charles Ogletree Jr. and Austin Sarat eds. New York: New York University Press, 2006.

Keenan, John F. "The Lindbergh Kidnapping Revisited." *Michigan Law Review* 84 (1986): 819–822.

Kennedy, John F. "Radio and Television Report to the American People on Civil Rights." The American Presidency Project. Gerhard Peters and John T. Woolley. n.d., (last visited 9 June 2012), http://www.presidency.ucsb.edu/ws/index.php?pid=9271&st=&st1=.

Kennedy, Randall L. "*McCleskey v. Kemp*: Race, Capital Punishment and the Supreme Court." *Harvard Law Review* 101 (1988): 1388–1443.

Kerns, Jeannie. "After 35 Years in Prison, One Time Death Row Inmate Rebecca Machetti Released." *Guardian* 3 July 2010, http://www.examiner.com/article/after-35-years-prison-one-time-death-row-inmate-rebecca-machetti-released.

"Killers in Arkansas. Texas Executed by Lethal Injection." *New York Times* 26 June 1990: A2.

Kim, Jessica. "North Carolina Lawmakers Nearly Repeal 'Racial Justice Act.'" *Talking Points Memo* 17 June 2011, http://tpmdc.talkingpointsmemo.com/2011/06/north-carolina-lawmakers-challenge-law-that-attempts-to-restore-racial-justice-to-death-penalty.php.

King, Gilbert. *Devil in the Grove.* New York: HarperCollins, 2012.

King, Jr., Martin Luther. "Advice for Living." The Martin Luther King, Jr. Papers Project. n.p., n.d., http://mlk-kpp01.stanford.edu/primarydocuments/Vol4/Nov-1957_AdviceForLiving.pdf.

King, Jr., Martin Luther. "Letter from Birmingham Jail" 16 April 1963, http://www.africa.upenn.edu/Articles_Gen/Letter_Birmingham.html.

King, Jr., Martin Luther. "Letter to G.W. Sanders." The Martin Luther King, Jr. Papers Project. n.p., n.d., http://mlk-kpp01.stanford.edu/primarydocuments/Vol5/15June1959_ToG.W.Sanders.pdf,

Kirchmeier, Jeffrey L. "Aggravating and Mitigating Factors: The Paradox of Today's Arbitrary and Mandatory Capital Punishment Scheme." *William and Mary Bill of Rights Journal* 6 (1998): 346–459.

Kirchmeier, Jeffrey L. "Casting a Wider Net: Another Decade of Legislative Expansion of the Death Penalty in the United States." *Pepperdine Law Review* 34 (2006): 1–40.

Kirchmeier, Jeffrey L. "Dead Innocent: The Death Penalty Abolitionist Search for a Wrongful Execution." *Tulsa Law Review* 42 (2006): 403–435

Kirchmeier, Jeffrey L. "Drinks, Drugs and Drowsiness: The Constitutional Right to Effective Assistance of Counsel and the Strickland Prejudice Requirement." *Nebraska Law Review* 75 (1996): 425–475.

Kirchmeier, Jeffrey L. "Let's Make a Deal: Waiving the Eighth Amendment by Selecting a Cruel and Unusual Punishment." *Connecticut Law Review* 32 (2000): 615-652.

Kirchmeier, Jeffrey L "Our Existential Death Penalty: Judges, Jurors and Terror Management." *Law and Psychology Review* 32 (2008): 55–107.

Kittrie, Nicholas N., Elyce H. Zenoff, and Vincent A. Eng. *Sentencing, Sanctions and Corrections*. New York: Foundation Press 2002.

Koenig, Thomas H. and Michael L. Rustad. "Book Review: Deciding Whether the Death Penalty Should Be Abolished." *Suffolk University Law Review* 44 (2011): 193–209.

Koestler, Arthur. *Dialogue with Death*. Chicago: University of Chicago Press, 2011.

Kosner, Edward. "An Infamous Crime Revisited." *Wall Street Journal* 14 June 2012, http://online.wsj.com/article/SB10001424052702303822204577466420187730062.html.

Kozinski, Alex and Sean Gallagher. "Death: The Ultimate Run-On Sentence." *Case Western Reserve Law Review* 46 (1995): 1–32.

Lacayo, Richard, Anne Constable, and Daniel S. Levy. "Clearing a Path to the Chair." *Time Magazine* 4 May 1987, http://www.time.com/time/magazine/article/0,9171,964240-1,00.html.

Laccetti, Susan. "McCleskey's Letters Showed 'A Deep Faith.'" *Atlanta Journal* 25 September 1991: A6.

Landsman, Stephen. "Legal History: History's Stories." *Michigan Law Review* 93 (1995): 1739–1767.

Lane, Mary Beth. "Celeste Commutes Eight Death Sentences." *Plain Dealer* 11 January 1991: 1-A.

Lassiter, Patrice Shelton. *Kennesaw and Marietta, Generations of Black Life in Georgia*. Charleston: Arcadia, 1999.

Lazarus, Edward. "Mortal Combat: How the Death Penalty Polarized the Supreme Court." *Washington Monthly* 1 June 1998: 2–3.

Lazarus, Edward. *Closed Chambers*. New York: Random House, 1998.

Lepore, Jill. "Birthright." *New Yorker* 14 November 2011: 44–55.

Levy, Ariel. "Prodigal Son." *New Yorker* 28 June 2010: 53.

Lewis, Nell Battle (ed.). "Capital Punishment in North Carolina: Special Bulletin Number 10." Raleigh: The N.C. State Board of Charities and Public Welfare, 1929.

Leyden, John G. "Death in the Hot Seat: A Century of Electrocutions." *Washington Post* 5 August 1990: D5.

Liebman, James S. "Slow Dancing with Death: The Supreme Court and Capital Punishment, 1963–2006." *Columbia Law Review* 107 (2007): 1–130.

Liebman, James S. "The New Death Penalty Debate: What's DNA Got to Do with It?" *Columbia Human Rights Law Review* 33 (2002): 527–554.

Liebman, James S. and the Columbia DeLuna Project. *The Wrong Carlos: Anatomy of a Wrongful Conviction*. New York: Columbia University Press, 2014.

Liebman, James S. and Lawrence C. Marshall. "Less Is Better: Justice Stevens and the Narrowed Death Penalty." *Fordham Law Review* 74 (2006): 1607–1680.

Liebman, James S., Shawn Crowly, Andrew Markquart, Lauren Rosenberg, Lauren Gallo White, and Daniel Zharkovsky. "Los Tocayos Carlos." *Columbia Human Rights Law Review* 43 (2012): 711–1151.

Liebman, James S., Jeffrey Fagan, and Valerie West. "A Broken System: Error Rates in Capital Cases, 1973–1995." *Columbia University* 12 June 2000, http://www2.law.columbia.edu/instructionalservices/liebman/.

Lifton, Robert J. and Greg Mitchell. *Who Owns Death? Capital Punishment, the American Conscience and the End of Executions*. New York: William Morrow & Co., 2000.

Lincoln, Abraham. "On the Perpetuation of Our Political Instiutions." *Teaching American History*. 27 January 1838, http://teachingamericanhistory.org/library/document/the-perpetuation-of-our-political-institutions/.

Lincoln, Judge James H. "The Everlasting Controversy: Michigan and the Death Penalty." *Wayne Law Review* 33 (1987): 1765–1791.

Lindsay, Sue. "Judge Resigns over Death Penalty Law: Heydt, on Panel Picked to Rule in 1997 Slaying, Says System Is Flawed, Statute 'Unworkable.'" *Denver Rocky Mountain News* 13 April 1999: 19A.

Liptak, Adam. "David Baldus, 75, Dies; Studied Race and the Law." *New York Times* 14 June 2011, http://www.nytimes.com/2011/06/15/us/15baldus.html.

Liptak, Adam. "New Look at Death Sentences and Race." *New York Times*, 29 April 2008, http://www.nytimes.com/2008/04/29/us/29bar.html.

Loring, Ed. "Warren and the Warden." 11 *Hospitality* January 1992: 1

Lovett, C.S. *Dealing with the Devil*. Baldwin Park, CA: Personal Christianity, 1967.

Lowry, Beverly. "The Good Bad Girl." *New Yorker* 9 February 1998: 60–70.

Lucas, Greg. "Poll Takes Snapshot of Californians' Views." *San Francisco Chronicle* 14 January 2000: A20.

Lynch, Mona and Craig Haney. "Looking across the Emphatic Divide: Racialized Decision Making on the Capital Jury." *Michigan State Law Review* 2011 (2011): 573–607.

"Lynching This Morning in Columbus." *Butler Herald* 13 August 1912: 5.

MacLean, Nancy. "Gender, Sexuality, and the Politics of Lynching: The Leo Frank Case Revisited." *Under Sentence of Death: Lynching in the South*. William Fitzhugh Brundage ed. Chapel Hill: University of North Carolina Press, 1997. 158–188.

MacQuarrie, Brian. *The Ride: A Shocking Murder and a Bereaved Father's Journey from Rage to Redemption*. Cambridge, MA: Da Capo Press, 2009.

Magzis, Laura, PhD. Report. 8 July 1987 [on file with author].

Mailer, Norman. *Executioner's Song*. New York: Little, Brown and Company, 1979.

Mandery, Evan J. *A Wild Justice: The Death and Resurrection of Capital Punishment in America*. New York: W.W. Norton, 2013.

Mann, Dave. "DNA Tests Undermine Evidence in Texas Execution." *Texas Observer* 11 November 2010, http://www.texasobserver.org/cover-story/texas-observer-exclusive-dna-tests-undermine-evidence-in-texas-execution.

Manson, Pamela. "New Chief Justice Hopes to Eliminate 'Unhealty' Tension." *Arizona Republic* (Phoenix) 15 December 1996: B1.

"Marietta Confederate Cemetery." City of Marietta, GA. n.d., (last visited 8 June 2010), http://www.mariettaga.gov/departments/parks_rec/cemeteries.aspx#3.

"Marietta's Shame: The Lynching of Leo Frank." *Cobb Online*. n.p., n.d., (last visited 8 June 2010), http://www.atlantanation.com/leofrank.html.

Marquart, James W. Sheldon Ekland-Olson, and Jonathan R. Sorensen, *The Rope, the Chair and the Needle*. Austin: University of Texas, 1994.

Marsel, Robert S. "Mr. Justice Arthur J. Golberg and the Death Penalty: A Memorandum to the Conference." *Southern Texas Law Review* 27 (1986): 467–492.

Marshall, Thurgood. *Papers of Thurgood Marshall*. n.p., n.d. MS. Library of Congress, Manuscripts Division, Container 530, Folder 5.

Marshall, Thurgood. "Remarks on the Death Penalty Made at the Judicial Conference of the Second Circuit." *Columbia Law Review* 86 (1986): 1–24.

Martelle, Scott. "The Faithful Report for Duty to the Boss." *Los Angeles Times* 22 May 2000: B3.

Martin, Vicke L. "Who Killed Frank Schlatt?" *Atlanta Voice* 21 October 1978: 1.

Marzullo, Amanda. "Last Man Out: People v. Taylor and Its Precursors in New York Death Penalty Jurisprudence." *University of Pennsylvania Journal of Law and Social Change* 11 (2007–2008): 271–272.

Masters, Brooke A. "Pat Robertson Urges Moratorium on U.S. Executions." *Washington Post* 8 April 2000: A1.

Masters, Brooke A. "Reforms in System of Capital Punishment Are Urged; An Unusual Coalition Joins the Debate Over 'Many Problems' in Meting Out the Death Penalty." *Washington Post* 12 May 2000: A31.

Masur, Louis P. *Rites of Execution: Capital Punishment and Transformation of American Culture, 1776–1865.* New York: Oxford University, 2012.

Mayer, Jane. "Attack Dog." *New Yorker* 20 February 2012: 42.

Mayer, Jane. "State for Sale." *New Yorker* 10 October 2011: 90.

McCartin, Donald A. "Second Thoughts of a 'Hanging Judge.'" *Los Angeles Times* 25 March 2011, http://www.latimes.com/news/opinion/commentary/la-oe-mccartin-death-penalty-20110325,0,2340912.story.

McClennen, Crane. "Capital Punishment in Arizona." *Arizona Attorney* October 1992: 18.

McCleskey, Warren. Letter to Rev. George Wirth. 29 December 1990.

McCleskey, Warren. Letter to Sister Reginald. 12 May 1982.

McCleskey, Warren. Letter to Sister Reginald. 7 July 1982.

McCleskey, Warren. "Warren McCleskey's Last Will and Testament." *Jackson State Prison.* 24 September 1991.

McEnteer, James. *Deep in the Heart: The Texas Tendency in American Politics.* Westport, CT: Praeger Publishers, 2004.

McEvoy, George. "Too Bad Most Last Meals Aren't Well Done." *Palm Beach Post* 10 April 1995: 13A.

McFeely, William S. *Frederick Douglass.* New York: W.W. Norton & Co., 1991.

McFeely, William S. "A Legacy of Slavery and Lynching: The Death Penalty as a Tool of Social Control." *Champion* (November 1997): 30–32.

McKenzie, Judge Sam Phillips, *Order of Judge Sam Phillips McKenzie, Georgia v. McCleskey,* No. A-40553 (Superior Court of Fulton County, GA. October 13, 1978).

McLaurin, Melton A. *Celia, A Slave.* Athens: University of Georgia, 1991.

McPherson, James. *Battle Cry of Freedom.* New York: Oxford University Press, 1988.

Mears, Michael, *The Death Penalty in Georgia, A Modern History 1970–2000.* Atlanta: Georgia Indigent Defense Division of Professional Education, 1999.

Mello, Michael. "Ivon Stanley and James Adams' America: Vectors of Racism in Capital Punishment." *Criminal Law Bulletin* 43 No. 5 (2007).

Mello, Michael. "On Metaphors, Mirrors, and Murders: Theodore Bundy and the Rule of Law," *New York University Review of Law & Social Change* 18 (1990/1991): 887–938.

Meltsner, Michael. *Cruel and Unusual: The Supreme Court and Capital Punishment.* New York: Random House, 1973.

Merlan, Anna. "Dallas County Judge Who Ruled Death Penalty Unconstitutional Is Forced to Recuse Herself." *Dallas Observer Blogs* 3 January 2012, http://blogs.dallasobserver.com/unfairpark/2012/01/judge_who_declared_death_penal.php.

Merlan, Anna. "Teresa Hawthorne: The Decider." *Dallas Observer Blogs* 24 June 2012, <http://blogs.dallasobserver.com/unfairpark/2012/06/judge_teresa_hawthorne_people.php>.

Miller, Bill. "The Execution of a Disabled Killer Rekindles the Debate on Capital Punishment." *The Washington Post* 2 February 1993: Z10.

Millsap, Jr., Sam D. "Your Turn: Until the System Is Fixed, Executions Must Stop." *Express-News* (San Antonio) 29 June 2000: 5B.

Minz, Howard. "Defeat of Proposition 34: California's Death Penalty Battle Will Continue." *The Herald* (Monterey County) 8 November 2012, http://www.montereyherald.com/politics-local/ci_21951068/defeat-proposition-34-californias-death-penalty-battle-will.

Mitchell, Kirk. "Gov. Bill Ritter Issues 29 Pardons, Commutations." *Denver Post* 8 January 2011, http://www.denverpost.com/search/ci_17040359.

Montgomery, Bill. "Both Sides of Debate Agree: Executions Aren't Pleasant." *Atlanta Journal and Constitution* 26 September 1991: D3.

Montgomery, Bill. "McCleskey-Case Informant Freed on Execution Eve." *Atlanta Journal and Constitution* 28 September 1991: B3.

Montgomery, Robert H. *Sacco-Vanzetti: The Murder and the Myth*. New York: Devin-Adair Co., 1960.

Moore, William "Billy" Neal. In Memory of Warren McCleskey. 25 September 1991 [on file with author].

Moore, William "Billy" Neal. *I Shall Not Die*. Bloomington, IN: AuthorHouse, 2005.

Moore, William "Billy" Neal. "Remembering Warren." 11 *Hospitality* January 1992: 5.

Moore, William "Billy" Neal. Telephone Interview. 5 July 2011.

Moran, Richard. *Executioner's Current*. New York: Alfred A. Knopf, 2002.

Moss, Debra Cassens. "The Statistics of Death." *ABA Journal* 1 January 1987: 51–55.

MSNBC.com News Service. "Del Governor Spares Murderer Facing Execution." *MSNBC.com* 17 January 2012, http://www.msnbc.msn.com/id/46026790/ns/us_news-crime_and_courts/#.TxYBJYHsbPo.

Mulkey, Bruce. "Time for a Moratorium on Death Penalty?" *Asheville Citizen-Times* (North Carolina) 8 July 2000: A6.

Musa, Aziza. "Board Approves Report on Willingham." *Texas Tribune* 15 April 2011, http://www.texastribune.org/texas-dept-criminal-justice/cameron-todd-willingham/board-approves-report-on-willingham-/.

Mustian, Jim. "Georgia Pardons Board Spares Condemned Killer Daniel Greene." *Ledger-Enquirer* 20 April 2012, http://www.ledger-enquirer.com/2012/04/20/2019904/georgia-pardons-board-spares-condemned.html.

Myers, Betty. Affidavit. 18 May 1987 [on file with author].

Nagourney, Adam. "Seeking an End to an Execution Law They Once Championed." *New York Times* 6 April 2012, http://www.nytimes.com/2012/04/07/us/fighting-to-repeal-california-execution-law-they-championed.html.

Nagy, Pamela S. "Hang by the Neck until Dead: The Resurgence of Cruel and Unusual Punishment in the 1990s." *Pace Law Journal* 26 (1994): 85–131.

"National Affairs: Capital Punishment: A Fading Practice." *Time Magazine* 21 March 1960, http://www.time.com/time/magazine/article/0,9171,894775-1,00.html.

"National Briefs: N.H. House Deals blow to Death Penalty." *New Orleans Times-Picayune* 11 March 2000: A9.

Nellis, Ashley and Ryan S. King. *No Exit: The Expanding Use of Life Sentences in America*. Washington, DC: The Sentencing Project, July 2009.

"New Resolution Approved by the U.N.: The Pro Moratorium Front Grows." *Hands Off Cain* 22 December 2010, http://www.handsoffcain.info/news/index.php?iddocumento=13317774.

Newport, Frank. "In U.S., 64% Support Death Penalty in Cases of Murder." *Gallup Politics* 8 November 2010, (last visited 20 June 2013), http://www.gallup.com/poll/144284/Support-Death-Penalty-Cases-Murder.aspx.

Newport, Frank. "In U.S., Support for Death Penalty Falls to 39-Year Low." *Gallup Website* 13 October 2011, http://www.gallup.com/poll/150089/Support-Death-Penalty-Falls-Year-Low.aspx.

Noah, Timothy. "Bush's Tookie: Remembering Bush's Worst Public Moment." *Slate Magazine* 2 December 2005, http://www.slate.com/id/2131451/.

Nuckols, Christina. "Gilmore Signs Bill Opening DNA Window." *Virginia-Pilot* 3 May 2001: A1.

Nugent, Karen. "Death Penalty Foes Aid Rep." *Telegram & Gazette* (Worcester, Massachusetts) 18 December 2000: B1.

Nuss, Jeannie. "Arkansas Turns to Different Lethal injection Drug." *Associated Press* 20 April 2013, http://abcnews.go.com/US/wireStory/arkansas-turns-lethal-injection-drug-19001808#.UXmtDKLU-86.

O'Brien, Barbara and Catherine M. Grosso. "Confronting Race: How a Confluence of Social Movements Convinced North Carolina to Go Where the McCleskey Court Wouldn't." *Michigan State Law Review* 2011 (2011): 463–504.

Ochs, Phil. "Iron Lady." *I Ain't Marching Anymore*. Rhino/Elektra, 2006. CD.

O'Connor, Justice Sandra Day. "Note from Justice Sandra Day O'Connor to Justice
    Lewis F. Powell of 13 November 1986, McCleskey v. Kemp Case File, No.
    811-6811, Basic File." *Justice Lewis F. Powell Jr. Archives, Washington and Lee
    University, Lexington, VA*. n.d., (last visited 28 June 2012), http://law.wlu.edu/
    deptimages/powell%20archives/McCleskeyKempBasic.pdf.
O'Connor, Justice Sandra Day. "Thurgood Marshall: The Influence of a Raconteur."
    Stanford Law Review 44 (1992): 1217–1220.
Office of Planning and Analysis of Georgia Department of Corrections. "A History of
    the Death Penalty in Georgia." January 2010, http://www.dcor.state.ga.us/pdf/
    TheDeathPenaltyinGeorgia.pdf.
"Officer Down Memorial Page." n.p, n.d., (last visited 4 April 2011), http://www.
    odmp.org/agency/177-atlanta-police-department-georgia.
Ogletree, Jr., Charles J. "Making Race Matter in Death Matters." In *From Lynch
    Mobs to the Killing State*. Charles J. Ogletree Jr. and Austin Sarat eds.
    New York: New York University, 2006.
Ogletree, Jr., Charles J. "Black Man's Burden: Race and the Death Penalty in
    America." *Oregon Law Review* 81 (2002): 15–38.
O'Hanlon, Kevin. "Bill Abolishing the Death Penalty Could Be in Peril." *Lincoln
    Journal Star* 13 May 2012, http://journalstar.com/legislature/bill-abolishing-
    the-death-penalty-could-be-in-peril/article_f8a967f5-f239-5486-aebf-
    93466fdfd369.html.
"Oklahoma Killer Is Put to Death." *New York Times* 11 September 1990: A15.
Olsen, Lise. "The Cantu Case: Death and Doubt." *Houston Chronicle* 24 July 2006,
    http://www.chron.com/disp/story.mpl/metropolitan/3472872.html.
Olsen, Lise and Maro Robbins. "Lawyers Join Chorus for an Outside Cantu Review."
    Houston Chronicle 25 July 2006: A1.
Olsen, Lise and Maro Robbins. "Tapes Spur Calls for DA to Relinquish Cantu Case."
    San Antonio Express-News 24 July 2006, http://www.mysanantonio.com/news/
    crime/stories/MYSA072506.1A.CantuFollo.14c6778.html.
Oney, Steve. *And the Dead Shall Rise*. New York: Vintage, 2004.
"Oral Agrument." *McKleskey v. Zant,*, n.p. 16 April 1991, http://www.oyez.org/cases/
    1990-1999/1990/1990_89_7024/.
O'Reilly, Bill. "Commentary: Worse than the Death Penalty." *2000 APBnews.com
    Online* 8 June 2000.
Oshinsky, David M. *Capital Punishment on Trial*. Lawrence: University Press of Kansas,
    2010.
Paden, Rebecca Nash and Joe McTyre. *175 Facts about Marietta Georgia*. Marietta: City
    of Marietta, Georgia, 2009.
Parrish, Michael E. "Revisited: The Rosenberg "Atom Spy" Case." *University of
    Missouri-Kansas City Law Review* 68 (2000): 601–621.
Paternoster, Raymond, Robert Brame, Sarah Bacon, and Andrew Ditchfield. "Justice
    by Geography and Race: The Administration of the Death Penalty in Maryland,
    1978–1999." *University of Maryland Law Journal of Race, Religion, Gender and
    Class* 4 (2004): 1–99.
Paulus PP. II., Ioannes. *Evangelium Vitae* 25 March 1995, http://www.vatican.va/holy_
    father/john_paul_ii/encyclicals/documents/hf_jp-ii_enc_25031995_
    evangelium-vitae_en.html.
Pazniokas, Mark. "At Petit's Request, Two Senators Stop Repeal of Death Penalty."
    Connecticut Mirror 11 May 2011, http://www.ctmirror.org/story/petits-
    request-two-senators-stop-repeal-death-penalty.
Pearson, Edmund. "A Reporter at Large: Hauptmann and Circumstantial Evidence."
    New Yorker 9 March 1935: 37–48.
Pena, Susan L. "A Cantata of Redemption: Warren McCleskey's Final Statement Set to
    Music." *Sojourners Magazine* May–June 1995: 61.
Persky, Anna Stolley. "Numbers Tell the Tale: North Carolina's Death Row Inmates
    Let Statistics Back up Bias Claims." *ABA Journal* May 2011: 18.

Pertman, Adam. "Judge's Obscurity after Vote a 'Tragedy.'" *Boston Globe* 19 May 1996: 2.

Pfeifer, Paul E. "Retire Ohio's Death Penalty." *Cleveland Plain Dealer* 26 January 2011, http://www.cleveland.com/opinion/index.ssf/2011/01/retire_ohios_death_penalty_pau.html.

Phillips, Scott. "Racial Disparities in the Capital of Capital Punishment." *Houston Law Review* 45 (2008): 807–840.

Piazza, Bob. "Opposing the Death Penalty; Relatives of Victims Join Call for Moratorium." *Richmond Times Dispatch* 30 April 2000: B–6.

Pikington, Ed. "Georgia Rushes through Executions before Lethal Injection Drugs Expire." *Guardian* 21 February 2013, http://www.guardian.co.uk/world/2013/feb/21/georgia-executions-lethal-injection-drug-pentobarbital.

Piscopo, Michelle. "*Provenzano v. Moore* and *Bryan v. Moore*: How These Two Challenges Finally Forced the Florida Legislature to Pull the Plug on Old Sparky." *Temple Political and Civil Rights Law Review* 10 (2000): 245–264.

Pittman, Craig. "'Dead Man Walking' Brings Nun's Crusade to Screen." *Star Tribune* (Minneapolis) 19 January 1996: E1.

Podgers, James. "A Break for Executions: New ABA President Calls for Push on Death Penalty Moratorium." *ABA Journal* September 2000: 99.

Ponsor, Michael. "Life, Death and Uncertainty." *Boston Globe* 8 July 2001: D2.

Poole, Shelia M. "Forgiven," *Atlanta Journal-Constitution* 30 March 2013, http://www.myajc.com/news/news/forgiven/nW6tj/.

Possley, Maurice. "Fresh Doubts Over a Texas Execution." *Washington Post* 3 August 2014, <http://www.washingtonpost.com/sf/national/2014/08/03/fresh-doubts-over-a-texas-execution/>.

Possley, Maurice. "Man Executed on Disproven Evidence, Experts Say." *Chicago Tribune* 2 May 2006, http://www.chicagotribune.com/news/local/chi-060502willingham,0,7161822.story.

Powell, Justice Lewis F. "Memorandum to Conference of 16 October 1986." *McCleskey v. Kemp* Case File, No. 811-6811. n.d., (last visited 28 June 2012), http://law.wlu.edu/deptimages/powell%20archives/McCleskeyKempBasic.pdf.

Powell, Jr., Justice Lewis "Memorandum to Leslie from Justice Lewis F. Powell, Jr. of 16 September 1986, *McCleskey v. Kemp* Case File, No. 811-6811, Basic File." *Justice Lewis F. Powell Jr. Archives, Washington and Lee University, Lexington, VA.* n.d., (last visited 28 June 2012), http://law.wlu.edu/deptimages/powell%20archives/McCleskeyKempBasic.pdf.

Powell, Jr., Justice Lewis. "Note from Justice Lewis F. Powell, Jr. to Chief Justice William Rehnquist of 31 March 1987, *McCleskey v. Kemp* Case File, No. 811-6811, Basic File." *Justice Lewis F. Powell Jr. Archives, Washington and Lee University, Lexington, VA.* n.d., (last visited 28 June 2012). <http://law.wlu.edu/deptimages/powell%20archives/McCleskeyKempBasic.pdf>.

Prejean, Helen. *The Death of Innocents: An Eyewitness Account of Wrongful Executions.* London: Canterbury Press Norwich, 2006.

Prejean, Helen. *Dead Man Walking: An Eyewitness Account of the Death Penalty in the United States.* New York: Random House, 1993.

Prettyman, Jr., Barrett. *Death and the Supreme Court.* New York: Harcourt, Brace & World, Inc., 1961.

Prial, Dunstan. "UN Receives Anti-Execution Petition." *AP Online*, 18 December 2000, 2000 Westlaw 30834462.

Protess, David. "Two Volunteers for Execution, Two Governors Who Would Not Let Them Die." *Huffington Post* 28 November 2011, http://www.huffingtonpost.com/david-protess/kitzhaber-death-penalty-moratorium-oregon_b_1113616.html.

Pryor, Judge Joel J. "Order by Judge Joel J. Pryor, Chief Judge Superior Court of Atlanta, GA Judicial Circuit." 25 June 1987.

Pusey, Allen. "Truman Escapes Assassination." *ABA Journal* November 2012: 72.

Radelet, Michael L. "Post-*Furman* Botched Executions." *LIFElines* 1991: 7.

Radelet, Michael L. "The Role of the Innocence Argument in Contemporary Death Penalty Debates." *Texas Tech Law Review* 41 (2008): 199–220.

Radelet, Michael L. and Hugo Adam Bedau. "The Execution of the Innocent." In *America's Experiment with Capital Punishment: Reflections of the Past, Present and Future of the Ultimate Penal Sanction*. James R. Acker et al. eds. Durham, NC: Carolina Academic, 2003.

Radelet, Michael L. and Hugo Adam Bedau. "Miscarriages of Justice in Potentially Capital Cases." *Stanford Law Review* 40 (1987): 21–173.

Radelet, Michael L. and Glenn L. Pierce. "The Role of Victim's Race and Geography on Death Sentencing." In *From Lynch Mobs to the Killing State*. Charles J. Ogletree and Austin Sarat eds. New York: New York University Press, 2006.

Radelet, Michael L., Hugo Adam Bedau, and Constance E. Putnam. *In Spite of Innocence*. Boston: Northeastern University, 1992.

Rakoff, Vivian. "The Death Penalty and Youth." *Family Practice News*. 15 May 2005, http://www.familypracticenews.com/index.php?id=2934&type=98&tx_ ttnews[tt_news]=43084&cHash=da03e20e36.

Ramo, Rene. "Ex-convict Works to Rebuild Life after Spending Years on Death Row." *Denver Post* 22 May 1998: A-32.

Ramsland, Katherine. "Gary Gilmore." TruTV Crime Library. n.d., (last visited 25 July 2014), http://www.trutv.com/library/crime/notorious_murders/mass/ gilmore/index_1.html.

Rankin, Bill, et al. "A Matter of Life or Death." *Atlanta Journal-Constitution* 22–25 September 2007, http://www.ajc.com/metro/content/metro/stories/ deathpenalty/dayone/dpdayone1.html.

Ratcliffe, R.G. "Ex-governor Urges Death Penalty Review." *Houston Chronicle* 18 October 2009, http://www.chron.com/disp/story.mpl/metropolitan/6673921.html.

"Recapping the Times' Election Endorsements." *Los Angeles Times* 4 November 2012, http://www.latimes.com/news/opinion/endorsements/la-ed-end-recap- 20121104,0,5024503.story.

Redlich, Norman. "Fighting the Death Penalty: A Thirty-Five Year Perspective." *Albany Law Review* 54 (1989–1990): 617–624.

Redlich, Norman. "'Out Damned Spot; Out, I Say.' The Persistence of Race in American Law." *Vermont Law Review* 25 (2001): 475–522.

Redmon, Jeremy and Craig Schneider. "Georgians React to Judge's Decision to Halt Parts of Anti-illegal Immigration Law." *Atlanta Journal-Constitution* 28 June 2011, http://www.ajc.com/news/georgia-politics-elections/georgians-react- to-judges-991342.html.

Redmon, Jeremy. "Georgia Lawmakers Pass Illegal Immigration Crackdown." *Atlanta Journal-Constitution* 14 April 2011, http://www.ajc.com/news/ georgia-lawmakers-pass-illegal-909988.html.

Reid, T.R. "Many Europeans See Bush as Executioner Extraordinaire." *Washington Post* 17 December 2000: A36.

"Report of the Circuit Attorney on the Murder of Quintin Moss and Conviction of Larry Griffin." *Death Penalty Information Center*. 12 July 2007, http://www. deathpenaltyinfo.org/finalreport_execsum.pdf.

Reske, Henry J. "Behind the Scenes." *ABA Journal* August 1993: 28.

Robertson, Gary. "Veto Override Scuttles N.C. Racial Justice Act." *Charlotte Post* 3 July 2012, http://www.thecharlottepost.com/index.php?src=news&srctype=de tail&category=News&refno=4765.

Robinson, Bill. "Robbery Victim: McCleskey Was 'Guilty as Sin.'" *Atlanta Journal* 25 September 1991: A6.

Robinson, Dr. Matthew. "The Death Penalty in North Carolina." n.d., (last visited 1 March 2011), http://pscj.appstate.edu/ncdeathpenalty/.

Robinson, Paul H. and John M. Darley. "The Utility of Desert." *Northwestern University Law Review* 91 (1997): 453–499.

Rockefeller, Winthrop. "Executive Clemency and the Death Penalty." *Catholic University Law Review* 21 (1971): 94–102.

Rogers, Alan. "'Success—at Long Last': The Abolition of the Death Penalty in Massachusetts, 1928–1984." *Boston College Third World Law Journal* 22 (2002): 281–353.

Rohatyn, Felix. "The Shadow over America." *Newsweek* 29 May 2000: 22.

Roper, Donald M. "Goldberg, Arthur Joseph." *The Oxford Companion to the Supreme Court of the United States*. Kermit L. Hall ed. New York: Oxford University Press, 1992.

Rose, David. "Dead Man Stalking." *The Observer* 21 April 1996: 8.

Rose, David. "The One Empty Seat in Atlanta." *The Observer* 14 July 1996: 3.

Rosen, Jeffrey. *The Supreme Court: The Personalities and Rivalries That Defined America*. New York: Holt Paperbacks, 2007.

Rosenfeld, David. "Ex-member of Clemency Board Alters Death View." *Mesa Tribune* 29 October 2000: A5.

Rusche, Georg and Otto Kircheimer. *Punishment and Social Structure*. New York: Columbia University Press, 1939.

Rush, Benjamin. *An Enquiry into the Effects of Public Punishments upon Criminals and upon Society*. Philadelphia: Joseph James, 1787.

Rush, Benjamin. "On Punishing Murder by Death." *The Selected Writings of Benjamin Rush*. Dragobert D. Runes ed. New York: Philosophical Library, 1947.

Ryan, Jr., Bernard. "Trials of Julius and Ethel Rosenberg and Morton Sobell: 1951." *American Trials of the 20th Century*. Edward W. Knappmann ed. Detroit: Visible Ink, 1995.

Ryan, Cy. "Governor Vetoes Bill Calling for Study of Death Penalty Costs." *Las Vegas Sun News* 9 June 2011, http://www.lasvegassun.com/news/2011/jun/09/governor-vetoes-bill-calling-study-death-penalty-c/.

Sachdeva, Anjali. "French Leader Says U.S. Should Abolish Death Penalty." *Pittsburgh Post-Gazette* 29 August 2000: D6.

Samuels, David. "American Mozart." *Atlantic Monthly*. May 2012: 72–83.

Sanburn, Josh. "Designer of Georgia's Confederate License Plate Doesn't Understand Why People Are Upset." *Time Magazine* 20 February 2014, http://nation.time.com/2014/02/20/confederate-flag-georgia-license-plate/.

Sanburn, Josh. "Report: Executioner Errors Led to Botched Lethal Injection." *Time Magazine* 13 June 2014, <http://time.com/2871154/clayton-lockett-botched-execution-due-to-iv-problems/>.

Sandlin, Erin. Interview with Clara Garrett Jenkins. Kennesaw State University Oral History Project, Cobb NAACP. Civil Rights Series. No. 33, 19 October 2009, (last visited 25 July 2014), http://archon.kennesaw.edu/index.php?p=digitallibrary/digitalcontent&id=36&q=menaboni.

Santos, Fernanda and John Schwartz. "A Prolonged Execution in Arizona Leads to a Temporary Halt." *New York Times* 24 July 2014, <http://www.nytimes.com/2014/07/25/us/a-prolonged-execution-in-arizona-leads-to-a-tempo rary-halt.html>.

Sarat, Austin. "ABA's Proposed Moratorium: Recapturing the Spirit of *Furman*: The American Bar Association and the New Abolitionist Politics." *Law and Contemporary Problems* 61 (1998): 5–28.

Sarat, Austin. "The Cultural Life of Capital Punishment: Responsibility and Representation in Dead Man Walking and Last Dance." In *The Killing State: Capital Punishment in Law, Politics, and Culture*. Austin Sarat ed. New York: Oxford University Press, 1999.

Sarokin, H. Lee. "Does a Botched Execution Constitute Double Jeopardy." *Huffington Post* 5 October 2009, http://www.huffingtonpost.com/judge-h-lee-sarokin/does-a-botched-execution_b_309751.html.

Schabas, William A. *The Abolition of the Death Penalty in International Law.* Cambridge: Cambridge University, 1997.

Schanche, Jr., Don. "Georgia's Electric Chair Has Grim History." Knight Ridder/Tribune News Service. 8 October 2001, http://www.accessmylibrary.com/coms2/summary_0286-6782784_ITM.

Scheidegger, Kent S. "Capital Punishment in 1987: The Puzzle Nears Completion." *Western State University Law Review* 15 (1987): 95–126.

Scheidegger, Kent. "Rebutting the Myths about Race and the Death Penalty." *Ohio State Journal of Criminal Law* 10 (2012): 147–165.

Scherzer, Aaron. "The Abolition of the Death Penalty in New Jersey and Its Impact on Our Nation's 'Evolving Standards of Decency.'" *Michigan Journal of Race and the Law* 15 (2009): 223–263.

Schwartz, Louis. Book Review of *Protest: Sacco-Vanzetti and the Intellectuals* by Felix, David. *University of Pennsylvania Law Review* 114 (1966): 1260–1264.

Schwartzman, Rebecca. "ABA Conference Brings Scrutiny to Ga.'s Capital Procedures." *Fulton County Daily Report* 17 October 2000: 1.

Scott, Thomas Allen. "Marietta." Cities and Counties." 19 December 2011. 8 June 2010, http://www.georgiaencyclopedia.org/nge/Article.jsp?id=h-765.

Scott, Thomas Allen. *Cobb County, Georgia and the Origins of the Suburban South: A Twentieth-Century History.* Marietta: Cobb Landmarks and Historical Society, 2003.

Seabrook, John. "Don't Shoot." *New Yorker* 22 June 2009: 36.

Seelye, Katharine. "Measure to Repeal Death Penalty Fails by a Single Vote in New Hampshire Senate." *New York Times* 17 April 2014, <http://www.nytimes.com/2014/04/18/us/in-new-hampshire-measure-to-repeal-death-penalty-fails-by-a-single-vote.html>.

Sellin, Thorsten. "Executions in the United States." In *Capital Punishment.* Thorsten Sellin ed. New York: J&J Harper, 1969.

Severson, Kim. "North Carolina Repeals Law Allowing Racial Bias Claim in Death Penalty Challenges." *New York Times* 5 June 2013, http://www.nytimes.com/2013/06/06/us/racial-justice-act-repealed-in-north-carolina.html.

Shannon, Brad. "GOP's Dunn Concedes to Bob Ferguson in AG Race." *Olympian* 8 November 2012, http://www.theolympian.com/2012/11/08/2312527/gops-dunn-concedes-to-bob-ferguson.html.

Shapiro, Bruce. "Dead Reckoning: A World Effort to Force an End to the U.S. Death Penalty Is Gaining Strength." *Nation* 6 August 2011: 14–18.

Shechter, Patricia A. "Unsettled Business: Ida B. Wells against Lynching, or How Anti-lynching Got Its Gender." In *Under Sentence of Death: Lynching in the South.* W. Fitzhugh Brundage ed. Chapel Hill & London: University of North Carolina Press, 1997.

Shuster, Fred. "Musicians Join Voices against Death Penalty." *Daily News of Los Angeles* 25 March 1998: L5.

Sickinger, Ted. "Coalition Opposes Executions." *Kansas City Star* 14 February 2000: B1.

Simon, Jim and Jack Broom. "Utter Quitting Supreme Court—Justice Says He Can't Be Party to State's Capital Punishment." *Seattle Times* 29 March 1995: A1.

Simon, Stephanie. "Benetton Sued over Death Row Visits." *Los Angeles Times* 24 February 2000: A5.

Simpson, Sandra L. "Everyone Else Is Doing It, Why Can't We? A New Look at the Use of Statistical Data in Death Penalty Cases." *Journal of Gender, Race & Justice* 12 (Spring 2009): 509–543.

Socolovsly, Jerome. "Germany Opposes U.S. Death Penalty." *AP Online* 13 November 2000, 2000 WL 29040420.

Soteropoulos, Jacqueline. "Ex-state Justice: Innocent Executed." *Tampa Tribune* (Florida) 12 February 2000: 1.

Spangler, Anthony. "Judge Expresses Concerns about Fairness of Death Penalty." *Fort Worth Star-Telegram* 24 July 2001: 4.

Staletovich, Jerry. "Justice Raising Voice to Bury Death Penalty." *Palm Beach Post* (Florida) 19 January 1998: 1A.

Stann, Kap. *Moon Handbooks: Georgia*. Emeryville: Avalon Travel, 2008.

"State by State Database." *Death Penalty Information Center* 8 June 2012, http://www.deathpenaltyinfo.org/state_by_state.

"State-by State Strategy Propelled Atkins to Success, Ellis Says." *University of Virginia School of Law* 3 March 2005, (last visited 25 June 2013), http://www.law.virginia.edu/html/news/2005_spr/atkins.htm.

"Statement from Governor Pat Quinn." *Illinois Government New Network* 9 March 2011, http://www.illinois.gov/PressReleases/ShowPressRelease.cfm?SubjectID=2&RecNum=9265.

Steiker, Carol S. and Jordan M. Steiker. "Annex B—Report to the ALI concerning Capital Punishment." *Report of the Council to the Membership of the American Law Institute on the Matter of the Death Penalty*. American Law Institute, April 15, 2009, (last visited 11 July 2013), http://www.ali.org/doc/capital%20punishment_web.pdf.

Steiker, Carol S. and Jordan M. Steiker. "The Seduction of Innocence: The Attraction and Limitations of the Focus on Innocence in Capital Punishment Law and Advocacy." *Journal of Criminal Law and Criminology* 95 (2005): 594–624.

Steiker, Carol S. and Jordan M. Steiker. "Sober Second Thoughts: Reflections on Two Decades of Constitutional Regulation of Capital Punishment." *Harvard Law Review* 109 (December 1995): 355–438.

Stein, Rob. "Ohio Executes Inmate Using Single Drug." *Washington Post* 10 March 2011, http://www.washingtonpost.com/wp-dyn/content/article/2011/03/10/AR2011031000737.html?hpid=topnews.

Stevens, John Paul. *Five Chiefs*. New York: Little, Brown and Company, 2011.

Stevens, John Paul. "On the Death Sentence." *New York Review of Books* 23 December 2010.

Stevens, John Paul. *Six Amendments: How and Why We Should Change the Constitution*. New York: Little, Brown and Company, 2014.

Stewart, Barbara. "Life and Death. It's a Living." *New York Times* 5 May 1996: NJ-4.

Stout, David G. "The Lawyers of Death Row." *New York Times Magazine* 14 February 1988, http://www.nytimes.com/1988/02/14/magazine/the-lawyers-of-death-row.html?src=pm.

Stratford, Michael. "Ark. Governor Reverses Course on Death Penalty." *San Francisco Chronicle* 21 January 2013, http://www.sfgate.com/default/article/Ark-governor-reverses-course-on-death-penalty-4199466.php.

Streib, Victor. "Death Penalty for Female Offenders." *University of Cincinnati Law Review* 58 (1990): 845–880.

Stroup, Robert H. "The Political, Legal and Social Context of the McCleskey Habeas Litigation." *Columbia Human Rights Law Review* 39 (2007): 74–96.

Stroup, Robert. Telephone Interview. 31 July 2012.

Strout, George M. *A Sketch of the Laws Relating to Slavery in the Several States of the United States of America*. Philadelphia: Henry Longstreth, 1856.

"Study: White and Black Children Biased toward Lighter Skin." *CNN U.S.* 13 May 2010, http://articles.cnn.com/2010-05-13/us/doll.study_1_black-children-pilot-study-white-doll?_s=PM:US.

Summers, Margaret. "The Death Penalty Gender Gap." *Womensenews.org* 21 April 2011, http://www.womensenews.org/story/crime-policylegislation/110424/the-death-penalty-gender-gap.

Sunby, Scott E. "The Loss of Constitutional Faith: *McCleskey v. Kemp* and the Dark Side of Procedure." *Ohio State Journal of Criminal Law* 10 (2012): 5–35.

Swofford, Stan. "State Law Could Affect McCarver Case." *News and Record* 7 August 2001: B3.

Tabak, Ronald J. "Capital Punishment." *The State of Criminal Justice 2012*. American Bar Association Criminal Justice Section, June 2012.

Tabak, Ronald J. "The Continuing Role of Race in Capital Cases, notwithstanding President Obama's Election." *Northern Kentucky Law Review* 37 (2010): 243–271.

Tabak, Ronald J. "Executing People with Mental Disabilities: How We Can Mitigate an Aggravating Situation." *Saint Louis University Public Law Review* 25 (2006): 283–306.

Tabak, Ronald J. "Finality without Fairness: Why We Are Moving towards Moratoria on Executions, and the Potential Abolition of Capital Punishment." *University of Connecticut Law Review* 33 (2001): 733–763.

Tang, Terry. "We Delude Ourselves about Barbarity of Death Penalty." *Seattle Times* 5 April 1995: B4.

Tarschys, Daniel. "Preface." *The Death Penalty: Abolition in Europe*. Council of Europe. Strasbourg: Council of Europe, 1999.

Taslitz, Andrew E. and Carol Steiker. "Introduction to the Symposium: The Jena Six, the Prosecutorial Conscience and the Dead Hand of History." *Harvard Civil Right—Civil Liberties Law Review* 44 (2009): 275–295.

Taylor, Marisa. "Study: Racial Disparities Taint Military's Use of Death Penalty." *The Kansas City Star* 28 August 2011, http://www.kansascity.com/2011/08/28/3104989/study-racial-disparities-taint.html.

Taylor, Jr., Stuart. "Glimpses of the Least Pretentious of Men." *Legal Times* 8 February 1993, http://stuarttaylorjr.com/content/glimpses-least-pretentious-men/.

Taylor Jr., Stuart. "The Politics of Hanging Judges." *Legal Times* 30 October 1995: 25.

Taylor, Stuart. "We Will Kill You Anyway." *The American Lawyer* December 1990, http://stuarttaylorjr.com/content/we-will-kill-you-anyway.

Tempesta, Anthony. Book Review. *The Lindbergh Case* by Fisher, Jim. *Military Law Review* 147 (1995): 293–296.

Temple, Sarah Blackwell Gober. *The First Hundred Years: A Short History of Cobb County, in Georgia*. Marietta: Cobb Landmarks and Historical Society, 1997.

Thomas, Jr., Robert M. "Fred Speaker, 66, a Crusader against Capital Punishment." *New York Times* 16 September 1996: B9.

Thomas, Evan. "Life of O'Reilly." *Newsweek* 12 February 2001: 29.

Thomas-Lester, Avis. "A Senate Apology for History on Lynching." *Washington Post* 14 June 2005, <http://www.washingtonpost.com/wp-dyn/content/article/2005/06/13/AR2005061301720.html>.

Thurston III, George L. "Propers Say Spenkelink Was Denied His Rights before Being Executed." *Washington Post* 21 September 1979: sec. A.

Timberg, Craig. "A Death Penalty Change of Heart; Va. Lawmakers to Weigh Legislation to Stop, Stall or Study the System." *Washington Post* 28 January 2001: C1.

Timms, Ed. "Terrell Unit Is Renamed." *Dallas Morning News* 21 July 2001: 32A.

Tirschwell, Eric A. and Theodore Hertzberg. "Politics and Prosecution: A Historical Perspective on Shifting Federal Standards for Pursuing the Death Penalty in Non-Death Penalty States." *University of Pennsylvania Journal of Constitutional Law* 12 (2009): 57–98.

Tomaso, Bruce and Christy Hoppe. "Tucker Execution Case Expected to Have a Lasting Legacy." *Dallas Morning News* 5 February 1998: 12A.

Toobin, Jeffrey. *The Nine: Inside the Secret World of the Supreme Court*. New York: First Anchor, 2008.

Totenberg, Nina. "Justice Stevens: An Open Mind on a Changed Court." *NPR*. 4 October 2010. http://www.npr.org/templates/story/story.php?storyId=130198344.

Trial Transcript, *Georgia v. Warren McCleskey*, No. A-40553 (Superior Court of Fulton County, GA October 9, 1978).

Tribune News Services. "Rome Honors Ryan's Execution Moratorium." *Chicago Tribune* 2 February 2000: 12.

Trindal, Elizabeth Steger. *Mary Surratt: An American Tragedy*. Gretna, LA: Pelican Publishing, 1996.

Trombley, Stephen. *The Execution Protocol: Inside America's Capital Punishment Industry.* New York: Crown, 1992.

Tucker, John C. *May God Have Mercy: A True Story of Crime and Punishment.* New York: W.W. Norton and Company, 1997.

Turner, Karl. "Judge Orders Killer's Death, Decries Death Penalty." *Plain Dealer* (Cleveland) 17 November 2000: 1A.

Tysver, Robynn. "Execution Suspension Approved; Senators Hand Johanns Life-and-Death Decision." *Omaha World-Herald* 20 May 1999: 1.

Tysver, Robynn. "Death Penalty Report Author Fires Back." *Omaha World-Herald* 8 August 2001: 1.

United Press International. "Charlie Brooks: First Execution by Injection." *Baltimore Afro-American* 14 December 1982: 6.

U.S. General Accounting Office. *Death Penalty Sentencing: Research Indicates Pattern of Racial Disparities.* Washington, DC: February 1990.

Udomoa, Ebong. "Connecticut Abolishes Death Penalty." *Chicago Tribune* 25 April 2012, http://www.chicagotribune.com/news/sns-rt-us-usa -deathpenalty-connecticutbre83o1cm-20120425,0,5387703.story.

Utter, Robert F. "Washington State Must Abandon the Death Penalty." *Seattle Times.* 11 March 2009, http://seattletimes.com/html/opinion/2008843232_ opinb12utter.htm.

Van Deerlin, Lionel. "History Casts Doubts on Tribunals." *San Diego Union-Tribune* 21 Nov. 2001: B7.

Van Deerlin, Lionel. "History Casts Doubts on Tribunals." *Union-Tribune* 2001 November 21: B7.

Van Gelder, Lawrence. "Footlights." *New York Times* 12 March 1998: E1.

Verhovek, Sam Howe. "Karla Tucker Is Now Gone, but Several Debates Linger." *New York Times* 5 February 1998, http://www.nytimes.com/1998/02/05/us/ karla-tucker-is-now-gone-but-several-debates-linger.html.

Verniero, Peter G. "Appealed to Death." *New York Times* 14 January 2007, http://www. nytimes.com/2007/01/14/opinion/nyregionopinions/14NJverniero.html.

Vila, Bryan and Cynthia Morris (eds.). *Capital Punishment in the United States: A Documentary History.* Westport, CT: Greenwood Publishing, 1997.

"Violence on Rise Despite Dip in Crime Rate." *Ottawa Sun* 20 July 2001: 7.

Vogel, Ed. "Assembly Committee Rejects Two-Year Suspension of Death Penalty." *Las Vegas Review-Journal* 17 May 2001: 1A.

Von Drehle, David. *Among the Lowest of the Dead.* New York: Times Books, 1995.

Von Drehle, David. "Retired Justice Changes Stand on Death Penalty." *Washington Post* 10 June 1994: A1.

Waldron, Thomas W. "Rawlings, Schmoke Call for a Moratorium on State Executions; Noting 'Uncertainties,' They Appeal to Glendening." *Baltimore Sun* 18 May 2000: 2B.

Walker, Peter N. *Punishment: An Illustrated History.* New York: ARCO Publishing Co., 1973.

Wallsten, Peter. "Chief Justice Criticizes Death Penalty." *Stuart News/Port St. Lucie News* (Florida) 2 January 1998: A1.

Walt, Kathy. "Death Penalty Support Plunges to 30-Year Low." *Houston Chronicle* 15 March 1998: A1.

Warchol, Glen. "Hi-Fi Torture Victim Dies 28 Years Later." *Salt Lake Tribune* 16 July 2002, http://www.freerepublic.com/focus/f-news/716825/posts.

Warden, Rob. "Reflections on Capital Punishment." *Northwestern Journal of Law and Social Policy* 4 (2009): 329–359.

Warden, Rob. "Uncertainty Principle Is Wrong Theory for the Death Penalty." *Chicago Sun-Times* 21 January 2006: Editorials 18.

Watkins, Tom. "Religious Leaders Seek Clemency for Georgia Man on Death Row." *CNN* 5 May 2011, http://articles.cnn.com/2011-05-05/justice/georgia. execution_1_religious-leaders-innocence-claim-martina-correia.

Weinberg, Arthur (ed.). *Attorney for the Damned: Clarence Darrow in the Courtroom.* Chicago: Univeristy of Chicago Press, 1989.

Weinstein, Henry, "Death Penalty Moratorium Attracting Unlikely Adherents." *Los Angeles Times* 17 October 2000: A5.

Weinstein, Henry. "Nebraska Governor Vetoes Moratorium on Executions Legislation." *Los Angeles Times* 27 May 1999: A4.

Weinstein, Henry. "Support for Death Penalty Drops Sharply in State." *Los Angeles Times* 2 November 2000: A1.

Weir, Ed. "A Time to Weep." *Hospitality* January 1992.

Weisberg, Jacob. "This Is Your Death." *New Republic* 1 July 1991: 23–27.

Wellstone, Senator Paul. Letter to Wayne Snow Jr., Chairman of State Board of Pardons and Paroles. 27 June 1991.

Welsh-Huggins, Andrew. "Ohio Executes Inmate with New Death Penalty Drug." *Huffington Post* 10 March 2011, http://www.huffingtonpost.com/huff-wires/20110310/us-ohio-execution/.

Wexley, John. *The Judgment of Julius and Ethel Rosenberg.* New York: Balantine Books, 1997.

White, Gayle. "Jailer Testifies He Can't Recall Who Sought Informant in Cell Adjacent to McCleskey." *Atlanta Constitution* 11 August 1987: A34.

White, Josh. "Sniper Trial Took Toll on Attorneys, Muhammed's Lawyers Shoulder Own Stress, Depression and Guilt." *Washington Post* 21 March 2004: C01.

Whitman, James Q. *Harsh Justice: Criminal Punishment and the Widening Divide between America and Europe.* New York: Oxford University Press, 2003.

Wice, Brian. "Capital Punishment, Texas Style." *Texas Bar Journal* April 1992: 386–389.

Will, George F. "Innocent on Death Row." *Washington Post* 6 April 2000: A23.

Williams, Carol J. "Death Penalty Costs California $184 Million a Year, Study Says." *Los Angeles Times* 20 June 2011, http://www.latimes.com/news/local/la-me-adv-death-penalty-costs-20110620,0,3505671.story.

Williams, Clint. "Paths Paved in Violence: Consequences of Abuse Evident on Death Row." *Arizona Republic* 21 November 1993: A25.

Williams, Paige. "Witness to a Botched Execution." *New Yorker* 30 April 2014, <http://www.newyorker.com/news/news-desk/witnesses-to-a-botched-execution>.

Wilson, Lawrence. "Declaration of Lawrence Wilson, Former Associate Warden of Custody at Folsom Prison and Former Warden at San Quentin." 14 April 1992.

Windlesham, Lord. *Politics, Punishment, and Populism.* New York: Oxford University Press, 1998.

Wise, Daniel. "Prosecutors Want Death Penalty; Qualms Voiced about Costs, Time, Training of Lawyers." *New York Law Journal* March 1995: 1.

Witham, Larry. "Faiths Vary Widely on Execution." *Washington Times* 7 February 1998: B8.

Witt, Howard. "Texas Urged to Probe Claims of Wrongful Executions." *Chicago Tribune* 7 July 2006: 6.

Wolfgang, M.E. "Racial Discrimination in the Death Sentence for Rape." *Executions in America.* W. Bowers ed. New York: Lexington Books, 1974.

Wolfgang, Marvin E. "Introduction." *Of Crimes and Punishments.* Cesare marchese di Beccaria. Marsilio Publishers, 1996.

Wolfgang, Marvin E. and Marc Riedel. "Race, Judicial Discretion and the Death Penalty." *American Academy of Political and Social Sceince* 407 (1973): 119–133.

Woodward, Bob and Scott Armstrong. *The Brethren: Inside the Supreme Court.* New York: Simon & Schuster, 1979.

Woodworth, George. Email Interview. 25 June 2013.

Wright, George C. *Racial Violence in Kentucky 1865–1940: Lynchings, Mob Rule and "Legal Lynchings."* Baton Rouge: Louisiana State University, 1990.

Zangrando, Robert L. *The NAACP Crusade against Lynching, 1909–1950.* Philadelphia: Temple University Press, 1980.

Zimring, Franklin. *The Contradictions of American Capital Punishment.*
New York: Oxford University Press, 2003.
Zimring, Franklin F. "Pulling the Plug on Capital Punishment." *National Law Journal*
7 December 2009, http://www.deathpenaltyinfo.org/legal-scholar-
calls-withdrawal-model-penal-code-quiet-blockbuster.
Zimring, Franklin E. and Gordon Hawkins. *Capital Punishment and the American
Agenda.* Cambridge: Cambridge University, 1989.
Zorn, Eric. "Prosecutors Deaf to Outcry against Death Penalty." *Chicago Tribune* 7
March 2000: 1.
Zorn, Robert. *Cemetery John: The Undiscovered Mastermind behind the Lindbergh
Kidnapping.* New York: The Overlook Press, 2012.

CASES CITED

Eddings v. Oklahoma, 455 U.S. 104 (1982), 175, 344nn25–26
Enis, People v., No. 86636, 2000 WL 1728576 (Ill. Nov. 22, 2000), 354n43
Enmund v. Florida, 458 U.S. 782 (1982), 262, 360n2
Evans v. Muncy, 498 U.S. 927 (1990), 344nn29, 31, 345n32
Feaster, State v., 757 A.2d 266, 295–296 (N.J. 2000), 354n45
Fierro v. Gomez, 77 F.3d 301 (9th Cir. 1996), 203, 349n30
Fierro v. Gomez, 865 F. Supp. 1387 (N.D. Cal. 1994), 349n30
Fowler v. North Carolina, 428 U.S. 904 (1976), 96, 332n23
Frank v. Magnum, 237 U.S. 309 (1915), 37, 318n16
Frey v. Fulcomer, 974 F.2d 348 (3d Cir. 1992), 358n3
Furman v. Georgia, 408 U.S. 238 (1972), 86–90, 87f, 91, 93, 94, 96, 97–98, 101, 102,
    105, 107, 111, 116, 119, 133, 135, 136, 141, 149, 152, 159, 161, 162, 173, 175,
    199, 208, 211, 216, 217, 218, 219, 226, 228, 230, 231, 232, 237, 240, 256, 257,
    261–62, 269, 272, 273, 274, 277, 279, 281, 284, 285, 288, 289, 292, 293, 295,
    296, 312, 313, 314, 324nn8, 16, 328n58, 331nn16–18, 20–21, 340nn44, 4, 344n20,
    349n49
Georgia v. McCollum, 505 U.S. 42 (1992), 145, 339n21
Georgia v. Warren McCleskey, Superior Court of Fulton County, GA Commencing 9
    Oct. 1978, Crim. Action No. A-40553, 319n19, 320nn22, 24–25, 29–30, 32, 35,
    320nn22, 24–25, 29–30, 32–33, 35, 321nn1–10, 14–15, 22, 25, 322nn2, 4–5, 9–10,
    20, 323n32
Giglio v. United States, 405 U.S. 150 (1972), 33–34, 322nn8, 11
Glass v. Louisiana, 471 U.S. 1080 (1985), 345n3, 347n50
Glossip v. Gross, 135 S. Ct. 2726 (2015), ix
Godfrey v. Georgia, 446 U.S. 420 (1980), 106, 332n38, 333n7
Gomez v. Fierro, 519 U.S. 918 (1996), 349n30
Gomez v. United States District Court, 503 U.S. 653 (1992), 202, 348n28
Graham v. Collins, 506 U.S. 461 (1993), 346n44
Grannis, State v., 900 P.2d 1 (Ariz. 1995), 352n36
Gregg v. Georgia, 428 U.S. 153 (1976), 97–102, 101f, 105–6, 107, 111, 141, 154, 159,
    161, 162, 171, 173, 190, 193, 203, 216, 217, 218, 219, 224, 226, 228, 231,
    241, 251, 252, 256, 257, 262, 274, 286, 288, 292, 293, 295, 307, 332nn30, 33,
    344nn22–23
Gregg v. State, 210 S.E.2d 659 (Ga. 1974), 332n26
Gregg v. State, 233 Ga. 117 (1974), 332nn29, 34
Haley v. Ohio, 332 U.S. 596 (1948), 67, 328nn57–58
Hall v. Florida, 134 S. Ct. 1986 (2014), 265, 361n14
Hardwick v. Crosby, 320 F.3d 1127 (11th Cir. 2003), 343n6
Harris v. Nelson, 394 U.S. 286 (1969), 37, 323n28
Herrera v. Collins, 506 U.S. 390 (1993), 228, 352n16
Hill v. Humphrey, 662 F.2d 1335 (11th Cir. 2011), 361n13
Holland v. Florida, 130 S. Ct. 2549 (2010), 270, 362n30
House v. Bell, 547 U.S. 518 (2006), 270, 362n34
In re Kemmler, 136 U.S. 436 (1890), 180, 345nn4–5, 10
Jackson v. Denno, 309 F.2d 573 (2d Cir. 1962), 331n17
Johnson v. California, 545 U.S. 162 (2005), 362n36
Jones v. Chappell, No. CV 09-02158, 2014 WL 3567365 (C.D. Calif. 16 July 2014), 273,
    362n46, 365n47
Jones v. State, 701 So. 2d 76 (Fla. 1997), 353n34
Jurek v. Texas, 428 U.S. 262 (1976), 97, 98, 99, 102, 204, 332n30, 366n8
Kansas v. Marsh, 548 U.S. 163 (2006), 246, 270, 357nn35–37, 362n32
Kemmler, In re, 136 U.S. 436 (1890), 180, 345nn4–5, 10
Kennedy v. Louisiana, 554 U.S. 407 (2008), 268, 269, 361nn23, 25–26
Knight v. Florida, 528 U.S. 990 (1999), 263, 360n6, 361n8
Korematsu v. United States, 323 U.S. 214 (1944), 63, 327n40
Lackey v. Texas, 514 U.S. 1045 (1995), 360n6

LaValle, People v., 817 N.E.2d 341 (N.Y. 2004), 280–81, 364n22
Lewis v. Jeffers, 497 U.S. 764 (1990), 332n40
Lockett v. Ohio, 438 U.S. 586 (1978), 106, 171, 230, 332n38, 333n6, 343n5
Louisiana ex rel. Francis v. Resweber, 329 U.S. 459 (1947), 182, 345n14
McCleskey v. Bowers, 501 U.S. 1281 (1991), 346nn40, 43
McCleskey v. Kemp, 481 U.S. 279 (1987), xiii–xv, 138, 149–50, 151–65, 179, 188,
    192–93, 210, 215–16, 217, 219, 222, 223, 225–26, 230, 231, 236, 237, 239, 241,
    242, 250–51, 261–64, 267, 270, 272, 274, 275, 276, 279, 281, 282, 283, 286, 288,
    289–90, 292, 293, 295, 296, 297, 298–301, 306, 307, 311, 312, 313, 314, 315,
    317n2, 321n17, 336n2, 337n13, 339n23, 341nn10–18, 342nn19–21, 23–26, 28,
    30–32, 36, 352n1, 362n1, 366n16
McCleskey v. Kemp, 753 F.2d 877 (11th Cir. 1985), 322n12, 340n38–39
McCleskey v. State (Superior Court of Butts County, Georgia 16 Feb. 1981), 320n38
McCleskey v. State, 263 S.E.2d 146 (Ga. 1980), 320nn26, 28, 322nn1, 7
McCleskey v. Zant, 496 U.S. 904 (1990), 323n25
McCleskey v. Zant, 499 U.S. 467 (1991), 36–40, 145, 179, 184, 188, 192-93, 215, 217,
    218, 240, 250, 256, 270, 306, 307, 322nn3, 13, 19, 323nn23, 29–31, 33–34, 351n9
McCleskey v. Zant, 580 F. Supp. 338 (N.D. Ga. 1984), 321nn13–14, 16–17, 19, 21, 322n13,
    339n20, 340nn35, 37
McCleskey v. Zant, 753 F.2d 877 (11th Cir. 1985), 322n15
McCleskey v. Zant, 890 F.2d 342 (11th Cir. 1989), 322n18
McGautha v. California, 398 U.S. 935 (1970), 84–85, 331n5
McGautha v. California, 402 U.S. 183 (1971), 84–85, 287, 331n6
Maples v. Thomas, 132 S. Ct. 912 (2012), 270, 362nn28–29
Marshall, State v., 613 A.2d 1059 (N.J. 1992), 364n24
Martinez v. Ryan, 132 S. Ct. 1309 (2012), 270, 362n31
Massey v. State, 195 S.E.2d 28 (Ga. 1972), 332n18
Massiah v. United States, 377 U.S. 201 (1964), 322n17, 323n31
Mata, State v., 275 Neb. 1 (2008), 347n67
Maxwell v. Bishop, 398 F.2d 138 (8th Cir. 1968), vacated 398 U.S. 262 (1970), 84, 141,
    338n7
Medellin v. Texas, 552 U.S. 491 (2008), 361n7
Miller-El v. Dretke, 545 U.S. 231 (2005), 270, 362n35
Miller v. Alabama, 132 S. Ct. 2455 (2012), 362n38
Minister of Justice v. Burns, No. 26129, 2001 S.C.C. 7, 2001 Can. Sup. Ct. LEXIS 9
    (Canada, 15 Feb. 2001), 255, 360n41
Miranda v. Arizona, 384 U.S. 436 (1966), 71, 93
Morgan v. Illinois, 504 U.S. 719 (1992), 172, 344n15
Nichols v. Heidle, 725 F.3d 516 (6th Cir. 2013), 362n42
Nichols v. Heidle, No. 06-6495, 2013 WL 3821537 (6th Cir. 26 July 2013), 362n42
Payne v. Tennessee, 501 U.S. 808 (1991), 312, 368n28
Penry v. Lynaugh, 492 U.S. 302 (1989), 264, 361n10
People v. See name of opposing party
Powell v. Alabama, 287 U.S. 45 (1932), 338n30
Powell v. Texas, 392 U.S. 514 (1968), 344n20
Proffitt v. Florida, 428 U.S. 242 (1976), 97, 98, 99, 102, 332n30
Quinn, State v., 623 P.2d 630 (Or. 1981), 333n22
Reece v. Georgia, 350 U.S. 85 (1955), 338n2
Ring v. Arizona, 536 U.S. 584 (2002), 314, 369n37
Roberts v. Louisiana, 428 U.S. 325 (1976), 97, 99–102, 332n35
Roe v. Wade, 410 U.S. 113 (1973), 94, 332n9
Romero v. Lynaugh, 884 F.2d 871 (5th Cir. 1989), 358n3
Rompilla v. Beard, 545 U.S. 374 (2005), 362n27
Roper v. Simmons, 543 U.S. 551 (2005), 265–66, 267, 357n25, 361nn16–18
Rose v. Lundy, 455 U.S. 509 (1982), 217, 351n9

Rudolph v. Alabama, 375 U.S. 889 (1963), 73–79, 80, 262, 330nn37, 40, 360n1
Santiago, State v., 122 A. 3d 1 (Conn. 2015), ix
Sawyer v. Whitley, 505 U.S. 333 (1992), 228, 352n15
Simmons v. South Carolina, 512 U.S. 154 (1994), 254, 359n30
Singleton v. Norris, 108 F.3d 872 (8th Cir. 1997), 234, 354nn46–47
Skinner v. Switzer, 131 S. Ct. 1289 (2011), 270
Smith v. Balkcom, 671 F.2d 858 (5th Cir. 1982), 338n9
Smith v. State, 581 So. 2d 497 (Ala. Crim. App. 1990), 358n3
Snider v. Cunningham, 375 U.S. 889 (1963), 330n37
Spencer v. Zant, 715 F.2d 1562 (11th Cir. 1983), 340n34
Stanford v. Kentucky, 492 U.S. 361 (1989), 263, 265, 360n5
State v. *See name of opposing party*
Stephens v. Kemp, 464 U.S. 1027 (1983), 154, 341n5
Stephens v. Kemp, 721 F.2d 1300 (11th Cir. 1983), 341n6
Stephens v. Kemp, 722 F.2d 627 (11th Cir. 1983), 341n6
Strickland v. Washington, 466 U.S. 668 (1984), 269, 362n27
Stripling v. State, 711 S.E.2d 685 (Ga. 2011), 361n13
Suffolk District v. Watson, 411 N.E.2d 1274 (Mass. 1980), 333n23
Taylor, People v., 878 N.E.2d 969 (N.Y. 2007), 363n20
Teague v. Lane, 489 U.S. 288 (1989), 217, 351nn9–10
Thompson v. Oklahoma, 487 U.S. 815 (1988), 263, 360n4
Timmendequas, State v., No. A-109, 2001 N.J. LEXIS 24 (N.J. 1 Feb. 2001), 233–34, 354n45
T. Makwanyane and M Mchunu, State v., No. CCT/3/94 (Constitutional Court of the Republic of South Africa 6 June 1995), 255, 359n32
Trop v. Dulles, 356 U.S. 86 (1958), 76, 81, 329n35, 332n29
Tucker v. Louisiana, 135 S. Ct. 1801 (2016), ix
United States ex rel. Jackson v. Denno, 309 F.2d 573 (2d Cir. 1962), 331n17
Valle v. Florida, 132 S. Ct. 1 (2011), 361n8
Wainwright v. Sykes, 433 U.S. 72 (1977), 217, 351nn9–10
Wiggins v. Smith, 539 U.S. 510 (2003), 269, 362n27
Wiles v. Bagley, 561 F.3d 636 (6th Cir. 2009), 362n41
Wilkerson v. Utah, 99 U.S. 130 (1879), 76, 200, 329n34, 348nn5, 17
Williams v. Taylor, 529 U.S. 362 (2000), 171, 343n6
Wilson, State v., 685 So. 2d 1063 (La. 1996), 267, 361n22
Witherspoon v. Illinois, 391 U.S. 510 (1968), 75, 329n30
Wogenstahl, State v., No. 1995-0042, slip op. at 3 (Ohio, Jan. 25, 2013), 362n43
Woodson v. North Carolina, 428 U.S. 280 (1976), 97, 99–102, 324n11, 332nn35–37

INDEX

executions, 58–59, 62, 63–64, 66,
108–9, 110, 176–77, 182–83,
189–91, 194–95, 220
faulty, 65–66
Florida, 194
Georgia use of the, 346n47
how death is caused by the, 183
infamous criminals executed in the,
182
Kentucky, 194
electric chair (Cont'd.)
and McCleskey, 181f, 183–95, 191f,
346nn22, 35, 38, 43–44, 47, 347n70
New York, 179–81, 181f, 195
Oklahoma, 194
at Sing Sing, 181f
South Carolina, 194
and Fred Speaker, 329n31
suffering from the, 183, 194
Tennessee, 194
Virginai, 194
women executions, 66
Electrocution. *See* electric chair
Elkey, Viki, 283
Elkins, Michael (execution), 205
Elliott, Robert G., 63–64
Ellis, James W., 264
Emmett Till Act (2008), 122
England abolition of the death penalty, 67
Enlightenment, The, 47, 48, 57
*Enquiry into the Effects of Public
Punishments upon Criminals and
upon Society, An* (Rush), 47
Equal Justice and the Death Penalty (Baldus,
Woodward & Pulaski), 142
Equal Justice Initiative, 311
Equal Protection Clause, 79, 132, 156, 159
See also Fourteenth Amendment
European countries abolition of the death
penalty, 66–67, 108, 255–56
European Court of Human Rights, 263
European Parliament, 256
European Union, 255
Evangelium Vitae (John Paul II), 236
Evans, Michael Wayne (execution), 115
Evans, Offie
deal with police, 32–36, 322n20
jail conversation with McCleskey,
22–23, 40, 184
release from prison, 192
statement to police, 164, 321n12,
322nn13, 20
trial testimony, 25, 32–33, 184
Evans, Wilbert, 176–77, 345n32
Evers, Medgar, 8

evolving standards of decency
and Eighth Amendment, 76, 98, 262,
264, 266, 269, 272
and electric chair, 194
and international law, 263
and juvenile executions, 266
on non-homicide crimes and death
penalty, 78, 267–69
excessive bail, 81, 366n8
exculpatory evidence of innocence, 33
execution
and burning, 193–94, 194, 197–98,
200, 202, 221, 300, 314
Civil War, 54–55
costs, 233, 235, 272, 273–74, 279, 280,
283, 284, 286–87, 289, 291, 315
frequency of, 73, 81–82, 90t, 110, 112,
211, 251
of the insane, 70
military, 46, 49, 54–55, 200, 311–12
mitigation and reform, 169–78,
343nn3, 6, 344nn18, 26, 28, 31,
345nn32–33
for non-homicide crimes, 73–74
private vs. public, 52, 64
public, 182–83, 199, 210, 240, 271
race based laws, 131–38, 337nn13, 15,
19, 26, 338n30
resuming in the 1970s & 1980s,
105–16, 333nn14, 16, 21–22,
334nn26, 30, 33–34
voluntary, 107–8, 110, 115, 218, 219,
285
by year, 90t, 115t, 222t, 288
See also death penalty history;
innocence; intellectual disability
and death penalty; *Specific states*
executioners, 55, 63–64, 190, 204, 205,
210, 211
Executioner's Song, The (Mailer), 107
execution methods
change in, 44
firing squad, 57, 107–8, 182, 200–201,
211, 348n17
guillotine, 71, 108
hanging, 57–58, 132, 182, 197,
198–200, 211
history, 197–98
humanizing, 61
impact on persons involved, 211
lethal injection, 203–10, 347n70,
349nn45, 49, 350nn58, 63
non-U.S., 210–11
twentieth century, 182
See also gas chamber

Exum, James, Jr., 232

Fallin, Mary, 208
Falwell, Jerry, 235
Farmer, Millard, 227
Farrell, Mike, 177, 236
Farwell, Leonard J., 51
FBI (Federal Bureau of Investigation), 140
FDA (Food and Drug Administration), 204, 209
Feamster, Tom, 109
Federal Bureau of Investigation (FBI), 140
Federal Death Penalty Act, 217
Felch, Alpheus, 51
Fifth Amendment, 56–57
Final Statement of Warren McCleskey, The (mini-opera), 236–37
Finch, Abraham, 46
Finland abolition of the death penalty, 67
Finley, Noah (execution), 133
firing squad, 57, 107–8, 182, 200–201, 211, 348n17
Florida
    Commission on Capital Cases, 287
    death row population, 89
    executions, 63, 66, 135, 194, 220–21, 288–89, 355n72
    exonerations, 287
    innocent on death row, 243
    intellectual disability and death penalty in, 257
    lynching, 124, 135, 337n19
    race and the criminal justice system, 150
    reinstatement of death penalty, 94
    Stewart's Supreme Court confirmation and senators from, 342n37
Food and Drug Administration (FDA), 204, 209
Ford, Gerald R., 96, 102
Ford, Timothy K., 160, 340n2
foreign/international law, 360nn37, 43, 6
    and Justice Breyer, 264, 265, 360n6, 361n8
    and Congress, 266
    death penalty, 255–56, 291, 360n43
    execution of foreign nationals, 255, 360n37
    juveniles and the death penalty, 263, 265–66
    and Justice Kennedy, 263–64, 265
    and Justice Marshall, 262
    and Justice Roberts, 266
    and Justice Scalia, 265, 266

and Justice Stevens, 360n6
    and the Supreme Court, 78, 200, 265–66, 360, 360n6
forgery, death penalty for, 49
Forni, Raymond, 255
Forrester, J. Owen
    and Baldus study, 148, 306
    career, 306
    decisions in McCleskey's case, 36
    and McCleskey's habeas corpus, 34
    and Offie Evans statement, 322n13
    stays of execution, 187–88, 306
Fortas, Abe, 82, 84, 93
Foster, Doris Ann, 114
Foster, Emmitt (execution), 351n30
Fourteen Days in May, 163
Fourteenth Amendment
    and Baldus study, 146, 148
    and death penalty for non-homicide crimes, 268–69
    and Eighth Amendment, 76
    equal protection guarantee, 132
    and *Furman v. Georgia*, 87
    and individualized consideration of mitigating factors, 332n38
    and *McCleskey v. Kemp*, 148, 154, 155–56, 159, 161, 261
    and *McGautha v. California*, 85
    Justice Powell on death penalty and the, 158
    purpose, 81
    See also due process
Fowler, Jesse T., 96
Fraim, William, 55
France, 47, 227, 255
Francis, Willie, 65, 182
Frankfurter, Felix, 62, 66, 67, 328n58
Frank, Leo, 6f
    and anti-Jewish sentiment, 119, 124, 223
    burial, 5–6
    case and habeas corpus, 7, 37
    crime, 5, 15
    historical marker, 308
    and Ku Klux Klan, 7, 308, 310
    lynching, x, 5–7, 95, 127, 135, 318nn14, 16
    Marietta citizens current feelings regarding, 308, 367n11
    and Thomas E. Watson, 7, 308–9, 308f
Franklin, Benjamin, 47
Franks, Bobby, 62
Freeman, Jeannace June (execution), 75, 329n26
French Revolution, 47

and David Duke, 337n13
and Leo Frank, 7, 308, 310
lingering presence of, 299
and McCleskey's execution, 191, 191f
parade in Marietta, 310
segregation and the, 12

LaGrand, Walter (execution), 201
Lambert, Bobby, 244
Lambert, Joseph, 233
Landis, Abraham Hoch, 317n4
Landis, Kenesaw Mountain, 317n4
Landry, Raymond (execution), 205
Lanham, Henderson, 140
Last Day of a Condemned Man, The (Hugo),
    227
last meals, 187, 223, 297, 366n13
Latinos, lynching of, 124, 125
law and order (campaign issue), 91–92
Lawes, Lewis E. (warden), 61
Lawson, David (execution), 202–3
Lawyers' Committee for Civil Rights
    Under Law, 148
lawyers. See defense counsel, See
    prosecutors
Layton, James R., 265
LDF. See NAACP Legal Defense and
    Education Fund
Leach, Kimberly, 220
League for the Abolition of Capital
    Punishment, 61
League of Women Voters, 283
Leard, Mary, 124
Le dernier jour d'un condamne. See Last Day
    of a Condemned Man.
Lee, Robert E., 54, 310
Legal Defense Fund. See NAACP Legal
    Defense and Education Fund
Lemon Street High School, 12, 13, 310,
    367n13
Leopold, Nathan, 61–62, 77
Lester, James, 94–95
lethal gas (execution method). See gas
    chamber
lethal injection
    adoption of, 203–4
    chemicals used in, 207–10, 257
    executions, 205, 208–9, 219, 221
    history, 108
    legal challenges to, 205–7, 208, 288
    non-U.S. use of, 211
    and physicians, 204, 206
    problems with, 201, 204–6, 208
    twentieth century use of, 182
    use instead of electric chair, 193–94
Let Justice Be Done (report), 313

"Let's Kill Gary Gilmore for Christmas"
    (song), 107
Levy, Lisa, 220
Lewis, Anthony, 162
Lewis, John, 122
lex talionis, 47
Leyva, Ed, 235–36
Liebman, James S., 161, 244, 245
Life and Death in Sing (Lawes), 61
life without the possibility of parole
    (LWOP)
    juveniles, 272
    New Jersey, 282
    North Carolina, 276, 277
    numbers serving, 312–13
    public opinion on, 293
    states with sentencing option of, 254,
        359n31
    Texas, 279
Lincoln, Abraham
    assassination, 240
    debates on slavery, 53
    execution of assassination
        conspirators, 55, 56f
    on lynching, 123
    military executions, 55
    pardoning Sioux warriors, 55
    and Harriet Beecher Stowe, 227
Lindbergh (Charles Augustus, Jr.) Baby
    Kidnapping, 63–64, 71, 327n44
Lindbergh, Anne, 63–64
Lister, Ernest, 59
Littlest Rebel, The (movie), 126
Livingston, Edward, 240
Lockett, Clayton (execution), 209–10,
    350n63
Lockheed Aircraft Company, 13, 319n16
Lockheed Martin Aeronautics, 308
Loeb, Richard, 61–62, 77
Loney, George, 121
Long, Virginia, 233–34
Look, 122
Lopez, Wanda, 243
Los Angeles Times, 273, 287
Loudres, Woodie, 110, 333n21
Louisiana
    abolition organizations in, 50
    child rape law, 267–68
    Dead Man Walking, 226
    discretionary sentencing, 132
    executions, 65, 113, 135, 182, 245
    innocent on death row/executions,
        242, 245
    lynching, 134, 135, 337n19
    noose tie worn by prosecutor in, 134,
        337n13

Markell, Jack, 278
Marsellus, Howard, 113
Marshall, Thurgood, 137*f*, 156*f*
   as attorney for death row man, 134
   capital punishment views, 188, 228, 295
   in Wilbert Evens execution, 176
   and foreign/international law, 262
   and *Furman v. Georgia*, 87*f*, 88, 173
   and *Gregg v. Georgia*, 98, 101*f*, 173
   and Willie Howard lynching, 123
   on innocent client, 239, 355*n1*
   lynching experience, 138
   and McCleskey's final apppeal, 188
   and *McCleskey v. Kemp*, 85, 138, 149, 152, 154, 158, 307
   and *McCleskey v. Zant*, 39–40
   and *Maxwell v. Bishop*, 84
   1976 death penalty cases, 100, 102
   on public knowledge about capital punishment, 257
   on racism and lynching, 134
   retirement, 189
   views on Supreme Court, 188–89, 346*n43*
Martin, Boyce F., Jr., 272
Martinez, Bob, 221
Martin Luther King Jr. Center for Nonviolent Social Change, 310
Maryland
   abolition of death penalty, 285, 288
   clemency/commutations, 114
   executions, 49, 198, 219
   moratorium, 252
   unequal imposition of death penalty in, 251
Massachusetts
   abolition of death penalty, 285, 288, 327*n38*
   clemency/commutations, 83
   executions, 46, 49, 181, 198
   Leo Frank lynching and Boston, 7
   reinstatement of death penalty, 111
   Sacco & Vanzetti, 62, 63, 182, 241, 327*n38*, 355*n6*
Massachusetts Council against the Death Penalty, 327*n38*
Massiah claim, 37–38, 38–39, 39, 40, 323*n31*
Mata, Luis, 257
Mather, Cotton, 48
Maxwell, William, 141, 338*n7*
May, Justin Lee (execution), 205
Maynard, Andrew, 364*n31*
Mayo, Charles, 55

Mayo, William, 55
Mears, Michael, 188, 346*n47*
Mease, Darrell (clemency), 360*n41*
media
   abolition of the death penalty and the, 74–75
   advocating for capital punishment and lynching, 66
   and Baldus study, 290
   bias reporting, 247
   on the electric chair, 180
   and high-profile/unusual crimes/ executions, 61–62, 176, 219–21, 281
   on innocent people on death row, 242–44, 250
   and Warrren McCleskey, 18, 40, 150, 163, 192, 299*f*
   and the moratorium movement, 253
   and reversal rate study, 254
   on Supreme Court, 231
   and victims and their families, 300
   viewing executions, 180–81
Meeropol, Abel, 127
Meltsner, Michael, 86
Mennonite Church, 75
mental illness and death penalty, 46, 63, 65, 267, 361*n20*
mental retardation. *See* intellectual disability
Methodist Church, 75
Mexican-Americans, 124, 140
Mexican nationals on U.S. death rows, 255
Michigan
   abolition of death penalty, 51, 57, 64–65, 74, 76, 280, 288, 325*nn33, 35*
   executions, 52, 64–65, 197
Michigan State University, 277
Micke, William, 86
Miliam, J.W., 122
military executions, 46, 49, 54–55, 200, 311–12
Milledgeville, Georgia, 123, 182
Miller, Benjamin Meeks, 137
Miller, Walter Monroe, 61
Miller, Zell, 192, 218, 223
Minnesota, 55, 59, 60, 76, 120, 288
miscarriage of justice (legal standard), 31, 38, 185
Mississippi
   executions, 135, 163, 182–83, 202, 208
   laws for slaves vs. whites, 132
   lynching, 122, 124, 135, 337*n19*

and the Thirteenth Amendment, 318n17

Emmett Till lynching, 122

Missouri
    abolition of death penalty, 59
    clemency/commutations in, 337n19, 360n41
    executions, 135, 201, 209, 351n30
    innocent on death row, 244
    intellectual disability and death penalty in, 257
    lynching, 135, 337n19
    reinstatement of death penalty, 61

Mitchell, Aaron (execution), 92, 330n59

Mitchell, William "Billy", 147, 340n34

mitigating evidence
    ALI model statute, 296
    categories of, 173–75, 334n26
    culpability, 147, 173, 174, 312
    discretion in evaluating, 230
    "Good Character", 174
    and individualized sentencing, 106, 332n38
    in McCleskey's case, 106, 171–72
    and mental illness, 267
    "Nature-Nurture", 174
    and reform, 169–78, 343nn3, 6, 344nn18, 26, 28, 31, 345nn32–33
    at sentencing hearing, 96, 98, 99, 100, 106

Model Penal Code, 98, 296

Monge, Luis (execution), 82, 108

Monroe, James, 48, 325n2

Montana, 219, 267, 286

Moore, William Neal "Billy", 113–14
    and Jack Boger, 190
    commuted sentence, 334n30
    friendship with Warren McCleskey, 169–70, 177, 187, 300
    opposition to death penalty work, 306
    parole, 306, 334n30, 346n38

Moral Consequences of Economic Growth, The (Friedman), 136

moratorium movement, 249–57, 286, 289, 293, 358n3, 359nn31, 33, 360nn37, 41, 43

moratoriums
    California, 72
    call for, 235
    Nevada, 252, 286
    New Jersey, 282
    Oregon, 278–79
    Tennessee, 365n48
    Washington, 279

Morgenthau, Robert, 235

Morris, Errol, 220

Morris, Newt, 5, 7, 318n14

Mother Theresa, 178

Mount Carmel Cemetery, 5

Muhammad, John Allen, 344n31

murder, death penalty for, 49, 52, 132, 133

Murder Victims' Families for Reconciliation (MVFR), 236, 283

Murphy, Frank, 65

mutilation, 48, 123, 124, 183, 193–94

Myers, Betty, 11, 26, 27, 193, 319n12

Myers, Carol, 109

NAACP (National Association for the Advancement of Colored People)
    and abolition in New Mexico, 283
    challenges to the death penalty by the, 79, 289
    and Juneteenth celebration, 310
    Henderson Lanham on the, 140
    lynching defined by the, 335n13
    lynching reform and the, 127, 128, 129, 337n26
    lynching statistics, 124–25
    on McCleskey Court of Appeals decision, 148–49
    Justice Marshall working for the, 138
    and protests in North Carolina, 276
    Eleanor Roosevelt and the, 337n15

NAACP Legal Defense and Education Fund (LDF)
    and Baldus study, 142, 146, 151
    death penalty abolition work, 224, 307
    and *Furman v. Georgia*, 91, 97
    and international law, 262
    litigation strategy, 79–81, 83
    and McCleskey's case, 147, 160
    1976 death penalty cases rehearing, 103
    on race and the death penalty, 140–42
    See also Amsterdam, Anthony, Boger, John Charles "Jack".

Nabrit, James M., III, 340n2

narrowing function of aggravating factors, 106–7, 157, 268–69

National Association for the Advancement of Colored People. *See* NAACP

National Campaign for the Abolition of Capital Punishment (Great Britain), 75

National Coalition Against the Death Penalty, 224, 256

National Coalition to Abolish the Death Penalty, 224, 284

National Committee to Prevent Wrongful Executions, 235

national consensus and Eighth
   Amendment, 266, 268
National Registry of Exonerations, 242
National Review, 242, 246
Native Americans
   and death penalty, 45, 46, 55
   and lynching, 55
   lynching of, 124, 125
   in Marietta, Georgia, 3
   Trail of Tears, 3, 310
"Nature-Nurture" mitigating factors, 174
Nebraska
   abolition efforts, x, 286
   electric chair, 194
   executions, 194, 219
   moratorium bill, 251
   unequal imposition of death penalty
      in, 251
   unicameral legislature, ix, 364n38
Nelson, Laura, 121–22, 121f, 123–24,
   335n7
Nelson, Lawrence, 121–22, 121f, 123–24,
   335n7
Nepauduck, 46
Neufeld, Peter, 242
Nevada, 201, 202, 252, 286
New Deal, 79, 128
New, Everett, 16
New Hampshire, 50, 200, 252, 286
New Jersey
   abolition of death penalty, 281–82,
      288
   Colonial ban on executions, 46
   executions, 49, 181, 312, 364n24
   reinstatement of death penalty, 111
New Jersey Supreme Court, 282, 312
New Mexico
   abolition of death penalty, 75, 76, 111,
      282–83, 284, 288
   clemency/commutations, 114, 251
   executions, 283
   reinstatement of death penalty, 111
New Mexico Coalition to Repeal the Death
   Penalty, 283
New Mexico Public Health Association,
   283
Newsome, John, 132
Newton, Christopher J. (execution), 205
New York
   abolition of death penalty, 281, 288
   abolition organizations in, 50
   executions, 46, 49, 52, 179–81, 195
   Leo Frank lynching and, 5–7
   laws for slaves vs. whites, 131
   limited death penalty, 74

reinstatement of death penalty, 223,
   280–81, 364n23
New York City, 49, 281
New York Committee to Abolish Capital
   Punishment, 75
New York Times, 163, 215
Nicaragua abolition of death penalty, 108
Nixon, Richard M.
   on abortion, 94
   and Caryl Chessman, 72
   crime as a campaign and governing
      issue, 91–92, 150
   "silent majority", 91
   Supreme Court appointments, 84, 86,
      89, 93, 101, 152, 231
non-homicide crimes and death penalty
   1958–1959, 73–74
   rape, 52, 59, 64, 74, 78, 79, 133, 135,
      205, 222–23, 242, 267–69, 332n47,
      361n21
North Carolina
   executions, 46, 49, 52, 135, 181, 202–3
   intellectual disability and death
      penalty in, 257
   lynching, 135, 337n19
   mandatory death penalty, 101
   moratorium resolutions, 252
   Racial Justice Act, 276–77
   Stewart's Supreme Court confirmation
      and senators from, 342n37
North Carolina Racial Justice Act, 276–77
North Dakota, 59, 76, 120, 288
Northern Mariana Islands, 288
North, The
   Leo Frank case and, 7
   racial tensions, 125
Northwestern University, 242
Norway abolition of death penalty, 108

Obama, Barack H., 269, 278
Ochs, Phil, 73
O'Connor, Sandra Day, 156f
   appointment to Court, 150
   on the death penalty, 232, 295
   on intellectual disability and death
      penalty, 264
   on juries and racism, 145
   and *McCleskey v. Kemp*, 149, 151, 152,
      154, 162, 164, 355n1
O'Dell, Joseph (execution), 245
Of Crime and Punishments (Beccaria),
   226 27
Ohio
   abolition organizations in, 50
   clemency/commutations in, 252
   death penalty laws, 233

Prague, Edith G., 364n31
Prejean, Helen, 226–28, 244, 245
presidential assassinations
    James Garfield, 56
    John F. Kennedy, 8
    Abraham Lincoln, 55, 56f, 240
    William McKinley, 58–59
    Franklin D. Roosevelt (attempted), 63, 326n18
    Harry S.Truman (attempted), 70
procedural default and habeas corpus, 270
Procedural Reform Study, 142, 148, 152, 338n10
    See also Baldus study
Proffitt, Charles, 102
Progressive Era, 53, 59, 240
Prohibition, 61
proportionality
    and Eighth Amendment, 78, 157
    New Jersey, 282
    race and, 50, 132
    review system, 234
Proportioning Crimes and Punishments in Cases Heretofore Capital, 47
prosecutors
    and aggravating factors, 25–26
    arbitrariness seeking death penalty, 273
    discretion of, 145
    and jailhouse informants, 242
    misconduct, 247
    race-based exclusion of jurors, 136, 146, 277, 311
    race-based meetings with victim's families, 146
Protess, David, 242
Protestant Episcopal Church, 75
public executions, 182–83, 199, 210, 240, 271
Public Justice, Private Mercy (Brown), 72
public opinion on death penalty
    African American, 145–46
    anti-death penalty activists focus on the courts and, 93, 105
    blue-collar vs. more affluent people, 93
    in California, 92, 108
    change over time, 43–44, 292–93, 297
    clemency and commutations, 252
    increased support of death penalty, 216
    innocent on death row and, 247, 257
    and juveniles, 271
    LDF and, 85
    moratoriums, 252

1930s–1950s, 69
1960s, 75, 80–81, 92–93
1970s, 93, 95–96, 105, 108
1980s, 150
1990s, 224, 352n39
and persons with intellectual disability, 271
post WW II, 67
in Virginia, 177
Puckett, Cheyenne, 178
Puerto Rico, 61, 62, 288
Pulaski, Charles A., Jr., 141, 151, 290, 307
    See also Baldus study
punishment
    Colonial, 46–47
    race-based punishment for rape, 131, 134, 140–41, 149
    race of victims and, 142–50, 250, 311, 338nn12–14, 339nn22–23, 25–26, 28, 340n34
    and Franklin D. Roosevelt, 65
    Justice Scalia on, 172, 246, 270
    for slaves, 123, 131–33
    Justice Stevens on, 293–95, 349n49
    utilitarian and retributive justification for, 172–73
    U.S. views on, 292
Putnam, Claude, 75
Putnam, Constance E., 241

Quakers (American Friends Service Committee), 46–47, 75, 80
Quinn, Pat, 283–84, 286

race/racial discrimination
    arbitrary application of death penalty and, 77
    in baseball, 11, 317n4
    Brennan on being "imprisoned by the past", 279, 298
    and the courts, 131–38, 137f, 337nn13, 15, 19, 26, 338n30
    current status regarding, 310–15, 369n38
    and death penalty application, 88, 112, 135–36, 346n44, 362n1
    effect of defendant's race, 78, 82, 88, 109, 116, 339n23
    effect of victim's race, 88, 109, 116, 339n23
    geography and lynching, 123–26, 335n13
    and innocence, 239–40

and abolition of death penalty
  (1950s–1960s), 76–82, 77f
and abolition of death penalty (1970s),
  83–89, 331n17
on constitutional requirements for
  capital trials, 26
on cruel and unusual punishment,
  198, 200
on death penalty for non-homicide
  crimes, 267–69
on discretionary sentencing, 133
and *Dred Scott v. Sandford*, 132
on the electric chair, 180, 182
and federal court review, 218
on the firing squad, 348n17
and foreign/international law, 262–66,
  265–66, 360n6, 361n8
on individualized sentencing, 106
and international opinion, 262
on lethal injection, 204, 206–7
on LWOP, 254
and McCleskey's final apppeal, 188
and *McCleskey v. Kemp*, 149–50, 151–65,
  153f, 156f, 340nn1–2, 341n9,
  342nn20, 36–37, 343n52
on mitigating factors, 171, 175, 343n6
political pressure on the, 93–94
on post-sentencing actions, 176
and punishment theories, 172–73
and return of death penalty (1970s),
  91–103, 101f, 332nn38, 47
role in history of the death penalty, 67
rule of four, 149
and Scottsboro case, 137
speeding up executions, 110
states rights and capital cases, 136
twenty-first century death penalty
  cases, 261–74, 360n6, 361nn7–8,
  10, 20–21
See also Specific justices
Surratt, John, 55
Surratt, Mary, 55, 240
Swanner, Jodie Schlatt. *See* Schlatt, Jodie
Switzerland abolition of the death
  penalty, 66–67
Szymankiewicz, Joseph, 108

Tafero, Jesse J.(execution), 183
Taft, William Howard, 136
Talby, Dorothy, 46
Tallahassee Democrat, 162
Taney, Roger, 132, 162
Tarver, Robert L. (execution), 347n63
Taylor, Fred, 191
Taylor, John A. (execution), 201

Taylor, John B., 281
Technology Review, 145
Temple, Shirley, 126
Tennessee
  abolition of death penalty, 59, 60
  abolition organizations in, 50
  discretionary sentencing, 132
  executions, 181, 194
  lynching, 135, 337n19
  moratorium on executions, 365n48
  reinstatement of death penalty, 60, 61
Terrell, Charles, 236
Texas
  death penalty laws, 106
  death penalty statute, 366n8
  death row, 236
  discretionary sentencing, 132
  electric chair, 61
  executions, 61, 66, 110–11, 112, 135,
    176, 181, 204, 205, 208, 243–45,
    254, 279, 297, 351n30
  innocent executions, 243–45
  last meals in, 366n13
  lynching, 124, 135, 183, 337n19
  Native Americans and extrajudicial
    mob violence, 124
  politics of death penalty in, 279
  problems with system for capital cases,
    254
  race and the criminal justice system, 150
  sentencing guidelines, 99
Texas Civil Rights Project, 254
Texas Forensic Science Commission, 245
Thayer, Webster, 62
Thibodeaux, Damon (exoneration), 242
Thin Blue Line, The (film), 220
Thirteenth Amendment, 81, 318n17
Thomas, Andrew, 65
Thomas, Clarence, 189, 207, 346n44
Thomas, Mamie, 22, 23–24
Thompson, Hunter S., 93
Thrash, Thomas W., Jr., 18, 306
Till, Emmett, 122
Timely Justice Act (Florida), 288
Time Magazine, 76, 162, 163
Toobin, Jeffrey, 268
Torresola, Griselio, 70
Trail of Tears, 3
Trail of Tears Association, 310
Trail of Tears National Historic Trail, 310
treason, death penalty for, 49, 51, 52, 59,
  74, 325n33
Treason Clause, 48
trial of Warren McCleskey, 21–29, 321n12
Tritt, Travis, 307

CPSIA information can be obtained at www.ICGtesting.com
Printed in the USA
BVOW03s0238061016

464311BV00002B/5/P

9 780190 653002